A SOCIAL HISTORY OF
ENGLAND, 1200–1500

edited by

ROSEMARY HORROX

and

W. MARK ORMROD

CAMBRIDGE
UNIVERSITY PRESS

CAMBRIDGE UNIVERSITY PRESS
Cambridge, New York, Melbourne, Madrid, Cape Town, Singapore, São Paulo

Cambridge University Press
The Edinburgh Building, Cambridge CB2 2RU, UK

Published in the United States of America by Cambridge University Press, New York

www.cambridge.org
Information on this title: www.cambridge.org/9780521789547

© Cambridge University Press 2006

First published 2006

Printed in the United Kingdom at the University Press, Cambridge

A catalogue record for this publication is available from the British Library

Library of Congress Cataloguing in Publication Data
A social history of England, 1200–1500 / edited by Rosemary Horrox and W. Mark Ormrod.
p. cm.
Includes bibliographical references and index.
ISBN-13: 978-0-521-78345-3 (hardback)
ISBN-10: 0-521-78345-3 (hardback)
ISBN-13: 978-0-521-78954-7 (pbk.)
ISBN-10: 0-521-78954-0 (pbk.)
1. Great Britain – Social life and customs – 1066-1485. 2. Great Britain – History – Medieval
period, 1066-1485. I. Horrox, Rosemary. II. Ormrod, W. M., 1957–
DA185.s63 2006
942.03 – dc22

ISBN-13 978-0-521-78345-3 hardback
ISBN-10 0-521-78345-3 hardback

ISBN-13 978-0-521-78954-7 paperback
ISBN-10 0-521-78954-0 paperback

Contents

Illustrations

Preface

This book is intended as a comprehensive and accessible account of the society of England between the early thirteenth and the late fifteenth centuries. The dates 1200–1500 conventionally describe the 'later middle ages' in England, but are obviously not impermeable: some of the contributions that follow necessarily take certain matters back to the eleventh and forward to the sixteenth centuries. The book is organised around five large chapters which provide analyses of the historiographical background and the debate about demography (chapter 1), the social hierarchy and attitudes towards it (chapter 2), the experience of life in towns (chapter 6) and in the countryside (chapter 7), the forms of religious belief current in the society (chapter 11) and the other kinds of identity, individual and collective, that built on and helped to inform social organisation (chapter 15). Around these chapters is a series of shorter, more specialised studies that develops further some of the major themes from war to work, law to literacy, consumerism to magic.

The book thus aims to respond to a new agenda of social history which has extended the range of the sub-discipline from a preoccupation with the material existence of the lower orders to include a range of non-material aspects of life including attitudes to work and to crime, the development of ideas about nationality, and the existence (or otherwise) of self-consciousness or 'individualism'. As such, this book draws no distinction between 'social' and 'cultural' history, and tries to represent the experience of those who lived in the later middle ages in as broad a manner as possible. An important part of this holistic approach involves an understanding that interpretation of historical evidence is often unstable, reflecting in turn the patchy nature of the evidence. This is particularly evident with regard to the estimates of the population of England before and after the Black Death, and we have aimed not to impose arbitrary figures but to allow different contributors to set out their own arguments on this important and still controversial theme.

In the notes the place of publication is London, unless otherwise stated.

Contributors

Richard Britnell	University of Durham
Janet Burton	University of Wales, Lampeter
Bruce M. S. Campbell	Queen's University of Belfast
Wendy R. Childs	University of Leeds
Peter Coss	Cardiff University
Eamon Duffy	Magdalene College, Cambridge
Valerie I. J. Flint	University of Hull
Robin Frame	University of Durham
P. J. P. Goldberg	University of York
Rosemary Horrox	Fitzwilliam College, Cambridge
Maryanne Kowaleski	Fordham University, New York
Philippa C. Maddern	University of Western Australia, Perth
Mavis E. Mate	University of Oregon
W. Mark Ormrod	University of York
Charles Phythian-Adams	University of Leicester
Michael Prestwich	University of Durham
S. H. Rigby	University of Manchester
Miri Rubin	Queen Mary, University of London
Paul Strohm	Columbia University, New York
†Simon Walker	University of Sheffield

Abbreviations

Ag. Hist. Rev.	*Agricultural History Review*
AmHR	*American Historical Review*
BL	British Library
EcHR	*Economic History Review*
EETS	Early English Text Society
EHR	*English Historical Review*
JEH	*Journal of Ecclesiastical History*
JMH	*Journal of Medieval History*
P&P	*Past and Present*
PRO	Public Record Office (The National Archives)
RS	Rolls Series
TRHS	*Transactions of the Royal Historical Society*

CHAPTER I

Introduction: Social structure and economic change in late medieval England

S. H. Rigby

In W. G. Runciman's words, 'all societies can be characterised in terms of the nature and degree of institutionalised differences of privileges among their members'.[1] However, the precise nature of the social privileges characteristic of pre-industrial societies such as medieval England has proved a controversial issue amongst historians and social scientists. For instance, can medieval English society be analysed in terms of the class divisions characteristic of modern societies, or should it be seen, like other pre-industrial societies, as stratified in terms of orders or estates? Was conflict inherent within medieval social relations or can instances of conflict be explained by more immediate, short-term factors? Such debates are linked to broader methodological questions such as whether historians should describe a society in the terms employed by members of that society or whether societies of the past can be analysed using the concepts of modern social theory. Here it will be argued that, rather than being stratified exclusively in terms of classes, orders or any other single form of social inequality, medieval English society was made up of a number of different axes of social inequality. Any one individual thus had a variety of social identities, including those of class, order, status group and gender. The first part of this chapter examines how these forms of social inequality came together to create the particular social hierarchy to be found in late medieval England; the second assesses the forces working to produce economic and social change in the later middle ages.

[1] W. G. Runciman, 'Towards a theory of social stratification', in F. Parkin, ed., *The Social Analysis of Class Structure* (1974), p. 56. I would like to thank Rosalind Brown-Grant, Bruce Campbell, R. C. Nash and the editors of this volume for their extremely valuable comments on earlier versions of this chapter.

SOCIAL STRUCTURE: CLASSES, ORDERS, STATUS AND GENDER

That modern social theory *can* be fruitfully applied to medieval social inequalities is shown by the 'dichotomic' social analysis offered by Marxist and Marxist-influenced historians such as Hilton, Brenner, Dyer and Razi.[2] The social hierarchy here is understood in terms of one or a number of binary oppositions, such as those between propertied and non-propertied, lord and peasant, employer and employee, exploiter and exploited. Whilst Marxists such as Hilton recognise the existence of a variety of groups within medieval society, their underlying assumption tends to be that 'feudal' societies such as medieval England were fundamentally determined by the relations between a landowning class on the one hand and a class of peasant-producers on the other. Similarly, for Hilton, medieval urban society should also be understood in terms of the relations between two main classes: the artisans and the mercantile elite. Marxists see the relationship between these dichotomic classes in town and country as necessarily antagonistic. We are thus presented with a 'dysfunctional' model of medieval society: one in which conflict is viewed as the inevitable outcome of the prevailing social relations.

For Marxists, conflict was generated within rural society by the lords' extraction of a 'surplus' from the peasant-producers in the form of rent. This rent could be paid in kind, as grain or livestock; but, far more frequently, it was rendered as labour services on the lords' demesnes (the land which they had not permanently leased out to tenants) or, most commonly of all, in the form of a money payment. This transfer of wealth was enforced by the legal and political powers enshrined in the landlords' manorial rights and, in particular, their power over their unfree tenants. Conflict between lords and peasants was inherent in this relationship, as tenants had a vested interest in minimising the level of rents and dues and the extent of manorial controls, while their lords stood to gain by maximising them. Similarly, as employers, the landlords had an interest in enforcing low wages whilst labourers and smallholders naturally sought higher wages. Such clashes of interest could generate intense struggle about levels of rent, wages and manorial restrictions. These struggles could be initiated from below, most dramatically in mass uprisings such as the Peasants' Revolt of 1381. Popular struggles could also take more local forms, such as claims to free status, refusals to carry out labour services, 'go-slows' when performing services, resistance to the

---

[2] For bibliographical details of works cited in general terms here and elsewhere, see Further Reading.

collection of manorial dues and demands for higher wages. However, social conflict could also be initiated from above. When, in the early fourteenth century, the estate administrators of the bishopric of Winchester systematically reduced the payments in grain to demesne employees, this effective cut in wages was just as much an example of class conflict as were the demands of labourers for higher wages in the era of labour shortage which followed the Black Death of 1348–9.

For Marxists, conflict was as inevitable within urban society as it was in the medieval countryside. Urban social conflict was generated by the appropriation of surplus from the producers, in this case the craft masters and journeymen, by the mercantile ruling elite, even if the appropriation of surplus in these circumstances was sometimes carried out by local taxation rather than by direct economic means. Although a variety of mechanisms existed within urban society to prevent social tensions from breaking out into open violence, 'those who sought unity and peace were often papering over cracks in a divided social structure'.[3]

With its stress on objective property rights as the basis of social stratification, the Marxist approach lays less emphasis on the subjective perception of social relations by medieval people themselves. If, in terms of the medieval social theory of the three orders,[4] the lay lords and church prelates were members of two different social orders (that is, those who fought and those who prayed) then, in class terms, these groups seem almost indistinguishable from one another, since together they constituted a single 'aristocracy' which derived the bulk of its income from its landed estates.[5] In this class perspective, the account of social structure offered by medieval preachers, theologians and poets in which the social hierarchy was presented in terms of interdependent orders was far from a faithful portrait of reality. Rather, it was an imaginary representation of society, an ideology that legitimated the wealth, power and status accorded to particular social groups.

One alternative to the Marxist emphasis on polarised social classes and sharp social distinctions is to see social hierarchies in terms of 'gradation': that is, as constituting a spectrum of quantitative differences of wealth, status and power. D. W. Robertson, for instance, claimed that medieval

[3] R. H. Hilton, *Class Conflict and the Crisis of Feudalism* (1985), p. 123; C. Dyer, *Standards of Living in the Later Middle Ages: social change in England, c. 1200–1520* (Cambridge, 1989), p. 25; R. H. Hilton, *English and French Towns in Feudal Society* (Cambridge, 1992), pp. 60, 150; C. Dyer, 'Small-town conflict in the later middle ages: events at Shipston-on-Stour', *Urban History*, 19 (1992), 184.

[4] See below, pp. 4–5.

[5] Dyer, *Standards of Living*, pp. 21–2, 25; C. Dyer, *Making a Living in the Middle Ages: the people of Britain, 850–1520* (New Haven, CT, 2002), p. 8.

England had no classes in the modern sense, but only a long series of degrees of social rank.[6] Certainly, as Bailey reminds us, it is misleading to talk of landlords and peasants as though they were 'homogenous and easily defined classes' since, in practice, these groups incorporated their own 'fine gradations of status and wealth'.[7] It is this internal stratification of the peasantry that has been the focus of the so-called 'Toronto school' of medieval historians. Whilst medievalists have traditionally concentrated on the relations between lord and peasant embodied in the *manor*, writers such as Raftis, the DeWindts and Britton have also stressed the need to examine the social life within the medieval English *village*. They have shown how an elite within the peasantry dominated landholding and, albeit to a lesser extent, the profits of ale-brewing, and have demonstrated how this elite enjoyed greater marriage opportunities and a wider geographical range of social contacts than those beneath them in village society. Indeed, this emphasis on differences within the peasantry even led Britton to present the sub-groups within the village as distinct social 'classes', each of which possessed its own internal cohesion and 'class-consciousness'. Whilst co-operation between the villagers in the form of pledging, concords and land exchanges tended to be *intra*-group, cases of social friction (assault, theft, defamation and raising the hue and cry) were more likely to be *inter*-group, although, as Britton himself shows, there is also substantial evidence for intra-group hostility, particularly between individuals within the village elite.[8]

In practice, an emphasis on social gradation rather than dichotomic social division is often combined with a third social perspective, that of functional interdependence. Here, the constituent groups of society are not seen as existing in some necessary opposition (as they are in the dichotomic approach), but are rather conceptualised in terms of a mutually beneficial division of labour. This approach is popular with many modern historians, for whom medieval society was not made up of classes but rather of estates or orders which were ranked in terms of the status or honour accorded to their functions by the subjective social evaluation of the day. However, this view also found expression within the medieval period itself in the famous doctrine of the 'three orders'. According to this theory, society was divided into three estates or orders,

---

[6] D. W. Robertson, *Chaucer's London* (New York, 1968), p. 4.

[7] M. Bailey, 'Rural society', in R. Horrox, ed., *Fifteenth-Century Attitudes* (Cambridge, 1994), p. 150. See also J. A. Raftis, *Peasant Economic Development within the English Manorial System* (Montreal, 1996), p. 130.

[8] E. Britton, *The Community of the Vill* (Toronto, 1977).

the *oratores*, *bellatores* and *laboratores*: that is, those who pray, those who fight and those who work. These social groups were defined not by their economic role or their property rights but by their social function. Society was therefore thought of in terms of a body, with the orders as the limbs or organs whose specialist tasks were necessary for the wellbeing of the whole. Each order needed the services of the others if it was to prosper and survive. As Langland's Piers Plowman says to the knight, 'For my part, I'll sweat and toil for us both as long as I live, and gladly do my job as long as you want. But you must promise in return to guard over Holy Church and protect me from those thieves and wasters who ruin the world.'[9]

In particular, the tripartite theory stressed the need for the third estate, the producers, to be, in the words of Thomas Wimbledon's famous sermon of *c.* 1388, 'subject and low' and in dread of displeasing their superiors.[10] All should accept their place in the divinely ordained hierarchy. Individually, each man should remain within the estate to which God had called him, accepting the need to work 'according to his degree' rather than aspiring to rise in society. Collectively, since each group needed the services of the others, each should know its place and perform its duties rather than upsetting the 'natural' order of things. Of course, medieval thinkers were well aware that social conflict and mobility existed and that reality did not always match up to their ideal. Nevertheless, this divergence between ideal and reality tended to be regarded as the result of personal sin, as a failure of individual reason, rather than as the necessary product of contemporary social relations.

Medieval thinkers could easily reconcile an account of society as divided into functionally defined orders with a conception of social structure as a gradated hierarchy by their recognition that each order had its own internal stratification. Thus, the secular clergy were ranked from archbishops and bishops at the top of the English ecclesiastical hierarchy down to local priests and chaplains. Within the lay aristocracy there was a growing distinction between the parliamentary peerage (eventually internally ranked as dukes, marquises, earls, viscounts and barons) and the gentry (which was itself divided into knights, esquires and gentlemen). Furthermore, whilst in theory the clergy as an estate was ranked in its entirety above the laity, in practice, contemporaries were quite capable of

---

[9] *Piers Plowman*, B-Text, Passus VI, lines 25–8, 159–66.
[10] I. K. Knight, ed., *Wimbledon's Sermon Redde Rationem Villicationis Tue: a Middle English sermon of the fourteenth century* (Pittsburgh, 1967), p. 67.

equating particular ranks within the clergy with those within the laity. For instance when, in his mid-fifteenth-century *Book of Nurture*, John Russell, marshal to Humphrey, duke of Gloucester, came to deal with the thorny problems posed by the order of precedence in the seating arrangements in a noble household, he divided potential guests into five hierarchically arranged groups. Each group had its own internal gradations according to birth, income and dignity. Within each group there was an equation between members of the clergy and of the laity, from archbishops and dukes through bishops and earls, mitred abbots and barons, unmitred abbots and knights, down to parish priests and esquires.[11]

The view of society propagated within the medieval period has had a profound influence on modern historians. Rather than dismissing medieval social theory as mere ideology, Keen argues that in order to understand late medieval society we must 'know something about the contemporary hierarchy as men then saw it'. For Keen, late medieval England can be described as 'what we nowadays call a deference society', one characterised by 'an ordered gradation' of the social hierarchy which regulated the respect and the kind of service which people expected to render to or to receive from their fellows. Even though social divisions were more flexible in England than those of continental Europe under the *ancien régime*, 'in the minds of men of that age, the relations of deference and service that persisted between the grades [of society] were the basis of social order, of its essence: they had not yet come to regard social distinctions as divisive, as forces with the potential to tear society apart'.[12]

That society should be seen in terms of its self-perception, and the consequent belief that (as one critic of this approach puts it) pre-industrial societies such as late medieval England were 'neatly ordered ladder(s), the rungs of which were demarcated primarily by status and held together by harmonious social relationships',[13] is now a common view amongst historians and sociologists. Its defenders include writers such as Mousnier, Fourquin and Crone. With a consensus in place amongst the members of society about the ranking of the different social groups, conflict is seen here as being paralysed from within by the power of some 'common culture' or 'dominant ideology': a view actually anticipated in

---

[11] F. J. Furnivall, ed., *The Babees Book* (EETS, os XXXII, 1868), p. 189–90. For further discussion, see below, p. 72.

[12] M. Keen, *English Society in the Later Middle Ages* (Harmondsworth, 1990), p. 1; see also S. L. Waugh, 'Closure theory and medieval England', *New Left Review*, 226 (1997), 126–7.

[13] S. McSheffrey, 'Conceptualising difference: English society in the late middle ages', *Journal of British Studies*, 36 (1997), 139.

early fifteenth-century England in Robert Rypon's claim that 'the unity of the state exists in the agreement of its minds'.[14] Certainly, in relation to medieval English towns, a number of historians – Thrupp, Reynolds, Palliser, Phythian-Adams and Rosser – have argued that urban political life was based on shared ideological norms such as the deferential belief that the rich should lead and dominate, so that to disobey one's social superior was to commit a sin. Similarly, for rural society, members of the Toronto school such as Britton and A. R. DeWindt have claimed that, in the thirteenth century, conciliation was 'much more common than conflict' in lord–peasant relations. Rather than the inevitability of conflict stressed by the Marxist model, it is the shared interests of lord and tenants which are emphasised here, feudal lords being seen as benefiting from the economic progress of their wealthier customary tenants and as bound by the responsibility to maintain local justice and to protect the orphans and widows within their power.

How are we to choose between these conflicting views of medieval English society? Although the dichotomic, class-based approach to medieval English social structure may seem to be in contradiction to the gradated and functional stress on orders, there is no reason why these models should necessarily be seen as mutually exclusive. Instead, the decision to emphasise classes or to put a stress on orders will tend to reflect our own immediate analytical concerns. If, for instance, we are interested in the manorial policies of the landlords, such as their abandonment of direct management of their demesnes in the late fourteenth and fifteenth centuries, we will tend to emphasise the class similarities between clerical landowners and their lay counterparts. If, on the other hand, we are interested in how individuals obtained their access to such property and how it was transmitted, we will be likely to stress the differences between the clergy and the laity as orders. Certainly, we do not have to swallow the doctrine of the three orders in its entirety in order to recognise that social status in medieval England was not solely the consequence of one's class position. Thus for the clergy access to the corporate wealth of the Church (both its temporal wealth as a landowner and the income from spiritual services drawn from particular ecclesiastical offices) was itself the consequence of their membership of, and ranking within, a particular status group, a group which was defined by functions

---

[14] A. J. Fletcher, '"The unity of the state exists in the agreement of its minds": a fifteenth-century sermon on the three estates', *Leeds Studies in English*, ns 22 (1991), 109.

that were not based on the production of goods or any other economic activity.

While it may be the case, as Doyle argues, that 'power differentials unrelated to wealth are quite inconceivable',[15] this does not mean that inequalities in the social distribution of power and status in medieval England were therefore simply the *result* of economic inequalities. On the contrary, the acquisition of wealth, the mode of its possession and the ability to transmit wealth to successors fundamentally differed between the lay and ecclesiastical magnates. While the lay landowners enjoyed a personal ownership of property which meant that they could pass it on to their heirs, the access to the institutional wealth of the Church enjoyed by the higher ecclesiastics was the result of success in specifically clerical career paths. Lay and ecclesiastical landlords in medieval England were themselves certainly aware of their shared *class* interests: for example, in using the law to keep down wages in the aftermath of the Black Death. But they were also aware of their conflicting interests as members of separate *orders*, as in the competition over land and wealth. By the thirteenth century the ecclesiastical landlords possessed almost half of all agricultural land in England, and the laity expressed its desire to set a limit on such acquisitions by persuading the state to issue 'mortmain' legislation regulating the conditions under which the Church might receive new grants. It is, therefore, perfectly possible to reconcile an analysis of medieval society based on classes with one based on orders, provided that we realise that these are matters of analytical convenience, and that both offer useful insights into the social reality of medieval England.

Once we see individuals as the members of multiple social groups, there is no need to limit the social groups of medieval England either to the classes of Marxist historiography or to the three orders set out in medieval social theory itself. As in other societies, individuals could also be ranked socially as the members of status groups defined by language, race, culture or religion. A classic example of this in medieval England is provided by the Jews, who, despite the individual wealth of a number of prominent Jewish moneylenders, never as a group enjoyed substantial political power or high social status. As a result, in the thirteenth century the Jews suffered increasingly from punitive royal taxation and restrictive legislation until, eventually, they were expelled from England in 1290 – a precedent that other European states were later to follow.

---

[15] W. Doyle, 'Myths of order and ordering myths', in M. L. Bush, ed., *Social Orders and Social Classes in Europe since 1500* (1992), p. 221.

In recent years, historians have increasingly devoted their attention to another of the social axes of medieval society, that of gender, a form of inequality which was central in determining access to wealth, status and power in late medieval England. Traditionally, if society has been seen as a pyramid, sociologists and historians have tended to see the family, not the individual, as its basic building block. It is membership of a family that is regarded as determining access to economic resources, power and status, and as the main mechanism for the transmission of such privileges. Certainly it has been argued that the family was the most basic social unit known to medieval society itself.[16] Yet writers within the medieval period were also aware of the social differences *within* families. As the legal treatise known as *Bracton* put it in the thirteenth century, 'Women differ from men in many respects for their position is inferior to that of men'.[17]

It is this inequality between the genders, the ways in which the biological differences between male and female were culturally and socially interpreted in historically specific ways, which has been emphasised by feminist social theorists and historians. For these writers, medieval society was profoundly patriarchal: that is, characterised by a systematic subordination of women to men and the consequent relative exclusion of women from wealth, status and power. While women may have enjoyed agency and initiative as individuals, their social position was also characterised by a structured inferiority to men of their own class in terms of inheritance and property ownership, economic opportunities, access to education, legal rights and enjoyment of formal political power. Such historians tend to stress the social disabilities common to all women. As Bennett put it, peasant women can be seen as facing 'limitations fundamentally similar to those restricting women of the more privileged sectors of medieval society'.[18] Similarly, Mate argues that shared disabilities and experiences were, at least in the sense that these combined to prevent any transformation of women's status, 'more fundamental' than those of class.[19] All women were confronted by the reality of their systematic social inferiority, even though women of different classes

---

[16] M. Keen, *Chivalry* (New Haven, CT, 1984), p. 160. The 'family', in medieval terms, could also be taken to imply the *familia*: the whole household, including servants. This is discussed further by Coss, below, pp. 46–50.

[17] G. E. Woodbine and Samuel E. Thorne, eds., *Bracton de legibus et consuetudinibus Angliae: Bracton on the laws and customs of England* (4 vols., Oxford, 1968–77), ii, pp. 29, 31.

[18] J. M. Bennett, *Women in the Medieval English Countryside* (Oxford, 1987), quotation at p. 6, also pp. 178, 185–9.

[19] M. E. Mate, *Daughters, Wives and Widows after the Black Death* (Woodbridge, 1998), quotation at p. 8, see also pp. 182, 192, 197.

experienced this subordination in different ways. In other words, not only peasants and landlords, or clergy and laity, but also men and women can be seen as distinct social groups whose members possessed a common position within the social distribution of power and privilege.

Once we see individuals as occupying a number of intersecting social positions, including those of class, order, gender and status group, the notion of late medieval England as a society of gradated orders can, in certain respects, be reconciled with the view that this was a society divided along class lines. However, where the two approaches remain funda-mentally opposed is in their assessment of the extent and significance of contemporary social conflict. This *was* an age of deference, as is shown by John Russell's concern with having each man literally in his proper place at the dinner table. But this could also be an age of ambition and of conflict, as Chaucer's Wife of Bath symbolised by her determination to enjoy first place when making offerings in church. Indeed, such 'quarrels for precedence seem at times less the occupational hazard of churchgoers in late medieval England than their principal occupation'.[20] One reason for emphasising the importance of conflict in medieval English society is that such conflict has been seen as a major determinant of long-term social change. It is to the forces that brought about social and economic change in medieval England that we now turn.

SOCIAL AND ECONOMIC CHANGE: TRADE, POPULATION, CLASS AND MONEY

If medieval English society can be understood in terms of a variety of overlapping forms of social inequality, how can we explain the long-term changes that this structure underwent? In particular, is it possible to identify a 'prime mover' of social and economic change in late medieval England? For the earliest historians of the medieval English economy and society, writing in the nineteenth and early twentieth centuries, the main determinant of social and economic change was the long-term growth of the market and an increasing division of labour within society, which allowed an increase in economic efficiency and productivity. This approach was based on the work of Adam Smith, for whom the market was the dynamic agent of economic growth in overcoming the stagnant 'natural economy' of the countryside, a growth embodied in the rise of

---

[20] S. H. Rigby, 'The Wife of Bath, Christine de Pizan and the medieval case for women', *Chaucer Review*, 35 (2000), 139–40; E. Duffy, *The Stripping of the Altars: traditional religion in England, 1400–1580* (New Haven, CT, 1992), pp. 125–7 (quotation at p. 126).

towns, trade, manufactures and the middle class. This model of economic development, in terms of the unilinear rise of a market economy, provided the framework within which pioneering historians such as Ashley, Cunningham, Lipson and Pirenne made sense of medieval economic development.[21]

For Lipson, medieval rural society could be analysed in terms of the 'classic' manor on which the landlord's demesnes were worked by the labour services provided by unfree tenants. This system 'was essentially adapted to an age of natural economy' since, when money was scarce, manorial obligations had to be rendered in other forms, such as labour services. It followed that the manorial system 'could only break down when the supply of money became sufficiently great and its circulation sufficiently rapid to familiarize men with its efficiency as an economic instrument'. Lipson did emphasise the impact of the Black Death and of late medieval population decline upon the evolution of the manor; without such a demographic downturn, the decline of the manor would have been 'an infinitely slower process'. Nevertheless, even his analysis of the impact of plague was couched in terms of the shift from a natural to a money economy, since a decline in population meant an increase in the money per head of the population. The greater prevalence of a money economy, encouraged also by plunder from the Anglo-French wars, by the growth of the woollen industry and by the expansion of towns and trade, stimulated the commutation of labour services and allowed the peasants to obtain their freedom.[22] Similarly, for Cunningham, Ashley and Pirenne, the impetus for the decline of the self-sufficient manor came from outside, from the growth of international trade and the consequent development of towns and of new urban classes of merchants and artisans. Agriculture was modernised under the impact of commercialisation, urbanisation and the shift to a money economy, all of which stimulated innovation by allowing landlords to assess the profitability of their estates. The decay of the seigniorial system advanced hand in hand with the development of commerce since the commutation of labour services and the rise of money rents were explicable only as the result of the contemporary growth of industry and exchange.

---

[21] W. J. Ashley, *An Introduction to English Economic History and Theory* (1888); W. J. Ashley, *The Economic Organization of England* (1914); W. Cunningham, *The Growth of English Industry and Commerce during the Early and Middle Ages* (Cambridge, 1915); E. Lipson, *The Economic History of England*, I (1915).

[22] Lipson, *Economic History of England*, I (6th edn, 1956), pp. 88–95, 102–29.

In this perspective, the dichotomic and the gradated approaches to social stratification do not necessarily constitute competing ways of conceiving of medieval society. Instead, these two forms of social stratification are seen as succeeding one another chronologically. As Du Boulay put it, by the fifteenth century 'the original exclusive contrast in western European society between warring noble and cultivating peasant had been all but overcome. It was destroyed by progress, that is the creation and then the redistribution of wealth, and the foundation of intermediate classes whose ambitions pressed ever upwards in imitation of supposedly aristocratic behaviour'. For those who hold this view, the doctrine of the three orders is seen as having still had some semblance of reality as a description of English society as late as the start of the fourteenth century, but by the end of the fifteenth century it had been replaced by a new picture of society, one which emphasised the emergence of new and diverse social groups.[23]

Yet while some writers, particularly literary scholars, continue to see the period after the Black Death of the mid fourteenth century in terms of the rise of a 'bourgeoisie' inhabiting a 'new world' of money, trade, profit and economic individualism,[24] this once dominant Smithian orthodoxy was, in the second half of the twentieth century, replaced by a new paradigm: one which offered an alternative chronology and explanation of medieval English social and economic development. This approach, associated with the work of historians such as Postan, Miller, Hatcher and Titow, differed from 'the rise of a money economy' model in three main ways. Firstly, instead of being based on the economics of Adam Smith, it appealed to the theories of Thomas Malthus and David Ricardo. Secondly, as a result, population replaced trade as the main dynamic underlying long-term development. Thirdly, as opposed to the unilinear conception of change offered by the Smithian school, the so-called 'neo-Malthusian' or 'neo-Ricardian' model emphasised the fluctuating and even reversible nature of economic and social development under the impact of the rise and fall of population.

Malthus argued that, in normal conditions, population will tend to grow in a geometric progression (2, 4, 8, 16, 32, 64, etc.). However,

---

[23] F. R. H. Du Boulay, *An Age of Ambition* (1970), p. 65. See also Keen, *English Society*, pp. 4–11; S. L. Waugh, *England in the Reign of Edward III* (Cambridge, 1991), p. 24; J. Bolton, '"The world upside down": plague as an agent of social and economic change', in W. M. Ormrod and P. G. Lindley, eds., *The Black Death in England* (Stamford, 1996), p. 21.

[24] D. Aers, *Chaucer* (Brighton, 1986), pp. 18–20; S. Knight, *Geoffrey Chaucer* (Oxford, 1986), pp. 74, 78, 127–8, 131–4; J. Coleman, *English Literature in History: medieval readers and writers* (1981), pp. 17, 129, 133.

because of what Ricardo identified as a tendency towards diminishing returns in agriculture, the food supply needed to support this growing population could only increase in an arithmetic progression (2, 4, 6, 8, 10, 12, etc.). Thus a trebling of the labour input in agriculture would not necessarily bring about a corresponding trebling in the output of food: the *total* amount of grain produced would rise, but per capita productivity would tend to fall. As a result, living standards would suffer as a surplus population came to press on the available food, land and employment opportunities. One solution would be to cultivate more land but, as Ricardo argued, since the best agricultural land tends to be occupied first, newly colonised land was likely to be less productive. Doubling the area under cultivation would not, therefore, lead to a doubling of agricultural output: once again society was faced with the problem of diminishing returns. Malthus believed that the growing pressure of population on resources would eventually be relieved in two ways. The first was the 'preventive' check of lower fertility, as poverty and lack of economic opportunities forced people to postpone marriage and so to produce fewer children. The second was the 'positive' check of higher mortality, as poverty made people susceptible to famine and disease. Eventually, by means of these self-correcting mechanisms, the surplus population would be removed and the pressure on resources would abate, allowing the whole cycle to begin once more.

For those who emphasise the rise and fall of population as the prime mover of social and economic change, the centuries before *c.* 1300 in England can be seen as a long phase of demographic growth (an 'A-phase' in Malthusian terms). The absence of regular censuses means that any estimates of the population of medieval England can only be extremely approximate. Nevertheless, it seems likely that at the time of Domesday Book in 1086, England had about two million inhabitants. Postan estimated that, by the start of the fourteenth century, this could perhaps have trebled to six million people, and his figure was widely accepted by economic historians working in the second half of the twentieth century.[25] To these neo-Malthusians, the results of population growth on such a scale were disastrous for the lower ranks of society in the later thirteenth and early fourteenth centuries. Firstly, although arable production did increase through land reclamation, the total supply of food did not keep pace with the growth in demand, resulting in a long-term tendency for grain prices to rise. The newly cultivated land was likely to

[25] For more recent and more conservative estimates, see below, pp. 25–7.

have been of poorer quality, while yields on the older land would tend to decline as a result of the growing shortage of animals, and thus of manure, as producers shifted from pasture to arable in order to feed the growing number of mouths. Secondly, with a growing demand for land confronting a relatively fixed supply, the average size of a peasant holding declined while the level of rents and of other renders such as entry fines rose. Thirdly, a rising population, many of whom were smallholders unable to feed themselves from their holdings, meant a glut of labour on the market and a consequent fall in real wages. However, if smallholders and labourers suffered during the generations immediately before the Black Death, landlords, whether ecclesiastical or lay, tended to benefit. Those lords who produced directly for the market from their demesnes were able to sell grain at a high price and to take advantage of low wages; those lords who preferred to lease out their land were able to obtain relatively high levels of rent as a result of the rising demand for land.

For neo-Malthusians, the imbalance between population and the resources available to support it could not continue for ever: by the early fourteenth century much of the population was on the edge of subsistence and the checks on population growth had come into play. The series of wet summers and widespread animal disease from 1315 to 1322 may have been an accident of nature, but in Malthusian terms their impact was socially determined by the existence of a large, 'disaster-sensitive' sector of the population. Perhaps 15 per cent of the population died in the famines of 1315, 1316 and 1317. For Postan, indeed, it was these years of crisis, rather than the arrival of the Black Death, that marked the onset of the late medieval 'B-phase' (in Malthusian terms) of declining population. The plague itself hastened such decline, the initial outbreak in 1348–9 perhaps killing as many as 45 per cent of the population. Further epidemics in 1361–2, 1369 and 1375 made this sudden shock into a long-term trend: Razi calculated, for example, that at Halesowen, in the West Midlands, the adult male population fell by almost 40 per cent between 1345–9 and 1371–5.[26] There followed at least fifteen major national epidemics in the century after 1375, quite apart from many local outbreaks. Whether these epidemics were actually outbreaks of bubonic and pneumonic plague, as most historians tend to assume, or whether they were the result of some other disease, such as anthrax or a viral fever, is a controversial issue. What is important for our purposes, however, is the impact of epidemic disease on late medieval population and, as a result,

[26] Z. Razi, *Life, Marriage and Death in a Medieval Parish* (Cambridge, 1980).

on the English economy and society. By the time of the first poll tax of 1377, England's population was, at most, around two and three-quarter million – less than half the figure that Postan calculated for *c*. 1300. Yet, as late as the 1520s, when recovery had already begun, England's population had still not regained its 1377 levels, with a figure of two and a quarter million or even less being likely.

In these circumstances, all the trends of the twelfth and thirteenth centuries went into reverse. With an excess of land for the level of population, arable land fell out of cultivation or was put to other uses. Secondly, the increase in land per capita meant a glut of land on the market with consequent lower levels of rent, entry fines and other renders. With lords competing for tenants, the English peasantry was able to demand concessions from the lords so that, by 1500, the villein (unfree) tenures once typical of over half the peasantry had virtually disappeared, having been replaced by new forms of free leasehold and copyhold.[27] Thirdly, there was now an over-capacity in grain production, which meant that, in the long term, grain prices fell – although this tendency only set in after 1376. Finally, high mortality rates from plague and the consequent availability of land for those who survived meant a reduction in the numbers of people offering their labour on the market and a consequent rise in real wages. With low grain prices, the withering away of labour services and high labour costs, many lords now leased out their demesnes or switched to pasture with its relatively low labour inputs. All these trends are well established. More problematic is whether the decline in total production and the squeeze on manorial profits in this period should be seen as signs of economic 'recession', especially as this recession was originally seen by its modern proponents as not necessarily having involved 'falling *per capita* output, falling living standards or rising unemployment'.[28] Most controversial of all has been the fate of England's towns and the question of whether, in contrast with the pre-plague expansion of town life, the late medieval fall in national population led to urban 'decline', 'decay' and 'desolation', or whether this was a period of rising living standards for townspeople in an era of geographical redistribution of wealth towards the towns.

In recent years, a gender dimension has been added to this population-based analysis. The later middle ages have been seen by some historians as not only an era of improved conditions for peasants and labourers but also

---

[27] These forms of tenure are discussed by Campbell, below, pp. 213–15.
[28] J. Hatcher, *Plague, Population and the English Economy, 1348–1530* (1977), p. 47. See, however, J. Hatcher, 'The great slump of the mid-fifteenth century', in R. H. Britnell and J. Hatcher, eds., *Progress and Problems in Medieval England* (Cambridge, 1996), pp. 261–3.

as a period of particular social advance for women. For historians such as
Goldberg, the century after the Black Death was one when women enjoyed
a growing economic independence. As tenants, women were, in an era of
high mortality and low male replacement rates, now more likely to acquire
land, either as heiresses or by their widow's right of dower. As labourers,
women shared in the general rise in real wages and, given the types of work
in which they were most likely to be employed, should have benefited from
the disproportionate rise in the wages of the unskilled and the reduction in
wage differentials. With skilled labour in short supply, women could find
employment in jobs which had once been the preserve of men, as smiths,
tanners, carpenters, tilers and so on. In a period of labour mobility, women
may have been particularly attracted to the towns as servants and as
workers in the expanding textile and other industries whose products were,
in an age of high wages and cheap food, in increasing demand. In a time of
labour shortage, householders may have attempted to guarantee themselves a supply of labour by the practice, familiar from the sixteenth
century, of using resident servants, often young unmarried men and
women. It is possible that the demographic effect of these increased economic opportunities was to delay marriage for women, with a consequent
reduction in marriage and fertility rates. We are accustomed to think of the
plague-ridden later middle ages as the 'golden age of bacteria' or, because
of the consequent labour shortage, as the 'golden age of the labourer'.
Now, historians such as Barron would also encourage us to think of this
period as a golden age for women.[29]

While still emphasising the centrality of the rise and fall of population
to economic and social change, this new approach to women's work
provides a challenge to the traditional Malthusian assumption that high
living standards would lead to earlier marriage, higher fertility rates and
population growth. By contrast, those who argue that high wages resulted
in deferred marriage would see the late medieval period as one in which,
in addition to high mortality rates, there was actually a decline in the
fertility rate. It would seem that late medieval people adopted what was,
by Malthusian standards, a 'perverse' response to rising living standards.
Historians such as Poos and Smith have suggested that late medieval
England may therefore have exhibited Hajnal's 'Western European'
marriage pattern, characterised by relatively low fertility produced by a
tendency to 'late' marriage and by a high proportion of women never

[29] C. M. Barron, 'The "golden age" of women in medieval London', *Reading Medieval Studies*, 15 (1989), 35–58.

marrying (perhaps similar to conditions in sixteenth-century England, when the average age of marriage was 27–8 for men and 25–6 for women, and when perhaps 10 per cent of women remained single).

However, even those who stress the gains made by women in the century after the Black Death remain pessimistic about their ability to hang onto these gains in the longer term. The problem for late medieval women was that, since the social position of any particular individual is the product of the meeting point of many different axes or dimensions of inequality, there was no reason why a reduction of the exclusion they experienced in one dimension of social inequality (such as economic opportunities) would necessarily result in corresponding gains in other spheres of their lives (such as political power). As in other pre-industrial societies, it is extremely difficult to speak of a single, unitary status of women in later medieval England. When women's position came under threat once more, whether through economic recession and a slump in demand in the mid to late fifteenth century or through revived population growth and an increase in the supply of labour in the late fifteenth and sixteenth centuries, the fact that their economic gains had not been accompanied by a growth of their legal rights or political power meant that they were ill-equipped to defend themselves. Rather than presenting pre-industrial society in terms of a unilinear growth or decline of women's social exclusion, the approach of historians such as Goldberg and Barron emphasises how women's wealth, status and power could fluctuate between and within the late medieval and early modern periods. Moreover, these fluctuations were caused by, yet also actively fed back into, contemporary demographic and economic trends.

The Malthusian/Ricardian model was a work of brilliance, which, in its stress on the rise and fall of population, provided a unified explanation of a mass of empirical information and established many long-term socio-economic trends. Inevitably, of course, its bold claims can be criticised in a number of ways. Firstly, it tended to treat the population growth of the twelfth and thirteenth centuries as the inevitable outcome of the continued availability of new land, of internal peace and of the absence of epidemic disease. The possibility that the growth of population was itself the consequence of other economic trends, such as the growth of markets and the impact of commerce, tended to be neglected (even though Postan himself raised this as an issue).[30] Secondly, the absence of registers of births,

[30] M. M. Postan, *Essays on Medieval Agriculture and General Problems of the Medieval Economy* (Cambridge, 1973), pp. 12, 16.

marriages and deaths before the sixteenth century means that it is extremely difficult to provide evidence to corroborate the Malthusian deduction that, by the early fourteenth century, the preventive check of deferred marriage had come into play. Indeed, whether the western European marriage pattern, with its late marriage and low fertility rates, already existed before the Black Death or whether women then married relatively 'early' (in their late teens or early twenties) has provoked much debate.

Thirdly, it is not clear that the famines of the early fourteenth century were a self-correcting, Malthusian positive check on a population that had reached the limits of sustainability. After all, any pre-industrial agricultural society would have found it hard to cope with three years of disastrous harvests. The poor yields, famines and animal disease of the years 1315–22 do not necessarily have to be seen as the consequence of over-population; rather, they may simply have been the product of what were, in economic terms, exogenous factors such as the deterioration of weather resulting from short- or long-term climatic change. Fourthly, even if we accepted that the famines did constitute a Malthusian check on population growth, it is by no means clear that England's population had entered a long-term decline in the decades before the arrival of the Black Death. It is quite possible that it stabilised after the famines. It is even possible, as Razi suggested for Halesowen, that the famines functioned as a safety valve which released the pressure of over-population and allowed population growth to resume. A fifth criticism of the Malthusian approach is that, even if population continued to decline, or at least failed to recover, after the second decade of the fourteenth century, this was not necessarily the expression of some Malthusian demographic 'oscillation'. Other, non-Malthusian factors may have affected living standards (and thus levels of mortality and fertility), such as the growth of royal purveyance and increasing demands for taxation to finance the Hundred Years War.

A sixth criticism of the Malthusian approach, at least in its original formulation, was that Postan was unwilling to ascribe a primary role in history to what, in terms of Malthusian theory, seems to be a historical accident: that is, the arrival of plague in England in 1348. Instead, at first, Postan presented the prolonged decline in population of the later middle ages as 'a natural punishment for earlier over-expansion', with long-colonised land exhausted, marginal land abandoned and new land not available to support any growth in population.[31] Yet, given that yields of

---

[31] *Ibid.*, pp. 12–16; M. M. Postan, 'Medieval agrarian society in its prime: England', in M. M. Postan, ed., *The Cambridge Economic History of Europe*, I (Cambridge, 1966), pp. 569–70.

wheat, barley and oats in 1400 were probably very similar to those of 1200, it is unlikely that late medieval England was a place where population growth was constrained by soil exhaustion. Certainly, in his later writings, Postan himself put an increasing emphasis on the role of the Black Death and of later epidemics in keeping down population in the later middle ages; and it is the impact of plague that has been stressed by historians such as Chambers, Hatcher and Platt. Even if population was already in decline before 1348 (which, as we have seen, is itself controversial), the arrival of plague did not simply accelerate a trend that was already in existence, or constitute a self-correcting mechanism brought into play by over-population. Rather, in the scale of its impact and the nature of its operation, the advent of plague signals the establishment of a new demographic regime in which there were persistently high levels of mortality despite marked improvements in living standards. The arrival of plague may have been related to the environmental and climatic disturbances of this period but, in economic terms, it was an exogenous or autonomous demographic determinant: one whose impact seems not to have been related to standards of living but rather, unlike strict Malthusian checks, affected rich and poor alike.

Finally, the extent to which women were able to take advantage of the population decline of the later middle ages has also generated debate. One problem is that any deductions about changes in the age of marriage, in fertility rates and in the numbers of women employed as servants must be extremely speculative in the era before the introduction of registers of births, marriages and deaths. Another is that historians such as Bennett and Mate have offered a far less optimistic interpretation of the social position of women in this period. They stress how, even during the late medieval labour shortage, women tended to work in low-skilled, low-status, low-paid jobs, and that they also tended to be intermittent workers, jumping from job to job or juggling several tasks at once.[32] Except in the largest towns, there is little evidence that women were ever formally apprenticed. In the countryside, women's paid work was often irregular and usually poorly rewarded: on the lords' demesnes dairy work was a female preserve but dairy managers were always male. The centralisation of the brewing trade in the hands of a small number of professional beer-brewers meant a reduction in the chances for women to earn money by selling their surplus domestic ale production. Women's

[32] J. M. Bennett, 'Medieval women, modern women: across the great divide', in D. Aers, ed., *Culture and History, 1350–1600* (New York, 1992), pp. 147–75.

work was vital to the household but its economic centrality did not bring about commensurate social power or legal rights. Neither did the decline in the male replacement rate and consequent increase in the number of female heirs mean that women enjoyed any more social power, since heiresses were particularly likely to be married at an early age and thus to surrender most of their property rights for life to their husbands. Among the elite, the rights of women who held property on a joint tenure with their husbands were admittedly more secure, but only a minority of women acquired land in this way. At a lower social level the greater availability of land may have made widows, who held a share of their husband's land for their lifetime, less attractive as marriage partners.

Yet, for all the criticisms that were made of the Malthusian/Ricardian approach, it was unlikely to be abandoned by historians until some more convincing alternative became available. Rival schools of thought thus sought to identify other candidates for the role of prime mover of late medieval economic and social development. In particular, the Marxist stress on class and class conflict was developed by Brenner into an alternative account of the underlying dynamic of social and economic change, one that is as comprehensive and as stimulating as the Malthusian approach which it sought to replace. Brenner offers two main criticisms of the demographic model. The first is that the Malthusian account is based on an inherent tendency of population growth to outstrip resources. Brenner thus seeks to provide a Marxist explanation for the lack of innovation in medieval agriculture, based on the nature of peasant agriculture and on the surplus-extraction relationship between landlords and peasants. On the one hand, feudal landlords had little incentive to innovate, as they had alternative ways of increasing their income through raising the levels of rents and dues rendered by the peasants, particularly those liable to the restrictions and obligations of unfree tenure. On the other hand, the existence of such renders meant that peasants had little incentive to invest or improve, and many who existed at the level of subsistence actually lacked the resources to do so. While he accepts the Malthusian description of the population of early fourteenth-century England as impoverished and under-employed, Brenner stresses that such over-population was not a natural phenomenon or the expression of some universal law of demography, but was rather the product of a particular system of class and property relations.

Brenner's second criticism of the demographic approach is that while the changing balance of supply and demand can offer an explanation of changes in, say, the relative prices of grain and pastoral goods, such an approach is less successful when it comes to explaining changes in social relations. The Malthusian model seeks to account for social change in terms of population-based changes in the supply and demand for land and labour: when population was rising, the landlords were able to impose their terms on their tenants and employees; when it was falling, peasants and labourers were able to demand better conditions and benefit from the social redistribution of wealth created by high wages and cheap land and food. Brenner's counter-argument to this population-based model of change is that although it seems perfectly logical when England is seen in isolation, it breaks down when seen in a comparative perspective: in other societies, identical population trends have been accompanied by exactly the opposite social results. He thus claims that, in the later middle ages, both eastern and western Europe had a *shared* demographic trend (population decline), yet experienced *divergent* social developments (the growth of peasant freedom in the west, including England, and the rise of serfdom in the east). Certainly, the low labour:land ratio which is traditionally used to explain the gains of the English peasantry in the later middle ages has also been invoked, paradoxically, to account for the social reverses experienced by eastern European peasants as their landlords resorted to serfdom to provide the labour needed to work their demesnes. For Brenner, falling population cannot explain *in itself* why serfdom or freedom prevails. Instead, such social outcomes have to be explained in terms of the relative ability of lords and peasants to mobilise to achieve their goals. He argues that, in the late medieval west, peasant communities were relatively powerful, with strong forms of collective production and social organisation, and so were able to resist the landlords and obtain their freedom. In the east, by contrast, peasants lacked this collective form of organisation and so were unable to resist the seigniorial offensive which, in tandem with the efforts of the state, resulted in their eventual enserfment.

Inevitably, Brenner's account of medieval social and economic change attracted a number of criticisms. For instance, far from the landlords' increasing appropriation of surplus from unfree peasants being the cause of the Malthusian crisis of the early fourteenth century, it would seem that the inelastic rents characteristic of unfree customary tenures may, ironically, have actually come to protect peasants against market forces by keeping rents below the level that reflected the real demand for land. Another criticism is that it is as difficult to provide a strictly Marxist explanation of the impact of plague as it is to give a strictly Malthusian account of it: both approaches have to recognise that plague, with its massive social and economic consequences, was an autonomous factor.

Nevertheless, even if we accept demographic fluctuations (or at least those caused by exogenous factors such as plague) as givens, Brenner's central claim that such trends have no *automatic* impact upon agrarian class structure is well made. After all, it does seem to be an inconsistency that when manorialism and serfdom in the earlier middle ages can be said to have 'evolved in response to a scarcity of people', a similar population scarcity in the later middle ages is seen as resulting in 'rising real incomes and the loosening and eventual dissolution of the bonds of serfdom'.[33] Brenner's point is that, in itself, the land:labour ratio will not tell us which of these two apparently logical outcomes actually occurs.

Both the Malthusian model and Brenner's Marxist approach stress the constraints on agricultural *supply* as the key to crisis and over-population in medieval England. However, more recent approaches to medieval economic change have turned our attention towards shifts in *demand*, which were not always based on the rise and fall of population. One such challenge to the population orthodoxy comes in the form of 'monetarist' accounts of price changes in terms of fluctuations in the money supply. For historians such as Mayhew, Spufford and Day, the level of prices, wages and rents does not simply reflect changes in population. Rather, the monetarist approach is based on the quantity theory of money, which claims that the value of money is inversely proportional to the quantity of it in circulation. Money is like any other commodity: the more there is of it, the lower the value of each individual piece of it. If there is a good harvest, the value of each individual unit of grain falls; similarly, if there is an increase in the money supply, each individual piece of money is worth less, and people have to offer more of it in order to obtain the commodity they wish to purchase so that prices rise. Conversely, a decline in the money supply will tend to be associated with a period of price deflation. Thus the stock of money in circulation is itself an independent variable which affects levels of demand and of prices and so has an impact on peasants' living standards and lords' manorial policies. For instance, Nightingale has argued that the economic recession of the mid fifteenth century was not simply the result of population decline, since earlier plague outbreaks had been followed by marked urban and commercial growth. Rather, this slump was the product of a decline in the money supply and an associated shortage of credit, the effects of which were to reduce demand, incomes and the number of commercial transactions. Monetary, urban and commercial depression brought about a corresponding slump in agriculture.

---

[33] J. Hatcher, 'English serfdom and villeinage: towards a reassessment', *P&P*, 90 (1981), 26–7, 37–8.

In turn, this slump then had social effects of its own, concentrating land-holding into fewer hands and so polarising village society into employers and wage-labourers.[34] Whereas the pioneers of economic history saw a unilinear tendency towards the growth of a money economy as eventually under-mining the manorial system, the final demise of manorialism is now seen as actually having occurred in an age of low prices caused by a decline in the money supply.

The importance of shifts in demand in the medieval economy is also stressed in the work of historians such as Britnell and Campbell, who have returned to the Smithian stress on commercialisation as a dynamic force for change in the countryside. Traditionally, historians have emphasised the centrality of subsistence grain production to medieval agriculture. With the economy geared to meeting the consumption needs of peasants and feudal households, the result was said to have been a relative uniformity across England in the types of grain and animals produced, a uniformity altered primarily by 'natural' factors such as soil, climate and topography. Of course, writers such as Postan were aware of the ways in which population growth could lead to a growing commer-cialisation of the economy with the emergence of markets for land, labour and food. Nevertheless, both the Malthusian/Ricardian approach and Brenner's Marxist model emphasise the lack of innovation and the inelasticity of agricultural supply within the medieval economy and its consequent tendency towards demographic crisis.

The thrust of more recent work has been to remind us of the extent of commercialisation (and hence of consumerism) and to emphasise its positive impact on agricultural production. In the twelfth and thirteenth centuries, agrarian society was being increasingly integrated into a market economy. On the one hand, particularly from *c.* 1180, the landlords adopted direct management of their demesnes so as to produce grain, wool and livestock for the market. On the other hand, even the meanest peasant-producers were obliged to sell grain and cash crops, such as wool, in order to pay their money rents, manorial fines and royal taxes. Literally thousands of weekly markets were formally recognised in the period 1200 to 1349, so that most villages would have had access to at least two or three nearby markets. Furthermore, much trading, including that of landlords with their own tenants, avoided any formal regulation. Whilst the tra-ditional view of those such as Lipson emphasised the post-plague period

---

[34] P. Nightingale, 'England and the European depression of the mid-fifteenth century', *Journal of European Economic History*, 26 (1997), 631–56.

as a 'new world' of trade, towns and money, historians such as Miller and
Hatcher, Bolton, Britnell and Christopher Dyer now stress the century
and a half *before* the Black Death as a key period for the evolution of an
English merchant class, a commercial economy and a local marketing
structure. Similarly, the main growth in the urban proportion of
England's medieval population seems to have been accomplished in the
two centuries after Domesday Book, when urban population rose from
perhaps 10 per cent of the national total to as many as 15 per cent or even
20 per cent by 1300. If national population had doubled or more, the size
of the non-agricultural population that had to be supported by the
countryside had increased even more rapidly.

With the growth of trade came the possibility of increased regional
specialisation whose benefits could, as writers such as Persson have
suggested, offset the Ricardian tendency to diminishing returns. Such
economic specialisation, rather than uniformity, can be seen within the
sub-regions of East Anglia, with the Fenland producing salt and dairy
goods, the Breckland concentrating on wool, rabbits and barley, southern
Suffolk shifting to dairying and textiles, and north-eastern Norfolk producing wheat and particularly malting barley. The urban growth of this
period also encouraged agricultural commercialisation and specialisation,
a specialisation that owed more to market factors than to local variations
in soil and climate. Pastoral goods were far more easily and cheaply
transported to market than bulky arable products. The annual export of
45,000 sacks of raw wool from England in the first decade of the fourteenth century, when the trade was at its peak, represented the wool of
over ten million sheep and provided a valuable source of income not just
to manorial lords but also to the peasant-producers whose flocks
accounted for the bulk of this high-quality wool output. Nevertheless, the
impact of growing demand was also felt in arable production. In particular, the demand generated by the London market had a marked
influence on the type of grains produced by manorial demesnes and upon
the intensity of arable production methods, whilst the capital also made
its influence felt on land use in terms of its demands for wood for fuel.
Historians now emphasise the innovations made in this period in response
to rising demand. New crops were introduced, such as vetches for fodder,
and intensive cropping systems were adopted, as in east Norfolk. There
were also improvements in vehicle design and in horse-harnessing and
shoeing, which meant that horses ceased to be primarily pack animals and
were increasingly used to haul produce to market by cart, so removing one
of the main constraints on the spread of the market economy.

Thus, whilst the Marxist model traditionally emphasised the post-plague period as the crucial era in the long transition from feudalism to capitalism in England, the commercialisation model stresses the twelfth and thirteenth centuries as the period when agriculture became oriented to the market, the size of units of production grew and dependence upon wage labour became more marked. Whether the commercialisation of the economy in the twelfth and thirteenth centuries was primarily generated by the population growth of this period or whether commercialisation was itself a key factor in stimulating such growth is a 'chicken and egg' issue. The important point is that, once it was called into existence, commercialisation became an active causal factor in its own right. As a result, when population fell back to its former levels after 1348, commercialisation and consumerism remained potent forces, even if in economic terms the pressures towards the specialisation and intensification of arable production were now reduced.

However, it is not just Marxist assumptions that are challenged by this new emphasis on the impact of commercialisation in the pre-plague era. Rather, Campbell's recent work on medieval English agriculture also questions Malthusian and Ricardian views about the insufficiency of English economic development in this period. For Campbell, whilst the traditional figure of around two million for England's population in 1086 seems plausible, the often-cited figure of six million or more for the early fourteenth century may be an over-estimate. He argues that, given the area under cultivation at this date, and assuming similar grain yields from peasant producers as were found on the landlords' demesnes, it is doubtful that English medieval agriculture could have supported more than five million people, and that the level of the population on the eve of the famines was perhaps four and a half million.[35] England's population may therefore have grown by 125 per cent between 1086 and 1300. Campbell suggests that, through colonisation and a more intensive use of the land, the area under crops had increased by about 89 per cent over the same period. If average yields per acre had increased by 20 per cent, the maximum that Campbell sees as possible, then agriculture would have been producing around 127 per cent more in 1300 than it had in 1086. On Malthusian and Ricardian assumptions, it would have been unlikely for a doubling of England's population to have been matched by a corresponding increase in output. Yet, on Campbell's figures, it would seem

---

[35] For these figures, and those that follow, see B. M. S. Campbell, *English Seigniorial Agriculture, 1250–1450* (Cambridge, 2000), ch. 8, and below p. 234.

that an increase in England's total population on this scale had been accompanied by a corresponding expansion in total arable output.[36] Others, such as Snooks, have offered even more optimistic assessments of English economic achievements and increases in this period.[37] It is therefore possible that rising population actually went hand in hand with increased food output and that population density was positively correlated with agricultural productivity, again challenging the logic both of the Malthusian/Ricardian model and of Brenner's Marxist assumption that feudal relations of production imposed an institutional constraint on matching increased demand with supply. Certainly, if levels of per capita productivity were roughly the same in 1300 as they had been in 1086, and the level of productivity at the time of Domesday Book had been compatible with a further two centuries of population growth, it would be difficult to see why England's population should be regarded as on the edge of Malthusian disaster at the beginning of the fourteenth century.

This 'neo-Smithian' approach has produced important work that has added much to our knowledge of economic change in medieval England. Nevertheless, the extent to which commercialisation stimulated agricultural development in pre-plague England remains a matter of controversy. As we have seen, the commercialisation model has certainly not raised previous estimates of the total population that English agriculture was able to support at the end of the thirteenth century. Moreover, all statistical calculations for medieval England are subject to wide margins of error. For example, the 20 per cent increase in per acre yields assumed by Campbell is actually the very maximum that is credible. If, as above, we postulate an increase in the sown area of 89 per cent between 1086 and 1300, but assume an increase of per acre yields on this larger area of 'only' 10 per cent, this would give us an increase in total grain output of 108 per cent with total population growth of 125 per cent, this would have put pressure on the food supply and on levels of per capita consumption. A final, and even more pessimistic, option would be to suggest that, since the lands added to the cultivated area after 1086 were likely to have been inherently poorer than those already in cultivation, even maintaining average per acre yields at their previous level would still have been quite an achievement, requiring either more intensive production on the old

---

[36] Net grain exports were probably less than 1 per cent of total grain production at this date and so can be ignored for the purpose of these calculations.

[37] G. D. Snooks, 'The dynamic role of the market in the Anglo-Norman economy and beyond, 1086–1300', in R. H. Britnell and B. M. S. Campbell, eds., *A Commercialising Economy: England 1086 to c. 1300* (Manchester, 1995), pp. 27–54.

lands or improvements to agriculture in the newly colonised areas. On the assumption that average per acre yields were similar in 1086 and 1300, an 89 per cent expansion of the sown area would give us a corresponding increase of about 89 per cent, compared with Campbell's posited growth in total population of 125 per cent.

Of course, all of these calculations would be cast in a more optimistic light if we adopted a figure for population in 1300 of as low as four million. But, equally, they would have far more pessimistic implications if we saw population as being as high as five million or more by that date. Campbell himself suggests that a shift away from brewing grains and fodder crops and towards bread grains and pottage crops would have yielded a higher food-extraction rate and produced an increase in processed grain kilocalories of between 100 per cent and 150 per cent. The lower of these figures would have allowed population to double from two million to four million without a decline in living standards, but would have posed more problems if England's population was nearer five million by 1300. The higher of the figures (150 per cent), however, would have been sufficient to support a population increase from two million to five million. Whether England's population doubled or trebled between 1086 and 1300 thus has extremely important consequences for how we assess its economic performance in this period.[38]

Early critics of the Malthusian approach to economic change, such as Russell and Harvey, centred their attacks on Malthusian claims about the impoverishment of the English peasantry in the late thirteenth and early fourteenth centuries. Yet, for all the criticisms of Malthusianism offered in recent work, a pessimism about the condition of much of the English peasantry at this date still seems plausible. As population grew, more and more of the rural population was made up of smallholders without sufficient land for subsistence and who were forced to offer their labour for declining real wages. The result was deteriorating mean living standards and relatively poor and monotonous diets for the majority. Whilst a small peasant elite would have benefited from high prices, cheap labour and rents set at below economic levels, many villagers would have been seriously malnourished. Poorer villagers may also have suffered from the tendency of smallholders to pay more rent per acre to manorial lords than those with larger holdings. They were also more likely to have been

---

[38] B. M. S. Campbell, 'England: land and people', in S. H. Rigby, ed., *A Companion to Britain in the Later Middle Ages* (Oxford, 2003), pp. 3–25; Dyer, *Making a Living*, p. 155.

paying an economic rather than a customary rent when they sub-leased land from other peasants.

For all the recent emphasis on the stimulus to agricultural production provided by rising demand, those areas which adopted new and more intensive methods of agriculture, such as eastern Norfolk, still seem to have been those that were blessed with exceptionally favourable geographical, economic and social conditions. One reason why such improvements remained the exception on the landlords' demesnes, despite the stimulus of increasing demand, was that the rising grain prices and ample supply of cheap labour characteristic of thirteenth-century England guaranteed high levels of income to landlords and provided them with little incentive to reinvest their profits. Besides, even though an intensified use of cheap labour made it possible for a growth in population to be accompanied by a growth in the output per unit of land, the output per unit of *labour* used to achieve this improvement would still tend to decline. Even if yields per acre did not fall, as the Malthusians suggested, then, output per capita was still in decline, with correspondingly negative implications for living standards. The real challenge for agriculture was to raise both land and labour productivity in a time of growing population; this goal was only to be achieved following the agricultural revolution of the post-medieval period.

For the Malthusians, Ricardians and Marxists, the inelasticity of supply characteristic of England's agriculture meant that it failed to respond to the growing demand created by the population growth of the thirteenth century. The pre-industrial economy had the potential to raise productivity, even without major technological change, but the institutional obstacles to realising this potential remained strong. In particular, the absence of the large, commercial farms using wage labour meant that medieval agriculture lacked the dynamism characteristic of agrarian capitalism. For Campbell, however, it is the lack of demand that was responsible for the failure of output to grow. This lack of demand was, in turn, based on the fact that medieval urban growth was rather limited, at least when compared to that of the early modern period when the massive expansion of London meant that much of England's agriculture had to be reorganised to meet the capital's appetite for food and raw materials. The problem facing pre-modern agricultural growth was thus one of a lack of incentives to produce, rather than of any inherent inability to match demand with supply.

But why was urban demand so restricted within the medieval economy? One answer – and one that takes us back to the supply-side of the economy – is that a low output of food per unit of land and per agricultural worker inevitably meant low living standards and set strict limits on the proportion of the population that could be supported in non-agricultural occupations. The economy was trapped in a vicious circle: a lack of demand limited supply; a low level of supply limited demand. An alternative approach, as we have seen, is to present the urban development needed to stimulate agricultural output as the product of 'exogenous' factors (that is, exogenous in terms of agriculture and population), such as long-distance trade, fiscal policy, monetary fluctuations and dynastic warfare. In itself, this approach is perfectly legitimate. It is simply that it would seem to confirm, rather than to undermine, the traditional view of the agrarian economy itself as lacking any systematic tendency to grow and so needing to be kick-started from outside.

Recent work thus still leaves us with a picture of an agricultural economy in which, from around 1260, population was continuing to rise but the arable area had reached its limits; in which yields per acre were static; in which intensified methods of agriculture were the exception and where even these were accompanied by a decline in per capita productivity; and in which real wages were falling and the population was pressing ever harder on the land. That these trends were to be experienced once more in the age of rising population of the sixteenth century does not make them any less real for the start of the fourteenth. It would therefore be misleading to polarise debate about England's agrarian economy in the pre-plague era as one about 'growth' versus 'stagnation' in agricultural production. Rather, the key issue is the extent to which the growth that undoubtedly did take place in total agricultural output, and which has been so emphasised in recent research, was adequate to meet the increasing demands placed upon it by an expanding population.

If historians are increasingly aware of the wide range of different forces working to produce change within medieval rural economic and social life, this is even more true for the sphere of industry and overseas trade where scholars have long stressed how non-economic factors, such as the consequences of royal policy, diplomacy and warfare, could have a decisive economic impact. A classic instance is the transformation of overseas trade in the later middle ages. Here, under the impact of the heavy royal customs duties on the export of wool introduced to pay for the Hundred Years War, England switched from being a producer of raw wool for the industries of Italy and the Low Countries to itself being a major exporter of manufactured woollen cloth to mainland Europe. Its cloth producers came to enjoy an unintended protection as the costs of the export duties on raw wool were passed on to foreign clothmakers in higher prices and to domestic wool producers in lower prices. This shift from wool to cloth was also associated with the growth of the trade of London, through which cloth exports were increasingly channelled, at the expense of the provincial ports. Once we accept this variety of factors at work in medieval agricultural, industrial and commercial development, the way is opened up for a far more precise chronology of social and economic change than that based on centuries-long phases of rising and falling population.

When we look at social and economic change in medieval England, as when we examined its social structure, we are confronted with a number of rival theoretical approaches. Inevitably, when historians from parti-cular schools of thought have struggled long and hard to identify some new piece of the historical jigsaw (population, class, the money supply, changes in demand or whatever), there is a natural tendency for them to proclaim theirs to be the most important piece of the puzzle. The sig-nificance of other explanatory factors is then downplayed as they come to be treated as analytical givens. Yet, in practice, the historical picture we eventually obtain is the product of all of the pieces of the jigsaw brought together. As with descriptions of social structure, so with explanations of social and economic change, it *is* possible to reconcile and combine particular aspects of apparently competing schools of thought. Once the initial heat of debate dies down, medieval historians have tended to opt for a theoretical eclecticism and to marry the strengths of each of the different approaches on offer. Once we abandon a quest for the prime mover of change, the theoretical frameworks adopted by historians become enabling rather than restrictive, opening up new areas of study (such as gender), suggesting new questions for us to ask of the empirical evidence, and reminding us of the importance of the multiplicity of causal factors (such as the money supply or class conflict) involved in any historical explanation. It is this encounter between theory and evidence that gives medieval social and economic history its fascination as, on the one hand, the need for empirical testing prevents theory from becoming circular and self-confirming whilst, on the other, the need to use evidence to test theoretical hypotheses prevents empirical research from lapsing into mere antiquarianism.

CHAPTER 2

An age of deference

Peter Coss

THE SOCIAL ORDER

At the beginning of the great treatise on the laws and customs of England known as *Bracton*, the anonymous early thirteenth-century author attempted a classification of persons.[1] His first and most basic division is between the free and the unfree, freedom being 'the natural power of every man to do what he pleases, unless forbidden by law or force'. A second division is between male, female and hermaphrodite. Yet another classification is between those who are in their own power (*potestas*) and those who are in the power of another. This power may be paternal, that is to say the power of the father, or it may be seigniorial power, which *Bracton* regards here as essentially power over bondmen (the unfree). This division is complicated by the fact that there are also people who may be said to be in the care rather than the power of others, and by wives, who are 'under the rod'.

These, then, are the basic divisions of mankind. But *Bracton* highlights a further difference. There are some men of great eminence who rule over others. In spiritual matters these are the pope and his archbishops, bishops and other lesser prelates. In temporal matters they are the king, earls and barons, magnates or vavasours – men, that is, 'of great dignity' – and knights. Kings, *Bracton* explains, associate such men in governing God's people, investing them with 'great honour, power and name' when they gird them with the sword, the sword signifying the defence of the realm. *Bracton* evidently sees the secular upper classes in essentially military terms and in terms of service to the king and to the state; there are echoes here of the traditional threefold division of mankind into those who fight, those who pray and those who work.

[1] G. E. Woodbine and Samuel E. Thorne, eds., *Bracton de legibus et consuetudinibus Angliae: Bracton on the laws and customs of England* (4 vols., Oxford, 1968–77), ii, pp. 29–38.

As an anatomy of contemporary society, this schema is manifestly inadequate. It is partial, in both senses of the word. The author of *Bracton* was a royal servant and an enthusiast for the emerging common law, and these factors inevitably determined his approach. Moreover, he omits significant sectors of society. No account is taken of the majority of the clergy, who may have constituted something in the region of 5 per cent of the total adult male population. Nor is there any reference to the growing urban population, which by 1300 accounted for perhaps as much as 20 per cent of English people. Furthermore, *Bracton* takes no account of the growing army of administrators – bailiffs, stewards and the like – who comprised an emergent group of 'professional people' in society.[2]

Yet, for all that it misses some of the more dynamic and sophisticated aspects of thirteenth-century society, *Bracton* nonetheless takes us into the very heart of the medieval social world. The social relations that governed the countryside conditioned so much of medieval life. The lack of freedom under the law – serfdom or villeinage – and the seigniorial power with which it was inextricably associated represented the most basic social relationship in the contemporary world: the relationship between lord and peasant. Behind the law and behind institutions, as *Bracton* implies, lay physical force. He reminds us of the military preparedness of the nobility and of the great emphasis which was placed upon honour and dignity. This was a profoundly unequal society, a world in which social distances were vast. Wherever one looks it was an assertive and highly status-conscious society.

The English common law, the basic features of which were in place by 1200, and of which the author of *Bracton* was both a product and a champion, had effectively excluded a large proportion of the rural population from access to the royal courts. Under the common law of villeinage, customary tenants were consigned to the jurisdiction of their lords, virtually assimilating them with the descendants of slaves and making the terms villein (*villanus*, inhabitant of a township or vill) and serf essentially interchangeable. The situation under the law is described starkly by a late thirteenth-century lawyer. Serfs, he tells us:

cannot acquire anything save to the use of their lord; they do not know in the evening what service they will do in the morning, and there is nothing certain in their services. The lords may put them in fetters and in the stocks, may imprison, beat and chastise them at will, saving their life and limbs. They cannot escape,

[2] A. Harding, *England in the Thirteenth Century* (Cambridge, 1993), chapter 4.

flee or withdraw themselves from their lords, so long as their lords find them wherewithal they may live, and no one may receive them without the will of their lords. They can have no manner of action without their lord against any man, save for felony. And if such serfs hold fees [tenements] of their lords, it must be understood that they hold only from day to day at the will of their lords and by no certain services.[3]

This reflected legal theory. In reality, there was much more certainty in peasant life – in the matters of tenure and services – than is implied here. Nonetheless, these beliefs were ideologically potent and had a general effect upon social attitudes. Freedom was by no means an abstraction. The disabilities faced by villeins were real enough and could be very considerable.[4] These disabilities, moreover, were regarded by the royal courts as tests of villeinage. They included compulsory labour services performed by tenants on their lord's demesne as a condition of tenure, and involved both weekly work and so-called boon works at peak times of the year. They included the payment of heriot (death duty); payment on the marriage of a daughter, and sometimes of a son, known as merchet; payment of a fine if a daughter was found guilty of fornication or became pregnant out of wedlock (leyrwite); payment of toll (a licence fee for the sale of stock); and payment of an annual aid or tallage. Villeins could not buy or sell their land without the agreement of the lord, and could not leave the manor. They could not send their sons to be educated or to enter the Church without the lord's permission. Moreover, they were liable to be amerced, that is to say fined, in the lord's court for mis-demeanours; they were asked to pay an entry fine when they 'inherited' or otherwise entered into holdings; and they were forced to pay multure, a proportion of their grain, as the price for using the local mill. From the lords' perspective, much of this was not only lucrative but wholly essential for the functioning of their estates. The fact that by the beginning of the early thirteenth century most lords were heavily involved in running their estates directly, cashing in on a buoyant market for foodstuffs, rather than leasing them out to farmers, added to the necessity for keeping a tight control both on the services owed to them by their tenants and on the integrity of the tenements on which those services were assessed. Land transactions between peasants had to be controlled. If a lord's tenants were judged to be unfree, the royal courts would have no cognisance of these matters, leaving such tenants to face their lord alone.

[3] W. J. Whittaker, ed., *The Mirror of Justices* (Selden Society, VIII, 1895), p. 79.
[4] For discussion of the extent to which these burdens were modified in practice, see below pp. 212–13.

By no means all peasants were unfree. In the second half of the thirteenth century, somewhere in the region of one-third of all rural tenants were free, though there were significant regional variations. Free tenants held their land on considerably better conditions than villeins, although their money rents could be noticeably higher. It should not be assumed that the free were economically better off. Many free tenants were cottars (cottagers), often holding less than five acres of land. As this was insufficient land on which to support a family, such people needed to supplement their incomes by wage labour and/or a variety of other occupations. England enjoyed an expanding economy in which there were opportunities, but it also experienced rural poverty.

When all the diversity has been allowed for, the relationship between lord and villein, institutionalised by the manor court and mediated through the lord's bailiffs and other agents, remains the most basic relationship in medieval society. It did much by its very existence to condition rural life. It was one expression of the subordination of man to man, which was a central feature of medieval society. It is no coincidence that the body of manorial tenants was known as the homage: that is, those who had pledged faith to the lord for their holdings. The greatest expression of this subordination is that a lord could sell his serfs singly, as well as part and parcel of an estate. Either way, they were sold with their goods, chattels and offspring. Nothing can convey the social gulf between lord and serf more clearly than this. As the great legal historian F. W. Maitland pointed out, the same Latin word (*sequela*) was used in the documents for the offspring of both cattle and unfree tenants.

Not surprisingly, then, the language of courtesy (which, as we shall see, was in full swing by the early thirteenth century) was matched by a language of deprecation. In courtly literature we find the adjective *vilein* and the noun *vileinie* to describe all that is vile, mean and unpleasant. This is, of course, the origin of our words villain and villainy. Their original meaning, however, is closer to similar words derived from Old English like churlish (from churl or *ceorl*) and boorish (from boor, *gebur*). The Latin word *rusticus*, both as noun and as adjective, could be used in the same sense. From the late twelfth century, artists began to depict the shepherds of the Christmas story 'as gross beings, with thick lips, leering mouths, and matted hair', whilst literary depictions of peasants showed them to be 'filthy and corrupt, cunning but stupid, immune, and even allergic, to the finer things in life'. One story had a peasant faint on sniffing the pleasant aromas coming from an apothecary's shop; he was revived by being thrown on to a dung-heap. It is hardly surprising that in

counties – 'little knights' or *milituli* as some contemporaries called them – as well as landless, or near landless, men attached to lordly households. The essence of knighthood was its military calling. But it also involved important civilian duties, including providing juries for the grand assize. There remained a strong service component to knighthood. By the early fourteenth century, by contrast, there were more like 1,500 knights across the whole of England. The knights had become a relatively small landed elite. The thinning of knightly ranks was a feature of the first half of the thirteenth century and was the consequence of a series of complex social changes involving increasing consumption and a growing spirit of exclusion among the higher reaches of secular society. The result was a fully fledged chivalric knighthood, which by the 1240s was beginning to operate as a powerful force within English society.[8]

By this time chivalry already had something of a history, and it is important to understand what is meant by fully chivalric knighthood. In its most primitive form, chivalry was a code of honour which developed around the bearing of knightly arms and was much influenced by the Church in its attempts to redirect the energies of the nobility away from wanton violence and towards the idea of Christ's *militia*; this was manifested most strongly in the crusades. During the last decades of the twelfth century, however, chivalry was transformed through its adoption as an ideology by the high nobility of northern France. In romance literature we see knighthood being invested with strong and explicitly exclusive values, values that were both social and moral. Chivalry became a matter of refined manners in civilian life, and by no means confined to war or to its counterpart, the tournament. One of chivalry's strongest ingredients was courtesy, and one of its most famous and enduring characteristics was noble love, or *fin amour*. A great deal of emphasis was placed on the knighting ceremony, which now became a lavish festival of initiation, symbolically charged and filled with mystique. In other words, there developed around chivalric knighthood a much stronger and more clearly expressed class-consciousness than had existed before. These new practices, and the values associated with them, passed naturally from France to England.

The changes are easy enough to observe; but they are, frankly, more difficult to account for. As far as England is concerned, the most probable explanation is that their adoption resulted from a reaction on the part of the magnates to knightly aspiration from below. In order to assert their

---

[8] Chivalry is discussed further by Prestwich, below, pp. 75–7.

superiority in the face of a lesser aristocracy, the nobility created what David Crouch has called a superior knighthood.[9] In doing so, they carried only a minority of erstwhile knightly families with them, for many could not afford to keep pace. By their very nature, the changes took some time to work through society; hence the gradual thinning of knightly ranks. The consequences for English society, however, were very great.

This new, more exclusive, chivalric knighthood was expressed by means of heraldry. Heraldry was to be found everywhere by the end of the thirteenth century – on buildings, on dress, on wall paintings, on tiled pavements, on seals, in manuscripts, on caskets and chests and on domestic plate. The majority of people, however, must have encountered it most often in churches, where it was found on monumental effigies and, increasingly in the fourteenth century, on brasses and in stained glass. Through heraldry, individuals and families expressed their identity, their pride in their lineage, their sense of association with other chivalric families and their sense of separateness from the non-armigerous. Heraldry was an expression of the social and cultural hegemony of the elite.

The deference which peasants were expected to pay their superiors is illustrated in the Luttrell Psalter, an extraordinary illuminated manuscript made for the landowner Sir Geoffrey Luttrell of Irnham in Lincolnshire, most probably between *c.* 1340 and 1345. The scene in question is a nativity scene where the three kings are shown meeting the shepherds out in the fields. With his left hand, the foremost shepherd points to the star. His right hand, however, is touching his forehead in what appears to be a gesture of deference, and his body is slightly bowed.[10] There is evidence to suggest that, where such deference was not forthcoming, peasants could find themselves facing their landlords' wrath. At Laleham in Middlesex, for example, an estate of the abbot of Westminster, a dairy servant was deprived of one bushel of the livery of grain to which he or she was entitled for the period 29 September 1330 to 25 April 1331 on account of his or her bad demeanour (*pro malo gestu suo*).[11] Nor was this an isolated incident on the estates of Abbot William de Curtlington. In dispute with the tenants of two of his manors over their traditional remission from servile work on feast days, he finally allowed them just

---

[9] Crouch, *Image of Aristocracy*, p. 153.
[10] M. Camille, *Mirror in Parchment: the Luttrell Psalter and the making of medieval England* (1998), p. 221.
[11] Westminster Abbey Muniments 27116. I am most grateful to Barbara Harvey for this reference.

two days off at each of the festivals of Christmas, Easter and Whitsun. As a good-will gesture, in 1321, he offered to forgo the money that they owed him as a result of the dispute. At Bourton-on-the-Hill, the tenants accepted. At Todenham, however, the offer was withdrawn because of the attitude of the reeve, Henry Melksop, who acted as spokesman. He was described by the abbot as a man with a fine face and a large snarl, who did not deign to open his mouth in thanks. In response to his grumbling, the abbot retracted his good will.[12]

It is hardly surprising that a common motif in medieval sermons is the disdain that the rich and high-born felt for their inferiors. As one might expect, this disdain was perceived most often through the prism of the seven deadly sins, the principal one in this context being pride, though it was often also linked to avarice. Such men, we hear, are 'prowde in lokyng, prowd in spekyng, prowde in heygh crying abovyn othere ... prowd in goinge, standyng and syttynge', 'grym in spekynge, heynes [heinous] in berynge ... sory in blamynge, loth to be undernome [reproved]'. They 'for pryde, deyneth noght to speke with a pore man, ne unnethes [nor scarcely] to loke on him. And if thei speketh with him, hit schal be overthwerte [askance] and despitousliche [scornfully]'. Pride of ancestry is a major factor in all of this. But the high-born were by no means the only culprits. People suffered as much, if not more, from the airs and graces assumed by bailiffs and the like. As one preacher says, those raised from a low to a high position 'will not deign to look upon their inferiors or the poor, save from a distance and from the tips of their eyes'. In the words of another, 'When he lokythe a-pon hymselve and a-pon his grete aray, his wif and his meyny [retinue], his rychesse, and all-so his place, his worschipp and his honour, mervell he may that he, that was so pore and so nedy, thus hygh now is brought'.[13]

The rich, moreover, were highly competitive amongst themselves: 'everi lord biholdeth othur, how he is arayed, how he is horsid, how he is manned; and so envyth other'. Medieval lords could be decidedly touchy where their honour was concerned. This is seen in periodic tussles over the right to a particular coat of arms. On campaign in Wales in September 1405, Sir John Dalyngrygg came across John Green esquire in the arms he considered to be his own and threw down his gauntlet, demanding that they settle the matter 'without delay'.[14] Such cases were

---

[12] B. F. Harvey, *Westminster Abbey and its Estates in the Middle Ages* (Oxford, 1977), pp. 230–1.

[13] G. R. Owst, *Literature and Pulpit in Medieval England* (1933), pp. 309–12, which is also the source of the next quotation (p. 311).

[14] M. Keen, *The Origins of the English Gentleman* (Stroud, 2003), p. 42.

often heard in the court of chivalry, which was in existence by the time of the battle of Crécy in 1346 and probably earlier: in the later fourteenth century, during the Scrope versus Grosvenor dispute over the right to bear the arms *azure a bend or*, large numbers of gentlefolk, including Geoffrey Chaucer, came to court to give evidence for one side or the other.

NOBILITY, GENTRY AND SERVICE

The world of lordship was neither monolithic nor unchanging. The creation of new earls was a matter for the king, and he needed to deal skilfully and to tread warily, for the consequences could be disastrous for him politically. It was vital that a man who was being considered for elevation to an earldom should be socially worthy as well as enjoying, or receiving, an income sufficient to sustain his new eminence. Edward II's promotion of the upstart Piers Gaveston to the earldom of Cornwall and Gaveston's subsequent judicial murder provides but one of a string of examples in which the promotion of men deemed unworthy of their new dignity was opposed by the established nobility. Nevertheless, new earldoms *were* created, and not only to fill the gaps left by families who failed in the male line. Between 1307 and 1397, twenty-four new earldoms were created outside the royal family. The fourteenth century, moreover, saw the introduction of additional titles into England. The first English duke was Edward, the Black Prince, elevated to the dukedom of Cornwall in 1337. The title of duke was normally, though not invariably, reserved for members of the royal family. Once again, insensitivity could have repercussions, as when Richard II's new creations of 1397 were hailed contemptuously as *duketti* (little dukes), even though most of them were related to the king. Richard II also created the first marquis in England (between duke and earl in descending order of rank) in 1385, and the first baron by royal patent in 1387. The first viscount (between earl and baron) followed in 1440.

This stratification was part of the emergence of the English peerage. In the thirteenth century, holding lands in barony did not convey an automatic right to a parliamentary summons, and those called to parliament did not necessarily come by right of tenure: what mattered primarily was a man's standing with the king. All of that changed in the fourteenth century. The higher nobility became progressively more exclusive, and the parliamentary 'baronage' was transformed into the peers of the realm. The term 'peers' was used in a parliamentary context as early as 1312.[15] The lords claimed the right to be tried only by their peers. Not that this would necessarily save them. It did not do the earl of March much good in 1330, when he was tried by his peers in parliament and then executed for treason. In 1341 their right to such trial was confirmed by statute. The notion of summons by virtue of precedent, and their own increasing spirit of exclusion, caused the parliamentary lords to pull away steadily from the rest of the nobility.

By the end of the fourteenth century, the increasing separateness of the parliamentary peerage had become the subject of elaborate ceremonial. Richard II's creations of 1385 and 1397 were marked by investiture in parliament with coronets, caps and gowns. By the end of the fourteenth century lords were wearing scarlet robes, with three bands of fur denoting dukes and earls and two denoting barons. Not surprisingly this period saw many quarrels over precedence. Where men were to be seated was a matter of great importance. The rolls of parliament record that, when John Beaufort was created earl of Somerset in 1397, he was

brought before the king in parliament between two earls, namely Huntingdon and the earl marshal, wearing a velvet cloak as a garment of honour, with his sword borne before him pommel uppermost. Then the king's charter of creation was read publicly … and afterwards the king himself girded the earl with the said sword, and caused him to be seated in his place in parliament, between the earl marshal and the earl of Warwick.[16]

It is hardly surprising that quarrels might ensue, as they did at a royal council in March 1405 when the earl of Warwick was given the right to higher precedence in parliament than the earl marshal, the earl of Kent was preferred over the earl of Arundel, and Lord Grey was placed higher than Lord Beaumont.[17]

By the fifteenth century only the peers were considered truly noble. In consequence, the rest of the nobility – the English gentry – enjoyed mere gentility, a watered-down version, as it were, of nobility. An intermediate distinction of banneret – the superior knight distinguished by the fact that he brought his own contingent, under his own banner, to the battlefield and who was often rewarded by the king with a personal summons to parliament – was phased out. These men had figured in the

---

[15] M. Prestwich, *The Three Edwards: war and state in England, 1272–1377* (1980), p. 140.

[16] J. E. Powell and K. Wallis, *The House of Lords in the Middle Ages* (1968), p. 414. See also S. H. Rigby, *English Society in the Later Middle Ages: class, status and gender* (Basingstoke, 1995), pp. 197–8.

[17] Powell and Wallis, *House of Lords*, p. 437.

sumptuary legislation of 1363, which sought to determine the quality of clothing which each estate, or social group, was entitled to wear, and again in the preamble to the graduated poll tax of 1379. At this time, they looked set to become a social category in their own right. Nonetheless they gave way before the increasing exclusivity of the peers.

During the first half of the fourteenth century the gentry crystallised out of the lesser nobility. County landowners as a whole became increasingly visible as members of the greatly expanding number of royal commissions, as holders of local office, including the important justice of the peace, and as members of parliament. Here they represented the county constituencies and exercised collective influence as the most powerful element within the emerging House of Commons. The knights now became the first rank of a graded gentry, as gentle society itself coalesced. Below the knights the newly armigerous rank of esquire took shape during the middle third of the fourteenth century. As the sumptuary legislation of 1363 makes abundantly clear, there were others, besides the knights and esquires, who were regarded as gentle. Local administrators and lawyers, too, played an increasingly prominent role in commissions and as MPs. From these beginnings the gentry continued to evolve. An act of parliament of 1413 recognised a new status of gentleman below the rank of esquire. Not all gentlefolk were male, of course, and wives were generally regarded as enjoying the same status as their husbands. They, too, participated in chivalric culture. It is worth remarking that, since marriage was a prominent means of upward mobility for men, there must have been many cases where wives were actually of higher birth than their husbands.

So far, we have talked of higher and lower lords and of the social gradations that developed within the nobility, or nobility and gentry. It is necessary, however, to say something of the relationships between different levels of this hierarchy. One important dimension to such relationships, especially at the beginning of our period, was tenure. One man would hold his land of another in return for service, most notably military service. The relationship between the two was cemented – theoretically speaking, it was inaugurated – by the performance of homage and the swearing of an oath of fealty. *Bracton* spends some time explaining this – as well he might, for the subordination of man to man was the basic cement of medieval society. The subordination of peasant to lord, discussed earlier, had its counterpart in noble society, although here of course the relationship was an honourable one, involving mutual respect and support. *Bracton* describes the act of homage at this level. The tenant, he says, ought to place both his hands between the two hands of his lord, by which there is symbolized protection, defence and warranty on the part of the lord and subjection and reverence on that of the tenant, and say these words: 'I become your man with respect to the tenement which I hold of you ... and I will bear you fealty in life and limb and earthly honour ... saving the faith owed the lord king and his heirs'.

Homage, moreover, 'ought not to be done in private, but in a public place and openly, in the presence of many, in the county or hundred court or the court of the lord'.[18]

During the course of the thirteenth century, however, lords came increasingly to reward their followers in cash and in kind rather than deplete their own resources by grants of land. They did so by written contracts, which 'preserved the ideals behind the acts of homage and fealty without insisting on their performance, and spelled out in detail the conditional, and time-limited, nature of the rewards offered for service'.[19] In the past historians tended to concentrate on military service; but this was not the only dimension of service. Lords needed followers to man their retinues in peacetime. They required service of varying kinds on their estates, in their households and to protect them at law. This was a world in which lords were always seeking clients to bolster their power and where men sought patronage for advancement and protection. Moreover, honourable subordination had valuable social cachet. To be shown respect, in a gentle manner, was a vitally important ingredient of esteem, for the lesser landowners as well as for the great. In the mid-thirteenth century the rising courtier, Sir Geoffrey de Langley, received a small piece of land in Somerset for the service of saying 'welcome' (*welkeme*) to the grantor whenever they both attended the local hundred court.[20] Even in the fifteenth century, in a world where contracts and legal obligations dominated, people could still enjoy public rituals of respectful subordination. In 1429 it is recounted that:

John de Nowell did his homage to Thomas Hesketh in this manner: that Thomas de Hesketh was seated on a great stone with his hat on his head, and John Nowell, kneeling bareheaded before him, turned his face to him squarely and held his hands between the hands of the said Thomas, and said thus, 'I become your man from this day forward and will bear you faith for the

---

[18] Woodbine and Thorne, *Bracton*, ii, pp. 231–2.
[19] M. Jones and S. Walker, eds., 'Private indentures for life in peace and war 1278–1476', in *Camden Miscellany*, XXXII (Camden Society, 5th ser. III, 1994), p. 13.
[20] P. R. Coss, ed., *The Langley Cartulary* (Dugdale Society, XXXII, 1980), no. 523.

tenements I hold from you in Harwood' ... and when John Nowell had said this Thomas kissed him: and then a book was set before him, on which John Nowell laid his right hand and said thus, 'Hear this, Thomas de Hesketh, that I John Nowell will be faithful to you and bear you faith for the free tenement that I hold from you in Harwood, and will perform loyally all the customs and services which I owe you to do at the times assigned, so help me God'.[21]

All forms of subordination involved service of one type or another. As Rosemary Horrox has written, 'Service has some claim to be considered the dominant ethic of the middle ages'.[22] The service relationship could be found at all levels of society. Employees in agriculture and industry were generally described as servants. Interesting in this context is the distinction made by the writer Bartholomew Anglicus between the slave, the bond servant or serf, and the servant who contracts freely. As his late fourteenth-century translator, John Trevisa, put it, 'The thridde manere of servauntes is bound frelich and byn here owne good wille, and serveth for mede and for hire, and this ben propirlich iclepid [called] *famuli*'. The word *famulus* is significant. This type of servant becomes part of the household, the *familia*, of his employer and is therefore under his juris-diction. A lord or employer had a right to expect high standards of behaviour. Indeed, as Robert Grosseteste made clear in his advice to the countess of Lincoln in the mid-thirteenth century, a lord or lady was likely to be judged on the quality of his or her servants. Nonetheless, in theory at least, the relationship was one of respect on both sides. Trevisa writes that a good lord 'loveth more to be iloved than idrade'. Most illuminating is the contrast he makes with the bond servant: 'Hit is a properte of ... hem that ben of bond condicioun to grucche and ben rebel and unbuxom [disobedient] to here lordis and ladies'. They must be 'iholde lowe with drede'.[23]

Service was also performed in more elevated contexts. Wherever we look, we see gentle persons in the service of the high born: in households, in the administration of estates, in military service and in raising troops, in giving counsel and so on. Such service conferred honour and prestige on both parties and, although it naturally involved a certain degree of deference, the relationship was essentially a symbiotic one. Much of the

[21] M. Keen, 'Introduction', in P. Coss and M. Keen, eds., *Heraldry, Pageantry and Social Display in Medieval England* (Woodbridge, 2002), pp. 3–4.

[22] R. Horrox, 'Service', in R. Horrox, ed., *Fifteenth-Century Attitudes: perceptions of society in late medieval England* (Cambridge, 1994), p. 61.

[23] P. J. P. Goldberg, 'What was a servant?' in A. Curry and E. Matthew, eds., *Concepts and Patterns of Service in the Later Middle Ages* (Woodbridge, 2000), pp. 9–10.

social terminology in use in medieval England has its roots in service: knight, esquire, valet, yeoman. Extra prestige was conferred by service in the royal household, as, indeed, by royal service in general.

The language of deference *within* the gentle classes became, if anything, stronger in the fourteenth century. It could be expressed, moreover, in very affectionate terms. Indeed, the mixture of affection and subordination with which a nobleman might address his lord can sometimes seriously mislead historians. A letter long thought to have been written by Lady Joan Pelham to her husband, John Pelham, from Pevensey on 25 July 1399, seeking news of how he was faring at Pontefract, has been shown recently to have been written by Sir John Pelham himself to Henry Bolingbroke, duke of Lancaster, at a critical juncture in the latter's return from exile. Pelham was holding Pevensey Castle for Henry and was to be lavishly rewarded when he became king. Pelham addressed Bolingbroke as '[M]y dere Lorde, derest and best yloved off all erthlyche Lordes': the strong sense of affection makes it clear why for so long the letter was thought to be a piece of correspondence between husband and wife. As Simon Walker has written, this document allows the historian 'to glimpse the strength of feeling, admittedly heightened and exaggerated by a moment of crisis, that could exist between lord and man'.[24]

Nor, of course, was the language of deference confined to letters to princes, or indeed confined to letters to men. A surviving fragment of a letter book of the 1390s shows the respect and courtesy with which a lady was addressed.[25] The letters are in French, still the language of gentility, and they are written from socially diverse people. They also indicate the extent to which women were involved in the culture of courtesy and the language of deference. The lady in question was Dame Alice de Bryene, daughter of Sir Robert de Bures of Acton in Suffolk and widow of the Gloucestershire knight, Sir Guy de Bryene the younger. One of the letters was probably written to her following the death of her father. It may have been from a relative or friend, or from one of her higher-ranking advisers. The letter is very conscious of her status, while at the same time offering advice. It begins: 'My very honoured and very sovereignly of right entire heart well-beloved lady [*treshonuree & tresoveraignement de droit entier coer biename dame*], I recommend me humbly to your very good nobility [*tresbonne noblesse*] as your subject [*suggit*] and servant readily prepared to do you service according to my power in

---

[24] S. K. Walker, 'Letters to the dukes of Lancaster in 1381 and 1399', *EHR*, 106 (1991), 75–9.
[25] For what follows see P. Coss, *The Lady in Medieval England* (Stroud, 1998), pp. 64–6.

honest manner'. After praying to God omnipotent for good news of her estate and her health, and for such increase in her honour as would be a joy and comfort to all her friends and servants to hear, the writer goes on to excuse himself to the very honoured lady (*treshonuree dame*) for not having come to her presence. Another letter seems to have been written by a supplier who has let the lady down. 'I recommend me', he says, 'to your ladyship [*seignuresse*] as much as I know how or am able to, desiring to hear and know ... of your gracious estate, which may God through his mercy long hold in honour and ease'. He then excuses himself for his failure to supply a *grant piece* (of what precisely is unclear) and finally signs off as 'your humble servant, William Maldon'.

Two other letters are from Alice's sons-in-law, John Devereux and Robert Lovell. John begins, 'Very honoured and very gracious lady, and my very reverent mother [*ma tresreverente Miere*], I recommend me to you', and continues in the same vein. Robert was decidedly more florid and gushing. He begins, 'My very honoured and with all my heart whole-heartedly well beloved lady and mother I recommend me to you as whole-heartedly as far as I know how and am most able, desiring sovereignly to hear and truly know good and joyous news of you and of your honourable estate'. Lady Alice may well have found this son-in-law charming, and one wonders whether his speech was as smooth as his writing. How far Robert Lovell was genuine in his sentiments is not of course the issue. The important point is the respectful and deferential manner in which people wrote to her, whether they were friend, relative, adviser, son-in-law, merchant or servant.

FAMILY AND HOUSEHOLD

Bracton noted two varieties of power: the power of the lord and the power of the father (*dominica et patria potestas*). Although he discusses the father's power mainly in relation to his male offspring, the implication is that his authority is exercised as head of his household.[26] *Bracton* points us to an important locus of power and authority, that of the family or *familia*, understood not in the modern sense but in the sense known since classical antiquity as all those persons who were subject to the authority of the *paterfamilias*.[27] In the medieval context this meant essentially servants, spouse and blood relatives. The family in this sense was synonymous with

[26] Woodbine and Thorne, *Bracton*, ii, p. 350.
[27] D. Herlihy, *Medieval Households* (Cambridge, MA, 1985), pp. 2–4.

the household, a unit of co-residents, with its own moral identity, under the authority of its (usually, though not invariably) male head.

Naturally, it is the noble household that we know most about. From their account rolls, in particular, we learn a great deal about the household economy, and about its membership, organisation and routine. The household existed primarily to satisfy the needs of the lord and his family, and among these needs was, of course, a well-ordered life. The *Rules* which Bishop Robert Grosseteste wrote in French for the countess of Lincoln in 1240–2 on how to guard and govern her household puts a great deal of emphasis on authority and the maintenance of order. 'Tell high and low', he instructs, 'and do this often, that they ought to execute all your orders ... fully, quickly and willingly and without grumbling or contradiction ... Order those who are in charge of your house, in the presence of your entire household, that they keep a careful watch that all your household, within and without, be faithful, diligent, chaste, clean, honest and useful'. Those who fail any of these criteria should be turned out of the household.[28]

A striking representation of the *paterfamilias* occurs in the Luttrell Psalter. A series of *bas-de-page* scenes depicts the household at work, elaborately preparing the food, conveying it to the hall and then waiting, efficiently and deferentially, at table. Sir Geoffrey Luttrell is depicted at the centre of the table, flanked by his spouse, family and guests. The table, like the service, creates an impression of great opulence. As Michael Camille points out, however, the 'focus of the scene ... is on Geoffrey as ruler of his house'.[29] Immediately above the depiction of the sober diners are the words of Psalm 115: 'I call upon the name of the Lord'. Everything emphasises the significance of lordship. The scene, moreover, seems to have eucharistic overtones, the effect of which is to register the divine authority underlining Geoffrey's role as *paterfamilias*. The household was also a religious community, in which the household chaplains carried responsibility for its moral and spiritual welfare. The overall authority, however, was that of its lord. Members of the household could be his spiritual kin. Sir Geoffrey Luttrell, for example, was godfather to the sons of his butler, of his cook and of another of his kitchen employees.

The authority of the *paterfamilias* was reflected in the operation of the law. Under the system of frankpledge, every male over the age of twelve

---

[28] 'The rules of Robert Grosseteste', in D. Oschinsky, ed., *Walter of Henley and other Treatises on Estate Management and Accounting* (Oxford, 1971), pp. 399–407.
[29] Camille, *Mirror in Parchment*, p. 105.

years, free or unfree, was supposed to be in a tithing, a group of (nom-inally ten) men who were responsible collectively for producing any one of their fellows in court. There were numerous exceptions, including magnates, knights (and their kinsmen) and clerics. Also excluded from frankpledge was anyone in the 'mainpast' of another.[30] The head of the household was himself responsible for the appearance in court of any of its members; or, as Maitland puts it, for 'those whom his hand feeds, his *manupastus* or *mainpast* – we may use a very old English word and say his loaf-eaters'.[31] At the 1249 Wiltshire eyre, for example, it was recorded that Sweyn Sturdi had been one of a group accused of battery, burglary and robbery. Having failed to appear, he was outlawed by the county court. As he was in the mainpast of James Huse, the latter was fined. Similarly Stephen the forester and Richard, his groom, were accused of robbery and consorting with evildoers. Stephen was also of the mainpast of James Huse and once again James Huse was fined for his failure to produce him. It may be that James Huse was exceptionally unlucky in his servants; or it may be that he kept an unruly household. The groom, incidentally, was hanged.[32]

But it was not only landowners, high and low, who kept households. The same eyre roll tells us that Osbert, a man of the parson of Pewsey, killed a woman and immediately fled. The jurors having declared him guilty in his absence, he was to be outlawed. As he was in the mainpast of Parson Solomon, the latter was fined.[33] As well as clerical households of various sizes, we have to think of the households of freeholders in the countryside and of burgesses in the towns. In these last, in addition to women, sons living with their fathers, and menial servants, there might also be apprentices, all constituting the mainpast of the burgess. The head of household was not, however, generally considered responsible for the *actions* of his servants, unless he had specifically commanded them.

The household was also there to serve and protect its lord. In this sense, the retinue was an extension of the household. Hence John of Gaunt could argue against parliamentary attempts to curb the conduct of liveried retainers on the grounds that it was up to a lord to discipline his men.[34] When a household turned against him, as sometimes it could, the

---

[30] This is part of the rich symbolism of hands discussed by C. Phythian-Adams below, pp. 370–2.

[31] F. Pollock and F. W. Maitland, *The History of English Law before the Time of Edward I* (2nd edn, 2 vols., Cambridge, 1968), i, p. 568.

[32] C. A. F. Meekings, ed., *Crown Pleas of the Wiltshire Eyre* (Wiltshire Records Society, XVI, 1961), nos. 288, 292.

[33] *Ibid.*, no. 347.

[34] J. A. Tuck, *Richard II and the English Nobility* (1973), pp. 145–52.

lord had little defence. This is what happened to Sir Thomas Murdak of Edgcote, Northamptonshire, who was murdered while he was staying with the greater part of his household at Stourton Castle in Staffordshire, on 11 April 1316. At least fifteen people were involved in the murder, most of them members of the knight's own household. The first blow was struck by William, son of Richard de Bodekisham, who was described as the victim's dispenser – that is to say, his pantry man, an important official in the provisioning of his household. He hit Thomas Murdak on the head with a staff as he lay in bed. When Thomas tried to rise, he was stabbed by Robert the Chaplain, his seneschal or steward, the man who looked after the household's financial affairs. The fatal blow, however, appears to have been struck by Roger the Chamberlain, who cut Thomas open above the navel. Roger is described as the chamberlain of Juliana, the victim's wife, so that he too was an important member of the household. The crime was abetted by William Shene, the knight's cook, and Adam the Palfreyman. Among others involved were Robert the Sumpter; John son of Juliana, chaplain; William le Taillour; and three women, Matilda de Hastang, Mabel de Blayworth of Edgcote and Mabel, wife of Hugh the clerk of Edgcote. These last seem to give us the ladies of the household. The name Hastang, that of a major gentry family in Warwickshire and elsewhere, reminds us that the children of one gentry family could often be brought up in the household of another. Mabel de Blayworth had property of her own, so that she was not an entirely insignificant figure. How many of the additional men were members of the Murdak household is unclear. Adam the Palfreyman and Robert the Sumpter were servants of John de Vaux, the constable of Stourton Castle, where the murder took place. In truth, the murder was plotted by John de Vaux and Juliana Murdak, who were lovers. Of all the perpetrators, only Juliana was executed.[35]

The prescribed penalty for a wife murdering her husband was not hanging but burning at the stake, for the crime was not murder but 'petty treason', analogous to the murder of a master by his servant or an abbot by one of his monks. In other words, the household modelled the state and the head of the household occupied a position equivalent to the king on his throne. Only thus could proper social order be preserved. Medieval authorities all agreed that it was up to a husband to discipline his wife, just as he should any other member of his household. At the end of the thirteenth century, Chief Justice Mettingham referred to the man's

[35] Coss, *The Lady in Medieval England*, pp. 131–8.

'primacy and mastery at the table and everywhere else'.[36] The lawyer's phrase 'under the rod' may literally mean 'under his authority', but it has unmistakable physical overtones. Though Thomas of Chobham, among others, instructed husbands to correct their wives moderately and discreetly, it was expected that they would inflict physical punishment when this was deemed necessary, just as they would when dealing with children and servants. The courts accepted this. On one occasion a man who twice assaulted his wife with a knife and broke her arm was found to be justified by her disobedience.[37] The man who failed to apply physical discipline to an unruly wife was thought to be in danger of being cuckolded.[38] This was not, of course, the only way to secure a wife's obedience. Peter Idley's 'Instructions to His Son' recommended thus:

> Thy wife thou love in perfect wise,
> In thought and deed, as heartily as thou can,
> With gentle speech the best thou can devise;
> This shall make her a good woman,
> And also to love thee best of any man,
> And dread thee also and loath to offend,
> Thy goods keep, neither waste nor spend.[39]

The intention, however, was much the same. A wife should be submissive.

So too should sons and daughters, even when they had grown up and left home. John Paston II wrote to his father thus: 'Most reverent and worschepful fadyre, I rekomawnd me hertylye, and submytt me lowlely to yowre good faderhood, besechyng yow fore cheryte of yowre dayly blyssyng'.[40] Recognition of the special authority of the head of the family is also implicit in a number of didactic works representing instruction and advice by fathers for their children. The direct threats that underpinned acts of paternal discipline are demonstrated not only in the physical violence meted out against children in their youth. Fifteenth-century fathers were not above cutting grown-up sons and daughters out of their wills.

---

[36] P. Brand, 'Family and inheritance, women and children', in C. Given-Wilson, ed., *An Illustrated History of Late Medieval England* (Manchester, 1996), p. 63.
[37] P. Fleming, *Family and Household in Medieval England* (Basingstoke, 2001), p. 58.
[38] B. A. Hanawalt, *The Ties That Bound: peasant families in medieval England* (Oxford, 1986), p. 206.
[39] Fleming, *Family and Household*, p. 56.
[40] Davis, *Paston Letters*, i, no. 231.

LORDSHIP AND AFFINITY

A second dimension to a lord's power was domanial lordship: that is, authority over his estates and over the people who lived there. The basic unit of this lordship was the manor. Manors came in all shapes and sizes, but they normally contained a demesne, land whose produce went directly to the lord for consumption or for the market, and tenanted land in the hands of villeins and/or free tenants. Some manors were large and coincident with the village, but most were small to medium-sized properties of less than six square miles. Jurisdiction over the tenants was exercised by the manor court, most often held in the lord's hall. Bailey has written that:

as the medium through which lordship was exercised on the ground, [the manor court] was also central to the organisation of social relations in the middle ages. Through the manor, the personal ties, services and obligations which bound a medieval peasant to a lord were defined and enforced, communal by-laws were agreed and implemented, and many economic and social dealings with neighbours and family were regulated and formalised.[41]

Bracton envisaged such seigniorial authority being exercised solely over bondmen, but in reality manor courts had some jurisdiction over free as well as villein tenants. In many ways this was problematic for manorial lords, since the free had access to the royal courts. The need to retain the loyalty of free tenants to the manor court led to many improvements in the records and procedures of those courts, especially during the second half of the thirteenth century. The battle to maintain authority over their free tenants was somewhat easier to wage if lords also held leet courts. Operating once or twice a year, these were derived from public authority either by royal grant or by usurpation. They constituted the lowest rung in a system of courts moving up to the hundred (or wapentake) and the county. It was at these courts that view of frankpledge was held to ensure that all adult males were in tithing, a responsibility otherwise undertaken by the sheriff in his tourn. With view of frankpledge went a variety of judicial and administrative responsibilities connected with the hundred and county courts. Greater lords, in particular, might also hold privatised hundred courts and exercise various other franchises, including the right to execute felons.

---

[41] M. Bailey, *The English Manor c.1200–c.1530* (Manchester, 2002), p. 2. See also pp. 97–8, 196 below.

To contemporaries, domanial lordship would not have seemed as distinct from familial lordship as it does to us. It is true that, in the higher-ranking households in particular, persons of gentle birth also provided service; and there was always a tendency for service in the noble household to confer gentility. Other household servants, however, were recruited from the families of the tenantry. Familial and domanial lordship were linked in other ways, too. In the *bas-de-page* scenes of the Luttrell Psalter, the labour in the fields complements the service provided in the household. These scenes have the effect of emphasising lordship over persons rather than over land. In the illustrations to a sequence of psalms concerned with God's provision for his people, there is again an accent on a form of lordship that connects divine authority with the power and protection provided by the secular lord. The entire depiction reflects Sir Geoffrey Luttrell's ideological position. What we have, as Camille neatly puts it, is 'a vivid portrayal of the customary labours on a fourteenth-century manor, that sought to cement social hierarchies and idealize feudal relations'.[42]

Over and above these forms of lordship lay the broader authority of the great magnate. A magnate's power was actually three-dimensional, for it rested simultaneously on his household, his estates and his affinity. All three were closely interlocked. However, it was the broader affinity that made the magnates' power distinctive, in that it gave them territorial predominance. Although we must be careful not to draw too stark a contrast between the twelfth and thirteenth centuries, in the former an individual magnate's power had been centred most often upon the military tenants who constituted the core of his honor and who owed suit to (that is, were obliged to attend) his honor court. Although historians no longer see the honor as a feudal kingdom in miniature, it remains true that the great lords of the twelfth century had enjoyed considerable authority, largely free from interference by the central authority. However, the legal reforms of the later twelfth century accelerated the erosion of this honorial power, as the royal courts took business away from baronial courts and protected the feudal tenant from arbitrary action by his lord. In the thirteenth century, when the reach of royal justice extended still further, the power of the great lord was therefore exercised less through his honor and more through his affinity, which may be described as the sum total of his followers. Increasingly, the

---

[42] Camille, *Mirror in Parchment*, p. 209.

relationship between the lord and his affinity was dominated by money, in the form of fees and annuities.

At the core of an affinity were men retained for their service, in peace and war, by means of a written indenture (a bilateral contract with copies kept by both parties). But the extent of a lord's affinity went beyond this. It is often represented by historians as a series of concentric circles. It included kinsmen, tenants and neighbours. It comprised menial servants, councillors, estate officials and local gentry. In other words the affinity was 'a sea of varying relationships' centred on service and loyalty to a lord.[43] As K. B. McFarlane famously wrote, 'Over and above his indented retinue (the hard core, as it were, of his affinity), a great man therefore was the patron and paymaster of a swarm of hangers-on, both men and women, not bound to do him exclusive service but in receipt of his bounty in ways both more and less permanent'.[44] Looked at from this perspective, medieval society was a world of patrons and clients bound together to mutual advantage: the power exercised by a lord and his retainers was, as McFarlane so perceptively put it, 'a joint-stock enterprise'.[45]

Important as the retinue and military considerations undoubtedly were in determining the contours of an affinity, it is important to recognise the other dimensions that existed. Moreover, the indenture took shape in a world in which contracts for service were becoming increasingly important. One dimension to this was the lord's household (in the narrow sense) and the need to put household service on a sounder basis. Another was the need for administrative service on a broad front, made doubly necessary by the introduction of the direct farming of estates and the necessity of employing a whole panoply of officials to secure the lord's interests. Over and above all of this was the growing need for expert legal advice. As Waugh has said, the contract for service 'evolved into a versatile tool of social organisation which could be used in many different circumstances'.[46]

In reality, however, the power of the later medieval magnate was not always as great as it may seem on the surface. The growing self-confidence of the gentry, with their employment on increasing numbers of commissions as well as in local office, the development of the parliamentary

---

[43] G. A. Holmes, *The Estates of the Higher Nobility in Fourteenth Century England* (Cambridge, 1957), p. 79.

[44] K. B. McFarlane, *England in the Fifteenth Century* (1981), p. 30.   [45] *Ibid.*, p. 32.

[46] S. L. Waugh, 'Tenure to contract: lordship and clientage in thirteenth-century England', *EHR*, 101 (1986), 839.

Commons and the steady expansion of royal justice all challenged
magnate power. From the thirteenth century onwards we find the nobles
responding to this challenge by penetrating public authority as never
before and by binding lesser landowners and local officials (who were
often one and the same) more closely to them. By a variety of means,
including indentures of retainer and the granting of annuities, great lords
drew men into their affinities. This was the essence of what historians
have called 'bastard feudalism'. By such means, and by virtue of the
interests and values they shared with lesser men, magnates could sometimes achieve considerable local power. However, they were not generally
in a position to act as successful monopolists. The gentry were an
independent-minded and potentially truculent lot and the great lords
lacked the resources to retain large numbers of them; not even John of
Gaunt, the greatest magnate of the late fourteenth century, could manage
to enrol or control all the gentry in all the regions where he had territorial
interests. Consequently, to maintain their power, magnates had to
operate through the gentry's own social networks, to offer arbitration in
their many disputes and to exercise effective patronage – in contemporary
parlance, to deliver 'good lordship'. This in turn raised the expectations
of the gentry and created difficult challenges for nobles. There was
the potentiality for conflict locally between competing magnates and the
members of their respective affinities, a fact that helps to explain
the concern that surfaced intermittently in parliament over the activities
of their liveried retainers. There was also the resultant rivalry for influence
at the centre of government. Even the most powerful lord could find
himself with problems.

John Watts has written that the 'dream of every nobleman was surely
the unchallenged rule of the locality, in which case everybody would be,
in some sense, a part of his following, because everybody would look to
him for justice. Such a lord would indeed have the "princypall rewle and
governance" next to the king, and the distinction between the affinity and
the local *communitas* [community] would all but disappear'.[47] For all the
wealth, power and authority of the later medieval magnate, this dream
was extremely difficult to realise. One of the magnates who came closest
to doing so was William de la Pole, earl (later duke) of Suffolk. His case is
instructive and will be used here as an example.[48] Although his own

---

[47] J. Watts, *Henry VI and the Politics of Kingship* (Cambridge, 1996), p. 67.
[48] H. Castor, *The King, the Crown, and the Duchy of Lancaster: public authority and private power,
1399–1461* (Oxford, 2000), part 2, *passim*.

estates were clustered in central and north-eastern Suffolk, his authority dominated the whole of East Anglia for a decade or so, from around 1437 when he reached an accommodation with the locally powerful but lesser figure, William Phelip, until his fall from power in 1450. His rule was made possible by the pre-existing network of association that was derived ultimately from the duchy of Lancaster, onto which his own authority was grafted, and by the (temporary) absence of any effective, alternative lordship. Pre-eminent in the region during these years were Suffolk's agents, John Heydon, Reginald Rous and Thomas Tuddenham: such was their perceived influence and authority that these men were themselves called upon to arbitrate in local disputes. Suffolk's lordship was thus quickly established as the driving force in local political life: as Margaret Paston wrote to her husband in 1449, 'Sondery folkys haue seyd to me that they thynk veryly but if ye haue my lord of Suffolkys godelorchyp qhyll the werd is as itt is ye kan neuer leven jn pese wyth-owth ye haue his godelordschep'.[49] What made Suffolk's rule in his 'country' virtually unassailable, however, was his control at the court of Henry VI. During the 1440s Suffolk did far more than simply enjoy access to royal patronage and thus dispense it to the benefit of his East Anglian retainers; he positively dominated the court. His case therefore demonstrates the interdependency between power in the localities and power at the centre. East Anglia gave Suffolk the power base from which his national power became possible, while his control of the centre impacted upon, and indeed cemented, his regional authority. Indicative of this symbiosis is the fact that his agent Thomas Tuddenham himself acquired court office, becoming keeper of the great wardrobe in 1446.

Predictably enough, Suffolk had to face challenges to his regional lordship. From around 1440 the young John Mowbray, third duke of Norfolk, sought to restore his family's erstwhile position in East Anglia; and from around 1447 the intrusive courtier, Thomas Daniel, posed a threat to the stability of Suffolk's power base. Given his entrenched position, however, Suffolk was usually able to keep his competitors at bay. Such struggles were, indeed, an accepted part of regional politics: as Helen Castor has stressed, the 'aim of every local magnate ... was to defeat or neutralize by accommodation the regional pretensions of his rivals in order to achieve or maintain control of his "country"'.[50] What destabilised Suffolk's affinity, then, was not so much the existence of two

---

[49] Davis, *Paston Letters*, i, no. 135.
[50] Castor, *The King, the Crown, and the Duchy of Lancaster*, p. 100.

challengers to his local power as the fact that his central control faltered in the later 1440s. The military and diplomatic failures in the war against France meant that he suffered a loss of support among the higher nobility as a whole, and became increasingly dependent upon a narrow clique within the king's household. Suffolk's power at the centre faltered and collapsed, leading to his downfall, disgrace and murder in 1450. The 'order' that he had established in East Anglia then fell away and the region suffered several years of marked instability, disaffection and violence – as the Paston letters graphically reveal. The Suffolk 'experience' illustrates both the potentiality and the fragility of a form of late medieval magnate power based in household, estate and affinity but requiring also continued influence at court and effective access to royal patronage.

HIERARCHY AND DISSENT

As Rosemary Horrox has written, medieval society 'to a degree which modern readers sometimes find disconcerting, was based on hierarchy. Human society, mirroring the whole created universe, was arranged in order of importance.'[51] At the heart of medieval social theory lay the doctrine of the three estates or orders, the divinely ordained threefold division of humanity into those who prayed, those who fought and those who worked. Together they constituted an organic community in which each was vital for the survival of the others. Like *Bracton's* classification, however, this ideology reflects only a stripped-down version of medieval society. Social commentators responded not by knocking it aside – indeed, it remained the stock-in-trade of both poets and preachers – but by elaborating upon it. Society continued to be seen as a hierarchy in which everyone (or nearly everyone) had their place and their function, a function necessary for the welfare of the community. Equally, each estate had its characteristic faults; these became the subject of an elaborate literature that found its highest expression in the work of Geoffrey Chaucer and William Langland. But because terrestrial order reflected the order of the universe, to transgress it was to invoke divine displeasure. An extremely powerful ideology had been constructed, and this was underpinned by, and reflected in, the institutions of the state and the Church.

With a descending concept of authority as powerful as this, resistance was difficult. And yet the potentiality for conflict in medieval society was great: one has only to think of the king's relations with his subjects, of the

---

[51] Horrox, 'Service', p. 61.

inequality in gender relations, or of peasant/landlord relations. The central problem of Angevin kingship and the whole point of Magna Carta, to which King John briefly subscribed in 1215, was to bring the king within the law – to bring the executive under control, as we would say in modern parlance. It was a problem that primarily concerned the highest of the king's subjects, but it was one that also involved an increasingly wide spectrum of society. Similarly, as peasant tenants were expected to hand over to lords a proportion of their labour and of the fruits of their labour – demands that were no part of the process of production from their point of view – the potentiality for conflict here was enormous. It is no wonder that, in the last instance, seigniorial demands were backed by force.

Obviously, people could, and did, rebel. But, equally obviously, rebellion was a dangerous enterprise. 'Wronged' barons could throw off their allegiance to their feudal lord by a formal act of *diffidatio* (defiance) or renunciation of homage, as Gilbert Basset and his companions did against Henry III in August 1233, for example, and Earl Simon de Montfort and his followers were to do again, with far more serious consequences, on the eve of the battle of Lewes in May 1264. Rebels could raise their banners in open aggression against the king, but in doing so they risked not only the loss of their inheritances but also the capital charge of treason. A battered wife could leave her husband and return to her kin. There are instances of this happening and, indeed, of kin rescuing a woman who was being maltreated, but it was probably very rare. Sometimes, no doubt, a woman resisted her husband physically. But medieval depictions of women beating their husbands, quite common on misericords and depicted in the Luttrell Psalter for example, should not be taken as mirroring life but as expressions of the abnormal, of what happens when the world is turned upside down. Occasionally, a woman took more drastic action and actually disposed of her husband, but we have already seen the likely consequences of this. Peasants could run away to towns and, if undetected, lead a new but uncertain life, or they could stay and resist their lord's demands. The records of manor courts offer innumerable instances of tenants refusing or avoiding work, or doing their work badly. But rebellion in the true sense was, not surprisingly, rare, for it brought the whole weight of authority down upon the rebels.

So, how could one temper authority? One could of course appeal to a higher authority. A wronged woman could invoke the church courts, where she might get her husband rebuked or even secure a judicial separation, known technically as 'divorce from bed and board'. Peasants in contention with their lord might also invoke a higher authority in the form of the royal courts. They are seen doing so from the end of the twelfth century onwards, when the records of those courts become available to us. But such assertive plaintiffs were also required to accept certain parameters. Primarily, they had to accept the fundamental distinction between free and unfree. Only by proving their freedom could they bring issues surrounding the level of their services to those courts. This, then, became the question before the courts, rather than whatever particular issue had sparked off the conflict. Alternatively, they could claim that they were tenants of the ancient demesne of the crown, which meant that their services could not be raised above their customary level. Such a case involved scrutiny of Domesday Book, since many estates that were once the king's ancient demesne were now in private hands. Cases based on this issue were common across the thirteenth and fourteenth centuries, and they remind us of the importance of custom in medieval life.

What was custom on the manor was generally outside the purview of the royal courts. But it played a very large part in peasant life. It was when lords raised their demands above the customary level that their peasants tended collectively to resist. Similarly, lords had the customs of their manors recorded so that they could exact the maximum services that they were due. 'Almost everywhere', writes Hatcher, 'custom triumphed over caprice'.[52] Custom, however, was not static. It represented the balance of compromise between landlord power and peasant resistance. Changes on the manor were by no means necessarily in the direction of freedom. Nonetheless, custom could in many circumstances operate as a check on the lord. Similarly, it was partly by calling upon precedent (which is another word for custom) that the tendency of royal governments to act arbitrarily was checked by action in parliament. It was by maximising the potential that was present in ascending as opposed to descending ideas of power that political changes could be made. The story of how primitive ideas of restraint were gradually extended in the course of conflict was the stuff of what used to be known as constitutional history. In order to make changes permanent, they were enshrined in custom.

Authority could also be tempered by the offering of officially sanctioned advice. Thomas of Chobham, writing in the early thirteenth century, instructed husbands to correct their wives moderately for they

---

[52] J. Hatcher, 'English serfdom and villeinage: towards a reassessment', *P&P*, 90 (1981), 10. For further discussion see below, pp. 212, 225.

should be dearer to them than all their possessions. But he also pointed out that:

it should always be enjoined upon women to be preachers to their husbands, because no priest is able to soften the heart of a man the way his wife can ... Even in the bedroom, in the midst of their embraces, a wife should speak alluringly to her husband, and if he is hard and unmerciful, and an oppressor of the poor, she should invite him to be merciful; if he is a plunderer, she should denounce plundering; if he is avaricious, she should arouse generosity in him, and she should secretly give alms from their common property, supplying the alms that he omits.[53]

Advice here was not only legitimated but also enjoined by the chief moral authority in society: the Church. It was designed to have a softening effect. Similarly, one can imagine situations in which the customary counsel which a vassal owed his lord might result in more temperate and appropriate action. Authority must also have been tempered by the practicalities of life. A king needed his subjects, a magnate needed his followers, a lord needed his peasants and a patriarch needed his family. Marriage itself was a partnership, however unequal, and the oft-quoted division between public (male) and private (female) spheres was belied in practice by the sheer range of activities carried out by wives. This partnership is observed most easily in the central role of the medieval lady in the running of both household and estates. The gentry letters of the fifteenth century provide a most useful corrective here, for they underline the relationship of co-operation that often existed between husband and wife. Similarly, lords required the co-operation of the tenants on their estates, not only to undertake tasks of some responsibility but also to ensure the functioning of the manor court. Indeed, these courts were in many respects dependent upon the greater tenants who staffed them.

Finally, authority was modified and conflict dampened by the desire for stability. Those with a greater stake in society desired social harmony most, but the strong sense of hierarchy was in some respects cohesive in itself and could mask potential lines of fracture. In any case, then as now, most people desired peace. Conflict was certainly latent in the structure of medieval society but there were also very strong forces working for cohesion. Historians who veer too far towards either conflict or harmony do so at their peril. It is important also that we recognise the power of affective bonds, especially between lord and man, and between husband and wife. Chaucer

[53] Coss, *The Lady in Medieval England*, pp. 92, 160–1 (quotation on p. 160).

points to the possibilities for genuine affection within medieval marriage and some of the evidence bears him out: as Eileen Power once said, there must have been many married friends in medieval England.[54]

However, if social harmony was maintained to some degree by desire and consent, it was also fostered in large measure by institutions and by ideology. It goes without saying that the latter were put under strain at times of social and economic crisis such as occurred in the second half of the fourteenth century. It is to this that we must now turn.

A CRISIS OF AUTHORITY

That there was a crisis of authority in the second half of the fourteenth century, in the wake of the Black Death, is hardly open to doubt. Its most obvious manifestations lie in the agrarian sector, in landlord–peasant relations, but it is apparent in towns as well as can be seen spectacularly in 1381 when the rural populace of Kent and Essex marched on London, burned property, executed some of the king's leading ministers, and presented their demands to him. Although the Peasants' Revolt was precipitated by the raising of a poll tax, the crisis in agrarian relations that underlay it went back at least a generation.

William Langland, who wrote the first major version of his great poem, *Piers Plowman*, during the 1360s, expressed quite graphically the breakdown in rural authority following the plague. Piers, functioning at this point as manorial reeve or seigniorial bailiff overseeing labour services, is faced by a section of the workforce unwilling to discharge their duties, and whose idea of ploughing is to imbibe ale and to sing 'hey, trolly-lolly'. Langland interpreted his social observation in terms of the traditional ideology of the three interdependent estates. Hence the defiant peasant becomes Waster, who will not work, and the landlord is presented as the Knight whose role in society is to protect both the producers and the clergy from their enemies (who, in this case, are the 'wasters' themselves). Langland's vision dissolves the idealised world of rural harmony depicted by the illuminator of the Luttrell Psalter. He shows us that the supposedly natural and courteous authority of the lords, which was thought to evince an equally natural respect, was in reality the product of an ideology. He reveals, too, that this respect had strong institutional

---

[54] E. Power, 'The position of women', in C. G. Crump and E. F. Jacob, eds., *The Legacy of the Middle Ages* (Oxford, 1926), p. 416.

backing. He shows how rural relations had been deeply poisoned by the introduction of labour laws in 1349 and 1351. These were designed to hold wages down to pre-Black Death levels, to give lords priority over the labour of their tenants, and to discourage mobility in search of better conditions. In the long run these measures were to prove a failure and the landlords were forced to abandon the system of demesne farming. In the meantime, however, a crisis of authority had been experienced in many areas of life.

This crisis can be seen in the challenge to priestly authority and interpretation that lay behind the religious movement known as Lollardy. With the aid of the state the Church set about devising a programme of repression. Underpinning clerical hostility was the fear of lay access to the bible. Heresy and sedition, as the Church consistently sought to remind lay rulers, were inextricably linked and would march hand in hand. As if to prove the point, the radical preacher John Ball taught at the time of the Peasants' Revolt that God had created all men equal and that servitude had been introduced against his will: 'Whan Adam dalf [delved] and Eve span', he said, 'Wo [who] was thanne a gentilman?'[55] There were manifestations of unrest in urban society, too. Some of the larger towns experienced revolts in 1381. Moreover, the crisis of authority within agrarian society spilled over into the many small towns, hitherto relatively easily controlled by lords and their agents. Here was a sector of the economy where landlord control seems to have been slipping badly.

Yet another symptom of crisis – or at least of a decline in social distance – is present (according to one interpretation, at least) in the earliest surviving literature of Robin Hood.[56] In *The Gest of Robyn Hode*, a compilation of tales that may well date from the end of the fourteenth century, the outlaws – or 'yeomen of the forest' – behave with marked and somewhat excessive courtesy, aping aristocratic manners. When Little John encounters the knight, Sir Richard at the Lee, he is 'full courteous' in his actions and in his acknowledgement of the knight's own status and qualities:

> Litell Johnn was full curteyes [courteous],
> And sette hym on his kne;
> 'Welcom be ye, gentyll knyght,
> Welcom ar ye to me.

[55] R. B. Dobson, *The Peasants' Revolt of 1381* (2nd edn, 1983), p. 374.
[56] P. R. Coss, 'Aspects of cultural diffusion in medieval England: the early romances, local society and Robin Hood', *P&P*, 108 (1985), 66–76.

> 'Welcom be thou to grene wode.
> Hende knyght and fre'.[57]

Robin Hood himself is also quite happy to befriend the knight, providing that he is a 'good fellow': that is to say, one who is not unduly conscious of his rank. What the *Gest* appears to advocate is a sort of commonwealth of the free, where corrupt administrators like the sheriff of Nottingham have been sent packing and where men have equal access to the rivers and the forests; a world, indeed, not unlike that envisaged by the peasants in 1381. The king, too, is expected to become part of this society, though he is to be treated courteously and dutifully. After Robin and the king meet in Sherwood Forest, they play a game of 'plucke buffet', an archery competition where the loser of each round receives a blow from the victor.

> And many a buffet our kyng wan,
> Of Robyn Hode that day:
> And nothynge spared good Robyn
> Our kynge in his pay.

The king took this in good part.

> 'So God me helpe', sayd our kynge,
> 'Thy game is nought to lere [hard to learn],
> I sholde not get a shote of the
> Though I shote all this yere'.[58]

In short, even the figure of the king is integrated into a scheme of 'good fellowship' in which social familiarity wins out over relative status and power.

SOCIAL GRADATION

These episodes are a reminder of the fact that traditional patterns of deference were under threat not only in the lowest reaches of society but also further up the social scale. The late fourteenth century has often been portrayed as an era of increased upward mobility – or perhaps of the *fear* of upward mobility, a topic discussed by Philippa Maddern below.[59]

---

[57] R. B. Dobson and J. Taylor, eds., *Rymes of Robyn Hode: an introduction to the English outlaw* (1976), p. 80 (stanzas 24–5).

[58] *Ibid.*, p. 110 (stanzas 425–6).   [59] See pp. 113–18.

Gentility and social aspiration appear prominently as themes in the literature of the age, pre-eminently in the *Canterbury Tales*. The tensions that Chaucer illuminates in this context are essentially those that existed on the middle rungs of society. While the innkeeper Harry Bailey, the leader of the pilgrimage, expresses contempt for the entire notion (or at the very least the Franklin's pretensions to it) – 'Strawe for your gentillesse', he says – the Wife of Bath argues at some length that gentility is a matter of virtue not of birth, and not even of a combination of the two. It is the Franklin, however, who is the pivotal figure when it comes to interplay over the issue. He is obsessed with gentility and with the image of gentility, both in relation to himself and to his wayward son. At the same time he conspicuously fails to show deference to the higher-born squire. His self-image is one of rich-living country 'gentleman', characterised by the aristocratic virtue of largesse.

> It snewed in his hous of mete and drynke . . .
> His table dormant in his halle alway
> Stod redy covered al the longe day.[60]

And yet, in his haughty and somewhat pompous manner and in the tale that he tells, the Franklin manifestly fails to appreciate the true nature of 'gentillesse' – at least, as seen from an aristocratic perspective. He believes, for example, that gentility is quantifiable: 'Which was the mooste fre [i.e. noble], as thynketh yow?'[61]

Given the social pretension that oozes from the Franklin and the tension that surrounds him, it is hardly surprising that scholars have sought to locate him within the social order. The graded poll tax of 1379 is helpful here. This was the second of the three poll taxes that immediately preceded the revolt of 1381. The basis of the tax, like that of 1377, was a charge of 4d per head. Every married man and every single person over the age of sixteen was to pay this basic sum. However, those who by rank or occupation could be expected to possess greater wealth were to be assessed accordingly. The assessors were given discretion to diverge from these guidelines as they felt appropriate, and often did so.

The preamble to the 1379 poll tax stipulates that each franklin should be assessed at 6s 8d or 3s 4d, according to his estate. Moreover, the poll tax returns themselves reveal a liberal sprinkling of franklins in the countryside. The (incomplete) Leicestershire returns, for example, reveal

---

[60] The Riverside edition, General Prologue, lines 345, 353–4.
[61] The Riverside edition, The Franklin's Tale, line 1622.

twenty-three franklins (or, in one case, the widow of a franklin).[62] Of these, seven were 'petty' franklins, paying only 1s or 2s, the remainder paying at the standard rate of 3s 4d. There were no Leicestershire franklins paying the higher rate of 6s 8d. By way of comparison, one banneret, ten knights bachelor and fifty esquires are recorded in the county; of the esquires, thirty-three paid 3s 4d, the sum required from those in service but without land or possessions. (There were also two women described as ladies, each of whom paid 3s 4d.) Franklins, then, were almost as thick on the ground as resident knights and esquires; they were also generally, but by no means invariably, less well off. The fragmentary returns for Warwickshire tell a similar story, with two franklins and two widows of franklins paying 6s 8d each and over half of the forty recorded franklins paying at the rate of 3s 4d.[63] One such man was Richard Cloude of Canley near Coventry. He belonged to a well-established freeholding family on the estate of Stoneleigh Abbey and seems to have held at least 150 acres of land. He was the descendant, moreover, of one Robert de Canley, who had tried to carve a manorial lordship for himself at Canley back in the thirteenth century. One can well believe that such men, being very significant figures in their villages – especially where there was no resident member of the gentry – could be both ambitious and pretentious.

The problem is that, even so, these real historical figures do not quite conform to Chaucer's fictional Franklin. Most importantly, and unlike the literary Franklin, Richard Cloude and men of his status tended not to hold the major offices in the county administration – roles that were normally reserved for men of the rank of knight or esquire, who formed the established or 'county' gentry. Nigel Saul has suggested that 'Chaucer may well have been commenting in a vein of gentle satire not so much on what franklins were as on what they aspired to be'.[64] However, there may be more than just satire of social pretension going on here. Perhaps Chaucer was alluding to the snobbery and the exaggerated fear that existed within the established order lest the pretensions of such *burel* (coarse, unlearned) men as the Franklin be allowed to get out of hand. After all, Chaucer also plays on social instability in his depiction of the emancipated woman, the Wife of Bath. The hyperbole that surrounds the Franklin thus takes us directly into the tensions and status confusions

---

[62] C. C. Fenwick, ed., *The Poll Taxes of 1377, 1379 and 1381* (2 vols., British Academy, nos. XXVII, XXIX, 1998–2001), i, pp. 514–87.

[63] *Ibid.*, ii, pp. 642–88.

[64] N. Saul, 'The social status of Chaucer's Franklin: a reconsideration', *Medium Aevum*, 52 (1983), 23.

that existed in later fourteenth-century England. There were real franklins who were knocking on the door of gentility, just as some of their fore-bears had long done. The difference was that, in the changing world of post-plague England, there appeared to be more chance of the door opening. Other satirists pointed to the same phenomenon:

> And I beheulde a faire hous with halles and chambres,
> A frankeleyn-is fre-holde al fresshe newe.
> I bente me aboute and bode atte dore
> Of the gladdest gardyn that gome [man] ever had.[65]

The late fourteenth-century franklin was thus an ambivalent figure; and his ambivalence cut deeply into the world of deference in later fourteenth-century England. On the surface, at least, that ambivalence appears to have been resolved by the Statute of Additions of 1413, which led to the central law courts recording 'the estate, degree or mystery' of each party to a legal action. This effectively established a line of demarcation between those of gentle status on the one hand and the highest of the non-gentle, the yeomen, on the other. The gentlemen (and their wives) became, in effect, the lowest rank of gentry. The franklins, it seems, were split in twain. Those who came through as gentlemen included men like John Hyde, whose family had long held a substantial property (a hide of land) at Denchworth in Berkshire, and whose father had managed to acquire further property there in the late fourteenth century. The reality, however, was more complex than this simple model might suggest. For one thing, there was no necessary consistency in usage, with individuals being varyingly described, and the new title of 'gentle-man' took some time to fully establish itself. Moreover, the divide between gentleman and yeoman did not result simply from upward mobility in the countryside. Many of those called gentleman in the early fifteenth century were civil servants and professional bureaucrats. Others represented those local administrators and wealthy freeholders who had long lived on the margins of gentility. It may be that, as society emerged from the period of crisis that characterised the second half of the four-teenth century, the line between the gentle and the non-gentle was drawn a little further down the scale. On the whole, though, it seems that the grade of gentleman resulted more from the need for sharper definition than from a widening of gentility. With this sharper definition, older and

---

[65] M. Day and R. Steele, eds., *Mum and the Sothsegger* (EETS, os CXCIX, 1936), lines 945–51.

imprecise social terms such as franklin fell away and the divide between gentleman and yeoman increasingly captured the imagination.

It is significant that Chaucer's aspiring Franklin rides to Canterbury with the Serjeant-at-Law. Great fortunes could be made from the law, as Philippa Maddern discusses below.[66] The Leicestershire poll tax returns reveal one serjeant of the law paying £2, one 'great' apprentice of the law (to use the terminology of the tax preamble) paying £1, and six men described as either attorneys or apprentices of the law paying 6s 8d each. Lawyers were one of the more destabilising elements in later medieval society because they tended to carve out lordships for themselves and because their rise was often resented, not least because they came from within local communities. The classic example is the Paston family. William Paston rose from rural (perhaps even unfree) stock to become a justice of the common bench. William was the son of Clement Paston, described in the fifteenth century as a 'good, plain husbandman' with 100–120 acres of land in Paston – much of it bond land – and a small water mill. William's uncle, Geoffrey Somerton, a lawyer and himself seemingly of lowly origins, sent William to school. Through his purchases William established a lordship, a 'seigneury', at Paston itself. In addition to land, he acquired unfree tenants of his own and set about turning the Paston home into a manor house. His improvements necessitated a royal licence to move the road from the south to the north of his house, affecting access to the church – positively in the case of the Pastons themselves, negatively in the case of the villagers. In the years following William's death in 1444, there surfaced repeated and strident hostility to the Pastons that reveals an enormous amount about the social tensions and jealousies that could result from the uppitiness of neighbours who were once equals and who now claimed to be lords. The ultimate insult to the Pastons was that they had servile origins; as Caroline Barron has stressed, there was 'more than a whiff of bondage' about the land that Clement Paston had held.[67] If the Pastons, with William's success and all the additional resources this brought, still found it difficult to persuade contemporaries of their status, then the suspicion engendered by those men of the law who rose never so high can only be imagined. Although resentment against lawyers had become traditional by Chaucer's day, there is every reason to suppose that it was sharper during the heightened social tension of the late fourteenth and early fifteenth centuries.

---

[66] See pp. 130–2.

[67] C. Barron, 'Who were the Pastons?', *Journal of the Society of Archivists*, 4 (1972), 534.

Before leaving the world of the 1379 poll tax, attention should be drawn to one further social category that figures there. 'Farmers' – that is, men who took leases on the demesne lands of lords – had been a longstanding feature of rural society. However, we catch them in 1379 at the beginning of a new phase in their history, one that brings us to the heart of changes that were taking place in the countryside during the later middle ages. According to the 1379 poll tax preamble, farmers of 'manors, parsonages and granges' were expected to pay sums ranging from 1s to 6s 8d, according to their estate. A glance at the Leicestershire and Warwickshire returns shows that the majority were paying the relatively modest sum of 1s (although it must be remembered that this was still three times the basic rate for this tax). A few, however, were paying high sums. Thomas de Kirby at Shepshed, John Mitchell at Marston Jabbett (an estate of Leicester Abbey), and John Bailey on the Coventry Priory estate at Southam, for example, all paid 3s 4d, while John de Barrow paid 6s 8d at Old Dalby, as did Thomas Cosford at Churchover. During the late fourteenth and early fifteenth centuries, such men became increasingly prominent. The years 1380–1410 witnessed a wholesale retreat from demesne agriculture, as the great lords – caught in the scissors of falling prices and rising labour costs – turned to leasing on a very large scale. It has been calculated that 'as the lords shed their demesnes, they were handing over to the farmers the management of agricultural production of perhaps a fifth or a quarter of the agricultural land in Britain'. In consequence farmers appeared as 'a powerful new force for change in the countryside'.[68]

The farmers came from a variety of backgrounds, but there seems no doubt that the majority were peasants, many of them customary tenants either of the manors whose demesnes they were leasing or of others nearby. They tended to come from the more substantial families of the villages whose members had often been active as reeves or manorial officials. Two well-documented examples come from Wiltshire. Both John Hickes, who leased Durrington from 1401 until his death in 1413/14, and Thomas Weylot alias Barber, who leased the demesne at Coombe Bisset during the years 1491–1523, came of long-established families who had held tenancies, manorial offices and public offices in Durrington. Both families were also of villein status. Even in Weylot's time, when the legal realities of unfreedom were becoming all but irrelevant, the mark of

[68] C. Dyer, *Making a Living in the Middle Ages: the people of Britain 850–1520* (New Haven, CT, 2002), p. 346.

villeinage still rankled, which may explain why Weylot used an alias.[69] Leasing seems to have provided a valuable opportunity for rising socially, as well as economically, above one's fellow villagers.

Some farmers had still higher ambitions. Since farming was an activity also undertaken by men of free peasant stock – and, indeed, by merchants, clergy and even members of the gentry (albeit often merely as contractors who then sub-let land to the peasantry), it is evident that the activity offered opportunities for considerable upward mobility and significant wealth accumulation. One socially aspirant farmer was John Andrewe who, in 1449, built the elegant property known as Hall House, which still stands at Sawbridge on the county boundary between Warwickshire and Northamptonshire. John and his brother Thomas were of local peasant stock and were the lessees of the Sawbridge demesne. They appear later in the records of the court of king's bench as gentlemen. In 1476 they were granted a coat of arms and fabricated an ancient pedigree for themselves. Other more hard-headed farmers have some claim to be regarded as among England's first capitalists. Roger Heritage of Burton Dasset, Warwickshire, for example, was farming around 500 acres of land by 1480 and paying a rent of £20 per annum to the lord of the manor. He produced for the market on a large scale, employed a considerable labour force and reinvested his profits in buildings and equipment. He seems to have lived frugally, was businesslike in outlook and indifferent to the social climbing of men like the Andrewe brothers. In the world of proto-capitalists, men like Roger Heritage stand alongside the famous merchant clothiers who were controlling the clothmaking processes and marketing the finished products.[70]

It is important, however, not to see these developments in isolation from other aspects of rural social life. Peasant families in general were increasing the size of their holdings by the fifteenth century. Everyone, it seems, was better off. The rural population as a whole was better fed and better housed in the fifteenth century, and enjoyed more and better personal possessions and household goods. At the same time, the new agrarian conditions did not lead to greater equality. For the more substantial peasant families the opportunities to accumulate land were greater

[69] J. N. Hare, 'The demesne leases of fifteenth-century Wiltshire', *Ag. Hist. Rev.*, 29 (1981), 1–15. Matthew Oxe of Staverton (Suffolk) changed his surname when he acquired manumission: M. Bailey, 'Rural society', in Horrox, *Fifteenth-Century Attitudes*, p. 158.

[70] N. W. Alcock and C. T. P. Woodfield, 'Social pretensions in architecture and ancestry: Hall House, Sawbridge, Warwickshire and the Andrewe family', *Antiquaries Journal*, 76 (1996), 51–72; C. Dyer, 'Were there any capitalists in fifteenth-century England?' in J. Kermode, ed., *Enterprise and Individuals in Fifteenth-Century England* (Stroud, 1991), pp. 10–15.

than ever before, and rural society became increasingly differentiated into the three categories of yeoman, husbandman and labourer. It has been calculated that, by the end of the fifteenth century, an eighth of rural householders held fifty acres of land or more – a vast difference over the period before the Black Death.[71] At the top end, the level of accumulation could be considerable, and the distinction between a prosperous yeoman and a demesne farmer was often blurred. John Mell of Bramfield in Suffolk, for example, who had inherited forty-eight acres in 1461, had increased his holding, through a combination of purchase and leasing, to 150 acres in 1478. His will contained bequests amounting to £26 13s 4d to the younger sons and daughters of his family. Such men were members of what Christopher Dyer has called 'the brave and ruthless new world at the end of the Middle Ages'.[72]

The fifteenth century saw the end of servile status, not through political revolt but largely through peasant migration as families and individuals moved in search of better land and better conditions. This was the age of deserted and shrunken villages, the combined effect of mortality and migration. Peasant families were now geographically mobile to a quite extraordinary degree, greatly reducing whatever affective bond may previously have existed between land and family. The distinction between tenures became blurred as leasehold expanded and as servile status was increasingly removed from customary land. The latter, in consequence, became more desirable, fuelling the land market. Villein tenure was replaced essentially by copyhold tenure, whereby a tenant could show title through a written copy of an entry in the manor court roll. Although landlords were far from powerless, peasants were often in a position to resist landlord exactions by rent strikes and by leaving, or threatening to leave.

Lords, then, were often forced to relax conditions – to offer incentives, one might say – to retain their tenants. It was necessary, moreover, for landlords to be alert to the needs of their tenants and to the fragility of the landlord–tenant relationship. This relationship could be particularly strained when lords faced claimants to their estates. Once again, the Paston letters can take us beyond the starkness of the usual run of records. In June 1465 John Paston, learning that one of his manors was likely to be under attack, advised his wife Margaret 'that ye conforte my tenantis and help hem til I com hom, and let hem wet [know] that I shall not lese it'; 'ye be a gentilwoman', he adds, 'and it is worshep for yow to confort yowr

---

[71] Dyer, *Making a Living*, pp. 357–8. [72] *Ibid.*, p. 362.

tenantis'.[73] Margaret may indeed have had some genuine compassion for her tenants, especially those of her ancestral manor of Mautby, which she had brought to her Paston marriage. In the same year, she wrote to her husband suggesting that the Mautby tenants be given rushes from the Paston marsh and the windfall wood 'that is of noo gret valewe' to help with the necessary repairs to their houses. A few years later she wrote to her eldest son that 'your lyffelod hath stond this ii yere in such trobill that ye myght right nought have of it, ner yet can take of it wyth-ought ye shuld hurt your tenauntes. Thei have so ben vexid be on-trewe means before this tyme'.[74] This sounds like an indictment, implicit if not explicit, of her late husband. As if to underline the point, Margaret remembered all her tenants in her will. Every household was to have 4d, 6d or 8d – or, at Mautby, 1s.[75] One is left to wonder just how rare, or just how common, such compassion was. One wonders, too, whether it was encountered before landlords found themselves coming upon hard times.

In this 'golden age of the English peasantry', as it is sometimes called, life in the countryside was undoubtedly 'freer' than it had been in the past. The increased bargaining power enjoyed by tenants and the ultimate failure of the landlord reaction after the Black Death ensured that this was so. With the end of demesne farming, the disappearance of servile obligations and the shortage of tenants, the landlords were relaxing their hold. The manor court went into steady decline. As one recent commentator has put it, 'The withering of serfdom and the transformation of villein tenure into contractual tenures reduced the range and volume of seigniorial business conducted in manor courts, which in turn may have resulted in more lax administration and greater slippage of cases'.[76] The decline of manor courts was hastened when the peasant tenants ceased to use them for their own suits against one another. The system of frankpledge also declined, and with it some of the power of the leet courts. However, this sense of rural emancipation should not be taken too far. These local courts did not disappear altogether. There was still a need to maintain order. Indeed, the system of by-laws, much used in the past to regulate agriculture, was greatly extended and actively used by the village elites as a means of maintaining harmony. Leet courts, too, continued to regulate behaviour. Above these courts were the quarter sessions held by the justices of the peace, who had

---

[73] Davis, *Paston Letters*, i, no. 73.   [74] *Ibid.*, i, nos. 178, 210.

[75] C. Richmond, 'Landlord and tenant: the Paston evidence', in Kermode, *Enterprise and Individuals*, p. 36.

[76] Bailey, *English Manor*, p. 184.

increasingly wide responsibilities entrusted to them. In the fifteenth century an increasing number of prominent men were appointed to the county bench, even if they did not invariably sit. It was in the sessions of the peace, more than anywhere else, that people directly encountered the status and power of the landowners.

If life was becoming freer in the countryside, the opposite seems to have been true in at least some of the towns. It is of course a truism that town air made a person free, although there is need for some qualification. Small towns were in large measure the product of seigniorial initiative, and the landlord's presence continued to be felt to a greater or lesser degree. In the larger towns there were numerous private jurisdictions. Nevertheless, in the royal boroughs and in the greater seigniorial towns, in particular, a large measure of autonomy was achieved. Despite a necessary array of civic officials, there was often a strong sense of freedom from oppression. In the fifteenth century, however, towns seem to have become more authoritarian and oligarchic. This was due, in part at least, to the decline in absolute levels of population and trade and the resultant fall in municipal (as opposed to personal) incomes. To maximise the income that remained, and to protect the privileges of the urban elite, more regulatory regimes were introduced. At the same time, there was a decline in popular participation in government and a greater concentration than ever on wealth as the chief qualification for office. There was an increasing tendency for aldermen to be appointed for life and for mayors to be chosen only from their number. There was greater emphasis now both on the dignity of office and on pomp and ceremony in government. At York, for example, the mayor now became 'my lord mayor' and was preceded in procession by a serjeant carrying a sword and a mace.[77] At Coventry, and elsewhere, an insult to a 'man of worship' was regarded as a dire offence.[78]

Urban society was therefore just as status-conscious as was rural. Chaucer portrays his town-based pilgrims in the *Canterbury Tales* – the Merchant, the five London guildsmen and the Wife of Bath – as richly, even ostentatiously, dressed, and makes it abundantly clear that this is largely for effect. The guildsmen's wives enjoy being addressed as 'madame' and leading the procession at church. The Wife of Bath was 'out of all charity' should anyone approach the altar to make their

---

[77] S. H. Rigby and E. Ewan, 'Government, power and authority, 1300–1540', in D. M. Palliser, ed., *The Cambridge Urban History of Britain, I: 600–1540* (Cambridge, 2000), pp. 309–12.
[78] M. D. Harris, ed., *The Coventry Leet Book* (EETS, os CXXXIV–V, CXXXVIII, CXLVI, 1907–13), ii, p. 569; M. D. Harris, *The Story of Coventry* (1911), p. 85.

offering before her, usurping her rank.[79] Urban society, then, was imbued with the notion of precedence and deeply affected by the language of gentility. The Statute of Additions and the recognition of the rank of gentleman penetrated urban society too. Neither living nor working in towns were necessarily bars to gentility and town-based lawyers and bureaucrats and office-holding merchants were often accorded the title of gentleman. That said, it is also true that many wealthy merchants who did not hold office preferred not to take up the title, possibly because it retained service connotations. The great Newcastle merchant of the fifteenth century, Roger Thornton, was called merchant on his magnificent Flemish brass, despite the fact that he possessed a coat of arms and that his family intermarried with the greatest families in the county. If Londoners are anything to go by, merchants – even if they adopted coats of arms – remained aloof from chivalric culture until well into the fifteenth century.[80]

COURTESY AND PRECEDENCE

While notions of gentility remained both fluid and contested throughout the later middle ages, fundamental notions about appropriate social behaviour were at once more constant and more broadly disseminated. Courtesy books – manuals of etiquette, dealing in the minutiae of good manners and deportment – were extremely popular in the fifteenth century and survive in large numbers. Some appear to have been aimed at the children of yeomen farmers and the like, although they were probably mostly read in households more elevated than that. They reveal a veritable obsession with precedence. John Russell, who was marshal to Humphrey, duke of Gloucester, was much exercised in his *Boke of Nurture* over the seating arrangements for the guests who might appear at a noble household.[81]

The persistence of a strong sense of hierarchy is also reflected in fifteenth-century letters. John Paston I began a letter to the duke of Norfolk, around 1455, with 'Right hy and myghty prynce, my right gode and gracyous lord, I recomand me to your godelordship'.[82] Such language was reserved for dukes, however, and they responded in a manner which

[79] The Riverside edition, General Prologue, lines 376–8, 449–52.
[80] C. Barron, 'Chivalry, pageantry and merchant culture in medieval London', in Coss and Keen, *Heraldry, Pageantry and Social Display*, pp. 219–41.
[81] F. J. Furnivall, ed., *The Babees Book* (EETS, os XXXII, 1868), pp. 185–94.
[82] Davis, *Paston Letters*, i, no. 51.

reflected their sense of position: 'Right trusti and right welbelovid, we [*sic*] grete ye hertily well'.[83] Lesser lords were not addressed in princely terms, nor did they respond with a ducal 'we'. John Paston wrote to Lord Grey, for example, as 'Right worshipfull and my ryght gode lord'.[84] 'Right trusty and well beloved', with variants, remained a standard mode by which lords addressed gentle inferiors. At the lower end of the scale Richard Calle, the Paston bailiff, addressed John Paston I as 'Ryght reverent and my mooste wurschipfull maistre'. James Gloys, the family chaplain, addressed John as 'right reverent and wurchepfull ser', adding on one occasion 'and my gode mayster'.[85] Letters could also be downright obsequious, as in a letter to John Paston III from the bailiffs of Yarmouth, which begins, 'Right reverent and wurshipfull ser and oure veray lovyng and curteys good maystir', and ends, 'Youre loveres and bedmen [bedesmen] the old Baliffis of Yermouth and the newe Balyffis that now shalbe'.[86]

Such elaborate terms of address were of course a matter of form. Although the marriage of Margery Brews to John Paston III had been a love match, she would still begin her letters to John, 'Right reverent and worshipfull ser, in my most umble vice [wise] I recomaunde me unto yow as lowly as I can'. But their continuing use, even in contexts where they are undercut by expressions of hostility or affection, is symptomatic of a society acutely conscious of hierarchy. They allow us to glimpse a consciousness of status that would also have been manifest in speech and (the most difficult of all to reconstruct) in body language. The illustrator of *The Beauchamp Pageant* – a biography of Richard, earl of Warwick composed for his daughter and heiress Anne in the later fifteenth century – was clearly well aware of the etiquette associated with doffing or removing headgear, or of the distinction between bending the knee and kneeling. It was this awareness of what was appropriate behaviour that allowed body language to be insulting. In the early fifteenth century Cambridge undergraduates went 'jetting' – swaggering through the streets – to the outrage of the townsmen. Deference could be denied, but its very denial was a sign of how much it still mattered.

---

[83] So wrote the duke of Norfolk to John Paston I; the duchess of Norfolk and the duke of York addressed him similarly: *ibid.*, i, nos. 464, 466, 504.
[84] *Ibid.*, i, no. 50.
[85] *Ibid.*, ii, nos. 443, 473–4, 532, 618, 632, 645.
[86] *Ibid.*, ii, no. 825.

CHAPTER 3

The enterprise of war

Michael Prestwich

The trappings of war were everywhere in late medieval England. Knightly families prided themselves on the military insignia of their coats of arms. Tombs showed knights in full armour. Seals displayed lords mounted on their chargers. Even a water jug might take the form of a fully armed and mounted knight. The concept of war was glorified in a world of chivalric values. War was not, however, a matter of colourfully caparisoned knights riding to battle in a glamorous cavalcade. It was a highly complex business. Resources were mobilised on a massive scale to ensure that armies were properly supplied and financed. Bankers gambled as they lent to competing monarchs. Fortunes were won and lost, notably in the ransom market that followed success on the battlefield. War was also a powerful engine for social change; fortunes could be lost and won, not only by those who fought, but also by those who financed and supplied the campaigns.

The intensity of war varied considerably. In the early thirteenth century England was a backwater in military terms. King John lost his continental possessions with the exception of those in south-western France, and by the end of his reign there was a very real possibility that Capetian France would absorb the English monarchy. Under his successor Henry III expeditions to France were few, and did little more than defend existing English possessions; there was no realistic hope of recovering Normandy. Civil war in the mid 1260s was fierce, but brief. There was a series of campaigns in Wales, which culminated in conquest under Edward I, but war was not a constant element in men's lives in the thirteenth century. Matters began to change in 1294, with a four-year-long French war that was the precursor of the frequent campaigns of the fourteenth and the first half of the fifteenth century. War against the Scots began in 1296; this was the one conflict that seriously spilled over into England itself. Hard lessons were learned in the Scottish wars, and applied to war in France. The so-called Hundred Years War began in 1337, and although the conflict was punctuated by some extended periods of truce, war not peace became the normal situation. English armies were the most formidable in Europe, and achieved astonishing successes at Crécy in 1346 and at Poitiers ten years later. In the fifteenth century, after Henry V's great victory at Agincourt in 1415, the momentum could not be maintained, even though hardly a year went by without an English expedition to France until the war ended in 1453. Sporadic civil war between the houses of Lancaster and York followed, along with intermittent campaigning in Scotland, notably in 1481–2. The possibility of English intervention in France also retained a powerful attraction. Edward IV invaded in 1475, and even Henry VII found himself drawn into military involvement on behalf of Brittany.

The scale of English involvement in war was as varied as its intensity. Large armies were the rule under Edward I. He had some 30,000 men involved in putting down the Welsh rebellion of 1294–5, and almost as many in the Scottish campaign of 1298. Edward III had roughly 30,000 men at the siege of Calais in 1346–7, but most of the armies of his reign were much smaller. Henry V had some 10,000 troops with him when he landed in France in 1415, but by the time his troops reached Agincourt sickness had substantially reduced the number of the 'happy few' who won that famous battle. Numbers in the final campaigns in France were very much smaller; it was rare for an expeditionary force in Henry VI's reign to exceed 2,000 men.

The higher up a man was in the social hierarchy, the more likely he was to fight. It was highly exceptional to find an earl who did not campaign; the case of two successive earls of Hereford in Edward III's reign who never fought in war is perhaps to be explained by some physical incapacity. Knights were expected to fight; in the course of an inquiry held in 1324 the sheriff of Buckinghamshire explained with some surprise that John Stonor was a man of arms who had never actually taken up arms – the explanation is that he was a lawyer. Arguments that another justice, Henry le Scrope, lacked nobility were countered in a lawsuit of 1386 by the fact that his father had been knighted at the battle of Falkirk. When Bartholomew de Lisle abandoned his duty defending the Isle of Wight in 1340, he was sternly rebuked: 'It is not becoming for belted knights to eloign themselves from places where deeds of war may take place, but rather to go to those places and stay there for honour's sake'.[1]

The number of knights in England changed radically in the course of this period. At the start of the thirteenth century there were probably up to 5,000, but in the relatively peaceful years of Henry III's reign there was

[1] *Calendar of Close Rolls, Preserved in the Public Record Office, Edward III, 1339–41* (1901), p. 444.

a rapid decline.[2] By the third quarter of the century numbers had fallen by over half, and in the early fourteenth century there were probably some 1,500 knights in England. Numbers then changed little until the third quarter of the fourteenth century; success in war no doubt encouraged men to take up knighthood. There was a truce in the French war from 1360 to 1369, and when fighting began again it became far more difficult to recruit knights than it had been earlier. In the fifteenth century the proportion of knights in English armies could be very low indeed. When the earl of Huntingdon took a force of over 2,000 men to Gascony in 1439, he had no more than six knights with him. As knightly numbers declined, so their place came to be taken by squires, who, by the later fourteenth century, were armed and equipped in a way that made them virtually indistinguishable from knights. Gentility, rather than specifically knighthood, became a key social distinction. When in 1433 an esquire serving in Gascony, William Packington, heard Thomas Souderne say that he was 'no sort of gentleman' and that he was really a haberdasher, he promptly killed him in hot blood.[3]

Fighting as a knight was not reserved for the young and fit. Many knights continued to campaign into what would now be regarded as their retirement years. Sir Thomas Ughtred fought at Bannockburn in 1314, and led his retinue in Edward III's campaign of 1359–60, in a military career lasting forty-six years. Hugh Calvely, a hero of Edward III's French wars, campaigned for over forty years. John de Sully claimed to have fought his first battle in 1333 and his last in 1367 – a thirty-four-year career. The earl of Shrewsbury was sixty-six when he was killed in battle at Castillon in 1453. No doubt there were some men of knightly and gentle rank who did not fight in many campaigns, but in the French wars many fought year in, year out. John de Lisle did not miss a single major campaign between 1338, when he was twenty, and his death on the Black Prince's expedition of 1355. He had a vested interest in the war, for the king had granted him £40 a year for as long as it lasted.

Knightly ideology was distinctive. Chivalry provided knights, and those who fought in knightly fashion, with a culture that helped to justify war. Men sought to emulate such heroes of myth and history as Arthur and Alexander. The values of generosity, courtesy, prowess and loyalty were promoted; great stress was laid upon honour. Women gave their

---

[2] Other possible reasons for the decline are discussed on pp. 36–8 above.

[3] D. A. L. Morgan, 'The individual style of the English gentleman', in M. Jones, ed., *Gentry and Lesser Nobility in Later Medieval England* (Gloucester, 1986), p. 23.

heroes tokens to wear in war, as a means of encouraging them to perform deeds of valour. The emblems of chivalry were highly prized. Heraldic devices had an obvious utility as a means of recognising men in battle, but became an important emblem of lineage, symbolising family honour and pride. The roof of Henry III's great new church of Westminster Abbey was seen as an appropriate place to display the coats of arms of the upper nobility. The way in which men sought to be remembered emphasised the importance of war and chivalry in their lives. Effigies of knights on their tombs showed them in full armour, even on occasion on horseback, and memorial brasses likewise perpetuated the military image.

Tournaments were great celebrations of chivalry and major social occasions. The government frequently tried to control or even prevent them from being held, for rather than providing useful training they offered a distraction from the hard business of war. They might also provide a cover for unwelcome political gatherings, as in Edward II's reign. Edward III, however, developed the tournament as a way of building support for his military enterprises. He even planned an Arthurian order of knights, with a great round table at Windsor, though in the event what was carried forward with the foundation of the Order of the Garter in the late 1340s was a cut-down economy version.

Chivalric attitudes both influenced, and were influenced by, contemporary literature. Brian FitzAlan, who fought for Edward I in Scotland, possessed a copy of the Arthurian romance *Perlesvaus*. James Audley, one of the heroes of Crécy, owned at least four volumes of what were termed romances. Tales of Arthur and Alexander emphasised the way in which war, as well as love, should be conducted with honour. The story of William Marmion, given a helmet with a golden crest by his ladylove in the early fourteenth century and told to make it famous in the most dangerous place in Britain, demonstrates the way in which the ideals of romance might be turned into distinctly dangerous reality. He charged into the Scottish forces besieging Norham Castle. Of course, in practice men did not always behave in a chivalrous manner. The annals of warfare are full of unchivalrous incidents. Dishonest *ruses de guerre*, attacks on enemies when they were unprepared, pillage, destruction and rape: these were the common currency of medieval knights as well as of those soldiers who were their social inferiors. Men found surprisingly little difficulty in accepting both the ideals of chivalry and the tough realities of war. The one no doubt helped to make the other more acceptable.

The way in which armies were organised had its effect on the changing structure of aristocratic society. English forces had never been fully feudal (that is, raised on the basis of service owed in return for tenure of land), and certainly could not be so described in this period. Even in the early thirteenth century there was no question of the king's tenants-in-chief going on campaign at the head of contingents formed from their landed tenants, and producing the service of over 5,000 knights that was their theoretical obligation. Geoffrey FitzPeter, for example, served on the Irish campaign of 1210 with ten knights, not the ninety-eight and a third that he was formally obliged to provide. Radically reduced new quotas were established by 1245, which meant that there could no longer be any expectation that the land making up a traditional knightly fee carried a burden of providing a knight for royal campaigns. Feudal service at the reduced level continued to be requested, though not for all campaigns, until it was effectively abandoned in 1327. In Edward I's Welsh campaign of 1277, 228 knights and 294 sergeants (two of the latter being equivalent to one knight) served for the forty days of feudal service. In 1322 about 500 troops performed feudal service on a futile campaign against the Scots. A late revival of feudal service, in 1385, was essentially fiscal, not military, in purpose.

Given the outdated and ineffective character of feudal military service, it is not surprising that the crown attempted to introduce other systems of military obligation, based on an assessment of men's wealth. Edward I's attempt to recruit all landowners worth at least £20 a year ran into acute political difficulties in 1297, but Edward II attempted the summons of all £50 landholders in 1316, and a radical reconstruction of military service was considered in 1324. Edward III introduced a graduated scale for assessing landholders' contributions to the army in 1344, but an attempt to recruit men on this basis in the following year was extremely unpopular. Obligatory service was effectively abandoned by the crown in 1352. The success of the war in France meant that pay and the prospects of profits from booty and ransoms were all the persuasion men needed to fight.

The main building blocks for the armies of the later middle ages were thus not feudal contingents, but aristocratic retinues. These might vary very considerably in size, from a small handful of men to a force numbered in hundreds. Formal agreements between lords and their followers for the provision of service in war and elsewhere survive from the late thirteenth century, although it is clear that the practice of retaining was much older than that. Retainers were granted fees and robes annually in return for their services; they were also paid wages and might receive other benefits. The evidence suggests that, while most men would have a small core of regular retainers, there was a considerable turnover of men in military retinues. Of the fifty-two men known to have been in the earl of Lincoln's retinue in Scotland in 1307, no more than eighteen had campaigned with him previously. In the case of the Yorkshire knight Thomas Ughtred, two-thirds of those he employed in his following in the second quarter of the fourteenth century cannot be shown to have served under him for more than a single campaign. The stability of retinues increased in time, but the military retinue was never identical with that of peacetime conditions. As discussed in the previous chapter, lords needed estate managers and lawyers just as they needed knights and esquires in their armed followings. The extent to which military retaining patterns conditioned the development of what is often termed bastard feudalism was, therefore, limited. Lords retained men by means of indentures and grants of annuity for many different reasons, of which the need for a military following was only one.

The general populace was far less involved in war than were the aristocrats and knights. Recruitment was at a higher level in some regions than others. Cheshire, for example, was called on with great regularity, with the result that a tradition of service built up in the county. Some of the archers and infantrymen must have been, in effect, professional soldiers during the campaigning of the Hundred Years War, but it is not possible to reconstruct their careers in the way that can be done for the knights. There is very little evidence to show what sort of training villagers received to turn them into soldiers, but an ordinance of 1363, frequently reissued thereafter, condemned the popularity of worthless games such as football, and ordered men to practise archery on every holiday. Records of musters at which commissioners of array recruited villagers for the wars suggest that most men possessed some appropriate equipment, but local communities had to bear the cost of providing them with the full accoutrements required. Under Edward I the cost to a village was about 5s for each soldier recruited, but by the 1330s, when lightly armed horsemen or mounted archers were requested, the sum rose to about £2. One indication of the burden on local communities is the bribes that they were prepared to pay to be let off. The men of Grantham, for example, paid £1 6s 8d for exemption from providing two archers in the late 1330s. Not surprisingly, many of those who were recruited came from the dregs of society. Edward I began the practice of filling the ranks of the army by emptying the country's gaols. Robert Knollys was said to have recruited for his raid in France in 1370 'various escaped men of religion and apostates, and also many thieves and robbers from various gaols'.[4] Desertion by the infantry shows that military service was not popular. Edward I's armies, especially in Scotland, suffered losses on a massive scale, and harsh measures were threatened against those who left the army without permission. Once in France, however, desertion was less of a problem, for it was far less easy to return home from overseas.

How were men rewarded for their service? Pay was one answer, but in the thirteenth century many magnates were ready to provide substantial numbers of troops at their own expense. It was beneath an earl's dignity to take pay from the king, and many barons followed the same line of thinking. There was a reluctance to accept the subordination implicit in accepting pay from the crown, and an expectation that the king would provide rewards in a different way, above all by granting out conquered land. Evidence suggests that about two-thirds of the cavalry in Edward I's Scottish campaigns served on a voluntary basis. The burden on noble budgets was considerable, and it is not surprising that Edward received complaints in 1297 from some great men, arguing that they lacked the resources to provide troops. Overseas campaigns were more expensive than those in Britain, and were therefore viewed differently; pay was acceptable abroad. Under Edward II, the powerful earl of Lancaster was not prepared to take pay from a king he despised. By Edward III's reign, however, noble attitudes had changed, and pay was universal.

Pay was intended less as a reward than as a means of covering costs. There was nothing new in the thirteenth century in paying troops. Mercenaries had been a very significant component in the Anglo-Norman armies of the eleventh and twelfth centuries. The knights of the royal household, who formed the core of many armies, were normally paid wages in addition to receiving fees and robes. In the initial phase of the Hundred Years War the king paid double wages in order to encourage men to join in what must have appeared a very risky venture. This proved too expensive, and became less necessary as enthusiasm built up for the war. The 1340s saw the introduction of the 'regard', a bonus paid quarterly, which enhanced the direct rewards men received. Pay was certainly not sufficient to meet the costs of buying horses to replace those lost on campaign, and until the later fourteenth century the crown paid compensation for any horses that were killed or found to be incapable of further campaigning.

The rates of pay for infantry troops were set at very reasonable levels. In the thirteenth century the normal rate was 2d a day; this rose in the

---

[4] V. H. Galbraith, ed., *The Anonimalle Chronicle 1338 to 1381* (Manchester, 1927), p. 63.

Hundred Years War, when mounted archers would receive 6d. In comparison with agricultural wages, these were good sums of money. It is striking, however, that whereas the Black Death of 1348–9 and the resultant labour shortages caused a substantial rise in agricultural and other wages in England, military wage rates were not affected in the same way. Wages had stood at the same levels for a long time, and recruitment was not so difficult as to make a change necessary.

Other forms of reward were probably more important than pay. Grants of conquered land were much sought after, particularly by the greater men. After his conquest of Wales in 1282–3, Edward I distributed major estates in North Wales to the earls and others who had made his success possible. The earl of Lincoln received Denbigh and Earl Warenne was granted the lordship of Bromfield and Yale. In Scotland, the king promised lands to his followers even before they had been captured, and a significant vested interest in the war was built up. The position in France was less easy, for there Edward III was fighting, as he saw it, to establish his rightful claim to the throne. He could hardly afford to alienate his potential French subjects by promising their lands to his English followers. Henry V, however, following his conquest of Normandy, had no scruples about granting Norman estates to his commanders and others in his armies. He made no fewer than 358 grants of Norman land, establishing a strong English interest in retaining the duchy. Grants of regular annuities to those who served well in war were also important, particularly under Edward III.

Captured prisoners might be ransomed. This was unlikely to yield much in the case of Welsh or Scottish campaigns, but in the fourteenth century the fruits of the ransom trade in France were ripe and ready for picking. Guy of Flanders, captured by Walter Mauny in 1337, was sold to Edward III for £8,000. At Crécy both sides were ordered to fight to the death, but even so some prisoners were taken. Poitiers was a very different story. A host of prisoners was taken, and huge ransoms demanded. Edward III bought three captives from his son, the Black Prince, for £20,000 and the earl of Warwick ransomed the archbishop of Sens for £8,000. The crown benefited greatly from the royal ransoms received as a result of the capture of David II, king of Scots, in 1346, and above all that of the French king, John II, in 1356. This latter ransom was worth £500,000, though in practice not all of it was paid. The ransom trade was not, of course, all one-way. The Scots benefited financially as well as militarily from their triumph at Bannockburn, with the capture of men such as the earl of Hereford and John de Segrave. The crown contributed

£3,000 towards the ransom of Henry Percy, taken prisoner at Otterburn in 1387. English defeats in France carried a heavy financial penalty. John Talbot could not afford the heavy ransom demanded after his capture at Patay in 1429, and received a grant of £9,000 from the crown to help him purchase his release. The crown was not always so generous. Henry IV's refusal to contribute to the ransom of Edmund Mortimer, captured by Owain Glyn Dŵr in 1402, led to Mortimer joining forces with his captor. Despite such examples, the English undoubtedly gained more than they lost from the business of ransoming prisoners.

Plunder was another way that soldiers profited from war. The purpose of the great raids or *chevauchées*, so characteristic of Edward III's French wars, was to ravage the countryside and to place intolerable economic pressure on the enemy, as well as to force them to battle. For individuals, there were splendid opportunities to capture valuables. It was later said that, after the capture of Caen in 1346, there was not an English matron who was not decked with splendid cloths taken from the French. There were conventions about the taking of plunder; the lord claimed a proportion. When the earl of Salisbury made an indenture with Geoffrey Walsh in 1347, it was laid down that the earl was to receive half the profits of ransoms and booty. By the 1370s, the normal proportion retained by the lord was one third; when the custom of paying for lost horses was given up, the proportion of booty men could retain was increased.

War was a major enterprise, which affected the English economy in a wide range of ways. Good-quality horses were needed, even when knights were expected to fight on foot in battle, as they were first asked to do in 1327, and the demands of war transformed horse-breeding. Records of royal stud farms show the great efforts put into this, and magnates must have also striven to improve the quality of their mounts. There was also a substantial trade in high-quality bloodstock from abroad, particularly from southern Europe. Edward I began importing horses at the time of his first Welsh campaign in 1277, and early in Edward III's reign horses were bought for the king in Sicily and Spain.

Armies needed to be fed, and this could have a significant impact on the agrarian economy. This was especially the case with campaigns in Wales and Scotland. Although there was a much greater expectation that soldiers fighting in France could live off the land, supply from England was important for them, too. In Henry V's reign there was a royal victualling office at Harfleur performing much the same function as Edward I's offices had done at Berwick and Skinburness; and even when supply systems within Normandy had been organised, some foodstuffs were still brought by sea from England. The quantities that were purveyed by royal officials might be very considerable. Late in 1296 Edward I ordered the seizure of 33,000 quarters of grain, and accounts from 1297 suggest that the king seized at least 10,300 quarters of wheat, 6,700 quarters of oats, 2,400 quarters of barley and malt, and 1,000 quarters of beans and peas for his armies. The calculation that London, with a population of up to 100,000, required some 165,000 quarters of grain a year helps to put these figures into perspective. The impact of such demands was not felt equally; regions near the campaigning areas, and the ports where the troops mustered, were especially hard hit. The eastern counties in particular suffered from demands for prises, as these compulsory purchases of foodstuffs were known. The process was highly unpopular. In contrast to the political conventions surrounding taxation, there was no principle of obtaining parliamentary consent for prises, and the process of collection itself was very open to corruption. In Edward III's reign the situation was eased, partly as armies were expected to live off the land in France and partly because increasing use was made of contracts with merchants to provide the foodstuffs needed by armies. In the fifteenth century commanders were largely expected to make their own arrangements to ensure that they had adequate supplies, thus reducing the burden on England and its government.

An army needed weaponry and other equipment. The work of armourers, fletchers, farriers, carpenters, wheelwrights and coopers was vital. Bows were simple weapons, but those of the highest quality could cost as much as 2s 6d each, though 1s 6d was a more normal price. Huge quantities of bows and arrows were accumulated by the crown in the middle years of the fourteenth century and stored in the Tower of London. In the late fifteenth century, by contrast, parliament was exercised by the perceived shortage and high cost of imported bow staves. Tents were needed. These might be splendid structures; early fourteenth-century accounts detail a seven-post 'hall' with two porches on each side. Carts were required for transport. On occasion major engineering projects were needed. Edward I had prefabricated pontoon bridges constructed, at very considerable expense, for the crossing from Anglesey to the Welsh mainland in 1282, and in Scotland to enable his forces to cross the Firth of Forth in 1303–4. The building of siege engines was another major undertaking. Edward I had no fewer than thirteen such pieces of equipment at the siege of Stirling in 1304, one of which, the great Warwolf, took some fifty carpenters three months to construct. It was less easy for the English to use large-scale siege equipment in the French wars;

big siege engines were difficult to transport across the Channel. Henry V, however, at the siege of Rouen in 1419, made full use both of trebuchets, huge throwing engines, and of artillery. The provision of all this equipment was a substantial burden.

Naval support was essential, even for campaigns within the British Isles; one of the keys to Edward I's successes was the proper co-ordination of land forces with support from the sea. The need for shipping in the Hundred Years War was great; in particular, it was not easy to transport large numbers of troops, with horses and equipment, to Gascony. It took at least one sailor for every two soldiers transported across the Channel. Some 300 vessels were needed to take Edward I's force of under 9,000 to Flanders in 1297. There was no permanent royal navy, but at some periods the crown possessed a number of vessels. Henry V owned about forty ships, but such a fleet came nowhere near meeting the needs of war. The great majority of ships used to transport troops, and for naval service, were merchant vessels, requisitioned by royal officials in an unpopular process. Although shipowners were usually rewarded for their service, seaports were badly affected by the demands made on them by the crown. Ships were frequently commandeered long before they were needed, and the prosperity of the ports, and indeed of English trade, undoubtedly suffered as a result, particularly during the fourteenth century. Yarmouth, for example, was hard hit by the crown's demands.

War was costly. Edward I conquered Wales in his campaign of 1282–3, and this meant expenditure of some £80,000, excluding the cost of the castles that were built to consolidate the achievement. The French war of 1294–8 saw about £165,000 spent on building up a grand alliance of continental princes. The defence of Gascony cost a further £400,000, and the king probably spent another £50,000 on his campaign in Flanders in 1297–8. The initial stages of the Hundred Years War saw relatively little fighting, and did not involve the recruitment of large English armies, but purchasing allies proved very costly. By October 1339 Edward III's debts were estimated at £300,000. In the early 1350s, which was not a period of especially heavy fighting, annual military expenditure ran at about £118,000, compared with £21,000 on domestic matters. In 1359–60, when Edward III conducted a large but ultimately unsuccessful campaign in France, the department of the royal wardrobe (which covered most of the war costs) incurred expenditure approaching £150,000. Defence was particularly expensive. The English success in capturing Calais in 1347 was a military triumph, but proved to be a financial disaster. Holding the town cost around £12,000 a year. The decision to adopt what was known as a 'barbican' policy in the late 1370s involved heavy expenditure on maintaining English-held fortresses on the French coast. The conquest of Normandy under Henry V was a superb military achievement, but it proved very costly to defend the duchy in the reign of his son. On a smaller scale, the English capture of Berwick in 1482 was thought by one disgruntled contemporary to have committed the country to more expense than it was worth.[5]

Taxation offered one solution to the problem of war finance, but even the combination of direct taxes and heavy customs duties might prove insufficient at such times of heavy expenditure as the 1290s and the late 1330s. The crown therefore needed loans to finance its campaigns. Italian merchant companies, notably the Riccardi and the Frescobaldi, provided funds under Edward I and his son. Such loans were a risky investment for hard-nosed men of business, for returns were very uncertain. Not surprisingly, the Italians regarded Edward III's military adventures sceptically, and failed to produce sums on the immense scale that the king required. The Bardi and Peruzzi companies did lend money in the early stages of the French war, but after both firms suffered major losses in the 1340s the way was left open to English financiers. The first great English merchant banker was William de la Pole, a Hull wool merchant by origin. Other merchants followed his lead, generally preferring to spread the risk by forming consortia. Courtiers might also lend to the crown. William Latimer, operating in partnership with the merchant Richard Lyons, was deeply involved in some distinctly questionable dealings with Edward III's government in the king's later years. In the fifteenth century Cardinal Beaufort did well for himself by lending to his nephew Henry VI in support of the war effort. Men of such eminence stood a good chance of being repaid. Smaller lenders were more vulnerable, and most vulnerable of all were the involuntary lenders: men who were not paid for goods and services supplied for the war effort.

War could have a profound effect on individual fortunes. It could make a man, or bankrupt him, and was an important determinant of social mobility. The cost of fighting was clearly a very considerable burden for magnates in the thirteenth century, especially if they did choose not to accept royal wages. Horses were expensive; a good warhorse might cost a knight a year's income. In 1297 William de Ferrers borrowed £200 from a merchant, William de Coumbmartin, to whom he mortgaged his manor of Newbottle, so that he could take part in the Flanders expedition.

---

[5] N. Pronay and J. Cox, eds., *The Crowland Chronicle Continuations 1459–1486* (1986), pp. 148–9.

On the same occasion, the earl of Arundel claimed that he was impoverished and received a royal licence to lease some of his lands for £100 a year so that he could meet his military costs. At the end of the Flanders campaign, William Martin lost all his equipment when his ship was wrecked in a storm, and the king promised him compensation of £510. Even in the successful years of the fourteenth century, fighting in France could prove costly for individuals. William Ferrers of Groby, for example, was exonerated in 1360 from paying any levy for the defence of Ireland from his Irish lands, since he had spent so much on the campaign in France in 1359–60. As the fortunes of war turned against the English in the fifteenth century, times became more difficult. In 1422 a merchant, Geoffrey Hebbe, enrolled in Henry V's army, perhaps in an attempt to restore his declining fortunes. He had to sell family property in his hometown of Chichester in order to fund his new career, which did not bring him the financial success he sought. Thomas Hostell, a man-at-arms who lost an eye from a crossbow bolt at Harfleur in 1415, went on to fight at Agincourt and at sea. Much later, he petitioned Henry VI, complaining that he was 'sorely hurt, maimed and wounded; as a result of which he is much enfeebled and weakened, and now being of great age has fallen into poverty'.[6] William Peyto was captured by the French in 1443, and had to mortgage his estates in order to pay his ransom. He was unable to obtain wages due to him from the crown, and by the time of his death in 1464 one of his manors was still in the hands of his creditors. At a higher level of society, the capture of Robert Hungerford, Lord Moleyns, in Gascony in 1453, and the need to pay a ransom of £6,000 for him, was a disaster for his family.

In contrast to the stories of financial disaster, there were many success stories. Men could make their fortunes as well as their reputations out of war. Thomas Rokeby was the lucky man who located the Scots and brought the news to the English army in 1327. For this he was knighted and received a promise of lands worth £100 a year. He prospered in the service of Edward III and became a major figure in the north. Walter Mauny, a Hainaulter, came to England at the start of Edward III's reign as a page to Queen Philippa. Through a mixture of royal patronage and the profits of campaigning, he established himself in England, eventually becoming a Knight of the Garter. Had his children not both been illegitimate girls, he would no doubt have established a new and powerful landed family in England. Walter Bentley was a Yorkshire knight of no

---

[6] A. Curry, *The Battle of Agincourt: sources and interpretations* (Woodbridge, 2000), pp. 435, 449.

great standing, but the confused situation in Brittany in the 1340s offered ample opportunities to someone of military skill and driving ambition. It was, however, marriage to a wealthy Breton widow, Lady de Clisson, rather than the direct proceeds of war, which enabled him to create a virtually independent lordship in the duchy. John de Coupland made his name and fortune after his success in capturing the Scottish king at Neville's Cross in 1346, receiving an annuity of £500 for life. In his case, success was cut short by his murder at the hands of a group of Northumberland gentry, angered by the methods he used to build up his landed wealth.[7] Thomas Erpingham's family were local Norfolk gentry of no great distinction. His military career began in Gascony in the late 1360s; he became a Knight of the Garter in 1400 and steward of the royal household under Henry V. His greatest moment came at Agincourt, when he was almost sixty; he was said in some accounts to have commanded the archers in the battle. Erpingham built up a substantial estate in his native county, partly through grants he received and partly by purchase. In spite of the difficulties encountered by the English regime in France following the death of Henry V, men such as John Fastolf were still able to do very well for themselves. Fastolf's inheritance had been worth about £46 a year, but with the profits he sent back to England, above all in the 1420s and 1430s, he was able to buy estates worth £775 a year. He also spent lavishly on jewellery, plate and books.

Men invested the fortunes of war in different ways, but many decided to put their winnings into stones and mortar. The great front of Warwick Castle stands as a very visible reminder of the success of the fourteenth-century earls of Warwick in the French wars. At a knightly level, John de la Mare's castle at Nunney in Somerset, John Cobham's at Cooling in Kent and Edward Dalingrigge's at Bodiam in Sussex all reflect the glories of fourteenth-century campaigns across the Channel, their battlements at least as much symbolic as practical. Walter Hungerford's castle at Farleigh Hungerford and John Fastolf's fine brick castle at Caister provide fifteenth-century examples. Raglan Castle on the Welsh border, with its great keep known as the Yellow Tower of Gwent, also reflects the profits of war gained by the Herbert family in the fifteenth century.

The successes of the aristocracy and gentry in bolstering their fortunes with the profits of war can be demonstrated much more easily than for soldiers of lower rank. There were not many who rose from the lowest status through their military achievements, and those who did could face

---

[7] Robert Salle, discussed below, is an analogous case, p. 88.

hostility. Robert Knollys probably began his career as a humble bowman. He acquired great fame fighting for Edward III in France in the fourteenth century, but his landed acquisitions in his native Cheshire were not on a large scale. Command in Brittany and elsewhere brought him power, but lasting wealth escaped him. Promises of land in Normandy did not amount to much. Nor did those of knightly birth who were under his command always appreciate his abilities; John Minsterworth, a Gloucestershire knight, led a mutiny against him. Robert Salle was another soldier of low birth, said to be of villein origins. He did well in the wars, became a knight, and acquired property in his native Norfolk. Resentment at his rise may explain his death at the hands of the East Anglian rebels in the Peasants' Revolt of 1381. 'We know you well, ye be no gentleman born, but son to a villein such as we be.'[8]

Most of the wars of this period were fought abroad, not on English soil. The immediate impact of war was, as a result, far less than in France. The regions bordering on Wales and Scotland, however, were directly affected. Welsh raids into England, and counter-raids launched from the marches, were a regular part of life before the Edwardian conquest. The holders of the marcher lordships established by the English crown in south and east Wales during earlier generations maintained a strong military tradition: it was their experience of war against the Welsh, indeed, that helped them to played a major part in the English civil wars of the mid-thirteenth century. Their lordships continued to be a fertile recruiting ground through the fourteenth century; this was a much more deeply militarised area than the peaceful areas of central, southern and eastern England.

The Scottish border was largely peaceful during the thirteenth century, but from 1296 the north of England experienced the agony of frequent foreign invasion, with all the horrors of burning and looting that entailed. The years of Edward II's reign in particular saw the north transformed as Scottish raiding parties destroyed swathes of territory with fire and sword, rendering previously profitable manors almost worthless. Men suffered greatly. In 1315 Robert de Reymes claimed that he had lost horses and armour worth 100 marks (£66 13s 4d), that he had paid a ransom of 500 marks (£333 6s 8d) to the Scots, and that his lands had been destroyed, at a loss of £1,000. Manorial accounts and valuations, even allowing for understandable exaggeration, provide testimony to the widespread damage done by the Scots. No defensive strategy seemed to work. The

---

[8] R. B. Dobson, ed., *The Peasants' Revolt of 1381* (2nd edn, 1983), p. 263.

great castles of the north, such as Warkworth and Alnwick, were no real obstacle to the Scots, and the best technique was simply to pay the latter off with heavy tributes. One response by the local gentry, notably in the later fourteenth century, was to build a large number of tower houses and small-scale fortifications to provide a measure of defence for their estates. When Aeneas Silvius Piccolomini, the future Pope Pius II, was travelling in the north in 1435, he dined one night in a village close to the border. After eating, the party became fearful that the Scots were approaching. The men went to take refuge in a tower some way off. The women remained; they said that they did not consider rape a wrong. This was a society hardened to the horrors of war. Yet recovery was possible. In periods of truce, the north showed a remarkable degree of resilience as lands were restocked. The Percy family, and to a lesser extent the Nevilles, rose to prominence in the fourteenth century, and a very different northern political society from that of the thirteenth century emerged in the north, toughened by the severe test of war.

War had many indirect effects on society in England. For example, it may have encouraged crime. Men's absence from their estates while they campaigned in France and elsewhere provided criminals with some opportunities. More importantly, the practice of granting men pardons in return for military service, initiated on a large scale by Edward I in 1294, was an easy method of recruiting tough soldiers, but did nothing for the preservation of law and order at home. The homecoming of men hardened by campaigning was not always welcome. Something of a crime-wave seems to have followed the return of Edward III's forces from the siege of Calais in 1347, and in 1361 the justices of the peace were empowered to force those returning from France since the treaty of Brétigny (1360) to take up work lest they be encouraged to continue the unruly ways of war. In the north, war came to be accompanied by a lack of respect for central authority, and offered openings for criminal activity.

It is impossible to provide a convincing balance sheet to demonstrate the success or failure of English military enterprises during the later middle ages. In some years, notably the 1290s and the late 1330s, there is no doubt whatsoever that war cost the country a great deal, with very little by way of gains to offset the huge sums spent in subsidies to foreign allies, on war wages and on preparations for campaigns. In other periods, above all in the years from 1346 to the late 1350s, the war was highly profitable. The impact of war varied according to social status. Some of the aristocracy undoubtedly gained much; their castles stand as testimony to their success. Knightly families as a whole did not prosper so obviously;

their declining numbers by the fifteenth century suggest that the strains of war may have been too much for some. There were, however, many success stories among the knights, men who gained wealth as well as reputation. Further down the social scale, it is much harder to see the benefits of war. The pressures of war taxation and of seizures of foodstuffs were heavy, and few of those recruited into the army from the ranks of the peasantry can be shown to have profited from campaigning. Despite all the glories of war, the ideal vision of society was one in which the king was 'dwelling in his own land in the seat of peace, desiring above all the quiet and tranquillity of nobles, lords and commons'.[9]

---

[9] *Rotuli Parliamentorum* (6 vols., 1783), ii, 283, cited by G. L. Harriss, *King, Parliament and Public Finance in Medieval England to 1369* (Oxford, 1975), p. 466.

CHAPTER 4

Order and law

Simon Walker

Notions of order and law were inseparably allied in later medieval England. Order, both the public order of civil society and the domestic order of the household, depended upon the maintenance of hierarchy through the conscientious discharge of their obligations by every rank of society. The nature of these obligations was clearly set out by John Stafford, archbishop of Canterbury, in his address to the parliament of 1433. The magnates of the realm must work to maintain unity and concord within the kingdom; the knights and middling men (*mediocres*) should administer justice with equity; it was the people's part to obey the king's will and his laws.[1] Disobedience of whatever kind, whether of servants towards their masters or of wives towards their husbands, was a kind of treason, the first step down the road towards general insurrection. Law was the means by which this authoritarian ideal of social harmony was regulated and enforced, acting like the sinews of the physical body as it turned 'a group of men ... into a people'.[2] In talking of law, theorists distinguished between divine, natural and positive law, but in the case of each, the purpose of the law was agreed to be declarative: it disclosed an existing state of justice. Actions and decisions that were against justice and universal right (*commun droit*) could not, therefore, be considered legal.

These ideas were articulated with greatest clarity by academic theorists and political moralists and there was, of course, often a significant difference between their precise formulations and the self-interested actions of legal 'consumers', the men and (more occasionally) women who saw in the law a means to achieving their own ends. Litigants expected a fair and equal judicial system, but they also demanded from it confirmation of

---

[1] *Rotuli Parliamentorum* (6 vols., 1783), iv, p. 419. This survey has benefited considerably from the comments of Paul Brand.
[2] N. Doe, *Fundamental Authority in Late Medieval English Law* (Cambridge, 1990), p. 47.

their own claims and complained bitterly if this was not forthcoming. Such theoretical formulations of order and legality nevertheless left their mark on popular expectations of justice. Codifications of local custom justified their usages by reference to the law of nature; the justices of the common law courts allowed arguments from 'reason' and 'conscience' to modify the severity of due process; and protests against misgovernment, such as the demand of Jack Cade's rebels in 1450 that 'every man should have his due, coming in due time to [the king] to ask justice or grace',[3] drew upon the textbook commonplaces of the civil law. Maintaining and enforcing justice was the principal duty of the sovereign. Every English king swore at his coronation to do equal right to all his subjects, and failure to keep this promise was the commonest source of political dissension. The king had consequently as much to lose from any failure to maintain the force of law as any of his subjects. Edward II was replaced as ruler because 'although he was bound by his oath to do justice to all, he wished to do so only for his own gain'; Richard II's enforced abdication was justified 'for default of governance and undoing of the good laws';[4] and the unrest, injustice, partiality and abuse of the law that supposedly characterised Henry VI's reign were taken by his supplanters to be evidence of a defective title to rule.

To preserve their own rights, and to provide the justice their subjects demanded, English kings had at their disposal a well-articulated framework of courts, capable of entertaining both civil and criminal pleas from every part of the country and from all sections of society. By 1200, a group of royal justices was already sitting permanently in the bench at Westminster, while a larger body of judges, the justices in eyre, were sent around the kingdom at irregular intervals, punishing criminals, enforcing the king's fiscal and feudal rights and settling private disputes brought before them. In 1194 the office of coroner was established, to provide for the regular keeping of crown pleas in each county between eyres. The county court, meeting usually every month and presided over by the sheriff, provided a local forum for royal justice, while the hundred courts, meeting every three weeks, dispatched much minor civil litigation and furnished the presentments on which the criminal work of the justices in eyre was based. Royal justice had begun the long process of dissociation from the person of the king, although many of the most important pleas

---

[3] I. M. W. Harvey, *Jack Cade's Rebellion of 1450* (Oxford, 1990), p. 189.
[4] S. B. Chrimes and A. L. Brown, eds., *Select Documents of English Constitutional History, 1307–1485* (1961), pp. 37, 191.

continued to be heard 'before the king' (*coram rege*), a phrase that implied the interest, if not the actual presence, of the king. From 1234, these pleas before the king were formalised into a separate court, the itinerant king's bench, with its own set of records and staff.

For much of the thirteenth century, this remained the pattern of royal justice, although the volume of litigation brought before the justices in eyre soon began to prove overwhelming. During the two months when the eyre justices were in Wiltshire in 1249, for example, nearly 500 civil actions were heard before them, almost 500 presentments were made by jurors concerning the infringement of royal rights and other criminal matters, and a further 275 persons were indicted and tried as suspect of a crime.[5] There was a further influx of business from 1278, as the justices began to entertain private complaints of trespass, initiated by written bill. As a result, new groups of justices were commissioned, in the first instance to reduce the pressure of business on the eyre, although eventually their sessions came to supersede it entirely. The work of the assize justices, who heard possessory pleas, was systematised into a series of county circuits in 1273, while the justices of gaol delivery, initially a mixed body of royal servants, justices of the central courts and influential local gentry, became exclusively professional in their composition after 1299. By 1328, when the assize and gaol delivery circuits became permanently associated, their combined judicial powers supplied the central supervision of local justice that had once been exercised, in a more deliberate but less wieldy fashion, by the justices in eyre.

Supervision was not, however, sufficient to satisfy the growing body of opinion disturbed by the apparent growth in lawlessness that contemporaries dated back to the later years of Edward I's reign. Complaints that 'the peace of the land was not kept as it ought and as it used to be'[6] became an increasingly frequent feature of political discourse in later medieval England, and successive kings sought to respond to it by a variety of more interventionist expedients. Some, like the special commissions of *oyer et terminer* ('to hear and determine') issued in response to individual complaints of injustice, enjoyed a brief vogue. Others, such as the revival of the general eyre attempted in 1329, were abandoned almost immediately. The solution that finally proved acceptable, the

[5] M. T. Clanchy, ed., *Civil Pleas of the Wiltshire Eyre, 1249* (Wiltshire Record Society, XXVI, 1971), p. 29; C. A. F. Meekings, ed., *Crown Pleas of the Wiltshire Eyre, 1249* (Wiltshire Record Society, XVI, 1961), pp. 37, 95.

[6] D. W. Sutherland, ed., *The Eyre of Northamptonshire, 1329–30* (2 vols., Selden Society, XCIX, 1983), i, p. 5.

commissions of the peace, extended the task of law enforcement beyond the small and overburdened corps of professional legal personnel, to whom the reforms of the Edwardian era had largely confined it, and sought instead to harness the vested interests of the landed class in the maintenance of social order. Knightly 'keepers of the peace', charged with a variety of military and police functions, had sometimes been employed in the counties since the mid-thirteenth century. By the early fourteenth century, some gentry keepers were also involved in the work of gaol delivery and their powers were further extended in 1329 to include the ability to determine indictments made before them (that is, to bring them to judgement and impose the appropriate penalties). Although this determining power, which effectively created an independent criminal jurisdiction, was withdrawn from the peace commissions several times over the next thirty years by a government still unsure of the most effective solution to the problem of disorder, it was the justices of the peace who eventually emerged in the late fourteenth century as the principal agents for the enforcement of the criminal law at local level. Required to sit at least four times a year, and charged with a growing portfolio of social and economic responsibilities, the combination of Westminster justices, local lawyers and substantial local gentlemen that customarily staffed the shire bench proved well suited to the demands of their task.

The short-lived experiments that characterised the royal administration of criminal justice for much of the fourteenth century were not replicated in the field of civil litigation, where the court system proved generally adequate to the demands laid upon it for more than a century after the demise of the eyre. Almost permanently located at Westminster, the common bench developed into the busiest of all the royal courts. During the thirteenth century, the business of the court increased as much as thirty-fold; by the 1330s as many as 6,000 cases were in progress there each year. The common bench dealt with 'common' pleas – those pleas in which the crown had no direct interest – and these were, in practice, overwhelmingly actions for the recovery of property or of debt. Although process in common bench was slow, the court proved flexible in its provision of remedies, as the royal chancery tailored the forms of action it offered to the circumstances of individual litigants with increasing precision. As a result, the business of the court expanded further in the late fourteenth century and showed no signs of consistent decline until the 1440s.

This decline, when it came, may have owed something to a temporary loss of confidence in the general effectiveness of royal justice under the uncertain direction of Henry VI, but it was no less the consequence of the crown's continuing ability to develop new institutional remedies. The court of chancery developed out of the general responsibility that the chancellor possessed, as head of the royal secretariat, for the supervision of the king's administration and, in particular, for the correction of any defects of justice that might occur in the due process of the common law courts. By the 1380s, the chancery had developed a distinctive procedure for dealing with such cases – based on the submission of bills of complaint, the interrogation of witnesses, and a judgement delivered, without a jury verdict, according to the requirements of conscience – that proved increasingly attractive to litigants by virtue of its speed and informality. In the early fifteenth century, the court began to take regular cognisance of real property cases, especially those involving the disposition of land through the legal device know as the enfeoffment to use (a form of trust), that could not easily be accommodated within the strict rules of argument demanded by the common law. The volume of chancery business grew further, although the absolute number of cases the court heard each year – perhaps 500 a year by the 1480s – was always less significant than the disproportionate representation of the most sensitive and intractable property disputes amongst them.

The maintenance of social order within later medieval England was not, however, dependent upon the effectiveness of the king's courts and the accessibility of royal justice alone. A dense network of subordinate jurisdictions in both town and countryside supplemented the work of royal justice in combating disorder, regulating conduct and enforcing certain social norms. The most pervasive influence in this respect was exercised by the ecclesiastical courts; the men of the bishopric of London complained in 1290, for example, that the ministers of the church courts were more oppressive to them in their exactions than all the lay courts.[7] In every diocese, the bishop and his officials maintained a hierarchy of courts, stretching from the chapters of the rural deans to the diocesan consistory court and the episcopal court of audience. These courts enforced the canon law, a codification of papal pronouncements and the decisions of church councils on matters of theology and morality held to be binding on all Christians, and their relationship with the royal courts was regulated by a series of more or less accurate statements of existing

---

[7] *Rotuli Parliamentorum*, i, p. 60.

practice, the best known of which was the writ *Circumspecte agatis* (1285). In the punishment of mortal sin, such as adultery and fornication, the jurisdiction of the church courts was largely unquestioned, while the regulation of marriage and the probate of wills was divided between secular and ecclesiastical tribunals. A significant source of further business was 'breach of faith' litigation, concerned with providing redress for an alleged act of perjury. This brought the enforcement of various contractual obligations, most typically for the repayment of small debts, within the remit of the church courts: two-thirds of the litigation in the Hereford consistory court during the 1490s was of this type, for example. Although the volume of business in the church courts never rivalled that in the king's, the nature of the suits they entertained gave them a particular potency as enforcers of contemporary conceptions of social order. Procedure in the ecclesiastical courts was divided between 'instance' and 'office' business: in instance cases, a plaintiff brought suit against a defendant; in office cases, the court initiated action on its own behalf, usually in response to a report of the 'common fame' of the parish, provided by the churchwardens or a group of selected inquirers (*inquisitors*). This allowed the more prominent members of the local community to play an active part in the maintenance of moral discipline by enforcing the punishment of scolds and prostitutes, the regulation of disorderly taverns, and the suppression of any other activity, such as gaming during mass, that seemed to threaten the effective conduct of Christian life.

Such concern for social regulation was at its most vigorous in the volatile and densely packed towns of later medieval England. To aid them in their task of enforcing the social and legal order, urban magistrates had at their disposal an especially extensive array of parallel, and sometimes competing, jurisdictions. The jurors of Stamford identified as many as eleven free courts in their town in 1274, serving the needs of no more than 5,000 inhabitants, besides the 'court of Stamford' itself, in which the lord of the town exercised regalian rights of justice by grant of the king. Most borough courts had begun, like Stamford's, as hundred courts, enforcing the king's peace, but the need to find a speedy resolution to commercial disputes, as well as the particular urgency that the general issues of public order and hygiene acquired in an urban environment, led to the development of further tribunals and the modification, in civil pleas, of the recognised procedures of the common law by the dictates of local custom and of conscience. In Colchester, for instance, regulation of urban life was shared between the hundred court, which dealt mainly with police matters, and a court of pleas, in which the town's bailiffs delivered judgement according to the flexible procedures of the law merchant. The level of litigation in towns was high by contemporary standards, chiefly because the greater availability of credit within urban society led to the widespread use of borough courts for the recovery of commercial debts. The London sheriffs' courts, which attracted a mixture of debt and trespass litigation, handled at least 1,000 civil actions a year during Edward IV's reign – roughly equivalent to the annual workload of the adjacent king's bench – and it seems that provincial towns like Nottingham and Shrewsbury could also generate substantial levels of debt-related activity in their borough courts.

For the great majority of the population, however, those who depended directly or indirectly on the cultivation of the land for their livelihood, experience of the law was shaped, though not wholly bounded, by the workings of the court of the manor in which they resided. The manor court was a private institution, usually presided over by the steward or bailiff of the lord of the manor, which had as its principal purpose the protection of seigniorial interests. It regulated the lives of all the lord's tenants, though it bore most heavily on the unfree, enforcing the labour services due from them and controlling the transfer of land between them. It served, in addition, as a forum in which the agricultural affairs of the community such as the grazing of the common fields could be agreed, and dealt with minor cases of assault, trespass and slander. Manorial courts met frequently – in theory, once every three weeks, though usually rather less often in practice; the eight sessions a year the court at Sevenhampton (Wilts.) managed between 1275 and 1287 is characteristic.[8] They discharged their business haphazardly, regularly mixing leet business with the control of husbandry: the creation of legal and natural order, respectively. Procedure in the manor court differed in certain important respects from that encountered in the common law courts: business was discharged by the 'whole court', all the tenants of the manor obliged to attend, rather than by a small group of jurors; the commonest form of trial was by compurgation, in which the accused swore formally to his innocence and had his oath confirmed by the oaths of a (varying) number of oath-helpers; and if a judgement of right had to be rendered, it was based upon the court's collective understanding of manorial custom rather than upon substantive principles of law.

[8] R. B. Pugh, ed., *Court Rolls of the Wiltshire Manors of Adam de Stratton* (Wiltshire Record Society, XXIV, 1970), p. 2.

Evidence for the existence of manorial courts stretches back no further than 1209, although there is no reason to think that they could not have operated effectively, granted their reliance upon oral testimony and collective memory, at a very much earlier date. The proliferation of surviving rolls of court proceedings from the 1270s implies, however, a new stage in the development of the manorial court. Better record-keeping bred more standardised procedures as landlords, anxious to retain the profitable legal business of their free tenants in the face of growing competition from the royal courts, sought to streamline and improve the range of services they offered. Judgements were no longer rendered by the whole body of suitors to the court but, instead, by trial juries; wager of law and compurgation gave way, as the dominant mode of proof, to jury verdicts; documentary evidence began to be preferred to the oral state-ment of custom. While presentments remained principally concerned with the enforcement of seigniorial obligations, private suits were also initiated in growing numbers to settle pleas of debt, claim damages for minor nuisances and try titles to land. By the early fourteenth century, the manorial court had consequently come to constitute, for many liti-gants, a swifter and substantially cheaper forum for the resolution of disputes than the hierarchy of royal courts. The changes in manorial organisation that followed the Black Death inevitably reduced the importance of the manorial courts as agents of seigniorial discipline but, in other respects, they retained their significance. The development of presentment procedure, in particular, gave the court a powerful new instrument of communal policing, deployed against those elements within a village whose behaviour appeared to threaten social harmony, like the Saffron Walden couple who were said, in 1384, 'by their insulting words, [to] bring dissension among the people'.[9]

The rich variety of courts active in later medieval England and the available indications of the levels of business they entertained therefore suggest a culture in which recourse to the law was seen as the most natural and convenient solution to many social and administrative difficulties. Litigation was expensive and time-consuming but it appeared to offer advantages to all those who could afford the associated costs. The social range of those seeking resolution of their disputes in the courts was consequently broad; at least three-quarters of Lincolnshire plaintiffs in king's bench between 1291 and 1340 were villagers, while an analysis of the status of litigants in common pleas in 1441 suggests that about a

---

[9] M. K. McIntosh, *Controlling Misbehavior in England, 1370–1600* (Cambridge, 1998), p. 60.

quarter were yeomen or husbandmen and another quarter were merchants, traders or artisans.[10] Recourse to the law played such a central part
in the conduct of relations at every level of society for several reasons.
Some were practical, for many routine administrative problems were
addressed through the agency of the law: the king's finances were audited
and investigated by a bench of judges, the barons of the exchequer; roads
were repaired and water-courses were kept clear by the authority of
commissioners armed with judicial powers to examine and punish
delinquents; land was most securely conveyed from vendor to purchaser
by engaging in a 'final concord', recorded before the eyre or bench justices. At a more general level, law offered the promise of binding
authority in a world that often lacked it. Appeal to the fixed and pre-
dictable norms of due process was especially attractive within a society in
which private authority, whether exercised legitimately by a franchise-
holder or illegitimately by those who took advantage of their local
influence to flout the king's peace, frequently appeared a more significant
force than the occasional intervention of a distant royal official. A
working knowledge of the law inevitably became a highly desirable skill
for anyone with a stake in landed society. For a minor gentleman like
Robert Godsfield of Sutton (Lincs.), who prosecuted and defended all his
cases without the aid of an attorney, procedural dexterity and some
formal legal training conferred the ability to confound more substantial
opponents in the courts.

This necessary familiarity with the law was further promoted by the
penetration of legal professionals deep into local society. A group of
specialist pleaders, known as serjeants, were active in the common bench
by the 1240s. Their appearance, the first step in the growth of a recognisable English legal profession, was a response to the increasing popularity of royal justice. In the twelfth century, when most litigation had
been pursued through the communal courts of the hundred and the
honor, knowledge of the technicalities governing the entry and subsequent conduct of a plea was apparently widespread among the suitors of
each court. The common bench had its own rules, however, in which
only the small group of pleaders who regularly frequented it were well
versed; their services consequently came to be highly valued by those

---

[10] B. W. McLane, 'Changes in the court of king's bench, 1291–1340: the preliminary view from
Lincolnshire', in W. M. Ormrod, ed., *England in the Fourteenth Century: Proceedings of the 1985
Harlaxton Symposium* (Woodbridge, 1986), pp. 158–9; C. W. Brooks, 'Litigation and society in
England, 1200–1996', in C. W. Brooks, ed., *Lawyers, Litigation and English Society since 1450* (1998),
pp. 77–8.

wealthy enough to use the court. A second group of legal specialists, the attorneys, who handled the paperwork on behalf of clients in the West-minster courts, emerged towards the end of the century, as the growth in levels of litigation generated sufficient business to allow the creation of profitable regional practices. By the end of Edward I's reign, serjeants could be found acting in most shire courts, while lawyers combining the role of serjeant and attorney were present in many major urban jur-isdictions; even in the manorial courts of St Albans, the abbot was forced to prohibit the employment of outside pleaders (*adventicii placitatores*) as early as 1275.[11] It was this growing band of provincial lawyers who did much to spread knowledge of the law and appreciation of its power among their clients, providing the precise references to statute law with which many private individuals chose to decorate their petitions to parliament and furnishing, for a price, the advice and expertise that allowed groups of tenants a new ability to resist the demands of their lords. At Titchfield (Hants.), the unfree tenants of the Premonstratensian abbey responded to the threat of heavier labour services by suing out a common law writ of *monstraverunt* against the abbot in 1271 and, when this action failed, appealed to the evidence of Domesday Book in order to preserve their privileged status. They maintained their resistance for a further five years and the final composition conceded some, at least, of the villagers' claims.

There were, then, definite advantages to be gained by the acquisition or purchase of some practical legal literacy; but it is a striking feature of the period that the legal professionals who furnished such advice – the soli-citors and conveyancers who operated in local courts as much as the justices, serjeants and apprentices at Westminster – were one of the least popular occupational groups in later medieval England. Wat Tyler's demand, during the Peasants' Revolt of 1381, that all lawyers should be beheaded was the most extreme statement of this antipathy but there were many more limited, and more practical, expressions of the same distaste. Lawyers were excluded from elections to parliament in 1404, for instance, while a later parliamentary petition sought to limit and regulate the activities of the allegedly excessive number of attorneys practising in Norfolk and Suffolk, who were said to be encouraging vexatious suits for their own profit.[12] Lawyers attracted this kind of opprobrium chiefly because, as discussed elsewhere in this volume, they were a new and

---

[11] A. E. Levett, *Studies in Manorial History* (Oxford, 1938), p. 192.
[12] *Rotuli Parliamentorum*, v, pp. 326–7.

strikingly successful social grouping within later medieval society.[13] An apprentice-at-law could expect to command a professional income of around £60 a year, enough to place him on a par with the established local gentry, while, at the top of the profession, a serjeant-pleader's earnings might be as much as £300 a year.[14] Such men used their command of ready cash and the knowledge of the land market acquired in the course of their professional lives to build up substantial landed estates that excited the envy, and disquiet, of their new neighbours: Robert Belknap, chief justice of common pleas, was thought to be 'most powerful in the county of Kent in those days';[15] and the scions of several legal dynasties, the Scropes, Stonors, Bourchiers and Pastons among them, came to exercise a similar authority.

Equally, the faith that individuals and communities invested in the law's ability to deliver them from oppression did nothing to prevent a growing chorus of complaint at the English legal system's perceived inability either to guarantee good order or to offer impartial justice. These complaints took innumerable particular forms but certain general themes ran through them all. One was alarm at the level of public disorder within the kingdom, which popular opinion periodically considered to be on the verge of anarchy: 'If the turbulence is not stopped, general warfare may result', warned the chronicler Peter Langtoft, during the troubled final years of Edward I's reign.[16] A second general grievance was the seemingly limitless degree of expense and delay that the royal courts, in particular, proved capable of inflicting upon litigants. Contemporaries ascribed this state of affairs to the venality of lawyers and court officials; an early fourteenth-century satire complains that judges were seduced from justice by bribes and partiality towards the powerful, while their clerks sat at their feet, 'like people half-starved, gaping for gifts'.[17] Finally, a widespread perception developed that the law had itself become an instrument of oppression, serving the turn of the powerful more readily than it protected the interests of the innocent. This was a view especially associated with the complaints of the parliamentary commons, who, throughout the fourteenth and fifteenth centuries, consistently identified

---

[13] See also pp. 66, 130–2.
[14] E. W. Ives, *The Common Lawyers of Pre-Reformation England* (Cambridge, 1983), pp. 321–5. Such figures put in context the level at which lawyers were taxed in 1379: see above, p. 66.
[15] T. F. Tout, *Chapters in the Administrative History of Mediaeval England* (6 vols., Manchester, 1920–33), iii, p. 422.
[16] T. Wright, ed., *The Chronicle of Pierre de Langtoft* (2 vols., RS, XLVII, 1866–8), i, p. 360.
[17] P. Coss, ed., *Thomas Wright's Political Songs of England* (Cambridge, 1996), pp. 225–6.

the protection afforded by certain sections of the nobility to their clients and dependants against the due process of the courts as the principal source of injustice within the realm.

These complaints had about them a significant degree of self-interest. 'Justice with favour' was what most litigants wanted and, if it was not forthcoming, they were quick to apportion blame. Nevertheless, there was much in the administration and execution of later medieval justice to give colour and substance to their grievances. Litigation was undoubtedly costly: every royal writ had to be paid for; learned counsel required both an initial retainer and further consultation fees; the clerks of the central courts expected further payments to record and file the resultant proceedings. An active suit in the Westminster courts cost around £2 a term to prosecute and, for those whose business required frequent recourse there, the cumulative expense could be very considerable. Such expenditure did not, however, guarantee either a speedy or an equitable outcome. In criminal cases, the main problem was to get the defendant into court. Continued non-appearance could only be countered by initiating the lengthy procedures leading to outlawry – a sanction that had become, in any case, largely ineffective by the later middle ages. In civil suits, too, there were vexing procedural delays to be negotiated; but the real problem often lay deeper, in the growing complexity of the common law itself. The customary rules of inheritance in England were augmented and modified during the later middle ages by the development of a series of legal devices, most notably the entail (a means of specifying inheritance rights within families) and the enfeoffment to use (a form of trust), that allowed landowners to make a more flexible disposition of their property but also rendered an unimpeachable title to land increasingly hard to acquire. In disputes over real property, appeal to the common law began to prove more effective as a means to create a claim rather than as a guarantee of existing rights. When each of the principal litigants possessed a defensible claim to the disputed lands, even a relatively routine property dispute, like that over the Kentish manors of Richard Lovelace, might take more than forty years to resolve.[18]

Still further disquiet was created by the routine exercise of private influence upon the progress of litigation. Among disappointed plaintiffs, the complaint that 'it is seldom seen that a poor man hath favour when a lord is party'[19] was understandably common. Until the late fourteenth

---

[18] P. W. Fleming, 'The Lovelace dispute: concepts of property and inheritance in fifteenth-century Kent', *Southern History*, 12 (1990), 1–18.
[19] C. Carpenter, ed., *The Armburgh Papers* (Woodbridge, 1998), p. 54.

century, it was customary for great magnates and the major religious houses to include a number of royal justices among their retained legal counsel. Edward III's trusted servant, Sir John Molyns, successfully concealed a career of violence and extortion from official investigation for many years thanks, in large part, to his close working relationship with John Inge, a justice of king's bench. Even when the direct retaining of royal justices ceased, gifts in kind, to encourage the judges towards a more favourable decision, continued to be considered acceptable. Such payments were only the most conspicuous element in a constant process of informal suasion designed to create the atmosphere of good favour (*benevolentia*) deemed necessary for successful litigation. Sheriffs' clerks were paid to empanel favourable juries, or to allow litigants access to the names of the jury panel; the jurors themselves were lavishly entertained as each party sought to convince them of the strength of its case; and suitably imposing groups of influential 'well-willers' were assembled to pack the courthouse when an issue finally came to trial. If all else failed, the threat of force that lurked behind many of these manoeuvres could be openly articulated. Edward Courtenay, earl of Devon, threatened to break the head of a royal commissioner if he continued proceedings against one of his retainers.[20] Although it was the illegitimate exercise of their social influence by great men like Courtenay that most concerned contemporaries, the pressure of 'lordship' upon due legal process was routinely encountered at every social level and within every jurisdiction. Outsiders complained, for instance, that the 'great acquaintance' enjoyed by the local merchants at Southampton gave them a decisive advantage in the borough court.[21] In many manorial courts, considerations of status and family interest meant that, while the jurors were prepared to present for a whole range of felonies and misdemeanours, the burden of conviction fell disproportionately upon the poorest and least powerful villagers.

In evaluating the quality of order and justice prevalent in later medieval England, therefore, the precocious development of a network of public and private courts, the elaboration of the common law, the growth of a group of specialised legal professionals and a demonstrable public appetite for litigation must be weighed against expressions of a widespread disenchantment with the effectiveness of royal justice and the

[20] I. S. Leadam and J. F. Baldwin, eds., *Select Cases before the King's Council, 1243–1482* (Selden Society, XXXV, 1918), p. 81.
[21] C. Platt, *Medieval Southampton* (1973), p. 176.

abundant surviving evidence for the partiality and intimidation of which contemporaries complained. Such complaints are, in one respect, as universal as the gulf between ideal and reality. Lacking the financial resources to maintain either a standing army or a permanent police force, English kings were dependent on the co-operation of their subjects for the maintenance of civil order and the doing of justice. For most of the time, this co-operation was freely given, as much by the village notables who staffed the juries of presentment as by the substantial gentry who acted as justices of the peace and took their turn in the onerous office of sheriff, but it carried with it an inevitable price: the pursuit of private interest by those charged with public office. Sir Thomas Metham, a justice of the peace in Yorkshire, was accused in 1387 of ransoming a rival landowner's tenants 'as if they had been prisoners in time of war'; a little earlier, Sir Thomas Bradeston was said to have used the powers of his office as constable of Gloucester Castle to conduct himself 'like a little saint in court, and like a raging lion in his own country'.[22]

Such incidents were commonplace, but they generated less outrage than the tone of many parliamentary petitions implied. In a society where most administrative or legal transactions depended to some degree upon the co-operation of friends and neighbours, lordship was recognised for what it was, less an abuse of power than its necessary condition, and regulated in its exercise by considerations of honour and 'worship' that ensured only the most headstrong or desperate magnate would risk open defiance of the law. Its management was as much a political as an administrative matter, involving calculations of relative advantage that stretched far beyond the judicial arena. Although the evolution of due process often provided the powerful with an additional means of enforcing their authority, it could also place some restraint upon its unfettered exercise. Influential support could keep a weak case open but it could not easily overcome a secure title, while even a well-connected peer like John, fifth Lord Lovell, might be thwarted by a lesser opponent prepared to use to the full the resources of publicity and delay the common law provided.[23]

Although England was no different from any other western European monarchy in the later middle ages in its reliance upon seigniorial initiative to shore up the edifice of royal authority, the consequences of

---

[22] PRO, KB 27/507, *Rex*, mm. 33–7; N. Saul, *Knights and Esquires: the Gloucestershire gentry in the fourteenth century* (Oxford, 1981), pp. 266–7.

[23] PRO, SC 8/23/1117, 1118; *Rotuli Parliamentorum*, iii, pp. 573, 633–4.

this reliance were rendered especially far-reaching by two distinctive developments. One was the expansion of the English state apparatus that inevitably accompanied the crown's pursuit of new military ambitions – in Scotland, France and Wales – during the late thirteenth and fourteenth centuries. The further delegation of royal authority that this necessitated, to the purveyors, arrayers and tax-collectors whose job it was to satisfy the king's demands for men and money, not only intensified expressions of discontent at the consequent levels of fiscal exaction – 'they hunt us as hounds do a hare on the hill', one contemporary complained of Edward III's tax-collectors[24] – but also made the task of supervising and restraining the actions of such lesser officials more difficult. The general investigations into complaints of official malpractice ordered by Edward I in 1290 and by Edward III in 1340 proved only temporary solutions, while commissions of *oyer et terminer*, established to provide a speedy response to specific complaints of injustice, soon became a favoured device of the powerful for harassing their opponents. Yet the resentment aroused by the abuses of such lesser officials ran deep, for they confounded contemporary expectations of social order by wielding an influence that their status did not warrant. William Chorlegh, under-sheriff of Lancashire during the 1370s, was said, for example, to have acquired so much wealth by his extortions while in office that, although his lands and rents were worth only £10 a year, it was well known that the annual expenses of his household exceeded £200.[25] The failure of successive kings decisively to address these concerns produced a new disenchantment with the effectiveness of royal justice and created an atmosphere of hostility towards its representatives that eventually threatened the rule of law itself. It was acts of disobedience towards the king's lesser servants, the chancellor argued in 1383, that had lain at the roots of the great rising of 1381.[26]

The second distinctive feature of English state development that served to define popular attitudes towards the issues of order and law was the unusually swift development of the system of public justice itself. By the late thirteenth century, the scholastic commonplace that the king was the fount of all law was, in England, becoming a reality. Litigants who wished to contest a title to land, to pursue a debt of more than £2, or even to enjoy the uncertain privilege of a jury verdict, were most likely to pursue their actions before the king's justices. Certain categories of cases initiated

---

[24] Coss, ed., *Thomas Wright's Political Songs*, p. 152.
[25] S. Walker, *The Lancastrian Affinity, 1361–1399* (Oxford, 1990), p. 163.
[26] *Rotuli Parliamentorum*, iii, p. 150.

in subordinate jurisdictions were now easily removed to the royal courts, and judgements passed in them routinely put under review, by securing a writ of *pone* or *recordari*. The consequences of this expansion in business for public perceptions of royal justice were not, however, always positive. The increased competence of the king's courts fostered an expectation of the speedy and final resolution of all types of dispute that it proved, in practice, impossible to fulfil. In part, this was a question of resources. The Westminster-based legal establishment was always small, amounting to no more than 400 active practitioners even in the late fifteenth century, and demand for royal justice outstripped the supply of suitable lawyers. Assize sessions were, for example, expected to be held three times a year in each county, but it soon became clear that this was too ambitious a provision: in Yorkshire, the justices of assize held only thirty-six sessions in the quarter-century between 1389 and 1413.[27] This shortage of qualified personnel also compromised the crown's periodic attempts to maintain a rigorous standard of probity among the judiciary: Chief Justice Willoughby, dismissed from king's bench in 1340 for selling the laws of England as if they had been sheep or cattle, was sitting once again in common pleas by November 1343; Chief Justice Thorpe, sentenced to death for accepting bribes in 1350, was acting as a baron of the exchequer a year later.

The real problem, though, lay deeper, in the nature of the common law itself. The king's courts attracted custom by their promise of speedy and effective justice but, in order to fulfil this promise, they imposed upon the concerns of litigants a necessary formalism, requiring plaintiffs to define their grievances in terms of a standardised set of pleas and juries to adjudicate upon a single 'issue' placed before them. The procedure was an antagonistic one, which deliberately excluded from consideration many relevant circumstances, yet aspired to deliver an uncompromising verdict in favour of one party or the other. The common law provided judgement more readily than justice and, within the context of communities in which litigants had to go on living with each other after judgement had been rendered, recourse to the royal courts could prove highly disruptive, stimulating accusations and recriminations that destroyed the social equilibrium upon which the maintenance of good order depended. On occasion, the availability of legal redress itself fanned the flames of local discord; the provincial itinerations of king's bench sometimes evoked a tenfold increase in the levels of trespass litigation

---

[27] PRO, JUST 1/1500, 1507, 1509, 1517.

brought before the court.[28] The growing sophistication of legal procedures further accentuated this tendency, for the emergence of the attorney
allowed litigants to remove their dispute from the cognisance of local
jurisdictions, where the social pressure towards compromise was strongest, and to pursue their case by proxy at Westminster instead. The
consequent proliferation of courts in which a suit could potentially be
pursued meant that, unless both parties to a dispute were wholeheartedly
committed to finding an acceptable settlement, a final resolution was hard
to achieve. New opportunities to delay an opponent, or to reopen an
apparently settled case, would always present themselves. When William
Paston, a justice of common pleas, clashed with a local esquire at the
Norfolk shire court in August 1424, their subsequent dispute was pursued
through seven different tribunals, from the manorial court of Forncett to
the king's bench and the court of exchequer chamber.

Neither order nor justice was, therefore, an inevitable outcome of
recourse to the law. It was this failure in what appeared a natural progression from cause to effect that most exercised and angered contemporaries. They ascribed it to the effects of sin within the body politic
and sought to extirpate the individual vices – of greed, anger and lust for
domination – they identified as responsible. A more fundamental
problem, however, was the clash between competing understandings of
the nature of order itself that played itself out in the daily execution of the
law. The king's justice embodied a positive and interventionist conception of order, which sought to reveal the natural harmony of a hierarchically ordered society and, where such a harmony did not exist, to
impose it. Although dominant ideologically, this positive ideal of order
was not necessarily the most prevalent in later medieval England. Besides
the vision of disciplined social harmony that the educated publicists of
the state advanced, the notion of order meant, for many people, simply
the desire to live at peace with their neighbours. Edward IV's ambition to
make things 'sit still and be quiet'[29] was one shared by many of his
subjects. In the close-knit communities of rural England, this was never
an easy task. The necessary co-operation that a shared agricultural livelihood required created many sources of tension, while the constant

---

[28] A. Musson and W. M. Ormrod, *The Evolution of English Justice: law, politics and society in the
fourteenth century* (Basingstoke, 1999), pp. 118–19.
[29] D. A. L. Morgan, 'The king's affinity in the polity of Yorkist England', *TRHS*, 5th ser. 23 (1973),
17.

availability of tools and knives, as well as the casual consumption of ale, meant that violence could easily flare.

As a result, later medieval society had evolved a variety of informal means, based on natural justice and common sense, for settling disputes without recourse either to violence or to litigation: by the mediation of respected individuals, like William Clowne, abbot of St Mary's, Leicester, who 'in his country and everywhere beyond was ever a composer of dispute and contention';[30] by communal self-regulation of the kind practised by many craft guilds and religious fraternities, whose statutes insisted that members should be accorded before the officers of the guild before litigating against one another; by holding lovedays, at which representatives of the disputing parties would seek to negotiate an acceptable agreement on their behalf; and by formal submission to the arbitrement and award of a third party, often a great magnate or a judge. These varied methods of dispute settlement had in common procedures that appealed to a set of communal values that the precocious growth of the common law had, in some respects, disturbed. The rigidity of the common law forms of action meant that royal judges could consider the circumstances of a dispute only in so far as they related to the legal issues at hand. Arbitrators could be asked to examine a broader range of issues and generally took pains to ensure that the process of negotiation over which they presided accorded due recognition to the social status and obligations of the disputing parties. Their aim was to frame a settlement acceptable to all sides and their awards sought to create or, more usually, re-establish social ties between the disputants. So strong was the pre-ference for settlement over judgement that many cases initiated in the royal courts were subsequently concorded before the parties joined issue, either by private treaty or by agreement arrived at in a lesser (and less costly) court; this was, for instance, the case for almost half the civil actions initiated before the eyre justices in Berkshire in 1248.[31]

The problem that the king and his subjects had to confront was that these two approaches to the task of maintaining order were, in certain respects, incompatible. The adoption of common law procedures in manorial courts increased seigniorial profits but diminished the degree of direct community participation in the legal process, delegating the task of rendering judgement from the whole court to a group of jurors, among

[30] G. H. Martin, ed., *Knighton's Chronicle, 1337–1396* (Oxford, 1995), p. 200.
[31] M. T. Clanchy, ed., *The Roll and Writ File of the Berkshire Eyre of 1248* (Selden Society, XC, 1973), pp. lviii–ix, cviii.

whom the better-off villagers were disproportionately represented; the growing popularity of presentment replaced a civil suit for compensation with a procedure that sought the punishment of the accused. In the enforcement of public order, local communities were sometimes unwilling to allow the common law its full disruptive force. Since the effectiveness of criminal justice largely depended upon the indictments made by the presenting juries, they were in a position to assert their preference. The preamble to the Statute of Winchester (1285) complained that, 'from day to day, robberies, homicides and arson are more frequently committed than they used to be' because jurors were reluctant to present certain types of offence.[32] Presenting jurors also enjoyed a certain degree of discretion in deciding, for example, whether a theft would be classified as a trespass (punishable by money penalty) or as a felony (punishable by forfeiture of life and limb). In taking that decision, their concern was with the offender more than with the precise nature of the offence. Only the habitual local criminals, such as the 'common malefactors in fairs and markets' identified by the Lincolnshire trailbaston jurors in 1328, were liable to be presented as felons; other offenders would be presented for trespass, punishable by a fine.[33] In cases of homicide, jurors often operated a distinction in degree of culpability that the formal legal rules did not draw, between killing by stealth and with premeditation (usually described as 'murder'), and other forms of violent death. They also proved consistently unwilling to credit the evidence of 'approvers', confessed criminals who now sought a stay of execution by informing on their accomplices; their proven bad character made them unpopular figures, whose testimony was not to be trusted.

The jurors' exercise of their discretion in such cases was a source of frustration to the king's judges but, as long as royal and communal attitudes towards public order issues remained approximately consonant, did little harm. Where social attitudes were at odds with the crown's legislative initiatives, however, the consequences could be less welcome. In the most serious cases, judicial or executive intention could be thwarted entirely. Henry V's attempts to enforce the provisions of a newly agreed maritime truce upon the shipmen of the south-west encountered considerable resistance, for example; the king was seeking to

---

[32] *Statutes of the Realm* (11 vols., 1810–28), i, p. 96.
[33] B. W. McLane, 'Juror attitudes towards local disorder: the evidence of the 1328 Lincolnshire trailbaston proceedings', in J. S. Cockburn and T. A. Green, eds., *Twelve Good Men and True: the criminal trial jury in England, 1200–1800* (Princeton, NJ, 1988), pp. 43–53.

condemn as piracy what local opinion regarded as legitimate self-help. As a consequence, the royal commissioners sent down to Exeter in 1414 managed to secure only four indictments from the forty separate juries summoned before them.[34] More characteristic was a differential pattern of compliance, as local communities picked and chose between the elements of a single legislative package. The clause in the Statute of Winchester (1285) requiring the clearing of woodland from beside the royal highway was widely welcomed, as a sensible precaution against thieves and robbers, whereas the provision that local communities make restitution to the victims of any unsolved robberies occurring within their jurisdiction was subject to a variety of ingenious delays. In general, communal implementation tended to impart to statutory enactments an idiosyncratic construction that conformed more closely to the locality's expectations of good order than to the crown's.

A clear instance of this is the paradoxical development of the law of rape and ravishment in later medieval England. For much of the thirteenth century, the crime of rape was, unless made the subject of an appeal by the victim herself, treated as a misdemeanour, punishable by a fine or by imprisonment. In the second Statute of Westminster (1285), however, rape was reclassified as a major felony, punishable by loss of life or limb. The immediate consequence was a drastic reduction in the number of convictions. Juries disliked the seriousness of the new penalties and refused to convict, with the result that the victims and their families turned instead to civil actions for damages in order to gain some sort of redress – a recourse that preserved the communal preference for reparation over revenge at the expense of the crown's legislative intentions. Presentments for rape continued to be made, but their purpose was now only indirectly punitive. Juries developed them, instead, into a flexible instrument for the imposition of social discipline, using the shame of a presentment as a sanction to be deployed against priests who kept mistresses, the clients of prostitutes and other offenders against agreed moral norms.

In coming to some final judgement about the nature and quality of order in later medieval England, then, it is important to accommodate both official and communal expectations of justice. The king's law was not a unique recourse; it was one among several concurrent jurisdictions, and proved most effective when deployed in conjunction with less formal

---

[34] E. Powell, *Kingship, Law, and Society: criminal justice in the reign of Henry V* (Oxford, 1989), pp. 201–8.

sanctions. Popular expectations and priorities constantly influenced the enforcement of royal justice, occasionally mitigating its force but more often giving purpose to a legal process that could appear, in formal terms, largely futile. Judged in terms of results, for example, the criminal law can only appear ineffective; the derisory conviction rates – about 30 per cent for theft and 20 per cent for homicide – for gaol deliveries at Newgate in London in the 1280s remained characteristic throughout the later middle ages.[35] But if the severe capital sentences of royal justice held little appeal to local jurors, common law procedures provided other sanctions, such as outlawry and abjuration of the realm, that more effectively enacted the preferences of communal justice for publicity and exclusion by identifying and expelling the offender from the community. Litigants continued to find that recourse to royal justice served their purpose, despite the usually inconclusive nature of its outcomes; the volume of East Anglian business in king's bench more than doubled between 1422 and 1442, although defendants appeared to answer the charges against them in only 11 per cent of all cases.[36] This was because their expectations of royal justice were not always those implied in the judicial record. Using the superior coercive powers of royal justice to afforce the traditional procedures of communal dispute resolution was a well-established pattern. A suit in the king's bench might not bring a result, but it could apply an informal sanction against unacceptable behaviour by threatening the perpetrator with the nuisance and dishonour of a court appearance, and brought useful pressure on an opponent to settle out of court. When such a settlement was agreed, collusive litigation between the parties provided essential confirmation of its terms by making the award enforceable in the common law courts. The public courts were thus chiefly valued for their ability to enforce and ratify private arrangements. Astute legal consumers, like the Townshends of Rainham, used common pleas to collect the many small sums owed them, while reserving the major property disputes in which they became entangled for the more flexible routines of arbitration.

Judicial procedures in later medieval England are, in these respects, best judged as a means to an end, rather than as an end in themselves. Royal justice worked most effectively as a regulatory device, reviewing the decisions of subordinate courts and co-ordinating the efforts of individuals and communities to police their own activities. Although the developing legal

---

[35] R. B. Pugh, 'Some reflections of a medieval criminologist', *Proceedings of the British Academy*, 59 (1973), 86–7; J. G. Bellamy, *The Criminal Trial in later Medieval England* (Stroud, 1998), p. 14.
[36] P. C. Maddern, *Violence and Social Order: East Anglia, 1422–1442* (Oxford, 1992), pp. 33–6.

establishment at Westminster was sometimes dismissive of the formulaic actions and traditional procedures of the communal courts, the king could not hope, in reality, to maintain the good order his subjects demanded of him without the considerable resources of time, learning and manpower that such tribunals provided. Accommodating the demands and pre-ferences of the local potentates who held sway in them might mitigate the force of royal authority, but it also served to impart a crucial responsiveness to the legal remedies the crown provided. Dilatory and uncertain though it could be in the delivery of justice, the king's law was developed, by this necessary co-operation, into a powerful instrument for the implementation of a broader conception of social order.

CHAPTER 5

Social mobility

Philippa C. Maddern

In 1970 F. R. H. Du Boulay famously dubbed the later middle ages an 'age of ambition'.[1] But did upward social mobility typify late medieval English society, and should we take social mobility to be the process by which whole classes of people benefited or lost from late medieval economic conditions, or as a matter of the success or failure of an individual? The possibility of a whole social group experiencing a shift in fortune is best represented by the case of the peasantry. It is now fairly certain that the living standards of whole classes of peasants declined towards the starvation line in the economic conditions prevailing before the Black Death, and that they rose significantly in the era of comparative shortage of labour and abundant availability of land between 1350 and 1500. But changes in the fortunes of a social group were often more complex than this. In the case of the gentry, high inflation and stiff economic competition in the thirteenth century may have led to the decline of some knightly families relative to the fortunes of noblemen and of lesser freeholders. Yet, as Peter Coss has discussed above, the composition of 'the gentry' was subject to change as the social ranks deemed to qualify for 'gentility' came to include first esquires and then gentlemen.[2] In shire administration, the later middle ages saw some of these lesser gentry take over positions which had been held almost entirely by knightly families in the thirteenth and early fourteenth centuries.

Changes in status terminology may not signal real rises in individual social status, and the fact that economic conditions at different times benefited or disadvantaged whole classes of people only barely illuminates the fates of their component individuals. It is also necessary, then, to analyse the careers of individuals and families who markedly improved the wealth and status to which they had been born. This kind of purposive individual

---

[1] F. R. H. Du Boulay, *An Age of Ambition: English society in the late middle ages* (1970).
[2] See above, pp. 36–7, 41–2.

pursuit of increased social and economic status has been aptly termed
'careerism'.[3] Studying it provides a sharper focus on some of the overall
social movements of late medieval England, and allows us to appreciate the
constellation of factors acting upon socially mobile individuals. However,
this approach can also mislead. Instances of successful careerism must be
balanced against those of individual social decline. The full story must also
take account of gender differences. Most importantly, we should question
the historical significance of individual careerism. Every age undoubtedly
boasts rags-to-riches stories. Were they more frequent and spectacular in the
later middle ages, and did opportunities for successful careerism vary within
the period 1200–1500? Finally, examining individual social mobility also
demands awareness of contemporary attitudes.

The criteria for class and status in late medieval England were not
simple. Undoubtedly wealth was a vital engine of careerism. As one poet
warned:

> . . . thou gettest no degree,
> Nor no worship abide with thee
> Unless thou have the penny ready to take to.[4]

But wealth alone could not determine status. John Townshend of Norfolk, the fifteenth-century son of a prosperous free tenant, accumulated
manors and lands worth around £40 a year (notionally enough to sustain
a knighthood), but remained a 'yeoman' all his life. The sixteenth-century
antiquary John Leland, neatly negotiating what he evidently perceived as
an anomaly of wealth and class, described Townshend as a 'mean man of
substance'.[5] Beyond income, many other factors – legal status, bloodline,
behaviour – determined social degree. The most prosperous serf remained
theoretically divided from free people by a deep status gap and its
attendant socio-legal disabilities. Many medieval thinkers held that
both villeinage and honourable status were entirely genetic in origin.
'A serf can beget in matrimony none but a serf', asserted Sir John Fortescue, while John Russell, writing on precedence, ruled that royal blood
conferred precedence on impoverished nobles.[6] No wonder, then, that

---

[3] M. Bennett, 'Careerism in late medieval England', in J. Rosenthal and C. Richmond, eds., *People, Politics and Community in the later Middle Ages* (Gloucester, 1987), pp. 19–39.

[4] R. T. Davies, ed., *Medieval English Lyrics: a critical anthology* (1963), p. 224.

[5] C. Moreton, *The Townshends and their World: gentry, law and land in Norfolk, c. 1450–1551* (Oxford, 1992), pp. 5–7.

[6] Sir John Fortescue, *On the Laws and Governance of England*, ed. S. Lockwood (Cambridge, 1997), p. 60; F. J. Furnivall, ed., *The Babees Book* (EETS, os XXXII, 1868), pp. 189–90.

rising families – the Pastons, the Townshends, the Hoptons – manu-factured pedigrees to match their newly acquired prosperity. By the fifteenth century, behaviour and lifestyle could determine status. A late fifteenth-century etiquette booklet urged readers to mind their table manners so that 'men will say thereafter / That a gentleman was here'.[7] Even the nature of one's income mattered. From 1429 onwards only income from freehold land enabled a man to vote for, or stand as, a knight of the shire. Thus social climbers craved land aside from its economic benefits. Careerists such as the successful exchequer official Hugh atte Fenne, descended from Yarmouth merchants and officials, knew that late fifteenth-century demesne agriculture was comparatively unrewarding; yet atte Fenne devoted some of his massive earnings to buying manors (with their attached status markers of manor courts and control of church livings), presumably to further his social elevation.[8] In view of this variety of status criteria, we should expect to see con-temporary comment on social mobility engaging with issues wider than mere economic advancement or decline.

But did late medieval thinkers recognise legitimate ambition or guilt-free demotion? Genetic theories of status could imply that social mobility was literally unnatural. 'It is a foul thing [for] beasts to act against their nature, so it is a fouler thing [for] men to act against their estate', declaimed one theorist.[9] Presumably if men never acted against their estate, society would remain immobile. Throughout the period, thinkers who espoused either the social ideal of the three orders (those who prayed, those who fought and those who worked), or the organic meta-phor of the body politic (the prince as head, the peasants as feet, and so on) also often assumed that the hierarchy was divinely ordained. Though individual status change would not necessarily destroy the hierarchy, it was preferably avoided. 'It is the best, early and late / Each man [to] keep his own estate', wrote the chantry priest John Audeley in the early fifteenth century.[10]

Significantly, commentaries on the familiar topoi of Fortune's wheel and the instability of the world were often concerned not with social mobility per se but with reflections on the brevity of life and the urgency

---

[7] Furnivall, *Babees Book*, p. 22.
[8] Roger Virgoe, ed., 'The will of Hugh atte Fenne, 1476', in *A Miscellany* (Norfolk Record Society, LVI, 1993), pp. 31–3.
[9] J.-P. Genet, ed., *Four English Political Tracts of the Later Middle Ages* (Camden Society, 4th ser. XVIII, 1977) p. 9.
[10] Davies, *Lyrics*, p. 171.

for all Christians to concentrate on remedying their fate in the next world. The early fifteenth-century author of *Dives and Pauper* used the image of Fortune's wheel to allegorise life cycle rather than social status. Wealth inevitably attended 'middle age', poverty characterised old age and death. From this standpoint, attempting careerism was simple folly. '[P]roud covetous folk' might 'waver in this world in wealth and worship, now higher, now lower', but all die, and many fall 'into the pit of hell'. The churchyard was a great leveller: 'thou shalt not know the bodies of the rich from the poor ... the free from the bond, but all they turn there to earth and ashes'.[11] Yet, paradoxically, Christian salvation offered (to the righteous) a form of lasting post-mortem social mobility that miraculously co-existed with perfect egalitarianism. 'That ever was thrall, now is he free', proclaimed one Christmas carol, while the author of *Dives and Pauper* promised that in heaven, 'every man and woman [shall] have so great lordship that all they shall have place enough without envy'.[12]

Secular texts consistently portrayed Fortune as deceitful and fleeting: as Chaucer put it, 'When Fortune chooses to flee, no man can hold her back'.[13] Images of Fortune's wheel invariably show it grinding some to despair and death while raising others to eminence. No-one could be certain that Fortune's irrevocable cycle would turn in their favour: as a fourteenth-century lullaby admonished its understandably distressed infant:

> Lollay, lollay, little child, thy foot is on [Fortune's] wheel
> Thou knowest not whither it turns, to woe or to weal.[14]

Worldly social mobility was therefore uncertain, ephemeral and double-edged, always invoking the possibility that one person's success was another's ruin. John Trevisa viciously lampooned richer social climbers as 'men ... hardly satisfied with their own estate', emphasising the deceptiveness and disconnectedness that resulted from social ambition: 'They that will take every degree are of no degree, for in bearing they are like minstrels and heralds ... in eating and in drinking gluttons, in gathering of goods hucksters and taverners'.[15] Popular vernacular religious texts represented such behaviour as literally fiendish; in the sequence of

---

[11] P. H. Barnum, ed., *Dives and Pauper*, I (2 vols., EETS, os CCLVXXV, CCLXXX, 1976–80), ii, pp. 270–1.
[12] Davies, *Lyrics*, p. 196; Barnum, *Dives and Pauper*, ii, p. 320.
[13] The Riverside edition, The Monk's Tale, lines 1995–6.   [14] Davies, *Lyrics*, p. 107.
[15] C. Babington and J. R. Lumby, eds., *Polychronicon Ranulphi Higden ... together with the English translations of John Trevisa* (9 vols., RS, XLI 1865–86), ii, pp. 169–70.

mystery plays known as the N-town cycle, it is the devil who incites a beggar's daughter to 'counterfeit a gentlewoman, disguised as she can'.[16]

A raft of late medieval legislation sought to quell attempts by working people to exploit increased economic opportunities after the Black Death or to adopt the behaviour and customs of their social superiors. Artisans in 1363 were ordered to 'hold them every one to one craft' and the Cambridge parliament of 1388 forbade anyone employed in agricultural labour up to the age of twelve even to attempt a more lucrative profession. Sumptuary legislation supposedly checked 'the outrageous and excessive apparel of divers people against their estate and degree', and a testy statute of 1390 imposed a year's prison sentence on labourers, artificers or servants who attempted to hunt 'gentlemen's game'.[17] This legislation was not especially successful. Nevertheless, these and similar developments in legal practice may have amounted to a cohesive programme by the upper orders, fearing the increased economic power of labourers after the Black Death, to retain existing social structures and force workers into social immobility.

In the period after 1350, prescriptive literature also censured downward social mobility, either as deriving from sinful behaviour or because it implied a wilful disregard for proper earthly social order. The author of the *Brut* chronicle castigated women widowed by the 1361 plague who, 'forgetting their own worship and birth ... married them with those that were of low degree'.[18] The figure of Pauper in *Dives and Pauper*, distinguishing between the deserving and undeserving poor, attributed reprehensible loss of fortune to wilful indulgence in expensive sins (lechery, gluttony, dicing) or vicarious social ambition: 'these days many folk disburden themselves of their own good and take it to their children to make them great'.[19] Guild statutes, like those of the late fourteenth-century guild of the Blessed Mary at Chesterfield, regularly refused charity to any member whose means were diminished by 'lust, or gluttony, or dice-play, or other folly'.[20]

Social mobility formed an ironic counterpoint to writings insisting that it was unacceptable: why castigate the socially mobile if they did not exist? Some late medieval lay people, themselves perhaps upwardly mobile,

---

[16] P. Meredith and S. J. Kahrl, eds., *The N-Town Plays: a facsimile of British Library MS Cotton Vespasian C VIII* (Ilkley, 1977), ff. 136–7.

[17] *Statutes of the Realm* (11 vols., 1810–28), i, pp. 311–13, 379–80, 380–2; ii, pp. 57, 65.

[18] F. W. D. Brie, ed., *The Brut* (2 vols., EETS, os CXXXI, CXXXVI, 1906–8), ii, p. 314.

[19] Barnum, *Dives and Pauper*, ii, pp. 286–7.

[20] Toulmin Smith, ed., *English Gilds* (EETS, os XL, 1870), p. 166.

possibly resented clerical moralising. Chaucer's Knight cut short the
Monk's tale of the fall of princes, demanding to hear instead the 'glad-
some' tale of someone who 'in poor estate ... climbeth up and waxeth
fortunate'.[21] Other writers, both before and after the advent of the Black
Death, actively instructed the socially ambitious. In the thirteenth century, Walter of Henley, observing that a man might fall 'by little and little
into poverty', claimed that his book on estate management would teach
the reader 'to order his life beforehand' and thus avoid such disgrace.[22]
Even the production of manuals purporting to teach gentle behaviour
presupposed socially mobile readers who, not being born to upper-class
manners, had to acquire them by study. Later medieval deeds record the
manumission of well-to-do serfs; and the means by which aspirants to
gentility consolidated their position were calmly acknowledged in
Edmund Paston II's discussion, around 1490, of his nephew's prospects of
attracting a rich marriage: 'Merchants or new gentlemen I deem will
proffer large'.[23]

Fears and hopes, however, tell us little about actual social mobility and
how it was achieved. How great (or slight) was the usual rise or fall? Did
successful careers affect only the individuals concerned, or their families
and lineages in the long term? All these questions remain to be addressed.
Let us survey briefly six families among whose members social mobility
can be observed. They have been chosen because enough material survives
for us to make some judgement as to how far they moved socially. They
are neither a representative nor a truly random sample.

William de la Pole is probably the most famous case of successful late
medieval careerism. His birth status is obscure, yet from 1319 to 1366, by a
combination of aggressively efficient wool-dealing, eagle-eyed opportu-
nism and lavish lending to the crown, de la Pole became by far the
leading merchant in the north of England. While still a merchant, he
acquired successively the status of king's yeoman, knight and baronet. His
son Michael became a distinguished soldier and civil servant, admiral
(1376–7) and ambassador to Milan (1378–9). He was created earl of
Suffolk in 1385. By the mid fifteenth century, Michael's grandson William
was duke of Suffolk and, as discussed by Peter Coss above, one of the
richest and most influential magnates in England. The marriage of this

---

[21] The Riverside edition, The Nun's Priest's Prologue, lines 2775–8.
[22] Walter of Henley, 'On husbandry', in D. Oschinsky, ed., *Walter of Henley and Other Treatises on Estate Management and Accounting* (Oxford, 1971), p. 109.
[23] N. Davis, ed., *Paston Letters and Papers of the Fifteenth Century* (2 vols., Oxford, 1971–6), i, p. 642.

William's son to a daughter of the duke of York was to make the family in-laws of the Yorkist kings and give them a claim to the throne.

The origins of the Penifaders of Brigstock, Northamptonshire were humble. Robert Penifader (*fl.* 1262–1318) was a relatively well-off free peasant and frequent manorial office holder. Two of his children apparently benefited from pre-plague overcrowding in rural England and the disastrous famine of 1315–20 to acquire land from desperate neighbours. Cecilia Penifader (*c.* 1295–1344) never married, but by the end of her life had purchased comparatively large holdings – a house and farmyard, over seventy acres of meadow and two of arable. Her brother William (*c.* 1285–1329) apparently gained sufficient schooling to enter at least minor clerical orders. He also prospered materially. By 1326 he had a house, two acres of arable, and nearly 140 acres of meadow and pasture. However, two other siblings, Robert and Henry, were less prosperous, and by the later fourteenth century the Brigstock Penifaders were living in considerably reduced circumstances.

The Townshends of Norfolk achieved more lasting success. Roger Townshend, who died *c.* 1435, was a well-off free tenant. His son John (d.1466) became a wealthy yeoman. John's children leapt to gentility. His daughter married a prominent Norfolk esquire and his son Roger II became a distinguished lawyer, a knight and a justice of the court of common pleas. Roger II made an excellent marriage – to Eleanor Lunsford of Suffolk, who brought with her £300, the reversion of lands worth 20 marks annually and enviable talents for estate management.[24] The family's rise continued through the sixteenth century. All Roger II's surviving children (except for a daughter who entered the prestigious abbey of Barking) married into the top class of East Anglian society. The income of his heir, Roger III, at £440 per annum, far outranked that of any other Norfolk knight in the 1524 subsidy assessment. Roger III was a royal courtier, created knight of the body by 1533. The distribution of his estate in 1551 allowed even his younger sons to found elite lineages.

The Folewoods of Warwickshire were of lesser gentry origin and remarkably stable status. At least eight generations lived and died as minor landholders in Tanworth-in-Arden, Warwickshire, between *c.* 1230 and *c.* 1500.[25] From the 1230s they appeared consistently as witnesses to deeds, and occasionally as small-scale buyers of rents and lands. Early

---

[24] Moreton, *The Townshends*, esp. pp. 5–45, and Appendix 4.
[25] The fortunes of the Folewoods can be reconstructed from the Archer Collection in the Shakespeare Birthplace Trust Record Office. The family is discussed by C. Carpenter, *Locality and Polity: a study of Warwickshire landed society, 1401–1499* (Cambridge, 1992).

family members (except for two who entered the Church) were given no status. But by 1436 the family's income was above the Warwickshire average for those of gentle status who were neither knights nor esquires. John Folewood was styled 'gentleman' in 1443, and by 1500 Richard Folewood had acquired the title 'esquire'. Yet fifteenth-century Folewood transactions remained humdrum: the family acquired rents of 2s 6d and 6s 8d, and bought one toft and two small crofts. Most probably, therefore, the Folewoods' newly acquired gentry titles reflected changes in bureaucratic practice, rather than real social advance.

The Vavasours of Yorkshire were of higher status. The main line, of Hazlewood, was established as a provincial knightly family before the fourteenth century, and continued so until 1524. Their most notable careerist, John Vavasour (*c.* 1440–1506) was the eldest son of a cadet branch of the family based at Spaldington. He became successively serjeant at law (1479), king's serjeant (1483), justice of pleas in the palatinate of Lancaster (1485) and justice of common pleas (1490). He was recorder of York from 1485, and was constantly named on peace sessions and commissions of enquiry from 1483 onwards. Knighted in 1501, he purchased manors in Yorkshire and left the staggering sum of £800 in gold at his death.[26] He died childless (he was estranged from his wife) and the bulk of his wealth went to his nephew Peter, whose marriage to Elizabeth, daughter of Andrew, Lord Windsor, may have resulted from his adventitious prosperity. Apart from Peter, no other family member demonstrably benefited from John's success.[27]

Finally, the various members of the Swillington family, also long-established Yorkshire knights, display a positive kaleidoscope of social mobility. Hugh Swillington (d.1304) acquired lands in East Anglia through his marriage. His son Adam (d.1328) was a retainer of Thomas of Lancaster, but Adam's eldest son died young and his grandson Robert (d.1379) lost most of his patrimony, possibly through incompetence, to a cadet line founded by his uncle Sir Robert, second son of Adam. Sir Robert had risen through baronial and royal service. A trusted retainer and chamberlain of John of Gaunt, he died in 1391 owning thirty-five manors and leaving substantial bequests to his heir, Sir Roger, and to his bastard son Thomas de Hopton. By 1420 Sir Roger and his two sons were

---

[26] Vavasour was the butt of contemporary jokes for his miserliness: J. Raine, ed., *Testamenta Eboracensia*, IV (Surtees Society, LIII, 1869), pp. 89–92.

[27] Emma Hawkes, "'I thanke God myne adversari . . . hathe had no wurshyp . . . in the cort to his great shame': honour, family and the law in late medieval Yorkshire' (Ph.D. thesis, University of Western Australia, 1997), pp. 106–14, 172–5, 301.

dead. Most of the Swillington inheritance came to John Hopton, son of the illegitimate Thomas. Thus John, consigned by dubious birth to the very fringes of gentility, became a substantial and reputable Suffolk landowner. His eldest son and grandson were knighted, his daughters married into established armigerous East Anglian families, and his descendants thereafter became fixtures in upper-class East Anglian society.[28]

What do these case histories suggest? Careers were made in husbandry, trade, the Church, the law and royal or magnate service. Marriage and the failure of male lineage all affected social mobility. Yet these tales also raise disquieting reflections. Were careerists – that is, individuals who purposively achieved a rise in status – numerous among the six lineages? Three families (the Penifaders, the main Vavasour line and the Folewoods) displayed almost no social mobility; two cadets of already upper-class families grew richer and more eminent (John Vavasour and Sir Robert Swillington); two individuals (Peter Vavasour and John Hopton) were whisked upwards by biological chance; and only two families showed sustained, significant and purposive social rise (the de la Poles and the Townshends). Significantly, perhaps, the same two families show the greatest individual status change, with William de la Pole and the younger Townshends rising significantly above their birth status.

Individuals' success thus did not necessarily translate into long-term advancement. The Hopton, Townshend and de la Pole families benefited from their forebears' luck and acumen, but none of William and Cecilia Penifader's younger kin was launched upwards by their success. The cadet Swillingtons flourished at the expense of the main line. Only one other Vavasour profited from John's career. The Townshend fortunes were enduring, but other success stories were curtailed by lineage failure. The role of incompetence is harder to determine. Ineptitude may have contributed to the property losses of the elder branch of the Swillingtons, but no one now can tell whether the unsuccessful Penifaders were inefficient or merely unfortunate.

One factor, however, is common: where it occurred, social mobility generally resulted from multiple causes. The de la Poles got their start through trade, but Michael de la Pole's aristocratic patrons paved the way to his earldom. William Penifader combined agriculture with ecclesiastical employment; the Townshends rose through a combination of agriculture, a legal career and good marriages; John Vavasour inherited property and made a professional fortune from legal and other forms of

---

[28] C. Richmond, *John Hopton: a fifteenth century Suffolk gentleman* (Cambridge, 1981), ch. 1.

service. John Hopton benefited not only from accidents of survival but also from his second marriage to a well-to-do widow.

Thus the question of the significance of social mobility in late medieval England becomes increasingly perplexing. Spectacular rises and falls undoubtedly occurred; but what if most families were like the Folewoods, whose status remained remarkably constant over 250 years? To make an accurate statistical survey of late medieval social mobility is impossible. Our sources allow no certainties; and any estimate based on a selection of examples will inevitably be biased by the undue prominence of brilliant successes, the difficulties of assessing the numbers of people who rose from very lowly origins, and the problems of following the histories of those dragged by social decline below record-keeping orbits. The story of Alice de Schischurst, daughter of a poor Halesowen family in the late thirteenth century, is a particularly poignant example of the last process. Alice came from a servant family, but lost status and was declared *persona non grata* on the manor in 1275. A further year's temporary employment in two successive houses provided only a brief respite. In late 1276 she stole some food, set fire to her employer's house, and fled the manor. Was her disastrous slide into poverty and crime irremediable? We will never know, since she disappears thereafter from the manorial record.

How then can we assess the importance of careerism in late medieval England? Two interconnected methods appear most promising. First, we can consider the various late medieval factors producing social mobility and their power to do so at different periods. Secondly, studies of social mobility in limited populations, such as those by Bennett and Carpenter, yield conclusions which may, with caution, be extrapolated to the rest of late medieval England.[29]

Six major routes to purposive social advancement influenced careers in late medieval England: agriculture; trade and industry; ecclesiastical preferment; the law and other forms of political or administrative service; military service; and marriage. But the impact of such opportunities was limited by the fact that most were barred, to a greater or lesser degree, to some sectors of the population.

Women especially were disadvantaged as careerists. Military service was open only to fit males. Women were barred from practising the law, gaining ecclesiastical preferment (other than in a nunnery), and (almost

[29] M. J. Bennett, 'Sources and problems in the study of social mobility: Cheshire in the later middle ages', *Transactions of the Historic Society of Lancashire and Cheshire*, 128 (1978), 59–95; Carpenter, *Locality and Polity*, ch. 4.

universally) from holding office. Neither did women form part of ruling urban elites, though a few – especially widows – ran businesses. Urban ale-brewing is a good example of an originally female-dominated trade; its profit levels were always low, and by the late fourteenth century moves to standardise the industry had decreased the participation of women. By 1500 further industrial changes, only partially associated with the introduction of beer-brewing, had pushed most women out of leading positions in the industry and into low-paid retailing jobs. Other urban occupations common to females – domestic service, huckstering, prostitution – held out minimal prospects of upward social mobility. Even successful husbandry demanded the ability to hold or own land independently, a capacity denied to married women. Admittedly, nothing barred widows or single women from husbandry or estate acquisition, and unmarried women, from peasants like Cecilia Penifader to great gentlewomen like Eleanor, widow of Roger Townshend II, used their temporary landowning status to advance their own, or their families', interests. But whether they changed their status by such means is very doubtful. Eleanor Townshend remained a gentlewoman and Cecilia Penifader a peasant. Careerism by means of these opportunities can, therefore, have affected at most only the male half of the population.

For the poor, too, empty pockets could curtail opportunities for social advancement. Expensive training was required to enter the law. To join the upper echelons of the military demanded years of practice in arms and expensive horses, swords and armour. Especially after 1350, good church livings were often monopolised by university graduates, putting them well beyond the reach of most poor people, while ordination demanded a prior guarantee of the candidate's financial security. From the fourteenth century, male and female monasteries alike demanded at least a £5 entry fee, and some levied additional payment for providing necessary gear for the novice. Such sums were within the reach of well-off yeomen, but hardly provided career opportunities for the poor. Only marriages – though not necessarily upwardly mobile ones – were available to both sexes and all social classes. And even among comparatively well-off males, none of the routes to advancement listed above, as far as we can tell, produced a large number of successful careerists.

War was perhaps the least likely source of social mobility. Dazzling examples of fortunes made in the Scottish and French wars can be found, some of them discussed by Michael Prestwich in chapter 3,[30] but wars

---

[30] See pp. 81–2, 86–8.

were only randomly available throughout the period 1200–1500, and relatively few took advantage of them. Even in the militarised society of late medieval Cheshire, professional soldiers formed only a minority, and most 'appear to have found it difficult to enter polite society ... with the profits of their service'.[31]

Urban trade may seem a more promising option for the socially ambitious. Immigrants from rural areas undoubtedly flocked to late medieval cities and the turnover among wealthy urban oligarchs was high, especially after the advent of the Black Death. It would seem a reasonable inference that rich merchants gravitated to the status of country gentry and were replaced by the upwelling of ambitious incomers. Individual instances apparently confirm both processes. In the early fourteenth century men of humble origins did become urban success stories. Richard Embleton, for instance, a newcomer and small-scale trader in Newcastle in the 1290s, became 'by far Newcastle's greatest merchant' by the early fourteenth century, serving as mayor twenty-two times.[32] An urban journeyman might hope to marry his master's widow and succeed to his business; and even servants might benefit from generous citizens. John Russell, servant to a plutocratic Exeter goldsmith, was bequeathed all his master's goods, properties and tools of trade, entered the freedom of the city in 1378, and succeeded to nearly the same offices and status as his former master. The Boleyns seemingly exemplify the complete cycle in one generation. Geoffrey Boleyn, who came from an obscure lesser gentry family of Salle, Norfolk, went to London, became a rich mercer, was elected mayor in 1457–8, bought large estates in Norfolk and Kent, built a substantial manor house at Hever, married, as his second wife, a lord's heiress, and founded the noble lineage that eventually produced Henry VIII's second wife.

But how common, and how great, were social rises in towns? Here we should be careful to distinguish geographical from social mobility, and between opportunities at different times in the later middle ages. In the period *c.* 1280–1340 towns undoubtedly exercised a magnetic attraction to an increasingly desperate rural proletariat; but, perhaps partly because of the numbers involved, signs of their success are discouragingly few. In Norwich between 1311 and 1333 a single urban quarter (Mancroft) recorded an average of over thirty adult male immigrants' names in its

[31] P. Morgan, *War and Society in Medieval Cheshire 1277–1403* (Manchester, 1987), p. 8.
[32] E. Miller and J. Hatcher, *Medieval England: towns, commerce and crafts 1086–1348* (1995), p. 337.

tithing roll each year.[33] Hence competition for a share in lucrative urban trades was exceptionally stiff. Only a tiny proportion of the hundreds of annual immigrants to Norwich could hope to become leading traders or prosperous freemen, and hence perhaps one of the four city bailiffs, or even a leet constable. Indirect evidence suggests that poorer immigrants generally stayed poor. Between 1311 and 1333 the proportion of the Mancroft population owning real property halved. As early as 1308 civic legislators were alarmed at the numbers of servants in the city whose only resource was a penny a day wage.[34] Almost certainly, therefore, Walter of Hicklemere and his brother, excused the 1s fine for not registering in a Norwich tithing because of their poverty, were more typical of urban immigrants in the period 1250 to 1350 than such spectacular successes as William de la Pole or Richard Embleton.[35]

What, then, were the possibilities for post-plague urban careerists? Disease reduced the ranks of urban elites – and probably the numbers of competing immigrants, too. Yet it seems likely, also, that urban economic conditions after the Black Death were harder for social aspirants than before 1348. Urban social mobility was by no means always upwards: traders and artisans failed, as reiterated guild provisions for charity to colleagues ruined by 'adventure of this world' testify.[36] The overseas wool trade that had benefited careerists such as William de la Pole went into long-term decline after the 1360s. In York, Beverley and Hull the numbers of large-scale merchants decreased between 1306–36 and 1460–1500, both absolutely and relative to those with much lower annual turnovers. Provincial cities were troubled by the tendency of Londoners to monopolise local markets as well as their own trade. Some fifteenth-century oligarchies remained dauntingly exclusive: in Exeter, only forty of 472 non-oligarchic heads of household in 1377 later joined the ruling group. In these conditions some fortunate individuals could still succeed. In the late fifteenth century Edmund Shaa, son of a Cheshire mercer, went from riding his father's packhorses to become a London goldsmith, mayor and (eventually) a knight. But, in general, tougher economic conditions probably curtailed social gains and tended to limit successful careerism to those individuals already sufficiently well off to purchase entry to

[33] E. Rutledge, 'Immigration and population growth in early fourteenth-century Norwich: evidence from the tithing roll', *Urban History Yearbook* (1988), 25.
[34] W. Hudson and J. C. Tingey, eds., *The Records of the City of Norwich* (2 vols., Norwich, 1906), i, p. 189.
[35] Norwich and Norfolk Record Office [N&NRO], Case 5, Shelf b/1 Leet Roll 16 Edward I (1287–8).
[36] Smith, *English Gilds*, p. 24.

lucrative and honourable trades. Shaa's father was a rich provincial merchant; the Boleyns were gentry before ever they moved to London.

What about the other sort of urban careerism – the proportion of city-dwellers who made a clear transition to rural aristocracy? The evidence is equivocal at best. It is not even clear that contemporaries perceived a move from burgess to gentry status as significant progress. Some writers classed substantial merchants as the social equals of – or even superiors to – gentlemen, and, as Peter Coss argues above, some armigerous townsmen preferred to be known as merchants.[37] Though many burgesses invested in county estates or interacted with magnate society, few, it seems, were prepared to resign their urban eminence. John Grey, Robert Wilford and John Webber, wealthy Exeter citizens, were also 'esquires' of the earl of Devon in 1384. Richard Buckland bought lands in Northamptonshire and sat as MP for the county in 1425 and 1431, yet continued to trade as a wealthy London fishmonger till his death in 1436.[38] Local studies show few urban plutocrats unequivocally leaving their towns and breaking into county society. In fifteenth-century Warwickshire only one merchant, William Botener of Coventry, successfully bought his way into landed gentility. In late medieval Exeter, '[t]here is no evidence that members of the ... oligarchy either worked for or desired the life of a country gentleman'.[39]

Was investment in agriculture – either by direct husbandry or by acquiring lands worked by others – a safer route to riches? After 1350, when land was cheap and labour dear, there is good evidence to suggest that the average size of peasant holdings rose, propelling many of those balanced precariously on the poverty line into comparative wealth and security. The favourable rent/wage nexus also allowed peasants to bargain on almost equal terms with landlords. Some of the resultant success stories are discussed by Peter Coss in chapter 2.[40] Nor were possibilities of upward mobility by land acquisition limited to peasants. Payling argues that high death rates among the male heirs of gentry families from the late fourteenth century onwards stimulated land sales and the distribution of lands between heiresses, creating opportunities for the upwardly mobile.[41]

---

[37] See p. 72.
[38] C. M. Barron and A. F. Sutton, eds., *Medieval London Widows, 1300–1500* (1994) pp. 118–20.
[39] M. Kowaleski, 'The commercial dominance of a medieval provincial oligarchy: Exeter in the late fourteenth century', *Medieval Studies*, 46 (1984), 381.
[40] See pp. 67–70.
[41] S. J. Payling, 'Social mobility, demographic change, and landed society in late medieval England', *EcHR*, 2nd ser. 45 (1992), 53–6.

But how many families rose significantly through agricultural success alone in the post-plague period? Local studies are not encouraging. In fifteenth-century Warwickshire only one family, the Spensers, achieved 'a significant social rise solely by agricultural enterprise'.[42] The Townshends seem similarly unmatched in fifteenth-century Norfolk. Agriculture itself therefore seems hardly likely to have produced widespread social mobility, though possibly small-scale agriculturalists, benefiting from comparatively favourable economic conditions from the late fourteenth century onwards, accumulated enough resources to propel their children upwards through education or trade. The profits of John Townshend's husbandry, for instance, clearly paid for his son's legal education. Agricultural success, therefore, may have produced a pool of prosperous yeomen in the late middle ages from which socially successful descendants could emerge.

But agriculture also produced its ruinous failures, especially at two periods in the later middle ages. Overcrowding, and the accompanying disastrous famines of the years 1290–1330, brought William Sclatter, originally a fairly prosperous Halesowen half-virgater, to debt, subletting, forced land sales and eventual poverty.[43] Then, in the later fifteenth century during a period of rising wool prices, landlords realised the value of reinventing arable demesnes and common pasture as pastoral enterprises and game parks. The practice involved evicting poorer cottagers and barring their livestock from common grazing lands. Between 1485 and 1517, so inquest jurors claimed, in Buckinghamshire alone over a thousand people were forced off nearly 8,000 acres.[44] Juries vividly evoked the sudden descent into destitution. In 1498, one jury alleged, the sixty occupants of 240 acres of arable in Wormleighton, Warwickshire, were driven out 'weeping, to wander in idleness' and subsequently 'perished of hunger'.[45] Among the gentry, however, fifteenth-century social decline does not seem unequivocally related to agricultural failure or mismanagement. Carpenter's study of all rural gentry families in Warwickshire shows that the commonest cause for a family's 'disappearance' was not economic mismanagement but failure in the male line.[46]

An ecclesiastical career appears, initially, to have been a sounder pathway to fame and fortune in later medieval England. All free men were theoretically eligible to study for the priesthood or to enter a

---

[42] Carpenter, *Locality and Polity*, pp. 136–7.
[43] Z. Razi, *Life, Marriage and Death in a Medieval Parish* (Cambridge, 1980), pp. 81–2, 146.
[44] I. S. Leadam, ed., *The Domesday of Inclosures, 1517–8* (2 vols., 1897), ii, pp. 570–9.
[45] PRO, C43/28 File 14.   [46] Carpenter, *Locality and Polity*, ch. 4, esp. pp. 138–46 and table 4.

monastery. Even ex-serfs, having gained manumission, could rise to comfortable ecclesiastical preferment. Once ordained, nothing (theoretically) barred a man from reaching the lordly heights of a bishopric. Walter Bronescombe, bishop of Exeter from 1258 to 1280, and Adam Orleton, successively bishop of Hereford, Worcester and Winchester between 1317 and 1334, provide two examples of successful churchmen whose origins were so humble as to baffle their modern biographers. The self-congratulatory account of Abbess Joan Wygenhale of Crabhous, Norfolk, shows that women from minor gentry families could also enjoy a rise to the comparative independence and comfort of an abbess's post.[47]

But in the clerical world, as in urban economies, aspirants to fortune almost certainly vastly outnumbered the available opportunities throughout this period. Samples from clerical poll tax assessments of the late fourteenth century show that well over half of all clergy – between 55 and 83 per cent – inhabited the poorly paid and fiercely competitive world of the unbeneficed. In these circumstances rich and well-connected clerical careerists were most likely to succeed. Gentry and aristocrats dominated the episcopate between *c.* 1350 and the Reformation. Royal relatives or protégés easily found lucrative ecclesiastical posts throughout the period: men such as Aymer de Valence, half-brother to Henry III and bishop of Winchester from 1253 to 1260, or Henry Beaufort, whose appointment to the see of Lincoln in 1398 was probably the result of the fragile political alliance between his father John of Gaunt and Richard II. Beaufort eventually achieved the bishopric of Winchester and a personal fortune of over £50,000. Clearly the higher a cleric's social origins, the greater chance he stood of achieving prosperity. Poorer candidates to the priesthood, like William Penifader, might never hold a benefice, relying instead on often badly paid work as supernumerary parish officers or casual mass priests. It seems likely, then, that the majority of men who entered the priesthood never significantly advanced their birth status. A similar argument applies to monasteries and nunneries. Bright boys from relatively modest (though landed) families could, like John Wheathamstead of St Albans, rise to an abbacy. But considering the entry price, it is no surprise to find that recruitment to monasteries apparently came largely from middle-class families – rural gentry and urban merchants – and that large, rich and prestigious abbeys attracted a disproportionate share of entrants from aristocratic families.

---

[47] BL, Add. MS 4733, ff. 50v–53v.

Successful careerism, then, may have been a comparative rarity in the late medieval Church, limited to those bright young men who managed to find patrons to fund their education and present them with benefices after ordination. Furthermore, any advance in status made by churchmen/women was almost necessarily limited to a single generation, since celibacy was enjoined upon them (although widows and widowers could enter the Church and the latter reportedly did so in large numbers after the Black Death). Any property they controlled was institutional, and could not be conveyed to other family members. Church patronage did allow successful ecclesiastics to benefit their kin, but it was unlikely to confer long-term advancement on the lineage.

Ecclesiastics apart, marriage was the most widely available of the possible strategies under discussion, but it is surprisingly difficult to find any but isolated instances of marriage producing social mobility. The story of Thomasine Bonaventure, a poor Cornish girl who caught the eye of a London merchant, became first his servant, then his wife, and finally achieved a richly dowered widowhood and two further marriages, is a striking but not representative case. Most families thought long and hard about the advantages of different matches, and unequal marriages, where one party stood to gain disproportionate wealth and status, were often reprobated and hard to achieve. The Pastons' steward, Richard Calle, son of a Framlingham grocer, achieved the posthumous title 'gentleman' through his marriage to his employers' daughter Margery. But at the time her family literally locked the door against her and tried to have the marriage set aside. Only Margery's steadfastness in the face of episcopal cross-examination kept the marriage alive. At the upper levels of society, heiresses were undoubtedly attractive partners; but their guardians commonly demanded such heavy prices for the alliance that only the wealthy could afford the investment. When in the late 1430s Sir William Chamberlain married Anne, only daughter and heiress of Sir Robert Harlyng of Norfolk, he had to provide, beforehand, a jointure worth £100 a year.[48] No wonder, then, that in fifteenth-century Warwickshire, though '[s]ome ... greater families grew greater still through fortunate marriages', social or geographical newcomers found it hard to break into the marriage market.[49] Furthermore, the requirement for the husband's family to supply a jointure meant that in the event of his early demise the family might find their heirs eclipsed in power and influence by the diversion of a substantial part of their income into the widow's coffers.

---

[48] Magdalen College, Oxford, Fastolf Papers, 17.   [49] Carpenter, *Locality and Polity*, pp. 115–16.

Among the peasantry there is some evidence that marriage was, at some periods, a strategy at least for preventing social decline. On the estates of the bishopric of Winchester in the late thirteenth century, young landless men sought as marriage partners older widows holding tenancies. After the wife's death, the survivor might inherit the holding and re-marry a younger woman, who in turn might became a marriageable widow. However, in better economic circumstances, where woodland or pastoral economies offered alternative livelihoods, and in the improved conditions after the Black Death marriage to widows apparently lost its attraction, which suggests that, even among the peasantry, marriage was not a pre-ferred pathway to social mobility. Undoubtedly, good marriages could provide general social and legal support for less capable or prosperous relatives of the couple. Both Cecilia Penifader and her sister Cristina benefited from their third sister Agnes's marriage to Henry Kroyle junior, a well-off peasant whose family backed up the Penifaders in their various transactions in the Brigstock manor court. But in this case, as in others, the marriage produced hardly any status shift at the time, and none in the longer term. In short, though a few marriages could produce rises in social status, in the majority of cases marriages operated more to maintain than to alter social status.

Possibly the best prospects for a male careerist throughout the period lay in the remaining option available to him: legal, political or admin-istrative service. Opportunities in this area were, perhaps, more numerous than in any other set of careers. Though the upper ranks of the legal profession – justices of the central courts, serjeants and leading appren-tices at law – comprised perhaps only 120 members at any one time, even this compares favourably with the small numbers of bishoprics or arch-deaconries open to ecclesiastical careerists. Below the pinnacle of central court appointments were literally hundreds, if not thousands, of places for men with some legal training: attorneys, solicitors and clerks in the royal courts and the courts of every liberty and borough in the realm; officers attached to every quarter sessions or shire court; holders of manorial courts; members of the 'counsel learned' of great (and sometimes lesser) landowners. Litigation was expensive and large sums of money flowed into the pockets of lawyers. Sir John Fastolf spent £1,085 in ten years on the legal defence of three manors.[50] Canon law and the civil service were alike pathways to successful ecclesiastical careers: John Waltham and

---

[50] A. R. Smith, 'Aspects of the career of Sir John Fastolf (1380–1459)' (D.Phil. thesis, University of Oxford, 1982), p. 12.

Robert Hallum, bishops of Salisbury in 1388–95 and 1407–17 respectively, were both of relatively obscure birth, but obtained bishoprics through careers in civil and ecclesiastical administration.

This great span of administrative employment opened up opportunities to men from many social levels. In the late fourteenth century, for instance, peasants holding manorial offices were well placed to take advantage of the new possibilities of renting demesne lands. The Giffards of Bibury (Glos.) were reeves of the manor in 1387 but became farmers of it in 1396. Furthermore, some offices were apparently opened to men of progressively lesser rank. Positions in county administration below the rank of sheriff were, by the later middle ages, commonly held by yeomen or husbandmen. William Dallyng of Fordham (Norfolk) was styled only husbandman in 1424, but by 1442 had achieved the label 'gentleman', a rise attributable to his legal skills, which brought appointment as under-sheriff (1422, 1429 and 1438) and sub-escheator (1439–40), as well as retainers for legal work from patrons such as the priory of Holy Trinity, Norwich.[51] Hence men from comparatively lowly families could prosper. Hugh atte Fenne of Yarmouth amassed huge wealth during his twenty-five years as an exchequer official: his will, proved in 1476, contained bequests of over £2,500 and references to extensive estates in Norfolk, Suffolk, Sussex and Middlesex.[52] Thomas Kebell was the son of Walter Kebell, steward to Joan, Lady Abergavenny. Thomas became a lawyer, served the family of Lord Hastings, attracted other clients, became serjeant-at-law in 1486, married three times (twice to heiresses) and died in 1500 owning estates in some twenty places in Leicestershire alone, including a luxuriously furnished mansion at Humberstone. Lawyers, of course, were well placed to find properties available for sale and good marriages. In general, then, as Carpenter concludes, it seems that 'the real avenues to the acquisition of land and to social advancement lay through the professions'.[53]

Yet even here we should pause and consider the magnitude of the phenomenon. Although lawyers and public servants prospered, it is doubtful that many achieved spectacular social success. The children of prominent lawyers in the fifteenth century did not often rise to the peerage – though the majority of late fifteenth-century serjeants-at-law at least ensured heraldic recognition of gentility for their descendants. Lesser

---

[51] P. C. Maddern, *Violence and Social Order: East Anglia 1422–1442* (Oxford, 1992), pp. 138, 142–3; N&NRO, DCN 1/1/76, 78, 82–4.
[52] Virgoe, 'The will of Hugh atte Fenne', pp. 31–3. [53] Carpenter, *Locality and Polity*, p. 137.

lawyers may have entered the profession hoping rather to stem social decline than to rise to greatness. Adam Mundford, for instance, was the younger son of an established, but lesser, gentry family in Norfolk, and could expect little by way of patrimony. His busy practice as an attorney in the court of king's bench in the first half of the fifteenth century maintained, without significantly advancing, his birth status.

So, is 'an age of ambition' an apt description of late medieval England, or even of England at any particular point in the period 1200–1500? Considering the overall effects of all known forms of social mobility, this seems doubtful. True, the class boundaries of late medieval England were never impermeable. Individuals migrated from one class to the next; incompetents and unfortunates sank below their birth status, while the enterprising and lucky (almost entirely male) advanced their own, and sometimes their children's, social standing. But the preconditions and opportunities for social mobility were not the same for all social groups at all times. In the period 1250–1350, advancement for peasant families was difficult to achieve and almost impossible to sustain. In these circumstances, different classes adopted varying strategies. Large numbers of poor peasants migrated to towns, though probably only a tiny proportion of them succeeded there. Others adopted marriage strategies to ease their path to a tenancy, or joined the throngs of unbeneficed clergymen. By the late fourteenth century, demographic and economic trends had produced a comparatively prosperous class of free peasants, yeoman and lesser gentry who may have provided a greater pool of potential careerists. In the fifteenth century men of yeoman background can be found taking advantage of both land and office. In some cases the offspring of such men profited from estates, education and marriages bought with their own hard-won acquisitions. This rise in the numbers of potential careerists possibly produced both a fear of successful careerism and some backlash; governments legislated against ambitious wage claims and inappropriate dress standards, moralists deplored the hunt for worldly fortune, satirists scarified would-be aristocrats. However, the actual possibilities for sustained social advancement were in some areas limited by fifteenth-century economic conditions. For those seeking their fortune in town from the 1350s onwards, the profits of urban trade were apparently lower than before. Not until the late fifteenth century did rising wool prices bring, again, potential prosperity to great landowning pastoralists and merchants (and that at the apparent price of destitution for those poor labourers forced from their land). The success of families such as the de la Poles can thus be read as the consequence of different generations, either by design or luck, adopting careers appropriate to their particular time and status: William de la Pole rode the wool boom of the early fourteenth century, while his son Michael made his name in the wars of the later fourteenth century. The only career option to remain attractive throughout the period was office holding, either ecclesiastical or secular, and even here the beneficiaries (male almost without exception) not infrequently faced suspicion and ridicule from the existing ranks of the political and social elite. In the end, then, it seems certain that throughout the period 1200–1500 successful careerists were the exception, not the rule, and that for the vast majority of people social *im*mobility remained the norm.

CHAPTER 6

Town life

Richard Britnell

THE URBAN ENVIRONMENT

Medieval English towns, though much smaller than those of today, were sufficiently distinct from rural communities to justify separate consideration. They were trading centres, where employment was heavily dependent on non-agrarian activities. Though this implies that they should be identified primarily by economic criteria, towns developed distinctive characteristics, and the largest ones created political and cultural institutions without parallel in rural communities. There was no medieval word corresponding closely to our word 'town', but most of the places that need consideration for their urban characteristics were described in contemporary documents as 'boroughs', a word packed with a complex amalgam of economic, legal and cultural significance. Many different aspects of development were apparent in the physical shape and appearance of towns, so that a survey of the urban environment leads some way to an appreciation of what it meant to be a medieval town-dweller.

Though towns varied greatly in population and complexity, their size and layout alone distinguished them from rural settlements. The principal street or streets were lined with a distinctive configuration of properties, often of half an acre or less, held by money rents and freely transferable by sale or lease. These were the characteristics of 'burgage tenure', the form of freehold most characteristic of the urban environment, and many boroughs were so called simply because they contained properties of this kind. In many towns, especially smaller ones, the shape of these plots remains to this day incorporated into property boundaries, sometimes in the form of long, stone-walled gardens stretching back behind each house. The residences and workshops of the very smallest towns comprised simply two rows of house plots facing each other across a main road, or a tight cluster centred on a marketplace, but the more successful towns spread into more complicated and irregular plans. Where different stages of urban growth were characterised by differences in the dimensions of burgage plots, the contrasts often remained to be recorded on modern maps. Historical reconstruction of settlement plans is most secure when such cartographic evidence can be matched with that of medieval rentals listing these properties. Their size and the ground rent varied from town to town, but annual rents of 6d or 1s were common. At Biggleswade in Bedfordshire, where a market charter was granted by King John early in the thirteenth century, there were subsequently 123 burgage plots occupied at a standard rent of 1s each. Situated near a trading area, burgage plots were adapted to the needs of families who depended upon manufacturing and trade for their daily subsistence. They allowed their tenants a house and outbuildings by the street, and enough space to grow vegetables and to keep hens, without implying any deeper commitment to agriculture. Since most craftsmen worked from their own homes, the sights, sounds and smells of manufacturing must have pervaded the streets through much of the day.

Adjacent to main town streets there commonly stood barns for storing harvested crops, and behind the houses lay fields and closes, for though many townsmen no longer lived an agrarian way of life, no hard line divided urban and rural economies. Particularly among the wealthier ranks of urban society there were landowning families, most noticeably in those older towns, such as Cambridge, that had extensive fields attached to them. Pasturing animals on town commons was a right whose importance to the burgesses of many towns is indicated by the number of disputes concerning enclosures that reached town courts, and sometimes went on to the king's justices. This meant that, quite apart from beasts of burden, and animals on their way to and from market, town streets were liable to be thronged at some times of day with the livestock of local residents being moved from place to place. Other animals got on to the streets by error. Stray pigs, a universal problem in medieval towns, not only endangered passers-by (especially children) but also damaged property and dug up road surfaces. Pig-keeping amongst the inhabitants of Southwark and Westminster was encouraged by the size of the London market, and even there pigs were liable to escape into the streets for want of proper attention. In 1408, twenty-seven people were charged with allowing their pigs to stray in Westminster. A town with walls might have some hope of restricting movement by farm animals; the town court at Ludlow tried in 1476 to exclude pigs from within the walls. This strategy was not usually available, however, and it is doubtful how effective it was.

Livestock around town inevitably complicated problems of waste disposal and public hygiene. The inevitable deposits of animal dung were complemented by the sweepings and emptyings of urban households, which accumulated particularly on patches of waste land and in back streets. Shitelane, in fourteenth-century Winchester, was appropriately named. During the fourteenth and fifteenth centuries public concern with the disposal of waste from private households increased. Those who deposited filth in unauthorised places were fined, and householders were made responsible for the street in front of their houses. There was also more public provision for the salubriousness of public spaces. Londoners had had a public latrine at Queenhithe as early as the twelfth century, and other towns had provided such facilities near central marketing areas by the fifteenth. Such measures could only expect a limited success, given the magnitude of the problems of waste disposal.

Townsmen commonly cleaned their clothing at common washing places in flowing water. Drinking water, by contrast, was most commonly drawn from wells. The shortage of wells was one of the reasons why the bishop of Salisbury moved the site of Salisbury from Old Sarum in 1219. Common wells were a consistent feature of urban topography. In Colchester, for example, Stockwell, St Helen's Well, a well in Trinity Lane and All Saints' Well were all within easy reach of the town centre.[1] Public supplies were augmented by the private wells of wealthier householders. Not until late in the middle ages is there widespread evidence of water brought into towns by conduits. About the years 1448–51, the inhabitants of Wells constructed a system to pipe fresh water into the marketplace, bringing water from a source in the grounds of the bishop of Wells. Maintaining clean water supplies was a task of the urban authorities that met with setbacks through the contamination of wells and streams by poor drainage, badly sited cesspits, and the careless disposal of waste products. The hand of urban authorities concerned with this problem was strengthened by statutory legislation of 1388 which, in order to prevent the spread of disease, prohibited the throwing of garbage into watercourses.

The principal town streets led past houses, workshops and outbuildings to the central trading area that was vital to a town's existence. Not surprisingly, new towns were often located on an existing road, especially

---

[1] Essex Record Office, Colchester and North-East Essex Branch, Colchester Court Rolls 38/2, 50/13v, 54/19v; Colchester Oath Book, fos. 165–6.

at the point where it crossed a river or formed a junction with another road. Urban trade encouraged bridge construction, though too little is known about the dates at which most bridges were first built to be sure how closely the two were connected. Numerous new towns and markets of the twelfth and thirteenth centuries have an Old English name ending in 'ford' – such as Chelmsford, Rochford, Romford, Stratford and Wolvesford (the modern Witham), all in Essex – but it was unusual for them not to have bridges by the thirteenth century, and in some instances it is possible to show a link between the development of towns and the development of communications in this way. At Durham, Framwellgate Bridge was constructed at the behest of Ranulph Flambard, bishop of Durham from 1099 to 1128, who also created an adjacent borough below his castle walls. The importance of good road communications for the trade of medieval towns was recognised in the king's special interest in preserving the peace along them. The Anglo-Norman *Leges Henrici Primi* (1113 × 1118) explain that roads to cities and royal towns were designated the king's highway, and that they should be wide enough for two wagons to pass; especially heavy penalties were imposed on those who assaulted anyone travelling. The same principle is implied in Edward I's Statute of Winchester of 1285, which provided that the verges of the king's highway were to be kept broad and clear to inhibit the ambushing of travelling merchandise.[2]

The marketing area was often a single open space in which various types of stalls could be set out. Late medieval evidence from Banbury, for example, shows a large central marketplace in which separate areas were consigned for corn (Cornhill), meat (Butchers' Row) and livestock (Pig Market, Cow Fair). Where there was no adequate open space, markets might be distributed between a few central streets, as in Stratford-upon-Avon, where there was a Sheep Street, a Swine Street and a Corn Street. Market authorities usually provided market stalls, from which they derived rents. The trade of such formal markets was chiefly to serve the needs of local households. In the simplest case small towns had a single market day each week, when outsiders would bring their goods into the town for the townsfolk to buy, and would take away such cash and urban produce as they needed. Sunday markets were abandoned during the early thirteenth century, in the face of clerical disapproval, and there were other restrictions on choice. Disputes could arise if two neighbouring markets

---

[2] L. J. Downer, ed., *Leges Henrici Primi* (Oxford, 1972), p. 248; *Statutes of the Realm* (11 vols., 1810–28), i, p. 97.

were held on the same day, and it was incumbent on the founders of new towns to avoid such clashes.

In larger towns the layout of public markets was more complex. Here markets were held on numerous days of the week, sometimes every day, to meet household needs. Different commodities were traded in different parts of the town. In late medieval York trading points had multiplied to the point that much of the central area was taken up with buying and selling. The chamberlains' accounts of the city of York record income from the two principal markets for provisions, the Pavement and the Thursday Market, as well as from the fish market on Foss Bridge.[3] The London system was even more complex, and there was no single market there for most commodities. By the thirteenth century there were two principal riverside corn markets at Billingsgate and Queenhithe, and two inland grain markets, where principal roads entered the city, the four together reflecting 'the regional origin of the grain sold in them, the means by which it was transported to London, and the other commercial interests of those who dealt in it'.[4] Southwark, outside the city's jurisdiction, was another terminus of the grain trade.

Many older towns were entered through gates in a town wall, but this was not true of newer ones except when there was some special problem of defence, as at Southampton, where walls were constructed during the thirteenth century. Where there were town gates they were often used for purposes of public regulation and control – as points for the collection of tolls on trade, for example. The *Leges Henrici Primi* assert baldly that 'every town has as many streets as it has main gates appointed for the collection of tolls and dues'.[5] Walls were often used to restrict movement at night, and it was common to prohibit the location of brothels inside them. The many towns without walls had to achieve similar objectives in other ways. Where walls existed, urban growth regularly implied the creation of suburbs, characteristically sprawling along the roads beyond the town gates, as at Gloucester. 'Suburbs were the growing edges of the town.'[6] Settlement densities could be every bit as high in some of these suburbs as in the inner precinct, especially if the

[3] R. B. Dobson, ed., *York City Chamberlains' Account Rolls, 1396–1500* (Surtees Society, CXCII, 1980), pp. 20, 70.
[4] B. M. S. Campbell, J. A. Galloway, D. Keene and M. Murphy, *A Medieval Capital and its Grain Supply: agrarian production and distribution in the London region c.1300* (1993), pp. 28–30.
[5] Downer, *Leges Henrici Primi*, p. 248.
[6] D. Keene, 'Suburban growth', in R. Holt and G. Rosser, eds., *The Medieval Town: a reader in English urban history, 1200–1540* (1990), p. 98.

walled area included the grounds of abbeys, cathedrals or castles, as well as the cemeteries attached to parish churches.

Any large town attracted suppliers of large quantities who wished to sell their wares in smaller lots either to individual households or to intermediaries of various kinds. When grain and fish were brought by sea (to port towns such as Newcastle, Lynn, Southampton and Bristol), by river (to riverbank towns such as York and Cambridge) or by road in wagons, it was advantageous for these goods to be sold near the point of disembarking or unloading, especially if the wharfs were away from the town centre. It would have been a major disincentive to supplying Exeter, for example, if shippers had had to transport cargoes from the wharves at Topsham on the Exe estuary to the town markets, four miles away. Most large towns therefore had bulk markets separate from the central retail markets, either on the waterside or at a point where a major street entered the town. These were subject to tight regulations about how trade was to proceed in order to prevent individual townsmen from cornering supplies.

All towns had shops as well as public markets. They varied in character from purpose-built buildings on main thoroughfares, built by landlords or speculators, to parts of the tradesmen's own homes. A shop was an intermediate space between the public world of the market and the private world of the family home, a space where craftsmen could both work and meet their customers. Shops were characteristically places where manufactured goods were made, but some traders specialised in repairs, like the cobbler who mended shoes. Others offered personal services, like the barbers' shops that were a common feature of town streets. Shops had to be secure and weatherproof buildings, and some were the lower floors of two-storey structures. Where land was very valuable in town centres, as in thirteenth-century Cheapside, they were often surprisingly small. The average Cheapside shop at the peak of London's growth around 1300 was 6–7 feet wide and 10–12 feet deep, and on prime corner sites they might be no more than 4 feet square.[7]

Another half-public, half-private context for trade was that of the taverns, alehouses and inns that were becoming a more regular and conspicuous feature of town streets from the thirteenth century onwards. By the fifteenth century inns and the larger alehouses had distinctive names and signs. Taverns sold wine, alehouses sold ale, and inns provided accommodation and maintenance for visitors and stabling for their

---

[7] D. Keene, 'Shops and shopping in medieval London', in L. Grant, ed., *Medieval Art, Architecture and Archaeology in London*, (British Archaeological Association, 1990), p. 34.

horses. It is common to find the keepers of these establishments listed in town court records, charged with the infringement of rules that universally regulated the price of bread, ale and wine. Besides conviviality, they supplied a context for certain sorts of trade especially between burgesses, who were less bound by urban regulations than outside traders were. Innkeepers were themselves often actively engaged in a wider range of business, assisted by the numerous contacts they gained through keeping open house.

With all these signs of activity, the importance of manufacturing and trade to town life would have been immediately apparent. The power structure would have been more difficult to interpret merely from evidence that met the eye. The relationship between the town's inhabitants and the owners or occupiers of its most impressive buildings varied considerably from town to town. A castle or an abbey could mean that the town had a powerful overlord, but it was not necessarily so.

Many towns had castles nearby, or even in their centre. In old towns they had been violently imposed on the townsmen as a repressive measure – probably not within living memory in thirteenth-century England, though the same could not be said of Wales. Larger towns might even have more than one; London had three and York had two, one on either side of the River Ouse. Superimposed castles had a substantial effect on the topography of the older towns. Sometimes, as at Stamford, they were constructed on sites away from principal centres of population, but – as at Gloucester, Colchester, York, Lincoln, Oxford and Norwich – they had often been placed within town walls on space already occupied, and their development had entailed the destruction of residential property. Other castles, in the course of time, had been built not in existing urban centres but in defensive positions in the countryside, and in these cases town life accompanied or followed castle construction rather than attracting it. There are numerous examples in southern England – as at Corfe in Dorset, Arundel in Sussex or Devizes in Wiltshire, and in the Welsh marches at Ludlow and Monmouth. New castle towns were also prominent in areas of late urban development, such as northern England, where there were imposing examples at Newcastle and Carlisle, as well as at smaller centres such as Barnard Castle, Warkworth and Alnwick. Such castle boroughs had continued to be founded, even in southern England, for a century after the Norman Conquest.

During the century before 1200 castles had been a real danger to the safety and continuity of urban life, since they drew towns into the thick of conflict in times of civil war. The conflict that followed King John's repudiation of Magna Carta (1215) was a sequence of sieges that saw action in Rochester, Colchester, Windsor, Barnard Castle, Durham, Lincoln and Dover. But during the thirteenth century urban castles dropped out of the picture as serious military installations. Large numbers were abandoned and fell into disrepair over the course of the following centuries. The castles at Bedford, Bristol, Cambridge, Canterbury, Exeter, Hereford, Lincoln, Norwich, Oxford, Salisbury, Shrewsbury and York, as well as at some smaller towns, were said to be in ruins by 1500. At Worcester the stones of the castle were used for repairing the town walls and gates in 1459. Where urban castles survived through the later middle ages, and remained prominent features of the urban landscape, they owed their survival to purposes other than defence. Some served as residences for royal, baronial or episcopal households, as at Windsor, Warwick, Ludlow or Durham, and in these cases they characteristically remained administrative centres as well. Another factor in the survival of urban castles was their adaptability for the purpose of royal justice. Castle halls could accommodate royal courts of law, particularly in county towns where they housed the assizes and the county court, and the towers and dungeons of the castle could be used as prisons. The most notorious example of a castle being taken over as a prison was the Tower of London. Many county towns relied on some part of their castle as a prison, as at Colchester, Carlisle, Chester, Exeter, Hereford, Newcastle upon Tyne, Oakham, Northampton, Rochester, Shrewsbury, Winchester and York.

Because abbeys have a longer history than castles, their relationship to the development of urban topography was more complex. Some were pre-Conquest foundations that had been founded on new sites and had been the primary reason for a town coming into existence, as at St Albans, Bury St Edmunds, Ely, Peterborough and Durham. In all these instances the abbey constituted a very prominent feature of the urban landscape. But since the founding of new abbeys near existing towns had remained common in the late eleventh and early twelfth centuries, there were many towns for which the monastic presence was a secondary feature, as at Colchester, whose two religious houses, both just outside the town walls, were founded around 1100. Either way it was common, especially for larger towns, to have at least one monastic house standing cheek by jowl with burgage properties, often constituting something of a threat to the interests of the townsmen.

Imposing though castles and abbeys were as part of the urban scene, as symbols of power they could be deceptive. Colchester, with a Norman castle and two substantial abbeys, nevertheless enjoyed a very substantial degree of administrative autonomy, and the effective centre of daily decision-making, in the hands of an urban elite, was a relatively incon-spicuous moot hall beside the town's central marketplace. Some towns were administered by leading burgesses in the thirteenth century and afterwards from a central guildhall, the name implying that self-government had developed through some understanding between the burgesses and the members of a merchant guild. Such lowlier buildings provided the space for town courts and council chambers. Here the money collected from tolls was guarded in a communal wooden chest, and here were stored the records that increasingly from the thir-teenth century onwards charted the growing scope and sophistication of urban government by townsmen. Most larger towns had such administrative headquarters, commonly situated near the central markets since the supervision of trade was one of the principal duties of town officers.

The cultural activities of townsmen were represented most visibly by church buildings. In older towns, especially those that had grown vig-orously before 1200, the early multiplication of churches founded by pious landowners and townsmen had created large numbers of tiny parishes with only slight endowments. London had over 100 parishes by 1200. No other town could compare with this, but Norwich and Winchester each had about fifty-seven, Lincoln forty-eight, and York over forty. In these towns, as in some smaller ones, the parish was a very local focus of interest that brought together people from a small range of streets. However, the proliferation of urban parishes came to a halt in the mid twelfth century. The development of ecclesiastical law then assigned defined territorial rights to existing parishes, so that any attempt to reshape parish boundaries meant a loss of income to the rector. Conse-quently, many newer towns, such Chelmsford, had only a single parish church. It was often difficult to achieve agreement even for this level of provision, which explains why many new towns of the twelfth and thirteenth centuries became chapelries in existing parishes rather than parishes in their own right. For example, the new town of Market Harborough in Leicestershire, founded about 1170, remained a chapelry dependent on the parish church of Great Bowden. The new town of Hartlepool, founded on the Durham coast about the same time, was similarly dependent on the older parish church at Hart.

Besides their parish churches, townsmen had recourse to other centres of instruction and devotion. The thirteenth century witnessed the foundation of friaries in many of the more prosperous towns of England. Unlike monks, who were at least supposed to turn their backs on the secular world, friars had an explicit mission to the laity that was best served in larger centres of population and thus they deliberately selected towns as sites both for their priories and for much of their work of evangelisation. Some towns had four or more houses of friars of different orders by 1300 – not only Winchester and Norwich, for example, but also Boston, Lynn and Newcastle. The friars commonly took over central urban spaces. The Franciscans (Greyfriars) came to Gloucester about 1230 and the Dominicans (Blackfriars) soon afterwards; both were given sites within the city walls. When the Carmelites (Whitefriars) came there in about 1268, however, they went outside the walls to the north-east.

TOWNS AND TRADE

The thirteenth century marked the conclusion of over three centuries of urban growth. Since the late Saxon period, the number, size and distribution of towns had developed impressively, to the point that by 1250 there was a framework of urban trading centres across the kingdom. Some towns continued to grow in response to increasing demand for the goods and services they produced, so that the urban population of medieval England attained a peak somewhere around 1300. The market demand sustaining this expansion derived in part from the expenditure of greater landlords, both secular and religious, but more significantly from the purchase of goods and services by lesser landlords and villagers. Urbanisation was also encouraged in some contexts by the long-distance trade across the North Sea and the English Channel, though before the later fourteenth century the principal English exports – wool, hides, grain, minerals and other raw materials – had little impact on urban employment outside the growing port towns.

As an example of growth in the kingdom's older towns, we may consider the borough of Gloucester, not yet a cathedral city, which perhaps had between 3,000 and 5,000 inhabitants in 1200. At that time the town already had three abbeys (St Peter's, St Oswald's and Llanthony), eleven parish churches, three hospitals and a castle that served as a centre of royal administration. In the following century the number of institutional households increased further with the establishment of the three friaries. This number and range of ecclesiastical institutions implies that Gloucester ranked among England's twenty principal towns. Gloucester benefited from the growing wealth of the surrounding countryside and smaller market towns. Its iron and cloth industries served local buyers, and other mundane manufactures included soap, needles, girdles, gloves and barrels. There was a fishing industry that supplied inland consumers. The town also offered commercial services for the marketing of Cotswold wool. Besides their capacity to participate in regional development, Gloucester people were also able to benefit from the expansion of long-distance trade because of the town's position on the River Severn. Ships engaged in trade along the river from the West Midlands to Bristol and South Wales, and also to Ireland. Migrants from as far away as Cornwall and Ireland responded to the growing commercial and manufacturing opportunities the town had to offer. All these developments encouraged an increasing density of settlement within the town centre and continuing physical expansion beyond. The development of suburbs continued into the earlier thirteenth century. To the north, houses and shops stretched beyond the old North Gate of the walled Roman city along Lower Northgate Street to a region called Newland. Beyond East Gate a suburb developed in what was called Barton Street. Beyond Westgate the suburbs stretched down to the river in part of the town called Home Bridge.

All over the kingdom, meanwhile, the number of towns had increased as a result of landlord enterprise, continuing a pattern of scattered urban development that had been vigorous since the eleventh century. The classic study of these new foundations, by Maurice Beresford, identifies at least forty-five towns founded on new sites between 1200 and 1299, with another twenty probably from the same period.[8] A further nine originated between 1300 and 1370. The thirteenth-century newcomers include many that attained a lasting importance as local market towns – such as Haslemere (Surrey), Weymouth (Dorset), Salisbury (Wilts.), Thame (Oxon), Chipping Sodbury and Northleach (both Glos.). Some achieved even greater heights in the course of later economic development, notably Leeds (Yorks.) and Liverpool (Lancs.), both of which were founded in 1207, and Hull (Yorks.), re-founded in 1293. Other new enterprises, closely analogous to Beresford's new towns, transformed existing rural settlements. Olney (Bucks.) was reconstructed as a town by the earl of Chester probably not long before 1237, and

[8] M. W. Beresford, *New Towns of the Middle Ages: town plantation in England, Wales and Gascony* (1967).

Lechlade (Glos.) was similarly developed during the 1220s by the abbot of Gloucester.

How urban did medieval England become as a result of these developments? Estimates of the proportion of the population that lived in towns depend on what we are prepared to think of as a town and what we are disposed to accept as a figure for the population of England as a whole. If we take a high estimate of total population (six million) and a low estimate of urban population (two-thirds of a million) around 1300, then the proportion of the total living in towns works out at 10 per cent; but if we work with a low estimate of total population (four and a half million) and a high estimate of urban population (just under one million), as can also be proposed for the same date, the proportion is over 20 per cent.[9] It is reasonable on this understanding to suppose that the urban population of England was between 10 and 20 per cent of the total around 1300; most writers on the subject tend to prefer the upper part of this range. The total urban population of the kingdom declined, as did the total population of the kingdom, between the early fourteenth century and the mid fifteenth, and it was still significantly lower in 1500 than it had been in 1300, but there is no reason to suppose that the urban proportion was reduced.

On any interpretation, England was a land of predominantly very small towns even at the height of its medieval urban development. In 1300 probably five out of six towns had fewer than 2,000 inhabitants. At most sixteen towns had populations over 10,000, and even in 1300 the proportion of the population in towns of over this size was less than 1 per cent of the total population of the kingdom. Only London, with a population in 1300 estimated at 60,000–80,000 (or 100,000 if we include its suburbs on either side of the Thames), would count as a large city by European standards; by 1300 its metropolitan dominance 'was already firmly established as a fact of English urban life'.[10] The heavy preponderance of little towns is chiefly attributable to the characteristically slight dependence of the English economy on long-distance or overseas trade, and the correspondingly low level of specialisation between them. It may also in part be related to the powerlessness of individual towns to exercise economic control over surrounding territories, which meant that it was difficult for towns to restrict the development of their neighbours by direct compulsion. This distinguishes the leading English towns from

---

[9] For these varying estimates of total population, see p. 25.
[10] Campbell et al., *Medieval Capital*, pp. 9–10.

some of their more powerful late medieval equivalents in northern Italy and Flanders. The English context was one in which urban growth was overwhelmingly competitive in response to the growth of local demand for basic services and manufactures.

By reducing the costs of trading, including the costs of risk and uncertainty, urban markets contributed benefits to traders of all sorts, and that was the principal reason why so many could be newly established in a period of expanding local trade. Families that depended upon commerce and manufacturing for a living would be attracted to town life precisely because of the lower costs of trading there, and no compulsion was needed to persuade people to move from country villages into prospering towns. Yet the growth of towns as centres of consumption, because of the range of new opportunities for trade and employment that they opened up, undoubtedly benefited social groups other than townsmen. The greater ease with which peasant families could sell their farm produce was a mixed blessing, because it laid them open to new forms of exploitation by landlords hungry for cash. Yet many families in country areas benefited from the wider range of consumer goods available, particularly in the context of rising real incomes after the Black Death. Greater dependence upon the market, with its attendant risks of indirectly transmitted crises, were to some extent compensated by the greater confidence with which people could trade in normal circumstances, through closely supervised institutions of trade. The price to be obtained for goods in an urban market was a competitive one that reflected relative scarcities of supply and pressures of demand, and was to that extent recognised as a just one.

The operations of townsmen in search of the most favourable sources of supply brought about considerable progress in the integration of the regional markets for food and raw materials, so that at any given moment grain and livestock were purchased most heavily where they could be acquired most cheaply, and large price differentials were rapidly eliminated. The scope for these institutional developments to bring about price stability in a small country like England was limited to the extent that climatic conditions affected all regions in much the same way. In the famine conditions of 1315–18 prices oscillated wildly, and thousands died of starvation both in towns and country villages. Although England was able to acquire some grain from the Baltic region or from France in years of dearth, the capacity of imports to alleviate hardship was modest in comparison with the benefits of international trade in more recent centuries. However, by 1300, at least for southern and eastern England, it is possible to discern the rudiments of a national market centring on London. A study of the grain trade of the home counties has confirmed in detail that in the later thirteenth century the city was a powerful enough centre to integrate the price structure over much of southern England, with particularly clearly marked price gradients from the city's major supply region along the Thames Valley.[11] Price formation was probably least structured in the north and west of England, where the impact of urban demand was more localised and where transport was more costly.

The pattern of urban supply varied in detail between towns, but local trade patterns had common characteristics. There was a limited distance over which peasants and farm managers were willing to transport grain and livestock by road if their sale required personal supervision, and this created a common structure in which each town was a local centre for marketing by small producers. The thirteenth-century lawbook *Bracton* conservatively defined $6^2/_3$ miles as the distance over which goods could be conveniently traded in a day, and perhaps that represents some sort of norm, although longer road journeys to market of ten or twelve miles are recorded.[12] The sale of farm produce was often the responsibility of women from peasant families, who carried their butter, poultry or other produce to town, sold it from the appropriate stalls, paid the tolls the town demanded, and took home the cash remaining from any purchases to pay rents, fines or taxes. Estate officers, too, were often responsible for selling their employers' produce in urban markets. By 1300 most countrymen had more than one centre within such a distance, and the marketing areas of different towns overlapped. If this had been the only pattern of supply it could easily be visually represented by locating towns on a map and drawing a regular circle around each one.

To the extent that middlemen supervened in supplying towns, however, marketing structures were more complicated, and the distance over which goods were traded was more extended. Wider catchment areas for bulky goods were facilitated if a town had good water communications, since transport by water was much cheaper than by land. London could not have been fed from lands and pastures within a 12-mile radius of the city, and the heightened role of middlemen there is evident both from the prominence of corn merchants, or bladers, in the thirteenth-century ruling elite, and from the city's dependence

[11] J. A. Galloway, 'One market or many? London and the grain trade of England', in J. A. Galloway, ed., *Trade, Urban Hinterlands and Market Integration, c.1300–1600* (2000), pp. 23–42.

[12] D. L. Farmer, 'Marketing the produce of the countryside, 1200–1500', in E. Miller, ed., *The Agrarian History of England and Wales*, III (Cambridge, 1991), pp. 362–5.

upon remote sources of supply. A large town might become regularly dependent upon a smaller one as a collecting centre. Henley-upon-Thames (Berks.) was a regular up-river resort of London grain merchants, and Faversham was a comparable source of supply down river.[13] Opinions are currently divided over the extent to which, outside London, urban growth depended upon such supply links between the larger and smaller towns. James Masschaele has stressed the role of smaller towns as part of the supply network of the fifty larger ones.[14] It remains to be empirically determined at which point down the urban hierarchy such networks in fact ceased to be significant. No complex dependence upon external markets was needed to supply foodstuffs to Colchester, with its population of around three or four thousand.[15]

The extent of interdependence between towns was not limited to the structure of agrarian trade. Other patterns of urban hierarchy resulted directly from differences of urban specialisation. Although it is difficult to distinguish significant variations in occupational structure between one little market town and another, there were definite contrasts between small towns and larger ones, especially when those larger ones were ports or were associated with some distinctive field of mercantile enterprise. Sea fish, and imported goods such as wine, salt, dyestuffs and millstones, required redistribution from ports to dealers in inland towns, and the growth of ports on England's southern, eastern and south-western coasts since the eleventh century – Newcastle, Boston, Lynn, Great Yarmouth, London, the Cinque Ports, Southampton, Poole, Plymouth, Bristol – implies that structures of dependence were part of more general urban growth. Superior manufactures – high-quality cloths and metalware, for example – also derived from particular towns, and depended upon mercantile networks for their distribution. The sort of development to be seen at Gloucester clearly depended upon the existence of distribution networks with other towns. Such differences of specialisation, which affected the decisions of large households about how to supply their different requirements, created a hierarchical distinction between the larger towns, where quality and speciality goods were obtainable, and the numerous smaller towns whose products were more ordinary. Busier towns were also able to offer a range of services – especially in law, finance

---

[13] Campbell et al., *Medieval Capital*, pp. 47–9.

[14] J. Masschaele, *Peasants, Merchants and Markets: inland trade in medieval England, 1150–1350* (New York, 1997).

[15] R. H. Britnell, 'Urban demand in the English economy, 1300–1600', in Galloway, *Trade, Urban Hinterlands and Market Integration*, p. 7.

and education – that were much less likely to be available in a smaller centre. Besides governing some patterns of trade and credit between smaller towns and larger ones, such specialisms inevitably influenced the movements of traders between town and town, and even to some extent patterns of inter-urban migration.

Following the demographic disasters of the fourteenth century, the famines of 1315–18 and the Black Death of 1348–9, it is likely that for at least a century and a half larger towns became less reliant on smaller ones as sources of cereals. As pressure on agricultural resources declined through reduced consumption, and as transport costs rose through scarcities of labour, supplies from the immediate locality became more preponderant. Henley and Faversham were of diminishing importance in London's grain supplies in this period, and it is unlikely that such a weakening of extended supply networks was unique to the capital. River traffic on the Thames contracted during the fifteenth century.

Meanwhile, the networking of towns for the distribution of pastoral products and manufactured or imported goods became more advanced as standards of living rose. The growth of urban textile industries in the later fourteenth century, and again in the later fifteenth, was not solely in response to export markets, important though these were. A higher standard of clothing was in demand in the home market, and new mercantile networks came into being to satisfy that demand. In the later fourteenth century a new structure of marketing was needed to distribute the cloth from the growing cloth towns – Coventry, Salisbury, Colchester, Norwich, York – to London, to the ports and to inland centres of distribution and consumption. In this period at Colchester there was a striking growth of commercial links both with London and with Hadleigh, another prospering centre of cloth manufacturing in Suffolk. In the later fifteenth century inter-urban mercantile networks became even more complex, especially between provincial towns and London, as the textile industry diffused to a large number of smaller towns all across the kingdom. The more widespread consumption of certain imported manufactures (pottery, linen) and raw materials (iron, dyestuffs) depended upon similarly intensified networks between towns, and especially those that linked the provinces to London. Those towns that could not benefit from the new networks for one reason or another – perhaps in some cases because of the very strength of their institutionalised autonomy – were liable to suffer a loss of trading advantage. The problems of York's textile industry in the later fifteenth century in competition with the up-and-coming textiles of Halifax, Wakefield and Leeds have been ascribed in part by Jennifer Kermode to the isolation of York merchants from London credit networks.[16]

The middle ages, though a period of urban growth, was not one in which all towns had even prospects of prosperity, and across the period from 1200 to 1500 there were numerous shifts in the relative position of different towns and different regions. In any circumstances urban fortunes could be expected to be volatile over so long a period, but all the more so because the towns were small; in a town of 10,000 it only needed two or three hundred incoming families to increase the population by 10 per cent. Opportunities for growth were to some extent determined by advantages or disadvantages of location. Not only were sites on main roads, river crossings and navigable rivers favoured in varying degrees by ease of access, but there were additional regional considerations. Different parts of the kingdom had differing urban potential, partly because of contrasting qualities of land and partly because of differences in access to wider trade patterns. The distribution of urban wealth partly reflects the distribution of agricultural resources in an age when it was expensive to carry grain over long distances. The uplands of northern and western England were more conducive to pastoral husbandry than to intensive cropping, and the proportion of the land under cereals was less than it was through much of the Midlands, East Anglia, the home counties and Wessex. The pattern of England's long-distance trade also favoured the south and east, both because trade along the coast was relatively cheap and because it could be directed to the continent of Europe. The western and more northern coasts of England, though capable of sustaining some trade through Chester, Carlisle, Newcastle and the small Northumbrian ports, were engaged with much poorer trading partners on the edge of the known world. Trade with Ireland was substantial, but could not compare in quantity with that connecting England to the richer populations of France, Spain, the Low Countries, Scandinavia and Germany. In 1200 the towns of southern and eastern England were already more populous, wealthier and better located for mercantile enterprise than those in the north and west, and notwithstanding the growth of towns everywhere during the thirteenth century the bias of urbanisation within Britain swung even more strongly to the south-east of the island during the late middle ages.

---

[16] J. Kermode, 'Money and credit in the fifteenth century: some lessons from Yorkshire', *Business History Review*, 45 (1991), 475–501.

At every stage, however, the fortunes of towns were shaped to varying degrees by the investment decisions made by individuals and groups, and this introduced a large element of unpredictability into the causes of urban growth in different periods. The decisions of landlords were important to a wide range of towns at different stages of their fortunes. They were particularly apparent, of course, in decisions to build new towns, governed as these were by the economic and political power of individual landlords, the location of their estates, and the amount they were prepared to invest. In the development of older towns, too, landlords' decisions concerning their physical and institutional infrastructure, the location of large households and the founding of abbeys, all had an impact upon commercial prosperity. Most smaller towns, lacking administrative autonomy, remained heavily dependent on the lords who owned them. Eleanor Carus-Wilson argued, for example, that the development of Castle Combe as a centre of clothmaking was attributable to the personal interest of Sir John Fastolf, who bought and developed the manor. Between 1415 and 1450 he needed cloth in large quantities to fit out his retinue of soldiers in France, and he directed his orders to his own tenants back home. About fifty new houses were built in Castle Combe in the war period, and new fulling mills were constructed for finishing cloth.[17]

The decisions of the king and other landlords concerning their urban property continued to have some impact on urban prosperity all through the middle ages. For example, the fortunes of Winchester from the thirteenth century were closely related to the abandonment of the city as the centre of royal administration and royal residence. Winchester's sluggish performance – after its brilliant start in the late Saxon and Norman periods – was partly attributable to the decline of royal interest in the town, and the transfer of government activity to Westminster. In 1200 the permanent administrative centre of the kingdom was already in Westminster, and around that time Winchester Castle stopped being used as a major repository for royal treasure. Kings continued to visit Winchester Castle, though the town's importance as a military and political centre took a knock with the loss of Normandy in 1204. In the course of time royal visits became less frequent, and the castle was abandoned as a major royal residence after a fire in 1302.

---

[17] E. M. Carus-Wilson, 'Evidences of industrial growth on some fifteenth-century manors', *EcHR*, 2nd ser. 12 (1959), 190–205.

Besides landlords, however, townspeople themselves were agents of urban development, especially in some of England's largest and proudest towns. The growth of the woollen towns of the later twelfth and early thirteenth centuries – Beverley, Lincoln, Stamford and Northampton being outstanding among them – seems to be explained more by the enterprise of merchants than by anything that landlords did. The remarkable international success of a handful of the older boroughs in promoting their woollen textiles in the later fourteenth century – York, Salisbury, Colchester, Norwich, Coventry – has similarly to be ascribed to the dynamism of their merchants in opening up new markets and building business connections abroad. This must be the principal reason for the success of particular towns, even if there were more general reasons, such as Edward III's heavy export duties on wool, to explain the success of English cloth exports at this time.

The operations of London merchants, in association with local elites, were critically important both in developing the city's volume of trade and in determining which other towns benefited from the expansion of cloth exports during the later fifteenth century. The changing level of property values in the city shows that it was not immune from the consequences of fifteenth-century recessions. It is possible that London's population had fallen between 1300 and 1524, and quite likely that the city had experienced prolonged phases of economic contraction. Nevertheless, relative to other English towns London's wealth showed a long-term increase, and in the fourteenth and fifteenth centuries this indicated an increasingly metropolitan status. The city was concentrating more of the kingdom's mercantile wealth and activity, and exercising more influence on the fortunes of other towns, so enhancing the southern and eastern bias of England's urban prosperity. This success owed a great deal to the business practices developed by London merchants, which gave them superior access to credit and superior networks of business contacts both in the English provinces and in the Low Countries. The analysis of merchant enterprise in larger towns focuses on groups, but the case for the importance of mercantile enterprise can be shown to rest in some instances on individuals. Men such as Thomas Spring III of Lavenham were of considerable importance in building up the trade of their respective towns.

One town that lost rank during the thirteenth century was Dunwich, which decayed from being one of the wealthiest ports in England in the late twelfth century as a result of sea floods and the deterioration of its harbour. The town was one of the top ten in the later twelfth century, on a level with Winchester and Lincoln, to judge from the tallage it paid to the crown, but it does not figure amongst the hundred wealthiest towns in 1334. Its defences against the sea were built up in the later thirteenth century after flooding in the 1250s, but renewed inundation in 1287–8 marked a turning point from which recovery proved impossible. Storm damage was cited in 1300 as a reason why the burgesses could not pay Edward I their normal fee farm of £65. A survey of 1325 showed that 269 houses and twelve other properties had been swept away by the sea. This amounted to about a quarter of the town. This is a clear case of a community being reduced severely as a result of natural disaster. Ports that did not suffer from Dunwich's problems were probably amongst the biggest success stories. Among the wealthiest twenty English towns in 1334 were Bristol (second), Newcastle upon Tyne (fourth), Boston (fifth), Great Yarmouth (seventh), Lynn (eleventh), Southampton (seventeenth) and Ipswich (nineteenth), and it is likely that all these rankings represent a significant advance over the position of these towns in 1200. The tallages and aids demanded by the crown from Newcastle, Southampton and Yarmouth rose relative to those from other towns in the course of the period 1154–1312.[18] These towns were benefiting from the combined effects of favourable location, supportive landlord investment and successful local mercantile initiatives.

For the period between 1334 and 1524 the evidence for changes in urban rank is better because of the availability of nationwide tax assessments from those years, and though the information has to be used with caution, some of the changes are sufficiently striking to be worth detailed comment (table 6.1). Of the twenty leading towns in 1524, some – Bury St Edmunds, Colchester, Coventry, Lavenham, Salisbury, Totnes – had benefited to varying degrees and at various times from the success of local merchants in promoting the growth of clothmaking. Exeter had developed as a port serving the exceptionally prosperous economy of the south-western textile region. Some of the other successes – Maidstone, Reading, Worcester – are less easily explained. Some of the twenty leading towns of 1334 had meanwhile dropped behind – notably Lincoln, Boston and Yarmouth. The relative decline of the latter two illustrates a malaise affecting a number of east-coast ports in the fifteenth century, chiefly under the impact of competition from London, showing that

---

[18] A. Dyer, 'Ranking lists of English medieval towns', in D. M. Palliser, ed., *The Cambridge Urban History of England*, I: *600–1540* (Cambridge, 2000), p. 754.

Table 6.1. *The twenty wealthiest English towns in 1524, with changes in ranking since 1334*

Town	Rank in 1524	Rank in 1334
London	I	I
Norwich	2	6
Bristol	3	2
Newcastle	4	4
Coventry	5	10
Exeter	6	28
Salisbury	7	12
Lynn	8	II
Ipswich	9	19
Canterbury	10	15
York	II	3
Reading	12	40
Colchester	13	53
Bury St Edmunds	14	26
Lavenham	15	–
Worcester	16	36
Maidstone	17	–
Totnes	18	–
Gloucester	19	18
Yarmouth	20	7

Source: R. H. Britnell, 'The economy of British towns, 1300–1540', in D. M. Palliser, ed., *The Cambridge Urban History of Britain*, I: *600–1540* (Cambridge, 2000), p. 329.

locational characteristics could affect towns quite differently in different economic circumstances.

THE EXERCISE OF POWER

All English towns were subject both to the apparatus of royal government and to rights of tenurial lordship, whether that of the king or of some other lord. Landlords' rights took many forms, but the most common gave them rents from burgage plots, market stalls and land in the town fields and pastures, together with the profits of petty jurisdiction and tolls on trade. How a landlord chose to manage his urban possessions could make a considerable difference to his relations with townsmen on his estate. The larger a town became, the heavier the administrative task of managing its affairs, since the collection of revenues, the supervision of markets and the managing of litigation all required ongoing attention through the year. Lords with large and complex urban revenues often (not always) divested themselves of the managerial burden by transferring responsibilities to an individual lessee, to a consortium, or to the townsmen as a body. This last practice necessarily implied some administrative autonomy on the part of those concerned, especially where the lease included revenues from markets and fairs. By 1200 the larger royal towns were leased out either to an individual royal agent or, increasingly commonly, to the leading inhabitants of the town, in exchange for an annual payment. Early in the reign of Richard I the right to lease the king's revenues had been conceded by charter in perpetuity to the townsmen of Bedford, Colchester, Hereford, Northampton and Worcester, and from then on such grants become more numerous than before.

Some towns on the lands of wealthy churches or lay landowners other than the king were similarly given charters by their lords, and were authorised to elect their own senior officers, though it was unusual for such officials to have powers as extensive as those in royal towns. It was no foregone conclusion that all townsmen should enjoy even this limited degree of independence. Bury St Edmunds, St Albans, Evesham and Durham – all towns founded at the gates of major monasteries – remained seigniorial boroughs, both because administrative costs were relatively low for a resident landlord and because abbeys wished to maintain a high degree of control over their immediate environments. Small towns, too, were often administered by nominees of their overlords rather than by elected officers, since they presented fewer administrative problems than large boroughs and had scanty reserves of competent administrators amongst their inhabitants. An estate steward commonly presided over their courts, and estate officials collected judicial fines and tolls. In the late fifteenth century the ordinary courts of the bishop of Durham's borough of Northallerton were held before appointed townsmen; but twice a year, at Michaelmas and Easter, the steward of the bishop's liberty presided over the chief sessions, which handled tenurial, economic and social regulation.

Towns varied greatly in their importance to landlords. At one extreme, we may take the case of Westminster, whose value to Westminster Abbey increased from about 2 per cent of the abbey's total revenue in 1086 to 13 per cent in 1530. This is an outstandingly impressive example of the possibilities. By contrast, if we take the small town of Clare (Suffolk), which was at the seat of the great baronial honour of Clare, its value in the 1330s was about £16, less than 1 per cent of the total value of the estate. If a landlord decided to retain direct control over a town, whatever the reason, the holding of courts became a matter of obligation that might not be a lucrative one: some town courts cost more to run than they earned in revenue. In the case of small towns, it is often difficult to see where the advantage in direct rule lay.

Many small towns had no institutions to distinguish them from the inhabitants of a rural settlement except that they held their property by burgage tenure. The existence of a market gave the inhabitants of a borough the right to trade without paying toll, but the same right was expected amongst the tenants of manors with ordinary village markets. Rights to put animals on borough commons, or to fish in particular streams, similarly have their plain analogies amongst the tenants of rural communities. However, particularly in larger towns, townsmen often showed active concern for the status of the towns in which they lived, and common patterns of expectation were born of the emulating of one town by another. By 1200 a variety of distinctive institutions had created a hierarchy of criteria by which a borough's inhabitants might consider themselves specially privileged. One of these was the formation of a body of borough freemen or burgesses distinct from urban householders, and even including 'foreign' burgesses, who were not resident in the borough but who were prepared to pay for urban privileges. The right to freedom of trade, to pasture animals on the town commons and to be considered for office in the borough were detached from rights of tenure, and were made dependent on free status in this distinctive sense. Free status could be achieved by birth (by being the son of a freeman), by completing an apprenticeship in the town, or by being formally admitted in return for a money payment. A further development of burghal status came at the point when burgesses leased urban revenues from the king or other landlord, and so engaged in a large degree of urban self-government. Other, less welcome, marks of status derived in the course of time from the interest shown in urban wealth by the king. Particularly from Edward I's reign some towns were taxed at a distinctive higher rate and so constituted a sub-group of 'taxation boroughs'. The summoning of urban representatives to parliaments, increasingly normal from 1295 onwards, created a different but overlapping category of 'parliamentary boroughs'. Neither of these categories was very fixed, but most of the larger boroughs could always expect to be included in both, and a few took their right to parliamentary representation seriously as an index of status. These various advances in borough status all gave increasing scope for urban elites to organise themselves and to regulate the daily life of the towns in which they exercised authority.

Self-governing boroughs had to have officials to answer for royal and seigniorial dues, and these were inevitably drawn from the leaders of the community, characteristically defined in terms of their wealth. Such boroughs rarely had much formal constitutional apparatus before the thirteenth century, and when boroughs were put in the hands of their burgesses, the break with the previous regime was initially not very marked. Townsmen, 'elected' by some far from democratic procedure, replaced royal or baronial nominees. Yet even this process of electing invited some institutional innovation. Charters of urban liberties often granted townsmen a merchant guild, empowered to secure the control of trade in a town to its members, and this too required formal procedures to establish membership and forms of control. In addition there had to be consultative processes. Many towns were small enough for open meetings of burgesses to be feasible, even if in practice only the more socially secure bothered to attend. Between 1200 and 1550, however, urban constitutions became more elaborate. It became common for borough affairs to be managed by elected councils, and the structuring of urban political elites through conciliar organisation became increasingly self-conscious. Borough constitutions depended on both written and unwritten rules to establish a hierarchical pattern of appointments that would restrict high office to a well-defined elite group. Through all these changes, medieval townsmen always expected a direct relationship between political and economic power, so that office was given to those who had most, even if towns differed in the extent to which lesser men were excluded.

Such a direct relationship between political and economic power may be explained without difficulty. The elite had an inevitable interest in controlling the financial and legal institutions of the town. The enforcement of trading regulations, especially in industries producing goods for trading over long distances, was something vital to trading interests. Urban elites needed to control urban crafts, and often did so through the monitoring and enforcing of craft regulations, subject to close supervision by the council. The guilds of fifteenth-century York were responsive to mercantile considerations, since the city's mercantile elite had the power to influence the crafts to its advantage. There were obvious and less obvious advantages to the elite in maintaining a regular system of urban courts. In Exeter during the last decades of the fourteenth century, the town courts seem to have favoured the interests of wealthy creditors.

A wealthy man might expect to benefit from the character of urban institutions without being personally involved in urban government. Indeed many were anxious to avoid public office, especially in the fifteenth century when urban financial problems became more urgent. Law suits in borough courts, unlike those in the king's courts at Westminster, were generally concerned with small debts or minor assaults, matters too small, and involving litigants too modest in their fortunes, to generate large sums in legal fees or back-handers. Few pickings were to be had from the town chest, since a borough's income from rents and tolls rarely generated much surplus over financial commitments, which included both sums due to the king and the costs of maintaining town walls, roads, bridges and quays. It is unlikely, in other words, that urban office was a significant source of income for those involved in it, however welcome the confirmation of status it may have conferred. In the fifteenth century town rulers had more reason to fear losing money in office than to hope for rich pickings. In Grimsby the chamberlains' receipts declined from £41 18s 0d in 1394–5 to only £11 18s 0d in 1469–70, so that the bailiffs and chamberlains faced real financial problems. In many towns during this period, office became sufficiently burdensome to deserve an increased formal status for those who held it, as at Grimsby. Many urban elites tightened their rules for election to high office. However, this did not imply that urban ruling groups were closed and hereditary as one might expect if urban office was really a potential source of personal enrichment. On the contrary, they were characteristically open to new wealth, as if their members valued the chance to share their responsibilities with incomers of sufficient standing to be considered for office.

From Exeter, a prosperous provincial town, in the late fifteenth century, Maryanne Kowaleski has described four ranks of townsmen: a minority of merchants who formed a governing elite, dominating high office; independent craftsmen and traders, who participated in urban elections; the more dependent townsmen, not necessarily freemen, who only occupied menial roles in the borough hierarchy; and, finally, those too lowly and poor to be eligible for any office.[19]

In the larger towns, the first of these categories (comprising only 1 per cent of the male population at Exeter) was made up variously of merchants, lawyers and urban property owners, who made their money by trade, fees or rents rather than in manufacturing. This was a category of wealth that barely existed in most places, but it figures prominently in the history of the towns whose history is best recorded. The households of men in this group employed servants, though rarely more than about a dozen people. Some merchants in the cloth industry operated more as

---

[19] M. Kowaleski, 'The commercial dominance of a medieval provincial oligarchy: Exeter in the late fourteenth century', *Mediaeval Studies*, 46 (1984), 360–3.

capitalist clothiers with dozens of employees, especially in the late fifteenth and early sixteenth centuries, but this remained unusual. Whatever their source of income, the heads of families in such an elite had to be urban freemen to be eligible for office. Their powers depended in detail on the way a town was governed. If the town remained a seigniorial one, they might exercise authority through co-operation with the landlord. On the other hand, their concern for personal status was often coupled with concern for the status of their town; they might form the vanguard of those seeking additional powers of self-government, and thereby enter into conflict with the landlords who would not concede them. Even in the absence of chartered freedoms, the elites of some larger towns acquired independent authority through their role in large fraternities (organisations originally created for religious purposes), which were able to take over some of the activities more normally assigned to courts of law. Where rights of self-government had been given to townsmen, it was from this social group that the principal officers were appointed, so that their elite status was formally recognised by the crown. In the course of time they devised forms of elaborate borough ceremonial to symbolise the independent status of their towns and their own lofty position within them.

Such an elite was not available in smaller towns, whose dominant groups were more like Exeter's second category: independent craftsmen and minor traders. Men of this kind constituted the bulk of the freemen in any borough, whether freemen were defined by tenure or not. The variety of occupations they and their families undertook depended upon the size of the town, but fifteenth-century evidence from Canterbury, York, Chester and Norwich suggests that 50 per cent to 60 per cent of townsmen had some manufacturing role, the remainder being engaged in construction, transport, service industries and trade.[20] The head of the family needed to be a freeman in order for its members to trade freely in the town without having to pay tolls. These ordinary burgesses were often vigorous in defence of their rights, even at the expense of conflict with their social superiors. It was they who in the course of the later middle ages formed craft guilds. Many of them combined manufacturing and commercial activities with subsistence farming in the surrounding fields, and in some cases they derived cash income, too, from the sale of farm produce. This explains why conflicts with local landlords over enclosures and common rights recurred in the history of many English towns. In the

---

[20] P. J. P. Goldberg, *Women, Work and Life Cycle in a Medieval Economy: women in York and Yorkshire, c. 1300–1520* (Oxford, 1992), pp. 60–1.

largest towns this group was a subordinate one, occupying lesser offices in the guilds, or serving on panels of jurors and electors, rather than holding the leading positions in borough administration. By contrast, in smaller towns, with no merchant class and no substantial body of resident lawyers or property owners, the ruling group was necessarily drawn from their number.

Below the ranks of the burgesses were those who were not freemen of the town, who therefore had no trading rights and were liable to punishment if they traded on their own account without licence. These people constituted the wage-earning class and the unemployed. Their presence implies the need for a significant qualification to the common assertion that urban residence made men free. Their particular form of unfreedom (which differed from that of the rural villein)[21] was defined by lack of economic and political rights in the urban context where they lived. They still had access to the town courts to defend their contractual dues, if they were bold enough to go so far, and some certainly did sue employers for unpaid wages. They could also, of course, be sued; they often occur in late medieval court records being sued by former employers for breach of contract. Members of many families in this category would be domestic servants or journeymen, employed by the artisans of the city. Others were casual labourers engaged in the construction and repair work that was inevitably going on all the time in bigger towns, sometimes because they could not find employment in their specialised craft. Their proportion of a town's population varied considerably: it could be substantial in a large city like London where there were many families living off charity. The conditions of this lower rank of townsmen tended to improve in the period 1348–1450 because of shortages of labour, which reduced the problem of unemployment and pushed up wages to very high levels. Even so, there was strong resistance to any formal organisation of such workers that might compromise their dependent status.

The structure of urban society, represented here in this formalised way, was far from being static. Changing economic conditions brought shifts in the relative importance of different groups of people and sources of income. This was nowhere more true than in the composition of urban elites. Urban elites, at least at the rank of office holders, had to be men who had time to spare from the business of earning a living. Managing borough courts took up at least two mornings a week in larger towns, and there were numerous other duties associated with the regulation of trade

---

[21] For villein status, see pp. 210–13.

and the handling of government business. Only those who derived their income from employing other people had sufficient freedom to give their attention to public business. Economic change between 1200 and 1500 brought new categories of wealth into being at different times, in different places, and so encouraged shifts in the type of townsman available to assume official responsibilities.

In 1200 England lacked a substantial class of long-distance merchants. Though there might be powerful traders in London, Bristol, York or Newcastle upon Tyne, in the government of most towns property owners, clerks, tradesmen and the wealthier craftsmen were more prominent. The historian F. W. Maitland drew attention not only to the importance of wealth in land amongst the burgesses of Cambridge but also to the number of landowners, the Dunnings, the Blancgernons and others, within the urban elite. Because this was not a major commercial town, landed families retained importance through the thirteenth and fourteenth centuries.[22] As native overseas trade grew, especially in wool and wine, the significance of mercantile wealth for urban government increased. Developments in institutional organisation allowed wealthier merchants to stay at home and trade through intermediaries, so that they became available for office in an increasing number of towns. From the mid fourteenth century the growth of the woollen textile industry in towns such as Colchester and Salisbury similarly increased the number of clothiers and cloth exporters who could assume a role in public life. Even in York, which had prominent merchants in government considerably earlier, the prominence of such men increased from the 1330s with the expansion of the city's textile trade. The weight of public responsibilities borne by merchants, together with their propensity to invest in property as they grew richer, contributed considerably to their rising social stature in the later middle ages. Leading members of urban elites, even if heavily engaged in commerce, often ranked as gentlemen in the late middle ages, and they characteristically shared interests, standing and family connections with the gentry of the surrounding countryside.[23] It is difficult to know what pressures or attractions drew wealthy men into public life, if it is true that there were few personal advantages. Social pressures of one sort or another are likely, but ultimately one suspects that many men were motivated more by a desire for status and authority than by any material lure.

[22] F. W. Maitland, *Township and Borough* (Cambridge, 1898), pp. 63–4, 164–7.
[23] For further discussion of urban gentry, see pp. 71–2.

Urban elites, of whatever character, mediated between external powers (notably the king) and their fellow townsmen, performing the royal business as instructed, but often exercising a considerable margin of discretion. They were bound to maintain the legal standard of weights, measures and coinage, and from time to time officers of the king's court checked up on their efficiency. In many other respects, however, laws were either so loosely phrased that numerous interpretations were plausible, or else drafted in such a way that the courts could choose whether to apply them or not. The statutory provision for enforcing just prices, introduced immediately after the Black Death, could be enforced spasmodically according to the particular whims of different groups of burgesses in different contexts. Practices even in royal boroughs varied in detail from place to place.

A second area of local discretion was the making of new by-laws. Local legislation, supplementing statutory legislation, was far from being a distinctively urban phenomenon. Manorial courts often introduced such laws to regulate, for example, the stinting of pastures or the gleaning of common fields. The range of matters to be regulated was particularly wide in towns, however, and in the course of the later middle ages local legislation developed vigorously. Even in seigniorial boroughs like Westminster the same effect was achieved by ordinances approved in the town court. The multiplication of local by-laws widened the differences between towns in detail. From the fourteenth century they were characteristically recorded in registers that were colour-coded – like the Black Book of Winchester, the Little Red Book of Bristol or the Red Paper Book of Colchester. Such volumes were vulnerable either to negligent custody or, in more recent times, to the predations of antiquarians. Where they survive, they show that the scope for urban regulation was vast.

A further area of discretion lay in the power to impose charges on burgess households for funding expenditure of common concern. Streets, bridges, town walls and quays all needed reconstruction or repair from time to time, and emergency funding was occasionally required to pay the fees of lawyers or royal servants. Such sums were often not capable of being met out of recurrent income from rents and tolls, and the imposition of new tolls required royal authorisation. Councils nevertheless had the right at their discretion to levy a sum, payable by each burgess household, in order to meet the cost. These were often called scot and lot, or tallages. Decisions of this kind would rest with the borough council in a self-governing borough, and with the borough's overlord in a seigniorial borough.

Finally, townsmen with elective constitutions had discretion to vary both the extent to which they admitted freemen to the status of free burgesses and the form of their government. There was no fixed principle to determine how large the number of freemen should be in proportion to the total urban population, nor how freemen should be chosen. Nor were there universal rules about the size of the council or its mode of election. In these respects, too, townsmen developed their institutions in different ways. The first of these issues affected the nature of a town, since it determined the freedom of trade there. A town that set low hurdles to entry to freedom of the borough would be one in which a large proportion of the trading population paid no tolls or fines in the course of its daily activities. Such was Colchester in 1488, when over half the householders of the town may have been free burgesses. A town that was more restrictive, by contrast, would be able to charge tolls on a higher proportion of market transactions, and would be able to exact money from traders either for licences to trade or as penalties for having traded illegally, as at Exeter, where in 1377 freedom of the borough was enjoyed by only 21 per cent of householders.

COMMERCIALISM AND URBAN CULTURE

The development of towns implied a growing dependence upon money and trade throughout medieval society, and urban institutions responded to the associated shifts in outlook. The most profound changes resulted from the restructuring of patterns of personal interdependence. In the countryside peasants must often have relied upon co-operation with their neighbours for the performance of many recurrent tasks – for ploughing, if they shared plough beasts, and for the care of livestock if they employed a common herdsman. Interdependence intensified with the growth of communities whose basic foodstuffs and raw materials could be acquired only through successful buying and selling, and the resulting anxieties lie behind many of the new institutions and regulations created by urban societies in the period 1200–1500.

Rules relating to marketing, to minimise the inevitable risks associated with market dependence, were central to the documented concerns of townsmen and their rulers, and had been from an early stage in urban development. The fact that town markets were subject to tight controls was one of their attractions to those who bought and sold there. Such markets had a definite starting time and closing time, generally signalled by the ringing of a bell. They were closely supervised to prevent the use of false weights and measures, and to inhibit would-be monopolists. There was usually a rule that wholesalers and food processors had to hold back to give individual consumers time to buy what they wanted. In Worcester, for example, regulations of 1467 specify that the bakers were not to buy grain until 11 o'clock in summer and 12 o'clock in winter.[24] Outsiders were similarly discriminated against, and were also expected to pay tolls from which resident townsmen were exempt. Market regulations were devised chiefly to inhibit the exploitation of consumers and artisans by large operators. The multiplication of rules governing activities in the marketplace illustrate these concerns well enough, but in fact they affected the way in which activities were regulated throughout urban society.

Urban commercial regulations had complex origins in early English royal traditions, in canon law, in the privileges of chartered boroughs and in ad hoc pragmatism. They multiplied in the course of time, and by the fifteenth century constituted a formidable body of controls. Their elaboration accompanied, and to some extent determined, the generation of a new market-related ethic, as rules of the market acquired moral force. Some market regulations of the middle ages, such as the assize of ale (the test for conformity to a minimum standard of production), were implemented as a way of raising cash without any penal intent or imputation of moral opprobrium: among urban alewives there were many women of respectable status who might be amerced year after year under the assize, without the authorities showing any real intention of deterring them from what they were doing. However, many rules were assigned moral force, so that townsmen were offended, even outraged, when they were broken.

The development of commercial morality can to some extent be demonstrated from sermons and literary texts denouncing the Seven Deadly Sins; but preachers usually chose the least complicated examples of greed and fraud they could think of, which are those of least historical interest. Literary writings of this kind, written to a preconceived agenda independent of the preoccupations of urban life, misrepresent the moral values of ordinary townsmen, both by exaggerating the seriousness of offences that mattered little to them, and by omitting offences that were central to their concern. Misdemeanours in the drink trades, for example, though rich ground for sermon writers, were on the whole of less moral

---

[24] L. C. Toulmin Smith, ed., *English Gilds* (EETS, os XL, 1870), p. 381.

significance to burgesses than more complex regulations that preachers were unlikely to mention.

Institutional rules relating to the pricing of goods in town markets, and the prevention of monopoly practices, had been extended well beyond simple ideas of fairness and had simultaneously gained the status of ethical norms by the later fourteenth and fifteenth centuries, if not earlier. The idea that the borough authorities monitored prices was widely accepted. A Coventry jury in 1473, for example, reported that victuallers were 'of malice' withdrawing wine and victuals from the city 'because they may not utter it after their own consents and prices'.[25] Rules relating to forestalling (the large-scale buying up of goods in order to push up local prices) are some of the most rewarding to study in this connection, for two reasons. In the first place the offence was unambiguously one created by rules and laws, and only came to be generally recognised as a punishable offence during the thirteenth century. In the second place, the offence was against the market community rather than against any specific individual, so that the way in which it was reported and punished constitutes a fair indicator of the level of communal indignation. It is not difficult to find examples of juries who regarded forestalling as more than a technical offence. In 1499, for example, the jurors of Nottingham reported a forestaller who commonly bought up eight to ten quarters at a time 'to the great enhancement of price in the same market, to the grievous detriment of the lieges of our ... lord the king, and against his peace'.[26] This example may stand for many in illustrating that a new and complex ethic had indeed been created between the twelfth and the fifteenth centuries and that its formulations stretched far beyond simple concepts of fraud and deception.

The commercial morality that developed between 1200 and 1500 had features deriving from status divisions amongst townsmen at the time. One of its principal characteristics was that it was burgess-centred. Many of the rules about which urban juries expressed themselves most strongly corresponded to definitions of burgess rights, or the rights of members of the merchant guild, and such strong feelings show clearly how a new commercial ethic was coming into existence on the back of urban institutional development. A long list of guild rules from Reading, apparently dating from the fourteenth century, is chiefly concerned to

---

[25] M. D. Harris, ed., *The Coventry Leet Book* (EETS, os CXXXIV–V, CXXXVIII, CXLVI, 1907–13), p. 387.
[26] W. H. Stevenson, ed., *Records of the Borough of Nottingham* (5 vols., 1882–1900), iii, no. 37, p. 54.

restrict the trade of outsiders. 'Item', reads one such rule, 'no outsider may bring tanned leather into Reading at any time except to fairs'.[27] Burgesses were inclined to be particularly aggrieved when rules designed to protect them were twisted to the advantage of others. There can be no doubt of the moral conviction with which breaches of these rules were pursued. In 1410 a Colchester jury reported a case where a burgess had collaborated with a north-country shipper by writing to him and advising him not to sell his barley below 3s a quarter. This communication of market information was attributed to malicious plotting. In 1429, another jury reported five fishmongers who compounded a breach of market regulations with contempt for the burgesses of the town; they reputedly held their best fish back from the open market and sold them privately to outsiders 'to the very great extorsion of the burgesses'. The word *extorsio* is unusual and somewhat odd here, but it evidently implies moral reproof. In 1436 a man of St Osyth was fined because he not only commonly forestalled oysters but he deliberately sold them to outsiders rather than burgesses 'even when the latter were in the greatest need of victuals'.[28] Again the slight departure from bare legal form conveys a real sense of disapprobation that hungry burgesses should have been deprived of their oysters.

Another feature of the new commercial regulations related not to conflicts of interest between burgesses and others but to occupational differences between the burgesses themselves, and was particularly marked in the period after 1350. It derived from the growth of occupational specialisation and the suspicions to which this gave rise, which could only be redressed by complex new rules relating to the responsibilities of different crafts. To control the relationships between different occupational groups implied identifying them and passing rules about them. Quality controls were a similar case; if searchers were to be appointed to enter artisans' premises and identify shoddy workmanship, it was essential that the men of each craft should be precisely defined. Urban records of the middle ages record a deep mistrust of specialist interests and a commitment to the idea that one of the essential roles of government is to bring them into harmony. This concern accounts for a very large amount of the increase in rules and regulations that was one of the most striking administrative consequences of urban growth. It also

[27] C. Gross, *The Gild Merchant* (2 vols., Oxford, 1890), ii, p. 205.
[28] Essex Record Office, Colchester and North-East Essex Branch, Colchester Borough Muniments, CR 37/14d, CR49/23r, CR 54/2r.

accounts for the drive to identify separate crafts and define their membership. This principle was expressed in a royal ordinance of 1363, which ruled that 'artificers [must] ... hold them every one to one mystery ... and two of every craft shall be chosen to survey that none use other craft than the same which he hath chosen'.[29] This statute was inevitably imprecise in its implications, since for practical purposes the definition of a 'single' craft often depended upon local circumstances. Nevertheless, the statute empowered local councils to insist on their right to demarcate between different crafts if they saw reason for doing so. Ironically, a suspicion of the effects of occupational specialisation had the effect of encouraging the demarcation of separate crafts by political fiat.

The idea that different occupational groups had different and conflicting interests is one that was prominent in medieval urban thought. It was supposed that, without regulation, individual trades would create monopolies, foul the environment and swindle or inconvenience customers. Occupational specialisation was a threat, in other words, to social unity and peace. Some of the new rules transcended the bounds of particular towns. One text known as the Statute of Winchester (not to be confused with royal legislation of the same name), which was written into a number of urban registers, is a compendium of rules relating to millers, bakers, brewers, butchers, fishmongers, cooks, innkeepers, taverners, tallow chandlers, spicers, weavers, tanners, cordwainers, curriers and tawers – all supposedly controlled by statute.[30] Some of these rules concern demarcation issues. A tanner, for example, is banned from tanning the leather of sheep, goats, deer, horses and dogs, while a tawer may only taw the leather of these animals. Tanning was a wet process that involved soaking hides in various liquors; tawing was a dry process requiring the rubbing of alum and oils into the hide. In other words, there were two different processes for preparing leather to be applied to different types of leather by different craftsmen. Meanwhile, most regulations in manufacturing industry were craft rules specific to the town, approved by the town council and administered by the craft guilds.

The craft guilds, which were prominent social organisations in many towns, were the direct result of these concerns. There were several different aspects of craft organisation that were liable to be specified in craft guild ordinances, and they may be summarised under five main

[29] *Statutes of the Realm*, i, pp. 379–80.
[30] Harris, *Coventry Leet Book*, pp. 395–401; C. A. Markham and J. C. Cox, eds., *Records of the Borough of Northampton* (2 vols., Northampton, 1898), i, pp. 344–9; W. G. Benham, ed., *Red Paper Book of Colchester* (1902), pp. 18–21.

headings: controlling standards of goods and services; specifying training requirements; defining complaints procedures; preventing environmental hazards; and limiting hours of work. Not all craft guilds were concerned with all of these issues, some of which were much more relevant to some trades than others. Because craft guilds were rule-enforcing bodies, they required appropriate constitutional apparatus, which normally meant providing for the annual election of supervisors or masters.

England was generally slower than the more industrial parts of Europe in establishing craft guilds. Few craft guilds are on record before the late thirteenth century, and they were mostly in the textile industry where numbers tended to be larger, or in London. By the late thirteenth century some of the London trades – fishmongers, goldsmiths, skinners, tailors, vintners, pepperers, drapers and mercers – had trade associations that were plainly of a craft guild kind rather than religious fraternities. Evidence for craft guilds as a normal aspect of town life becomes abundant only in the fifteenth century. The late formation of craft guilds is chiefly attributable to the small size of towns. Unless there were a fair number of craftsmen all in the same craft in a town, there was little scope for such organisation. Yet that cannot be the whole story, since many towns were smaller in the fifteenth century than in the thirteenth. The formation of craft guilds needs additional explanation in terms of cultural developments characteristic of the late middle ages. The earlier spread of religious fraternities was probably a contributory factor, since in some cases groups of craftsmen meeting for pious reasons started to use their organisation for economic as well as more general social purposes. Another reason must be the spread of ideas about urban policing from one town to another. In this process the 'best practice' of London and the larger towns was very influential. Thirdly, the multiplication of guilds in the late middle ages was perhaps a response to a more competitive environment and the need for tighter quality controls.

RELIGION AND URBAN CULTURE

Given the importance of the Christian religion as a source of beliefs and practices, and as a means of their diffusion through formal and informal instruction, it is hardly surprising that churches were prime sites for the forging of urban culture. Throughout the period 1200–1500, townsmen were more likely to be instructed by preaching than country people, especially after the coming of the friars.[31] By 1300 some friary

---

[31] See also pp. 299–301.

churches were being designed especially to accommodate sermon audiences. Many works of later medieval literature, such as Margery Kempe's autobiography, demonstrate that townspeople listened to sermons both for edification and for entertainment, and that overlap was even more apparent in the dramatic performances available in towns where biblical or instructional plays were a normal part of the church year. More formal instruction was available in many towns from the twelfth century onwards as a result of the foundation of schools of various kinds, often associated at first with the principal churches, which derived an income from the fees they were able to earn. Schooling soon became more independent of the ecclesiastical establishment, but it nevertheless remained primarily in the hands of the clergy and supplied an additional source of clerical incomes. Even the small market town of Witham in Essex had the advantages of a 'Scolhus' about 1262.[32] These schools were able to benefit from the growing use of written legal instruments for the conveyance of property, but the scope for clerical employment in secular affairs expanded considerably from the twelfth century onwards as a result of increasing litigation and, even more importantly, new habits of legal and financial record-keeping. These required a grounding in the reading and writing of basic Latin, and such a training also served as a foundation for those who aimed for an ecclesiastical career.

Acknowledgement of the centrality of the Church and church-related education for laymen, whatever their aspirations, is implied by the burdens they bore, with varying degrees of willingness, in supporting their churches and the associated clergy. In return for administering the sacraments and teaching their parishioners the rudiments of the Catholic faith, priests were supported from the tithes as much on the profits of commerce and manufacture as on the fruits of the soil. Tithe was a complex system that had first evolved to suit rural, agricultural conditions rather than the urban, but it was for the most part collected in towns without opposition. The laity discharged what was expected; disputes where reckoning tithe proved difficult were relatively rare, even in large urban areas. The evidence of the surviving wills strongly suggests that the parish church continued to be the principal focus for urban lay piety, and that is where most townsmen and townswomen chose to be buried, often near other members of their families. Townspeople commonly left bequests for the benefit of the church, either in the form of payments for candles on particular altars at particular times, or as contributions to church fabric, or as personal gifts to

---

[32] PRO, DL 43/14/1, m. 1.

parish clergy. Such wills clearly indicate the structure of parish organisa-tion. The rector, who was entitled to tithes and certain fees, was often recognised in bequests to settle the mortuary fee of the deceased and to compensate him for any tithes or other dues forgotten. But the principal cleric with whom parishioners had contact was the priest, vicar or parish chaplain, who often received a separate personal gift. When Roger Petman, a shipmaster of Lynn, made his will in 1499, he bequeathed 3s 4d to the high altar of St Margaret's church 'for my forgotten offerings and tithes' and a further 13s 4d 'unto Master John Robsonne parish priest of Saint Margaret'.[33] Wills also remembered supplementary chaplains attached to the parish for the saying of masses, and parish clerks, even sub-clerks, were sometimes given small bequests of a few pence each.

In addition to supporting the personnel who might, by vocation and ordination, teach and administer the sacraments, the laity had obligations both towards the buildings in which the cure of souls was accomplished and towards providing the equipment necessary for the seemly discharge of parish services. Roger Petman's will also provided 3s 3d 'to the reparation of the said Saint Margaret's church' and 3s 4d 'to the reparation of St James's chapel'. The administration of such funds provided a source of leadership complementing that of the priest in some parishes. In practical terms, as a result of ecclesiastical legislation passed in the thirteenth century, the maintenance of church buildings (or at least nave and tower) and provision of requisite equipment rested with the laity and, in time, specifically with churchwardens, pairs of laymen serving for a year or two at a time, who were responsible on behalf of all parishioners for the efficient discharge of agreed responsibilities. Churchwardens managed certain aspects of the parish income, levying collections, rates and dues, and managing property endowments devised by deceased parishioners. They also managed certain expenditures: for instance, overseeing building repairs, arranging cleaning, maintaining vestments and liturgical equipment, and procuring new items when necessary. Finally, and depending on the parish, they might also have the responsibility for collecting and administering the revenues which supported auxiliary clergy, like the parish clerk. Churchwardens are less frequently mentioned in wills than clergy, but in 1467, for example, Robert Ase the tailor bequeathed a plot of land and a garden in Walmgate, York, to Robert Appilby and Thomas Kilwik 'wardens of the

---

[33] D. M. Owen, *The Making of King's Lynn* (1984), no. 292, pp. 253–4.

fabric of St Laurence's church', and to their successors, for the future benefit of the parish.[34]

The development of the doctrine of purgatory from the twelfth century further encouraged the initiative of the laity in the activities of the parish through their involvement in the founding and administration of chantries and obits.[35] A chantry was an arrangement which provided a priest to celebrate a daily mass at a specified altar, usually an existing altar in a parish church, for the benefit of nominated individuals, sometimes in life, much more frequently after death, almost always including the soul or souls of the man, woman or family footing the priest's stipend. A less wealthy man might endow an obit, an annual celebration of the mass with prayers for his soul and those of others related to him, usually timed for the anniversary of his decease. Once a chantry priest had celebrated the daily mass, he was available to assist in pastoral duties and other tasks in the parish, so any chantry founder was providing his or her parish with a free auxiliary. In this way private endowments benefited much wider groups.

Some foundations were for only a limited duration. A year or two was the most common, but ten, fifteen or even twenty-year durations were feasible. Temporary chantries could be paid for with a lump sum set aside in the founder's will, but were commonly funded by heirs who were obliged to set aside part of the income deriving from the inheritance they received from their progenitors, effectively paying a death duty on the estate to provide for the souls of their parents. Perpetual chantries, and even the lesser endowments needed for an annual obit, required provisions for long-term management. Their revenues were sometimes entrusted to the churchwardens of the parish where the chantry was founded, as in the case of John Nasyng's chantry in the parish of St Mary at Hill, London: the accounts for 1517–18 record rents totalling £4 9s 2d.[36] On other occasions the management of chantries and obits was in the hands of the urban community and so created extra work for town officials. Some men who had been the leaders of the urban community in their lifetime expected the town treasurers and auditors to administer their chantries after their deaths. For example, in 1496 the Southampton corporation was administering lands set aside by three former members of the town elite for their obits.

---

[34] R. H. Britnell, 'York under the Yorkists', in R. H. Britnell, ed., *Daily Life in the late Middle Ages* (Stroud, 1998), p. 193.

[35] For belief and practice relating to purgatory, see pp. 309–10.

[36] C. Burgess, 'London parishes: development in context', in Britnell, *Daily Life*, p. 166.

Sited in parish churches, smaller-scale intercessory arrangements had a profound impact, affecting local regimes by reducing or shaping the obligatory response incumbent on parishioners. They added to parish liturgies, providing extra services and equipment, devotions and observances. They increased the parish's role as a focus for batteries of intercession. Because they added to the number of priests in the parish, they bolstered the pastoral capacity of the parish and added to the solemnity with which liturgy might be performed; by the later fifteenth century, if not earlier, the presence of chantry priests had stimulated more ambitious musical performance in some urban parishes. In addition, chantries and perpetual anniversaries might also add to parish revenues, reducing the sums that parishioners were obliged to pay for services and repairs, or conversely enabling them to consider more ambitious outlay and provision. The benefits were great enough to ensure that parishes took their duties seriously, especially when churchwardens and the parish clergy exercised a supervisory role. Founders were often at pains to stipulate that failure to ensure that all was being carried out as required would mean transfer to another parish. The duties accompanying intercessory services therefore demanded a regular investment of time and effort.

Another area in which townsmen could initiate pious activities relatively independently of both urban government and ecclesiastical authorities was in the formation of fraternities. These were often called guilds, and so risk confusion with merchant guilds and craft guilds whose benefits were primarily commercial. The distinction between fraternities and these other sorts of guild was not absolute, since many craft guilds had religious and ceremonial functions. Nevertheless it is not usually difficult to decide whether a guild was a fraternity rather than a craft guild, since the rules and political status of the two forms were different. If a guild's members were occupationally specific, and if its ordinances included regulations for a particular trade, then it was a craft guild. A fraternity usually had members from numerous different occupations, its objectives centred on piety, sociability and mutual support, and it did not concern itself with any particular occupational regulations.

Fraternities were numerous in towns, and so well worth attention in any discussion of urban society, though they were far from being an exclusively urban phenomenon. In some parts of the country, such as East Anglia, most villages of any size in the later middle ages had at least one fraternity for their inhabitants.[37] Their presence would be most noticeable

---

[37] For an example of the guilds supported by rural settlements, see below, pp. 313–14.

inside a parish church. Fraternities were dedicated to a saint or to some other focus of religious devotion such as the Corpus Christi, the Holy Ghost or the Holy Trinity, and this implied special religious duties, such as the maintenance of lights on the altar of their patron saint in a particular church, and attendance together at mass at the patronal festival. For example, the Fraternity of St Thomas of Canterbury at Lynn (founded in 1376) was begun 'to maintain and find, before a certain image of St Thomas in the church of St Nicholas of the foresaid town of Lynn, one candle of 2lb of wax for to burn in service time each festival day in the year'.[38] Beyond this primary purpose, the objectives of fraternities stretched to include social provisions. One of these – a bridge between the religious and the social – was the obligation to attend the funeral of a deceased member, or at least to provide for prayers for his or her soul. In addition, members were inhibited from wronging each other by theft or slander, on pain of expulsion. There was usually some provision for mutual assistance in case of individual misfortune. The members of the Fraternity of St Thomas of Canterbury, for example, would contribute to the assistance of members impoverished 'through loss on the sea, or through fire, or any manner other sent of God'.[39] Fraternities can to this extent be regarded as providing some functional substitute for accident insurance, though of course one that depended on charity rather than any legal claim. The religious fraternity had more scope for development in England than the craft guild, partly because of the more open nature of its membership.

POLITICS AND URBAN CULTURE

Relations between the different ranks that made up urban society were normally peaceful. Such conflict as occurred had different causes and characteristics in different towns, so that it is not feasible to generalise from a single case study. On the other hand, the discussion so far will be adequate to explain many features of the tensions to be observed in moments of crisis, since the potential fault lines in urban society corresponded to social divisions that were found in many towns. These conflicts have been interpreted as examples of the sociological phenomenon of 'usurpationary closure', which occurs when those excluded from economic or political power aim to improve their relative

[38] Smith, *English Gilds*, p. 47.
[39] *Ibid.*, p. 48.

position, often 'by mass mobilisation and direct action and an appeal to some alternative standard of distributive justice'.[40]

One source of conflict was the division that separated powerful landlords from townsmen. The range of possibilities here is well illustrated in the events of the Peasants' Revolt of 1381, which was far from being an affair of peasant insurgents only. In Bury St Edmunds and St Albans, townsmen took up arms against landlords who claimed lordship over them. The burgesses of Cambridge, despite royal charters granting them considerable freedoms, clashed with a university that had grown up in their midst as a powerful complex of property-owning interests. Conflicts against landlords could create severe problems for particular townsmen, since it was only to be expected that some merchants, tradesmen, clerks and lawyers would look to wealthy local patrons for their custom. In 1315, in a period of conflict over common rights between the burgesses of Colchester and the abbot of St John the Baptist's Abbey, Hubert Bosse of Colchester was persuaded to renounce his rights to various pastures in contention and to become their friend for life, 'to serve ... both in counsel and in aid, and to work personally about their business, at the expense of the monks whenever I am given sufficient notice', supporting the abbey in all its doings except against the burgesses of Colchester.[41] Such men could be useful in patching up quarrels through arbitration, especially if (like Hubert Bosse) they were members of the urban ruling elite.

A second potential source of conflict, in any town with a powerful ruling elite, was between its members and the main body of the burgesses. Again, the disturbances that occurred across parts of England during the Peasants' Revolt of 1381 illustrate this hazard, particularly in the northern towns. York had for some years been riven with faction between the supporters of John Langton and John de Gisburne. In Beverley there were conflicts over both the institutions of urban government and elections to office. This source of tension was especially characteristic of the largest towns, where the rewards of political power were greatest; political life in London was frequently disturbed by party divisions, and there were deep-seated tensions in Norwich between the commons and the elite that broke out into open conflict during the 1430s.

Conflict between landlords and burgesses, and between burgesses and their ruling elites, does not exhaust the possibilities for clashes in urban society. There was also periodic conflict between the masters of different

[40] S. H. Rigby, *English Society in the later Middle Ages* (Basingstoke, 1995), pp. 10, 145–77.
[41] Essex Record Office, Colchester and North-East Essex Branch, St John's Abbey Register, f. 239.

crafts and their men. Craftsmen could use their freedom, buttressed with secondary self-protective rights as members of craft guilds, to control their employees and apprentices. The fixing of periods of apprenticeship, for example, though presented as a means of ensuring a high level of training, was also a device for ensuring a dependent work force. Craft guilds regulated wages to stop members from offering higher wages in an attempt to entice men to work for them. Other guild ordinances sought to control the conduct of journeymen, and might require an oath of good behaviour. Conflict was only to be expected, and is explicit in the terms of the Ordinance and Statute of Labourers enforced after the Black Death to inhibit wage increases resulting from scarcities of labour. Conflict over conditions of employment and broken contracts is more apparent in the records than conflict over wages, but that is partly because of the form of the labour laws. Wage earners attempted collective action of various kinds on numerous occasions, often under the form of a religious fraternity, as in the case of the journeyman weavers of Coventry in 1424. London wage earners, evidence of whose collective activities pre-dates the plague, joined together to raise wages from at least the 1290s.[42] Interesting though such movements are, they are seriously under-recorded, and usually find a mention in the records only at the moment when they were outlawed by the borough authorities. That was, it seems, their inevitable fate.

Besides these conflicts between the different urban social strata, occupational difference too gave rise to conflict, in spite of all the institutional attempts by town authorities to prevent them. It might be very difficult to maintain the peace between overlapping or closely adjacent crafts. In fifteenth-century York, for example, there was a running battle between the marshals (responsible for caring for horses) and smiths, who were said to be 'many days and years in variance ... [so] that many ... mayors and the chamber were hugely vexed with them'. There were also conflicts in York, notably in 1428, between tanners and the cordwainers (shoemakers) over the standard of leather that was being produced and the inadequacy of regular quality controls.[43] Such bilateral disputes were not the main concern of town authorities. Much more common in practice was the multi-lateral conflict that arose from the failure of particular crafts or occupations to respect the interests of their fellow burgesses. In 1359, for example, the

---

[42] Harris, *Coventry Leet Book*, pp. 91–6; E. Miller and J. Hatcher, *Medieval England: rural society and economic change, 1086–1348* (1978), p. 371; G. Unwin, *The Gilds and Companies of London* (1963), pp. 224–5.
[43] H. Swanson, *Medieval Artisans: an urban class in late medieval England* (Oxford, 1989), pp. 55–6, 68.

court rolls of Colchester record that six bakers were fined for conspiring with the town millers in order that all their wheat would be ground before anyone else's – a clear case of restrictive practice.[44]

Against the background of these multiple layers of conflict, we can better appreciate some of the symbolism relating to urban government and society. Many towns fostered a distinctive identity and civic pride through the perpetuation of stories and images founded in myth. Colchester attributed its walls to King Coel, the reputed founder of the town; a bastion on the west wall was called King Coel's Castle. His supposed daughter, St Helen, was recalled not only in the name of one of the borough's common wells, but also in the name of a lane and the dedication of an ancient chapel near the centre of the town. She was also the patron saint of the borough's most prestigious late medieval guild, and the early fifteenth-century borough seal commemorated her association with relics of the true cross of Christ. The name of London was reputedly corrupted from the name of the warrior King Lud, who had rebuilt its walls. York had King Ebrauk as its legendary founder; Coventry remembered the naked Lady Godiva for having freed the city from tolls; and Southampton remembered Sir Bevis for saving the town from the giant Ascupart. Such stories were not the preserve of a narrow elite, but entered as folklore into the common culture of these towns and contributed both to the dignity and the entertainment of their inhabitants.

Ideals of social unity were also promoted through urban ceremonial. Perambulating the bounds (walking, and therefore maintaining, jurisdictional boundaries) was as much a feature of urban life as it was of rural communities. Christian symbolism was also called upon to exemplify the social harmony desired by urban authorities. In particular, the public processions and other formalised celebrations attached to the feast of Corpus Christi symbolically harmonised differences of social rank and occupational distinctions. Other kinds of social division – differences of gender or age, for example – were acknowledged in this ceremonial, to the extent that women and children were assigned the passive role of spectators rather than an active role as participants. But the structuring principles that towns chose to ritualise most formally were those that were most problematic. The roles of women and children could be regarded as founded in divine ordinances and age-old tradition. The duties of councillors and burgesses, tradesmen and artisans, however, were open to political negotiation.

---

[44] I. H. Jeayes, ed., *Court Rolls of the Borough of Colchester* (4 vols., Colchester, 1921–*c*. 1941), ii, p. 83.

The feast of Corpus Christi was authorised in a papal letter of 1317 and introduced into England the following year. By the fifteenth century co-operation between the crafts in setting up its ceremonies was mandatory and defaulters were subject to heavy penalties. In Winchester it was set down that 'if any craft or crafts within the city aforesaid fail of their torch or torches of their craft, or refuse to keep the old order and ordinance upon Corpus Christi Day, [they are] to forfeit for every default 6s 8d to the use of the chamber'.[45] The biblical plays that accompanied these ceremonies were also a matter of enforcement rather than voluntary good will. In 1461 the burgesses of Coventry introduced a fine of £5 on any craft that failed to produce its play according to custom.[46] This feast meant a great deal to the civic awareness of many late medieval townsmen.

Corpus Christi means literally 'the body of Christ', whose continuation in earthly form was not understood as a mere metaphor. Medieval teaching stressed the identity both of the consecrated bread consumed in the mass and of the Church itself with the body of Christ. The power of the body imagery for political purposes lay in the way in which it conflated status and function. Those who used this idea had no doubt that some members of the body had higher status than others. The head is of higher status than the foot. At the same time, however, there are divisions of function between eyes, ears, noses, and so on, which are quite independent of status distinctions, and which can be thought of as purely functional. We have here simultaneously a divine justification for differences of power and differences of occupation and a recognition of the essential unity of humankind regardless of rank or function. When this imagery was developed for use in an urban context, it could justify the status distinctions between the leaders of the borough community and the rest. It could also justify the imposition of functional distinctions within urban society. The Corpus Christi festivals that many fifteenth-century towns organised were able simultaneously to idealise obedience to borough officers, as a duty of subordinate members to the head, and to draw attention to the need for co-operation and interdependence between different crafts as a political requirement, to be imposed by laws if necessary.

This latter symbolism was most explicit, perhaps, in the mystery plays that were organised in some towns – notably York, Wakefield, Chester and Coventry. These play cycles carried further the idea that the prevention of craft wars required regulation, by symbolising the additional

---

[45] W. H. B. Bird, ed., *The Black Book of Winchester* (Winchester, 1925), p. 131.
[46] Harris, *Coventry Leet Book*, p. 312.

need for co-operation and charity. The responsibility for mounting these plays sometimes became a reason in itself for defining the membership and functions of craft guilds: in York, the mystery play seems to have been the chief reason for the very existence of some craft guilds, if we are to judge from the prominence of provisions regarding the play in those crafts' rules and regulations. Unlike processions, which emphasised hierarchy of status, the play cycles of medieval towns epitomised the interdependence between members of a craft and between different crafts if the festival was to proceed according to plan. Often there was some direct connection between the subject matter of a play and the craft chosen to play it. At York the goldsmiths were responsible for the play of Herod and the Three Kings, since this required a lot of glitter to be convincing. Such considerations meant that the play cycle cut across the principle of hierarchies; the play of Herod and the Three Kings could not be performed before the nativity play, even if the goldsmiths were more important than the shepherds. Several crafts might have to co-operate to produce a single play. Even in this respect, however, the city council was always there to step in with regulations if good will broke down. Some crafts had to be compelled to contribute, as in 1435, when the Coventry records reveal the saddlers and painters being compelled to contribute to the card-makers' pageant.[47]

The economic, political and cultural development of town life between 1200 and 1500 had resulted in a wide range of new social practices and institutions that were both impressive in their own right and important for subsequent social development. In many ways it is possible to see complementarities between the different aspects of change: between the multiplication of crafts, the constitutional structuring of an urban hier-archy, and the growing lay participation in religious ceremonial, all of which contributed to shaping late medieval Corpus Christi festivities; or between growing dependence on trade, the growth of urban autonomy, and the creation of a distinctive commercial ethic. But for all the mutual reinforcement achieved by these adaptations to urban life in the course of time, medieval townsmen were never able to take social harmony for granted. Any account of urban life that ignores the recurrent antagonistic divisions gives a misleading impression of the degree to which economic interdependence, political structure and cultural innovation could over-come the clashes of interest endemic to English urban life during the later middle ages.

---

[47] Harris, *Coventry Leet Book*, p. 172.

CHAPTER 7

The land

Bruce M. S. Campbell

Today, at the beginning of the third millennium, agriculture employs only
2 per cent of the United Kingdom's workforce and contributes less than
0.1 per cent to the national income.[1] Agriculture and land use, like so much
else, are matters of government policy: regulated, subsidised and monitored. In the middle ages it was otherwise. Then, agriculture dominated
the economy. At least three-quarters of England's national income came
from agriculture, and agricultural products, processed and unprocessed,
accounted for the vast majority of all exports. To achieve this required most
of the land, the bulk of the labour force, much of the capital, and a great deal
of the management talent available within the national economy. For many,
farming was an occupation; for some, it was a business pursued for profit;
but for none was it as yet an industry. In an almost exclusively organic and
animate age, the mechanisation and industrialisation of agriculture
remained a long way in the future. Without direct government intervention, it was up to individual producers how they coped with problems and
responded to opportunities. There was no welfare system to cushion those
overwhelmed by the challenges and misfortunes that periodically confronted all who strove to make a living from the land. Although land was
prized primarily for its capacity to produce the essentials of life, its amenity
value was not unappreciated. Above all, throughout the middle ages control
and ownership of land conferred power, wealth and prestige.

Townsmen were as much affected by these considerations as countrymen. Then, as now, London was the most urban and least rural place
in the land, as William fitz Stephen's glowing account of the city at the
end of the twelfth century makes plain.[2] Even so, medieval Londoners

---

[1] I am especially grateful to Steve Rigby for his close critical reading of earlier versions of this chapter.
Mark Bailey, Christopher Whittick, Margaret Yates and the editors also provided many useful
suggestions and comments. Responsibility for the views expressed and any errors remains my own.

[2] D. C. Douglas and G. W. Greenaway, eds., *English Historical Documents, 1042–1189* (2nd edn, 1981),
pp. 1025–30.

lived at only one remove from the countryside and the world of nature.
As yet the city was still largely provisioned with food grown within its
immediate hinterland. Domestic heating, cooking, baking and brewing,
smithies and a host of other craft activities all relied upon faggots and
charcoal produced by the many intensively managed coppice woodlands
that would long remain a distinctive feature of land use in the surrounding countryside. The capital's need for building timber as well as
fuel ensured that the immediate home counties remained among the most
wooded in lowland England. Corn-mongers and wood-mongers were
thus among the city's most essential traders. In due course other dealers in
agricultural produce would also rise to prominence, particularly the wool
merchants who, as the textile-manufacturing centres on the continent
expanded, drew in wool from all across England for export through
London. Some of these commodities were brought to London by river-
boat down the Thames and sea-going vessels up the Thames. More
arrived overland on packhorses and horse- and ox-drawn carts. Horses,
ridden, driven and led, thronged the city's streets, creating a massive
need for both stabling and fodder. Cattle, sheep, swine and even geese
were also driven in numbers to the city's great livestock market at
Smithfield for sale and slaughter. The sights, sounds and smells of the
countryside penetrated the very heart of the city.

   Of necessity, provisioning urban populations promoted close and regular intercourse between town and country. In the case of London, villein
tenants of the many manors of St Paul's Cathedral were charged with
carrying grain to the city, in some cases as many as eight times a year.
Country accents could thus frequently be heard in the capital's streets,
those of Welsh and north-country drovers alongside those of home-
counties carters. Moreover, as enrolments of apprenticeships demonstrate,
many of those who lived and worked in the city had actually been born and
reared in the countryside, in villages and small towns. Significant numbers
of London mercers, for instance, hailed from the linen-producing countryside of east Norfolk. Those who achieved success in the city often used
their wealth to acquire rural property. Some Londoners, like Alderman
John Feld, who in 1474 was buried at Standon in Hertfordshire, did well
enough to purchase manors and make gentry of their sons: John Feld junior
was titled 'esquire' in the epitaph which he shared with his father.

   In the fourteenth century both the poets William Langland (born at
Malvern in Worcestershire) and Geoffrey Chaucer (born in London) lived
for long periods in the capital, yet *Piers Plowman* and the *Canterbury Tales*
have more to say about the countryside and those who lived there than they

have about the city. The rural imagery employed by both of these works was all-pervasive and would have been widely understood. In the visual arts, realistic scenes from contemporary rural life were used to illustrate episodes from the Bible. Townsmen may have despised husbandmen for being rustic, but none would have denied the indispensable nature of the latter's work. '[L]ook you do no husbandman harm that tills with his plough', was Robin Hood's injunction to Little John.[3] 'God speed the plough and send us corn enough', prayed one and all.[4]

The seasonal sequence of agricultural activity structured even the financial, legal and school years. This activity commenced each autumn with a new round of ploughing and sowing, rested at Christmas, resumed in early spring with a further round of ploughing and sowing, continued with lambing and calving, then culminated in late spring and summer with the harvests of wool, hay and grain. It was for good reason that the reeves and bailiffs appointed by lords to oversee the management of their rural estates mostly rendered their accounts at Michaelmas (29 September), as one cycle of reproduction ended and another commenced. Seasons of toil and indolence and of glut and shortage were consequently unavoidable facts of medieval life. Prices often varied more from season to season than they did from year to year: hence even the metropolis bought, sold and consumed to the rhythm of the farming year. Grain prices invariably peaked in early summer, as supplies from the previous harvest became depleted and storage costs mounted before the next harvest could bring relief. To bridge this hungry gap Langland, reared during the lean years of the early fourteenth century but writing in more abundant times, recommended a diet comprising bread baked from beans and bran, dairy produce, legumes, vegetables and fruit.[5] What people ate therefore varied seasonally. This was recognised and ritualised by the feasting and fasting prescribed by the Church, which made a Christian virtue out of economic necessity.

The Church also advocated charity as the Christian response to years of general scarcity, although in genuinely hard times this was rarely equal to the need. When harvests failed, Londoners of at least some means tended to fare better than their land-locked rural cousins because the concentration of purchasing power in the city served as a magnet to those

[3] R. B. Dobson and J. Taylor, eds., *Rymes of Robyn Hood: an introduction to the English outlaw* (Gloucester, 1989), p. 80.

[4] A. McRae, *God Speed the Plough: the representation of agrarian England, 1500–1600* (Cambridge, 1996), pp. 1–2.

[5] G. Russell and G. Kane, eds., *Piers Plowman: the C version: Will's version of Piers Plowman, Do-Well, Do-Better and Do-Best* (1997), pp. 365–6.

with surpluses to sell. Thus, a Genoese speculator responded to the exceptional prices prevailing during the Great European Famine of 1315–21 by shipping 1,000 quarters of wheat to London and selling it to an agent of the king. Great landlords, like the bishop of Winchester, whose broad acres ensured that they had surpluses to sell, reaped bumper profits from these abnormal market conditions. London corn-mongers also emerged enriched from the crisis. Indeed, in the home counties the superior prices pertaining on the London market siphoned grain out of rural markets and thereby exacerbated the scarcity of food; on several Essex manors mortality rose steeply in 1315–18. Here, as elsewhere in the countryside, normal coping strategies proved unequal to the challenge presented by such a prolonged run of catastrophic years. Nor did the government, preoccupied with the recent military reversal in Scotland, do anything to relieve the situation. Even Christian alms shrank in supply. As a direct result of the inadequate institutional response to this natural disaster, probably between a quarter of a million and half a million people perished of starvation and starvation-related diseases in England's worst recorded subsistence crisis. Until this reversal the population and economy had both been expanding; thereafter, for the remainder of the middle ages, they contracted and stagnated.

QUANTITIES AND TYPES OF LAND

Medieval England had a potential agricultural area of over 25 million acres (10 million hectares). In 1086, on the evidence of the Domesday survey, less than a quarter of this – amounting to approximately 5.9 million acres (2.5 million hectares) – was under arable cultivation. Some areas were already closely and fully settled – the fertile district of Flegg in east Norfolk, for instance, probably supported as large a population in 1086 as it would do in 1801 – but nationally there was much room for expansion. Over the course of the twelfth and thirteenth centuries many of these opportunities would be exploited, as more land was brought into agricultural use and exploitation of existing agricultural land was intensified. The impetus behind this movement came from several sources. First and most impor-tantly there were the needs of a population which at least doubled in size between 1086 and 1315.[6] Then there were the demands of the growing

---

[6] For the population estimates used here, see B. M. S. Campbell, *English Seigniorial Agriculture 1250–1450* (Cambridge, 2000), pp. 399–406. For further discussion of demographic patterns and estimates, see the Introduction, pp. 12–20.

craft-working and urban sectors: sectors which until the mid-thirteenth century almost certainly increased faster than the population at large. Finally, there were the mounting requirements of an export trade which may have trebled in value over the course of the thirteenth century, with over 90 per cent of that value contributed by agricultural products, principally in the form of raw wool.[7] To support these developments, agriculture and those engaged in it had to become more productive.

Demand peaked in the early fourteenth century. This was when medieval agriculture was at fullest stretch and pressure upon the land was at its greatest. Never again would so many people be so exclusively dependent upon domestic agriculture for their daily needs and for their employment. Nor would trade in agricultural produce bulk so large in the commercial life of the nation. The achievement is impressive and had been made possible by a range of strategies. First, and most obviously, more land had been brought into production by a widespread and largely piecemeal process of reclamation. Typically this entailed upgrading existing agricultural land to more productive uses, through the conversion of woodland to pasture, marsh to meadow, and grassland to arable. In the process, arable gained relative to pastoral output and certain products gained relative to others (such as milk relative to meat production). With a greater supply of labour, production methods were intensified. This facilitated the development of more productive husbandry systems, particularly through the closer integration of arable and pastoral production on the same land, vital ingredients of which were the intensive management of hay meadows and the incorporation of fodder cropping into arable rotations. Lastly, aggregate gains in productivity were achieved through greater specialisation at the level of the individual farm and farming region. This, of course, was contingent upon fuller involvement in market exchange.

In 1315, on the eve of the Great Famine, reclamation, clearance and the conversion of grassland to tillage had increased the arable area to perhaps 10 million acres (not much less than the 10.5 million acres under the plough in 1800). Some areas tilled at this time – parts of Dartmoor, the sandy East Anglian Breckland, and the heaviest midland clays – would never again be under the plough. In other areas, however, expansion was stemmed by institutional barriers in the form of royal forest jurisdiction, private hunting grounds, and rights of common pasture. Although the land thus reserved was often of poor quality, the experience of later

---

[7] E. Miller and J. Hatcher, *Medieval England: towns, commerce and crafts 1086–1348* (1995), p. 214.

centuries demonstrates that some of it would still have been worth bringing into cultivation had these obstacles not existed.

Whatever the quality of the arable, maintaining its fertility and containing weed growth usually required regular fallowing. This was when the land was rested and allowed to recharge its nitrogen balance. Fallowed land was also used as a vital source of temporary pasturage, and dung from grazing animals further contributed to the recycling of nitrogen. Before being returned to cultivation, such land was ploughed repeatedly to improve soil structure, destroy the root systems of weeds, and stir in any manure. Exceptionally, in a few very intensively cultivated areas such as east Norfolk and east Kent, cropping was virtually continuous, and husbandmen laboured hard to sustain productivity. At the opposite extreme, in areas of poor soil, the land might be rested for several years in succession before it was sown again. Throughout the greater part of lowland England, however, the arable was left fallow every second, third or fourth year. Consequently, only half to two-thirds of all arable was under crop each year, a total of perhaps 6.7 million acres when cultivation was at its maximum extent.

It was upon this cropped area that the nation had to rely for the grains and legumes that comprised its staple diet (there being little carryover of grain stocks from one year to the next). The same area also had to supply the fodder crops – principally oats, vetches, peas and straw – that helped sustain the draught animals that were the single largest source of the kinetic energy deployed within the economy. Draught animals were fundamental to most aspects of food production and distribution (as were water and wind power to food processing – at least 12,000 mills of all sorts may have been in operation by 1300) and their extensive use was one of the most distinctive features of west European agriculture in this period. On the evidence of the Domesday survey, England had a population of perhaps 162,500 working horses and 650,000 working oxen in 1086. Two centuries later, demesne stocking densities imply an enlarged draught animal population of perhaps 400,000 horses and 800,000 oxen. In terms of energy supply, this was equivalent to a labour force of 10 million men, at a time when the total population may have been less than 4.5 million and the adult male population less than 1.5 million.[8] Maintaining the nation's working animals, including the

---

[8] B. M. S. Campbell, 'The uses and exploitation of human power from the 13th to the 18th century', in S. Cavaciocchi, ed., *Proceedings of the XXXIV Settimana di Studi, 'Economy and Energy'*, Istituto Internazionale di Storia Economica 'F. Datini' (Prato, 2003), pp. 183–211.

breeding of replacements, was therefore as vital as feeding its population. Any failure of draught power would have serious consequences for the economy at large, as was demonstrated by the devastation inflicted upon cattle herds by a highly contagious outbreak of rinderpest in 1319. As one horrified contemporary reported, 'all the cattle died straightaway, and made the land all bare, so fast, come never wretch into England that made men more aghast'.[9] Thereafter it took twenty-five years to rebuild the nation's herd to its former capacity. Depleted dairy herds were temporarily offset by boosting swine numbers; the latter had higher rates of reproduction and could more rapidly be brought to maturity. Replacing working oxen posed a far greater problem and until the losses could be made good arable cultivation was perforce curtailed. Significantly, those arable producers least affected by this catastrophe tended to be those who had already made the switch from oxen to horses.

The vital economic importance of the pastoral sector requires fuller acknowledgement. Because grain consumed as bread, pottage and ale was the staple of diets, there has been a tendency to assume that arable was the only land use that mattered. Contemporaries knew otherwise. Nationally, there was always at least as much grassland as arable, and in parts of the north and south-west tillage was never more than a minority land use. Arable was the predominant land use in only a few closely settled and intensively exploited regions, most notably eastern Norfolk, southern Cambridgeshire and Huntingdonshire, and the Vale of Evesham in Worcestershire. Many areas had as much grassland as tillage and during the century and a half that followed the Black Death England became even greener and grassier, since there was less need for grain and less labour to produce it.

The 'Great Pestilence', as contemporaries called it, reached England in June 1348 and within eighteen months 30–40 per cent of the total population – at least one and a quarter million people – had perished (more in the worst-hit communities). Never has agriculture had to adjust to so profound a demand shock. In 1349 contemporaries recorded with amazement the depressed prices, inflated wages, unharvested fields, and abandoned and straying livestock. Edward III and his advisers responded immediately with the Ordinance of Labourers, which attempted to peg prices and wages at their pre-plague level and press labourers into employment whether they wished it or not. This temporary legislation

---

[9] Quoted in I. Kershaw, 'The Great Famine and agrarian crisis in England 1315–22', *P&P*, 59 (1973), 14.

was confirmed by the Statute of Labourers, enacted by the first parliament to follow the plague in 1351, and this, augmented by the Statute of Artificers of 1363, was to remain the basis of English labour legislation until the early eighteenth century.

It took thirty years or more for the processes of post-plague economic adjustment to work themselves out. It was not just that demand for land and its products contracted massively. The improved ratio of population to resources brought better living standards, with the result that the composition of demand also shifted. More people were now better able to afford their dietary preferences: superior-quality bread and ale and more animal products in the form of dairy produce and meat. As William Langland bewailed, even beggars refused 'bread that had beans therein but asked for the best white, made of clean wheat; nor none halfpenny ale in no wise would drink, but of the best and brownest for sale in the borough'.[10] Meanwhile, land and capital became cheaper and labour dearer, prompting significant shifts in production methods.

By 1377, after four successive national bouts of plague, the population had been reduced to 2.25–2.5 million, and would dwindle still further over the next hundred years. The net result was a significant expansion of permanent grassland and a notable realignment of settlement and population. In the process many villages became deserted and their tilled fields turned over to pasture. At Maidenwell (Lincs.), for example, where there had been perhaps 150 villagers in 1327/32, there were twenty-five adults in 1377 and fewer than ten families fifty years later; twenty-five years later its tax quota was halved, and by 1500 the village had been more or less abandoned.[11] It was almost as though the crowded countryside of the late thirteenth century had never been. If there was now a problem, it was that there were too few, rather than too many, people on the land – for the country's population may now have been smaller even than at the time of the Domesday survey at the end of the eleventh century.

The fifteenth century therefore reversed the trend of the thirteenth century, when much grassland had perforce been converted to arable on account of the higher returns which the latter gave. Nevertheless, even during the thirteenth century clearance and reclamation had probably added more in aggregate to the grassland than to the arable area. Most ditching and embanking of low-lying valley bottoms, fenland and marshland was for grass rather than tillage. Similarly, the extensive

---

[10] Russell and Kanes, *Piers Plowman: the C version*, p. 366.
[11] K. J. Allison, *Deserted Villages* (1970), p. 32.

reclamation and land improvement that took place around England's upland margins, especially that undertaken by the many Cistercian abbeys which received extensive land grants in these areas, aimed primarily at the creation of pasture farms. These became key sources of replacement working animals for lowland mixed-farming areas with more circumscribed pastoral resources. Thus, insofar as there was a shortage of pasturage, this was local and regional rather than national and could in some measure be redressed by inter-regional transfers of animals and their products. It was largely to service this growing livestock trade that so many fairs were founded during the twelfth and thirteenth centuries.

Nationally, by 1300 there was at least one acre of permanent grassland for every acre of arable; by 1500 this ratio had changed, with almost two acres of grass to one of arable. Additionally, several million acres of temporary pasture were annually available on the fallow arable. The presence of so much pasturage explains why the country's international comparative advantage lay in the production of wool, for sheep were a predominantly grass-fed animal. At the opening of the sixteenth century a visiting Venetian was impressed by the 'enormous number of sheep, which yield [the English] quantities of wool of the best quality'.[12] The fleeces of 5.25 million sheep were at that time being shipped overseas either as raw wool or processed into cloth. Two centuries earlier, when the wool export trade and population pressure were both at their peak, eight to ten million sheep were producing wool for export. Plainly, medieval husbandmen were well aware of the economic value of their meadows and pastures.

Meadow was by far the most highly prized and carefully managed type of grassland, since it could be mown to yield a hay crop. Often artificially created by the ditching and dyking of poorly drained ground, it required close supervision and careful management. Typically, livestock were admitted to meadows only after the hay crop had been removed. Ecologically, their specialised function and privileged management ensured that meadows were a tapestry of *mille fleurs*, rich in insects, reptiles, mammals and ground-nesting birds. They were a distinctive man-made component of the rural scene. John Leland was struck by the 'exceeding fair and large meadows on both sides of [the River] Welland' when he travelled from Northamptonshire into Leicestershire in the late 1530s.[13]

---

[12] C. A. Sneyd, ed. and trans., *A Relation, or rather a True Account, of the Island of England* (Camden Society, os XXXVII, 1847), p. 10.

[13] L. Toulmin Smith, ed., *The Itinerary of John Leland in or about the Years 1535–1543* (5 vols., 1907–10), i, p. 13.

Here, as elsewhere in the broad river valleys of the English midlands, a good supply of low-lying, well-watered, alluvial land coincided with sufficient rain to nourish grass growth and enough sunshine to facilitate the mowing and drying of hay. Areas deficient in meadows either had to obtain hay from elsewhere or rely upon other types of feed to keep their animals through the winter. London, for instance, obtained much of its hay from extensive commercial meadows in the Lea Valley, the River Lea itself providing a cheap and convenient means of boating this most bulky of commodities to the city. And it was as a surrogate for hay that vetches and other legumes were increasingly sown from the late thirteenth century.

Throughout England, some land was always set aside as permanent pasture. Since pasture was not normally mown, it was less productive and usually less valuable than meadow. The most highly prized pastures were those that were enclosed, since they could be grazed most systematically without the supervision of a herdsman. Useful but less valuable were the many odd scraps of pasture on wayside verges and the headlands of arable strips upon which animals could be tethered. The most extensive pastures, however, were typically those that were common to an entire township or village. In a famous article Garrett Hardin argued that common resources were prone to over-stocking, giving rise to what he called 'the tragedy of the commons' whereby the resources thus managed became degraded by over-exploitation.[14] In fact, they were such an indispensable part of the agricultural system, and were so carefully supervised, that such degradation rarely materialised, except, paradoxically, when pastures were in such relative abundance that a 'slash and burn' approach prevailed. Normally rules were developed for managing the land in the common interest. Lords through their courts helped enforce these rules, resolve disputes, and provide a forum for collective decision-taking. Over many centuries, common pastures therefore remained a stable and essential component of land use. Co-operation was something to which most medieval husbandmen were accustomed, especially in many aspects of pastoral husbandry including the pooling of draught resources to create plough teams. This, after all, was the social world from which sprang the team sport of football.

Sometimes, specific environmental circumstances created particular pastoral opportunities. Dry, sandy and acidic soils often gave rise to

---

[14] R. Hardin, 'The tragedy of the commons', *Science*, 162 (1968), 1243–8.

lowland heath, notably in parts of Norfolk, Suffolk and Dorset, where it was an integral component of sheep-corn systems of husbandry. As well as supplying grazing, heathland was carefully managed to yield bracken, furze and ling, used variously for fodder, bedding and fuel. Heaths, moors and rough pastures were nevertheless nutritionally poor. Marshland, both freshwater and saltwater, was nutritionally far richer and therefore capable of supporting much higher stocking densities. Valuable freshwater marshlands rich in a range of grass species were a particular feature of the Broadland and Fenland regions of East Anglia and the Somerset Levels; salt-marshes with their more limited flora bordered the Thames estuary. So vital were these marshlands to the local economy – not just for grazing but also for rushes, turf, fowling and fishing – that 'upland' manors at some distance away often held rights in them. Woodland, too, could be used for grazing, provided that this was compatible with coppicing and felling regimes and the leaf canopy was not so dense that grasses and other ground-level plants were shaded out. Beechmast and acorns were also an important seasonal source of food for swine. Woodlands thus used were typically relatively open, since the browsing of animals prevented the regeneration of saplings and suckers. Not unusually, royal forests and private hunting grounds served both as a source of pasturage for livestock and as a reserve for game.

Woodland had two prime functions. The first was to supply timber for construction and craft production, since iron was as yet too expensive to provide a viable substitute. The second, except in those few localities where use was made of peat and coal, was as a source of fuel for heating, cooking and a range of manufacturing processes. During the century and a half that followed the Black Death meeting these functions was not a problem, for there was much regeneration of woodland on land abandoned in the general retreat from cultivation. By the 1530s, when Leland was recording his topographical observations, trees had become a conspicuous feature of the landscape in many parts of England. Two centuries earlier the countryside had worn an altogether less wooded aspect. Clearance for cultivation had greatly reduced the nation's stock of woodland and what remained was under constant pressure. The many major building projects of the age also made heavy demands upon the supply of mature timber. In the second quarter of the thirteenth century structural timbers for the roof of the new cathedral at Salisbury were obtained from as far away as Ireland. Woodland, like other land uses, therefore became the subject of ever closer and more intensive management. Typically that meant carefully regulated felling and coppicing cycles. In effect, woodland was cropped in much the same way as meadow and arable but on a longer cycle due to the greater time required for regeneration.

In areas of strong commercial demand, coppice woodland could be a very valuable asset and was jealously controlled. This was especially the case in the counties of the south-east, where a strong local demand for wood was reinforced by the more powerful regional demand of London and, in the case of Kent and Sussex, by demand from the thriving coastal towns and cities of northern France and Flanders. Undoubtedly, these were among the most intensively managed woodlands of medieval England and they must have generated a significant amount of employment. In contrast, England's extensive wolds and downs were relatively lacking in woodland. So too were the most closely settled areas of common-field husbandry and most areas of marshland. All were almost as treeless as they were hedgeless, and their inhabitants had to be both thrifty and resourceful in their use of fuel. The more fortunate had access to the woodland resources preserved in the forests, chases and parks primarily set aside as private hunting grounds. Nationally, between a tenth and a fifth of the agricultural area was probably reserved in one form or another to the production of trees and wood.

Little of the land of England served no agricultural purpose whatever. Wastes, moors and heaths supplied feed to sheep and free-range cattle, and during the thirteenth century development of commercial rabbit warrens turned the most barren sands into gold. Not all agricultural land was equally closely managed and the way in which resources were utilised changed over time as pressure upon the land waxed and waned. Leland's *Itinerary*, compiled at the very close of the middle ages, is a reminder of how many distinctive farming landscapes were to be observed and how striking were the contrasts between upland and lowland, vale and wold, light soils and heavy, champion and enclosed country, and areas close to and remote from major towns. Mark Bailey's perceptive study of the East Anglian Breckland shows the valuable insights that can be obtained from close examination of one such distinctive farming environment.[15]

TYPES AND SIZES OF MANOR

How people lived on the land was as much shaped by institutional as by environmental factors. Of those institutions none was of more universal significance than the manor. Manors constituted the basic units of

[15] M. Bailey, *A Marginal Economy? East-Anglian Breckland in the later middle ages* (Cambridge, 1989).

seigniorial landownership and lay at the very core of agrarian life. They had three elements: land, divided between the lord's demesne (that is, land reserved to the lord's own use which he might either cultivate directly or lease out) and the land held by others; a dependent tenantry (both free and unfree); and juridical rights. Manors had their own courts whose profits were a source of revenue to the lord, as were the various seigniorial rights and prerogatives. Manors also had their own customs, chiefly concerned with the inheritance and transmission of land; these were typically upheld by tenants, for custom provided one of the principal defences that they had against their lords and was rigorously asserted. Manors also provided a framework for managing resources and supervising the conduct of those aspects of agriculture undertaken in common. There were, in fact, few aspects of agrarian life upon which the manorial system did not impinge.

Manors varied enormously in their size, value and relationship to the village community. 'Classic' manors were territorially coterminous with vills. These are the simplest to comprehend and hence feature most prominently in textbook accounts of the period. Cuxham in Oxfordshire, from 1271 a possession of Merton College, Oxford, is an excellent and well-documented example.[16] In reality, however, only a minority of manors were so neat and tidy. At one extreme of the spectrum were territorially extensive manors containing several vills, such as Halesowen in Worcestershire, owned from 1217 by the Premonstratensian abbey of Halesowen. It occupied a more or less continuous area of 10,000 acres within which, in addition to the small market town of Halesowen, there were twelve rural townships or settlements. Lords of such extensive manors naturally enjoyed considerable local influence and power; small wonder, then, that in the middle years of the thirteenth century tenant opposition at Halesowen to the increased rents and dues imposed by the abbey eventually came to naught.[17] At the other extreme were manors like that at Hevingham in Norfolk held in 1279 by Henry le Cat.[18] At that date Hevingham was unevenly divided between no fewer than seven lords, who had created a complex web of sub-manorial units by feudally sub-dividing their holdings – a process known as subinfeudation. Cat's manor was one of the largest, with a total of perhaps 300 acres of demesne

[16] P. D. A. Harvey, *A Medieval Oxfordshire Village: Cuxham 1240–1400* (1965).

[17] Z. Razi, *Life, Marriage and Death in a Medieval Parish: economy, society and demography in Halesowen, 1270–1400* (Cambridge, 1980).

[18] B. M. S. Campbell, 'The complexity of manorial structure in medieval Norfolk: a case study', *Norfolk Archaeology*, 39 (1986), 225–61.

and tenanted land, spilling over into the territories of neighbouring vills. Where lordship was so fragmented, tenants naturally tended to enjoy greater independence and freedom of action, not least because they were in a stronger position to play one lord off against another. This was a manorial structure that bred tenant individualism.

In the early fourteenth century, lay lords received just over two-thirds of their revenues from whole manors and the remainder from fractions of manors and an assortment of sub- and non-manorial tenements. The greater the lord and his estate, the larger and more valuable the manors he was likely to own. The contrast between great and minor landlords was further compounded by differences in the composition of these manors. It was on the smallest manors, for instance, that demesne revenues bulked largest: demesne lands accounted for over 40 per cent of revenues on manors worth less than £10, compared with approximately 25 per cent of revenues on manors worth £80 or more. Rents and services, in contrast, tended to make their greatest relative contribution on manors of middling size: those worth £10 to £60.

On the whole, it was on the largest manors that seigniorial prerogatives and monopolies – including entry fines, multure (payment for obligatory use of the lord's mill) and tallage (a seigniorial tax) – were most lucrative, for it was on these manors that lords – themselves often of superior social status – were in the strongest position to promote and exploit their rights. Almost a fifth of the value of large manors worth £80 or more in total came from this source. Other valuable rights, among them knights' fees (military sub-tenancies in the gift of a lord) and advowsons (the right to appoint the incumbent of a church), were similarly most significant on these manors, lending their lords additional prestige and patronage. Conversely, lords of the smallest and least valuable manors possessed far more limited juridical powers and hence profited much less from these rights and privileges. They also received relatively less from rents. Instead, it was their demesnes that supplied them with the single most important source of revenue, notwithstanding that these were poorly supplied with customary tenants obliged to pay part of their rent as labour services.

Demesnes evidently occupied a more prominent and independent position in the economy of small manors than of large. Very likely the bulk of these demesnes were kept and managed in hand by resident lords and worked for the most part with hired rather than servile labour, for by the late thirteenth century the typical tenant on a small gentry estate was a freeman rather than a serf, who paid money rents and owed no labour services. On such estates the lord was an immediate presence. Where a great lord like Roger Bigod, earl of Norfolk (proud possessor at his death in 1306 of almost a hundred manors scattered through eighteen English counties plus manors, castles and boroughs in Wales and Ireland), can have had little or no personal acquaintance with his tenants, Henry le Cat of Hevingham must have known almost all of his by name, for he personally presided over his manor court, supervised the workers on his demesne, and feasted with them when the harvest was gathered in.

It was on the largest manors that servile rents and services were of the greatest relative and absolute value. Such manors were disproportionately concentrated in the hands of ecclesiastical institutions, and above all were a feature of long-established episcopal and Benedictine estates.[19] These were the manors most likely to be operated with servile labour in the thirteenth century and upon which the conversion of labour services into money rents (a process known as commutation) tended to proceed the most slowly in the fourteenth and fifteenth centuries. The fact that they belonged to undying institutions seems to have reinforced this tendency towards continuity and inertia. It is ecclesiastical estates that have left the most copious legacy of manorial records, analysis of which has had a disproportionate impact upon the historiography of the period. Seduced by the quality of these records, historians have tended to stress the lot of servile tenants on large and highly feudalised manors, to the neglect of those (and there were many) whose circumstances and experience were different.

Of the many ecclesiastical manors that have been investigated, none are better documented – or were more exceptional – than those of the bishop of Winchester.[20] By the thirteenth century, his already ancient episcopal estate ranked among the most feudalised in the land. A disproportionate number of the bishop's manors were large, and the most valuable of them – East Meon and Taunton – were on a par with many a good-sized barony. Most of the manors were coterminous with a vill, and on most a majority of the tenants were personally unfree and held customary holdings by villein tenure. On such manors, there could be no escaping the bishop's authority. His villein tenants were legally tied to the land, could not dispose of their holdings as they pleased, and were denied

[19] E. A. Kosminsky, *Studies in the Agrarian History of England in the Thirteenth Century*, ed. R. H. Hilton, trans. R. Kisch (Oxford, 1956), pp. 103–16.
[20] B. M. S. Campbell, 'A unique estate and a unique source: the Winchester Pipe Rolls in perspective', in R. H. Britnell, ed., *The Winchester Pipe Rolls and Medieval English Society* (Woodbridge, 2003), pp. 21–43.

access to royal justice. Through his courts, the bishop policed tenant access to customary land and much else besides. Fines levied in his manor courts yielded over £550 in the accounting year 1301–2, equivalent to over 10 per cent of the bishop's gross income; his mills netted him a further £200; and from his tenants the bishop received rents, the monetary element of which accounted for a further 31 per cent of gross cash revenues.[21] In addition, most servile tenants paid substantial rents in kind, notably carrying services plus week-works and boon-works performed as labour services on the bishop's extensive demesnes, which were mostly managed to yield a cash income.

Equally distinctive but very different were the current and alienated manors of the crown, which comprised perhaps one in eight of all manors. These 'ancient-demesne' manors, like the rest of the crown's estate, had come to acquire a privileged legal position during the thirteenth century. Considerable jurisdictional powers had been bestowed upon their manorial courts and, in return for the right to charge tallage (a periodic seigniorial tax) more heavily and impose parliamentary taxes at the maximum rate, the crown had conceded exceptional rights to its tenants. This is clearly exemplified by case studies of the ancient-demesne manors of Havering and Writtle in Essex, and Godmanchester and King's Ripton in Huntingdonshire, which also testify to the wealth of information contained in the court records thus created. When the tax burden was heavy, as in the early fourteenth century, ancient-demesne status could be a disadvantage. At other times, the quasi-free status of the villein tenants – which made it difficult to raise rents and increase labour services – was clearly regarded as beneficial. Thus protected, the tenant population of Havering in Essex grew almost six-fold between 1086 and 1352, with most of that growth occurring before 1251. Havering's tenurial profile of a large number of quasi-free smallholders enjoying secure tenure, owing light labour services and paying low and relatively fixed rents, able to buy, sell, lease or sub-divide their land at will, entitled to employ a royal writ to defend their land, exempt from market toll, and able to come and go as they pleased, is symptomatic of the distinctive character of these ancient-demesne manors.[22] Not surprisingly, tenants on a number of manors attempted to claim ancient-demesne status in order to benefit from such privileges.

---

[21] Calculated from M. Page, ed. and trans., *The Pipe Roll of the Bishopric of Winchester, 1301–2* (Hampshire Record Series, XIV, 1996).

[22] M. K. McIntosh, *Autonomy and Community: the royal manor of Havering, 1200–1500* (Cambridge, 1986).

To whom manors belonged thus mattered a great deal to their tenants. Whether the lord was resident or absentee, an individual or an institution, made a difference. Strong and weak lordship determined the ease with which tenants gained tenure and occupancy of the land and the readiness with which they could exact concessions from their lords and assert custom. Manors thus shaped relations on the land and exercised a powerful institutional influence upon the course of rural development. Nor were they rigid and fixed, for the constant fission and fusion of estates arising from death and marriage, the recurrent turnover of estates between generations and families, and the progressive granting of property to the Church ensured otherwise.

PROPERTY RIGHTS IN LAND

Land was not a chattel. At no point in the middle ages was it owned exclusive of the rights of others. When land changed hands, by conveyance or inheritance, the rights of those with claims upon it had to be respected. Under feudal tenure, all land was ultimately held from the king in return for homage and service. Lay tenants-in-chief of the crown usually held by duty of giving military service and their property was subject to crown rights of wardship and marriage. Even ecclesiastical tenants, who generally held their land free of secular obligations, were expected to provide spiritual services in the form of prayers and charity. Other forms of tenure were sergeanty, whereby land was held in return for non-military service, and socage. The latter was the tenure of the legion of lesser freeholders, who held their lands in return for fixed rents. Those who were personally unfree held by various forms of customary tenure, typically from their lords rather than directly from the crown. Towards the close of the middle ages, as personal servility declined, these customary tenures became liberated from the taint of servitude and transformed into copyhold tenures. Irrespective of tenure and ownership, the Church claimed for itself a tenth of all the fruits of the soil as tithe.

In addition to its feudal rights, the crown claimed specific rights over lands falling within the royal forests – 'forests' here defined not by their vegetation but by the nature of royal jurisdiction within them.[23] Private lords likewise often enjoyed rights of free warren over the lands of others. At a lower social level men might have grazing rights over arable and

---

[23] The royal forests are discussed further below, pp. 199–200.

meadow land otherwise held in severalty; considerable tracts of land were held and managed in common by village communities; and everywhere there were rights of way. So well developed, and so well policed, were many of these rights that they acted as an institutional barrier to fuller economic exploitation of the land. It was not that these land uses failed to yield a range of agricultural products, but rather that rates of productivity were bound to remain low until more effective means of management and exploitation could be put in place. In most cases the latter were contingent upon disafforestation (the dissolution of forest jurisdiction) and enclosure, which first began to have a big impact during the fifteenth century when pressure upon the land was at its lowest. It has recently been estimated that possibly only a third of land still remained subject to common rights by 1500.[24] Seemingly, private and piecemeal enclosure had already made great progress, a good deal of it consequent upon the voluntary or forced desertion of settlement.

These property rights were variously upheld by law and by custom. At a local level, communities of cultivators typically used manorial courts to enact and enforce by-laws relating to common rights and common resources. The same courts dealt with disputes between customary tenants concerning customary land, since these were excluded from the common law, to which, from the late twelfth century, free tenants could take their disputes concerning free land. Over the course of the thirteenth century the royal courts attracted much business by developing cheap and effective legal procedures for resolving the growing number of disputes which arose from the rapidly expanding market in free land. A market in customary land developed more fitfully and unevenly and was mostly handled by manorial courts. The justice and, more particularly, the procedures offered here were, however, increasingly influenced by those offered by the crown. The latter's progressive acceptance of the rights of entail – which allowed the grantor to stipulate how land should descend – meant that the principle also became accepted in manorial courts. At Coltishall in Norfolk, for example, at the court of the manor of Hakeford Hall held on 25 November 1317, Agnes of Holme conveyed $6\frac{1}{2}$ rods of customary land to Robert of Dokingges, her husband to be. Robert was granted tenure 'for himself and the heirs of his body born in matrimony to Agnes', with reversion to Agnes if the marriage was childless.[25]

---

[24] G. Clark and A. Clark, 'Common rights to land in England, 1475–1839', *Journal of Economic History*, 61 (2002), 1027.
[25] King's College Cambridge, E32.

Land held at death could not be bequeathed by will but instead was subject to defined rules of inheritance. For tenants holding directly from the crown strict rules of primogeniture applied. In a stable population sons were likely to inherit in approximately 60 per cent of all cases; in default of sons, the inheritance would pass to daughters (20 per cent) or to lateral relations (20 per cent). In a growing population, such as that of the thirteenth century, the proportion of inheriting sons might approach or exceed 70 per cent; but in a contracting population, such as that of the late fourteenth century, inheritance by daughters and lateral kin tended to exceed inheritance by sons. The biological lottery was such that it was a rare family that sustained direct inheritance in the male line over more than three generations, especially after the Black Death. Property ownership by perpetual institutions was, of course, spared such discontinuities: whereas lay estates were prone to amalgamation and disintegration, conventual and episcopal estates were remarkably stable over time.

Women played an important role in the transmission of landed property. Even during the boom years of demographic growth between 1200 and 1327, when there should have been no shortage of sons, only 61 of the 192 baronies studied by Scott Waugh descended exclusively through males, and in only 36 cases was this in the direct line from father to son.[26] All others passed at some stage through women. Moreover, whereas at this social level male inheritance was invariably impartible, female inheritance was partible. In practice, of course, there was often only one female heir. Nevertheless, there were enough instances of co-heiresses to ensure that there was much sub-division of property. In the case of baronies the largest recorded number of co-heiresses was six. By the early fourteenth century approximately 16 per cent of tenants-in-chief were female; at that point women probably owned about a tenth of all landed property. When inheritance by females increased after the Black Death this proportion increased with it.

Women of the landowning classes also received land upon marriage in the form of a dowry, intended to support them and their children, although after 1300 this marriage portion was increasingly paid in cash. In addition, widows had an automatic right of dower in their husband's lands – which usually amounted to a third of the estate – for the duration of their lives. Serial widows – such as Isolda, the daughter and eventual sole heiress of William Pantolf, who outlived all five of her husbands

[26] S. L. Waugh, *The Lordship of England: royal wardships and marriages in English society and politics 1217–1327* (Princeton, NJ, 1988), p. 19.

between 1180 and 1223 – could accumulate significant amounts of land in this way. Rights of jointure also ensured that widows retained any land previously held in joint tenancy with their husbands. Dower and jointure made these women very eligible, and remarriage of widows was common, until the high male mortality of the later middle ages reduced the supply of eligible men.

Where female inheritance and widowhood were responsible for much fission of property, both temporary and permanent, marriage was more likely to lead to the fusion and growth of estates. A famous instance of this occurred when John of Gaunt's first wife, Blanche of Lancaster, inherited half her father's estate in 1361 and then, on the death of her sister the following year, the remaining half. This made Gaunt the wealthiest subject in the realm. Not surprisingly, both crown and lords were keen to control the marriage and remarriage of heiresses. Following the Statute of Westminster in 1285, those anxious to limit the impact of female inheritance upon the descent of land began to use entail to ensure that land would pass only in the male line, although this was a strategy that could generate major legal disputes, as in the fifteenth-century struggle over the Berkeley inheritance.

At a non-aristocratic level it was the growth and development of the common law during the thirteenth century that pioneered the definition of female property rights in land. If freeholders were the first to avail themselves of these rights, customary tenants soon followed. Nor were women backward in asserting their rights. When, in 1317 at Coltishall, William Snoudoun sold without the consent of his wife Agnes half an acre of customary land held by them in jointure, she sued and received 3s 4d in compensation.[27] Female property rights in land were sometimes at their strongest at this level. Local custom might entitle a widow to more than a third of her husband's land, for instance, and she might inherit it outright rather than just for life. Under the latter circumstance remarriage by widows often led to much lateral transfer of land from one family to another. Inheritance customs in general showed wide local variation. Among the peasantry, male as well as female inheritance could be partible, thereby increasing the frequency of sub-division. Alternatively, sometimes it might be the youngest rather than the eldest son who inherited all (a custom known as Borough English). This was on the assumption that the youngest was most in need of an inheritance because they had had least opportunity to make their own start in life.

---

[27] King's College Cambridge, E32.

In default of heirs, land held in chief from the king escheated to the crown (and land held by tenants reverted to their lords). In this way the crown sometimes made substantial windfall gains, as in 1306 when the aged Roger Bigod, earl of Norfolk, died childless. Where an heir was under age (usually defined as under twenty-one in the case of males, fourteen in the case of females), the crown could exercise rights of wardship: just as widows of tenants-in-chief could not remarry without his consent, so the king had a right to arrange a marriage for the heir. For obvious reasons, rights of wardship and remarriage did not apply to the lands held by the Church. Nevertheless, the crown exploited the superior real property right that it exercised over these lands and claimed the revenues of bishoprics and abbacies when they lay vacant, a claim that might extend to asset-stripping the estate of livestock and timber.

The royal forests were a further significant source of revenue to the crown. At their maximum extent, in the first half of the thirteenth century, they embraced over a quarter of the land of England, including, for instance, the whole of the county of Essex. Hunting was the sport of kings and the royal forests were dedicated to this recreational use. Under forest law, owners were restricted in the use to which the land could be put and penalties were imposed for felling timber, clearing woodland or killing the beasts of the chase. An inherent conflict therefore existed between the king, who was keen to uphold the amenity value of the forests, and private landowners holding property within their bounds, who were more interested in the utility value of these lands. Resentment against the forests was widespread, which is one reason why tales about outlaws who sheltered in the greenwood and poached the king's deer were so popular. Poaching was also rife in private parks, as much for the excitement that it offered as for the illicit source of food and profit that it provided. In the fifteenth century one enterprising Augustinian canon of Blythburgh Priory, Suffolk, offered a 'rent a ferret' service to those who poached rabbits in the local warrens.[28]

Hunting conveyed status and was a recreation to which many aspired. Magnates, in emulation of the crown, maintained their own private forests, usually described as chases. Royal permission was required for their creation, and this tended to be granted only to the greatest magnates. Licence to create smaller parks was more readily obtained but still remained socially selective. Insofar as minor landlords hunted it thus tended to be in the parks and chases of their social superiors. These were

[28] M. Bailey, 'The rabbit and the medieval East Anglian economy', *Ag. Hist. Rev.*, 36 (1988), 17.

securely enclosed, as much to keep the deer and other animals of the chase in as to keep intruders out. Such parks proved to be more enduring than the more extensive hunting grounds of the crown. By 1500, clearance had greatly eroded the extent of woodland within the royal forests and diminished its hunting potential; extensive areas had also been dis-afforested and thus no longer constituted a legal barrier to the advance of the plough and the growth of settlement.

OWNERSHIP OF THE LAND

Throughout the middle ages no more than 20,000 individuals and 1,000 institutions effectively controlled the land of England. As a class, land-owners and their households (including those in religious orders) accounted for no more than 5 per cent of the population. Yet it was this narrow elite who determined tenure, levied rents and exercised lordship over those who occupied and worked the land. Local justice and administration were also their responsibilities. Their courts provided a means of resolving disputes over land and enacting and enforcing agrarian by-laws. Many lords used their influence and superior command of capital to invest in local infrastructure, by building bridges, maintaining ferries, constructing mills, initiating drainage schemes, re-planning set-tlements, establishing markets and fairs, and founding and endowing churches. In effect they performed many of the functions nowadays discharged by local government, planners, the Nature Conservancy Council and the Forestry Commission.

Lords were custodians as well as owners of the land, and those with the most land had the potential to exercise a considerable environmental influence. Through their courts and their officials they stewarded such scarce resources as meadows, pastures and woods, while their forests, chases and parks served as protected reserves of plants and animals. One purpose of their estates was to provide them with revenue (lords were well aware of the utility value of the land), but they also derived political power and status from the acres that they owned and pursued country sports as one of their principal pleasures; so they were acutely conscious that land also had an amenity value. How lords chose to balance the utility and amenity values of the land depended upon their inclination and individual circumstances. Neglect and under-investment typically accompanied minorities, vacancies and forfeiture. Years of careful man-agement could be undone in no time by the asset-stripping of a cash-strapped lord or an unscrupulous executor or escheator. War could be even more devastating. At times during the fourteenth and fifteenth centuries Scottish raids proved a major disincentive to investment in buildings (apart from purely defensive structures) and stock throughout much of the north of England.

Less than a thousand great landlords – comprising the crown, earls and barons, archbishops and bishops, and over 800 religious houses – owned over half the land (See table 7.1). Their estates ranged in scale from 2,500 to 100,000 acres of land, up to a third of which was generally kept in demesne. Some or all of the demesne land was managed directly to supply the lord and the lord's household with provisions and cash; the remainder was leased out. M. M. Postan claimed that during the heyday of direct demesne management in the thirteenth century the greatest estates were managed as 'federated grain factories'.[29] In the less certain economic times of the fourteenth century there was a piecemeal and spasmodic retreat from direct management, gathering momentum as the century drew to a close. By the opening of the fifteenth century most lords had exchanged the role of direct producer for that of rentier, and direct seigniorial involvement in agriculture persisted on demesnes managed only as an immediate source of provisions for their households.

No estate was greater than that belonging to the crown. In 1086, on the evidence of the Domesday survey, the king held land in approximately 1,800 vills, about 14 per cent of the total; but because its manors were above average in size, the crown actually controlled roughly a quarter of the landed wealth of England. By the thirteenth century much of this huge landed endowment had been granted away. Nevertheless, the crown still retained enough land to ensure that its own estate remained the largest and geographically most widely spread, containing perhaps one thirtieth of all the land in the realm (table 7.1). Scale had its disadvantages and the royal lands consistently failed to produce the income that they ought. Even so, at the opening of the fourteenth century the crown's estate probably contributed £13,000 to £14,000 to its annual peacetime revenue of £30,000. In the fifteenth century several aristocratic estates were re-annexed by the crown, although the crown estate's use as a source of patronage meant that its net yield did not increase proportionately.

The next greatest estates in the land in 1300 were those of the earls. The wealth they generated was very considerable. In 1311 one of the greatest, the earldom of Lancaster, yielded a princely £8,700, though the average income of such estates was considerably lower, at under £2,000. Like

---

[29] M. M. Postan, 'Revisions in economic history: IX. The fifteenth century', *EcHR*, 9 (1939), 162.

Table 7.1. Estimated English seigniorial landed incomes in the early fourteenth century

Social group:	Estimated number of households	Mean annual landed income per household to nearest £1	Total landed income to nearest £50	% of total landed incomes	Approximate % of land owned
LAY LANDLORDS:				**41.0**	**51**
Crown:	1	£13,500	£13,500	2.5	3
Nobility: Earls	13	£1,600	£20,800	3.8	5
Barons	114	£260	£29,650	5.4	7
Women	22	£255	£5,600	1.0	1
Gentry: Knights	925	£40	£37,000	6.8	9
Lesser gentry	8,500	£12	£102,000	18.7	23
Women	1,675	£9	£15,100	2.8	3
ECCLESIASTICAL LANDLORDS:				**59.0**	**49**
Greater clergy: Archbishops and bishops	17	£1,590	£27,000	4.9	6
Religious houses	826	£194	£160,000	29.3	37
Lesser clergy: Beneficed clergy	8,500	*£16	*£136,000	24.9	6
ALL LANDLORDS:	**20,593**	**£27**	**£546,650**	**100.0**	**100**
GREATER LANDLORDS:	**993**	**£258**	**£256,550**	**46.9**	**59**
Crown:	1	£13,500	£13,500	2.5	3
Nobility:	149	£376	£56,050	10.3	13
Greater clergy:	843	£222	£187,000	34.2	43
MINOR LANDLORDS:	**19,600**	**£15**	**£290,100**	**53.1**	**41**
Gentry:	11,100	£14	£154,100	28.2	35
Lesser clergy:	8,500	£16	£136,000	24.9	6
ALL LANDLORDS:	**20,593**	**£27**	**£546,650**	**100.0**	**100**

*Approximately one fifth from the glebe, the rest from tithes.

Sources: N. J. Mayhew, 'Modelling medieval monetisation', in R. H. Britnell and B. M. S. Campbell, eds., A Commercialising Economy: England 1086 to c.1300 (Manchester, 1995), pp. 55–77; B. M. S. Campbell and K. Bartley, England on the Eve of the Black Death: an atlas of lay lordship, land and wealth, 1300–49 (Manchester, 2006). Data on the beneficed clergy are taken from: M. R. Livingstone, 'The Nonae: the records of the Taxation of the Ninth in England 1340–41' (Ph.D. thesis, Queen's University of Belfast, 2003), pp. 250–1 (I am grateful to Marilyn Livingstone for permission to cite these figures).

those of the crown, these estates were usually widely dispersed. At the end of the thirteenth century the earldom of Cornwall comprised forty-six manors, which for administrative purposes were divided into nine groups, each under its own steward. At his death in 1315 Guy de Beauchamp, earl of Warwick, held an estate of at least 50,000 arable acres divided between a hundred different manors. Although the earldoms are among the most conspicuous of medieval estates, collectively they probably comprised only about a twentieth of the land of England. In aggregate the smaller but far more numerous estates of the barons were much more important. The greatest barons rivalled all but the richest earls in their landed wealth. Henry Percy died possessed of an estate worth at least £2,276 in 1314; Giles, the 'rich', Lord Badlesmere had landed property worth over £1,489 in 1338. Lesser barons included men like Henry de Bodrigan, whose clutch of Cornish manors together with one out-lier in Bedfordshire were valued at £113 in 1309. Between them the earls and barons, who comprised the lay nobility, owned and controlled roughly an eighth of all the land.

For every acre owned by the lay nobility there were probably at least three owned by the greater clergy. Episcopal and conventual landlords between them owned well over a third of the land in England. Their estates had an enduring integrity that was often ancient in origin: hence the force of tradition and custom tended to weigh heavily upon both the managers and the managed. The bishop of Winchester drew an annual net income of approximately £2,000 to £3,000 from an estate of almost sixty manors spread across seven counties in southern England whose origin largely derived from the generosity of its early benefactors, the Anglo-Saxon kings of Wessex. With its arable, meadows, pastures, woods and hunting grounds, this, the greatest of the episcopal estates, must have comprised little short of 100,000 acres and thereby rivalled in its territorial extent the wealthiest of the earldoms. Only in geographical terms did these great episcopal estates differ significantly from their lay counterparts, for they tended to be concentrated in the region where the bishop himself held ecclesiastical jurisdiction. Together, the two archbishops and fifteen bishops owned approximately a sixteenth of all the land.

The 800-plus religious houses owned six times as much. Their massive stake in the land, terminated by the dissolution of the monasteries in the 1530s, is one of the most distinctive features of landownership in this period. If episcopal estates were the ecclesiastical counterparts of the earldoms, the monasteries were the counterparts of the barons. Their constitution ensured the stability of their estates, and continuing lay benefactions meant that they tended gradually to accumulate property – to such an extent, indeed, that in 1279 Edward I enacted the Statute of Mortmain in order to control the continued one-way transfer of land to the Church. The greatest and most ancient of the monastic estates were those belonging to the Benedictines. In the 1330s Glastonbury Abbey, the wealthiest Benedictine monastery in England, had just under forty demesne manors. It is estates such as these that have bequeathed the most complete and detailed archives. Much less is known about the estates of younger and poorer monastic foundations, of which there were a great many. Their property portfolios were generally much more miscellaneous and rarely contained many plum manors. This was especially true of Cistercian estates, many of which had been built up later from grants of relatively poor and marginal land reclaimed through the enterprise of the monastic communities themselves.

Histories of the land are often told solely from the perspective of the great, high-profile estates and of those who lived and worked on them, notwithstanding the fact that 40 per cent or more of the land was owned by the 20,000 minor landlords – knights, the lesser gentry and the beneficed clergy. Certainly, the combined landed income – if not the amount of land owned – of these minor landlords matched, and very probably exceeded, that of the greater landlords. It was to help small landowners extract, honourably and honestly, the greatest profit from their estates that Walter of Henley had written his *Husbandry* some time in the 1270s or 1280s. Among landlords they were the most directly involved in managing the land (and many of them deployed their expertise as stewards on the estates of their social superiors), yet how and to what ends they managed their own estates awaits systematic historical enquiry, especially in the period before the Black Death.

Knights ranked as the topmost tier of the gentry. Around 1300 there are reckoned to have been approximately 1,100–1,500 knights. Collectively, they owned approximately one twelfth of the land. The largest knightly estates were those held directly from the crown: these had an average value of £40 in the first half of the fourteenth century. Smaller and less valuable were the innumerable knights' fees, which the greater landlords had created by subinfeudation in return for military service. Men holding significant knightly estates in chief might rightly be confused with barons. For instance, Thomas de Audley (d.1308), Matthew FitzJohn (d.1309) and Robert de Wylughby (d.1317) all enjoyed landed revenues in excess of £250 and wanted only a royal summons to attend parliament in their own right to qualify formally as barons. By contrast, over half of knightly estates held in chief were worth less than £25, and many of them comprised only one manor.

Members of the lesser gentry, of whom there are likely to have been at least 10,000, almost by definition held one small manor or less. This class is very difficult to define until its membership began to be specified during the fifteenth century.[30] At the start of the fourteenth century individuals corresponding in status to the later esquires and gentlemen probably enjoyed annual incomes of about £12. What they lacked in individual wealth they made up in numbers: collectively they controlled more land than the crown, earls, and barons combined. They held this land primarily as mesne-tenants (i.e. middle tenants) rather than as tenants-in-chief, sometimes of several lords. In 1279 Henry le Cat of Hevingham held land from John le Marshal, the earl of Gloucester, the bishop of Norwich and the prior of Gislingham. A manorial account of 1287–8 for the sub-manor of Cats shows Henry holding his own modest manorial court and personally supervising the cultivation of a demesne comprising 122 sown acres.[31] A century later Henry's descendants would assume the title 'esquire'.

Clerics, unlike Henry le Cat, had no heirs to consider. A parson's glebe lands and his tithes were intended to provide for him during his lifetime so that he could discharge his parochial duties. On the evidence derived from the royal tax of a ninth in 1340–1, the average glebe contained about 100 acres of land of all sorts, of which roughly three-quarters was held in demesne. The provision for some parsons was, however, far more generous. At Carisbrooke on the Isle of Wight, the glebe comprised approximately 600 acres of land together with a dovecote and mill and yielded an income reckoned at £23 16s 0d in 1340–1; in addition, the rector received rents and services worth £15 and tithes valued at £16 5s 0d, providing him with a total revenue of over £55.[32] The rector of Carisbrooke was unusual, insofar as most parsons received far more from their tithes than their glebe lands. Indeed, being able to count upon such a reliable source of net income lent parsons considerable financial and economic clout. As recipients of more grain than their mostly modest bachelor households could ever require, many became important suppliers of grain to the market. Additionally, perhaps a sixteenth of all the land was in the hands of parsons – including institutions such as colleges and monasteries, to whom rectories, with their assets, might be

---

[30] See pp. 65–6. [31] Campbell, 'Complexity of manorial structure'.
[32] PRO, E 179/173/11. I am grateful to Marilyn Livingstone for this example and reference.

granted.[33] When combined with the far more extensive land holdings of the greater clergy, this meant that ecclesiastical landlords of one sort or another owned almost half the land of England. Small wonder that lay landlords grew increasingly critical and covetous of the great landed wealth of the Church or that in 1381 the rebellious peasants reportedly demanded the redistribution of Church land among the commons.

TENANTS AND OCCUPIERS OF THE LAND

Members of the landowning class did not themselves cultivate the land. Their demesnes were worked by a combination of hired and servile labour, even if supervised on most small estates by the landowners themselves. The sole major exceptions were the Cistercians, who claimed to live by their own labour and whose granges were staffed by lay brothers (until recruitment of lay brothers failed in the altered demographic and moral climate of the fourteenth century). Yet even in the heyday of direct demesne management in the thirteenth century, rents were the largest single component of the income of the majority of landowners. Probably at least two-thirds of all the land was occupied by tenants of one sort or another. The Domesday survey records almost a quarter of a million such tenants in 1086, but the real figure may well have been higher for tenants, mostly free, who paid money rents appear to have been under-recorded. Two hundred years later, after much economic change and growth, the tenant population had grown to two-thirds of a million or even three-quarters of a million. Thereafter, as a result of population decline, the number of tenancies contracted once more, until by 1500 there may have been fewer than in 1086.

Prior to the Black Death, the proliferation of tenancies had been achieved by a combination of colonisation and sub-division. This meant that, although holdings expanded in number, on average they shrank in size. The manor of the prior of Norwich at Martham in east Norfolk affords a dramatic example. Here the opportunities for bringing more land into cultivation were decidedly limited. Nevertheless, the number of tenancies increased from 107 at some point in the late twelfth century to 376 in 1292, with the result that the mean amount of land per tenant declined from ten acres to less than three acres. Whether this was all the land these tenants held is a moot point, for many may well have held additional land in the neighbourhood from other lords; what is clear is

---

[33] In these cases the rector's duties were usually performed by a salaried vicar.

that the proliferation of tenancies on this manor was taken to an extreme rarely matched elsewhere.[34] By 1279, within that slice of midland England covered by the extant Hundred Rolls, the mean size of 21,436 holdings was fifteen acres.[35] This was probably above the national average, which by 1315 was approximately ten acres of arable.

After the Black Death, the opposite trends prevailed. The number of smallholdings shrank dramatically and the most successful and acquisitive tenants seized the opportunity to build up very substantial holdings. The size range of holdings thereby widened, yet this was no return to the holding structure of the twelfth century, for there was no precedent for the new elite of substantial tenants who gradually emerged. Thus, at Martham by 1497 not only had mean holding size quadrupled, but half of all the land was now held by less than a fifth of all the tenants. Thereafter these larger tenancies would continue to grow at the expense of the small – a process known as engrossing. This was less a product of landlord initiative than of the enterprise of the tenants themselves. The process was driven by the fortuitous accumulation of land by inheritance, the strategic annexation of land by marriage, and the systematic acquisition of land by purchase. It proceeded unevenly, for the initial social distribution of land varied a great deal from place to place, inheritance practices differed, and the land market was as yet imperfectly developed and subject to local variation. At Chippenham (Camb.) the 143 tenants recorded in 1279 had been replaced by forty-five tenants in 1544, eleven of whom held more than fifty acres and one of whom held more than a hundred acres.[36] The emergence of these incipient yeoman holdings was a widespread phenomenon and one whose momentum would be maintained, notwithstanding the renewal of population growth in the sixteenth century.[37]

Lords, who had once resisted the concentration of land into fewer hands for fear that this would diminish their revenues, were now prepared to countenance it. If lords adopted too hard a line they could lose scarce tenants to other, more indulgent, lords. Demographic change had empowered tenants relative to their lords, whose own political and

[34] B. M. S. Campbell, 'Population change and the genesis of commonfields on a Norfolk manor', *EcHR*, 2nd ser. 33 (1980), 174–192; B. Cornford, *Medieval Flegg. Two Norfolk hundreds in the middle ages: East and West Flegg, 1086–1500* (Dereham, 2002), p. 87.

[35] J. Kanzaka, 'Villein rents in thirteenth-century England: an analysis of the Hundred Rolls of 1279–80', *EcHR*, 2nd ser. 55 (2002), 593–618.

[36] M. Spufford, *A Cambridgeshire Community: Chippenham from settlement to enclosure*, Department of English Local History Occasional Papers XX (Leicester, 1965).

[37] See also above, pp. 67–71.

judicial muscle had been enfeebled by the rise of royal justice. Some lords, like the prior of Bicester at Wretchwick (Oxon) and William Cope at Wormleighton (War.), seized the initiative, dispossessed their few remaining customary tenants, and created large sheep and cattle ranches on land now permanently laid down to grass; others systematically converted freehold and copyhold tenements to leasehold over which they had more control. This was the seigniorial route to agrarian capitalism. The alternative peasant route involved the creation of substantial, consolidated, tenant farms from processes largely internal to peasant society. Sometimes communities of middling peasants emerged. Alternatively, the engrossment of land by a few was accompanied by the growing landlessness of the many. The latter created a legacy of poor cottagers and commoners – a quasi-proletariat – who laboured for a living and whose ranks in the sixteenth century were further swollen by the resumption of population growth.

Prior to the emergence of agrarian capitalism it is customary to describe the tenantry of medieval England as 'peasants'. This can be misleading. The most substantial of them had considerable wealth and occupied positions of trust and responsibility within rural society. It was a villein tenant, after all, who as reeve was charged with supervision of the day-to-day running of the demesne, including the purchase of replacement stock and sale of produce. Tenants both hired labour and sold it. They also engaged in a range of by-employments and craft activities. Given the limited size of their land holdings, self-sufficiency was rarely an option. Many key agricultural inputs – tools, implements, horseshoes, replacement working animals – were more conveniently purchased than produced on the farm. Textiles, pottery and buildings were also better bought from specialist producers. Buying and selling further helped to make good shortages, dispose of surpluses, and acquire the cash required to pay rents, fines, taxes and a range of other dues. All therefore participated in the market. Few may have done so to pursue profits per se but tenants certainly were well aware of their own self-interest and were active in their pursuit of it.

Those with limited amounts of land from which to support their families adopted strategies aimed at minimising risk. Typically, they were mindful of the superior authority of their lords and sensible of the legal and financial restrictions by which they were bound. This was one of the defining features of the medieval English 'peasantry', together with the predominantly small scale of peasant production and commercial transactions. For instance, those who could (for this depended upon seigniorial policy and local custom) bought and sold land; but until the fifteenth century the individual amounts involved were often tiny – typically a single strip, plot or parcel in the open fields. This active buying and selling of land demonstrates that there was no indissoluble emotional bond between a family and its land. Instead, the strategic acquisition and disposal of land was part of the complex strategy by which, in an age that lacked institutionalised welfare provision, individuals maintained themselves and their families through good times and bad. It was also a means of circumventing the rigid rules of customary inheritance.

Tenants may have been legally subordinate to their lords and restricted in their actions by their limited economic resources, but it should not be imagined that they were either mute or passive. They asserted custom in order to protect their interests and did so to considerable effect. When economic opportunities offered, they were well able to seize and exploit them. Indeed, they displayed an ability 'to adapt and develop, even in the face of harsh financial and legal restraints'.[38] The more prosperous among them were probably the most active agricultural innovators in the English countryside. Peasants rather than lords led the substitution of horses for oxen, and it was peasants rather than lords who produced most of the wool for export. The values and attitudes that shaped their social and economic behaviour varied a great deal from place to place, changed over time, and as yet are imperfectly understood.

There were obvious differences between closely regulated common-field villages, where much hinged upon maintaining the status quo, and those areas which allowed greater scope to individual initiative. Order, hierarchy and neighbourliness were associated with nucleated villages rather than dispersed hamlets and farms. Seigniorial influence was potentially tighter and stronger where manor and vill were coterminous than in multi-manorial vills of fragmented lordship. Closed, stable communities and open and expanding communities engendered contrasting mentalities. Whether tenants and tenures were free or unfree counted for a great deal. Those in regular contact with large towns and cities were obviously exposed to influences from which those at a distance were sheltered. Factors such as these help explain why active involvement in the Great Revolt of 1381 was so selective; why in the fifteenth century religious dissent took firm and vigorous root in only a few radical localities; and why in 1536 the Pilgrimage of Grace remained largely

---

[38] J. Whittle, 'Individualism and the family-land bond: a reassessment of land transfer patterns among the English peasantry c.1270–1580', *P&P*, 160 (1998), 63.

confined to the socially and religiously conservative north. Irrespective of whether they engaged in popular protest or private dissent, those who occupied and worked the land were always a force to be reckoned with and socially and economically were anything but homogeneous.

[Of the many distinctions of status and wealth by which tenants were differentiated the legal distinction between whether they were free or unfree was the most fundamental. If free they were entitled to the protection and justice of the royal courts; if unfree they were subject to the sole jurisdiction and justice of their lords. It was in reaction to this institutionalised discrimination that in 1381 the rebellious population demanded that 'there should be no more villeins in England, and no serfdom nor villeinage but that all men should be free and of one condition'.[39] The distinction drawn between serfdom and villeinage was a distinction between the personal status of being unfree (serfdom) and the tenure of unfree land (villeinage). By 1381 there were those who were free by blood (the majority), servile by blood (a large but dwindling minority), and those who regardless of whether they were free or servile held former villein land by various forms of customary tenure. As serfdom decayed, so customary tenure was transformed into copyhold tenure, the land in both cases being held at the will of the lord (rather than outright) and subject to the custom of the manor, with proof of title being recorded in the relevant manorial court roll.]

Although serfdom gave legal sanction to the subordination and exploitation of serfs by their lords, it was rarely as punitive in practice as it was in the common law of villeinage as elaborated by thirteenth-century jurists. Prudent lords recognised that they benefited from a prosperous and co-operative tenantry and hence did not object to their serfs owning goods and money. Provided that lords were paid an appropriate entry fine when a tenant took up a holding and a heriot when a tenant died and relinquished the holding, serfs enjoyed property rights in the holdings for which they paid rent. Insofar as they could not be evicted arbitrarily, serfs enjoyed considerable security of tenure. Lords valued serfs as a source of rent and labour and were therefore anxious to retain them. Indeed, strictly, a serf needed the permission of their lord in order to leave the manor. Serfs may have been liable to a wide range of rents, fines, dues and obligations – some of them personally demeaning – but these were more or less fixed by custom and were not easily renegotiated by lords. Nor, even in the thirteenth century, was the lot of the serf immutable.

---

[39] R. B. Dobson, ed., *The Peasants' Revolt of 1381* (2nd edn, 1983), p. 165.

Increasing numbers of lords allowed serfs to buy, sell and mortgage land provided that transfers were reported to the manor court and a licence fee or fine paid.

Seigniorial policy towards manorial tenants varied a good deal between estates. Much, of course, depended upon whether lords saw their serfs as assets to be stripped or as a human resource to be motivated and maintained. Serfs were always vulnerable to the risk that a change of lord could lead to the imposition of a harsher policy, and in material matters the law discriminated against them. For instance, at the Norwich assizes held in January 1313, Henry Carbonel of Rockland and Robert his son were acquitted of robbing John and Emma Kynernol of goods and cash to the value of 12s 6d because John was a serf of Henry and the goods were therefore deemed to be Henry's property. They had been confiscated because John Kynernol did not want to accept the jurisdiction and customary service that he owed to Henry Carbonel as his villein.[40] In this case insubordination by a villein precipitated retaliatory action by the lord. Such actions were not uncommon and clearly indicate that by the fourteenth century many customary tenants found their servile status irksome, restrictive and humiliating. Nevertheless, the tenant poverty that was such an increasing problem at this time tended to be more a product of deteriorating socio-economic circumstances than of inferior legal status per se.

In 1086, on the evidence of the Domesday survey and even allowing for the under-recording of free tenants, the vast majority of tenants were unfree. The new breed of rapacious Norman landlords were keen to extract as much as they could from estates won by conquest and were uninhibited by any established or cultural bond with the occupying tenantry. Yet, relative to its agricultural potential, England in the eleventh and early twelfth centuries was under-populated. Resort to extra-economic coercion consequently represented the surest way to recruit a labour force and extract more in rent than the land would have been worth if rents had been freely negotiable (i.e. a 'feudal' rather than market rent).[41] Resisting such impositions was difficult, for the new Norman lords were as yet unchecked by royal justice, were scant respecters of

---

[40] B. Hanawalt, ed., *Crime in East Anglia in the Fourteenth Century: Norfolk gaol delivery rolls, 1307–1316* (Norfolk Record Society, XLIV, 1976), p. 59.

[41] Those rents charged at more than the current market value of the land are known as 'feudal' rents, since exacting their payment depended upon a degree of coercion. Rents determined by market competition are known as 'rack' rents. 'Customary' rents are those that were traditionally paid and typically bore little relationship to the market value of the land.

custom, and had little compunction about resort to physical force. As a result, England's new Norman lords were probably more ruthless and successful at extracting rent than any of their successors.

Two centuries later the relative lot of serfs had changed significantly. Lords had put down roots and developed a close association with their estates and tenants. Seigniorial over-exploitation was self-evidently counter-productive. Population growth and commercial development meant that there was less need of coercion to recruit a labour force and extract rent. Property rights and the law were both more clearly elaborated and far greater use was being made of written records to define rents, rights and obligations. Custom had crystallised and become a force to be reckoned with. As a result most servile tenants now paid less than a feudal rent, and less even than a rack rent. There were still plenty of textbook examples of manors dominated by villein tenure and operated by serf labour. Many of the bishop of Winchester's manors were of this type. Villein tenants worked on the bishop's demesnes as ploughmen, labourers, harvesters, carters, cowherds, shepherds, swineherds and smiths, and filled the offices of reeve, beadle, hayward and park-keeper that were so necessary to the running of his manors. Life on these manors was remarkably well regulated and self-perpetuating but it did not constitute the norm. Manors dominated by free tenures existed in even greater numbers, especially on the estates of lay landlords and above all on those of the gentry. In fact, even when ecclesiastical manors are taken into account, it seems likely that nationally by the opening of the fourteenth century more tenants held by free than by villein tenure and there was marginally more freehold land than customary land.

One of the hallmarks of serfdom was forced labour. No other aspect of the institution has incurred more opprobrium. Consequently, the requirement to perform labour services on the lord's demesne has loomed disproportionately large in accounts of the period. In fact, labour services were neither as widespread nor as onerous as has sometimes been represented, for all that some tenants were undoubtedly burdened with them. Virgators (those with standard villein holdings of thirty acres) on the bishop of Winchester's manor at Downton (Wilts.), for example, were expected to work for 218 days on the bishop's behalf as well as cultivate their own holdings. Only the deployment of family members or farm servants could have met both requirements. In practice, however, many of these works were never claimed. Some were acquitted in lieu of other services rendered, a good many went by default due to sick days and holy days, and substantial numbers were commuted for cash. It has been calculated that on the manors of Ramsey Abbey only a tenth of the labour resources of villein tenants were actually expended in the performance of services upon the demesne.

On many other manors villein rents were paid either largely or entirely in cash. Everywhere north and west of a line from the Humber to the Severn, as well as throughout the greater part of Devon and Cornwall and in most of Kent, money rents were at least twelve times more valuable than labour rents. Nationally, on the manors held by lay tenants-in-chief, money rents were on average seven times more valuable than labour rents by the early fourteenth century, and this takes no account of those services that were commuted for cash. On a clear majority of manors, labour services were not only one of the least common components of rent; when priced at their commuted value they were also often the least valuable. These traits were more pronounced on small manors than on large ones, on lesser estates than on greater, and on estates in lay hands than those in episcopal and Benedictine ownership. For most servile tenants, labour services were more irksome than burdensome and tenant resentment at them was fuelled more by what these services represented than what was demanded. Most manors were so ill-provided with labour services that lords had to rely in the main upon hired labour to operate their demesnes. Even when direct demesne production was at its zenith, lords were more likely to employ than coerce labour. Hired labour probably accounted for over 90 per cent of demesne output. The labour sold to lords by tenants far exceeded that paid to them in rent.

Serfdom and its attributes persisted on the most conservatively run estates until the very end of the middle ages. On a few mighty monastic estates – such as those of the abbeys of Glastonbury and Tavistock in the south-west – a dwindling minority of tenants was still being required to perform labour services in the twilight of direct demesne management at the end of the fifteenth century. The last residual serfs by blood were obliged to purchase their manumission in the reign of Elizabeth I. Such continuity is impressive but exceptional. Within the country as a whole, freehold tenures and free tenants gained steadily on their villein and servile counterparts throughout the thirteenth, fourteenth and fifteenth centuries. Status and tenure were also progressively divorced from one another, allowing the transformation of villein tenure into copyhold tenure. Freed from the stigma of serfdom, copyhold land became much more desirable and free tenants, gentlemen and even townsmen began to acquire it.

Serfdom contracted by a process of attrition, a process that gained considerable momentum from the demographic collapse of the mid fourteenth century. On this occasion, and in the altered circumstances of a more commercialised world, labour scarcity enabled many born unfree to better their status if not their lot by deserting the manors of their birth and emboldened others to face down the demands of their lords. Labour services and other defining tests of servility simply lapsed or were commuted because policing and collecting them ceased to be tenable. Freehold tenures, in contrast, owed their sustained expansion to a more dynamic set of processes. Already in the twelfth century they were multiplying in areas of active colonisation and weak lordship: hence the superior demographic and economic dynamism of the once wooded hundred of Stoneleigh in Warwickshire compared with the more strongly manorialised and anciently settled hundred of Kineton in the same county; hence, too, the transformation of the East Anglian fens from under-populated marshland at the time of Domesday into the area with the densest concentration of relatively highly assessed taxpayers in the country by the early fourteenth century. Even outside these areas, however, the map of England was increasingly sprinkled with small manors dominated by free tenants paying cash rents. These were as characteristic of the age as the great, ecclesiastical, serf-dominated manors about which so much more has been written.

Once tenants became personally free, they could avail themselves of royal justice to resolve disputes over land. They could also come and go as they pleased. Lords continued to hold manorial courts, but the function of those courts was increasingly restricted to the registration of changes in the ownership of copyhold (former customary) land. All of this strengthened the legal position of tenants when they negotiated with their lords the terms upon which they held land. Yet winning their freedom did not necessarily mean that tenants had secured outright ownership of their holdings. The new copyhold tenures were still subject to the superior proprietorial interest of the manorial lord, who would continue to profit from that interest by charging entry fines and ground rents now 'quit' of the obligation to perform labour services. In this way, lords maintained their influence upon the occupancy of land, an influence that would revive and strengthen with the resumption of population growth in the sixteenth century. Taking advantage of the renewed competition for land, many sixteenth-century lords imposed higher entry fines and converted much freehold and copyhold land to leasehold, whose terms of tenure were more easily renegotiated as economic conditions changed.

RURAL LABOURERS AND CRAFT WORKERS

By 1300 well over half of all tenant households lacked enough land to feed themselves 'and those with larger holdings found it convenient to buy their bread, ale, joints of meat, pies and puddings from neighbours or from local markets'.[42] In fact, within the countryside agricultural commodities of just about every description were regularly bought and sold. A well-developed market in labour, without which the rural economy could not have functioned, accompanied this widespread marketing of commodities. Average annual wage rates can be calculated for a range of agricultural tasks throughout the thirteenth, fourteenth and fifteenth centuries and these can be compared with prices for a standard range of agricultural products, thereby establishing the real purchasing power of agricultural wages (figure 7.1). This provides an impartial measure of the changing economic fortunes of wage earners within the rural economy. Life for those who endeavoured to earn part or all of their living in this way was a struggle, but, as the trend in real wages demonstrates, sometimes the struggle was very much harder than at others.

Ascertaining the purchasing power of wages is one thing; identifying those who earned them is another. Wage earners are among the most anonymous members of rural society. Notwithstanding their tangible social and economic presence, they are hard to identify and harder still to count. Manorial accounts record their employment but rarely their names. Nor do manorial court rolls, with the conspicuous exception of the rolls of the Eastertide courts held on the estate of Glastonbury Abbey, shed much light upon them, for it is those landed villagers who dominated manorial life whose careers and families are most readily reconstituted. Poor labourers usually feature only fleetingly and their families too seem to have been short-lived. Typically, those with labour to sell were cottagers, commoners, squatters and sub-tenants and these are the very groups least well represented in extents and surveys. Their poverty in movable goods also means that they are rarely enumerated in contemporary tax lists, which, except in the case of the per caput poll taxes of 1377, 1378, and 1381, and the 1522 Muster Returns of able-bodied males, rarely enumerated those poor in movable goods. Such invisibility

---

[42] C. C. Dyer, *Everyday Life in Medieval England* (1994), p. 285.

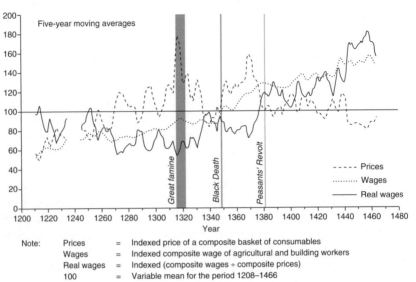

Note: Prices   =   Indexed price of a composite basket of consumables
            Wages   =   Indexed composite wage of agricultural and building workers
            Real wages =   Indexed (composite wages ÷ composite prices)
            100   =   Variable mean for the period 1208–1466

Source: B. M. S. Campbell, *English Seigniorial Agriculture 1250–1450* (Cambridge, 2000), p. 5.

Figure 7.1   Agricultural prices, agricultural wages and real wages in
England, 1208–1466 (five-year moving averages).

is unfortunate, for this is the rural socio-economic group that expanded
most before 1315, most bore the brunt of famine, economic recession
and plague, and contracted most thereafter. Upon their numbers largely
hinges the debate over the size of England's medieval population:
the higher the estimate of population the greater must their numbers
have been.

Vagrants and indigents apart, agricultural labourers were the poorest
members of rural society, and for the greater part of the thirteenth and
early fourteenth centuries their poverty increased. Initially, for the first
half of the thirteenth century, the real value of their wages appears to have
held up reasonably well. This was a period of economic expansion, and
while prosperity lasted the prospects for labourers were good. Commencing with the famine of 1257–8, however, their fortunes took a turn
for the worse. Expansion of the rural economy slowed down and the
supply of labour increased more rapidly than the demand for it. Real
wages fell, and by the mid-1270s would buy only half what they had
bought at the start of the century (figure 7.1). Wage earners either had to
settle for a lower material standard of living or work longer and harder to
maintain their existing standards. As the number of poor families rose,

most had little choice but to accept the first option and thereby increase their consumption of leisure rather than goods. For the next fifty years it was only when harvests were abundant and food prices low, as in the late 1280s and early 1300s, that real wages registered any improvement. Such gains were invariably wiped out as soon as harvests reverted to or sank below normal, as in the mid-1290s and, most traumatically, during the agrarian crisis of 1315–22.

In 1316 prices soared to 150 per cent above, and real wages plummeted to 75 per cent below, their respective long-term averages. This was the worst year for wage earners in the entire middle ages. Their predicament was greatly compounded by the sudden and massive contraction in wage-earning opportunities precipitated by the reduced harvests. Those without work and earnings, and especially those who held little or no land, undoubtedly suffered the highest mortality during these terrible years. Following this dreadful culling of the labouring poor, real wage rates recovered almost to the level of the mid thirteenth century. The substantial reduction in population, the tardiness of any demographic recovery, a chance run of good harvests, and, above all, the onset of price deflation arising from bullion scarcity, all contributed to this improvement in real wages. It did not last. Poor harvests in the mid 1340s brought the return of higher prices and drove real wages down again. The lot of rural wage earners on the eve of the plague was again a deteriorating one.

At least two to three times as many people died during the Black Death as had died during the Great European Famine. The magnitude of the demographic impact is apparent in an unprecedented 45 per cent collapse in prices and 24 per cent rise in cash wages, which, together, briefly sent real wages soaring. Unfortunately for workers, this windfall gain lasted little longer than the plague that had delivered it. Adverse weather and bad harvests in the early 1350s, coupled with the massive per capita increase in currency brought about by the great reduction in population, returned prices to their level at the opening of the fourteenth century. Worse was to follow. In 1369–70 the combination of dearth and plague pushed prices up to levels exceeded only in the grimmest years of the famine. Meanwhile, government curbs upon increases in cash wages – hurriedly imposed in 1349 and confirmed by statute as soon as the immediate crisis had passed in 1351 – proved remarkably effective. Para-doxically, therefore, from 1350 prices again pulled ahead of cash wages, with the result that for two decades after the Black Death real wages remained at or below their immediate pre-plague level.

Wage rates do not, however, tell the whole story. Other aspects of employment certainly improved during this period. Work was easier to get, there was a greater choice of employers, and those who wanted fuller employment undoubtedly enjoyed it. Wage rates may not have improved but actual earnings did. Women, in particular, were drawn into the labour market, to the benefit of household incomes. Some employers infringed the statute and paid illicitly higher wages, usually revealed only when they were prosecuted. In 1350 Roger Swynflete, keeper of the abbot of Selby's manor of Stallingborough, used higher wages with a range of tempting fringe benefits to lure the ploughman John Skit out of the employment of Sir John d'Argentene.[43] Others, ostensibly conforming to the statute, required less work for the same pay. As in the case of John Skit, the non-cash elements of remuneration were also increased and enhanced. Workers expected and increasingly demanded better food and drink. The diet received by harvesters working on the prior of Norwich's demesne at Sedgeford in Norfolk improved significantly at this time, with more meat, fish and ale and less bread and cheese, and continued to improve until the end of the century, as the bargaining power of labour progressively strengthened.[44]

As the supply of labour dwindled, and land holding became an increasingly attractive and available alternative proposition, the Statute of Labourers could not restrain the mounting upward pressure on wages. The plague mortality of 1375 intensified that pressure and the bumper harvest and consequent price collapse of 1376 raised it further, by delivering windfall gains in living standards and thereby raising material expectations. Real wages improved more dramatically during the 1370s than any other decade on record, and for the first time rose significantly above their medieval long-term average. The more the lot of wage earners improved, the more popular discontent with the government's policy of wage restraint and the justices of the peace who enforced it mounted. Dissatisfaction surfaced in the events of May and June 1381, when those who enforced the statute became some of the prime targets of the rebels. Thenceforth attempts to enforce the labour legislation were relaxed, and the way was opened for wages to approximate to their natural market level.

---

[43] R. Horrox, ed., *The Black Death* (Manchester, 1994), p. 319.

[44] C. C. Dyer, 'Changes in diet in the late middle ages: the case of harvest workers', *Ag. Hist. Rev.*, 36 (1988), 21–37.

For the next hundred years, real wages drifted steadily upwards and rural wage earners steadily bettered their lot. No longer was the countryside awash with under-employed, malnourished, impoverished labourers. Instead, employers found recruiting and retaining workers increasingly difficult and costly. Lest workers abscond in the middle of the farming year, more and more employers took advantage of the labour legislation and hired their farm servants on annual contracts. Typically, these servants lived in and, to judge from practice in later centuries, this was a common form of employment for young adults who had yet to acquire property of their own. It was a convenient arrangement for employers, since it guaranteed them a labour force for a full twelve months. Employees gained regular employment and a degree of security but were denied the full advantages of a free labour market. Once contracted, they could not leave their employment without the risk of falling foul of the justices of the peace (themselves usually employers of labour). Even so, for those who could get work – which was not always easy during the middle years of the fifteenth century, when the economy was depressed and demand for labour was slack – this was the golden age of the wage-labourer (figure 7.1). The real wages paid in the 1470s would not be bettered until the 1880s. Moreover, it was the least skilled workers who benefited most. As labour became ever scarcer and lower interest rates made it cheaper to invest in the acquisition of skills, the differential steadily narrowed between the wages of manual workers and those of skilled craftsmen and officials.

Those who worked as wage labourers did not as yet constitute a rural proletariat, in the sense of being wholly dependent upon wage earning for a living. Individuals may have been landless, but households rarely were. Together, land and family were the prerequisites for survival. Those who lived by their labour alone, unsupported by landholding in any form, were as yet a minority. Employment opportunities varied too much from season to season and year to year for wage earning by itself to provide a reliable livelihood. Without at least some land, be it only a cottage and a garden with a cow on the commons, it was difficult for labourers to survive slack seasons and poor years. The principal suppliers of wage labour were therefore young adults from established tenant households and those cottagers and smallholders with labour in excess of their own needs. The truly landless were always liable to succumb to destitution and vagrancy, becoming beggars and thieves rather than workers. Vagrants were the most vulnerable members of rural society and those who were able-bodied were the object of much contemporary social disapproval.

For as long as lords managed their estates directly, the demesne sector was probably the single largest source of paid agricultural employment. The sector as a whole was inadequately supplied with servile labour and, besides, hired labour was better motivated, cheaper to supervise, and often gave superior returns. Accordingly, prudent and progressive lords increasingly commuted labour services and substituted hired workers. Typically, a core of full-time labourers – the *famuli* – was hired by the year. They lived on the demesne, received a large part of their remuneration in kind, and were the forerunners of the 'servants in husbandry' of later centuries. In many respects they were the aristocracy of labour, for they enjoyed considerable security of employment and were relatively well looked after. There were also many small ways in which they could profit at their lord's expense. In 1367 Westminster Abbey's auditors discovered that *famuli* on its demesne at Kinsbourne (Herts.) were getting significantly better yields on those plots set aside for their own use than those reserved to the lord. During peak seasons of the year, such as spring ploughing and lambing, additional hired workers often augmented these permanent *famuli*. Other casual workers might be hired, as required, on a daily or piece-rate basis. The more intensive the husbandry system, the greater was the use made of casual labourers.

Without waged labour, few rectors would have been able to cultivate their glebes, and the same applied to the most substantial tenant producers. Many villeins lacked sufficient family labour to work a yardland of thirty acres and fulfil their labouring obligations on the demesne, and therefore hired workers to make good the shortfall. By 1300, it has been estimated that wage labour may have accounted for about a fifth to a quarter of the total labour expended in producing goods and services within the economy at large (with family labour providing the lion's share of the remainder). This includes the urban sector, so the contribution of wage labour to the rural economy is likely to have been somewhat smaller. Even so, the depressed level of real wages prevailing for almost a hundred years before the Black Death demonstrates that there were more wage earners seeking work than there was employment for them. Rural under-employment was rife and went hand in hand with the sub-division and sub-letting discussed below. When, as a result of commercial recession and bad harvests, the demand for labour actually contracted, those attempting to make a living by combining smallholding with wage earning were particularly hard hit.

Labourers were thus the most conspicuous casualties of the fourteenth-century crisis, but in the longer term demographic collapse opened up new opportunities for them. Many gave up labouring and availed themselves of the opportunity to obtain larger holdings. Most people wanted land if they could obtain it, because of the superior economic security that this provided and the higher status that it bestowed. The shrinkage in the supply of wage earners was therefore greater than the contraction in the total population, which is why there was such strong pressure to pay higher wages. Craft-working also offered an increasingly attractive alternative to agricultural labouring.

Smallholders had long displayed great ingenuity in augmenting inadequate farm incomes in this way. In the thirteenth century, fishing, turf-cutting, salt manufacture, textile production from hemp, flax and wool, and mineral extraction and working were all to be found as part-time occupations in various parts of the country. A few of these rural industries provided employment on a relatively large scale. The manufacture of linen and worsted cloth for domestic and overseas markets bolstered high population densities in north-east Norfolk, and in Cornwall and Devon thousands of tin miners were employed in the stannaries. More widespread were those non-agricultural crafts integral to the rural economy. Occupations listed in the 1381 poll tax returns for the hundred of Tunstead in Norfolk include baker, butcher, carpenter, cooper, draper, dyer, fuller, glover, leatherworker, locksmith, miller, pedlar, plumber, skinner, smith, tailor, thatcher and weaver.[45] Most were practised in combination with small-scale farming. Probably the same applied to many of the clerks who served the growing reliance by all levels of rural society upon written records. Zvi Razi and Richard Smith believe that 'England, certainly between 1250 and 1349, contained a larger proportion of its rural population in possession of practical literary skills than was to be found in any of her European neighbours'.[46]

Non-agricultural employment may have contributed roughly a tenth of rural incomes by 1300. Two centuries later this proportion had probably doubled, as manufacturing fastened more vigorously onto rural labour. In an age of rising wage rates, reduced aggregate demand, and stiffer market competition, rural labour offered advantages of cheapness, freedom from guild restrictions, and relative abundance. For smallholders, industrial

---

[45] PRO, E 179/149/57.
[46] Z. Razi and R. M. Smith, 'The origins of the English manorial court roll as a written record: a puzzle', in Razi and Smith, eds., *Medieval Society and the Manor Court* (Oxford, 1996), p. 67.

earnings and agricultural incomes complemented and subsidised each other. From the late fourteenth century the most prosperous rural economies were typically those that sustained expanding industries for the deepening consumer demand of the times. In particular, the manufacture of cloth for home and overseas markets transformed the rural economies of much of the south-west of England, the Weald of Kent, parts of East Anglia, and the Pennine dales of Lancashire and the West Riding of Yorkshire. At the same time, the area around Birmingham emerged as a major centre of leather and metal-working.

Once proto-industry took root within a locality, expanding industrial employment stimulated new household formation and helped stem the decline of population. In such areas, immigration and higher fertility counteracted the high mortality of the age. Earnings from manufacturing sustained incomes among small-scale producers and boosted the local demand for agricultural produce and industrial raw materials, notably textile fibres, hides and charcoal. Local towns and markets prospered. Around 1540 Leland declared Birmingham to be 'a good market town' and commented, 'A great part of the town is maintained by smiths [who] have their iron out of Staffordshire and Warwickshire and sea coal out of Staffordshire'.[47] Via migration, these proto-industrialising rural econo- mies gained at the expense of those that remained exclusively agricultural. Slowly but surely, a pronounced redistribution of population and wealth was brought about. For those intent upon escaping the shackles of serf- dom, an area of expanding industrial employment free of seigniorial interference, where work with or without a smallholding was easily obtained, provided an attractive destination. From these modest begin- nings in the late middle ages, major branches of manufacturing would in due course develop that would eventually transform both the regional and national economies.

LANDLORD–TENANT AND INTER–TENANT RELATIONS

For the lords who owned it, land bestowed status and power, generated revenues, and provided opportunities for recreation. For the tenants who occupied and worked it, land was primarily the source of their liveli- hoods. They needed it to produce food, raw materials and commodities for sale. It provided security for loans, could be leased as a source of income, and in hard times could be sold to raise cash. Typically, the more

---

[47] Toulmin Smith, *Itinerary of John Leland*, ii, pp. 96–7.

land tenants held the greater the buffer against adversity and the higher their standing in rural society. Yet the right to hold land was contingent upon the payment of rent to landlords. For this reason, Marxist historians have stressed 'the essentially antagonistic nature of lord–peasant relationships'.[48] Outward manifestations of this antagonism are not hard to find. One of the best-documented and most frequently recounted is the protracted dispute between the abbot of Halesowen and his tenants in the thirteenth century, which in 1282 resulted in the deaths of Roger Ketel, one of the ringleaders of the resistance, and Alice Edrich, the pregnant wife of another.[49] The tenants of the abbey of Bury St Edmunds were more successful. In October 1328, after months of disturbance in West Suffolk and the town of Bury, they abducted the abbot: he was carried to London, moved from house to house to escape detection, and then smuggled overseas to Diest in Brabant where he was confined in mean conditions without books until April 1329.[50] Most famous of all is the revolt of 1381. This culminated in the execution by the rebels in London of Simon of Sudbury, archbishop of Canterbury and chancellor of England, and Robert of Hales, prior of the English Hospitallers and royal treasurer, and climaxed in the famous confrontation at Smithfield between the fourteen-year-old Richard II and the rebel army led by Wat Tyler.

The grievances by which these protests were sparked were invariably specific in both time and place. This was true even of the revolt of 1381, which was on a far larger scale than any of the other protest movements; roughly 10,000 insurgents may have assembled on Blackheath outside London on 11 and 12 June 1381 and significant numbers were also active in the other main centres of protest in Cambridgeshire and Norfolk. On this occasion specific grievances coalesced into general demands. As reported by contemporary chroniclers, the rebels wanted freedom from the legal restrictions of serfdom, freedom from arbitrary lordship, freedom from what they regarded as high and unjust rents, and an end to the labour laws. In short, the rebels wanted to retain for themselves the fruits of their own labours and have the liberty to enjoy them. More radically, they wanted a general redistribution of the extensive landed property of the Church and

---

[48] R. H. Hilton, *Bond Men Made Free: medieval peasant movements and the English rising of 1381* (1971), p. 234.
[49] Z. Razi, 'The struggles between the abbots of Halesowen and their tenants in the thirteenth and fourteenth centuries', in T. H. Aston et al., eds., *Social Relations and Ideas: essays in honour of R. H. Hilton* (Cambridge, 1983), pp. 151–68.
[50] H. E. Hallam, 'The life of the people', in H. E. Hallam, ed., *The Agrarian History of England and Wales*, II: *1042–1350* (Cambridge, 1988), p. 851.

powers of lordship to be vested in the king alone. Significantly, eviction was not as yet a bone of contention, for lords remained proprietorial about their tenants, and consolidation, clearance and enclosure lay in the future. Not until the sixteenth century did grievances against enclosure and the extinction of common rights erupt into popular protest, notably in Kett's Rebellion of 1549.

The protracted disputes between the abbeys of Halesowen and Bury St Edmunds and their tenants and the briefer but more dangerous 'national' revolt of 1381 were no isolated acts of protest. They sprang from the tensions and frictions to which all rural societies are prone. These were stoked by the build-up of population pressure on the land during the hundred years or so before the Black Death and then further heightened by the expectations aroused by the dramatic release of that pressure as a result of the plagues of 1348–9, 1361–2, 1369 and 1375. This biological culling of the population ought to have brought windfall gains to those who survived. Yet these rarely materialised as fast or as fully as wished. The sudden labour shortage encouraged the more reactionary lords to clamp down on their serfs in order to preserve their supplies of servile labour and maintain their incomes from the rights of lordship. To keep down the cost of labour, a government of landowners adopted and pursued a statutory policy of wage restraint. To compound matters, although land values fell, landlords did their best to ensure that customary rents remained at their established level. For the first time since the twelfth century, increasing numbers of villein tenants found themselves paying rents that approached or even exceeded the current competitive market rent. Hence the demand of the rebels in 1381 that rents should be set at a maximum of four pence an acre. Meanwhile, tenants of ancient freeholds continued to pay a low fixed rent, typically half that paid by their villein neighbours, and such wide discrepancies naturally fuelled a powerful sense of injustice.

This was especially true among those substantial villein tenants who occupied positions of influence within rural society. These were the men who discharged the key manorial offices, acted as jurors and principal pledges in the manor courts, and served as heads of tithings at the view of frankpledge. In maintaining the manorial status quo they served their own interests as well as those of their lords. In changing times, it was their strong vested interest in the manors of their birth that inhibited them from selling up and migrating to seek land and work on better terms. Accordingly, they were the very tenants who presented lords with the easiest target for extracting payments. Knowing that they could take most liberties with these tenants, lords such as the abbot of Bury St Edmunds refused to abolish labour services and hit their villeins with high entry fines and heriots.[51] Tenants responded by seeking tenurial reform, and, when this was not forthcoming, cast prudence aside and became actively involved in the revolt of 1381. They, no doubt, were the brains behind the systematic destruction of manor court rolls, the documents that bore explicit testimony to their servility. In this they were joined by far greater numbers of labourers and craft workers, whose equally powerful frustrations stemmed from the constraint placed upon a free market in labour by the Statute of Labourers. This was why such resentment was vented by the rebels against the persons and properties of those members of the gentry who, as justices of the peace, tried cases of trespass against the statute. Behind the violent events of May and June 1381 lay expectations thwarted by serfdom, intransigent lords, restrictive labour legislation, and a government and judiciary that were on the side of landowners.

Yet over the entire period from 1200 to 1500, what is most striking about landlord–tenant relations is the rarity with which resentment ignited into violence. Many manors, estates and parts of the country appear to have been entirely untroubled by either popular protest or open confrontation. This does not mean that tenants were entirely contented with their lot, rather that they used non-violent means to express their dissatisfaction. Landlords' rights may have been backed up by the law, and in the last resort by force, but tenants, including servile tenants holding by villein tenure, were far from powerless in the defence and assertion of their own rights. Custom was on their side and even the law upheld the immutability of the assize rents paid by most free and many unfree tenants. Tenants also had the advantage of numbers and the knowledge that it was upon their work and co-operation that landlords ultimately depended in order to operate their demesnes and manors.

This had always been the case, but the leverage they could achieve by passive withdrawal of co-operation or outright obstruction became even more marked after the demographic collapse of the mid fourteenth century. Labour services could be grudgingly and poorly performed, payment of rents and fines withheld, suit of mill and court evaded, demesne produce embezzled, and parks and warrens poached. Lords could, of course, retaliate; but this, at a time of increasing tenant scarcity, could prove counter-productive by driving tenants away and inviting further insubordination. Nor did closer supervision necessarily provide an answer to the problem. Following the Black Death manorial officials proved hard to

---

[51] I am indebted to Mark Bailey for these points.

recruit, dilatory in the discharge of their duties, and fraudulent in their dealings. When Robert Oldman – who for thirty-eight years had served Merton College, Oxford, loyally and dependably as reeve of its manor of Cuxham in Oxfordshire – succumbed to plague in March 1349, he proved irreplaceable. Over the next ten years, none of the seven individuals, including Robert's son John, who took on the job either survived the plague or proved equal to the task. Eventually, in 1359, the college abandoned direct management and leased out the demesne.[52] To a landed audience familiar with the problem of recruiting trustworthy manorial officials, Oswald, Chaucer's cunning and self-serving reeve of Bawdeswell in Norfolk, would have been instantly recognisable.[53] By the time that Chaucer was writing, tenants were not only refusing to assume onerous manorial offices; they were also refusing to take up vacant holdings except on their own terms. Thereafter, for landlords, the situation went from bad to worse. By the 1430s, tenants on the estate of the bishop of Worcester were refusing payment of a whole range of fines and dues and repudiating their servility. The bishop and his officials had little option but to acquiesce.[54]

In the long run, co-operation was cheaper for lords than coercion, especially for those with limited jurisdictional powers. Tenants – always inclined towards caution – likewise found co-operation involved less wear and tear than resistance. Lords, after all, were always a force to be reckoned with and were not to be crossed with impunity. Nor was fleeing the manor for better opportunities elsewhere entirely cost-free. For tenants who had made substantial investments in their holdings, it was an option of last resort. Mutual co-operation consequently offered advantages to both landlords and tenants. Prudent landlords therefore worked with, rather than against, their tenants. By pursuing such a policy successive abbots of Ramsey Abbey largely avoided the strife and indignities meted out to their brother abbots of Halesowen and Bury. The same was true of other categories of landlord, and especially those gentry landlords who could ill afford to alienate their tenants, for they lived among them. The latter's identification with their tenants is exemplified by the active participation of several members of the gentry in the revolt of 1381, of which great landlords and especially ecclesiastical landlords were the most conspicuous targets.

[52] Harvey, *Medieval Oxfordshire Village*, pp. 63–74.
[53] Riverside edition, the General Prologue, lines 587–620.
[54] C. C. Dyer, *Lords and Peasants in a Changing Society: the estates of the bishopric of Worcester, 650–1540* (Cambridge, 1980), pp. 264–82.

It is also important to remember that tensions between tenants could be stronger than tensions between tenants and lords, especially when livelihoods were straitened and competition for resources intense. Court rolls demonstrate that quarrels and fights were a feature of manorial life. Disputes between tenants over land could become particularly bitter and heated. Thus, in 1312, Robert le Parker of Starston in Norfolk threatened his brother Thomas with a knife and tried to persuade him to give up a piece of land left him by their father; Thomas retaliated by grabbing a cart shaft and killing Robert, subsequently claiming that he did so in self-defence.[55] Pieces of land were worth a good deal in Norfolk's congested countryside at this time, and inter-tenant competition for them could be intense. Although symptomatic of the problems prevailing at the time, such disputes are generally passed over with less comment than those between tenants and landlords over tenure and status, since they are not deemed to have been a source of structural social change.

Without a succession of massive climatically and biologically induced shocks it is, nevertheless, improbable that structural change would have occurred when and on the scale that it did. Between 1315 and 1353 landlords and tenants were hit by failures of crops and mortalities of cattle, sheep, and, eventually, humans, of a magnitude and with a frequency that were outside their experience, beyond their comprehension, and in excess of the capacity of any pre-industrial socio-economic system to withstand. Conditions were further exacerbated by a marked escalation of warfare and the mounting costs of waging it, especially following the military victory of the Scots in 1314 and the outbreak of war with France in 1337. In the midst of hard and uncertain times, taxes on movable goods and the forced purveyance of provisions for the army struck at the very commercial activities and credit relations upon which so many had become dependent for their economic survival. 'A market economy and a subsistence level of production – this could be a most unfortunate combination, and those who lived with it lived dangerously'.[56] Creditors squeezed by both harvest failure and tax demands found themselves obliged to foreclose on debtors. This triggered surges of sales of pathetically small pieces of land by those liquidising portions of their assets in order to pay off debts. Desperation also drove many of the poorest to sell off land in order to buy food, vainly hoping to make good these losses

[55] Hanawalt, *Crime in East Anglia*, pp. 51–2.
[56] B. F. Harvey, 'Introduction: the "crisis" of the early fourteenth century', in B. M. S. Campbell, ed., *Before the Black Death: studies in the 'crisis' of the early fourteenth century* (Manchester, 1991), p. 15.

when better times returned. During the seven lean years of 1315–21 people begged, borrowed and stole in order to survive. Crimes against property mushroomed. As order and social control disintegrated, manor courts, hundred courts, and gaol delivery sessions became swamped with business. In the bulk of cases, both the victims and perpetrators of crimes were tenants. Yet although this was when material conditions in the medieval countryside sank to their nadir, these grim years are notable for the lack of overt confrontation between landlords and tenants. Full rather than empty bellies were a precondition for protest.

When tenants had the stomach for it, what were most at issue between them and their lords were personal status and rents. Serfdom tied rent-paying tenants to the manors of their birth and excluded them from access to royal justice while rents provided landlords as a class with their single largest source of revenue. Landlords always had heavy demands on their income. They, too, had households to support and children to provide for, owed payments to their feudal superiors, and paid taxes to the crown. In a status-conscious age, upholding their lifestyle also became increasingly expensive as material culture steadily advanced in sophistication. Unless they could maintain the real income received from their estates, many, especially those of limited means, could not both meet these obligations and remain solvent. The sustained price inflation of the long thirteenth century was potentially as damaging to the incomes of landlords as it was to the incomes of their tenants, unless the real value of rents and other revenues could be maintained. That meant ensuring that rents did not lag too far behind rising land values. Tenants, however, had every incentive to resist and limit such initiatives, and retain for themselves the benefits accruing from higher land values. Landlords, consequently, found themselves with little room for manoeuvre. Even so pugnacious a landlord as the abbot of Halesowen had to content himself in the thirteenth century with merely doubling the entry fines for inheriting sons compared to the far greater increase that he was able to impose upon non-hereditary tenants.

In an increasingly bureaucratic age, lords found that, once the rents and services that tenants should pay had been agreed and set down in written custumals and extents, they were effectively unalterable. Consequently, during the thirteenth century, 'it is not the breaching of custom which is most striking but the observing of it'.[57] Significantly, neither the bishop of Winchester after 1208, the abbot of Westminster after 1225,

---

[57] J. Hatcher, 'English serfdom and villeinage: towards a reassessment', *P&P*, 90 (1981), 22.

nor the abbot of Peterborough after 1231 endeavoured to raise their villein rents, even though each was a power in the land and the *potential* rental value of their tenanted lands subsequently rose significantly. Instead, they raised their incomes as best they could by exploiting other sources of revenue. They engaged in direct demesne production. They also derived as much as they could from manor court fines, mill and market tolls, and by levying the periodic seigniorial tax known as tallage. Much as peasants may have protested at these seigniorial initiatives, the enlarged revenues thereby generated were no compensation for the income forfeited from rents that were effectively fixed. Moreover, in their scramble to profit from mills and markets, lords over-invested in them and ended up in competition with each other, to the benefit of their tenants.

For these reasons, until the mid fourteenth century demographic collapse fundamentally altered the economic status quo, rents of villein land – no matter how onerous they may have appeared to those who paid them – consistently lagged behind the current market value of the land. Notwithstanding the supposedly coercive powers of their feudal lords, throughout the thirteenth century few direct tenants found themselves paying the going rack-rent for the land. Landlords were obstructed by custom from raising the rents for villein land and were even less able to raise the rents for freehold land, whose immutability was upheld by the royal courts. As a result, rents almost everywhere remained sticky. With villein and free holdings alike, it was usually only the one-off entry fine paid by the incoming tenant that might remain negotiable. On the bishop of Winchester's great manor at Taunton in Somerset, the entry fines paid for villein holdings rose dramatically during the thirteenth century but nonetheless provided the bishop with inadequate compensation for annual rents that remained fixed. As a result there was no shortage of tenants ready to take holdings on these terms.

The abbot of Ramsey, too, demanded high entry fines for substantial villein holdings, possibly in order to exclude tenants who lacked the capital and credit necessary to make a success of managing them. Rather than themselves investing heavily in agriculture, successive abbots of Ramsey aimed at discouraging sub-division, opposing sub-letting, and facilitating and encouraging investment by tenants with the knowledge and capital to do so. In effect, sub-market rents served as a subsidy enabling the occupying tenants to accumulate capital and invest in their holdings. The same men helped maintain social control by assuming positions of responsibility in the operation of the abbey's manors. This strategy paid off, for the servile status attached to these holdings did not deter men of means from taking them and the estate itself long remained relatively untroubled by adversarial landlord–tenant relations.

Wealthy and powerful as they were, neither the bishop of Winchester nor the abbot of Ramsey was very efficient – let alone punitive – in extracting rent from their servile tenants. Nor do other landlords seem to have been more successful. Freehold land, which amounted to perhaps half of the tenanted total, was in fact almost immune to rental increases. Because of the prevalence of sub-market rents, at the beginning of the fourteenth century tenants successfully retained between 75 per cent and 80 per cent of rural income, leaving landlords as a class with between a fifth and a quarter. This was a significantly smaller share than would be enjoyed by landlords in the post-feudal world of the late seventeenth and eighteenth centuries when there were many more contractual tenancies and rents and land values were more closely aligned. In these later centuries of emergent agrarian capitalism a third or more of rural income went to landlords.

The failure of most medieval landlords to extract the full market rent for the land left enticing rent-seeking opportunities for their tenants. In particular, it encouraged head tenants to sub-let all or part of their holdings for the full rack rent. On the ancient-demesne manor of Havering, a substantial stratum of small sub-tenants are recorded in surveys made in 1251 and 1352–3; some of these sub-tenants even had sub-tenants of their own.[58] Because this was an ancient-demesne manor, land thus sub-let was permanently alienated; but elsewhere sub-letting was more usually a temporary or fixed-term arrangement and, for all that it must have been rife, is rarely so explicitly recorded in the documents. Widows, especially, are likely to have sub-let their dower lands to others. Substantial tenants, too, undoubtedly employed sub-letting as a means of recruiting and remunerating labourers to help work their holdings and substitute for them in the performance of labour services. In inflationary times, letting for relatively short periods would have been essential if rents were to be kept competitive. In such instances tenants can have had little compunction about demanding the full market rent from those to whom they sub-let. Peasant society was commonly highly stratified and analysis of court rolls demonstrates that its more affluent members were hard-headed in their dealings with those less advantaged than themselves.

---

[58] McIntosh, *Autonomy and Community*, pp. 109–11.

Inter-tenant leases of villein land are occasionally recorded in court rolls, but the manorial authorities must have found them very hard to monitor. Probably many lords turned a blind eye to sub-letting provided that they continued to receive the manorial rents and services to which they were entitled. For the poorest and most marginalised groups within rural society, this was almost their only means of gaining access to land, and the means thereby of scraping a livelihood. They clung tenaciously to their holdings and resisted all attempts to dislodge them, thereby divorcing lords from direct tenurial relations with those who actually occupied and worked the soil. Some lords, therefore, refused to condone it and insisted that the integrity of standard villein holdings – so central to maintenance of the established fabric of manorial life and the social order that rested upon it – remained inviolate. Over the extensive areas of freehold land, however, they could exercise no such tight control. At Bishops Cleeve (Glos.) in the late thirteenth century, one indebted free tenant whose lands were taken back by the lord turned out to have no fewer than twenty-one sub-tenants.[59] Sub-letting on this scale was hard to eradicate.

For tenants the alternative to sub-letting was sub-division. The wider the divergence between rents and prices, the lower the threshold size at which holdings remained economically viable. Fixed rents, rising land values, and inflating prices thus spurred the proliferation of ever smaller holdings, as at Martham. This outcome was especially likely where seigniorial control of tenures was weak. In fact, the more pragmatic lords may have placed greater value on a large tenant population than large tenant holdings: it meant more entry fines, more business for their courts, and an abundant supply of labourers for their demesnes. Land held by ancient freehold, over which lords had least control, seems to have been especially prone to sub-division. Whereas Merton College was able to maintain the 'long-term indivisibility of customary holdings' at Thorncroft (Surrey) between 1279 and 1349, free tenements were subject to 'rapid disintegration'.[60] Consequently, freeholders became disproportionately represented amongst the smallest and poorest tenants. It was one of the ironies of medieval life that many freeholders were materially less well off than significant numbers of servile tenants. The effect of rampant farm fragmentation was to drive up rural population

[59] C. C. Dyer, *Standards of Living in the later Middle Ages: social change in England c. 1200–1520* (Cambridge, 1989), p. 120.
[60] R. Evans, 'Merton College's control of its tenants at Thorncroft 1270–1349', in Razi and Smith, *Medieval Society*, pp. 236–7.

densities and trapped excess population on the land. By the opening of the fourteenth century the most crowded parts of Kent, Norfolk and the East Anglian fens supported rural population densities more than twice the national average. Here inadequate holding sizes forced many to turn to wage earning and a range of craft and other activities. It is tempting to interpret this economic diversity as a symptom of prosperity when in reality it arose from the struggle of impoverished smallholders to eke out an existence.

Under circumstances such as these, the demographic collapse of the fourteenth century may have been more of a boon than a misfortune. Once, as a result of reduced demand, the value of land fell, sub-letting lost much of its economic rationale; the rent differential between customary and competitive rents narrowed, and at the same time the supply of potential sub-tenants was greatly diminished. The incentives and opportunities now existed to accumulate land, and in this way the protracted and painstaking process of amalgamating plots and strips and engrossing holdings began. From these early beginnings the yeoman farms and enclosed fields of the sixteenth century would eventually emerge. Before then, as land values sagged, the point was reached when competitive rents were lower than customary rents. When this happened lords rather than tenants had most to gain from asserting custom, since custom justified maintaining rents and fines at their time-honoured levels. What tenants now wanted were lower rents and lower fines and, with them, greater personal freedom. That meant the elimination of villeinage and serfdom and their replacement with a new tenurial relationship on the land. This was the number one demand of the rebels in 1381.

Rebellion did not in itself achieve the reforms that servile tenants wanted, but the warning it gave landlords did not go unheeded. Lords ceased to obstruct change, and tenurial reform came about quietly through a process of renegotiation between lords and tenants in which the latter often took the initiative. In the altered economic climate, former demesne land was converted to leasehold and farmed out either piecemeal or en bloc. This greatly increased the supply of land available to tenants and meant that leasehold became much more common as a type of tenure. It also became more attractive as legal developments rendered leasehold tenure more secure under the law. For landlords, the greater negotiability of leasehold rents encouraged the conversion of villein and freehold land to leasehold whenever the opportunity presented itself. On the downside, lords found that for as long as land remained abundant and tenants scarce, letting such land was invariably on the lessee's terms. In 1466 Sir James Gloys advised Sir John Paston not to overcharge his farmers if he did not want to be left with unlet land on his hands.[61] Tenants could now play one lord off against another and lords as a class were insufficiently co-ordinated to resist them. When it came to recruiting tenants in this under-populated age, one lord's loss was another lord's gain.

By the middle of the fifteenth century a new demographic and economic equilibrium had become established which took much of the former heat out of inter-tenant and landlord–tenant relations. Lords remained in possession of the land but with the decay of serfdom tenants were left in full possession of their labour, while the terms upon which land was held were transformed. Grievances there undoubtedly were, but they remained localised and rarely got out of hand. Case studies of individual manors reveal a high turnover of tenants and the disappearance of many hitherto long-established families. Some died out as a result of the high mortality that was such a feature of the age. Many more simply moved away. In the process, the social fabric of communities changed beyond all recognition. Most settlements shrank in size and some became deserted. Settlement decay presented lords and tenants with stark choices. Lords seeking to improve the return on their land could do best by clearing it, enclosing it, and creating a few large pasture farms held directly from them by leasehold. Tenants on the receiving end of these actions found themselves stripped of their hereditary common rights, dispossessed of their ancestral holdings and evicted. When tension flared between landlords and tenants during the fifteenth century, this tended to be the issue that provoked it. Even in a high-waged and land-abundant age, rationalising land use in this way could not be achieved without social cost and friction. What is notable, however, is how quietly, at least in the fifteenth century, this process proceeded. In the sixteenth century, as competition for land revived, it would become altogether more antagonistic.

LAND AND PEOPLE C. 1180–C. 1540

Between the 1180s, when William fitz Stephen wrote his eulogy of London, and the late 1530s and early 1540s, when John Leland travelled around England and recorded his impressions of its subtly varied topography, profound changes took place on the land. One way of interpreting these changes is in terms of the rise and fall of population and the

---

[61] N. Davis, ed., *Paston Letters and Papers of the Fifteenth Century* (2 vols., Oxford, 1971–6), ii, p. 377.

associated build-up and release of pressure upon agrarian resources. This chapter has been based on the premise that, between 1180 and 1315, the national population grew from roughly 2.5–3 million to around 4.25–4.5 million. Even though this is a smaller increase than some historians would calculate, it still meant that raising production and accommodating more people on the land were paramount priorities. A succession of crises during the fourteenth century then brought this phase to an end. Between the onset of the Great European Famine in 1315 and the end of the fourth plague outbreak in 1375, the population was halved and the aggregate scale of economic activity correspondingly reduced. Then ensued a prolonged downswing, characterised by processes of rationalisation and reorientation that extended until well into the sixteenth century. Notwithstanding improved land availability and living standards, there was no demographic recovery. On the contrary, in the 1520s the population still numbered less than 2.5 million and possibly no more than 2 million.[62]

Those, like Leland, who saw and knew the countryside at the close of the middle ages – amply furnished with woodland and pastures, replete with livestock, and with such a sufficiency of arable land – can have had little if any notion of the far more congested and poverty-stricken world that had prevailed two centuries earlier, into which both Langland and Chaucer had been born. Only the many shrunken and deserted villages and other signs of dereliction bore testimony to once more populous times. And just as Leland and his contemporaries had comparatively little sense of what had gone before, so in the late twelfth century, when fitz Stephen was writing, surely no-one can have had any inkling of what was to come. For fitz Stephen and his contemporaries, the auguries had been good. Silver and money were more abundant than ever before; the economy was expanding fast, and England, along with most of the rest of Europe, stood on the threshold of a remarkable era of 'efflorescence' and growth that would last, indeed, for the greater part of the thirteenth century.[63] People as yet were relatively well off because – as later, in Leland's day – in per capita terms there was an abundance of agricultural resources. Scarcity of people was a greater economic problem than scarcity of land.

Historians, with the advantage of hindsight, have been able to recognise and describe the great waxing and waning of humanity and human

---

[62] Campbell, *English Seigniorial Agriculture*, pp. 399–406.
[63] J. A. Goldstone, 'Efflorescences and economic growth in world history: rethinking the "rise of the west" and the industrial revolution', *Journal of World History*, 13 (2002), 323–89.

activity that occurred over the course of the thirteenth, fourteenth and fifteenth centuries. This was the important insight afforded by Postan in the 1960s, when he formulated his celebrated 'population and resources' model of the period.[64] Nevertheless, if the sole dynamic had been demographic and cyclical, the countryside of Leland's day would have been little different from that of fitz Stephen's – which it was not. Roughly as many people may have lived upon the land in the 1530s as in the 1180s, but how and where they did so had been significantly altered.

There were good reasons why change did not come full circle. Soil and terrain, economic and political location, field systems and manorial structures, the nature and power of lordship, and the types and terms of tenure, all shaped how the processes of change worked themselves out. The ebb and flow of economic activity was therefore characterised by much regional diversity whose pattern is far more complex than can be explained by any simple Ricardian model of resource exploitation. It was the responsiveness of a population to changing opportunities that mattered, rather than the relative fertility of the soil. This was shaped by many things, including the selective stimulus of market demand, the nature of manorial institutions, the policies pursued by lords and their agents, the strength and character of custom, and the personal status of the occupying tenantry. As historical social theorists have rightly emphasised, tenure and status were always central concerns of those who lived in the countryside because, by determining the conditions upon which land was held, they influenced incentive structures and the distribution of rewards.

How tenures were redefined and renegotiated over these three centuries was material, as Robert Brenner has demonstrated, to the manner in which the land was owned and occupied and thus to the nature and outcome of the balance struck between population and resources.[65] The growth of royal at the expense of seigniorial justice, the expansion of free relative to unfree tenures, the progressive separation of personal status from tenure, and the legal redefinition of property rights, together made possible the establishment of new socio-property relationships on the land. Whereas in the 1180s a clear majority of those who occupied the land were serfs holding by villein tenure, by 1540 serfdom had largely disappeared and villein tenure had been transformed into copyhold

---

[64] As discussed in the Introduction, pp. 12–15, 17–19.

[65] R. Brenner, 'Agrarian class structure and economic development in pre-industrial Europe', *P&P*, 70 (1976), 30–75; R. Brenner, 'The agrarian roots of European capitalism', *P&P*, 97 (1982), 16–113.

tenure. Landlords had largely given up direct management of their demesnes and as a result leasehold had emerged as an important tenure in its own right. In the process, the nature and burden of rents had been transformed. In these respects a powerful sequential imperative was superimposed upon the underlying cyclical dynamic.

The demise of serfdom and the relative weakening of seigniorial power were already in progress during the expansive years of the thirteenth century. Almost certainly the share of rural revenue pocketed by lords fell over the course of the century, to a quarter or less of the total, as rents lagged behind inflating land values. This was when coercive 'feudal' rents were metamorphosed into fixed 'customary' rents. Lords would find that customs and concessions acceded to during this era of increasing labour abundance and buoyant land values could not prudently be breached or rescinded in the altered economic circumstances that followed the demographic collapse of the fourteenth century. True, the Black Death triggered an immediate seigniorial reaction, but this met with only temporary and uneven success, partly because of the tenacity of tenant resistance but also because most lords had the wisdom not to resist change.

Without far greater co-ordination than lords as a class could muster, attempting to reimpose serfdom was futile. As tenants almost everywhere were in increasingly short supply, many voted with their feet and sought out those holdings that could be held on the best terms. Haltingly, as tenure and personal status became progressively divorced from each other, tenures became 'contractual' rather than 'manorial' and rents began to become 'competitive' rather than 'customary'. These developments were achieved more by consent than by conflict, and possibly made earliest and most vigorous progress on the small estates and manors that have so far escaped the systematic historical attention that they so clearly merit. Thereby the way was opened to the establishment from the close of the middle ages of a new and economically more fruitful working relationship between lords, tenants, and semi-landless labourers. Already the foundations had been laid for the precocious emergence of agrarian capitalism in favoured parts of the country, whereby occupying tenants, holding by copyhold, leasehold or freehold tenures, accumulated land, invested in their holdings, hired labour, and sought profits by producing for the market. These were the forebears of the yeomen who so dreaded the low prices arising from abundant harvests that, according to Shakespeare, they would 'hang themselves on the expectation of plenty'.[66] For

---

[66] William Shakespeare, *Macbeth*, iii.i.

them prospects in the 1540s were propitious, whereas for the growing numbers of cottagers and commoners they were bleak. Decay of the old manorial structures, dissolution of the monasteries, the increasing enclosure of common land, and the advent of a more aggressive and acquisitive class of landlord prepared to evict tenants and ratchet up entry fines and rents, had removed many of the old securities and created a brave new world that was harsher and more competitive. During the sixteenth century vagrancy became a far greater problem than it had ever been in the thirteenth century.

Agrarian change almost always proceeded slowly and unevenly. New technology needed to be tried and tested and adapted to specific farming environments. Advance was often contingent upon the implementation of many small but inter-related changes across a comparatively broad front. Adoption of agricultural improvements was often dependent upon changes taking place elsewhere in the economy. Above all, tenurial reform was invariably long in gestation. Developments on the land were consequently more evolutionary than revolutionary, yet their significance should not be underestimated. If the key to England's eventual economic rise lay in its early transition from feudalism to capitalism, it is now clear that the genesis of that transition lay well before the Black Death in the vigorously commercialising and expanding world of the twelfth and thirteenth centuries. The long era of retreat and retrenchment that then followed created the opportunity for a fundamental rationalisation and reconfiguration of productive forces and a redefinition of socio-property relationships. It also allowed the relaxation or removal of several key constraints, of which the elimination of serfdom was one of the most important. In a very real sense the end of this medieval agrarian cycle was marked by the dissolution of the monasteries – the greatest revolution in English landownership since the Norman Conquest – for their estates had long been the greatest bastions of serfdom and the old manorial order. Almost at a stroke, continuities of ownership and management often many centuries old were severed. Thereafter, another similar but less dramatic agrarian cycle ensued, its course profoundly shaped by these earlier medieval developments. The land, and those who owned, occupied and worked it, would long remain of crucial economic importance; never again, however, would that importance be so absolute as during the middle ages.

CHAPTER 8

A consumer economy

Maryanne Kowaleski

Most discussions of the pre-modern economy focus on supply and production and analyse such factors as the volume of exports and imports, agricultural yields and industrial output. Demand, which is much harder to measure, has received far less attention, although the early and late modern periods have been the subject of a veritable explosion of scholarship on consumption and consumer society in the last twenty years. Few medievalists have taken up this challenge, however, due largely to the paucity of sources to explore the patterns and meanings of consumption. Indeed, the medieval sources are scarcely adequate to analyse the supply-side economy. Another stumbling block is the conventional chronology that locates a 'consumer revolution' in the eighteenth century but traces its first manifestations back to the late sixteenth and seventeenth centuries.[1] In this scenario, the middle ages tend to be regarded as an undifferentiated period in which people were 'users' not 'consumers' and operated in a world of unchanging material poverty where objects were 'things' not 'commodities'.

Yet considerable research now challenges this viewpoint, particularly work by Christopher Dyer on the standards of living within different social ranks during the middle ages. Richard Britnell and Bruce Campbell, among others, have traced growing commercialisation in the medieval economy, which made demand a more important motor in economic development. Historians of aristocratic and gentry spending, especially Christopher Woolgar, have spelled out in some detail the consumption practices of elite households. Archaeological research has also provided much new data about the consumption patterns of particular goods, such as dress accessories, pottery and household goods, while recent syntheses analysing developments in the size, distribution of space,

---

[1] S. Pennell, 'Consumption and consumerism in early modern England', *Historical Journal*, 42 (1999), 549–64.

and material construction of housing and public buildings have deepened our understanding of how architecture responded to consumer demand. Studies on clothing now claim that the most significant changes in clothing styles – indeed, the 'invention of fashion' – began in the fourteenth century. This chapter aims to bring together this research by focusing in particular on the transformations that occurred in consumer spending between the high and late middle ages.

In so doing, I will argue that the early modern 'consumer revolution' actually began in the late middle ages, when the unusual economic conditions following the demographic devastation of the Black Death stimulated higher per capita expenditure and fostered spending on a growing diversity of goods and services, which in turn promoted development in several commercial and industrial sectors. Many of the key factors of the early modern consumer revolution – the appearance of new consumer goods, the attraction of novelties, changes in attitudes towards spending, increases in the amount and diversity of possessions, and the penetration of consumer demand further down the social ladder – can all be identified in the late middle ages. The experience and occasions of consumption also widened, whether as citizen, villager, parishioner, guild member, patron, mourner or student. The changes in consumer thinking during the late middle ages, moreover, were radical enough to prompt new discourses about consumption, such as the anxieties evident in the promulgation of sumptuary laws, critiques of luxury and waste, and legislation governing leisure pursuits.

When people spend money to buy goods or services, they are acting as consumers; when they have sufficient surplus income to increase their range of choices about where, when and on what to spend, they develop consumption strategies that can greatly influence the course of the economy. It is worth considering, therefore, what factors influenced the amount of money consumers had to spend. In the early middle ages, when peasants grew most of their own food and produced other goods (such as cloth) themselves, when urban demand was low because there were so few towns, and when even aristocrats tended to live off their estates, the consumer economy was not particularly vibrant. But as agriculture improved and trade expanded from the eleventh to the thirteenth centuries, towns multiplied, the number of markets and fairs increased, and agriculture became increasingly oriented towards production for the market. By 1300, somewhere around 15 to 20 per cent of the population lived in towns, where consumer demand was strongest because townspeople depended largely on the market for the necessities of life. Along with a rising population, which more than doubled during this period, the volume of commercial transactions increased, fuelled in part by a notable growth in the amount of coinage in circulation. To understand the impact of these developments on the consumer economy, however, we need to know whether they raised living standards enough to provide sufficient disposable income to allow even peasants, who represented over 80 per cent of the population, to exercise choice and taste when spending money. To stimulate the consumer economy, moreover, their expenditures needed to be on goods or services, not on taxes and rents, which were also rising at this time.

Although commercialisation certainly fostered economic development before the Black Death, studies of prices and wages indicate that it did not significantly raise living standards because the population was growing as fast or faster than available resources. Population pressure drove up rents and eventually outstripped the land suitable for farming, which contributed to lower agricultural yields as poorer lands were taken into cultivation. Grain prices rose under pressure from a growing population and lower yields, a problem aggravated by the climatic difficulties that led to the Great Famine of 1315–22. The rising population also supplied an over-abundance of labour, which kept wages low, particularly in relation to the more rapidly rising prices and rents. Many peasants and waged labourers, therefore, were caught in a price scissors that led to stagnating or lower standards of living by the late thirteenth and early fourteenth centuries. In contrast, the revenues of many in the landed elite rose during the thirteenth century as they reaped the benefits of higher prices for their agricultural output, higher rents for the lands they owned, and lower wages for the help they hired. Yet major landowners, which included the aristocracy and gentry, together with monks, nuns and beneficed clergy, only accounted for about 2 per cent of the country's population. And even their revenues began to decline during the early fourteenth century when famine, low agricultural productivity and other problems prompted prices and rents to fall.

The picture changed dramatically after the Black Death of 1348–9, which wiped out between a third and a half of the country's population and, together with recurrent epidemics, led to massive labour shortages that persisted until towards the end of the fifteenth century. Despite legislation to keep wages stable, they continued to rise, particularly in relation to agricultural prices, which plunged as demand for cereals slackened because there were so many fewer mouths to feed. Farmers responded to lower grain prices by diversifying into other types of agriculture, particularly livestock, a transition that helped to raise agricultural productivity. Rents also tumbled because there was more land than people able to farm it. This confluence of rising wages and falling prices and rents continued for over one hundred years, significantly increasing the purchasing power of the majority of the population. Some idea of the scale of this increase can be seen in the amount of waged work needed to purchase a standard basket of consumables (table 8.1). Buying these consumables required 27 units of agricultural labour and 35 units of building work in the first decade of the fourteenth century, but by the 1370s workers – particularly those in the building industry – had to work far less to acquire these same goods. By the 1460s, these consumer goods required only 12 units of agricultural work and 14 units of building work. In other words, workers could buy roughly twice as much food in the 1460s as they could in the early fourteenth century. Since rents were also falling, this means that disposable income after buying the necessities of life was considerably more than it had been in the pre-plague period.

Table 8.1. *The changing labour cost of a basket of consumables, 1220–1500*

Decade	Cost of basket of consumables (in shillings)	Units of agricultural work needed	Units of building work needed
1220s	24.89	24	
1240s	25.20	26	27
1270s	36.82	36	36
1300s	34.45	27	35
1330s	33.16	23	32
1340s	30.12	22	30
1370s	39.03	19	27
1400s	34.77	17	22
1430s	34.52	17	20
1460s	28.02	12	14
1490s	26.60		13

Source: D. L. Farmer, 'Prices and wages', in H. E. Hallam, ed., *The Agrarian History of England and Wales*, II (Cambridge, 1988), pp. 715–817 (p. 778); D. L. Farmer, 'Prices and wages', in E. Miller, ed., *The Agrarian History of England and Wales*, III (Cambridge, 1991), pp. 431–525 (p. 491). The basket of consumables includes 4 quarters of barley, 2 quarters of peas, one-tenth of an ox, half a wether, half a pig, $\frac{1}{4}$ wey of cheese, one stone of wool, and one-tenth of a quarter of salt. The 'unit of agricultural work' is the work required to thresh and winnow $\frac{1}{4}$ quarters each of wheat, barley and oats; to reap and bind one measured acre of grain; and to mow and spread one measured acre of meadow. A 'unit of building work' is a day's work as a carpenter (unaided), one day's work as a thatcher (with helper) and one day's work as a slater or tiler (with helper). The work value does not include food or drink given out. Note that the 1340s includes the years 1340–7 and that there is insufficient data on building work in the 1220s and farm wages after 1470 to calculate work values.

Not all shared equally in these improved standards of living. The landed elite and richer peasants who depended on selling grain or renting lands for their livelihood were faced with declining revenues at the same time as they had to pay more in wages to their hired help. But this group represented a small percentage of the total population, and many adjusted by diversifying into less labour-intensive livestock husbandry, or by managing their estates more efficiently. And the landed elite continued their role as the country's most prominent and conspicuous consumers, despite their financial difficulties. Nor did other developments, such as the ongoing Hundred Years War and the shortage of coin in the mid fifteenth century seem to have had particularly long-lasting effects on overall purchasing power or consumer demand. Indeed, some argue that England was enriched by ransoms and booty during the war. The tightening credit markets during the 'bullion famine' were also eased somewhat by new and more efficient legal devices for debt recovery, as well as by the steady penetration of credit transactions further down the social ladder. In the long run, these problems did little to influence the remarkable rise in purchasing power experienced by the great majority of English people – particularly the middling peasantry and working class – during the late fourteenth and fifteenth centuries, a rise that in relative economic terms was not paralleled until the twentieth century.

Much of the new purchasing power of the late middle ages was spent on food and drink. Particularly marked was the rising consumption of meat and ale by peasants and towndwellers. These dietary improvements are evident in the food that manorial lords offered during the harvest to lure workers at a time of intense labour competition.[2] In the thirteenth century, harvest workers feasted largely on bread and cheese with smaller amounts of ale, fish and meat. As the competition for labour increased, however, lords had to satisfy the demands of workers for higher-quality food. Improvements began by the 1340s but accelerated thereafter so that by the fifteenth century the percentage value of meat and ale given to harvest workers more than doubled. Other substitutions in the harvest workers' diet – ale in place of cider, beef instead of bacon – also reflected employers' efforts to satisfy tastes for higher-quality food and drink. The bread that was offered, moreover, was of higher quality, made of wheat rather than barley or rye. Indeed, throughout the late middle ages, the sharper price fluctuations for wheat compared to other grains indicates

---

[2] C. Dyer, 'Changes in diet in the late middle ages: the case of the harvest workers', *Ag. Hist. Rev.*, 36 (1988), 22–37, reprinted in C. Dyer, *Everyday Life in Medieval England* (1994), pp. 77–100.

that consumers were willing to pay more to acquire wheat, rather than settle for other grains such as rye or oats.[3] In towns, wheaten bread became the norm. Faunal evidence (studies of animal bones) also shows rising consumption of beef and mutton in late medieval towns, villages and castles, with new preferences in towns and gentry establishments for young meat, such as veal.[4] One effect of this rising demand for greater quantities and types of meat was the emergence of butcher-graziers to supply the market.

Increased purchasing power also allowed peasants and town residents to drink more ale, a development spurred not only by taste (medieval literature is replete with references to people's fondness for ale), but also by the reduced price of the grain used to make ale (mainly barley). But the most notable transformation in the market for drink was the introduction of beer from the Low Countries in the late fourteenth century. The hops used in making beer not only gave it a distinct flavour but also helped to preserve it for months and enabled transportation over long distances – in contrast to ale, which spoiled within a week. Beer drinking increased rapidly during the fifteenth century, although ale continued to be the drink of choice into the sixteenth century. The introduction of beer, however, gave rise to a new occupation. Beer-brewers were usually male and more heavily capitalised and organised than ale-brewers who tended to be women practising the craft on a part-time basis.[5] The increased availability of both ale and beer at reasonable prices (a gallon of ale cost no more than 2d in the fifteenth century) was also responsible for the growing popularity of ale-houses and taverns, particularly in towns. Taverns were one of those 'spaces of consumption' that attracted men and women of all but the highest social ranks because of the sociability and conviviality that drinking together provided to customers.

The aristocracy and gentry responded differently to rising per capita expenditure since their diet had always contained more expensive fare, such as meat, fish and luxury items like wine and spices.[6] Their meat consumption did grow in the late middle ages, particularly fresh meat and higher-quality cuts of beef, but their expenditure on fish appears to have fallen. When they purchased fish, moreover, they increasingly favoured

---

[3] D. L. Farmer, 'Prices and wages', in Miller, *The Agrarian History of England and Wales*, III, p. 445.

[4] A. Grant, 'Animal resources', in G. Astill and A. Grant, eds., *The Countryside of Medieval England* (Oxford, 1988), pp. 149–87.

[5] J. M. Bennett, *Ale, Beer, and Brewsters in England: women's work in a changing world, 1300–1600* (Oxford, 1996).

[6] C. M. Woolgar, *The Great Household in Late Medieval England* (New Haven, CT, 1999), pp. 111–35, esp. 132–3.

salted marine fish (such as cod, haddock, pollock and hake) over herring and stockfish or dried fish, perhaps a reflection of the widening choice of fish coming onto the market as English marine fishing diversified in the late middle ages.[7] Wine consumption also dropped, particularly among the gentry, although not because they had lost their taste for wine. Rather, the ongoing Hundred Years War disrupted the supply of wine from France and considerably raised its price. To compensate, ale consumption rose among the gentry, but perhaps more notable was the increasing popularity of another new product: sweet wine such as malmsey and romney from the Mediterranean. Expensive imported spices, always a prominent feature in the upper-class diet, remained important, but the nobility's use of one spice, sugar, increased greatly during the late middle ages, both as a sweetener and in medicinal concoctions.

Food had always served as a marker of status, but this trend strengthened during the later middle ages as the aristocracy searched for ways to distinguish themselves from the rising bourgeoisie. In past centuries, high-status foods – such as spices from the Orient, freshwater fish, wine, venison and game birds – were scarce, expensive and generally unavailable to those below the ranks of the elite; legal prohibitions on the exploitation of lords' fishponds and streams, their hunting preserves and parks also limited commoners' access to many of these foods. As purchasing power expanded, however, these items increasingly fell within the reach of a broader section of the population. Early sumptuary legislation in the fourteenth century aimed to stymie this social emulation by restricting the number of courses to two in each meal and the types and costs of food served in each course, but such legislation was unenforceable.[8] To distinguish social ranks many noble households began to differentiate the types of food to be served to guests, pointedly reserving special wild fowl or freshwater fish for the lord, while serving beef, mutton or herring to other members of the household. The aristocracy also seems to have avoided food commonly eaten by the peasantry, including greens, bacon, domestic poultry, boiled pottages, and brown bread. Social distinctions were also emphasised in the conspicuous consumption that characterised spectacular feasts with numerous courses of rich and elaborately prepared foods in which the quantity and appearance

---

[7] M. Kowaleski, 'The expansion of the south-western fisheries in late medieval England', *EcHR*, 2nd ser. 53 (2000), 429–54.
[8] *Statutes of the Realm* (11 vols., 1810–28), i, pp. 278–9.

of the food (including its colour, lustre and symbolic message) was more important than texture or how it tasted.[9]

Superimposed on these class distinctions were regional variations in diet that were often reflected even in the preferences of the local elite. For example, those residing in upland pastoral districts enjoyed more beef and mutton, while those near the sea had access to abundant supplies of fresh sea fish and shellfish. Within coastal districts, species such as hake, found only in the western fisheries, were more common in south-western England, while whiting was generally eaten fresh around the Wash, but more often consumed as preserved buckhorn in the West Country.[10] At least until the later middle ages when wheaten bread became more popular, rye bread was more common in parts of Norfolk and Worcestershire and oat cakes especially prevalent on the Scottish borders.[11] Cider was ubiquitous in the West Country, and ale brewed from oat malt was regularly drunk in Devon and Cornwall.

Seasonal influences, including the cycle of religious observances, had an even more powerful effect on patterns of food consumption. Peasants and wage earners were particularly affected by the cyclical rhythms of the farming year. Grain was more plentiful after the harvest but grew scarcer in the spring and summer months, especially if the harvest had been poor. Disastrous harvests, such as the string of failures during the early fourteenth-century Great Famine, left many on the edge of starvation because of the astronomical price of grain. Fresh meat was available year round to those who could afford it, but poorer people made do with bacon during the leaner months of winter and spring. Vegetables and dairy produce were abundant in the summer months, fruits in the late summer and autumn, and lamb in the early summer. Even imported goods followed seasonal rhythms: vintage wines arrived from Gascony in the late autumn and early winter, racked wines (off the lees) in the early spring. By the summer, what little was left was of a lower quality since medieval wine did not have much of a shelf life.

At times the liturgical calendar coincided with seasonal supply. Lenten fasting, for example, took place when supplies of grain, vegetables, fruit

---

[9] C. M. Woolgar, 'Fast and feast: conspicuous consumption and the diet of the nobility in the fifteenth century', in M. Hicks, ed., *Revolution and Consumption in late Medieval England* (Woodbridge, 2001), pp. 7–25.

[10] C. M. Woolgar, '"Take this penance now, and afterwards the fare will improve": seafood and the late medieval diet', in D. J. Starkey, C. Reid and N. Ashcroft, eds., *England's Sea Fisheries: the commercial sea fisheries of England and Wales since 1300* (2000), pp. 36–44, esp. 40–1.

[11] C. Dyer, 'Did the peasants really starve in medieval England?' in M. Carlin and J. T. Rosenthal, eds., *Food and Eating in Medieval Europe* (1998), pp. 56–8.

and fresh meat would have been low. But the demand for fish during the weeks of Lent occurred when fish were not readily available in local waters; by the eleventh century, this incongruence had stimulated the expansion of the domestic fishing industry, particularly the herring fisheries off Yarmouth. In the later middle ages, expanded purchasing power gave rise to tastes for a wider variety of fish which in turn seem to have stimulated the western fisheries off Ireland, Wales and south-western England, as well as English penetration of the cod fisheries off Iceland.[12] The incompatibility of seasonal food supply and the Christian Church's strictures against meat consumption on over 150 days of the year also fostered innovative techniques of fish preservation, which by the late middle ages offered consumers choices between dried, salted, pickled, brined and smoked fish.

Nowhere was the religious cycle of feasting and fasting more influential than within the monastery, where it determined the number and types of meals consumed by monks and nuns. At Westminster Abbey, the monks ate dinner every day, but enjoyed an evening supper only from Easter to mid-September and not on Wednesdays or Fridays after Pentecost.[13] On saints' days, however, extra dishes and meals were placed on the menu, a trend that seems to have accelerated as standards of living rose. The monks, moreover, found ways around the Christian prohibition on eating flesh on the many fasting days of the year by de-classifying fowl, all entrails and organs, and salted, pre-cooked or chopped meat from this forbidden category. Numerous exemptions were also made for those in the infirmary, office holders and students. By the fifteenth century, the monastic diet on non-fasting days (or for the many monks who evaded the fasting strictures) included an allowance of about two pounds of meat, one gallon of high-quality ale, two pounds of wheaten bread, five eggs and lots of cheese. Indeed, the monastic diet had become so rich that obesity was a greater threat than hunger.

The most visible sign of social rank in the middle ages was the clothing people chose to wear; the richness and amount of fabric, the type of fur adornment and decorative embellishments all signalled one's station and wealth. Clothing also had the power to convey other messages; the plainness of monastic apparel signified renunciation of worldly goods, insignia and heraldic devices distinguished military orders and noble

---

[12] W. Childs, 'The eastern fisheries', in Starkey et al., *England's Sea Fisheries*, pp. 19–23; M. Kowaleski, 'The western fisheries', in *ibid.*, pp. 23–8.

[13] B. Harvey, *Living and Dying in England 1100–1540: the monastic experience* (Oxford, 1993), pp. 38–71.

retinues, crowns and coronation robes emblematised power, and university hoods reflected the level of education attained.[14] The colour of clothing also carried significant meaning, as evident in the association of the liturgical calendar with vestments of particular colours. Sometimes these meanings derived from the cost of particular dyes, such as the very expensive scarlet (made from the body of a crushed insect found only in the Mediterranean), but at other times the meanings are less clear, as in the pejorative connotations of the yellow badges or arm bands that prostitutes and Jews were sometimes ordered to wear.

The style of men's and women's clothing altered little over the course of the twelfth to the early fourteenth century. But dramatic changes were introduced in the 1340s that first took hold in aristocratic clothing and affected bourgeois and even peasant dress by the end of the fourteenth century. Tailoring innovations in the shaping and sewing of cloth produced much more tight-fitting clothes which replaced the loose garments of previous centuries. By the late fourteenth century, the loosely-belted tunic-like gowns of women had given way to more fitted dresses that hugged the waist, torso and arms. The extent and rapid pace of change in men's clothing was even more notable, particularly among the young men who populated the royal court. They adopted a tight-fitting tunic that initially reached to the mid thigh or knees, but by the fifteenth century this had grown so short that it skimmed the buttocks. To fasten these garments, buttons and especially laces became much more common on both male and female clothing. During the mid fifteenth century, tailors produced sumptuously full, pleated and fur-lined over-garments for both men and women, headgear became larger and more prominent, and men's tunics became shorter but equipped with stuffed pads to broaden the outline of the shoulder.[15] All of this clothing was more extravagant in its use of fabric, as older, economical rectangular cuts were replaced by the cutting on the cross needed to shape the new garments. These styles also used many new and more expensive cloths – silks, velvets and brocades, many of them imported – and much more elaborate decoration, such as embroidery worked with pearls, or luxurious linings for hoods.

Dress historians rightly point out that the fourteenth century gave birth to 'fashion' in the sense that novelty began to dominate taste, stylistic

---

[14] F. Piponnier and P. Maine, *Dress in the Middle Ages* (New Haven, CT, 1997), pp. 115–41.
[15] A. Sutton, 'Dress and fashions *c.* 1470', in R. H. Britnell, ed., *Daily Life in the Late Middle Ages* (Stroud, 1998), pp. 5–26.

changes were frequent and sophisticated, and keeping up with new modes of dress became important.[16] In contrast to preceding centuries, the pace of stylistic changes – including the cut of cloth, types of fabric and designs, decoration, drapery and new shapes of articles of clothing – was exceedingly rapid during the late middle ages. The speed with which variations were adopted, as well as what was viewed as the extreme novelty of many of the new fashions, occasioned an outpouring of criticism on several fronts. Chroniclers and moralists in the mid fourteenth century decried the shortness and narrowness of clothing and attributed English political and economic troubles to the evilness of the new fashions. Negative reactions continued into the fifteenth century when the immodest brevity of male tunics, the absurdly long and pointed shoes worn by gallants, and the aping of every new fashion by even lowly yeomen and servants drew particularly harsh criticism. These critiques were paralleled in a series of (largely ineffective) sumptuary laws promulgated in 1337, 1363, 1463, and 1483.[17] All the laws attempted to control the type and cost of clothing according to social rank; in 1363, for instance, servants and artisans were restricted to cloth costing less than 2 marks the length, while ploughmen, agricultural workers and others with less than 40s of goods were restricted to wearing only blanket and russet wool cloth costing no more than 12d the length. Some scholars have interpreted these laws as protectionist in their restrictions on the use of imported fabrics, and as moralistic because of their attacks on inordinate dress, but they are best read as expressions of anxiety over the way upwardly mobile groups were blurring social distinctions because they could afford to keep pace with the new fashions. The laws essentially aimed to regulate desire – particularly among the middling sort, made up of the prosperous urban elite and the gentry – by establishing a new cultural order of dress that reflected social distinctions in a time of rapid social mobility. Thus the law recognised the upward mobility of rich urbanites in allowing merchants and wealthy artisans with goods worth more than £500 to dress like gentlemen possessing land worth £100 per year.[18]

Awareness of clothing fashions also drifted downwards, as evident in the liveries of cloth and clothing given to members of noble retinues and

---

[16] S. M. Newton, *Fashion in the Age of the Black Prince: a study of the years 1340–1365* (Woodbridge, 1980), pp. 8–13. For fifteenth-century critiques, see Sutton, 'Dress and fashions', pp. 11–17.

[17] *Statutes of the Realm*, i, pp. 280, 380–2; ii, pp. 399–402, 468–70.

[18] C. Sponsler, 'Narrating the social order: medieval clothing laws', *Clio*, 21 (1992), 265–83. On sumptuary legislation and contemporary critiques, see also A. Hunt, *Governance of the Consuming Passions: a history of sumptuary law* (New York, 1996).

city guilds whose annual allotments kept pace with stylistic variations in colour, fabric and cut but still acknowledged the wearer's place in the social hierarchy. London guilds, such as the Mercers, were concerned enough about their apprentices' quest for fashion to prohibit them from wearing stuffed garments and long pointed shoes, using silk or camlet, and even cutting their hair 'like a gallant or a man of court'.[19] The new styles even percolated down to the peasants, whose desire for more fashionable clothing was disturbing enough to occasion legislative prohibitions against their purchase of higher priced fabrics and decorative adornments such as fur linings.[20] Nonetheless, peasants' adoption of new styles lagged some ten or twenty years behind and, in many instances, their increased purchasing power was still not enough to buy the fancier and more elaborate styles, such as the newly fashionable *houpelande* (a high-collared gown fitted at the top but with tubular folds kept in place by a belt at the waist, with decoratively cut sleeve ends) that a shepherd yearns for in a poem by Froissart.[21]

There were also changes in footwear, headgear, furs and dress accessories. In the late fourteenth and fifteenth centuries, fashion made popular particularly pointed shoes for men, as well as leather pattens (clogs), long boots for walking as well as for riding, and belted gowns with leather purses or pouches slung from the belt. Over-garments of leather also became more common, including a short leather jacket (the 'jerkin' of the sixteenth century) worn over a doublet by many in the gentry and middling ranks of society.[22] At lower levels there were improvements in quality as shoe uppers increasingly employed tanned cattle hides (instead of inferior sheep or goat hides)[23] because the expansion of pastoral husbandry had increased the supply and lowered the price of hides. The fashion changes in fanciful headgear for both sexes – decorated with plumes, showy textiles and furs, and shaped into strange configurations, from padded rolls to the elaborate turban head-dress or towering cones favoured by women in the fifteenth century – became so frequent that scholars can precisely date late medieval illustrations by reference to the hats or hoods worn. Imported furs, usually the prerogative of the wealthy

[19] A. Sutton, 'Order and fashion in clothes: the king, his household, and the city of London at the end of the fifteenth century', *Textile History*, 22 (1991), 268–9.

[20] C. Dyer, *Standards of Living in the later Middle Ages* (Cambridge, 1989), pp. 176–7.

[21] Newton, *Fashion in the Age of the Black Prince*, pp. 74–5, 127–8.

[22] C. W. Cunnington and P. Cunnington, *Handbook of English Medieval Costume* (rev. edn, Boston, 1969), pp. 136–41, 174.

[23] F. Grew and M. de Neergaard, *Shoes and Pattens* (Medieval Finds from Excavations in London, II, 1988), pp. 44–6.

because of their cost, became a more ubiquitous feature of the clothing of the urban elite and even well-to-do peasants. Indeed fine squirrel skins, considered the height of elegance in the thirteenth century, were passé by the fifteenth century because so many more people could afford to wear them. The more costly skins of sable and marten became popular in their stead because of the value added by their scarcity as well as the way their colour and texture suited the new fashions.[24]

It is harder to date and document the pins, buttons, buckles, brooches, head-dress frames, laces and jewellery that accessorised medieval clothing.[25] Higher-status people possessed these items in abundance, and often paid dearly to have them manufactured from precious metals or decorated with beads, jewels or inlaid metals. Many were imported, particularly pins and aglets, the metal tags at the end of laces or ribbons. Buckles, perhaps the most ubiquitous of these accessories, appear to have undergone some innovations at the end of the fifteenth century when a process involving folded copper-alloy sheeting allowed production of a cheaper product on a large scale. Market demand also stimulated the emergence of the domestic pin industry as well as imports from abroad.[26] Probably the biggest change was in the proliferation of buttons, used for decoration as well as fastening the tunics and sleeves of the new, tighter-fitting clothes of the late middle ages. Laces grew more common for the same reason. Increased purchasing power also made jewellery more available, such as the inexpensive wire-wound rings so popular at the end of the fifteenth century. Most significantly, the late medieval market for dress accessories responded to wider consumer demand by producing a much wider choice of styles for all of these items, offering customers of all incomes the opportunity for fashionable self-expression.

Consumer demand for clothing also stimulated the import trade in textiles (particularly linen, used for undergarments, bed linens and napery) and goods such as pins, laces, aglets, caps and girdles,[27] as well as the domestic development of the textile and leather trades. The late medieval

---

[24] E. M. Veale, *The English Fur Trade in the Later Middle Ages* (Oxford, 1966), pp. 133–43.

[25] G. Egan and H. Forsyth, 'Wound wire and silver gilt: changing fashions in dress accessories c. 1400-c. 1600', in D. Gaimster and P. Stamper, eds., *The Age of Transition: The Archaeology of English Culture 1400–1600* (Society for Medieval Archaeology monograph, XV, 1997), pp. 215–38; G. Egan and F. Pritchard, *Dress Accessories c. 1150-c. 1450* (Medieval Finds from Excavations at London, III, 1991).

[26] C. Caple, 'The detection and definition of an industry: the English medieval and post-medieval pin industry', *Archaeological Journal*, 148 (1991), 241–55.

[27] H. S. Cobb, 'Textile imports in the fifteenth century: the evidence of the customs accounts', *Costume*, 29 (1995), 1–11.

expansion of the English woollens industry is well known, fostered not only by relatively cheap supplies of wool, but also by increasing affluence in all social ranks. Consumer demand was also responsible for the industry's diversification into lighter and less costly cloths (such as straits, kerseys and worsteds), as well as a growing emphasis upon more colourful fabrics. The availability of cheap hides, a by-product of the growth in pastoral husbandry and increased meat consumption, also helped to keep the price of manufactured leather goods relatively low. Used for footwear, gloves, hose, doublets, belts, purses and hats, as well as animal harness, saddlery, tents, buckets, cups and infantry armour, leather was the most water-proof material available in the middle ages. The rising consumption of a host of leather products, many of them inexpensive, also stimulated increased specialisation in the leather trades, with the emergence of new guilds for bottle-makers and coffer-makers, among others.[28]

The greater concern for social distinctions also left its mark on domestic architecture as the wealthy searched for greater privacy, comfort and status during the late middle ages. Whereas the hall had housed most members of the noble household in the twelfth and thirteenth century, separate chambers assigned to individuals and their servants became increasingly common in the later middle ages. Most of these chambers were bedrooms, but parlours – public rooms for smaller gatherings, often restricted to members of the family and high-status guests – also appeared more frequently by the fifteenth century.[29] The withdrawal of the lord into a comfortable private parlour provoked negative comments from contemporaries such as William Langland who recalled better days when lords dined in the hall with their whole household.[30] There was also a tendency to partition the hall with screens, whose more decorated surface faced the 'high' end of the hall reserved for the lord, another example of how architectural changes enhanced social divisions. To magnify their reputations, many lords opted for higher-quality materials and decorations in their palaces and great manor houses, expenditures made possible because the household was less mobile than in previous centuries and could concentrate its resources on fewer residences.[31] There were also improvements in comfort, including the use of glazed tiles for floors, glass

---

[28] M. Kowaleski, 'Town and country in late medieval England: the hide and leather trade', in D. Keene and P. J. Corfield, eds., *Work in Towns 850–1850* (Leicester, 1990), pp. 57–73.

[29] J. Grenville, *Medieval Housing* (1997), pp. 89–120.

[30] W. Langland, *The Vision of Piers Plowman: A Complete Edition of the B-Text*, ed. A. V. Schmidt (1978), p. 103.

[31] Woolgar, *Great Household*, pp. 61–82.

windows instead of wooden shutters or stretched linen, fireplaces and chimneys instead of smoky open hearths, and fixed beds instead of pallets. Status was also displayed in the number of retainers and servants kept by great lords. To house this growing band of retainers, castles and manor houses increasingly reserved ranges of lodgings for household officers and retainers of gentle status to separate them from lower-ranking servants.

The urban housing of wealthy merchants also witnessed a shift towards greater privacy and comfort with the multiplication of bedrooms, parlours, fireplaces and glazed windows from the fifteenth century onwards.[32] It is unlikely, however, that many of these developments trickled down past the level of wealthy artisans. Small shopkeepers and artisans generally lived in simple two-storey homes with only one or two rooms per floor, with the shop or workshop occupying the ground floor. Regardless of the wealth of the inhabitants, however, the demands of urban living left its mark in several ways: in the transfer of the hall and other domestic functions to the first floor in order to retain the ground floor for valuable commercial space; in the construction of jettied, multi-storeyed buildings (which in turn stimulated the construction of stairs and staircases) to increase the amount of space available; and in the alignment of the gable-end to the street with the house and its associated structures built far back into the plot to make the most of narrow street frontages. During the late middle ages, higher disposable income also encouraged first institutional landlords and then many urban dwellers to adopt higher-quality (and more fireproof) building materials such as brick and roof tiles.

Poorer urban residents usually rented accommodation, either small cottages containing one or two rooms located off the main streets in an alley or courtyard, or a single room perched atop shops. Although the total stock of urban housing declined in the face of reduced population levels during the late fourteenth and fifteenth centuries, landlords heightened their investment in 'rows' of small dwellings or shops with solars above that they rented out to wage earners.[33] This expansion in the stock of low-end housing (often called 'rents') must to some extent have been stimulated by the growing ability of wage earners, many of them recent immigrants to the town, to afford their own accommodation,

---

[32] S. Thrupp, *The Merchant Class of Medieval London* (Ann Arbor, MI, 1948), pp. 130–41; J. Schofield, *Medieval London Houses* (New Haven, CT, 1994), pp. 66–133; J. Schofield, 'Urban housing in England, 1400–1600', in Gaimster and Stamper, *Age of Transition*, pp. 127–43.

[33] D. Keene, 'Landlords, the property market and urban development in medieval England', in F.-E. Eliassen and G. A. Ersland, eds., *Power, Profit and Urban Land: landownership in medieval and early modern northern European towns* (Aldershot, 1996), pp. 108–9.

albeit of the cheapest sort. Such inexpensive housing drew many widows and single women who previously may not have been able to afford to live independently, but the design of 'rents' – small, cramped, lacking commercial space or kitchens, with communal latrines – also emphasised the lack of power and wealth of those who resided there.[34]

Prosperity in the countryside also seems to have prompted some improvements in peasant housing, although scholars now acknowledge that even thirteenth-century peasant buildings were fairly solid constructions built by professional carpenters.[35] The messuages of prosperous peasants contained not only a house, but also a barn and frequently other small buildings such as kitchens, bakehouses and pigsties. In many regions both the number and size of these agricultural buildings increased during the late middle ages, reflecting the peasantry's growing ability to afford capital improvements. Two-storey houses began to appear in the mid-fourteenth century and had become common by the end of the fifteenth century in regions such as eastern England, while elsewhere the once-popular longhouse (in which animals lived on one side and humans on the other) was often replaced by separate housing for animals and people. Perhaps most significant, however, were improvements in the materials and carpentry that made peasant buildings more solid and durable. The emergence of the yeoman farmer is also heralded in the appearance of larger, multi-storeyed houses such as the Wealden type found in Kent and East Sussex which had an open hall flanked on both sides by storeyed end bays. But few peasant houses were equipped with glazed windows, fireplaces and other marks of comfort until well into the sixteenth century.

The number and specialisation of items of furniture and the quality of interior decorations also rose during the late middle ages, although this growth occurred only slowly and was limited to the upper and wealthier middling ranks of society. Imported tapestries as well as cheaper domestically produced wall hangings began gracing the walls of gentry and merchant homes, while innovations in fifteenth-century carpentry produced more finely joined chairs, stools, beds, tables and cupboards. Beds in wealthy households became increasingly elaborate and curtained, and tables were often adorned with cloths such as the fine imported

[34] S. Rees Jones, 'Women's influence on the design of urban homes', in M. C. Erler and M. Kowaleski, eds., *Gendering the Master Narrative: women and power in the middle ages* (Ithaca, NY, 2003), pp. 190–211.

[35] C. Dyer, 'English peasant buildings in the later middle ages (1200–1500)', in Dyer, *Everyday Life*, pp. 133–65; Grenville, *Medieval Housing*, pp. 121–56 for this and what follows.

diaper or damask linen that became so popular at the end of the fifteenth century.[36] The biggest change in household goods, however, and the one that affected even the peasantry and wage earners, was the expansion and diversification of tableware during the late middle ages. This so-called 'ceramic revolution', stimulated by rising consumer demand and improvements in kiln and manufacturing, produced not only a plethora of new shapes, but also introduced new materials and glazes.[37] The popularity of durable Rhenish stoneware in a variety of forms (jugs, pitchers, drinking vessels) and tin-glazed earthenware from the southern Netherlands and Spain was particularly important in fostering domestic production of a wide range of cheaper alternatives, including lead-glazed earthenware. The demand for a variety of fine tableware is also evident in the rising use of pewterware, a development accompanied by the proliferation of pewterers' guilds and the growing export of English pewter, considered the finest available by the end of the fifteenth century.[38] The use of other metals, particularly brass, in the manufacture of tableware and other household goods (such as pots, washbasins and candlesticks) also expanded in the late middle ages.

These developments also reached downwards as peasants and wage earners increasingly replaced their wood vessels with ceramic or metal. By the fifteenth century, most peasant households owned a brass pot or pan, as well as domestically produced earthenware cups, bowls, jugs and plates.[39] The greater availability of ale and beer probably stimulated the market in cups and large jugs, while the increased consumption of meat may have spurred purchases of dripping and frying pans. It does not appear, however, as if there were any notable improvements in farming equipment during this period, although it is possible that peasants were able to take advantage of the increasing availability of domestically produced iron (aided by the use of mechanisation in forging and the introduction of the blast furnace into England by 1496) to acquire iron-bound wheels for their carts or tools. Yet consumer demand probably spurred the development of labour-saving devices such as fulling mills, windmills for grinding grain and horse-powered pumps to drain coal mines, which all helped to produce cheaper goods.

[36] Woolgar, *Great Household*, pp. 149–50.
[37] D. R. M. Gaimster, 'Cross-channel ceramic trade in the late middle ages: archaeological evidence for the spread of Hanseatic culture to Britain', in M. Gläser-Muhrenberg, ed., *Archäologie des Mittelalters und Bauforschung in Hanseraum. Eine Festschrift für Günter Fehring* (Rostock, 1993), pp. 251–60.
[38] J. Hatcher, *English Tin Production and Trade before 1550* (Oxford, 1973), pp. 31–6.
[39] Dyer, *Standards of Living*, pp. 169–75.

The increased purchasing power of the late middle ages was also directed towards the consumption of services, many tied to religious practice. Growing concern about shortening one's time in purgatory, for example, prompted rising investment in post-mortem masses and prayers during the late middle ages. Instead of founding a monastery as they had in earlier centuries, the landed elite favoured perpetual chantries to support a priest to celebrate masses for their soul, a movement responsible for the proliferation of chantry chapels in many English cathedrals and parish churches. Some wealthy town dwellers followed the lead of the nobility and gentry, but more channelled their funds into less expensive fixed-term chantries. Other rural and town dwellers paid for an annual obit or anniversary mass, or joined a parish or craft fraternity that provided such services to all members. Indeed, one reason for the burgeoning popularity of parish fraternities was the funeral services they offered to members too poor to afford such services by themselves.

Other expressions of late medieval piety also stimulated consumer demand. Indulgences (the remission of time in purgatory) became more easily available after 1350 in return for a wide range of good works, including visiting a particular shrine, fixing a bridge, repairing a church or funding an unfortunate individual. Their price varied widely, but could be only a few pence, in part because they were being mass-produced even before the invention of printing. The size of the demand is evident in the massive sums collected on behalf of a London hospital: £500 each year, which factors out to about 30,000 donations for just this one institution.[40] The spiritual benefits earned by pilgrims also gave rise to considerable expenditure on travel, accommodation and food, as well as on alms, votive offerings and souvenir badges. By the late middle ages, cap-badges and pins commemorating a visit to a holy shrine were being mass-produced, as were the certificates and indulgences to verify one's visit. Funerals were also occasions of consumption, and often conspicuous consumption when it came to the wealthy whose lavish funeral processions and cash handouts to hundreds of mourners (many of them unknown to the deceased) made them memorable events. The higher clergy, nobility and gentry spent large sums on tomb effigies and memorial brasses in displays of competitive consumption. These funerary adornments, particularly brasses and incised alabaster slabs, also became increasingly popular amongst the newly affluent merchant class (such as the Cotswold wool merchants) and lower gentry during the late middle

---

[40] R. Swanson, *Church and Society in late Medieval England* (Oxford, 1989), pp. 227–8.

ages, which in turn stimulated the expansion of the industry into provincial centres.

The distribution of food and cash to the poor at funerals in order to secure more prayers was also a form of charity, which itself underwent changes during the late middle ages. Attitudes towards the poor were hardening, due in part to the shortages and rising cost of labour in this period. Outrage against beggars who refused to work was particularly high, so the 'deserving poor' were increasingly distinguished from undeserving beggars and vagabonds. At the same time, however, the doctrine of purgatory and Christianity's call for good works encouraged charitable giving, while the range of pious expression was widening. These influences, when combined with increased purchasing power, meant that even ordinary people were faced with numerous choices in deciding when, how much, and to whom to give. The fabric of the parish church seems to have been a major beneficiary of charitable donations, as indicated by the 'great rebuilding' of parish churches during the late middle ages, particularly in regions where prosperity was particularly marked (such as the cloth-manufacturing areas of Devon and Wiltshire).[41] The laity's concern with the souls of the dead also stimulated the manufacture of larger and more expensive bells (and sturdier towers to hold them) that were so much a part of funerals and anniversaries. Donations, moreover, were increasingly channelled through the hands of lay people, particularly parish churchwardens and officers of parish guilds. Older forms of charitable giving, such as church-ales and help-ales, became more widespread as a means to raise money for such projects as church repairs, funds for poor relief, or simply to help out neighbours in need. Feasting and drinking together in a convivial atmosphere also helped to provide charitable relief without emphasising social distinctions.[42]

Charitable impulses and a growing demand for education also stimulated the foundation of many new schools and colleges during the fifteenth century. The highly prized ability to read and write was moving down the social ladder during the late middle ages because more people could afford to send their children – both boys and girls – to school. The rising literacy rate in turn fostered demand for books, more of which were written and made during the fifteenth century than ever before. Besides

[41] A. D. Brown, *Popular Piety in Late Medieval England: the diocese of Salisbury 1250–1550* (Oxford, 1995), pp. 111–31.
[42] J. M. Bennett, 'Conviviality and charity in medieval and early modern England', *P&P*, 134 (1992), 19–40.

providing employment for a growing number of illuminators, scriveners, bookbinders and stationers, the English market for reading material helped to promote the import of manuscripts, such as Flemish books of hours, and the introduction of the printing press in 1476. Devotional works, particularly primers or books of hours, were the most sought-after works in manuscript and in print; between 1485 and 1530, about a quarter of a million of these were printed.[43] Even poor female servants could possess one of these works, which, if unillustrated and unbound, might cost no more than 3d or 5d in the 1490s.

The late middle ages was a great age of 'do-it-yourself' books, such as guides to health or veterinary medicine for the householder. Legal manuscripts, such as collections of recent pleadings, statutes and tracts, were also being produced in much greater numbers during the late middle ages, not only in response to the demand from lawyers, whose services were increasingly sought as the legal system became more complicated, but for others who found a smattering of legal knowledge useful in a litigious world. Among them were scriveners, who were increasingly playing a para-legal role. Recourse to the law can itself be seen as a form of conspicuous expenditure. Consumer demand may have driven the rapid growth in the types of writs available to initiate a legal action, which rose from around fifty in the early thirteenth century, to 900 a century later, and 2,500 by the early sixteenth century.[44]

Because the preceding discussion has documented evidence for the growing strength of consumer demand in the late middle ages, the general tone has been optimistic. It is important to acknowledge, however, that despite the increased purchasing power of wage earners, many still lived close to the edge of subsistence, scraping by with only the bare essentials. Nor did all artisans, merchants and gentry cope successfully with the high labour costs, low rents and tightening money supply of the fifteenth century. The demands of taxation, particularly the regressive poll taxes of the late fourteenth century, also siphoned off surplus income, as did tithes, court fines, rents and market tolls. Yet it is also true that burdensome seigniorial dues and labour services slackened during this period as lords were forced to relax obligations in order to retain tenants. The greater availability of land as well as agricultural diversification drew more peasants into the market where they earned sufficient profits to invest

---

[43] M. Erler, 'Devotional literature', in L. Hellinga and J. B. Trapp, eds., *The Cambridge History of the Book in Britain*, III (Cambridge, 1999), pp. 496–7, for this and what follows.

[44] A. Musson and W. M. Ormrod, *The Evolution of English Justice: law, politics and society in the fourteenth century* (1999), pp. 116–27.

further in farm buildings and equipment. This growing market involvement, along with the challenge of coping with the difficulties of the
fifteenth-century economy, also helped to create a 'capitalistic' mind-set,
typified by the emergence of the yeoman farmer and entrepreneurial
clothiers of small towns and villages.[45]

The appearance of such occupations as beer-brewer, butcher-grazier,
pewterer and pinner, and increasing specialisation in the leather, cloth
and clothing trades, reflect the impact of growing consumer demand on
the industrial and commercial service sectors of the late medieval economy. New products such as beer and the 'new draperies' propelled some
of these industries, but most were stimulated by consumer demand for
the goods they made. Although rising wages heightened the price of
goods that required substantial labour input, the sharply reduced costs of
many raw materials, including grain (for bread and ale) and livestock (for
meat, dairy produce, wool and leather goods) kept the price of many
finished goods stable or even lowered them. Mass-production techniques
also made cheaper goods available to a far wider section of the economy;
these included earthenware (much of which consciously copied the style
and decoration of more expensive imported ceramics), pewterware, dress
accessories (pins, mounts, buckles, badges) and printed material such as
books and single-leaf sheets with indulgences or woodcuts. Satisfying the
home market, moreover, also raised demand for an enormous range of
imported goods, from luxury fabrics and linen to tableware, dress
accessories, sugar and sweet wines, while consumer demand abroad
fuelled English exports, particularly cloth.

The service sector also benefited from the surplus cash that people had
to spend. The late medieval consumer's ability to invest in different forms
of pious expression, including fraternity membership, masses and prayers
for the dead, charitable donations and pilgrimages, all helped to stimulate
employment and the production of goods. The number of people taking
up careers in education, law and the production of manuscript and
printed material also rose markedly. And late medieval people had access
to more celebratory occasions, from parish church-ales and May Day
celebrations to grandiose civic processions and Corpus Christi dramas
calculated to release social tensions and reinforce the social order at the
same time. Business also increased for ale-houses and taverns and for
minstrels and actors as expenditure on entertainment became a more

---

[45] C. Dyer, 'Were there any capitalists in fifteenth-century England?', in J. Kermode, ed., *Enterprise
and Individuals in Fifteenth-Century England* (Stroud, 1991), pp. 1–23.

common feature of the average family's budget. Indeed, many contemporaries believed that wage earners in particular were taking advantage of their higher pay to spend their time on less worthwhile pursuits such as drinking, gambling and sporting events. But, as Dyer argues, the widening consumption possibilities of the late middle ages were likely to have motivated wage earners and peasants to work more, not less, as evidenced by increased agricultural productivity, contemporary references to the work ethic of peasants, the proliferation of industrial by-employment in the countryside and the absence of sharp distinctions between employers and employed.[46] The vastly increased earning power of all wage earners, the appearance of cheaper, mass-produced goods targeted to the less well-off, and even the rise in ale-houses and gaming, all provided strong incentives to earn in order to spend.

The late medieval critiques of leisure and waste, which were backed up by local ordinances and national legislation, are themselves a reflection of the new tensions fostered by the emergence of a more consumerist society explicitly concerned with accumulation. At a time of rapid and confusing social change, when increased purchasing power enabled servants to own books and ape the fashions of their superiors, when the 'middling sort' of parish gentry, yeomen farmers and wealthy merchants were eager and often able to emulate the lifestyle of the elite, competitive consumption was an anxiety-provoking effect of the breakdown of social and cultural hierarchies by new types of consumer culture. Sumptuary legislation attempting to harness social emulation, and contemporary critiques of the lure of fashionable clothing – much of it considered so novel as to be outrageous – are also symptoms of the new (often multiple) meanings being given to consumer objects during the 'consumer revolution' of the late middle ages.

---

[46] C. Dyer, 'Work ethics in the fourteenth century', in J. Bothwell, P. J. P. Goldberg and W. M. Ormrod, eds., *The Problem of Labour in Fourteenth-Century England* (Woodbridge, 2000), pp. 21–41.

CHAPTER 9

Moving around

Wendy R. Childs

The ease and amount of travel within medieval England is still often underestimated. Over a hundred years ago, Jusserand showed that medieval roads teemed with herbalists, jugglers, messengers, pedlars, wandering workmen, peasants, preachers, friars, pardoners, pilgrims and the like; and in 1936 Stenton described in detail the medieval road network and provided plenty of examples of journey speeds. Beyond those works, which were specifically on travel, the many studies showing England as a much governed country and one with vibrant trade, markets and towns also presuppose an effective transport system within which people and goods could travel regularly and in safety. It is not surprising that England's roads and rivers should be busy, since there are no great physical obstacles to movement. Although English terrain can sometimes be bleak, as in the Pennines or Dartmoor and Exmoor, the terrain itself did not make travel prohibitively difficult. Moving around in the middle ages was essentially no more difficult for most people than it remained until the improved roads and canals of the eighteenth century and the trains of the nineteenth. Even at the end of the nineteenth century the usual local form of transport for many people was by foot or horse and journey times would not be much shorter than in the middle ages.

The speed of travel in the middle ages depended on the size and purpose of the travelling group and the fitness of man and horse.[1] Those on foot might expect to cover fifteen to twenty miles a day, and more if they were in haste. If conditions were adverse or animals were being driven, normal speeds might be not much more than six to ten miles a day. Goods were transported by people, pack-animals or carts. They might be simply put in baskets, sacks and bags, wrapped more carefully in oiled or waxed cloth or in leather, or placed in boxes and barrels.

---

[1] M. Harvey, 'Travel from Durham to York (and back) in the fourteenth century', *Northern History*, 42 (2005), 119–30.

Packhorses might normally carry about two hundredweights, but large bulky packs (perhaps full sacks of wool, weighing 364 lb) and large barrels (such as pipes and even full tuns of wine) would need a cart.

Pack-animals – horses, ponies or mules – would normally go at the same speed as a walking group but were fast enough to deliver fresh fish some way from the sea, and are known to have been capable of thirty miles a day. The large two-wheeled carts, capable of carrying up to a ton, were slower, probably normally making about twelve miles a day. In the worst winter conditions they might make only five to eight miles a day, but in fair weather, on good roads and drawn by horses they were capable of over twenty miles a day in the fifteenth century. By 1200 most major improvements in harnessing draught horses had already occurred: padded collars and harnessing in single or double file for maximum pull were common instead of several animals abreast. However, further improvement in cart design in the fourteenth century, especially for two-wheeled carts, undoubtedly helped speed and manoeuvrability by the fifteenth century. Double shafts between which the animals walked, rather than a single pole between two animals, facilitated single-file harnessing, which would increase traction; shafts also allowed the cart to be reversed and the horse to act as a brake downhill; the introduction of a postillion increased control over big teams; spoked wheels were less prone to bog down and were stronger for load carrying. These improvements were more important than any move towards larger four-wheeled carts. Large estates and households owned their own carts, but carts could also be hired for occasional use, and part loads or smaller packages could be sent by the regular carrier services that ran between the main towns. Women in the richest households might also use personal carriages, unsprung and no doubt uncomfortable, but often with magnificent cushions and hangings. The distances travelled in these conditions were sometimes surprisingly high. Eleanor de Montfort in 1265 travelled between fourteen and thirty-eight miles in a day, averaging twenty-six miles; Joan de Valence in 1296–7 travelled (often cross-country rather than on the main roads) from five to thirty-two miles a day, with most daily rates falling in the range of ten to twenty-three miles.[2]

Unaccompanied riders travelled fastest of all. Those who could not afford to keep their own horses would find no difficulty in hiring them, especially in the larger towns where inn-keepers often ran stables of horses for hire. However, unless frequent changes of horses were organised, a

[2] C. M. Woolgar, *The Great Household in Late Medieval England* (New Haven, CT, 1999), p. 187.

rider using one horse continuously over a long distance might still choose to cover not much more than about twenty to twenty-five miles a day if he or she wanted to keep the horse in good condition. On the other hand, the rich and others such as sheriffs and royal messengers on official business, who could change horses and were in some haste, could regularly travel thirty to forty miles a day; some reached over fifty. In 1375 William Percehay rode from York to Westminster in five and a half days, averaging thirty-six miles on the full days, and rode home in four and a half days, averaging forty-four miles on the full days.[3] In exceptional cases diplomats and messengers are known to have covered around 100 miles a day; one diplomat took only six days to cover the 600 miles from London to Milan in 1406. Once post services were organised by governments towards the end of the fifteenth century, speeds of seventy to eighty miles a day could be more frequently reached. But if speed was not essential, then the most comfortable ride was on an ambling horse, specially trained to move both right legs forward together, then both left legs. Chaucer's Wife of Bath is shown astride an ambler in the Ellesmere manuscript, written and illuminated *c.* 1400. Riding astride was more secure and may have been the preferred style for some women, but side-saddle seems always to have been considered more seemly. The Virgin in the flight to Egypt is always depicted in this way; the Ellesmere manuscript shows Chaucer's more refined prioress riding side-saddle; and it was also clearly the favoured aristocratic practice even for hunting by the early fifteenth century.[4] In extreme conditions, however, aristocratic women rode astride. Fleeing from Winchester in 1141, Empress Matilda rode 'male-fashion',[5] although it seems to have exhausted her and once out of danger she completed her flight by litter.

The speed of travel did not, of course, depend wholly on time spent on the road. Animals had to be fed and watered; time was also taken up in loading and unloading them; rest days might also extend the time taken on a long journey. Maximum distance might willingly be sacrificed in favour of particularly good shelter for the night. The rich might stay comfortably with relatives or friends; rich and poor alike could use monastic hospitality, although the Church was anxious to curb abuses of this. The majority of travellers probably stayed at inns. These could vary widely in size and comfort, from good-sized stone buildings to little more

---

[3] F. M. Stenton, 'The road system of medieval England', *EcHR*, 7 (1936), 17.
[4] See the calendar for May in *Les Tres Riches Heures du Duc de Berry*, ed. J. Longnon and R. Cazelles (1969); see also G. W. Digby, *The Devonshire Hunting Tapestries* (HMSO, 1971), plates I, II.
[5] P. McGurk, ed., *The Chronicle of John of Worcester*, III (Oxford, 1998), p. 301.

than poor rooms in taverns, marked by their pole or 'ale-stake' pro-
truding into the highway. The rich might be lucky enough to hire a
private room; others had to share not only rooms but also beds. Complaints of over-charging and poor service were sometimes vociferous
enough to reach parliament and resulted in statutes to control prices. In
accommodation, if in little else, Margery Kempe's experiences probably
illustrate those of many travellers. She stayed in monastic guest-houses, in
private houses and at a wide variety of inns, including one run by a
German in Canterbury and another in Leicester big enough to have
upstairs rooms for its guests. Time might also be deliberately sacrificed by
travelling in a larger group to ensure safety from brigands. Robbery was a
constant problem. The Statute of Winchester in 1285 decreed that the
king's highways were to be cleared of brushwood for 200 feet on either
side to deter brigands, and authorities for the St Giles fair at Winchester
actively policed the notoriously dangerous stretch of the London–
Winchester road at the time of the fair.

Land travellers had a whole network of highways and byways at their
disposal, from major through routes based on prehistoric tracks and
Roman roads to more recent pathways linking settlements. The Gough
map of *c.* 1360 indicates some of the major routes, and studies of royal
itineraries have suggested others. Landscape archaeology has helped to
identify medieval roads that sometimes survive as hollow ways, as at
Weekley in Northamptonshire. It can also identify the network of
alternative local routes that helped to spread traffic and wear and tear on
the roads.[6] Road surfaces are generally assumed to have been poor, deeply
rutted in summer and quagmires in winter with holes so deep that the
unwary could drown in them.[7] However, there was a significant amount
of regulation of roads. The label 'king's highway' was given to roads of
acknowledged importance, which at least from the time of the *Leges
Henrici Primi* had a recognised minimum width and which fell under the
king's direct protection. For example, in 1362 it was alleged that the king's
road to York, which ran between a park and a wood at Escrigg, was
overgrown and narrow. The defendants counter-claimed that the road
was only a local track and was sufficient for that purpose, and that there
were two alternative routes. The jury agreed, but nonetheless decreed that
the track should be enlarged and repaired.[8] Local lords and communities

[6] C. Taylor, *Roads and Tracks of Britain* (1979), pp. 116–23.
[7] H. S. Bennett, *The Pastons and their England* (Cambridge, 1951), pp. 130–7.
[8] C. T. Flower, ed., *Public Works in Medieval Law* (Selden Society, XXXII, XL, 1915–23), ii, p. 240.

had acknowledged responsibilities for road maintenance. Assize records provide plenty of evidence of unwillingness to fulfil these responsibilities, but there is no proof that this was the norm. Certain stretches might have been particularly difficult and expensive to maintain; certain people may have been reluctant to spend money; as the fortunes of towns and markets rose and fell, so the quality of local roads may have waxed and waned. But there is no proof that for the majority of lords and communities support for land transport had to be forced. Some, indeed, were always willing not only to support but to improve communications, to pave roads and build causeways and bridges to encourage access to their markets and thus increase their incomes from tolls.

Church support also helped. Travellers were considered worthy of charitable help. Hospitality was one of the duties of monastic houses, and laymen were encouraged by offers of indulgences or by admonition to help travellers. In Langland's *Piers Plowman*, Truth promises grace to merchants who do good works, including having bad roads mended and rebuilding broken bridges. Robert Holme of Hull took this idea to heart and in 1450 left over £46 for road building between Hull and Cottingham and between Hull and Anlaby.[9] The numerous examples of surviving medieval bridges testify to the skill and resources invested in them. Some, such as those at Rotherham, Wakefield and St Ives (Cambs.), still have bridge chapels attached, which served to invoke saintly protection – and, of course, to solicit financial offerings. The bridge at Rochester was maintained by endowments and other bridges by intermittent grants of pontage, but upkeep was a problem and sometimes when a bridge decayed a profitable ferry was installed instead. Wider rivers had to be crossed by ferry, which could be tiresome. The Humber ferrymen were accused of taking excess fares, making travellers wait until the boat was full and digging holes in the river-bed to make fording at low water impossible.[10]

Finding the way along the roads could be difficult. Medieval maps were not primarily designed to show routes, although itineraries did exist.[11] Some signposts were put up, such as those in 1352 at the bridges over the Colne in Buckinghamshire 'by which the way might be known'.[12] Way-marks were also used to guide travellers through woods (although these might be altered by those intent on theft). Local guides

---

[9] J. Raine, ed., *Testamenta Eboracensia*, III (Surtees Society, XLV, 1865), pp. 182–3.
[10] Flower, *Public Works*, ii, p. 306.   [11] For medieval *mappae mundi* see below, pp. 437–9.
[12] L. F. Salzman, *English Trade in the Middle Ages* (Oxford, 1931), p. 197.

could be hired or directions could be sought at the inn. A popular English–French phrase book of the fifteenth century includes just such a phrase for those going abroad: 'A quelle porte ysseray ie, et a quelle main prenderay ie mon chemyn?' (Which gate should I take to leave, and which way should I turn to get onto my road?).[13] Margery Kempe once simply knocked at a private house in Dover and successfully hired the owner and his horse to take her to Canterbury. Often the traveller could join those already familiar with the route. The number of regular commercial travellers and of common carters probably made this the easiest path of all.

Many goods, of course, were carried by water if possible and the cost advantage of water transport over land transport is well known, especially over long distances. Water transport needed fewer men to move bulk, and had no train of pack-animals to be loaded and unloaded every day, eating their heads off every night. The emphasis on rivers on the Gough map of *c.* 1360 underlines the acknowledged importance of river transport. A commentator in 1675 quantified the difference: packhorses were one-third dearer than carriage by cart; the cost ratio of carts to river carriage was 12 : 1 and that of carts to sea carriage was 20 : 1. Cost differences in the middle ages were similar: it cost more to send wine fifty miles on land than to carry it nearly 1,000 miles from Bordeaux to London.[14] The advantage of water over land is particularly marked for cheap bulk goods: the cost of carting at 3d a quarter over ten miles might mean an increase in the selling price of 100 per cent for coal but only 5 per cent for wheat. Many rivers were navigable (with flat-bottomed boats) far above modern navigable limits. Goods passed up and down the Humber and the Trent in small keels, and boats rode up the Ouse to York, but such water transport was not necessarily easy. In the Ouse, piles were needed to mark the forty-foot wide safe passage at Barlby and boats had to stop over at Selby to catch a second tide in order to reach York. In deeper waters boats were hindered by fish weirs and in shallow ones by fords and silting. York jurors in 1394, after stating that 'the water of Ouse is a highway and the greatest of all the king's rivers ... and is for the use of merchants in ships with diverse merchandise from the high seas to the city of York', went on to claim that goods were frequently endangered by fish weirs and fish nets, and that eight lives and fifteen ships with cargoes worth over £766 had been lost over a period of fifteen years. Navigation on the Trent was

[13] W. Caxton, *Dialogues in French and English*, ed. H. Bradley (EETS, es LXXIX, 1900), p. 49.
[14] M. K. James, *Studies in the Medieval Wine Trade* (1971), p. 149.

similarly threatened by weirs, and the Foss Dyke running between the Trent and Lincoln was so shallow that cows were driven across in summer.[15] Shallow water encouraged the use of fords; this problem could be offset by more expensive bridge-building, but too low a bridge could itself impede boats. To overcome this, lifting bridges were devised, such as the one called 'Turnbrigg' on the stream called the Dike at Snaith which was rebuilt after 1442 with a four-foot drawbridge in the middle; ship masters could lift the drawbridge at 1d a time to let their ship-masts through.[16]

Coastal transport was also very important for the distribution of local and imported goods, although it is generally too poorly recorded in the middle ages to be quantified. Heavy or bulky cheap goods, such as coal from Newcastle, were hardly worth moving at all except by water, and boats delivered it all down the east coast to London and beyond. In the West Country, Exeter received coastal cargoes on boats from ports all along the south coast from Dartmouth to the Cinque Ports, and sometimes received deliveries of herring on board ships from Great Yarmouth; similarly boats from Topsham, Fowey and Dartmouth could be found delivering slates and small timber to Southampton. Many coastal vessels were probably very small, but slightly larger ones of twenty to thirty tons were versatile. Not only could they carry substantial cargoes between local harbours and England's great international ports but they could also operate as off-shore fishing boats, and they could even undertake short international journeys. By way of such vessels, the merchants of Lynn could export ale, and south-east England could export firewood to Flanders. Larger ships of 100, 200 and even 300 tons dealt with the longer journeys to the Baltic, Gascony and Iberia. Although such trade was often in expensive goods, the cheapness of sea transport also ensured, for example, that timber could be imported from the Baltic to Hull or Lynn more cheaply than it could be obtained overland from English forests. Local investment, charitable gifts and royal grants (of quayage and cranage) maintained and improved the facilities for water transport just as they did for land transport. Open harbours were improved with jetties and quays, first of timber and then of stone; docks were built in London; cranes had appeared on quays at London, Southampton, Bristol, York and elsewhere by the fifteenth century; and warehouses, cellars and customs houses were built. To find the way in and out of ports and round

---

[15] Flower, *Public Works*, ii, pp. 112, 253–5, 358, 368; *Calendar of Patent Rolls Preserved in the Public Record Office, Henry VI, 1429–36* (1907), p. 202.

[16] *Rotuli Parliamentorum* (6 vols., 1783), v, p. 44.

the coasts local pilots, sailing marks (ranging from stakes stuck in the foreshore in order to define safe channels to cairns, church towers and steeples) and even lights were used. Sounding leads, lodestones and compasses, and sand-glasses helped pilots and masters to navigate at sea. Written sailing directions or 'rutters', which survive from the fifteenth century, incorporate information on directions, tides, currents, rocks and sandbanks, land-marks and the state of the sea bottom.

Sea transport, of course, carried higher risks than did land transport; it could also be slow whenever seamen prudently waited for good weather. Speeds at sea often averaged three to six knots, but were much more variable than on land, as ships were wholly dependent on weather and tides. A voyage from Poole to Brittany was expected to take four days, but once took seventeen; and the *Margeret Cely* took twenty-two days to sail from London to Plymouth (making an average speed of about half a knot).[17] In sea transport as in land transport there were technical improvements. In the thirteenth century side steering oars gave way to stern rudders; in the fourteenth century compasses were increasingly used; and in the fifteenth century multiple masts with mixed square and lateen sails improved manoeuvrability. This encouraged the building of even larger ships, which could carry more goods more cheaply and were also less vulnerable to attack; by the mid fifteenth century English shipowners were building ships of up to 300 and even 400 tons. Better ships might mean a greater margin of safety, but no greater comfort. There are several graphic descriptions of storms, terror and the overcrowding, theft, seasickness and stench on board medieval ships.[18] The rich could hire a whole ship and specify conditions; a lucky single merchant on a cargo ship might have a small deck cabin; but pilgrims packed on a passenger ship crossing the Bay of Biscay to Santiago would be lucky to have even temporary shelter.

In the thirteenth century most English ships went only as far as Ireland, Gascony and Flanders – where, at the great northern entrepôt at Bruges, they could sell wool and find goods from all over the known world – but a few already went as far as Norway. In the fourteenth century they began to sail into the Baltic and to Iberia. By the mid fifteenth century they can be traced making safe and regular journeys year after year to Iceland, Danzig, Bordeaux, Lisbon and Seville, and English merchants could trade into the Mediterranean using Spanish and Italian ships. Once across the

[17] M. Letts, ed., *The Travels of Leo of Rozmital* (Hakluyt Society, 2nd ser. CVIII, 1957), pp. 59–60, 62–4; I. Friel, *The Good Ship* (1995), p. 85.

[18] Letts, *Rozmital*, pp. 59–60, 62–4; F. J. Furnivall, ed., *The Stacions of Rome and the Pilgrims Sea-voyage* (EETS, os XXV, 1867), pp. 37–40; H. F. M. Prescott, *Jerusalem Journey* (1954), pp. 59–62.

Channel or into the Baltic, English goods and English travellers made their way by roads or great rivers such as the Gironde, the Rhine or the Vistula to Bordeaux, Avignon, Cologne, Santiago, Rome, Jerusalem or wherever their business took them.

Reasons for travel were many – economic, political, religious and social. Among the most important economic ones were not only trade but also employment and migration. Specialists such as masons, fine carvers and sculptors followed work from church to church or castle to castle. Fishermen too had to be on the move to follow the fish in season. But peasants and local craftsmen also needed to travel as part of their normal work. As the economy expanded, so markets and fairs grew in number and size to serve rural communities. Here producers from peasants to the bailiffs and estate managers of large estates sold grain, livestock and wool, and small craftsmen sold their goods. In return they might hope to buy non-local iron, salt and other essentials. Such local markets drew people from no more than a few miles away, but whether on foot or with carts and pack-animals they still needed adequate local roads, fords and bridges. Rural links, moreover, were not exclusively with one nearby market. Village contacts by the fourteenth century were wider spread and not simply economic. Peasants and craftsmen identified common political interests over a large area, as is made clear by the speed with which the news of the Peasants' Revolt spread in 1381.

The twelfth- and thirteenth-century expansion of the economy and population also brought about growth in the size and number of towns. Demand for food and other goods inevitably had an impact on movement in urban hinterlands. A small town such as Colchester drew its grain from a radius of about eight miles, but it drew raw wool for its cloth industry from a much wider area. Larger towns made even larger demands and some of the greatest might also begin to encourage the development of nearby rural markets as regional 'feeder' markets. The demands of London, the largest town of all, produced an integrated market for grain in southern England around 1300 and spawned contacts all over the country through the trade in wool, cloths, dyes and other industrial and consumer goods.

Towns not only depended on the temporary movements of marketing but on the permanent movement of migration. Migration was substantial and essential both before and after the Black Death. Much of it was relatively short-range and depended on local push and pull factors: local land hunger might push, while hopes of work and fortune in the towns pulled. The normal distance travelled by migrants was about ten to twenty miles, although some larger towns drew a noticeable number from a wider area. In small, rural Stratford-upon-Avon, only 10 per cent of immigrants came from beyond a radius of sixteen miles, but Exeter, as a port and one of the most important towns in the region, drew 46 per cent from beyond a radius of twenty miles and 15 per cent from over sixty miles away. Similarly Colchester, although small, attracted migrants from as far away as Bristol, Gloucester, Lincoln and York. London was exceptional and drew larger numbers from all over England.

In the thirteenth century urban migration can have caused little economic difficulty in the countryside and indeed might have been a relief to local over-population. Lords, like the earl of Devon at Plympton in 1242, might forbid their own serfs from claiming liberty as burgesses in the newly chartered towns without purchasing licences, but in most cases they encouraged immigrants. Few seem to have chased villeins who went further afield, although they might prosecute those who returned. One spectacular case concerned Simon de Paris, a freeman of London since 1288, who was arrested by his lord when he went home to Norfolk in 1306.[19] A number of initiatives were taken to stop villein migration after the Black Death, but their overall impact is uncertain. Migrants also included free peasants, small craftsmen and traders over whom lords had little control. Such migration brought further opportunities for travel because, even if journeys home were not regular, links with home were maintained.

Much movement also came from the demands of long-distance trade, which in time spawned some of the best transport organisation. In the thirteenth century international trade produced what might be called a 'cycle' of great fairs selling English cloth to foreign merchants, starting in spring with Stamford fair, which was followed by St Ives (Cambs.), Boston, Winchester and Northampton. To Winchester came merchants from as far away as Yorkshire, Herefordshire and Devon to trade with merchants who had travelled in from Flanders, the Empire, Spain and Provence. The importance of these fairs, and of others such as the one at Stourbridge, outside Cambridge, faded at the end of the thirteenth and in the first decades of the fourteenth century, just as that of the great Champagne fairs did in France, but trading mobility continued. It was concentrated now in the more permanent urban markets, which became the foci for much wholesale trade. Merchants in these towns, and especially in the major ports, kept up significant commercial contacts over a wide hinterland and abroad. Wool travelled to Hull from Yorkshire,

---

[19] H. S. Bennett, *Life on the English Manor* (Cambridge, 1937), pp. 300–1.

Lincolnshire, Derbyshire and even as far away as Shropshire in the fourteenth century; wool from the Cotswolds and the Welsh Marches was sent to Southampton and London in the fifteenth century. At that time Southampton exported cloth brought from Devon, Wiltshire and Gloucestershire as well as Hampshire. London sucked in cloth not only from nearby Essex and East Anglia but also from Yorkshire, Gloucestershire and Devon; at the beginning of the fifteenth century its commercial contacts spread over almost all counties, and these steadily grew stronger even in the more distant provinces. Clearly, London's prosperity depended to a significant degree on an extensive and well-organised transport system.

A regular and efficient transport system was also essential for international traders. The 30,000 to 40,000 sacks of wool exported annually at the height of the wool trade weighed some 4,875–6,500 tons, which would need at least that number of large carts or some 48,000–65,000 pack-animals to take it to the ports if it all went by road. The roads into Boston (Lincs.) alone would have had to cope with around 1,600 carts or 16,000 pack-animals carrying 10,000 sacks of wool in the three months or so between the shearing in June and the normal export season beginning in September/October. Roads and any alternative water routes would be packed. At the peak of European economic expansion, ports were crowded with ships: Hull needed 142 ships to move its wool to Flanders in 1304–5; Scarborough received over 300 fishing boats in the summer of 1305; and there were 300 English ships among over 950 ships loading wine at Bordeaux in 1304–5. The absolute volume of trade decreased after the Black Death but increased per capita, so that the cloth industry, for example, developed a strong export trade in the later fourteenth and fifteenth centuries. The industry depended not just on local wools but also on imported raw materials – woad, madder, alum, oils – which had to be transported from the ports to the production areas. Moreover, while all stages of manufacture might take place within towns such as Bristol or Salisbury, in country areas the cloth itself kept moving. Wool might be spun in one area, woven in another and the cloth moved again for dyeing and finishing. What happened can be seen in the business of John Stoby of Cirencester in 1459. He had thirty-six 'Bristol reds' woven and dyed in Cirencester and then had these cloths delivered by packhorses to six fullers at Stroud, eight miles away. After watering, washing, fulling, teasing and shearing the cloths were returned to him at Cirencester for onward transport to suitable markets. The cloths, however, were then seized on the grounds that Stoby had not paid ulnage (the duty charged on cloth exposed for sale) and were sent up to Westminster as exhibits in the case against him, transported by a regular Wiltshire carter passing through Cirencester at the time.[20]

Regular carting services were widespread in the fifteenth century, and no doubt long before. The Paston family relied on regular carriers between Norfolk and London for the delivery of letters and goods, and 'common carriers' served routes all over England. John Baron operated as a carrier 'for many years' between Bristol and Exeter; the common carriers of Oxford regularly carried scholars' possessions and books. The scale of the carting business around ports is visible through tolls paid at Southampton: in 1443–4 over 2,600 outward cart journeys distributed goods over a wide hinterland.[21] Carting was a regular livelihood, but had its difficulties and responsibilities. John Joce pleaded in 1448 that when he was carrying a pipe of the king's wine to Eltham, his horse fell coming down Blackheath Hill, the pipe rolled out of the cart, killed the horse, broke, and spilled the wine. He was liable for the damage and loss, but with his chief means of livelihood (the horse) dead, he could not pay.[22]

Traffic for economic reasons (marketing, migration, long-distance trade) may have formed the greater part of that on the roads and rivers, but travel for religious, political and administrative reasons was also high. The Church, as a pan-European organisation, demanded extensive travelling in the middle ages. Archbishops and bishops frequently went to Rome (or Avignon) to receive the pallium, symbol of their office, or on other church business; monastic orders sent representatives abroad; the mendicant orders regularly moved their members between universities throughout Europe; and clergy at any level might be called to the papal court. At home, archbishops and bishops travelled within their dioceses and attended convocations. They were often royal servants and balanced diocesan work with presence at the king's court and at Westminster. Travelling preachers such as the friars and unbeneficed priests in search of the next casual employment swelled the numbers of clergy on the move.

The Church also made demands on its lay members. Within the diocese, a steady stream of people might be called before church courts for spiritual offences. The Church also encouraged pilgrimage.[23] Many pilgrims went to nearby shrines, and the majority probably travelled no more than about forty miles, but some major shrines maintained a strong

---

[20] PRO, E 159/236, Recorda, Michaelmas m. 16.

[21] Bennett, *Pastons*, pp. 160–4; PRO, C 1/11/467, 19/469, 29/417, 46/60, 61/499; O. Coleman, ed., *The Brokage Book of Southampton, 1443–4* (Southampton Records Series, IV, VI, 1960–1), *passim*.

[22] PRO, E 28/78, 14 Oct. 27 Henry VI.   [23] Discussed in more detail below, pp. 314–18.

attraction over a wide area. While there were probably no more than a handful of pilgrims each week at many shrines, there might be thousands at major ones. Pilgrim numbers seem to have peaked around 1300, and donations declined at almost all English shrines thereafter, but new cults could pop up at any time, as at the tombs of Thomas of Lancaster after 1322 and Edward II after 1327. In the fourteenth and fifteenth centuries pilgrimage abroad increased in popularity, or at least is better documented. Pilgrims on their way to Rome and Santiago would be particularly conspicuous on the roads to Dover and Plymouth in Jubilee years, when exceptionally generous spiritual benefits were offered. In both 1350 and 1390 around 400 pilgrims and others acquired licences to go to Rome, and in 1428 and 1434 English shipowners bought licences to transport up to 3,000 pilgrims to Corunna for Santiago.

Soldiers made up another very large body of travellers. Kings mustered troops from all over England to serve in Scotland, Wales and overseas, mainly in France. In 1296 there were about 25,000 infantry on the payroll for Edward I's Scottish campaign and an additional Irish contingent of nearly 3,000 men. Such armies were accompanied by carts and pack-animals with supplies, although local suppliers were also used and where possible supplies were sent by sea. Even in years without campaigns, small forces moved to and from garrisons within the border areas. The conquest of Wales brought thousands of English soldiers on to western roads in 1277 and 1282; troops for Gascony were mustered at Plymouth and Winchelsea in 1294 and 1296; and over 8,000 travelled to Flanders in 1297. Although later armies were on the whole smaller than those of Edward I, the Hundred Years War with France led to yet more thousands of Englishmen thronging the roads as they made for southern ports to await embarkation for France. On return they again choked the roads, inns and billets round the ports, waiting for late pay before finally setting off for home. Since troops were drawn from all over England, most villages experienced the stories of returning soldiers.

The political world also demanded constant movement. The royal court remained peripatetic, although as time went on kings increasingly spent longer at their favoured places: King's Langley in the case of Edward II or Sheen in the case of Richard II. Royal itineraries show that kings rarely spent more than two or three weeks in one place and could be on the move for several weeks at a time. Many of the king's greater subjects also led peripatetic lives travelling between their estates and on political, diplomatic or military duties. Their itineraries are harder to establish, but in Edward II's reign Thomas earl of Lancaster (who rarely went abroad) can be traced moving between his estates when he was not in London or Westminster, and Aymer de Valence, earl of Pembroke, travelled energetically on the king's business between southern England, the Scottish borders, and France (sometimes twice in a year) as well as to his own estates in Pembrokeshire and Norfolk. Peripatetic households carried much baggage with them, sometimes even including house fittings such as glazed windows. The number of carts and packhorses needed could be high, but households such as those of Joan de Valence and Eleanor de Montfort in the thirteenth century kept costs down by owning only two or three vehicles themselves and borrowing or hiring more as necessary.[24]

The growth of government was almost constant throughout the period and, once the law courts and greater offices had settled at Westminster, an increasing number of people came there. Plaintiffs, defendants, witnesses and juries were summoned to the law courts there. From the fourteenth century many lesser cases were heard in the counties by keepers and justices of the peace and by ad hoc commissions of enquiry but they still demanded local travel. The Chancery drew many petitioners to Westminster and the Exchequer also brought all manner of accounting officials there. Sheriffs, for example, routinely travelled three times a year to the Exchequer. Back in the counties the stream of instructions to sheriffs and other officials demanded large numbers of royal messengers to deliver them. The estimate that the sheriff of Bedfordshire and Buckinghamshire in thirteen months in 1333–4 received about 2,000 letters and writs requiring action (sometimes requiring onward transmission of instructions to others) points not only to his burden of work but also to the immense mileage covered by messengers.[25] Government service also took officials to Wales, Ireland and Gascony. The development of parliament added a further group to the regular travellers. From Edward I's reign parliaments were held on average once a year (less frequently in the fifteenth century), and from Edward III's reign the commons were always there. By then a parliament meant the assembly of about 120–30 lords (earls, barons, officials, bishops and abbots), some 220–40 knights and burgesses, and up to sixty clerical proctors if they came. This group of 340–430 people brought with them retinues and servants in varying numbers. Accommodation for such numbers, even if temporary, was

---

[24] Woolgar, *Great Household*, pp. 184–6.
[25] H. Jenkinson and M. H. Mills, 'Rolls from a sheriff's office of the fourteenth century', *EHR*, 43 (1928), 24.

difficult to find in smaller towns and it is not surprising that parliament was increasingly called to London or Westminster. We know little of exactly where lords or commons stayed, but in the crisis parliament of 1321 the rebel lords found lodgings at the house of St John, Clerkenwell, St Bartholomew's priory, Smithfield, the New Temple, the earl of Lancaster's house in Holborn, and elsewhere around Smithfield, Islington and Holborn.

How significant was all this movement? Should we envisage later medieval England as a collection of regions or already as a country with a conscious identity as a whole? It was a commonplace of medieval literature to identify 'nations' and laugh at 'national' characteristics. The English were widely seen as emotional, violent and equipped with tails. But how strong was the awareness in England of a common 'Englishness'? As Robin Frame explores in his chapter on 'The wider world', those who travelled abroad (merchants, soldiers, sailors) and those who had lived on the unsettled northern borders were undoubtedly conscious of some sort of common identity, or at least of not being one of 'them' – the 'other'; but those elsewhere at home may have been less strongly aware.

Recent studies of inland trade discuss how far it is already possible in the middle ages to speak of an integrated economy. Integration has always been clear for the goods in international trade: wool and cloth came to trading centres from all over England and commanded very similar prices; high-value imports reached all parts of England and likewise commanded similar prices everywhere. Homogeneous prices are less evident for cheaper bulkier goods. Cheap heavy imports such as tiles and bricks probably did not move far from the ports and the internal grain trade was more regional than national, but even here there is some indication that the population pressure of the late thirteenth century brought about linked price movements especially in London's hinterland. Despite this partial economic integration England was still a country with a distinctive economic regional diversity, shaped by local terrain, climate and resources. This can be seen in regional exports of coal from Newcastle, lead through Hull, ale through Lynn from the barley fields of Norfolk, horses from Dorset, and beans and peas through Bridgwater. Yet, on balance, it might be fair to see the unity of the wool and cloth trades and the move to specialist industrial areas in England (as in Europe) as more significant than the regionality.

The most telling argument against over-emphasis on English regionalism is in political history. England was run as a single political unit, with one legal system, one parliament and a highly centralised government administration. This promoted a great deal of inter-regional travel and close links between London and the regions. It was the commonality of experience through movement to and from London and the royal court that helped in the fourteenth and fifteenth centuries to promote the use of eastern midland or London English as the most common variety in vernacular literature and Chancery law suits. The manageable size of England, the relative ease of travel and the highly centralised government mean that a political approach to the question of integration will always emphasise communication and common experience.

Over 300 years there were inevitably changes in 'moving around'. Changes are clear in technical and physical matters, such as in harnessing, cart design, ship-building and increased bridge-building; all made moving around easier, cheaper and safer. Changes also took place in patterns of movement and these made different demands on the routes used. As fairs gave way to more permanent urban centres, surges of seasonal activity gave way to more evenly spread traffic. As towns rose and fell in importance, activity on the roads leading to them changed and local hostelries or bridges flourished or decayed. The development of rural cloth industries spread industrial traffic wider as half-finished cloth and dyes moved around the local roads; the development of a cloth export industry in the West Country increased traffic to western ports; and the growth of London as a commercial, political, legal and administrative centre pulled in yet more travellers eastwards. There were changes in the volume of traffic on the roads and rivers, although these are hard to quantify. The demographic decline of the fourteenth century meant that there were fewer people to travel and a smaller volume of bulk trade to be carried. Yet these falls were partly offset by a rising standard of living, which encouraged greater trade in newer consumer goods and provided more time for social travel, and by the inexorable increase in administrative, governmental and industrial activity.

The overall conclusion must be that moving around in this period was frequent and not too difficult. Probably the majority of poorer country dwellers rarely went beyond the local market, but a large minority travelled further for work or for religious, political and social reasons. Further up the social hierarchy greater mobility appears among the merchant classes, the clergy, gentry, nobility and royal officials. Against such a background of constant movement it is probably irrelevant to argue whether the condition of roads was good or bad: travelling conditions did not in themselves suppress either the need or the desire for travel.

CHAPTER 10

Work and leisure

Mavis E. Mate

The teaching of the Christian Church on work and leisure was distinctly ambivalent. On the one hand Adam and Eve, after eating the forbidden fruit, were doomed to a life of perpetual toil, Adam tilling the ground and Eve bearing children in pain. Yet labour was also a means of developing the spiritual life of an individual. With labour, a man could produce goods that enabled him to give rather than receive charity. The willing adoption of labour, as in the case of monks, served as a form of penance. Above all, not working rendered men and women spiritually vulnerable and prey to the devil. Discussion of the sin of *acedia* (sloth), from the time of its earliest interpretation by Cassian, included both the internal, psychological state of spiritual dryness and the behaviour that might flow from such a state – the failure to perform one's spiritual duties to God. Over time, however, the aspect of laziness in the religious life came to predominate. By the end of the middle ages what had started as a monastic and spiritual vice had become the plain laziness of Everyman. As part of this transformation, the state of not working (*otiositas*), which in the eighth century had been almost synonymous with *acedia*, came to mean both idleness and time spent on pleasurable activities known as leisure.

Both social class and gender affected the work that people did and the amount of time that they had for leisure. The fighting and political activity that was the province of the nobleman and the round of religious services – the work of God (*opus Dei*) – that consumed the time of the monk, provided different rewards from the work undertaken by the agricultural labourer and urban craftsman. Men, whatever their social class, did not engage in tasks such as childcare, spinning or washing clothes, which were seen as women's work. Although aristocratic women generally hired wet-nurses to take care of young children, the responsibility for the children's welfare remained theirs, and they alone faced the dangers of repeated pregnancies. Many tasks were not gender-specific: aristocratic women, in their husbands' absence, successfully managed the family estates; peasant women worked in the fields alongside their menfolk, especially at harvest time; and townswomen frequently helped their husbands in business. Work carried out by women, however, was seen as less valuable than that done by men. Fighting was more highly regarded than child-bearing; ploughing was seen as more important than spinning; and when men were away working, women often brought their midday meals to them, rather than men interrupting their work to return home.

The distinction between work and leisure was extremely fluid. The aristocracy's activities – hunting, feasting, dancing – were pleasurable rather than arduous. But they also performed useful functions. Hunting provided food and, according to treatises such as the *Boke of St Albans* (printed in 1496), strengthened participants both physically and morally. Tournaments (where two teams of knights met in combat), and jousts (single combats) prepared the participants for war. Social activity such as a formal feast, whether in a baronial or a town hall, emphasised the status of the participants and fostered their sense of community. Even though the work of the lower classes was undoubtedly hard, it could also be pleasurable. When people worked together they generally talked to each other, adding enjoyment to an otherwise boring or arduous task. Soldiers, for example, patrolling castle walls in the hours before dawn, might wile away the time with tales of past exploits. Market women, chatting to their fellows while they waited for customers, were often criticised for idleness and gossip, but what they were doing cannot be neatly categorised as either work or leisure.

A number of pastimes and sports were neither class- nor gender-specific. Since Roman times, people had been willing to try their luck at dice. Various board-games, resembling backgammon and utilising dice, were common. The boards for the upper classes were often highly decorated but ordinary folk could play very well on a board scratched in stone. Water-related pastimes – boating, fishing, swimming, ice-skating and water-tilting – were particularly popular but could be dangerous: out of sixty-six fatalities involving sports and recreations recorded in thirteenth-century eyre and coroners' rolls, twenty-eight (43 per cent) involved water sports. Young women as well as men drowned while swimming alone.[1] Bowls had a long history, being played at least from the thirteenth century. The player used a round, usually stone, bowl which was rolled towards targets. Bowling could be done on any piece of flat ground and

[1] J. M. Carter, *Medieval Games: sports and recreations in feudal society* (Westport, CT, 1992), p. 84.

the equipment could be elaborate or simple, depending on the status and the resources of the men and women playing. In the late middle ages, gentlemen began providing covered bowling alleys as part of the amenities of their manor houses.

At some point in the early fifteenth century, playing cards made their way into England. Early cards were often individually handmade and therefore expensive; accordingly, card-playing may at first have been primarily an aristocratic pursuit. German, Swiss and French card-makers, however, produced packs in thousands and some of these were imported into England. In 1480–1, 13,866 packs of cards entered via London.[2] By the end of the century card-playing had clearly spread among all social classes and was enjoyed by women as well as men. The privy purse expenses of Elizabeth of York for 1502 record the grant of £5 to the queen's grace upon the feast of St Stephen (26 December) 'for her disport at cards'.[3]

The concept of 'disports', activities that brought both pleasure and some rejuvenation of the spirit, had arisen in the late middle ages. As aristocratic men were increasingly drawn into the everyday business of government, certain pursuits came to be seen as work. Offices such as justice of the peace or commissioner for walls and ditches, while they conferred status and power on the men involved, were also time-consuming. As a result a sharper distinction arose between these burdensome duties and other more pleasurable activities: the latter, according to Jean-Luis Marfany, were then morally legitimised as 'much needed compensation for and relief from the exacting gravity of the former'.[4] Suitable activities for gentlemen in their free time included not only their traditional pursuits but also the new pastimes of tennis and fly-fishing. Tennis, played with rackets, was familiar enough for Chaucer to mention it in *Troilus and Criseyde*. In the 1480s the jurats of the town of New Romney were allowed to play tennis on holy days but not on work days. The game, however, does not seem to have become popular among the gentry until after Henry VII, and Henry VIII had special courts constructed at six royal palaces.[5] Fly-fishing had been enjoyed in France and Germany since the thirteenth century, but there is no reference to it in

[2] H. S. Cobb, ed., *The Overseas Trade of London, Exchequer Customs Accounts, 1480–1* (London Record Society, XXVII, 1990).

[3] N. H. Nicolas, ed., *Privy Purse Expenses of Elizabeth of York: wardrobe accounts of Edward the Fourth* (1830; facsimile edn, New York, 1972), p. 84.

[4] J.-L. Marfany, 'Debate: The invention of leisure in early modern Europe', *P&P*, 156 (1998), 177; see also P. Burke, 'The invention of leisure in early modern Europe', *ibid.*, 146 (1995), 137–44, and his 'Reply to Marfany', *ibid.*, 156 (1998), 192–7.

[5] S. Thurley, *The Royal Palaces of Tudor England* (New Haven, CT, 1993), pp. 179–86.

England before the early fifteenth century.[6] Unlike the fishing with nets that artisans did for the daily increase of their goods, fishing with an angle was not necessary for earning a living and involved nothing laborious. It was thus a suitable disport for the well-to-do and helped to distinguish them from the common folk.

Wealth and leisure allowed the aristocracy to develop a distinctive class culture that was reflected in the clothes they wore, the food they ate, their manners (the use of handkerchiefs, for example) and above all in their recreations. Women played an integral part in this development. They were an essential audience for the displays of prowess at tournaments and they watched the 'disguysings' (masquerades) that were such a popular and regular part of Christmas entertainment. They played all the indoor games and engaged in needlework that was subsequently worn or displayed. But their participation in outdoor activities may have been limited. Women hunted with falcons and some may have participated directly in the hunting of large game, but how regularly is not clear: many hunts were all-male affairs. The new sports of tennis and fly-fishing were not immediately taken up by women. On the other hand, women may have spent more time than their brothers and husbands playing musical instruments, singing and, by the late middle ages, listening to books being read aloud or reading themselves.

In contrast, the life of many rural inhabitants before the Black Death was one of almost constant toil. It has been estimated that on arable farms in the midlands or the south of England it would take about 420 'work days' to cultivate a holding of thirty acres (that is, an economic unit large enough to supply sufficient food for an average family with a small surplus for sale). If the householder still performed 'week work' to a lord as rent for the land, that would add another fifty to one hundred days.[7] To survive, all family members needed to contribute their labour. Sons might be left in charge of pigs, or they and their fathers would work in the fields. The female members of the household, in addition to undertaking childcare and domestic tasks, would look after poultry, milk cows and ewes, make butter and cheese, and clean, card and spin wool. When required, they could weed crops, plant the garden and shear sheep.

---

[6] M. Keen, *English Society in the Later Middle Ages, 1348–1500* (1990), pp. 184–5; R. C. Hoffman, 'Fishing for sport in medieval Europe: new evidence', *Speculum*, 60 (1985), 877–902.

[7] C. Dyer, 'Leisure among the peasantry in the later middle ages', in *Il tempo libero: economia e società secc xiii–xvii*, Istituto Internazionale di storia Economica, F. Datini (Prato, 1995), pp. 294–7; H. Fox, 'Exploitation of the landless by lords and tenants', in Z. Razi and R. Smith, eds., *Medieval Society and the Manor Court* (Oxford, 1996), pp. 518–68.

Some women also brewed ale for the household's use and sold any excess. Everyone would help bring in the harvest. So too everyone took advantage of the resources of the wild, men trapping birds or small animals and women and children gathering firewood, fruit, nuts and, in estuarine areas, shellfish.

Families with smaller holdings of ten or five acres – by far the most common type – would not require so many work days to cultivate their land but, unless it was farmed very intensively, it would not provide sufficient food.[8] Children after the age of twelve would usually leave home and work as servants on the demesne, for fellow villagers or in a nearby town. Adult smallholders could add to the family resources by working as agricultural labourers or carrying out skilled occupations such as tailor or building craftsman. In wood pasture regions, care of pigs and cows could be combined with weaving or other industrial occupations. But wages were low, and in the late thirteenth and early fourteenth centuries food prices were high, so men probably took employment whenever it was offered, working as harvesters in the autumn and as craftsmen or labourers at other times of the year. Some women took advantage of rising prices by selling eggs, capons, butter and cheese in local markets, but their yearly profits are unknown. While their husbands were employed elsewhere, wives could work their land. Occasionally they might be hired by a lord or neighbour to milk, weed or stack hay, but such work was intermittent and could not be relied upon. Likewise, some women might spin thread for others, but in many parts of the country the cloth industry was still in its infancy. Smallholders in particular lived from hand to mouth in what Judith Bennett has well described as an 'economy of makeshifts'.[9] As was the case with the more affluent yard-landers (those with thirty plus acres) the contributions of both husband and wife were essential to the family's wellbeing – which is why most widowers quickly remarried.

Yet not every day was a work day. At least once a year people could visit the local fair and watch entertainers such as jugglers and sword-swallowers. During the winter months inclement weather could force men to stay at home. On Sundays and feast days servile week work and other labour services would not be required. Day labourers likewise abstained from labour on these days and frequently did not work on

---

[8] H. Kitsikopoulos, 'Standards of living and capital formation in pre-plague England: a peasant budget model', *EcHR*, 2nd ser. 53 (2000), 237–61.
[9] J. Bennett, *A Medieval Life: Cecilia Penifader of Brigstock c. 1295–1344* (New York, 1999), p. 88.

Saturdays and the vigils of feasts either. Only the demesne *famulus* was likely to work year-round with little respite. These non-work days (or holy days) could add up to 115 days a year. How were they spent? Essential work must still have been carried out on the family holding. Chickens needed to be fed and cows milked whether it was Easter Sunday or not. But community resistance to harvesting on feast days was so widespread that few farmers would have dared to flout the disapproval of their neighbours. Much free time was clearly devoted to leisure activities. Wrestling, casting stones and archery contests seem to have been common. During the spring and at the time of the midsummer bonfires, both men and women would dance and play games like blind man's buff. Time was also spent drinking and socialising. Yet in the thirteenth century a large number of ale-brewers brewed just once or twice a year. The ale they produced was either drunk within their houses or taken away in jugs. Since brewing was an intermittent activity, brewers had no incentive to provide special facilities such as extra trestle tables and forms. The drinkers were likely to imbibe standing up and have very little to spend. The ale-house as a social centre had not yet come into being.

The great loss of life that resulted from the Black Death and subsequent outbreaks of plague profoundly altered working conditions. The value of money wages rose. Government authorities reacted by passing the Ordinance and Statute of Labourers, which sought to roll wages back to the level of 1346–7 and to restrict the occupational and geographical mobility of workers. Vigorous enforcement of these measures does seem to have prevented 'official' wages from rising as high as they might otherwise have done. John Hatcher, however, has argued convincingly that many employers, in order to attract workers, supplemented authorised wages with unquantifiable extras such as gifts in cash and grain, free meals, housing or allotments of former demesne land.[10] Moreover the rule that workers should accept a yearly contract proved unenforceable. Presentments before the justices of the peace show that, despite the legislation, workers in the late fourteenth century preferred the freedom of short-term contracts and exhibited considerable occupational flexibility. An individual, for example, might be described as a carpenter and fisherman, and a ploughman might also work part of the year as a mower and thatcher. Unmarried workers, especially building workers and harvesters, became increasingly mobile, travelling perhaps as

---

[10] J. Hatcher, 'England in the aftermath of the Black Death', *P&P*, 144 (1990), 3–35.

much as seven miles or more in search of the best possible terms of employment.[11]

These increased opportunities affected women as well as men. As the cloth trade began to expand, so did the demand for female spinners and carders. When arable land was converted to pastoral husbandry it opened up jobs for women in the dairy and sheepfold. More women than in the past were hired to carry out tasks that were not gender-specific, such as weeding, harvesting and hay-making. In addition, in a few places, a woman was employed to do work that had formerly been the province of men. In Leicestershire in 1400, for example, women were mowing, driving plough oxen and breaking stones for road mending.[12] But this situation seems to have been atypical. In general women in the country-side were hired to fill traditional female jobs, all of which had a distinctive feminine word form: brewster, spinster and webster. Thus in Somerset in 1358, although one in four of the 419 workers presented before the justices were women, they were primarily spinsters and brewsters. There were seven websters and a few female common labourers. The other occupa-tions were all filled by men.[13] In many places women functioned as a reserve pool of labour, to be called upon only when male workers were scarce. In a few places female workers received the same wages as the lowest paid male workers, who might be young boys. or old men, but overall they were paid at a lower rate than adult males, although at a higher rate than in the past.

The higher earnings and more flexible work patterns aroused the ire of moralists. Single women living away from home escaped the authority and guidance of a father or husband, and a common labourer moving from employer to employer had no-one to control him or to answer for him. Preachers denounced the laziness, greed and arrogance of the working man who either refused to work or, when he did, did so in a slipshod manner. Mobile workers became classified, and thus denounced, as vagrants and idle beggars. At the same time the poor were assured that disciplined work for the accumulation of goods was pleasing to God. In *Piers Plowman*, William Langland observed that only hunger can goad the poor on to labour. In his own day, when hunger was sleeping, labourers were drinking and singing instead of working and beggars had become the dangerous drones of society. Although there is evidence that some

---

[11] S. A. C. Penn and C. Dyer, 'Wages and earnings in late medieval England: evidence from the enforcement of the labour laws', *EcHR*, 2nd ser. 43 (1990), 356–76.

[12] R. H. Hilton, *The English Peasantry in the Later Middle Ages* (Cambridge, 1975), p. 102.

[13] Penn and Dyer, 'Wages and earnings', 360.

people did refuse employment when it was offered, it is not always clear why they did so. They may have been unwilling to accept the low standard rates or they may have already earned enough for their basic subsistence needs, and, as the critics thought, been deliberately choosing more free time. Contemporary legislators became concerned that higher wages allowed people not only to dress better and eat better but also to engage in unsuitable leisure pursuits. In 1388 a statute forbade servants and labourers to play at unlawful games: tennis, football, quoits, dice, casting of stones and skittles. These games were not seen as particularly sinful in themselves, since they were allowed to the better-off, but they were held to be an encouragement to idleness and a distraction from more suitable pursuits such as archery.

Within urban society, the amount of available leisure time and how it was filled varied according to one's place in the hierarchy. The wealthy mercantile elite, who governed the towns, shared a number of characteristics with the gentry. Many of their activities, like attendance at civic banquets, combined elements of both work and pleasure. Hunting was equally important to them. London citizens, for example, had special hunting rights by charter in Middlesex, Surrey and the Chilterns, and some of the wealthier merchants had their own parks. London houses contained small gardens that provided herbs and fruit but were also designed 'for consolation and pleasure'.[14] The leading merchants in small provincial towns may not have hunted with the same regularity, but citizens of Canterbury, Colchester and Swansea enjoyed similar privileges to those of London. Merchants also kept substantial numbers of domestic servants who would take care of the most arduous tasks, leaving their employers free, if they wanted, to socialise with their peers or spend time in the evenings playing chess, backgammon and dice. Furthermore, the spread of permanent shops within towns by 1300 made it possible to buy perishable goods such as bread, butchered meat and dairy produce on a daily basis. Urban households had no need to be self-sufficient. Thus servants, both male and female, probably spent more time shopping for provisions than they would have done earlier. In the process they could take time to chat with their fellows or eye the manufactured goods for sale, so, like their betters, combining both work and leisure.

The traders and craftsmen who made up such a large part of the urban population fell into many different categories. In Winchester citizens were engaged in at least sixty different occupations and in York it was

[14] S. L. Thrupp, *The Merchant Class of Medieval London* (Ann Arbor, MI, 1962), pp. 136–45.

nearly a hundred, divided among traders, manufacturing crafts and providers of services such as shipmen, barbers and scriveners. In many cases these people worked out of their own houses or rooms and controlled their own time, each family making its own decision on the balance it allocated to work or leisure activities. As in the countryside, it was definitely a household economy with all family members contributing. Among the traders, daughters and wives would help out in the shop and engage in ancillary trades. Thus the wives of the bakers would frequently brew and sell ale as well as selling bread, and the wives of the butchers might make and sell tallow candles and/or cooked meats. So too, with the manufacturing crafts, the female members of the household would be left in charge of selling the finished product or could help with the craft itself, operating a second loom for a weaver or undertaking preparatory sewing for a shoemaker or glover. Since the work was primarily carried out indoors, it was not affected by the weather, but some craft guilds restricted work on feast days. Victuallers were allowed to supply the needs of citizens and strangers whatever the day of the week, and at Beverley barbers were allowed to shave men early on feast days. Work patterns must have depended on the time of year and the state of the market. When demand was strong, household members could take advantage of all available light and in the summer work from sunrise until late in the evening. During the dark winter months, work days were inevitably shorter. In slack times, work even in the summer may have stopped earlier and been carried out at a slower pace. The number of journeymen and servants that the family was able to afford would also affect the number of hours worked by individual members.

Most building workers were hired on a daily basis and paid a wage, usually in money but sometimes a combination of money and meals. Except on a few major building projects, they could not rely on year-round employment. Nor were they hired for a full six-day week. Workers on repairs to Cambridge Castle in 1278, for example, were paid for a five-day week; when two feast days fell in a week, one day's pay was deducted from the weekly wage.[15] Unlike rural tilers and carpenters, they did not usually have any landholding to absorb their free time and energy and provide some of their food needs. What they did with their free day is not recorded. But when wages were low, workers may have had little choice but to seek other employment. Since building craftsmen spent most of their working hours away from home, their wives could not provide any

[15] M. Rubin, *Charity and Community in Medieval Cambridge* (Cambridge, 1987), p. 39.

assistance, but occasionally fathers and sons would work together as teams. The family did not usually have the resources to support brewing, but both married and single women could work as tapsters, selling the ale produced by others. They might also sell a wide variety of other goods from fish and dairy products to ribbons, laces and second-hand clothes. They too could work as labourers, cleaning streets and sewers or carrying water, stones, sand and gravel. They might also be hired to wash clothes and napery for the wealthy, or vestments and altar cloths for churches. Many engaged in spinning and carding on a piece-work basis. It is not known, however, how much income such activities produced or whether any of them were carried out full-time, using nearly all the hours of the day, or whether they were primarily sandwiched between domestic tasks.

After 1348 the wellbeing of townspeople improved. Servants received a larger yearly stipend, but they, like the demesne *famulus* earlier, may still have had little free time. Building workers and labourers were paid at a higher daily rate but, except on a few large-scale building projects, were not paid for feast days. Nonetheless when food prices fell in the 1380s their real wages began to climb significantly. For the first time they faced a choice about whether to stop working when their basic needs had been met or to continue working in order to improve their lot. In many cases they decided to eat more meat and to drink more and better-quality ale, thus increasing the demand for the services of butchers and brewers.

In the second half of the fourteenth century brewing was becoming commercialised and professionalised. Instead of a large number of women brewing intermittently, a few women brewed all the year round as common or public brewers. The degree of commercialisation, however, varied from place to place, and in towns such as Colchester and Maidstone ale-brewing remained the province of a large number of female brewsters well into the fifteenth century. The ale was either delivered to tapsters or sold on the premises, often in a cellar provided with tables and benches. Taverns, which sold wine, likewise provided seating. In 1376 the London tavern called 'La galeye of Lombard Street' contained seven tables with seats, plus another table, two trestles, one long bench and a stool.[16] Smaller establishments might have just one or two tables and several benches, but they did provide a place where patrons, in addition to drinking and socialising, could play licit games such as chess and backgammon as well as illicit ones like dice and other forms of gambling.

---

[16] E. Rickert, ed., *Chaucer's World* (1948), p. 238.

Townspeople clearly enjoyed what free time they had. William fitz Stephen, in the twelfth century, writes lyrically about how Londoners flocked into the fields outside the city to engage in javelin throwing, wrestling, mock battles, archery practice and ball games. In the winter they would take advantage of the frozen marsh to slide and skate, using animal bones under their feet. Such activities were not peculiar to London. In the didactic poem 'How the Goodwife Taught her Daughter' a young woman is warned that if she wants to guard her good name, she should not watch wrestling or 'shooting at cock' (in which a cockerel is used as an archery target). After the Black Death, more and more time was spent frequenting ale-houses and taverns. But the customers may have been primarily men. Women were clearly allowed to go in and they worked there, dispensing drink. Such establishments, however, were good places for a prostitute to pick up casual clients and respectable women who spent time there risked losing their reputations.

The work ethic propounded by the moralists did not always fall on deaf ears. As entry fines and rents gradually dropped throughout the country in the late fourteenth and early fifteenth centuries, land became more readily available. Some cottagers who had survived with just half an acre or an acre built up a holding of five or six acres and former small-holders acquired thirty or more acres. So too urban craftsmen or traders, who earlier had no land at all, bought up small rural holdings. More work was needed in order to deal with these new acquisitions, even if it was just in terms of organising labour. By the late fifteenth century, knitting with four or five needles had spread into England and the production of knitted caps, stockings and socks became a further useful by-employment for both urban and rural women. Consequently many labourers, small-holders and their families, who were often under-employed before 1348, worked much harder in the next century, combining work on their own land with paid employment. Extra earnings could be spent not only on better food but also on better housing, clothing and consumer goods such as pottery, belts and buckles. The expansion of the home cloth market and the relative prosperity of many small market towns in the early fifteenth century all attest to this increased demand.

Earnings, however, did not always rise together with wage rates. In the case of the landless, annual income and wellbeing were determined by how many days they actually worked. During the mid-fifteenth-century recession, full-time employment could not be relied upon. Much agricultural work was distinctly seasonal. William Capell, who farmed the manor of Porter's Hall in Essex, hired fifty-two day labourers over the course of

1483–4. Almost two-thirds of the person-days worked by these people were expended during the harvest, in other words within a few weeks at the end of the summer.[17] At other times of the year workers might be hired for just a few days. In the summer of 1491–2 the steward of the Battle Abbey manor of Alciston in Sussex hired ten men to fill carts and carry out other works of husbandry. The longest period worked was forty-seven days, the shortest ten days. As in Essex, some of these agricultural workers had holdings of ten to sixteen acres on which they could work when not being paid, but others appear to have been landless. They could have worked for other villagers or sought building work, but there too work was often intermittent. Full six-day weeks were by no means the norm and many building workers were hired by the same employer for three days one week and four or five days other weeks. At Broadwater (Sussex) in the early sixteenth century a carpenter was hired for ten weeks, but each week he worked only three to four and a half days.[18] He, and men like him, may have deliberately chosen this part-time employment, since it gave them more free time, but in other cases it may have been all that was available. When inflation started in the early sixteenth century, these families became very vulnerable. During the 1520s overall prices within London rose by 7 per cent from the previous decade, but during the dearths in 1520–1 and 1527–8 cereal prices and, to a lesser extent, meat and poultry prices skyrocketed.[19] Wages did not follow. Workers who had to purchase all their food and who were totally dependent on what they and their families could earn were hard hit.

Free time, whether involuntary or deliberately chosen, was often spent playing games, including illicit ones. Marjorie McIntosh has shown that in smaller communities the laws were implemented only when those leisure-time activities banned by statute constituted a threat to good order.[20] At Winchester, however, between 1411 and 1455 repeated court presentments were made against dice-playing, bowling, handball, 'tales' and penny prick (throwing knives at a peg). The accused came primarily from the lower echelons of society and included a number of servants. Derek Keene has suggested that these were people who were compelled to seek their recreation in the street and other public places rather than in the privacy of their own house and garden.[21] In Surrey and Sussex in the 1440s fines were

[17] L. R. Poos, *A Rural Society after the Black Death: Essex 1350–1525* (Cambridge, 1991), pp. 207–30.

[18] Westminster Abbey Muniments 4023.

[19] S. Rappaport, *Worlds within Worlds: structures of life in sixteenth century London* (Cambridge, 1989), p. 131.

[20] M. K. McIntosh, *Controlling Misbehavior in England, 1370–1600* (Cambridge, 1998), pp. 96–7.

[21] D. Keene, *Survey of Medieval Winchester* (2 vols., Oxford, 1985), i, pp. 392–3.

levied in some villages against groups of young men playing at handball.[22] So too, throughout East Anglia and north-east England, ball games are recorded more frequently after 1450, and in some places a separate camping close can be found, where men not only practised archery but played the game of camp-ball (a blend of football and handball).[23] These games may have encouraged rowdy behaviour and even at times escalated into violence, thus disturbing the peace of more sober residents. Games accompanied by betting could eat up resources that should have been used for other things. In Castle Combe (Wilts.) in 1452, jurors insisted that from henceforth no-one should play at handball 'for any silver'.[24]

Within towns, and especially in unregulated suburbs, games could be enjoyed in public recreational facilities. At Westminster tennis was being played in the 1440s, and in the 1460s bowling alleys and archery butts began to appear.[25] Although in Southwark there is just one reference to a tennis court and bowling alley before 1500, other sites may well have existed without finding their way into the records. In the first half of the sixteenth century, however, such facilities appear to have multiplied, with at least five new bowling alleys recorded in Southwark, one of which housed gaming tables as well.[26] Bowling alleys could also be found in some smaller towns. At Chichester a Frenchman, John Francis, sold bread and ale from 1509 until 1517 and kept a 'bowle-alley'. At Sandwich in 1517–18 an affray arose in the bowling alley of William Ive. At Coventry the bowling alley was located on Whitley Common, a mile to the south of the city.[27] Yet by far the most important venue for game playing was the tavern and the ale-house. Hosts were continually being fined for allowing within their houses men who played at tables (*ad tabulas*). At other times, as at Battle in 1509, the ale-house keeper was accused of keeping card-players in his house.[28] In 1528 a taverner at Dover was told that if he allowed dice-players in his house he would be fined 10s.[29]

[22] M. Mate, 'The economic and social roots of medieval popular rebellion: Sussex in 1450–1', *EcHR*, 2nd ser. 45 (1992), 669; B. Hanawalt, *The Ties that Bound: peasant families in medieval England* (Oxford, 1986), p. 218.

[23] D. Dymond, 'A lost social institution: the camping close', *Rural History*, 1 (1990), 165–92; M. Bailey, 'Rural society', in R. Horrox, ed., *Fifteenth-Century Attitudes* (Cambridge, 1994), p. 164.

[24] McIntosh, *Controlling Misbehavior*, p. 102.

[25] G. Rosser, *Medieval Westminster, 1200–1540* (Oxford, 1989), p. 216.

[26] M. Carlin, *Medieval Southwark* (1996), p. 60.

[27] Lambeth Palace Library, ED 891, ED 899–905; Centre for Kentish Studies (Maidstone), Sa/Ac 2 fo. 249; C. Phythian-Adams, *Desolation of a City: Coventry and the urban crisis of the late middle ages* (Cambridge, 1979), p. 79.

[28] Huntington Library (San Merino, CA), BA 766.   [29] BL, Egerton MS 2092, f. 279v.

The main concern behind these prohibitions was obviously not morality, since all these games were allowed at Christmas and on special occasions such as the money-raising festivals known as church-ales, at which ale was sold for the benefit of the local parish church. Nor were all social classes forbidden to play. As the statutes issued in 1488 and 1495 make clear, it was apprentices and men on yearly contracts, such as servants, who were seen as the main offenders. When these men played games they were in effect stealing time that belonged by right to their employers. Thus one of the Southwark bowling alley keepers was accused of allowing the servants of his neighbours to play in 'the morning and in the evening', during time when they should have been working.[30] Similarly in 1491–2 Simon Jacob of Little Downham (Cambs.) was presented for allowing servants into his ale-house and causing them to 'subtract their service from their masters'.[31] If they gambled in conjunction with their game or by playing at dice they risked impoverishing themselves, and might thereby end up wasting the goods of their master as well as his time. An apprentice of a Southwark merchant, sent to trade at St Thomas's fair in Canterbury, passed the time in the evening after supper by playing at cards and dice with the others in his lodging. He lost four or five pounds of his master's money in one night's play, but in subsequent play by 'setting moche' and 'casting at lytle' he recovered his losses.[32] Other men were obviously not so fortunate. Drinking and gambling, moreover, could easily escalate into a violent confrontation and lead to 'many murders, robberies, and other heinous felonies'.[33] Coroners' rolls reveal confrontations that started in a tavern or inn and did lead to the death of one of the parties.

A wide range of licit pastimes, however, was also available. Secular and religious processions punctuated the year. In towns such as Coventry, York and Beverley mystery plays organised by guilds and municipal authorities combined with the more common procession for the feast of Corpus Christi. In London royal occasions such as coronations or the triumphal return of Henry V from Agincourt were marked with elaborate tableaux as well as lengthy processions. At Leicester and Stratford-upon-Avon the processions which marked St George's Day (23 April) were enlivened by some representation of the traditional fight with the dragon. Other towns and villages celebrated Hocktide (the second Monday and

[30] Lambeth Palace Library, ED 969. He also allowed people to play at dice.
[31] McIntosh, *Controlling Misbehavior*, p. 76.   [32] PRO, C 1/834/7.
[33] *Statutes of the Realm* (11 vols., 1810–28), ii, pp. 462–3.

Tuesday after Easter) with plays or games in which women symbolically vanquished men. Everywhere at midsummer and on St Peter's Day (1 August) houses and halls were decorated with boughs and blossoms, bonfires blazed in the streets and drink flowed freely. The musicians, minstrels, jugglers and players who served the households of the aristocracy would periodically visit towns in their area, providing entertainment for all. Dancing bears, bull-baiting and the public punishments meted out to wrongdoers also provided amusement. Outside the large cities church-ales were an important fund-raising activity. After 1450 an increase in such events led to the emergence of a new kind of community centre, the church-house, many of which contained baking and brewing facilities. In Devon, for example, sixty-four such houses can be documented.[34]

Women shared in these activities but more often as onlookers than as active participants. They did not play tennis or go to public bowling alleys. On the other hand, they danced around the bonfires and in the streets. They attended church-ales, but perhaps in lesser numbers than men. Their participation in the social and religious functions of trade and craft guilds was extremely selective. Although they might march in procession as members of fraternities and attend associated religious ceremonies, they did not usually participate in pageants and plays. In medieval London the wives and widows of masters in the most influential city guilds did attend important banquets, but at Coventry it was unusual for women to be present.[35] Women, as much as men, discovered the pleasures of shopping: fifteenth- and sixteenth-century shops were often larger and carried more stock than pre-Black Death ones.

The invention of mechanical clocks made it easier to calculate time by the hour and even by the minute. Clocks can be documented all over Europe, including southern England, from the second quarter of the fourteenth century although it may have been another hundred years before most towns had one. Hours of variable length according to the season were gradually replaced by hours of regular length. As towns acquired their own clocks, the urban day came to be regulated by the bell. Goods could not be sold in the market before and after certain hours. Town gates opened and shut at specific times rather than at sunrise or

---

[34] B. A. Kumin, *The Shaping of a Community: the rise and reformation of the English parish c. 1400–1560* (Aldershot, 1996), p. 60.

[35] M. Kowaleski and J. M. Bennett, 'Crafts, gilds and women in the middle ages: fifty years after Marian K. Dale', in J. M. Bennett et al., eds., *Sisters and Workers in the Middle Ages* (Chicago, 1989), pp. 11–25; Phythian-Adams, *Desolation of a City*, p. 90.

sunset. Finally the length of the working day was set down by local and national authorities. The Statute of Labourers of 1495, reissued in 1512, legislated that between mid March and mid September workers should be ready to start by 5am, should take breaks of no more than two to two and a half hours, and should remain at work until 7 or 8pm.[36] In many places in the north of England, however, the summer starting time was 6am.[37] At Coventry, although unemployed carpenters, tilers, masons, daubers and labourers had to appear with their tools by 5am, journeymen cappers were not expected to start until 6am and may have finished work at 6pm. Since the curfew was set at 9pm, when the city gates were locked, there was not much time for outdoor leisure activities on a regular work day if the set hours were actually followed.[38]

From the time of the earliest labour laws, concern had been expressed about able-bodied beggars who refused to labour and gave themselves instead to idleness and vice. Yet before the mid-fifteenth century this concern did not manifest itself in the form of presentments for vagrancy before local courts. Thereafter the number of accusations increased, reaching a peak in the 1520s and 1530s. In addition, in early fifteenth-century attacks on the friars, a sharp distinction was made between the truly poor – the 'feeble ... crooked and blind' – and able-bodied mendicants, who by their clamorous begging took money away from those who most needed it.[39] When making charitable bequests in wills and in endowing almshouses, benefactors similarly began to distinguish between the respectable poor, who were ashamed to beg and who had fallen on hard times through no fault of their own, and the undeserving – beggars and vagrants – who did not work and wasted what little they had in the ale-house. By the end of the fifteenth century, constant labour was clearly seen as a virtue in itself. The proclamation of 1495, for example, contained complaints about the work habits of employed artificers and labourers: they were late coming to work; they departed early; they sat for a long time over their breakfast, dinner and noon meal; and they slept too long at the afternoon siesta. Even more troubling were those who, with no private means to support themselves, lived without working and with no-one in authority over them. Destitute, rootless and masterless, beggars

---

[36] *Statutes of the Realm*, ii, p. 586; iii, p. 125.
[37] D. Woodward, *Men at Work: labourers and building craftsmen in the towns of northern England, 1450–1750* (Cambridge, 1995), pp. 123–5.
[38] Phythian-Adams, *Desolation of a City*, p. 75.
[39] M. Aston, 'Caim's Castles: poverty, politics and disendowment', in R. B. Dobson, ed., *The Church, Politics and Patronage in the Fifteenth Century* (Gloucester, 1984), pp. 45–81.

and vagrants were seen as conspiring to destroy society. In 1495 they were to be punished by three days in the stocks with bread and water and then sent away; in the sixteenth century they were to be whipped.

In both the fourteenth and the sixteenth centuries the prime concern of government authorities was the maintenance of order and stability. Yet though the rhetoric was the same, the underlying economic tensions were not. After the plague there seems little doubt that poverty had generally been reduced and jobs were plentiful. Indeed, a motivating factor behind the labour legislation was the fear that essential work was not getting done. Labourers who moved from place to place could have found work where they were but preferred to seek better terms elsewhere. In the sixteenth century labourers were often moving to secure any kind of employment at all, as they migrated from areas where industry and trade were decaying to places where employment was expanding. Even so, jobs were not always easy to find, especially in towns such as Coventry which were experiencing an economic crisis. Not all the beggars were lazy, thriftless drones; some were genuinely poor.

Although the allocation of time between work and leisure pursuits obviously varied from person to person, and between one time period and another, one fact seems clear: all social classes enjoyed and took advantage of whatever free time they had. Before the Black Death, with so many people living on the edge of subsistence, pleasures for ordinary folk had of necessity to be simple: swimming, boating, wrestling, archery, dancing and the occasional drinking and dice-playing. After 1348, when wages rose, more money was available for drinking and gambling. In the fifteenth and sixteenth centuries the spread of playing cards and the erection of urban bowling alleys and tennis courts added new opportunities for structured leisure. Some wage earners, rather than seeking employment six full days a week, chose more free time. Servants, in particular, relieved the drudgery of their days with games. Other men, however, chose to maximise their income in order to buy more land, to build a better house or to acquire more goods. Yet full-time employment, and with it the opportunity to improve one's standard of living, was not always available. A sluggish economy, not the failure of the work ethic, was at least partially responsible for the 'time-wasting' leisure pursuits that so worried the moralists.

CHAPTER II

Religious belief

Eamon Duffy

By the year 1200 most of England had been Christian territory for half a millennium: Christian beliefs and Christian attitudes shaped all its institutions and defined its identity. The Christian calendar determined the pattern of work and rest, fasting and feasting, and influenced even the privacies of the bedchamber, deciding the times of the year when men and women might or might not marry, when husbands and wives might sleep together or must abstain. Everyone, in principle at least, subscribed to the Christian creed. This taught that the world was not a random heap of blind circumstances, a cosmic accident, but that it was a meaningful whole, which had been created out of nothing by a good God. The life of that one God, utterly other and superior to his creation, had revealed itself not as a unitary power, but as a threefold energy, a Trinity – the creating omnipotence from which everything took its origin, the articulate wisdom which shaped history and gave form and coherence to all there was, and the unitive love which drew all things back in joy towards their source – Father, Word and Spirit. Mankind, created in a state of innocent friendship with God, had wilfully alienated themselves from him by sin, and as a consequence sickness, sorrow, disorder and death had come into the world. To remedy this situation and rescue his creation, God himself had entered his world as a vulnerable human creature. The Second Person of the Blessed Trinity, that Word by which everything had been made, himself took flesh and became a man, Jesus the Jew, the Son of God. Under the first-century Roman governor Pontius Pilate he had endured the brutal death of the cross, absorbing all the world's hostility and evil, returning in its place life and goodness. Raised from the dead and ascended into heaven, he would return at the end of time to restore the perfect justice and harmony which was God's will.

In the meantime, human beings were invited into unity with him in the Church he had left behind as an inspired vehicle for the teaching of truth, the source of healing and forgiveness, and the means by which his risen life could be communicated to men and women through the sacraments. These were ceremonies which gave new meaning to the fundamental bodily experiences of human kind – birth and marriage and dying, light and water, food and drink – transforming these things into channels of access to the Godhead, in which sin and its consequences were wiped away and the material order was spiritualised and renewed. For those who accepted this offer and conformed their lives to the will of God in holiness, there would be an eternity of blissful union with God; for those who rejected it and remained in sin, there would be an eternity of misery and self-inflicted suffering. Salvation was social, not solitary, an integration into the community of love which was the Church, militant here on earth, suffering in purgatory, triumphant in heaven. Men and women were thus surrounded by and dependent on not merely their living fellow Christians, but the countless hosts of the holy dead, human beings who had achieved holiness in this life and were now saints in heaven. These saints might themselves be invoked and relied on as vehicles of union with God. Their prayers were powerful to help, and, in anticipation of the final resurrection in which the whole created order would be transfigured and perfected, even their bones were already in this life a source of healing and blessing.

This was the overarching framework of belief that shaped medieval European society, the foundation myth whose narratives and symbols were endlessly invoked and replicated in carving and painting and coloured glass. Communities poured vast sums of money and years of labour into embodying it in the design and decoration of mighty cathedrals, monasteries and churches. The order of heaven was the pattern to which all earthly institutions must seek to approximate. Kings sought legitimacy by being anointed and crowned before the Church's altars and everyone agreed that the first duty of a ruler was to protect and advance the purposes and personnel of the Church. The most solemn promises men and women made were taken on the gospel books which told the Christian story, on the cross, on the relics of the saints, or before the altar where the sacramental body of Christ was consecrated. Civilised Europe was 'Christendom', baptism not only the entrance to the Church but the mark of true humanity.

Brotherhood, it has been said, always implies 'otherhood'. There were of course outsiders to this universal community of belief. In England at the beginning of our period, as everywhere else in Europe, there were substantial urban communities of Jews, whose presence was felt religiously as well as commercially. St Anselm's theological masterpiece, the treatise on the Incarnation known as *Cur Deus Homo* (Why did God become Man?), written in the 1090s, purports to have originated in debates with the London rabbis. But Christian sentiment, both elite and popular, was increasingly intolerant of this 'alien' religious presence. Protected by the crown as a valuable tax resource, twelfth- and thirteenth-century English Jewry was nevertheless increasingly beleaguered. The first European 'blood libel', the accusation that Jews murdered children as part of a perverted worship, was fabricated in twelfth-century Norwich. One of the most magnificent survivals of English romanesque sculpture, the twelfth-century East Anglian ivory cross now in the Cloisters Museum in New York, is encrusted with imagery depicting the Jews as God-slayers and blasphemers. The Jews of York were butchered in a pogrom in 1190, English Jews were forced to wear a yellow badge from 1217, and in 1290 the entire Jewish community was ejected from England. Thereafter any individual Jews wishing to settle in England had to undergo instruction and convert formally to Christianity.

Beyond Christendom, there were the formidable forces of Islam. To the east there were the Christians of the Byzantine world, whose teachings, and especially their rituals, differed from those of Latin Christendom, and who were therefore assumed to be wrong. And closer at hand, within the churches of the west themselves, were a secret host of heretics who rejected one aspect or another of the Church's teaching, and who were therefore perceived as pseudo-Christians, an enemy within the gate, though until the late fourteenth century England was to remain uniquely and remarkably free of the heresies which troubled the other churches of Europe.

As the fate of the English Jews reveals, although these others might (sometimes) be tolerated, they were never welcomed. Since faith was conceived of not as a state of mind but as a grace-inspired response to the call of God, unbelief was no mere matter of difference of opinion or even of confused understanding: it was stubbornness, a perversity of will. Not to be a Catholic Christian was to be damned. The thirteenth century would see in institutions such as the Inquisition the systematic implementation of a policy of repression against internal dissent, and the older theory and practice of the Crusade embodied a policy of armed confrontation with the external enemies of Christendom.

If there can be no doubt about the hold of Christianity over society as a whole, the beliefs of individuals are inevitably more elusive. A handful of medieval people have left autobiographical writings that provide insights into the privacies of belief. In England the most remarkable of these are by women: the *Shewings* of Julian of Norwich, a female recluse attached to one of the city's parish churches, and the *Book* of Margery Kempe, a housewife of Lynn (Norfolk). The precise extent and nature of Margery's contribution to her book, 'dictated' to male scribes, has been questioned, but the *Book* undoubtedly incorporates first-hand accounts of her visionary devotional life and journeyings round the shrines of England and continental Europe. Whoever its real 'author', it offers an unrivalled picture of an extreme but in important respects conventional religious imagination. Such documents of course are rare and by their nature atypical, and both were produced late in the middle ages, around the turn of the fourteenth and fifteenth centuries, as part of a remarkable flowering of vernacular religious culture. For earlier centuries we have no such sources, and must rely on inferences from less intimate documents – the devotional texts and regimes devised by clerics for (mostly aristocratic) lay clients, or the records of ecclesiastical scrutiny in the form of visitations of parishes or religious houses which chart what may be amiss but rarely inform us about the routine and satisfactory. Wills made by lay people survive from the fourteenth century, and their religious preambles and provisions provide evidence about lay religious preferences and expectations. Initially surviving only for royalty and aristocracy, wills become increasingly abundant for people lower down the social scale – minor country gentry and urban elites, even modest yeomen and townspeople – although, as always, the opinions of the poor remain largely hidden from us. The fifteenth century offers records of Lollard trials, providing an insight not only into the attitudes and opinions of religious dissenters, but, in the depositions of their offended neighbours, a sense of the contours of more conventional religious sensibilities. From the fifteenth century the records of parishes and guilds survive more copiously for England than for any other European country. And from the fourteenth century onwards the surviving traces of the material culture of medieval Christianity multiply – tomb inscriptions and effigies in stone and brass, wall and panel painting, painted glass, carving and church buildings themselves. Much of this expenditure of money and artistry, especially in towns, is richly documented and all of it bears witness to the massive appropriation and endorsement of the teaching of the late medieval Church, a symbol system valued and manipulated by an increasingly prosperous and religiously informed laity. If we cannot explore lay religious psychology in the detail we would like, we have at any rate abundant evidence of an enthusiastic and widespread conformity.

RELIGIOUS ENTHUSIASM: RECLUSES AND FRIARS

Our first major medieval source for the religious life of English people other than monks and nuns is a treatise of guidance written in English, and for women. Sometime during the second quarter of the thirteenth century an anonymous male member of a religious order composed a devotional manual for three sisters. We can deduce from what he wrote that these women were daughters of a gentry household, who had renounced the world and were living together in modest comfort as recluses, attended by their maid-servants and under the financial protection of a local lord, perhaps a relative. Nothing else is known for certain of the author or his first readers, though to judge by the dialect in which the treatise was written he lived in the west of England, somewhere near the Welsh border. *Ancrene Wisse* (A Guide for Anchoresses), was, so far as we can tell, the first sustained guide to the devout life to be written in English, though its original audience of genteel secluded ladies were clearly accustomed to saying their prayers in Latin, and, as their spiritual director's instructions make clear, had access to at least a simple form of the Latin book of hours, which was already becoming the favoured devotional tool of the well-to-do.

For much of the first millennium renunciation was the characteristic form of Christian zeal, dedication to celibacy and withdrawal from worldly occupations as a monk or a nun considered the surest guarantee of salvation. Although, as Janet Burton discusses in her chapter below, this ideal held its appeal, slowly but decisively the emphasis was to shift in the centuries after 1200, as a more positive value was placed on the religious dignity of ordinary people and ordinary lifestyles. For Christianity lived with tension here above all: its central doctrine of the Incarnation, and its emphasis on the material symbols of the sacraments, not least the fact that marriage itself was a sacrament, affirmed the goodness of creation and the value of the quotidian. The most feared and detested heresy of the middle ages was the dualism of the Cathars, who equated evil with the material world, denying in the process the spiritual dignity of ordinary lives involving sex and marriage. But mainstream Christianity was also suspicious of sex, in two minds about worldly occupations and the chances for salvation of the ordinary man or woman. The vocation of the recluse was therefore a venerable one, stretching back to the desert fathers, and having a long pedigree in Saxon England, as well as notable post-Conquest English exponents in Godric of Finchale and Christina of Markyate. In the twelfth century Ailred of Rievaulx had drawn up a Latin *Rule* for his own sister, which the author of *Ancrene*

Wisse knew and made use of, among many other sources. *Ancrene Wisse*, for all its disarming grace of style and vernacular directness, is therefore a learned work, deeply rooted in the ascetical and theological tradition of the Latin west. But it looks forward rather than back, its spiritual style anticipating and embodying many of the features that were to characterise lay religion in later medieval England.

Anchorites and hermits were of course to be found all over medieval Europe. In late medieval England, however, the vocation retained a more resolutely lay and independent character than elsewhere. English recluses by and large resisted the European trend to absorb them into formal religious orders, as Christina of Markyate had been absorbed. *Ancrene Wisse* is certainly a work aimed at a religious elite: vowed women living in chastity, immured in an anchorhold or hermitage abutting the wall of a church. But the spiritual regimen it advocates has a moderation and humanity notably lacking in much of the spiritual direction emanating from early medieval monastic circles. The author disapproved of cruel and unusual vows or ascetical exercises, and warned against excessive use of penitential practices involving self-inflicted pain, like flagellation or the wearing of hair shirts or belts: 'I would rather you well endure harsh words than harsh haircloths'. He encouraged his recluses to wash regularly and often ('Dirt was never dear to God, though poverty and plainness are precious to him'), advised that there was no reason for them to wear wimples like nuns, and thought the keeping of a cat a good idea. The piety he commended to them had no hint of mysticism or the arcane about it, and its component elements were destined to become the familiar elements of lay devotion until the Reformation. The recluses were to recite the Hours of the Virgin, to reflect on and recite prayers in honour of the joys of the Virgin or the pains and wounds of Christ in his passion, to protect themselves with holy water against the attacks of the devil, and to bless their bed at night by invoking the sign of the cross, using a Latin form of words which regularly occurs in magical charms of the period. He takes it for granted that each of the recluses has an altar in her bedroom, on which there stand the familiar pious paraphernalia of the later middle ages: a crucifix, images of the Virgin and other saints, and an assortment of relics. The women were especially to venerate the sacrament of Christ's body and could observe the elevation at mass through a window into the church.[1] And

---

[1] For this and what follows I have used the translation in Anne Savage and Nicholas Watson, *Anchoritic Spirituality* (Manwah, NJ, 1991).

though the three sisters for whom *Ancrene Wisse* was first written were apparently literate in Latin as well as English, the author seems from the beginning to have had a wider and more socially varied audience in view. He widened the book's appeal in revisions directed to 'you anchoresses of England, very many together, twenty or more', some of whom he thought would be illiterate, and to whom he recommended the recitation of Our Fathers and Hail Marys in place of the written devotions of the first version. He assumes too that the devotional props of the recluse's life will have a wider interest and appeal, and that an anchoress would be likely to have lay visitors, men as well as women, in search of counsel and comfort.

The anchoritic ideal involved a flight from the world as decisive in its own way as entry to a monastery or convent. But the fact that *Ancrene Wisse* was written for women who were not nuns, and in English, alerts us to a fundamental new fact about religion in thirteenth- and fourteenth-century England: the thrust towards the creation – or emergence – of an informed and devout laity. That thrust is evident not least in the attitude of the author of *Ancrene Wisse* towards the arrival in England of the religious revolution represented by the mendicant orders. The author of *Ancrene Wisse*, whoever he was, ardently supported both the Franciscans and the Dominicans, recently arrived in England, urging the devout women for whom he wrote to 'trust secular priests little and religious [i.e. monks] still less' and instead to choose 'our preaching friars and our begging friars' as spiritual guides and confessors. Friars were to be the only men allowed to eat with the anchoresses.

This enthusiasm for the friars is remarkable, for neither order had been established in England much more than ten years when *Ancrene Wisse* was first written. But the appeal of the friars to English society from the moment of their arrival had been spectacular. The Dominicans arrived in 1221, and were joined in 1224 by the Franciscans. Thomas of Eccleston's vivid account of the early years of the Franciscan mission to England gives an unrivalled sense of the breadth of the social appeal of the friars minor. After a brief period in a house in Cornhill in London, a city merchant (who later himself became a friar) gave them a tenement on the insalubrious fringes of Newgate, in Stinking Lane, close to the Shambles, where they settled. At Oxford in the summer of 1225 they were given a house by another merchant, Robert the Mercer. When it became too small for the rapidly expanding community they were given the use of a larger house and garden by Richard the Miller, a site later confirmed to their use by the city authorities.

These benefactions, and the names of the donors, make clear the appeal of the early fraternal movement to prosperous townsmen. But the glamour exerted by the friars reached beyond merchants, artisans and town officials. Many of the early recruits were from aristocratic or well-to-do backgrounds, as names like Fitzwalter and Fitzralph make plain. By the 1240s recruits included a former abbot of Osney and a former bishop of Hereford, and the order's leading Oxford figure, Adam Marsh, recruited in 1232, had been a successful career clerk, and a favoured nephew of the bishop of Durham. By 1244 they were established in both universities, fifteen out of nineteen cathedral cities, and in twenty-five of the towns which were or would become the county towns of England. By 1255 they had forty-nine houses in all, with an average of twenty-five friars in each – the London Franciscan house alone had up to eighty brethren at any one time. By the middle of the century, bequests to the four main orders of friars had become one of the most familiar inclusions in the wills of late medieval town-dwellers. Royal patronage was also directed to the friars: Henry III offered to clothe and shoe all London's friars in 1233, and the Dominicans, his special favourites, were supplied with building materials from the works at Westminster Abbey. Dominicans were to act as royal confessors from Henry III's reign until that of Henry V.

The appeal of the new orders was manifold: the first generations of English friars, and especially the friars minor, were noted for their strict observance of the rule and spirit of poverty. The friars minor declined the king's offer of shoes in 1233, and Eccleston's narrative is full of vivid stories of extreme hardship joyfully borne. For newly rich merchants such exemplary renunciation had a vicarious charm. The widespread medieval aspiration 'to transform my earthly goods into heavenly assets'[2] had a special urgency in the towns, where the gulf between wealth and poverty was starkest, and where consciences might well be queasy about the machinery of usury which accompanied mercantile prosperity. But the friars had a great deal else to offer: their special talents as preachers appealed to an increasingly sophisticated lay audience eager for religious instruction, edification and entertainment. By the late thirteenth century the barn-like urban preaching-churches to which the humble early fraternal buildings had given way were attracting large and eager lay audiences. The friars also established themselves as sensitive and understanding confessors and spiritual directors, with an appeal which, as we

---

[2] The phrase comes from the will of Cardinal Beaufort (d.1447): G. L. Harriss, *Cardinal Beaufort: a study of Lancastrian ascendancy and decline* (Oxford, 1988), p. 378 n. 8.

have seen, extended from rural recluses to the royal court. And the dead as well as the living crowded the churches of the friars, as urban elites sought burial, or at any rate commemoration and prayers, in the friary precincts.

REFORMING BISHOPS AND THE LATERAN DECREES

Recluses and friars represented varieties of religious voluntarism destined to have profound implications for the character of religion in later medieval England. But the quickening of lay piety which both movements tapped and aimed to foster was also a preoccupation of the thirteenth- and fourteenth-century episcopate, and was finding increasingly focused institutional expression. The pastoral agenda was set by the decrees of the fourth Lateran Council of 1215. England was well represented at the Council, with nine bishops or bishops-elect present, including the archbishops of Canterbury and York. In the wake of the Council, the English participants took the conciliar decrees back to their dioceses, where the more active embodied them in episcopal constitutions and in the *acta* of provincial and diocesan synods, commencing with the Council of Oxford, summoned in 1222. The first and most influential of these episcopal constitutions were those of Richard Poore, successively bishop of Chichester, Salisbury and Durham, which were very widely imitated and adapted by others. In this way the central pastoral emphases of the Lateran Council came to be embodied in the statutes of reform-minded bishops who had not been at the Council. The episcopal statutes which Robert Grosseteste issued for the diocese of Lincoln in 1237 recapitulate most of the key issues, directing that parish priests should have an understanding of the ten commandments, seven deadly sins, seven sacraments and the creeds, that they should preach on all these to their people, instruct them in the reverent use of the sacraments and especially in the veneration of the eucharist, and that they should both catechise children and scrutinise the religious knowledge and the moral health of their adult parishioners.[3]

This scrutiny was to be achieved through confession. Lateran IV's most influential decree, contained in canon 21, *Omnis utriusque sexus* (all of either sex), commanded that every Christian who had reached years of discretion must confess his or her sins at least once a year to the parish

---

[3] There is a convenient translation in J. Shinners and W. J. Dohar, eds., *Pastors and the Care of Souls in Medieval England* (Notre Dame, IN, 1998), pp. 87–94.

priest, who must judiciously apply the right remedies for sin. Canon 27 enjoined bishops to procure educated men for ordination since 'the art of arts is the government of souls'. These two decrees provided the framework and rationale for the recasting of the medieval parochial clergy as teachers, preachers and pastors of souls. Throughout the thirteenth century, therefore, reform-minded English bishops produced or commissioned sets of instructions and manuals designed to equip the clergy for these tasks, from Robert Grosseteste of Lincoln's *Templum Domini*, a manual for confessors, to Peter Quinel of Exeter's synodal statutes and *Summula* for priests (1287). The efforts of individual bishops were gathered up at the Council of Lambeth in 1281. The ninth of the council's decrees, directed at 'priests of simple learning', crystallised the rationale for the whole enter-prise in its famous opening words: 'the ignorance of priests plunges the people into the ditch of error'. The Lambeth decrees formulated a cate-chetical programme for the instruction of the laity in the essentials of their religion, to be taught by every parish priest four times a year.

In the century that followed, these thirteenth-century initiatives would be consolidated and extended in the production of a series of priestly handbooks such as the *Oculus sacerdotis* (The Eye of the Priest) of Wil-liam of Pagula, an Oxford-trained canonist who was also a working parish priest. His treatise was divided into three parts: a confessor's manual, a set of instructions on the Christian life and an exposition of the sacraments. This was abbreviated and revised by the Cambridge theologian John de Burgo in his *Pupilla Oculi* (Pupil of the Eye) (1385). These were Latin treatises, trade manuals for professionals, but a vernacular version of the curriculum devised at the Council of Lambeth was commissioned in 1361 by Archbishop Thoresby of York, which came to be known as *The Lay Folks' Catechism*, and which, as that title suggests, was to find a wide lay audience. Further vernacular resources for country priests were provided at the end of the fourteenth century by John Mirk, in his versified *Instructions for Parish Priests*, and in the model sermons for the liturgical year published under the title *Festial* (*c.* 1400).

It is striking that on the whole this push for pastoral reform came from the secular clergy. The spiritual dynamism of the eleventh- and twelfth-century English Church had been essentially monastic, most of its greatest bishops monks. The thirteenth century ended that monastic dominance. Monasteries went on attracting the loyalty and benefactions of the laity, and there were still towering monastic leaders and builders like Henry of Eastry, prior of Canterbury (1285–1331), under whom monasteries would be extended and adorned. But the great age of monastic creativity was over: the last great Cistercian foundation was Hailes in 1251. Monks might still become bishops, but by and large they occupied minor and usually monastic sees, and few of them were pastoral or theological originators. By contrast, from Stephen Langton (archbishop of Canterbury 1207–28) onwards the great episcopal reformers were secular clerks trained in the universities or in the royal household, or both. Many were ardent admirers of the friars, like Grosseteste, who resigned his university lectureship in Oxford to teach in the Franciscan school there, and who filled his diocese with Dominican and Franciscan preachers and confessors. Two archbishops of Canterbury, Kilwardby (1272–8) and Pecham (1279–92), were themselves friars. The thirteenth century, indeed, saw a revival in interest in the cult of the saint-bishop, stimulated perhaps by the reputation of Becket and the more recent canonisation of William of York. Three thirteenth-century secular bishops, Edmund of Abingdon, Richard Wych and Thomas Cantilupe, achieved formal canonisation, while at least half a dozen others, including Robert Grosseteste, William Bytton and Walter Cantilupe, enjoyed a contemporary reputation for sanctity and were the objects of local veneration after their deaths.

The thirteenth century saw a general consolidation and strengthening of the secular church, in diocese and parish. The codification of the customs of Salisbury Cathedral by Richard Poore (bishop 1217–28) provided a model for the efficient ordering of cathedral life, and the liturgical 'use' or customs of Salisbury (the Sarum rite) gained ground steadily elsewhere in the later thirteenth century. Its adoption was virtually complete in the parish churches of the province of Canterbury by 1350. Cathedral churches themselves, the monastic cathedrals excepted, were to prove more conservative and to cling for longer to their own ritual customs. The consolidation of the administrative structure and clerical culture of the cathedrals was reflected in a good deal of rebuilding, notably the great eastward extensions and lady chapels which are a feature of so many of the major churches of the thirteenth and fourteenth century, designed to supply the need for more liturgical space and reflecting the growing cult of the Virgin.

A PLACE FOR BELIEVING: THE CONSOLIDATION OF THE PARISH

By 1200 the parish structure which was to survive into the nineteenth century had more or less crystallised. The ancient minsters and estate churches which had preceded and helped shape the geography of the parish system had largely given way to churches funded by tithe or other forms of ecclesiastical levy and managed by local people. Appointment of clergy to serve these parishes was mostly in ecclesiastical hands, either those of the bishop or, in something like a quarter of the 9,500 or so parishes, in the hands of monasteries to whom the parish had been 'appropriated' by gift. This in effect made the religious house the rector of the parish, and necessitated the appointment of a vicar to carry out the parochial duties. In England's largest diocese, Lincoln, Hugh of Wells stabilised clerical provision by creating nearly 300 vicarages between 1209 and 1235, which, among other advantages, gave the clergy concerned a freehold in their benefices. Attempts were also being made to organise something approaching a minimum annual wage for parish clergy, set by the Council of Oxford at five marks (£3 6s 8d).

This institutional settlement was reflected in a corresponding effort by the episcopate to see the parishes properly served by the priests appointed to them. That concern showed itself in the first place in the campaign for a better-educated clergy. It is difficult to assess the role of the universities in that effort. The universities of course transformed the nature of theology and the role of canon law in the life of the Church, and university-trained bishops included many ardent teachers and legislators. Learned bishops might fill their cathedral chapters and diocesan administrations with graduates, as Simon of Ghent (1297–1315) did at Salisbury. No less than a sixth of the clergy instituted in the diocese of Exeter by Bishop Quinel at the end of the thirteenth century were university graduates. From the later fourteenth century bishops anxious to raise clerical standards would found schools and university colleges for poor clerks, of which William of Wykeham's twin foundations at Winchester and New College, Oxford in the late fourteenth century are the most striking. But it is a moot point how far university studies directly improved the standard of clerical ministry at a parish level. Graduates by and large had their eyes on a different sort of career, in royal or ecclesiastical administration, or within the universities themselves. The benefices of university clerks were designed not so much to put a theologian into the parsonage, as to launch and subsidise a career which would take the beneficiary permanently out of parochial duties. In pastoral terms, the more modest efforts of bishops to implement Lateran IV's vision of a competent non-graduate clergy, unskilled in theology or canon law but able to teach and confess their parishioners, was probably a good deal more effective, and certainly a good deal more realistic.

Just as importantly, bishops sought a better *behaved* clergy: celibate, decently tonsured (to make clear their status and mark them off from their parishioners), sober, resident and attentive to the spiritual and (in the case of the poor) the material needs of their parishioners. Their behaviour mattered most in the celebration of the liturgy and sacraments, and episcopal regulations gave a high priority to the decent ordering of worship. The statutes of Bishop Quinel of Exeter (1287) list the objects parishioners were required to provide: a silver chalice, a decent pyx to reserve the eucharistic bread, and another to carry the host to the sick, a chrysmatory of metal for the holy oils, a censer and incense-boat, a 'pax-brede' to be kissed at the kiss of peace, a stone altar and all its hangings and cloths, a font with a lockable cover, altar and processional candlesticks, especially the great triangular candle-stand used in the service of *Tenebrae* in Holy Week, a paschal candlestick, processional and altar crosses, a pall to cover the corpse at funerals, bells, a lantern to be carried before the priest when he took the *viaticum* (literally, 'journey money', a metaphor for final communion) to the dying, two sets of vestments, for work days and feast days, two surplices, and a small library of liturgical books and instructional manuals to enable the priest to perform his duties properly.

Uniformity in such matters was an aspiration, never a reality, though it was an aspiration that moved perceptibly towards realisation. By the end of the thirteenth century it was generally expected that the parish would provide the materials, books and furniture for worship, and maintain the nave of the parish church and the churchyard in good repair, while the patron or parson was responsible for the chancel. The office of churchwarden, elected by and acting on behalf of the parish community, would emerge in the course of the thirteenth and early fourteenth centuries to discharge the parishioners' obligations, and the wardens would accumulate a host of other communal responsibilities, both religious and secular. For most people below the ranks of the upper gentry, the parish was to establish itself not merely as the basic administrative unit of ecclesiastical responsibility, but as the principal focus of lay religious identity, and the parish church became the main object of the escalating devotional investment of the later middle ages. Through the fourteenth and fifteenth centuries most of the parish churches of medieval England were elaborated and adorned, the naves in particular enlarged and supplemented with aisles, initially perhaps to accommodate a rising population, but increasingly to house the growing number of guild and chantry altars, and to provide routes for the elaborate processions which were a feature of Sunday and festal liturgies in the Sarum rite.

RELIGIOUS ENTERPRISE AND THE 'VOLUNTARY SECTOR'

But if parish churches were at the heart of lay religion, the parish and its building contained rather than constrained the sometimes divergent energies which made up that religion. Reliance on the evidence of the statutes of synods and reforming bishops might convey the impression that medieval English Christianity was regimented and dragooned. The reality was very different. Most churches were examples of 'complex space', based not around a single focal point – the high altar or the pulpit – but subdivided into a series of distinct but overlapping enclaves, some more important or more private than others, and representing different subgroups and interests within the broader community. This complexity reflected the nature of the medieval parish itself, which was rarely a single hierarchical unit, but rather a constellation of groups, families and individuals who often co-operated and sometimes conflicted.

From the mid fourteenth century, and in many places earlier, most urban and many rural parishes contained at least one religious guild. These were voluntary religious bodies dedicated to a saint or religious mystery (such as Corpus Christi or the Trinity). Guild members met for mass on their patronal day, when they elected officers for the year, held a feast at which all the brethren and sisters were expected to be present (women were often members, but very rarely officers) and distributed alms to the poor. Members attended their fellow members' funerals and obits (commemorative services), often wearing the guild livery or hood, and provided the candles and torches that were an important part of such occasions. Churchwardens' accounts from all over the country show that guilds often contributed significantly to devotional, charitable and building projects within the parish. Many Corpus Christi guilds, for example, paid for the candles burned around the Easter Sepulchre in Holy Week, or maintained lights before the reserved sacrament, or paid for torches to burn at the elevation of the host at the parish mass on Sundays. Others contributed to the clerical manpower available to the parish by employing their own chaplain. Guilds offered ordinary people not merely an opportunity to express a shared devotion but a form of sanctified sociability, which often had a strong emphasis on respectability. As the ordinances of the London guild of St Anne at St Lawrence Jewry put it, the guild existed 'in maintenance of good love and for to nourish good and true company in destruction and amendment of men of wicked fame and of evil bearing, by way of alms and of charity'.[4]

---

[4] C. Barron and L. Wright, eds., 'The London English guild certificates', *Nottingham Medieval Studies*, 39 (1995), 121.

As that last phrase suggests, guilds might offer more quantifiable benefits too. In both town and country they were often substantial property-owners, able to lend money or to rent out real estate, land or livestock to members at attractive rates. In many places guild office was one of the recognised ways of establishing or consolidating one's weight in the community, and could function as an apprenticeship for more demanding parochial, manorial or civic office. Many urban guilds offered modest sickness benefits to ailing members, in London by the 1380s ranging from 6d to 14d per week, in other communities often based on quarterly penny levies or benefit collections from the guild brethren and sisters. Quite apart from the religious benefits of prayers for the souls of dead brothers and sisters, guilds ensured respectable burial for members too poor to provide for themselves. In scattered rural communities or large towns guilds might also maintain meeting-halls or even chapels which could serve as a local focus of identity, and their stipendiary clergy might function as assistant parish priests, providing crucial religious services, especially in winter, when travel to a distant parish church was difficult. In towns, craft guilds in particular might meet in convent or friary churches rather than in a parish, or might maintain lights or images in friary churches in addition to those they supported in the parish, for the friaries provided much of the clerical manpower guilds needed to celebrate the 'trentals' or groups of thirty masses for the dead they offered for each deceased member. The social composition of guilds varied greatly: some were craft guilds, and some, like the Holy Trinity guild at Luton, or the Jesus guild at St Lawrence Reading, were consciously exclusive instruments of oligarchy, dominated by the urban elite and their gentry or aristocratic allies and patrons. But although most guild membership registers are sparing with information about the occupations of their brethren, the indications are that most guilds, whether in town or country, at least aspired to be socially inclusive, and seem to have drawn their membership from all but the very wealthy and the very poor.

Motives for founding or joining a guild varied hugely, as a glance at some of the many documented guilds of fourteenth-century Bishop's (now King's) Lynn reveals.[5] Lynn had almost seventy guilds by the later fourteenth century. Five are known to be craft or occupational guilds: the clerks (dedicated to St John the Baptist), the young scholars (St William of Norwich), the shipmen (Exaltation of the Holy Cross), the young

[5] The following Lynn returns are from L.C. Toulmin Smith, ed., *English Guilds* (EETS, os XL, 1870), pp. 45–109.

merchants (Nativity of St John the Baptist) and the coifmakers (appropriately, the Decollation – beheading – of the Baptist). Some of the Lynn guilds had straightforwardly 'religious' reasons for their foundation. The Corpus Christi guild was begun in 1349, when three townsmen decided that the single candle they saw carried before the sacrament to dying plague victims was insufficient and founded the guild to provide additional lights 'for the period of their lives', thereby shrewdly providing the Almighty with a motive to preserve them from the pestilence. There were at least five guilds of St Thomas Becket in the town (which possessed a major secondary relic in the form of the archbishop's staff). One was founded by six men who had made the pilgrimage to Canterbury and one of its rules was that each year one member would go on behalf of the rest to the martyr's shrine. The Holy Trinity Guild in All Saints church, South Lynn was founded to fund a light in front of the image of the Trinity 'where there is often a great number of people because of the miracles which often take place there and because so many have been healed there of their infirmities and diseases'. The young merchants' guild of the Nativity of John the Baptist was formed in order to fund repairs to the north side of St Margaret's parish church, which looks like a piece of parochial piety to the town's main church, but they were afterwards joined by young merchants from other towns, and established a merchant chapel on the north side of the church. Lynn was a large and crowded community with one vast parish church, four houses of friars and a handful of parish-church-sized 'chapels', the largest of which by the late fourteenth century was agitating for independent parochial status. So the town's many guilds may have provided the citizens with smaller and more manageable units of religious belonging. The members of the guild of St Mary in Dampgate, at St James's chapel, for example, all lived in the same street. Guilds might serve as focuses of community awareness and identity in more fraught circumstances too. In urban communities like Bury St Edmunds, Dunstable or Cirencester, where monastic overlords hindered or prevented the attainment of civic or economic autonomy, prestigious guilds supported by the town's elites might offer a collective identity over against the monastic community, or even serve as shadow town councils. The precise relationship between guild and parish therefore varied from place to place, but it should rarely be conceived in terms of rivalry: the official, 'compulsory', religion of the parish and the voluntary religion of the guild were complementary, seldom opposed.

Guilds, which seem to have multiplied in the second half of the fourteenth century, were not the only contributors to the complexity of the late medieval parish. The elaboration of the doctrine of purgatory and the growing concern of lay people to provide for their own swift passage through its cleansing fires was in many ways the most influential development in late medieval Christianity, for it turned the monasteries, cathedrals and perhaps above all the parish churches of England into ante-chambers of purgatory, shaping the religion of the living to beliefs about the dead. From the doctrine of purgatory flowed a massive inflation in clerical numbers, to meet the growing demand for requiem and votive masses. From it, too, flowed an avalanche of pious donation to the churches, designed to honour God and the saints and to assist the devotion of one's neighbours, and which constituted therefore meritorious acts of charity that would help speed the soul of the donor through purgatory. From the later thirteenth century, a favourite expression of these concerns among the very wealthy was the foundation of perpetual chantries. A chantry was a service endowed by one or more benefactors for the celebration of masses and prayers for the dead. A chantry might be housed in a cathedral or monastic church, at a side altar in a parish church, in a specially constructed chapel in a churchyard or on a bridge, or in a collegiate church with a team of priests and singers. The establishment of even the simplest perpetual chantry employing only one priest involved setting aside a large enough endowment in land to support the priest and to maintain the altar. Even where the chantry was placed in an existing foundation, such as a monastery, the host institution would normally expect to make a significant profit over and above the running costs of the chantry, or at least be securely indemnified against loss. Under the mortmain legislation of 1279 the gift of land required the purchase of a royal licence and these were granted increasingly grudgingly in the later middle ages because of the crown's resistance to the permanent alienation of land into ecclesiastical hands. For all these reasons, the foundation of a perpetual chantry was an expensive business and, until the Black Death, the exclusive prerogative of the rich. Chantry chapels, blazoned with their founders' coats of arms and containing effigies in marble, brass or stained glass, were extravagant gestures of conspicuous consumption, often dominating the buildings in which they were located.

Cathedral chantries were largely the preserve of bishops and higher clergy, but monasteries, with an abundant supply of clergy to celebrate offices and masses and offering institutional stability, remained a favoured setting for long-term aristocratic and upper gentry chantry provision. In Norfolk, although the overall numbers of new chantry foundations declined after the Black Death, the proportion of perpetual chantries established after 1350 in religious houses, as opposed to purpose-built chapels or parish churches, increased from just over 40 per cent to almost 70 per cent, and remained high until the reign of Henry VIII. This was presumably because the mortality among the secular clergy in 1348–9 (when up to half the parish clergy in the Norwich diocese died) made founders horrifyingly aware that a community of priests or monks offered a better guarantee of permanent commemoration than an institution which might perish with its lay executors or chantry priest.

Nevertheless, chantry foundations in parish churches grew in number, with members of the urban elite as well as country gentry featuring as founders. In York during the first third of the fourteenth century almost every prominent aldermanic family, including six mayors, established chantries in one or other of the city's parish churches. Chantry foundation fell out of fashion among York citizens sooner than in many other communities, as testators increasingly favoured the employment of short-term stipendiary priests rather than the establishment of far more costly perpetual chantries. Nevertheless the York chantry priests formed in effect an official corps of auxiliary clergy, many living a common life in collegiate institutions and having their finances administered by the city chamberlains. By the later fifteenth century chantry foundation almost everywhere had declined, not, as some historians have imagined, because the doctrine of purgatory was losing its hold on the lay religious imagination: on the contrary, almost everyone who made a will at all made some provision for post-mortem prayers for their souls. But the overwhelming majority of intercessory benefactions were now short-term – for a year, five years, twenty years – an arrangement requiring no licence and a far smaller capital investment.

TOWN AND COUNTRY: TWO PARISH CHURCHES

Intercessory benefactions were everywhere in late medieval England, and the army of stipendiary priests who existed to fulfil them ensured that by the late fourteenth century every parish church in England had at least one altar in addition to the high altar. Some of these were tucked away in screened-off gentry chapels, and staffed by chaplains paid to pray primarily for their employers. But even private chantry priests were expected to assist in the religious activities of the parish at large, and many of them played key roles in the parish, training the choir, playing the organ or writing out the parish liturgical books and the wills of parishioners. Clive Burgess has demonstrated the extent to which private devotional initiative and collective parochial provision were interdependent in medieval Bristol, and the exceptionally well-documented parish churches of fifteenth-century Bristol offer an unrivalled window into the character of that collective Christianity.[6]

Between the death of her husband Henry in 1470, and her own in December 1485, the wealthy Bristol widow Alice Chester showered a series of major benefactions on her parish church of All Saints, in the heart of the city. She continued and extended the chantry established by her husband 'for the loving of almighty God and the augmenting of divine service' – the latter by providing the parish with the services of an auxiliary priest, who conducted masses and prayers of intercession for Alice Chester's family every Friday in the year and on the anniversary of Henry's death. Mistress Chester also paid for the installation of a riverside crane for loading and unloading merchandise by the Marsh Gate, a crucial amenity in this city devoted to maritime trade. Above all, she funded an extensive programme of renewal of the church's liturgical furnishings and devotional imagery. She commissioned a statue of the Trinity 'over the image of Jesus', standing in a gilded tabernacle covered with a curtain which could be closed or drawn back 'when it shall please the vicar and the parishioners'. She gilded the lady altar, paid for a painted frontal and commissioned a carved tabernacle with three of the most popular late medieval representations of Mary: the pietà (the representation of the Virgin with her dead son in her lap), the annunciation and the assumption. She had the rood altar gilded and carved with images of the saints – St Anne, St Mary Magdalene, St Giles, St Erasmus and St Anthony – and she provided another painted veil to cover these images 'at certain times'. She presented a long linen towel or 'houselling-cloth' to be held under the chins of her fellow parishioners as they knelt in rows to receive their annual communion on Easter Day.[7] She gave a great brass basin for the ritual washing of the church's relics on Relic Sunday and a new cross of enamel and silver gilt to be carried in the weekly processions before the main Sunday mass. And 'taking to her counsel the worshipful of this parish with others having best insights in carving, to the honour and worship of almighty God and his saints, and of her special devotion unto this church', she commissioned a new rood-loft, the great partition separating the chancel and high altar from the

---

[6] What follows derives from C. Burgess, ed., *The Pre-Reformation Accounts of All Saints' Bristol*, part 1 (Bristol Record Society, XLVI, 1995), pp. 15–17 and *passim*.
[7] For another gift of a houselling towel, see below, p. 335.

body of the church, filled with twenty-two carved and gilded images, arranged in pairs on pillars and tabernacles round the principal image of the Trinity, which was flanked by statues of St Christopher and St Michael the Archangel. Finally, considering that 'there was no hearse cloth in the church of any reputation in value . . . for the love and honour she had unto almighty God and all Christian souls, and for the ease and succour of all this parish unto whom she owed her good will and love in her day', she presented the church with a black pall, decorated with her own and her husband's initials and an inscription in Latin asking for prayers for their souls, for use at the funerals of other parishioners.

Mistress Chester's bounty epitomises many of the preoccupations at the heart of late medieval lay piety. It was a Christianity rooted in the concrete, nourished by the sight of images and the touch of relics and of sacramentals (sacred objects, such as holy water), focused on the passion of Christ and the intercession of the saints, above all the Virgin Mary, but also practical helper saints like Christopher, protector of travellers, Michael, protector of the death-bed, or Erasmus, protector against disorders of the stomach and bowels. It was a piety much concerned with death, with the power of prayers and pious works to ease the souls of the departed through purgatory, and with the mutual obligations of prayer and charity that bound the living to the dead. It was a ritual piety, intensely reverential towards the sacraments, above all the eucharist. It was keyed to the annual cycle of the liturgy, processions and masses, the feasts of the saints and their relics, and the Church's seasons: Lent, when the many images in the church were concealed behind veils painted with tokens of the passion, and Easter, when the community celebrated and consolidated its often fragile unity by reconciling quarrels and kneeling shoulder to shoulder to receive communion together. It was a Christianity which coloured, and was coloured by, the structures and values of society, emphasising the virtues of neighbourliness and hence attributing religious merit to practical benefactions like the riverside crane, acutely conscious of rank and precedence, endearingly and competitively sensitive to appearances and respectability. Planning her munificence, Mistress Chester had consulted the vicar and the leading parishioners, the 'worshipful' of the parish. The element of pride of wealth and conspicuous consumption in her giving is manifest in the gift of the hearse cloth or pall prominently embroidered with her own and her husband's initials. Through Mistress Chester's benefactions we catch a vivid glimpse of the social dynamics of an urban community, in which even lavish benefactors were expected to observe the courtesies of consultation and group decision-making. We glimpse too the physical layout of a prosperous late medieval church, crammed with altars and images and lights: the theatre for a liturgy which sanctified matter by blessing and venerating it, which sanctified space by processing around it or dividing it into holy corrals with decorated screens and partitions, and which sanctified time in the cycle of fast and feast, penitence and celebration, that made up the ritual year.

Chantries, like that of Henry and Alice Chester, were private institutions, attached to individuals or their families. In many parishes, especially rural parishes whose main income was derived from the activities of the living rather than the property of the dead, age- or gender-specific groups – the wives, the young men or grooms, the maidens – organised themselves for festal and religious activity, and maintained their own religious symbols in their parish church. These were rarely altars – more often candles in front of favoured images – but they include one of the most famous collections of stained glass surviving from the early Tudor period: the windows paid for by the young men, the maidens and the wives of the western end of the Cornish parish of St Neot. These groups were often organised geographically. Within the sheep-grazing Norfolk parish of Salle groups at Marshgate, Kirkgate, Lunton and Steynwade maintained 'ploughlights' and 'maiden-lights' in the church. Such groups were regularly remembered in local wills, like that of Alice Martyn who left 6d to the ploughlight and 'to the dancing lights of the maidens, to each of them 3d',[8] or that of William Kechyn, parishioner of Sloley in Norfolk who left 1s 8d to 'the ploughlight of the street there I dwell in' and 1s 'to every of the other seven ploughlights in the same town'.[9]

Salle, with a population in the mid fifteenth century of about 500, had seven guilds: of the Blessed Virgin Mary (the Assumption gild); St Thomas; St Paul (the parish dedication); St John the Baptist; St Margaret; the Trinity, which had its altar and priest in Thomas Roos's chapel; and St James, which had its altar in the chapel of the south transept. This chapel was built by Thomas Brigg (d. 1444). His initials are on bosses in the roof and on the outside cornice of the chapel, which is filled with Brigg burials, while Thomas and his wives kneel before St Thomas Becket, his name saint, in the upper registers of the stained glass. It was therefore very much a family chapel, partitioned from the rest of the

---

[8] N[orfolk] [County] R[ecord] O[ffice], archdeaconry of Norfolk wills, 222 Gloys. See also, based on evidence mainly from the south–west, K. L. French, 'Maidens' lights and wives' stores: women's parish guilds in late medieval England', *Sixteenth Century Journal*, 29 (1998), 399–425.

[9] NRO, N[orwich] C[onsistory] C[ourt], 444 Ryxe.

church as Briggs' land, no doubt, was fenced off from that of his neighbours. But the chapel was also the St James guild chapel, and along with the Brigg family name, the scallop shell of St James can be seen carved on its parapet. Similar sharing arrangements between guilds and local gentry operated in the north transept.[10]

We need to beware of deducing too much from these arrangements. It remains true that late medieval gentry were less closely involved with parish and guild than their humbler neighbours. Often guild members, they were rarely guild officers, and almost never served the parish as churchwardens. But in many parishes the gentry remained a significant and influential presence, initiating or supporting parish projects, part of the social complexity that was reflected in the physical complexity of the parish church building itself. The interior of Salle church, now a vast, cathedral-sized auditorium without partitions, was never conceived as a single open space, but an interconnecting network of sacred zones based round a multitude of altars and images, some privately owned, some the property of guilds in which many parishioners were sharers, many adorned with lights paid for by young people's gender-groups, all of them in some sense part of a common symbol system and set of resources, and manned by a transient population of salaried chaplains, many of them sons of local families, financed by guilds, by local land owners and by short-term benefactions like that of the yeoman Robert Pull who left eight marks (£5 6s 8d) in 1510 as wages for 'a priest that shall be able to sing [mass] in the church of Salle a year'.[11]

PILGRIMAGE

In 1986 work to strengthen the south-east tower pier in Worcester Cathedral uncovered a shallow late medieval grave. It contained the skeleton of a stocky man who had died in his sixties, clad in a lined woollen tunic and thigh-length walking-boots. By his side was a stout metal-shod wooden staff, once painted bright red, and a pierced cockle-shell, the conventional sign of a late medieval pilgrim. The expensive walking-boots had been almost new when they were slit along their length

---

[10] For medieval Salle see W. L. E. Parsons, *Salle: the story of a Norfolk parish, its church, manors and people* (Norwich, 1937); F. Blomefield and C. Parkin, *An Essay towards a Topographical History of the County of Norfolk* (5 vols., 1739–75), iv, pp. 421–6; T. A. Heslop, 'The visual arts and crafts', in B. Ford, ed., *The Cambridge Guide to the Arts in Britain*, II: *The Middle Ages* (Cambridge, 1988), pp. 194–9; R. Fawcett and D. King, 'Salle church', *Archaeological Journal*, 137 (1980), 332–5.

[11] NRO, NCC, Spyltimber 291. Pull also left 6d to each ploughlight.

to dress the corpse and the metal double-spike which shod the staff showed little sign of wear. The state of the skeleton's knee and hip joints, by contrast, suggested a man who had walked long and far, and archaeologists concluded that the boots, staff and shell represented a deliberate symbolic evocation of one or more pilgrimages which had retained deep significance for the dead man and those who buried him.

The symbolic language here is plain: death itself is being presented as the last long pilgrimage, the culmination of the Christian life conceived as a journey away from the familiar towards the divine. Such symbolism had its biblical sources in Abraham's abandonment of his homeland at the command of God, in Israel's journeyings in the wilderness, in the biblical idealisation of the holy city of Jerusalem and in Christ's homeless wandering with nowhere to lay his head. All this was evoked in the liturgy of death itself ('Go forth Christian soul, go from this world'), and in the very name given to the dying Christian's last communion – *viaticum*.

Understandably, this is the set of resonances and associations which have found most favour in modern discussion of the symbolic meaning of late medieval pilgrimage, and which in fact were to survive the practice of pilgrimage in England to re-emerge as a literary metaphor in the hands of Protestant writers like John Bunyan. The work of the social anthropologist Victor Turner in particular has encouraged historians to think of pilgrimage as a 'liminal' phenomenon, a religious rite which temporarily liberates pilgrims from the constraints and boundaries of the familiar by removing them physically and socially from their normal environments, across geographical and social thresholds, and which thereby creates a new and wider community in which social class, wealth and convention give way to a wider common identity and equality. Yet all this raises questions for the historian, aware that the single most important energy in late medieval English religious practice was its drive towards localism evident in the flowering of the parish and the guild. In fact, for many medieval Christians going on pilgrimage was not so much like launching on a journey to the ends of the earth, as of going to a local market town. Shrines were features by which they mapped the familiar, as much as signposts to other worlds and other social realities: a local, not a liminal, phenomenon.

There were of course national shrines like Walsingham or Canterbury which throughout the middle ages drew visitors in their thousands from all over England, and a steady stream of English men and women made their way even further afield to Rocamadour and Compostella, Jerusalem and Rome. But most fourteenth- and fifteenth-century pilgrimages were to sacred sites within one's own region: journeys that might take one no further than the next parish, and rarely further than the nearest market town. The first thing to grasp about late medieval pilgrim centres is that they were legion, and most of them were localised or regional in their appeal. Many, perhaps most, of these local shrines were centred not on a body but on an image, for images were easier to come by than holy bodies. Image shrines could loom just as large and serve the same functions as grave shrines. Rocamadour and Walsingham were image shrines. Below these great international image shrines were thousands of lesser images which attracted local loyalty. The 'good rood of the north door' of St Paul's in London or the rood of Boxley were matched by hundreds of lesser roods, in niches or tabernacles above side-altars in country churches, like the 'good rood upon the north side' of Blythburgh church to which John Brown left £2 in 1533 'to make him a new coat', or the good rood on the north side of Bramfield church whose decorated niche is still visible.[12] The cluster of shrines to which the early fifteenth-century Alice Cooke of Horstead in Norfolk declared 'I will have a man to go ... pilgrimages' – Our Lady of Reepham, St Spirit of Elsing, St Parnell of Stratton, St Leonard without Norwich, St Wandred of Bixley, St Margaret of Horstead, Our Lady of Pity of Horstead, St John's head at Trimingham and the Holy Rood of Crostwight – were all local image shrines, some of them known only from this single mention. All over late medieval England the local shrines of the Virgin were based on images, some of which achieved a regional status that put them on a par with more famous shrines.

Our Lady of Woolpit in Suffolk was an image in a chapel on the north side of Woolpit church. By the early thirteenth century the offerings of pilgrims were significant enough for Bury Abbey to demand a share. By 1286 a fair had sprung up, held on the main pilgrimage day, 8th September, the feast of the Nativity of the Virgin. By the fifteenth century local people were lavishing gifts on the shrine, like the diamond ring bequeathed by Dame Elizabeth Andrews of Baylham in 1473, one of a pair, the other of which went to Our Lady of Walsingham, or the 'pair of beads of thrice sixty garnished with silver and three gold rings set thereto, with a cross and heart of silver' offered to the shrine by Robert Reydon of Creeting in 1505, on condition that they remained always round the neck of the image of Our Lady of Woolpit. From the 1450s to the late 1520s testators from many of the surrounding villages and towns – Thorndon,

---

[12] NRO, NCC Punting 31.

Thurston, Otley, Gislingham, Wetheringsett, Kelsale and Fornham – made arrangements for pilgrimages on their behalf to Our Lady of Woolpit, and the shrine had clearly become a focus of regional identity.

This made it an appropriate forum for the exemplary punishment of local religious deviants. In 1499 a group of parishioners from the village of Great Ashfield, four miles from Woolpit, were found guilty of magical practices. They were required to perform public penance not only in their parish church, but at Norwich Cathedral, Bury St Edmund's marketplace and during the procession at the shrine of Our Lady of Woolpit, where they were required to offer candles to the image of St Mary in the chapel. More positively, regional aristocrats, and even kings and queens, made a point of identifying themselves with such local shrines. John Lord Howard of Stoke by Nayland, future duke of Norfolk, made several benefactions of money, lights and silver-gilt votive images to Our Lady of Woolpit in the early 1480s, and Woolpit was one of the five East Anglian shrines (alongside Our Lady of Walsingham, Ipswich, Sudbury and Stoke by Clare) to which Queen Elizabeth sent a pilgrim to pray for her in Lent 1502.

The devotee, like Elizabeth of York, who pays someone else to go on pilgrimage is clearly happy to dispense with the symbolic value of journeying, of abandoning the safe and familiar things of home, in favour of a transaction in which a transferable benefit is obtained. The point of the pilgrimage here is not the journeying but the spiritual benefit to be secured. This often took the form of an indulgence: the remission of penance and a consequent reduction of the time to be spent by the beneficiary in purgatory. Even pilgrimage literature might present the benefits of pilgrimage in this resolutely practical and unadventurous way. William Brewyn's guide to the Roman pilgrimage, listing the indulgences available at the Lateran, commented that 'if people only knew how great are the indulgences of the Lateran church, they would not think it necessary to go across the sea to the Holy Sepulchre'.[13]

The role of indulgences as a motive for pilgrimage in late medieval England hardly needs demonstration. The whole pilgrim-literature genre represented by *The Stacyons of Rome* turned on it – all such books were essentially trainspotters' guides to the best and most powerful relics and indulgences. The episcopal registers of Edmund Lacy provide dozens of examples of indulgences granted to local chapels, hospitals and churches

---

[13] C. Eveleigh Woodruff, ed., *A XVth Century Guide-Book to the Principal Churches of Rome, compiled c. 1470 by William Brewyn* (1933), p. 25.

to help defray the costs of building or repair work. Donors wanting the indulgence had to go to the parish in question, penitent, confessed and contrite, and make an offering.[14] Spiritual health rather than physical healing was the object of such pilgrimages, which perhaps formed the majority of pilgrimages in fifteenth- and sixteenth-century England.

Pilgrimages might be undertaken out of pure devotion or as the consequence of a vow. Vows of pilgrimage were by and large treated very seriously, and promises of pilgrimage to the major shrines of Rome, Compostella and Jerusalem could be dispensed from only by the pope himself. Pilgrimage vows might be undertaken as an act of devotion to a saint or to secure help or healing in emergency. When the ship in which the Norfolk priest Sir Richard Torkington was travelling back from the Holy Land was caught in a January storm, the crew and passengers pledged themselves to pilgrimage, 'some of us pilgrimages to our blessed lady of Loretto in Italy, and some to our lady of Walsingham and some to St Thomas of Canterbury we that were Englishmen'.[15] Vows of this sort had to be fulfilled one way or another, and if sickness or circumstances prevented it, then it had to be done by proxy. Margaret East, widow, of the Norwich parish of St Martin in the Bailey, made arrangements for her executor, her 'right trusty and well beloved cousin Thomas Thurkell, shoemaker in Beer street' to go on her behalf

certain pilgrimage, that is to say, in my life to the holy St Wandred, and after my decease he shall go unto St Thomas of Canterbury, and there to pray for me to release me of my vow which I made thither myself. And from thence the same Thomas shall go for me on pilgrimage unto the abbey of Chertsey where King Henry lieth, if my goods will stretch so far for his costs. And so by his pilgrimages that I may be released of my vows.[16]

For all its associations of launching into the unknown, therefore, in practice late medieval pilgrimage tended to be assimilated to the locality. Pilgrimage *might* take one beyond the familiar, and might offer temporary release from the ties that bound. But most late medieval pilgrims were consolidating, not dissolving, their social and religious world.

---

[14] J. H. Parry and A. T. Bannister, eds., *Registrum Edmundi Lacy, episcopi Herefordensis A. D. mccccxvii–mccccxx* (Canterbury and York Soc., XXII, 1918), pp. 21, 24, 28; G. Dunstan, ed., *The Register of Edmund Lacy Bishop of Exeter 1420–1455* (3 vols., Torquay, 1963), i, pp. 51, 107, 300, 315; ii, pp. 25, 314, 403; iii, pp. 14, 38, 39, 136, 210.

[15] R. B. Wheeler, ed., 'Torkington's pilgrimage to Jerusalem in 1517', *Gentleman's Magazine*, 82 (1812), 313.

[16] H. Harrod, 'Extracts from early wills in the Norwich Registries', *Norfolk Archaeology*, 4 (1855), 338.

VERNACULAR PIETY AND THE MIXED LIFE

We have seen that one mark of the success in England of the reforms initiated by the fourth Lateran Council was the steady burgeoning of parochial life, not merely as a forum for the passive absorption of clerical instruction, but as a vigorous and versatile outlet for lay religious concerns. A corresponding development was the growth of a vernacular religious culture, which reached its apogee in the reigns of Edward III and Richard II. In 1357 Archbishop Thoresby of York instructed his archdeacons to ensure that parish clergy every Sunday at least should teach the people 'in English, without any far-fetched subtlety of words' the articles of faith, the commandments of both old and new testaments, the works of mercy, the virtues, sacraments and deadly sins. Lay people, thus instructed, were in their turn to teach all this 'to their little ones, boys and girls, and compel them to learn them', and the clergy were to use the annual Lenten confessions of their parishioners to check whether the adults knew the fundamentals of their faith, and were teaching the children in their turn.[17] It was to facilitate this process that he commissioned *The Lay Folks' Catechism.*

We have no way of quantifying the success of Thoresby's programme, but it clearly assumes what it also seeks to promote: a vigorous lay interest in religion, expressed in the English tongue by men and women well enough grounded in the essentials of the faith to be able and willing to teach them to their children. At least at the upper levels of society, this religious interest went beyond simple catechesis. It has already been suggested that *Ancrene Wisse* was a major source or at any rate a symptom of this developing English religious tradition, though at a point where it was still largely the preserve of specialists, like women recluses. An even more central text might be St Edmund of Canterbury's *Speculum Ecclesiae* (Mirror of the Church), written originally in French but which circulated widely in Latin and in English. The *Mirror* was highly schematised, its sections arranged round the familiar pattern of seven sins, seven beatitudes, seven gifts of the Holy Ghost, seven sacraments and so on. Almost certainly intended for an audience of religious, it was manifestly the work of a clerk trained in the university. To this extent it resembles a long succession of didactic treatises in English prose and verse which stretch into the late fourteenth century and of which Robert Mannyng of Brunn's *Handling Sin* (1303) or Dan Michel of Northgate's *Ayenbite of*

---

[17] S. Powell, 'The transmission and circulation of the Lay Folk's Catechism', in A. J. Minnis, ed., *Late-medieval Religious Texts and their Transmission* (Cambridge, 1994), p. 67.

Inwit (The Prick of Conscience) (1340) are fair examples. But, like them, its circulation history suggests that it reached far beyond the circle of religious professionals, to a larger lay audience. Sharing a good deal of didactic material with the flow of episcopal constitutions and pastoral manuals produced in England in the long wake of Lateran IV, the *Mirror* added a distinctive element, a scheme of devotion in the form of a series of guided meditations on the life of Christ and especially his passion, to be undertaken at the canonical hours. This sort of pious exercise, emphasising ardour of feeling and imaginative empathy with the sufferings of Christ, would in due course be elaborated in English versions of Franciscan writings like the *Meditationes Vitae Christi*.

The ardent devotional atmosphere represented and encouraged by works of this sort was to find its richest expression in some of the 'mystical' writers of the English fourteenth century, starting with the Yorkshire hermit Richard Rolle (d.1349). Rolle wrote an enormous amount, in Latin and English, from scripture commentaries and glossed paraphrases of the psalms to devotional lyrics. Though he is most celebrated for his advocacy of a form of devotional rapture that aimed to fill the heart with 'the fire of love', he also wrote a prose treatise in Latin for priests, which drew heavily on William of Pagula's *Oculus Sacerdotis*. Many of his writings were in the form of 'little books' designed for the edification of his neighbours, and much of his prolific output was aimed at that traditional devout audience, women recluses. But Rolle's writings achieved a wider celebrity even in his own short lifetime, and found a ready lay as well as religious or clerical audience. He himself had aristocratic protectors among the Yorkshire nobility, and his works circulated both in wealthy lay households and in the Yorkshire monasteries and nunneries. His first entry into the life of a hermit is instructive here. Dressed in a bizarre costume improvised from two of his sister's kirtles and an old rain-hood of his father's, he appeared unannounced in the Dalton family chapel in the parish church of Pickering one summer day in 1318. John Dalton was bailiff of Pickering, keeper of the forest and constable of the castle, a considerable man. Rolle's father had probably been in his service, and Rolle himself had known Dalton's sons at Oxford. Though Rolle was a layman, the parish priest permitted him to preach an English sermon, and the Daltons were sufficiently impressed to take him into their house, and to clothe him properly as a hermit. The whole incident suggests a religious culture hospitable to the extraordinary, and not by any means slavishly subordinated to clerical control. Rolle does not seem to have had or sought official approval for his adoption of the eremetical life. Nor were the Daltons the only lay people impressed by Rolle's eloquence. His last work, the *Form of Living*, an English devotional treatise written for yet another female recluse, his disciple Margaret Butler, circulated very widely, and the colophon of one manuscript runs 'Here endeth the information of Richard the Hermit that he wrote to an anchoress, translated out of the northern tongue into southern that it should the better be understood by men that be in the Selby country'.[18]

Rolle's impact was a measure of growing interest in what another hermit-writer, Walter Hilton, called the *medeled* or mixed life: the search for a lay piety which combined action in the world with some degree of contemplativity. Hilton's *Epistle on the Mixed Life* was written for a nobleman anxious to save his soul. It adapted to lay use a venerable genre of devotional advice for bishops: spiritual men whose calling required them to be engaged with worldly things. Classical Christian teaching on the religious life had divided the Christian vocation into two parts, that of Martha and Mary, active and contemplative, with the contemplative, Mary's part, infinitely superior to Martha's. Hilton did not doubt the superiority of the contemplative life, but insisted on the prior claims of charity on those whose vocation lay in work for the world. Such men and women must therefore embrace both states of life as best they can: 'Take these two lives, active and contemplative, since God hath sent both, and use them both, the one with that other'. Thus the nobleman interrupted at prayer by the needs of his dependants or neighbours must not fret, but 'leave off lightly thy devotion, whether it be in prayer or in meditation, and go do thy duty and thy service to thine even-Christian [neighbour, fellow Christian] as readily as our lord him self bade thee do so, and suffer meekly for his love, without grudging if thou may'.[19] Seeking perfection in the world, 'you shall mix the works of active life with ghostly [spiritual] works of life contemplative, and then you do well'.[20]

The growth of a lay devotional tradition was at one level the product of episcopal and parochial endeavour, and of the activity of the friars as preachers, writers and confessors. But in the course of the fourteenth century both the episcopate and the friars became the target of increasingly vocal lay criticism, and vernacular piety, which was also driven by the burgeoning of lay literacy, took on a critical and questioning edge which, in England at any rate, was new. There was ample cause for

[18] H. E. Allen, ed., *English Writings of Richard Rolle* (Oxford, 1931), pp. xvi–xvii, 84.
[19] Quoted in M. Glasscoe, *English Medieval Mystics: games of faith* (1993), p. 125.
[20] S. S. Hussey, 'The audience for the middle English mystics', in M. G. Sargent, ed., *De Cella in Seculum: religious and secular life and devotion in late medieval England* (Cambridge, 1989), p. 112.

criticism. The episcopate was itself changing. Though the proportion of graduates remained impressively high, scholars and theologians, prominent among the bishops of the thirteenth and early fourteenth centuries, increasingly gave way to lawyers and administrators. Moreover, a combination of royal influence and papal provisions inexorably shifted the balance of the episcopate not only towards royal administrators but also towards the younger sons of the aristocracy. In the century after 1350 there would be twenty aristocrats in the key sees of Canterbury, York, London and Lincoln – William Courteney, Thomas Arundel and Henry Beaufort among them. Courteney was made a bishop at twenty-five, Arundel at twenty-one and Beaufort at twenty-three. Translation from one see to another became a routine device to reward service to the crown, and secular politics exercised an increasing influence on the Church.

The fresh bloom had come off the mendicant ideal too. Dominant in the two universities, and increasingly conforming to the patterns of the older religious orders, the radical simplicity and austerity of the early friars had given way to establishment status. From about 1270 the buildings of the Franciscans in England had become increasingly monasticised and increasingly grandiose. The London Franciscan church, begun in 1279, was three hundred feet long, eighty-nine feet wide and sixty-four feet high. Among the great and the good buried there in the thirteenth and fourteenth centuries, whose monuments thronged the building, were not only grandees of the city companies and former lord mayors but also a bevy of earls and duchesses. Burials (which would continue unabated until the house was dissolved by Henry VIII) also included the heart of a queen of England and the body of a queen of Scotland. In a devastating commentary on the erosion of the Franciscan ideal of poverty, the London house was robbed in 1355 by one of its own friars. His loot included gold, silver and jewels worth £200. The friars were increasingly clericalised too. Many of the earliest English Franciscans were lay brothers, but of the 144 friars whose deaths are recorded between 1328 and 1334, only nine were laymen.

Langland's *Vision of Piers Plowman*, the first version of which probably dates from the late 1360s, is the most extraordinary witness to this powerful, sophisticated and often sharply critical vernacular religious culture in later fourteenth-century England. Langland was almost certainly a clerk in minor orders, and many of the early manuscripts seem to have belonged to monasteries or to secular priests. But the poem, though saturated with liturgical echoes, displays a Christianity often at odds with the clerical establishment. Langland returns again and again to the value of a simple faith enacted in charity, not in empty profession. At one of the climactic moments in the poem, the opening of the pardon, the symbolic figure of a priest condescendingly rebukes Piers for presumption in expounding scripture. In this exchange, the reader is clearly meant to side with the ploughman, taught his ABC not by any 'diviner in divinity', but by 'Abstinence the abbess' and by Conscience.[21] Elsewhere Langland condemns the over-subtle preaching of the friars and other great clerks, who 'move matters immeasurable to tell of the Trinity', so that often the common people doubt their belief. They should abandon such teaching 'and tell men of the ten commandments, and concerning the seven sins'.[22]

In successive revisions the poem is increasingly informed by anger at the ills of the contemporary church, seen as compromised by slackness and corruption from top to bottom: unlearned parish priests who lead their parishioners to perdition; worldly prelates motivated by pride and greed; 'a heap of hermits' wending to Walsingham 'and their wenches after'; above all the friars, covetous deceivers, peddling cheap grace to eager hearers, and dumbing down the demands of religion in order to line their own pockets:

> ... all the four orders
> Preached to the people for profit of themselves,
> Glossed the gospel as they well liked
> For covetousness of copes, construed it as they would.[23]

Covetousness was central to Langland's powerful and pessimistic analysis of the state of the fourteenth-century English Church. He targeted clerical greed as one of the root evils, and looked to the secular arm for remedies; as Conscience declares:

> Sir king, by Christ, unless clerks amend
> Thy kingdom through their covetousness will fall from its nature,
> And holy church through them be harmed for ever.[24]

FROM RADICAL ORTHODOXY TO POPULAR HERESY: THE PROBLEM OF THE LOLLARDS

The views expressed by Langland were widely held in the 1360s and 1370s. The wealth of the higher clergy, and their resistance to royal attempts to tax them, was a constant irritant to secular landowners who felt that

---

[21] W. W. Skeat, *The Vision of William concerning Piers the Plowman in Three Parallel Texts* (2 vols., Oxford, 1886), i, B text vii.129–38 (pp. 244, 246).
[22] *Ibid.*, i, B text xv.68–80 (p. 440).   [23] *Ibid.*, i, B text prologue.57–61 (p. 6).
[24] *Ibid.*, i, C text iii.245–8 (p. 61).

clerical immunities increased their own tax burdens. Churchmen themselves were often the most vociferous critics of clerical abuse, but in the
last years of Edward III there was a mounting aristocratic call for con-
fiscation of the wealth of clerical proprietors. It was this issue that was to
bring the Oxford theologian and philosopher John Wyclif to the notice of
John of Gaunt, duke of Lancaster, early in 1377. Borrowing ideas from
older contemporaries like Richard Fitzralph and Marsiglio of Padua,
Wyclif formulated a potent cocktail of idealism and canniness, in which
denunciation of corrupt bishops and friars was used to underpin the
claim that sinfulness deprived a man, and especially a churchman, of any
right to property or rule, and that princes, not prelates, were the divinely
ordained instrument of reform for the Church. It was consequently the
duty of secular lords to heal the ills of the Church by confiscating its
revenues and putting them to proper use.

Wyclif's ideas, a useful element in the anticlerical campaign Gaunt was
orchestrating in the mid 1370s, rapidly attracted a following at court.
From 1378, however, he moved beyond these delicious and useful
teachings on clerical property to deny some of the fundamental
assumptions of late medieval Christianity. Locating all authority in the
text of scripture, literally understood, he rejected the value of ecclesiastical
traditions, and denied the authority of pope or bishop. The Church
consisted only of the elect, and so the visible Church, which contained
many children of Satan, had no authority to bind or loose, and no
coercive power. Since dominion came from grace, the true pope was
simply the holiest Christian, and not the man in Rome or Avignon, who
was indeed anti-Christ because of his exorbitant claims. Churchmen
could own nothing, and must depend purely on the free gifts of the
faithful. The friars and religious orders were instruments of Satan and
should be abolished. Above all, from about 1380 Wyclif denied the central
teaching of the medieval Church on the mass. Though he accepted that
the bread and wine of the eucharist were in some genuine sense the body
and blood of Christ, that sense could only be figurative and symbolic, for
the body of Christ was in heaven.

Wyclif was one of Oxford's most eloquent and celebrated teachers, and
in the 1360s and early 1370s had been perceived as the champion of the
oppressed secular clergy against the dominance of the religious orders in the
university. Even among the friars he was admired for his teaching on
clerical possession and poverty. But as his views radicalised, and specifically
after 1378 as he openly rejected the doctrine of transubstantiation, lynchpin
of so much late medieval piety, he lost support. The young Austin friar,

Adam Stockton, at some point had written admiringly in the margin of one of Wyclif's diatribes against the papacy, 'Hec venerabilis doctor, magister Johannes Wyclyf'. Sometime in 1380 or 1381, however, he crossed out *venerabilis doctor* and wrote instead *execrabilis seductor* – 'cursed seducer'.[25]

Stockton's change of heart probably reflected the dramatic upheavals of 1381, which marked a decisive watershed in the reception and reputation of Wyclif's theology. Though Wyclif's teachings on the eucharist, clerical authority and possessions, and on mendicancy and the religious life, had been condemned by Pope Gregory XI as early as 1377, a combination of papal disputes with the crown, the jealousy of the University of Oxford for its own independence and the reputation of its most famous teacher, and the protection of John of Gaunt prevented any drastic consequences. In 1381, however, the Peasants' Revolt sent shock-waves through the English religious and political establishments. Wyclif's theology had in fact contributed little or nothing to the disorders of that year, but his opponents were swift to assert connections between sedition and heresy, and his ideas were comprehensively condemned at a provincial council of the English Church held at the London Blackfriars in May 1382.

In the wake of the Blackfriars condemnation, however, it became clear that Wyclifism had escaped from the university and the court, and had found a popular audience. Though Wyclif himself seems to have written exclusively in Latin for a learned readership, a clutch of ardent and eloquent young Oxford disciples had taken his teachings out into the parishes, and had begun to preach them in English to receptive lay audiences. Philip Repingdon, Augustinian canon of St Mary's Abbey, Leicester, John Aston, secular clerk, and Wyclif's amanuensis John Purvey were all active in Leicestershire, and Purvey also in Bristol, in the early 1380s. Nicholas Hereford, a younger colleague of Wyclif at Balliol, was preaching Wycliffite sermons in Oxford, Northampton, Nottingham and Worcestershire; William Thorpe in London and in the north. The parochial patronage of the Oxford colleges allowed the scatter of Wyclif's ideas across the country, and Repingdon used the influence of his abbey to entrench Wycliffite teaching in Leicestershire. This spread was also assisted by the protection and patronage of a small handful of so-called 'Lollard knights' and gentry, whose chaplains and parish priests carried Wyclif's teachings into the pulpit and confessional.

---

[25] A. Hudson, *The Premature Reformation: Wycliffite texts and Lollard heresy* (Oxford, 1988), p. 86 n. 161.

The character and popular appeal of 'Lollard' teachings (the word Lollard is apparently a Dutch word suggesting a mumbler or grumbler) is vividly suggested by the hold it established in Leicester in the early 1380s. The movement there was centred on the disused leper-hospital of St John the Baptist, just outside the city, converted into a hermitage by a local layman, William Smith, who was joined by a chantry chaplain named Richard Waytestaythe, and by the hermit-priest William Swinderby, a protégé of Repingdon. Swinderby's teaching included attacks on the doctrine of transubstantiation, but seems to have focused especially on the injustices of tithe and the invalidity of the ministrations of unworthy priests. Waytestaythe and Smith focused on the evils of the cult of images, denouncing the shrine images of the Virgin of Walsingham and of the mother church of the diocese at Lincoln as 'witches', and giving a practical demonstration of the powerlessness of holy images by cooking a meal with the broken fragments of a statue of St Catherine. This cocktail of anticlerical, anti-sacramental and anti-symbolic teaching seems to have attracted a good deal of support in the town, including that of the mayor and some of the town council. Ten years on there would be a similar body of support among the urban elite of Northampton, where the chief Lollard ring-leader was another hermit, Anna Palmer, anchoress at St Peter's church.

Lollardy would remain a disturbing religious and political problem for another generation, from the posting of the manifesto known as the 'Twelve Conclusions' on the doors of Westminster Hall during the parliamentary session of 1395, through the shambolic rebellion of Sir John Oldcastle in 1414, to the even more amateurish Lollard plot of 1431. In 1401, prompted by a new dynasty eager to bolster its legitimacy by demonstrating its orthodox piety, parliament would pass legislation imposing death by fire on a relapsed or stubborn heretic. The act *De Heretico Comburendo* retrospectively legalised the burning earlier that year of a Norfolk Lollard, the priest William Sawtre, and placed in the hands of the ecclesiastical and civil authorities a powerful deterrent in the fight against what they perceived as a rising tide of heresy.

Just how extensive was lay support for Lollardy, and how wide its social spread, however, is difficult to say. Under Henry IV more Franciscan friars were executed for seditious preaching against the Lancastrian usurpation than Lollards were for heresy. Even in Oxford support for Wyclif's ideas could not indefinitely resist the hawkish scrutiny of successive archbishops of Canterbury, and in particular Archbishop Arundel's draconian legislation against heretical writing in 1407–9. Moreover, the Oldcastle revolt permanently linked Lollardy with treason, and in the process killed stone dead whatever vestiges of elite support the movement still retained. In any case, the so-called 'Lollard knights' had by no means been all equally committed heretics. They included individuals such as Sir Thomas Latimer, Sir Lewis Clifford and Sir Richard Sturry, who were certainly actively committed to the full Wycliffite programme, promoting its doctrines and protecting its clerical preachers. But the condemnation of 1382 scared off many early sympathisers, and Wyclifism must have been in any case for many of its early enthusiasts not much more than the left wing of a generally 'reformist' piety, which emphasised the value of vernacular religious texts, the dangers of a sterile or hypocritical ritualism, and the evils of a worldly clergy. The *Pore Caitiff*, a much copied and much read devotional compendium of *c.* 1400, drew on Lollard materials and shared much of the same reformist platform as Lollard writings and preaching, but was itself entirely orthodox. The characteristics of the 'Lollard wills' identified by K. B. McFarlane as the unifying mark of Wycliffite gentry – a loathing of the physical body and an insistence on simple burial characterised by alms to the poor in place of funeral pomp – are replicated in the wills of testators of impeccable orthodoxy, not least those of Archbishop Arundel and the ex-Lollard Philip Repingdon, bishop of Lincoln, who was to prove himself a determined opponent and persecutor of his former associates.[26] Denied the oxygen of educated clergy leadership and of gentry protection, Lollardy declined inexorably into mere negativity, a form of refusal of the dominant sacramental and symbolic expressions of contemporary Christianity, drawing its constituency from artisans and a handful of lower clergy. From about 1430 it was in recession, surviving tenaciously but largely as a clan tradition of dissidence in a handful of rural communities; significantly, no new Lollard texts were produced to nourish it.

The religious attraction of Lollardy is in any case elusive. It must certainly have centred on its biblicism, the draw of the vernacular scriptures which would long survive the movement. That draw helps explain the fact that most fifteenth-century owners and readers of Wycliffite bibles were impeccably orthodox Catholics, like the Suffolk wool magnate John Clopton of Long Melford, who built himself a tomb which doubled as the Easter Sepulchre for the adoration of the reserved sacrament at Easter. Lollardy shared with the Franciscan movement it so much detested a

[26] J. A. F. Thomson, 'Knightly piety and the margins of Lollardy', in M. Aston and C. Richmond, eds., *Lollardy and the Gentry in the Later Middle Ages* (Stroud, 1997), pp. 95–111.

powerful critique of the extravagant excess of much contemporary ritual provision and the consequent neglect of the poor. Many sensitive late medieval Christians suspected that gold lavished on statues would be better spent feeding and clothing the hungry and naked, that the real image of Christ was not the carved crucifix but the flesh of suffering humanity. Hence Lollard insistence that 'it were better to give a poor [person] or lame man a penny than to bestow their money in pilgrimage going and worshipping the images of saints, for man is the very image of God which ought only to be worshiped and no stocks nor stones', went unerringly to the nerve-centre of medieval Christianity.[27] Lollardy appealed also to a desire for simplicity that must often have been felt amidst the lavishness of late medieval Catholicism. Many laymen would have approved the Lollard sentiment that 'a simple *pater noster* of a ploughman that is in charity is better than a thousand masses of covetous prelates and vain religious full of covetousness and pride and false flattering and nourishing of sin'.[28]

It is characteristic of Lollardy that that insight articulated itself primarily as a polemic against the sins of others: as a critique of religion rather than an alternative religion. Especially after 1414 it displayed an unstoppable tendency to slide into the ideology of the village know-all, its character (admittedly memorably) preserved in ale-house belly-laughs at the expense of 'Our Lady of Foulpit' or 'Our Lady of Falsingham', rather than in any more positive folk wisdom. The same is true of Wyclifism even at its most sophisticated. The Wycliffite Sermon Cycle is the largest and most systematic body of Lollard teaching, a stupendous and learned labour providing 294 sermons for the whole year, produced in Oxford or in some aristocratic Lollard household in the last years of the fourteenth century.[29] But it is a chilling and dispiriting body of material, all too obviously infected by the spiritual dyspepsia of the movement's founder, monotonous in its moralism and its relentless polemic against the religious orders and the 'folly of prelates', entirely lacking in the affective warmth and devotion to the suffering humanity of Christ which is the distinctive mark of late medieval mainstream Christianity. It is hard to imagine this sour diet satisfying anyone's religious hunger for long.

The struggle with Lollardy dominated the history of the Church in England for two generations, a period which ran almost exactly from the outbreak of the papal schism in 1378 until the settlement of the western

---

[27] Isabel Dorte of East Hendred (Berks.) in 1491, quoted in D. Webb, *Pilgrimage in Medieval England* (2000), p. 233.

[28] Hudson, *Premature Reformation*, p. 196.

[29] A. Hudson and P. Gradon, eds., *English Wycliffite Sermons* (5 vols., Oxford, 1983–96).

Church in the pontificate of Martin V, which ended in 1431. In England as elsewhere this was a turbulent half-century, which witnessed the deposition of a king and the establishment of a new dynasty, and which saw too an astonishing flowering of literary and religious creativity with few parallels before or since. These were the years in which William Langland, Geoffrey Chaucer, the Gawain poet and John Gower were all writing, while the great religious texts of the period include the works of Walter Hilton and the *Cloud of Unknowing*, the *Shewings* of Julian of Norwich, the earliest York and Chester mystery drama cycles and, not least, the *Book* of Margery Kempe. Lollardy was undoubtedly the greatest single challenge the English Church faced in this period, but the threat it posed turned out to be less than contemporaries feared, and the importance of Lollardy in determining the agenda of fifteenth-century English Christianity has been grossly exaggerated by historians and literary critics alike. Fifteenth-century bishops remained vigilant against heresy, and there were what amounted to concerted campaigns in the Lincoln diocese in the 1460s, and in London in the 1490s. But for most dioceses for most of the century Lollards were less of a nuisance than village cunning men or withholders of tithe, a resounding absence rather than a brooding presence. Anti-Lollard polemic informs two of the key instructional and devotional texts of Henry IV's reign, Mirk's *Festial* and Nicholas Love's *Mirror of the Life of the Blessed Jesus*; lay behind Richard Fleming's foundation of Lincoln College, Oxford in 1427 as a seminary for orthodox preachers; and inspired both Thomas Netter's monumental Latin defence of the sacraments and Reginald Pecock's ill-fated and ill-judged vernacular polemics, whose rationalising treatment of the authority of scripture and tradition were to bring about his own condemnation for heresy. But it is hard to avoid the conviction that heresy had ceased to be a serious threat long before Pecock set pen to paper, and it is a mistake to see Lollardy or anti-Lollardy as the continuing key to fifteenth-century English religion. Attempts to detect a polemic against Lollardy in the N-Town mystery cycles are unconvincing, and Lollardy is strikingly absent even where one might most expect to find worry about it, for example in the East Anglian *Croxton Play of the Sacrament*. Christianity in Lancastrian, Yorkist and early Tudor England set great store by the sacraments and on the veneration of images, but these emphases were not a response to Lollardy. They are a feature of the ebullient Christianity of late medieval western Europe, as is also the punctilious concern for orthodoxy and interest in catechesis represented by the ubiquitous imagery of the four Latin doctors (Sts Ambrose,

Augustine, Gregory and Jerome) found on pulpits, rood screens and
fonts, or by the fashion for baptismal fonts depicting the seven sacraments
which spread through eastern England in the reign of Edward IV. Two
such fonts were erected in the Norfolk parish churches of Martham and
Loddon, which were also filled with the imagery of the saints. Fifty years
earlier, vociferous Lollard artisans and their wives had denied the value of
baptism and denounced the sacraments as a clerical swindle, but two
generations on it is less likely that the parishioners were exorcising their
community's Lollard past than that they had simply forgotten what had
never been more than a plebeian minority among them.[30]

It has, however, been suggested by Nicholas Watson that the measures
taken against Lollardy did have a profound effect on English religion for
the rest of the fifteenth century. Archbishop Arundel's Constitutions of
1407 outlawing the translation of the bible and restricting lay readership
of the scriptures in English, Watson believes, had a sterilising effect on
English religious thought, and led to the dumbing-down of English
religious writing. The intellectual daring of Langland and Julian of
Norwich gives way to a religious literature which no longer dares to
wrestle with knotty theological problems, but contents itself instead with
the confection of bland but safe devotional pap.[31]

There can be little doubt that official censorship had an impact on the
ethos of fifteenth-century English religion, which was reflected in artistic
and religious self-censorship. Already in the 1380s and 1390s revisions
carried out by writers as different as Langland and Julian of Norwich
manifest a growing nervousness about overstepping the tightening
bounds of orthodoxy, and an anxiety to distance the writers from suspicions of heterodoxy. But it would be a mistake to attribute too much to
ecclesiastical repression. It is not just religious literature that dumbs down
in fifteenth-century England, but writing in general. No fifteenth-century
poet comes within measurable distance of Chaucer or Langland, just as
no fifteenth-century English work of art comes within measurable distance of the de Lisle Psalter or the Wilton Diptych.[32] This apparent
decline may be an optical illusion, produced by accidents of survival or

[30] I dissent here from the interpretative framework adopted in Anne Nichols' magisterial study of the
seven sacrament fonts: *Seeable Signs: the iconography of the seven sacraments 1350–1544* (Woodbridge,
1994). For Loddon and Martham, *ibid.*, pp. 106–7.

[31] N. Watson, 'Censorship and cultural change in late medieval England: vernacular theology, the
Oxford translation debate and Arundel's Constitutions of 1407', *Speculum*, 70 (1995), 822–64.

[32] For accounts of the literary culture of the period with different emphases from those argued here,
see Paul Strohm's chapter, below, and J. Simpson, *Reform and Cultural Revolution 1350–1547*
(Oxford, 2002).

shifts in patronage, but golden ages of art and writing are often followed by what C. S. Lewis called 'drab' ages, and the slide towards affective devotionalism in English religious writing is a European and not merely an English phenomenon. It would be absurd to attribute what is arguably a generalised drop in cultural temperature to religious repression. England never had anything remotely like the Inquisition, and though bishops kept a weather eye open for Lollards throughout the century, there is little evidence of sustained persecution: fifteenth-century England had no thought-police. And Arundel's Constitutions did not in any case entirely stifle either religious exploration or theological daring. The decades that produced both *The Book* of Margery Kempe and the writings of Reginald Pecock cannot be considered either entirely barren or religiously unadventurous.

CEREMONY AND SINCERITY: CORPUS CHRISTI

If it cannot seriously be maintained that the religion of fifteenth-century England was paralysed by fear of censorship it has been more persuasively argued that it was sapped by complacency. In this account, the real weakness of the English Church was its domination by aristocracy, gentry and urban elites far too much at ease with the official religion, who saw in the monasteries, convents and cathedral prebends of the church not spiritual power-houses so much as genteel lodgings for unmarriageable younger children; who paid their chaplains less than their cooks; and whose pieties, however real, were genteelly tepid expressions of respectability and status. Similar criticisms could be levelled at most of the churches of late medieval Europe, but certainly England experienced none of the fervour of religious revivalism associated in Italy with the urban preaching missions of reformed Franciscans like Bernardino of Siena, and as Colin Richmond has observed, 'there was only one Margery Kempe'.[33]

Arguments about the extent of religious zeal or sincerity are notoriously subjective, and at the highest level at any rate the claim that the leaders of society lacked religious seriousness would be hard to sustain. Henry V has a fair claim to have been the most devout English king since Henry III, who built Westminster Abbey to be the focus of a series of Christological and saints' cults promoted by the monarchy. Religious seriousness need not

---

[33] C. Richmond, 'Religion', in R. Horrox, ed., *Fifteenth-Century Attitudes: perceptions of society in late-medieval England* (Cambridge, 1994), pp. 183–201, quotation at p. 195. A similar perception pervades the third and final volume of D. Knowles, *The Religious Orders in England* (3 vols., Cambridge, 1956).

necessarily manifest itself in revivalist preaching or mob hysteria at shrines. Henry V's reign saw notable developments in three defining areas of English religion: the appointment of an effective and vigilant pastoral episcopate; the promotion of greater religious interiority and asceticism; and an ebullient expansion of cultic activity, directed at the eucharist, the passion of Christ, and the saints. The episcopate under Henry V and his successors contained many courtly careerists, but also episcopal administrators and reformers of the calibre of Henry Chichele and Robert Hallum. This was an age of administrative consolidation, liturgical renewal and pastoral focus, represented by Lyndwood's great compendium of canon law and by the compilation of the Sarum *Manuale*, a pastoral tool of the first importance to ordinary parish priests. Henry V's twin Thames-side religious foundations – the Carthusian house at Sheen and the Bridgetine convent of Syon – would become power-houses of devotional writing and, at the end of the century, publishing. Many of the devout of London and the court would look to the clergy there for confessors and spiritual guides, and, at a more popular level, both houses offered annual indulgences which attracted flocks of pilgrims eager for pardon. This was no mere 'popular superstition'; notes on how to gain the Sheen and Syon indulgences are jotted down inside the front cover of the book of hours used by Margaret Beauchamp, wife of the earl of Shrewsbury. Henry personally interested himself also in the promotion of new or revived saints' cults – St Edward the Confessor, St John of Beverley (on one of whose feast days the battle of Agincourt was fought), and the growing civic and patriotic observance of the cult of St George.[34]

All that attests the resolutely public and social character of fifteenth-century Christianity, nowhere more in evidence than in the luxuriance of the cult of Corpus Christi. The feast of Corpus Christi was introduced into England in 1318; by the 1390s it had become universal and its texts and observances were a target for Lollard polemic. Corpus Christi indeed became a touchstone of orthodox belief and practice, and as bishop of Lincoln the former Lollard Philip Repingdon rigorously enforced its observance in England's largest diocese. But in fifteenth-century England enforcement was hardly necessary. The feast's central theme of community in and around the sacramental body of Christ made it an ideal vehicle for the proclamation of communal values and social hierarchy, and elaborate Corpus Christi processions, in which civic officials and craft

---

[34] J. Catto, 'Religious change under Henry V', in G. L. Harriss, ed., *Henry V: the practice of kingship* (Oxford, 1985), pp. 97–115.

guilds took their place, became a feature of the feast in many towns. By the 1380s the city of York had added to the liturgical procession an elaborate processional cycle of plays, responsibility for which was devolved to the city guilds, and precedence within which became an important element in jockeying for power and influence within the community. Ritual here was an arena in which the strains as well as the bonds of community could be displayed and negotiated. Co-operation with the city's celebration of the feast became a mark of good citizenship: thus York householders were required to hang their best hangings or bedspreads out of their windows to beautify the processional route.

The same union of citizenship and religious observance is visible everywhere in fifteenth-century England. The Corpus Christi procession at Bristol was a 'religious' not a 'civic' occasion, the civic authorities leaving its organisation to the city clergy and religious houses, but the mayor and corporation processed in scarlet gowns to the city churches on the other major summer liturgical feasts of the year such as Easter and Whitsun, and on many saints' days. The most distinguished Bristol mayor of the century, William Canynges, became a cleric himself in the last weeks of his final term of office as mayor, and for the last six years of his life played as large a role in the religious life of the city and diocese as he had in the city's secular affairs. His effigy, robed as a canon, was placed as a memorial in Westbury collegiate church, where he was dean, but he was buried alongside his wife in St Mary Redcliffe, his effigy here robed in secular dress as mayor, a one-man embodiment of the interweaving of religious and civic life in late medieval England.

The eucharist and its attendant public observances offer us a way into the difficult question of lay religious understanding and religious orthodoxy. It is tempting to assume a gulf between public observance and internal conviction, and difficult in any case to gain access to lay religious opinion. The mass, however, was no mere symbol of power and hierarchy, and if we seldom encounter non-formulaic lay confessions of eucharistic faith, there is plenty of evidence from lay manipulation of the symbolic language which surrounded the eucharist to suggest that it was widely understood and valued. The communal dimensions of the mass could readily be deployed in defence of popular community values in the face of overbearing authority, and also as a means of creating or repairing social bonds, in an exercise of what John Bossy has called the 'social miracle'.[35] Two examples of lay manipulation of the symbolism

---

[35] J. Bossy, *Christianity in the West, 1400–1700* (Oxford, 1985), pp. 57–75.

surrounding the distribution of the 'holy loaf' on Sundays will illustrate
this aspect of the social character of late medieval Christianity. The holy
loaf, not to be confused with the eucharistic host consecrated at the
central point of the mass and normally received by the laity only once a
year, at Easter, was a loaf of ordinary bread ceremonially presented to the
priest each week before the main parish mass by a householder – there
was a rota to determine whose responsibility this was. The loaf was
blessed by the recitation of the opening verses of St John's gospel over it.
At the end of mass it was cut up, and the pieces were distributed to the
congregation as a communion substitute, and as a symbol of the unity
and blessing that flowed from the mass. The pieces of blessed bread were
believed to have protective and healing powers, and in some communities
they were carefully graded by size, the larger pieces going to the parishioners of greatest consequence. As was the case with another peace
ritual, the kissing of a small devotional plaque known as the pax-brede
after the priest's communion, disputes over precedence during this ritual
were common, a mark of its key role in determining or signalling the
social pecking-order within many communities.

The Peasants' Revolt of 1381 had eucharistic resonances. It broke out,
surely by pre-arrangement, on the feast of Corpus Christi, 13 June 1381,
and historians have recently become intrigued by the interplay between
the social dimensions of that feast and the social breakdown expressed in
the rising.[36] The revolt is particularly well documented at St Albans,
where the chronicler Thomas Walsingham was an eye-witness. The
grievances of the commons at St Albans were varied, but one important
issue was the abbey's much resented monopoly on the milling of flour.
An earlier abbot had succeeded in forcing the local tenantry to surrender
their millstones and, in token of the abbey's control over milling, had set
the confiscated millstones into the floor of the monastery parlour. During
the rebellion, therefore, a mob armed with the implements of their trades
broke into the abbey, marched to the parlour and dug the stones out of
the floor. They proceeded to break the stones up, and distributed a piece
each to the men present to take home. The chronicler was much struck by
their action, and recognised it as a deliberate reference to the holy loaf
ritual. The commons took the stone particles home, he declared, so that
'seeing the pieces, they might remember that they had once triumphed in
this dispute with the monastery'. He went on to lament the damage to the

---

[36] For example, M. Aston, 'Corpus Christi and Corpus Regni: heresy and the Peasants' Revolt',
P&P, 143 (1994), 3–47.

monastery in a cluster of phrases from the psalms that rang the changes on eucharistic images of bread, corn and sheaves.[37]

One of the most striking features of this incident is the extraordinary and assured power of the commons' deployment of a familiar para-eucharistic ritual to express their sense of injustice and its setting to rights. The sensitivity to social order and decorum that normally characterised holy bread rituals was here heightened to reflect an idealised notion of the just ordering of society. In it the fragment of stone became what the Corpus Christi antiphon *O Sacrum Convivium* calls the consecrated particles of the eucharist: a *pignus*, or token, sign and down-payment of a hoped-for reality, at once a reminder of liberation achieved and a standing testimony to the power of that victory in the present and the future. For the commons of St Albans in 1381 the victory and justice celebrated in the mass was in some sense reflected in their protest against the oppression of the abbey that put an unjust price on their daily bread.

A similar sense of lay sophistication in manipulating the symbolic language of the mass emerges from an account of the resolution of an internal parish dispute in the small Bristol city church of St Ewen in the early 1460s. St Ewen's derived much of its income from the rent of shops and tenements in the town centre, and the churchwardens were locked in an expensive and long-drawn-out dispute with one wealthy parishioner, the corn-merchant John Sharp, over the rental of one of these properties. It was finally resolved in January 1464, and in token of restored charity Sharp changed his will to include a handsome donation to parish funds, in return for which he, his wife Elizabeth and deceased members of their family were entered in the church's bede-roll to be prayed for publicly as benefactors. On the following Sunday, as it happened, it was the turn of the Sharps to provide the loaf to be used in the holy bread ritual. There was a prescribed ritual for presenting this bread, which happened before matins and mass began. On the Sunday in question Elizabeth Sharp turned up in pomp, accompanied by a maid who carried the bread and the candle that was offered with it, and also a long embroidered linen towel. This was a 'houselling towel', the long cloth held under the chins of parishioners when they made their annual Easter communion, to prevent crumbs of the eucharistic host falling to the ground. Having duly presented the loaf, Mistress Sharp summoned the parson and the chief parishioners. She expressed her great joy at the restoration of unity and

---

[37] H. T. Riley, ed., *Gesta Abbatum Monasterii Sancti Albani a Thoma Walsingham* (RS, 3 vols., 1867–9), iii, p. 309.

charity within the parish and between her family and the rest of the community, and she donated the towel as a sign of that unity. Up till now, the parish, which did not own a single long towel, had improvised by pinning three short towels together. The unity of the new towel symbolised that the peace which had just been concluded was no patched-up affair, but a seamless whole, and the towel was to be used on the one day in the year when the whole parish celebrated and cemented its unity by receiving communion together. There are a lot of sub-texts here, and Mistress Sharp's gift was clearly designed in part to recover a lost authority in the community. She stipulated that till her death the towel was to remain in her keeping, and would be fetched at Eastertide by the parish clerk: holding on to the towel, she sought to exercise power in the community. But however that may be, once again, there is no mistaking the assured lay deployment of a eucharistic symbol and its accompanying language of unity and charity.

RELIGION AND THE INDIVIDUAL

Problems of evidence, the perennial silence of the common man (and even more, the common woman), make generalisations about plebeian religion difficult. But we can say with certainty that lay people of the middling and upper ranks were intensely and increasingly interested in religion. Religious texts to serve their needs abounded, above all the book of hours. This Latin prayer-book, composed of psalms, hymns and prayers, was divided into the seven monastic 'hours' of prayer and arranged round two themes: devotion to the Virgin Mary (and hence to the incarnation and death of her son Jesus Christ) and prayer for the dead. Books of hours, sumptuously illuminated and bound, had been at first the prerogative of royalty and aristocracy. By the early fifteenth century, however, they were being mass-produced by commercial stationers all over Europe, not only for the gentry, but also for prosperous urban guildsmen and their wives, and they had moved decisively down-market. Supplemented by regional calendars and a range of Latin and vernacular devotions added to order or written in by the owners themselves after purchase, they became the most important religious books of the later middle ages, handed on from parents to children and setting the tone of much lay piety. With the advent of printing their mass-production reached new heights, and almost 120 editions of the Sarum book of hours were printed for the English market before 1530. The early fifteenth-century Lynn merchant's wife and aspiring visionary, Margery

Kempe, is often thought of as illiterate, and she certainly could not write, but she owned and used a book of hours, taking it to church to 'say her Matins ... her book in her hand'.[38]

Margery's search for sanctity, modelled on the lives of continental women visionaries, was extraordinary by any standards, but she shared the main features of her devotional landscape with her more conventional neighbours. Even after she began her restless journeyings to the great shrines of Christendom, her parish church of St Margaret, Lynn, was one of the focal points of her spiritual life – she went there to pray and to hear notable visiting preachers, reported on the emotional impact of its Holy Week liturgy, knelt as the sacrament was carried from it through the streets to the sick during pestilence in Lynn, and took (and sometimes gave) spiritual advice from (or to) the local clergy and from notable members of the four orders of friars active in the town. Like her neighbours she travelled to regional holy places as well as to national shrines like Canterbury, Walsingham and the Holy Blood of Hailes. She and her husband made a special journey to see the Corpus Christi plays at York and to pray before the relics in the minster. She collected indulgences, attended her neighbours' death-beds, and listened to or read conventional saints' lives and popular devotional treatments of the passion. Between the religion of this aspiring saint and that of her bourgeois neighbours there was a difference of degree and intensity, rather than of kind.

The popularity of the book of hours among the gentry and the urban bourgeoisie has been associated by some historians with other manifestations of 'privatisation' in religion, such as the licensing of private chapels for mass, or the emergence within parish churches of the gentry pew. Built inside the parish church yet not altogether part of it, such pews or family chapels constituted, it has been suggested, a private enclave in which the gentry could get on with the practice of an elite religion increasingly remote from the public religion of the parish: 'they were, so to speak, getting their heads down, turning their eyes from the distractions posed by their fellow worshippers, [and] at the same time taking them off the priest and his movements and gestures'.[39] It has even been suggested that the spread of the book of hours posed a 'challenge' to 'institutional, parish-orientated religion'.[40]

---

[38] S. B. Meech and H. E. Allen, eds., *The Book of Margery Kempe* (EETS, os CCXII, 1940), pp. 212, 216.

[39] C. Richmond, 'Religion and the fifteenth-century gentleman', in R. B. Dobson, ed., *The Church, Politics and Patronage in the Fifteenth Century* (Gloucester, 1984), p. 199.

[40] J. Hughes, *The Religious Life of Richard III* (Gloucester, 1997), p. 123.

But this is perhaps to confuse personalisation with privatisation. Devotional use of these books certainly represented a search for greater interiority, a more engaged lay piety, but the contents of the book of hours were highly conventional, and mostly closely related to the liturgy and the widely shared repertoire of symbols which the liturgy made familiar. The very idea of a book of hours was to provide lay people with a simplified version of a clerical or monastic breviary, and so to enable them to share the official prayer of the Church. A fundamental component of all such books was the *dirige* or Office of the Dead, celebrated before most funerals and hence one of the parts of the medieval Church's worship most familiar to the laity. Most religious guilds celebrated *diriges* for deceased members, and encouraged or enforced attendance by guild members (those who could not read said the rosary). The additional prayers bound into or written in the margins of so many of these books were just as familiar – prayers to be recited at the elevation of the host at mass, or while gazing at such universal devotional emblems as the cross, the vernicle (the wounded face of Christ), the pietà, and the image of pity (the half-figure of the dead Christ, displaying his wounds and surrounded by the instruments of the passion). All these emblems were endlessly repeated in the decoration of churches as well as in devotional books and prints.

Nor was there a sharp distinction between the religion of the image and the religion of the devotional text. Many medieval churches provided placards or 'tables' on which were written prayers designed to accompany and focus attention on the images before which parishioners might pray. The London city church of St Christopher le Stock had twelve such 'tables' in March 1488. One contained the ten commandments; one, hanging beneath the statue of the pietà had 'divers good prayers of our lady and the psalter of charity'; and another depicted the image of pity – 'St Gregory's pity of James Well's gift' (an indulgenced representation of the wounded Christ seated in or on his tomb). The rest contained 'divers good prayers' directed to the various saints whose statues stood over the church's various altars and in the aisles. These were a characteristic late medieval assembly, which included the parish patron St Christopher, but also the plague saint Sebastian, St Anne, patron of child-bearing and family, St Erasmus and the popular pilgrim saint, St James. The church itself thus became a sort of three-dimensional book of hours.[41] As all that

---

[41] C. Richmond, 'The English gentry and religion, *c.* 1500', in C. Harper-Bill, ed., *Religious Belief and Ecclesiastical Careers in late Medieval England* (Woodbridge, 1991), p. 122.

suggests, individual focus on the public symbols that nourished *everyone's* interiority cannot sensibly be considered a symptom of privatisation.

The image of pity is a case in point. Reproduced in myriads of fifteenth-century devotional books, in blockprints, engraved on funeral brasses, carved on bench-ends and altars, and displayed on panel and wall-paintings, it was a powerful evocation of the suffering of Christ in the passion. It was also closely associated with the mass, the wounded body of the Man of Sorrows being equated with the bread of the eucharist. Hence it was a favourite choice all over Europe for the decoration of eucharistic vessels such as pyxes, and for the doors of the sacrament-houses and tabernacles used for storing the consecrated bread.

In the late fifteenth century the Chudleigh family, landlords of the parish of Ashton in Devon, decorated their burial chapel at the east end of the north aisle there. The panels of the screens which separated their chapel from the body of the church and from the high altar were decorated with figures and scrolls illustrating the liturgy of the new feasts of the Transfiguration and the Visitation, in a style derived from contemporary woodcuts, and markedly superior to the doll-like figures of the saints with which the parish had painted its rood screen. The Chudleigh chapel had its own altar and carved or painted images, and probably its own priest. The dominant religious image in the chapel, however, was a large representation of the image of pity, painted on the north wall above the family burial vault, where it could be seen through the screen-work, and therefore prayed before, by any parishioner. Gentry and plebeian piety, private and public, here converged and overlapped round one of the most resonant emblems of late medieval Christianity, the wounded and eucharistic Jesus.

To direct a devotional gaze on such an image of the passion, 'piteously to behold' it, was an act which was widely believed to bring with it rich spiritual blessings. Many versions of the image carried written promises of lavish indulgences granted by successive popes. In that ratification by church authority, and its corresponding guarantee of pardon and blessing, in its appeal both to elite and plebeian devotional taste, in its linking of sacramental orthodoxy to interiorised piety, in its lachrymose attention to the suffering of Christ as the heart of the Christian message, and finally in its revealing location in a private chapel set within a parish church, the Ashton image of pity, blurred and obscured now by the wear and whitewash of centuries, brings into sharp focus many of the most characteristic and convergent features of English religion at the end of the middle ages.

CHAPTER 12

A magic universe

Valerie I. J. Flint

The late medieval universe as viewed from England could be described as a magic one in many senses. If we may define magic as 'the exercise of a preternatural control over nature by human beings, with the assistance of forces more powerful than they',[1] it was indeed magic, for much of the surviving evidence expresses a sincere belief in the activity of supernatural powers superior to man, yet sometimes answerable to him. Such belief was central to Christian orthodoxy, to the establishment of the Christian priesthood, to its liturgy and its sacramental system, and to much of its judicial system. It was also helpful to the survival of much 'popular' magic. To the people of late medieval England, clergy and laity alike, supernatural influences underpinned all the most important aspects of human life. They were the food of love, the salve for anxieties, the source of healing and the means both to worldly success and to the ruination of enemies. Religious leadership worthy of the name must therefore prove that it had a beneficent relationship with these influences. The universe was magic also in accordance with a more restricted understanding of the word: through the fact, that is, that magicians were to be found operating within it, many of them loudly condemned by the orthodox Christian Church.

The existence of this state of affairs may call into question the application of the term 'magic' to both, for the latter appears to be the enemy of the former. Certainly this single modern term can do little justice to the complexities that beset the Church's efforts to claim sole command of supernatural enterprise. My excuse for using it here is threefold. Firstly it allows us to see how thoroughly supernatural influences – 'white magic' perhaps – were thought to pervade the late medieval English Christian universe. Secondly, it will let us look into the person and practices of the condemned late medieval English magician. Thirdly, and perhaps most interestingly of all, it will assist us to investigate a most singular process: one

[1] V. I. J. Flint, *The Rise of Magic in Early Medieval Europe* (Oxford, 1991), p. 3.

whereby many forms of apparently condemnable magic were in fact given licence within the Church at both a popular and a learned level.

The competition of 'black', or perhaps blackened, magicians could not be ignored. Indeed, if the orthodox failed to offer supernatural solace and the possibility of a result, then the disappointed might be driven to consult the unorthodox. Arguably, therefore, there were advantages in legitimising at least some magical practices. The tests that decided which supernatural influences might be accepted, and which might not, seem to have become ever more inclusive as the end of the middle ages drew near. It is possible, indeed, that the late medieval Church positively sought to incorporate a great deal of 'magic'; although adopted magic of this order could not be described as *magia*, nor its practitioners as *magici*, for such words were generally reserved for the prohibited arts and their adepts.

Against the background of these caveats about the application of the single term 'magic', we may now turn to discuss each of the three aspects of the magic universe in order, starting with the Christian universe. The stimulus for Christians to describe the universe came from the need to explain the first book of the bible, Genesis, especially its first three chapters. Here are found the fundamental ingredients of the Christian story: the creation of the cosmos and all within it in six days, the malevolence of the wicked spirits, the guardianship of the good angels, the ejection of mankind from paradise and the hope that this lost happiness might one day be regained. The model of a cosmos of three parts above the earth – the first a sub-lunary region reaching from earth to moon and peopled by demons, the second the upper air peopled by superior spirits usually termed angels, and the third inhabited by God himself – reached the later middle ages by many vehicles, not least Augustine's *City of God*.[2]

This same extremely widely read text provided for the acceptance of the four elements – earth, water, air and fire – as constituent parts of the universe (distributed in different proportions on earth and in the regions above it) and encouraged the adoption of the ancient notion of the four humours. According to this, human beings are distinguished in make-up and temperament by a different distribution of these four elements and the associated pairs of the four contraries – dryness, moisture, coldness and heat – within their bodies. Excess fire was assumed to produce a choleric personality, excess water a phlegmatic one, excess earth a melancholic one and excess air a sanguine one. Different human ages also brought about a

---

[2] St Augustine, *City of God* XXII, xi, ed. and trans. W. M. Green (Loeb Classical Library, 7 vols., 1957–72), vii, pp. 258–65.

diminution of certain elements and an increase in others. Childhood, for example, was thought to be characterised by heat and moisture, middle age by a cold dryness. The seasons and geographical climates in which persons were born also affected the balance of elements and their properties within them. So did the motions of the heavens, especially those of the seven known planets, which had their own humours. Saturn was melancholic, for example, Jupiter jovial and sanguine. Man's body was thus a microcosm of an enormously complex universe, and sensitive to all movement within it. Christians, however, had to be careful to find a place for divine providence and human free will in this complexity. The influence of the planets could not be seen as a determining one, but only as one part of the great panoply of powers guided by God.

The influx into England of translations into Latin of Arabic, Greek and Hebrew cosmological writings, at its height in the twelfth and thirteenth centuries, was prompted by, and further intensified, the existing interest in the universe. The works of Aristotle brought great refinement to the construct, and provided both for its embellishment and for a deeper understanding of nature. Such texts were exciting to schoolmen, astrologers, doctors and experimental scientists such as alchemists, but, though much discussed, they did not radically alter the way in which the universe was in general portrayed. Thus, the universe Chaucer spoke about in the late fourteenth century was not fundamentally different from that described by Augustine at the beginning of the fifth century.

Many treatises had carried this description into late medieval England, of which the *De Naturis Rerum* by the English Augustinian canon Alexander Neckham (d.1217) may stand as an example. Alexander took the first chapter of Genesis as the basis of his own account. He painted a vivid picture of fiery and splendid angels at home with Christ in the highest heavens, and of the dark angel Lucifer and the malign spirits who fell with him. This division and opposition of supernatural forces was, he argued, implicit in Genesis 1:4–5, which describes God dividing the light from the darkness and the day from the night. Thus, day rightly distinguishes the good angels, enfolded in perpetual brightness and up among the stars and planets. Night (*nox*) is proper to the harmful ones (from *nocere*, to hurt, a dubious but memorable etymology).[3] We have here in outline all we need for the perpetuation of a magic universe, together with some hint as to what may divide the 'white' supernatural forces from the 'black'. The harmfulness of the latter is exhibited in pride,

---

[3] Alexander Neckham, *De Naturis Rerum Libri Duo*, ed. T. Wright (RS, XXXIV, 1863), pp. 17–22.

envy, telling lies, sowing discord, and that dislike of true wisdom that leads to foolishness. Their dwelling place in the sub-lunary region above the earth gives them, furthermore, an affinity for dark and murky regions. The goodness of the former lies in precisely the opposite: humility, generosity, truthfulness, an appetite for peace and reconciliation and the proper cultivation of the mind, and a penchant for openness and light.

This view of the universe provided a template for the good and bad human 'magician'. The good one would call humbly upon the powers in the heights of heaven; the bad would arrogantly seek to command the demons of the lower air. Augustine again lent his authority to this distinction, and warned too against the Christian charlatan.[4] The latter was a complicating peril. Questions needed constantly to be asked about man and his relations with the supernatural. How wisely and humbly meant *is* a given means of approaching the powers of the universe? How truthful? Whom may we trust to say so? The making of the distinction between the good magician and the bad one, and the identification of the charlatan, will depend of course upon how these virtues and their contrary vices are defined in any given situation, and upon exactly who does the defining and identifying. Should it be scholars, should it be bishops, or should it (as in a later age) be left to the community? Given agreement upon such matters, however, Alexander's universe provides great scope for the acceptance of certain kinds of apparently 'magical' practice.

When Alexander turns to discuss the effect of the planets upon human endeavour, he allows that some aspects of the art of astrology may be legitimate. Thus, he adumbrates a solution to the problem of the conflict between astrological determinism, divine providence and human free will that would become widely acceptable. Should astrologers pretend that they could reveal a pre-determined future, or that the heavenly bodies could override divine providence or human free will, then their activities were of course illegitimate. Should they seek only to interpret the signs God had placed in the heavens, however, as farmers or sailors or doctors or miners might do (the last as they searched for precious metals born of the planets), then their efforts were to be commended, for they might help to direct persons to a righteous course of action.[5] Many other

---

[4] 'Magicians [perform miracles] through private contracts, good Christians through a public righteousness and evil Christians through the "ensigns" or symbols of this public righteousness': St Augustine, *Eighty-Three Different Questions*, ed. and trans. D. L. Mosher (Washington, 1982), p. 203 (qu. 79.4).

[5] *Speculum Astronomiae*, ch. 17; P. Zambelli, *The Speculum Astronomiae and its Enigma* (Dordrecht, 1992), pp. 270–3.

English scholars found it possible to reach an accommodation with astrology, among them Bartholomeus Anglicus in his *De Proprietatibus Rerum*, written *c.* 1262. The far more sophisticated *Opus Maius* of Roger Bacon (d. *c.* 1292) expressed a belief in the effects of the disposition of the heavens and of climate upon character, and explained how the signs of the zodiac partook of the elements and humours. Roger could also find much to recommend in judicial and medical astrology. Such views found support in continental works well known in England: in the *De Natura Rerum* of Thomas of Cantimpré (d. *c.* 1290), for example, which incorporated a whole work on image magic, as well as in the *Speculum Astronomiae*, which used to be attributed to Albertus Magnus.[6]

Alexander also seems to have believed in incantation and the evil eye. He is convinced of the magical properties of precious stones; some (the agate, for instance) induce love, some (the lodestone) prompt confession of wrongdoing, some (the allectory, found in the belly of the cock) ensure victory in war. Such stones could presumably be rightly employed by proper persons. Alexander was also happy to repeat many popular legends about the magical acumen of the poet Virgil, who could cast spells, conjure up ramparts and fabricate aery bridges wherever it pleased him to travel. We have no means of knowing how tongue-in-cheek this repetition was, but Virgil was still well respected in the schools and Alexander refrains from all moral comment upon his extraordinary abilities. Alexander also accords some credence to the popular prophecies of the great Welsh magician, Merlin.[7]

Alexander Neckham's *De Naturis Rerum* and allied treatises show how very open the English medieval Church could be to activity that might be described as magical. Science, in one sense, stands at an opposite pole from magic, for as the laws of nature become better understood, so the need for preternatural ways of controlling nature seems to diminish. One might expect, then, that 'scientists' would remain strictly aloof from magic. That many did not says much about their deep trust in the supernatural, and also about their views upon the employment and limits of the purely rational powers of mankind. Nature was not to be investigated for itself, but as a means of ascending 'from the study of natural properties to their Creator'.[8] In this way science helped to create a neutral

---

[6] B. Roy, 'Richard de Fournival, auteur du *Speculum Astronomie?*', *Archives d'Histoire Doctrinale et Littéraire du Moyen Age*, 67 (2000), 159–80.

[7] Neckam, *De Naturis Rerum*, pp. 39–44, 177–9, 237, 310–11.

[8] R. W. Southern, *Robert Grosseteste: the growth of an English mind in medieval Europe* (Oxford, 1986), p. 101.

territory between itself and magic in which effects apparently, or long thought to be, magical could be claimed as part of nature on its way to supernature, and in which, pending decisions about it, much 'natural magic' could be preserved.

In spite of this toleration of 'magic', there is lots of evidence – in the rulings of church councils, and in visitations, sermons and trials – that it alarmed many in late medieval England. Such evidence is not an infallible guide to attitudes towards magical practice. Legislative condemnations and sermons could be issued or reissued verbatim: Pecham's 1281 prohibitions, for instance, were simply reissued by Lyndwood in his *Provinciale* of *c.* 1422–30. Also, trials for magic were notoriously exploitable as a means of disposing of political enemies (including popes), and accusations of magical practice offered a ready means whereby members of professions, including doctors, might find scapegoats for their own failures. There was, moreover, little uniformity in the punishments imposed, which suggests that the persecution of magicians was as yet neither wholehearted nor well organised. Ralph of Coggeshall, for instance, tells of a council held by Archbishop Stephen Langton in 1222, in which an old woman was accused of being so adept at the magical arts as to enchant a young man and make him mad. She was not sentenced to death as a witch, but to life imprisonment.[9] *Sortilegium* (which originally meant divination by lots but acquired a more negative sense) was in general unacceptable, but excommunication seems to have been a more normal first step towards its punishment. It seems that a charge of magical practice had to be allied to one of treason or heresy to merit the severest penalty. Such charges should, in short, be seen rather as a coded means of making life uncomfortable than as an indicator of the real incidence of magic, or of the opposition to it, and one should treat the evidence of condemnation warily and strictly within its context. Accusations of magic were credible, but they were not necessarily taken very seriously.

At certain turbulent moments accusations of sorcery became particularly prominent in politics. Thus, Alice Perrers, mistress of King Edward III, was attacked successfully for sorcery in the parliament of 1376 and Queen Joan of Navarre was similarly accused (of 'sorcerye and nygromancye' with the help of friars) by her stepson Henry V in 1419. In 1441 Eleanor Cobham, the wife of Duke Humphrey of Gloucester, was accused of attempting to predict when King Henry VI would die, and in

---

[9] F. M. Powicke and C. R. Cheney, eds., *Councils and Synods and other documents relating to the English Church, 1215–1313* (2 vols., Oxford, 1964), ii, pp. 105–6.

1469 Edward IV's mother-in-law, Jacquetta of Luxemburg, was accused of using magic to procure the marriage of her daughter, Elizabeth Woodville, to the king. The late fourteenth and fifteenth centuries were remarkably prolific in such accusations, which may suggest that recourse to magic was, in those centuries, more frequent than it had been. Though women were clearly prominent among those attacked, men might also be accused.

Very occasionally we are told more precisely where and why people felt called upon to consult magicians, and what these magicians did. In a synod of 1287, Bishop Quinel of Exeter denounced conjuring and divination by means of reflecting surfaces such as sword-blades or water in basins, or through names written down and buried in the ground or put into holy water. The Becket miracles speak of looking into sword-blades, writing in strange characters and tying rings and charms round the necks of ill people as magical activities to be rejected.[10] Sorcerers indulged in lot-casting too, and made sacrifices to demons, most particularly to procure the love of a woman for their infatuated clients. A mandate for the repression of the magicians of his diocese, issued in 1311 by the bishop of London, explains that magicians are being asked to find lost objects, divine future events and interpret past ones, and cast spells. To do this they meet in secret and conjure up demons by means of tallow cakes or spinning tops, nail-parings, mirrors, stones or rings.[11] Finger-nails could be used as reflecting surfaces for the conjuring of images. Juliana of Lambeth, put on trial in 1314, was reported to have used wax images and secret books, and dressed in special black robes.[12] In 1371 one John Crok was accused of conjuring with a Saracen's head in a bag.[13] As well as procuring love, magicians seem also often to have been asked to interfere with marriage-making: hence the credibility of the charge against Jacquetta of Luxemburg.[14]

Several English scholars, and scholars whose works were popular in England, made it clear that obloquy might attach to persons accused of magical practice. And there were certainly magical books fitting none of the criteria for legitimated magic proposed above. The mid-thirteenth-century treatise *Picatrix*, which enjoyed a singular revival in the late

[10] J. C. Robertson and J. B. Sheppard, eds., *Materials for the History of Thomas Becket* (7 vols., RS, LXVII, 1875–85), i, pp. 199–200, 380–1.

[11] Powicke and Cheney, *Councils*, ii, pp. 1062, 1349.

[12] W. Stubbs, ed., *Chronicles of Edward I and Edward II* (2 vols., RS, LXXVI, 1882), i, pp. 236, 275–6.

[13] F. Getz, *Medicine in the English Middle Ages* (Princeton, 1998), p. 79.

[14] Powicke and Cheney, *Councils*, ii, pp. 88, 444, 457.

fourteenth century, was one such. The *Theorica Girgith Artium Magicarum*, which Chaucer may have seen (and condemned in the Franklin's Tale) was another.[15] The late fourteenth-century library of Thomas Erghome was replete with works labelled *Prophecie et Supersticiosa* in its catalogue, like the *Sworn Book of Honorius*, the *Liber Lune*, the *Tractatus de Penthagono Salomonis* and the *Ars Notoria*.[16] Some of the practices they described were designed to hurt and destroy, and in that respect came very close to the forbidden *nigromantia* (a word originally coined to describe conjuring with dead bodies, but which came to encompass other forms of forbidden occult practice).

The essence of contemporary objection to such texts, apart from the opportunities for charlatanry and mumbo-jumbo they clearly afforded, lay in the fact that they subverted the Church's own rituals by deploying elements such as the eucharistic host, the gospels, holy water and oil.[17] The prose treatise *Dives et Pauper* (c. 1405–10) told how candles from the Candlemas liturgy might be used by witches to harm their enemies by dropping wax upon their footprints. It also suggested that conjuring with dead bodies was still current practice among initiates.[18] The water in baptismal fonts was thought especially liable to attract magicians, so fonts should have covers that could be locked.[19] Anything that seemed to parody the liturgy and its celebrants was particularly suspect.

Many 'magical' texts did deploy liturgical practice. The *Ars Notoria*, for instance, made use of prayers, ascetic practices and mystic signs. It called upon the names of God and of angels in several languages, and (in some versions) the Virgin Mary as well. The aim was to secure the adept mastery of the liberal arts, thereby short-circuiting the educational demands of the contemporary Church. Hot-lines of this sort can be extremely dangerous to order and hierarchy, and the danger is compounded if they are popular, as the *Ars Notoria* undoubtedly was.

It is hard to decide exactly why texts of this kind were copied. Were they for illicit and clandestine use or were they thought useful to the orthodox (for example, by enabling wrongful magic to be quickly identified and quelled)? Whichever solution we prefer for individual codices, the fact that so many have survived is surely proof of a continued interest

[15] J. D. North, *Chaucer's Universe* (Oxford, 1988), pp. 252–4, 437–9.
[16] F. Klaassen, 'English manuscripts of magic, 1300–1500: a preliminary survey', in C. Fanger, ed., *Conjuring Spirits* (University Park, PA, 1998), pp. 3–31.
[17] Powicke and Cheney, *Councils*, ii, pp. 68, 76 (notes m and n), 210.
[18] P. H. Barnum, ed., *Dives and Pauper* I:1 (EETS, os CCLXXV, 1976), pp. 162–5.
[19] Powicke and Cheney, *Councils*, ii, pp. 453, 635.

in the genre as a whole. The magnificence of the fifteenth-century copy of the *Ars Notoria* now in the Bodleian Library, Bodley MS 951, suggests that this, at least, was made for a purpose larger than mere record. It is laid out, moreover, like a great glossed bible, with central text and marginal commentary, almost as a mockery of that learning it promised to infuse. Another Bodleian Library manuscript codex, MS Rawlinson D 252 (also of the fifteenth century), pocket-sized and neatly set out, appears to have been the handbook of a working necromancer. The practitioner is expected to summon demons to his aid and to command spirits, and the book is full of classic conjurations of angels by means of reflecting crystals (f. 6–6v), with rings (f. 80), with blood (f. 73v) and by burning herbs and incense (ff. 23, 34v). It purports to provide means for finding thieves and hidden treasure (f. 156–156v), for success in law-suits (f. 73v), for avoiding scandal, for healing and for inflicting harm (f. 125). The whole seems to provide an exemplar of all the English Church wished to outlaw. The reality, however, is less simple. There is much calling upon the Trinity in these invocations (ff. 37, 100v), and, even more confusingly, upon the memory of the 'magical' powers Christ himself conferred upon the apostles (f. 3). Such prayers, seemingly humbly meant, lack all sense of that power to compel which is sometimes thought to distinguish the 'black' magician from the 'white'. The handbook also contains (ff. 49–51) a confessional formulary ending, rather touchingly, with a prayer for protection against evil spirits.

Such codices show how complex the problem of magic in fact was in the late middle ages. The necromancer of Rawlinson D 252 seems to have been anxious to remain at least in touch with orthodox prayers and protections. He may, indeed, have been a cleric.[20] Not all the human needs the necromancer sought to satisfy were illegitimate ones, nor were all his invocations unacceptable. The range of requests and means of intercession suggest that the levels of anxiety and the appetite for ritual control were very great. The problem of magic was ever-present; but it was also, in essence, unresolved. The English Church and its clergy, we know, remained exceedingly 'ritualist' as the middle ages drew to a close, and some clergy stepped over the boundaries between acceptable and unacceptable practice. We may perhaps best understand these phenomena, however, as resulting from a desire to attend to these unsatisfied

---

[20] This codex fulfils, for example, the criteria for clerical necromantic codices set out by R. Kieckhefer, *Forbidden Rites* (Stroud, 1997), pp. 12–13.

anxieties and appetites as extensively as possible, rather than as a simple and cowardly capitulation to the superstitious.

Many of the authorities and scholars who were active in the condemnation of magicians showed themselves even more enthusiastic for the encouragement of magic, though not, of course, under this name. The encouragement took many forms, of which we may perhaps single out three. Firstly, we have miracles, most especially miracles which were thought to stem from sanctity, and which were associated with those great shrines that became such a feature of the English ecclesiastical landscape in the later middle ages. Secondly (especially perhaps in collections of miracles), we can discern a profound and orthodox interest in substances supposed to be magical, such as blood, or particular metals and jewels, or water. We may allow that these two manifestations fall within the category of 'popular magic' in so far as this elusive entity can be defined at all. Thirdly, we have evidence that 'magic' could be received as wisdom and as the proper cultivation of the mind, especially in the form of the learned arts of astronomy, astrology, medicine and alchemy.

The distinction between 'miracle' (good) and 'magic' (bad) was well recognised in England in the period. The compilers of the *Liber Memorandorum* of St Edmund of Canterbury (d.1240), for example, argued explicitly that St Edmund's miracles could not be ascribed to magic because they were performed only for the best of reasons.[21] There was clearly some confusion about the exact place of miracles vis-à-vis magic, a confusion occasionally registered in surviving manuscript compilations. The Rawlinson necromancer's handbook offers conjurations *ad habendis miraculis* (f. 156v), for instance, and a fourteenth-century manuscript, now Oxford, Corpus Christi College MS 221, is made up of a 'magical' text (Thetel, *On Images*), the miracle-filled *Dialogues* of Gregory the Great, and two saints' lives. Occasionally the *Miracles of the Virgin* are found in company with the *Ars Notoria* and Solomonic treatises, almost as though the one might compensate for, or even sanction, the other. The many strictly orthodox late medieval miracle collections that have survived can, therefore, be seen as a form of good magic to counter-balance the less good. They may also furnish us with excellent evidence as to the possible ingredients of good magic.

I shall draw illustrations from two English miracle collections, one made towards the beginning of the period, the other towards the end.

---

[21] 'Historia Translationis S. Edmundi', in E. Martène and U. Durand, eds., *Thesaurus Novus Anecdotorum* (5 vols., Paris, 1717), iii, p. 1872.

The first is the collection made, in 1307, for the canonisation of Bishop Thomas Cantilupe of Hereford (d.1282).[22] The second is the famous *Miracles of King Henry VI* (d.1471), a collection put together in the last years of the fifteenth century.[23] The miracles of Cantilupe register a sensitivity to forbidden magic directly. Could the death of little Roger of Conway have been precipitated by a woman sorcerer? Could any cures and resuscitations have been brought about by forbidden incantations, sortileges or magic words?[24] Yet they also allowed Cantilupe to be effective in many of the spheres in which necromancers were asked to operate: for example, victory in lawsuits, resuscitation from the dead, 'conjuring' with the help of blood or threads, and the special use of metals (particularly bent pennies). The fabrication of waxen images, too, was permitted in hope of, or thanks for, supernatural favours.[25] The same is true of the *Miracles of King Henry VI*. Cures and resuscitations are again prominent in these, often achieved through measurings with threads and the bending of pennies, and there are also victories in judicial proceedings.

Most interestingly of all, Henry's miracles include accounts of the successful foiling of thieves, one of which actually compares the modus operandi of the miracle-worker with that of contemporary magicians, much to the disadvantage of the latter. The owner of a stolen treasure recovers it, but is determined, nonetheless, upon revenge. He proposes to go to London to consult diviners, astrologers and soothsayers there, in order to find the thief. The dead King Henry appears, and warns him that he will himself die unless he desists, for God does not require the death of a sinner (Ezekiel 33:11). Rather than pay magicians, the owner should make an offering at King Henry's tomb instead.[26]

Bishop Thomas and King Henry did not succeed by calling upon spirits, and they never sought harm or revenge. Rather, they were helped by a holiness even greater than theirs, by their innate goodness and by their responsiveness to the humble prayers of others. There is a world of difference between the range of action allowed to the Christian miracle-worker

[22] This is available in fallible printed form in Society of Ballandistes, *A[cta] S[anctorum]* (68 vols., Antwerp and Brussels, 1643–1940), Octobris i, pp. 541–705, and also in an early manuscript copy: Vatican City, MS Vat. Lat. 4051. I am much indebted to Ronald Finucane for the loan of a microfilm of the latter.

[23] P. Grosjean, ed., *Henrici VI Angliae Regis Miracula Postuma* (Brussels, 1935); they are partially printed and translated by R. Knox and S. Leslie, *The Miracles of King Henry VI* (Cambridge, 1923).

[24] MS Vat. Lat. 4051, ff. 66v, 131, 133, 201v, noted in R. Finucane, *The Rescue of the Innocents* (Basingstoke, 1997), p. 133.

[25] *AS*, Octobris i, pp. 581–2, 611–13, 634.   [26] Grosjean, *Henrici VI*, pp. 33–4.

and that claimed by the condemnable necromancer, a difference consisting principally of personal qualities and intentions, just as Augustine had said it should. There is some sign that the Christian miracle-worker's hierarchical position in society was beginning to matter as well. Once these requirements had been met, however, many of the services asked of both miracle-workers and magicians were much the same. The same point could be made of other compilations: for example, the many late medieval collections of folk-charms and cures. The differences between them and the incantations of the Rawlinson necromancer's handbook are sometimes very hard to find. Many Christianised folk-cures required the use of special metals, or knives, or rings, or particular characters written on parchment, or even magic squares. We can find Christianised charms for victory in lawsuits and against thieves and, in one spectacular case, mystic characters including the tetragrammaton are called upon to defend the Christian practitioner from wicked spirits.[27] The compelling distinction between the art of the necromancer and that of the Christian enchanter seems to rest once again more in the attitude and aims of the practitioner than in the methods used.

Miracle collections and folk-charms such as these do not furnish evidence of good learned magic. For this we must turn to more sophisticated texts. Again, we may not call these 'magical', and many of the practices licensed in them were thought to be scientific, or at least to inhabit the neutral territory between the scientific and the supernatural. The art of making images, or talismans, mentioned briefly above, is a good example of learned neutral practice. This art depended directly upon contemporary views about the universe, for it drew upon the belief that the heavenly bodies emanated harnessable powers. These powers were transmitted by stellar rays, and were harnessed by being drawn into images which were themselves fashioned with careful reference to the prevailing dispositions of the heavenly bodies. The images, or 'signatures', might be engraved upon stones or gems or rings or metal plates. Information about image magic reached medieval England by many routes, including translations into Latin of the treatises *On Images* by Thàbit b. Qurra and by Thetel, or by means of the *De Radiis Stellarum* of Al-Kindi and of Hermetic texts. They usually circulated in company with other 'scientific' works. The author of the *Speculum Astronomiae* was prepared to take images seriously. One might bury images to avert pests, or use

---

[27] T. Hunt, *Popular Medicine in Thirteenth Century England* (Cambridge, 1990), pp. 79–99, notably p. 98 n. 86.

them to obtain love or profit, for example, provided only that one did not employ evil spirits, improper incantations, suffumigations or mystic signs.[28] Any hint of such behaviour and the practice was evil; but simple image magic might be helpful and therefore good. Roger Bacon took a similar line. Certain forms of divination, such as geomancy, hydromancy, aeromancy or pyromancy (conjuring by means of mystic symbols written in earth or sand, or through images seen in water, air or fire) were, he thought, almost certain to involve evil spirits, and so must be outlawed. Other very similar practices, however, might be entirely legitimate.[29]

Image magic was a branch of astrology, and astrology, reinforced by that influx of translations mentioned above, might now be as respectable as astronomy. Splendid workmanlike collections of astrological texts demonstrate both the practical relevance of astrology and the status it enjoyed in England. A thirteenth-century manuscript in the Bodleian Library, Selden Supra 76, from Winchester, is one such. This nicely written and professionally produced little book contains a number of works on astrology, including Roger of Hereford on judicial astrology, Al-Kindi *De Radiis*, some alchemical receipts and (f. 109v) a treatise on the drawing of omens from sculptured gems. Of course, astrology had its enemies, but the very ferocity of some of the opposition is itself evidence that many were in favour of the art. By the fifteenth century astrology had come to enjoy a remarkably wide range of support, not least, perhaps, because other forms of magical practice, such as conjuring with demons, now appeared to be so very much worse.

The English medical profession was especially quick to take advantage of the acceptance of astrology. Relations between the Church and the medical profession were often strained in the middle ages, and the inefficacy of doctors is a recurring theme in miracle collections and saints' lives (though usually as a means of throwing the saint's superior healing powers into greater relief rather than as a way of belittling doctors per se). Physicians are given powerful support in the bible, notably in Ecclesiasticus 38:1–15; but then comes the rub. They are to be honoured only as representatives of that God who stands behind all healing. The Paris medical faculty made the same point in their report on the plague in 1348, the first part of which ended by emphasising the need to return humbly to God but added '[T]his does not mean forsaking doctors. For the Most High created earthly medicine, and although God alone cures the sick, he

---

[28] *Speculum Astronomiae*, ch. 11; Zambelli, *The Speculum Astronomiae*, pp. 246–9.
[29] A. G. Molland, 'Roger Bacon as magician', *Traditio*, 30 (1974), 459–60.

does so through the medicine which in his generosity he provided'.[30] This need for a sign of their deference to God may underlie some of the enthusiasm doctors felt for astrology. The stars and planets were, after all, set in the heavens by God (Genesis 1:16–18). If man was subject to God's heavens, the stars, planets and elements, then greater knowledge of the secrets of these might reasonably distinguish and justify God's *medici*, and preserve the place of the profession within the Christian Church.

Thus, doctors admitted the 'magical' into their world. A method of assigning parts of the body to particular signs of the zodiac played an integral part in the diagnosis and treatment of disease, and so did a knowledge of the disposition of the heavens at a person's birth. A conscientious practitioner would take care, then, to register the birth-dates of his patients, and we have evidence that many did. Astrological medicine of this kind gained additional popularity from the fact that a simplified version was tolerably easy for amateurs to learn. Other forms of prognosis such as onomancy (the adding of the letters of chosen names together), geomancy, or scapulimancy (prognostication from the shoulder blades of sheep) gained a place on the coat-tails of medical astrology. The author of the *Speculum Astronomiae* allowed that geomancy and chiromancy (palmistry) might help in the understanding of man's medical state. King Richard II, fearful as he was of sorcery, commissioned a book containing simple medical astrology and geomancy, which still survives (Bodleian Library, Bodley MS 581). Although much late medieval English medical material was believed to deserve the name of science, therefore, it took great care to preserve elements of Christianised magic. The fact that there were objectors to this process renders it a complex one to assess, and we have as yet no means of estimating accurately the incidence of 'magic' in medicine. That it was present, however, there is no doubt.

One further branch of learned magic prevalent in the period deserves discussion: alchemy. This too took strength from Genesis. Paracelsus (d.1541), for instance, saw God's act of dividing light from darkness as the act of an alchemist separating gold from base matter. The belief that base matter might be turned to gold by the application of heat was found in other parts of the bible (for example, Proverbs 17:3, 27:21). Alchemy also called into service those notions about the universe which supported astrology, including the belief that all bodies are made of the four elements and four contraries, and the idea that there was a correspondence between the movement and composition of the seven planets and the

---

[30] R. Horrox, ed., *The Black Death* (Manchester, 1994), p. 163.

growth of the seven chief metals in the earth. The concept of the transmutation of elements led to the hope that gold might eventually be produced by a speeding up of that heat in the earth. This, it was believed, changed metals from their rudiments in mercury and sulphur through intermediate stages, such as lead, to silver and gold. Heat produced the transmutations in the earth; heat might, then, reproduce them on earth, perhaps with the help of a special elixir or quickener, sometimes known as the 'philosopher's stone'. No such summary account can do justice to the science or art of alchemy, but it may serve at least to show how attractive such possibilities might be. Many of the necessary techniques, such as distillation and the production of elixirs, were common to both alchemists and doctors. Indeed, they attracted the latter not least because alchemical procedures might lead to better medicines.

Thus, alchemy too formed an important part of that 'magic' which came into late medieval England. One of the most popular accounts of alchemy, Discourse X of the *Secreta Secretorum* (translated into Latin from the Arabic), survives now in over sixty English manuscripts and in several Middle English adaptations. Roger Bacon produced a version and Chaucer's yeoman knew the power of the text.[31] Again, the acceptance of alchemy was not unquestioned. The yeoman pointed to the gambling and greed it encouraged and to the need to remember that God's guidance was necessary to all such enterprises; but, at the end of the middle ages, the practice of alchemy was still built firmly into the social fabric of the country.

Charms, prayers, miracles, image magic, judicial astrology, medical astrology and even alchemy sought to answer many of the same questions, and to allay many of the same anxieties, which might take an individual to a 'black' magician. That the Christian picture of the universe could make room for such a range of ways of meeting human problems may have worked to its advantage. This may, indeed, have prompted Christian scholars to take to such defensible forms of magic with all the greater enthusiasm. Their efforts to do so were still being praised at the very end of our period. Thus, in his *Apologia* (written in 1487), Pico della Mirandola numbers Roger Bacon among those who knew the nature of good, non-demonic magic, and, fortunately, knew also how to encourage it.[32]

---

[31] J. D. North, 'Chaucer: The Canon's Yeoman's Tale', in Z. R. W. M. von Martels, ed., *Alchemy Revisited* (Leiden, 1992), pp. 85–7.

[32] Molland, 'Roger Bacon', 445–6.

It was once fashionable to view the final decades of the middle ages in England as a period of decadence and superstition, in great need of the purifying waters of the Reformation. Such a view does scant justice to the true state of affairs. The universe with which the late medieval English Church grappled was shot through with such a complexity of supernatural forces that a deficiency of means of harnessing the good in them, and of neutralising the bad, was far more to be feared than a superfluity. It was imperative that the supernatural forces of darkness be countered by the forces of light; and the variety and power of these dark forces rendered it essential that their counters be equally varied and powerful.

The enthusiasm for 'white' magic that protected so many levels of magical practice in late medieval England seems also to have protected its practitioners. Even those who transgressed the boundaries of the acceptable seem to have escaped the full violence of persecution. It has been astutely remarked that:

In so far as necromancers contributed to the plausibility of claims about witches, they bear indirect responsibility for the rise of the European witch trials ... To the extent that these early witch trials focused on female victims, they thus provide a particularly tragic case of women being blamed and punished for the misconduct of men.[33]

True; but there is a world of difference between the inclusiveness and tolerance of the late medieval magic universe and that which empowered the witchcraft trials and punishments. The sweeping away of the angels and saints and shrines and miracles and masses and prayers and sanctuaries and 'magic' of the medieval Church made space for demons; just as Augustine had feared it would.

---

[33] Kieckhefer, *Forbidden Rites*, p. 12.

CHAPTER 13

Renunciation

Janet Burton

Renunciation is a theme that ran through a wide variety of religious experience in medieval England and touched the lives of many people. It drew on a long Christian tradition of self-imposed separation from the world, which had begun in the third and fourth centuries when the hermits of Palestine and Egypt had shunned the city in favour of the desert. The many men and women who sought to emulate the lives, values and aspirations of the desert monks did so in the retreats of monastery, nunnery, hermitage and anchorhold: that is, in communities centred on the religious life or in a solitary existence.

By 1200 there was in England a well-established monastic order. There were monasteries that took as their code of life the Rule of St Benedict. There were others, like the Cistercians, who remained Benedictine but formed their own order. There were the regular canons, who since the late eleventh century had become a vital part of the English monastic scene; and there were nunneries of all orders and congregations, both large and wealthy Anglo-Saxon foundations and the smaller, often poor, houses of eastern England and the northern moors. But almost paradoxically the life of renunciation was made possible by those who lived in the world: by the material support offered to the monastic order by lay benefactors, who provided land on which a monastery could be built and endowments to yield income to maintain the community. If benefactors did not themselves live the life of renunciation, they received benefits from the monastic order, chiefly the spiritual benefits of vicarious intercession, commemoration and sometimes burial. Monks were seen as powerful intercessors for those who remained within the world, 'cowled champions [who] may engage in ceaseless combat against Behemoth for your soul'.[1]

By 1200 some of England's monastic houses were long-established, while others were a product of the great expansion of the twelfth century.

---

[1] M. Chibnall, ed., *The Ecclesiastical History of Orderic Vitalis* (6 vols., Oxford, 1968–80), iii, p. 147.

Although there was a brief flowering of the Carthusian order in the later middle ages, the era of growth was over by 1200 and religious houses, large and small, were by then a familiar part of the English townscape and countryside. But renunciation within a monastery or nunnery was not the only form of renunciation. There were, in particular, radical new developments in religious practice from the early thirteenth century, as the friars moved to England from their nerve centres in France and Italy. Unlike monks, friars actively sought to combine a pastoral and social mission with a devotion to poverty in an innovative concept of the religious life.

For all these monks, canons, nuns and friars, who collectively formed the monastic order of medieval England, the religious life was social: they shared a way of life in a community. But there were also those for whom renunciation was an individual experience: the hermits, anchorites and anchoresses of medieval England, and those, such as vowesses, who lived a religious life subject to vows but within the world. Because hermits were not part of an institution and lived alone, they did not leave records such as those generated by the great monastic houses. But we should not too quickly discount their presence and their importance in medieval religion and culture.

One of the central forms of renunciation was the giving up of material goods. St Matthew's gospel records Christ's advice to the rich young man who asked how he might obtain eternal life: in order to achieve perfection he should sell all that he had and give to the poor (Matthew 19:21). This created a powerful argument that material wealth and salvation were incompatible. But there were other forms of renunciation which came to be associated with the religious life of the middle ages, and one way in which we can approach the question of what the monastic, religious and eremitical life meant in medieval society is by looking at the vows which monks and canons, nuns and friars, made on their entry into the religious life and at the symbolism connected with that entry.

The religious life was first and foremost about renunciation of self and individual identity. This is highlighted in the document that formed the basis of monastic life in the medieval west, the Rule of St Benedict. On taking his vows the novice professed 'stability, conversion of his life, and obedience'.[2] The last meant total obedience to the rule and to the abbot. By obedience to the rule, monks were bound to the routine of a day organised into periods of prayer, work and reading, much of the time

[2] J. McCann, ed. and trans., *The Rule of St Benedict* (1972), ch. 58.

being spent in silence. They were to have no will of their own but become cogs in what was increasingly a liturgical wheel, praying for the salvation of humankind.

The Rule linked the profession of obedience to humility. In Benedict's eyes the second degree of humility is 'that a man love not his own will' and the third 'that a man for the love of God subject himself to his superior in all obedience'.[3] Up to the twelfth century many entrants to the religious life had no choice as to their future: these were the oblates, offered as children by their parents to the service of God and the mon- astery.[4] From the twelfth century greater emphasis was laid on the importance of the individual will in the decision to enter the religious life, and the centuries-old practice of placing children in monasteries for entry into the religious life at an appropriate age came to an end. However, the renunciation of self-determination – if not of the personal ambition to rise through the hierarchy of the monastery or nunnery to high office – remained an essential of the monastic life. This form of renunciation was open to everyone: 'personal standing is merged in the equality of each and all'.[5]

The demands of obedience are perhaps most clearly discerned within the framework of a community, but even those who lived a solitary life had to subordinate their own wills. The *Ancrene Wisse*, discussed by Eamon Duffy above, stressed the need for the solitary women to obey a superior: 'each anchoress must observe the outer rule according to the advice of her confessor'.[6] Members of the religious orders were not the only members of medieval society to live within a framework where some were in authority and others were not. The monastic community was, however – in theory at least – one where status disregarded birth and social rank; the authority that normally came with these markers was abandoned at the point of entry.

At the end of his year-long preparation for entry into the monastery, the first vow taken by Benedict's novice was stability, the renunciation of freedom to move. The Church had always been suspicious of wandering religious, who placed themselves outside the establishment and beyond the control of a rule or a superior. Monks and nuns were expected to remain in the cloister for life. Although stability was the ideal, it was practised in different ways. The practicalities of monastic life meant that

[3] *Ibid.*, ch. 7.   [4] *Ibid.*, ch. 59: 'The offering of the sons of the rich and of the poor'.
[5] Walter Daniel, *The Life of Ailred of Rievaulx*, ed. F. M. Powicke (1950), p. 12.
[6] H. White, trans., *Ancrene Wisse: Guide for Anchoresses* (1993), p. 3.

temporary absences were unavoidable. Abbots were figures of political, social and economic importance, and might travel widely; some monks had to leave the cloister to attend the general chapters of their orders or to study at university; and both monks and canons might serve in parish churches or hospitals. However, attempts were made to limit contact with the outside world and to ensure that absences from the monastery were minimised. The introduction by the Cistercians of the class of half monk, the *conversi* or lay brothers, had removed the need for monks to leave the monastery for the practical purposes of estate management and commercial enterprise. The *conversi* remained a significant group throughout the twelfth century, though a decline in numbers set in thereafter and this group dwindled fast after the Black Death. The external needs of cloistered women, who were thought to be particularly vulnerable, were met by lay brothers, masters or guardians, who ensured that their vocation and purity were not threatened by contact with those outside the nunnery walls.

It was thus one of the revolutionary aspects of the friars that they challenged and overturned this cornerstone of medieval monastic life. In their search for the apostolic life of mission and preaching as well as poverty, they turned their backs on fixed places to live and wandered. For the friars, the religious life meant the imitation of Christ, preaching and teaching. They were not the first to see preaching as a component of the monastic life, but never before had this resulted in the rejection of stability. By the time the friars reached England, the main orders, the Dominicans and Franciscans, had begun to establish priories as centres for their evangelical activity, but it was still a cardinal point of their existence that they did not settle but moved from place to place preaching the word of God in town and countryside, church and marketplace. Alongside this peripatetic existence, and in some ways contrary to it, was the growing dominance of the Dominicans and the Franciscans in the teaching of theology. For the Dominicans this was perhaps the logical outcome of the need for academic learning as a means to combat heresy – the purpose for which they had been founded. The effect was to promote and enliven that important medieval intellectual and social institution, the university.

At the opposite end of the scale from the friars were the anchorites and anchoresses, not just recluses from the world but *inclusi / incluse*: physically shut away from it. Their cells might be found attached to parish churches (for example, the anchorhold founded by Henry, duke of Lancaster, in the parish church of Whalley), in towns (such as the

Pontefract *reclusarium*, established before 1240) or on bridges (the anchorhold on Doncaster bridge in the patronage of the Fitzwilliam family).[7] The author of the *Ancrene Wisse* counselled that the anchoress profess stability, 'that she shall never more change that place, except out of necessity only (such as violence and fear of death, obedience to her bishop or his superior)'.[8] The service for the immuring of anchorites and anchoresses, as also for the entry of lepers into *leprosaria*, was the office of the dead, symbolising that they were thenceforth 'dead to the world'.

If monks and nuns professed stability and anchorites and anchoresses, walled in their cells, were restricted from travel, this was not necessarily the case with hermits. Some hermitages were firmly established in a particular location, but many hermits were free to wander. This was taken increasingly as a threat to the stability of Church and society, and measures were taken to regulate and control movement. This might involve placing hermits and hermitages under the authority of nearby religious houses, or increasing episcopal supervision. William Langland was typical of late fourteenth-century attitudes in his fierce criticism of false hermits: those who sought an easy life under the guise of holy men. The legislation of 1389 that ordered hermits to carry letters of accreditation from their local bishop was part of an anti-vagrancy statute.[9] There were clearly tensions over stability in concepts of the monastic life and this is reflected in lay society, which by the fourteenth century was suspicious of those who in the widest sense lacked stability, whether they were hermits or beggars, or, indeed, single women living outside a family.

Benedict's novice also promised 'conversion of life': the commitment to change his or her life. This was often marked by a change of name. It was also accompanied by a change of clothes: adopting a monastic habit was symbolic of the renunciation of society, property and personality. Conversely, if a monk rejected the monastic life and left the monastery, his old clothes would be returned to him. Part of the service of the making of a hermit involved the blessing of his clothes by the bishop. The brown habit and white scapular of the hermit, illustrated in the pontifical of Bishop Clifford of London (d.1421), 'signified humility of heart, chastity and contempt for the world and worldly things', and the words spoken by the bishop were, 'The Lord put on thee the new man, which

---

[7] J. Hughes, *Pastors and Visionaries: religion and secular life in late medieval Yorkshire* (Woodbridge, 1988), pp. 64–126, esp. p. 66. See also A. K. Warren, *Anchorites and their Patrons* (Berkeley, 1986).
[8] *Ancrene Wisse*, p. 3.
[9] V. Davis, 'The Rule of St Paul, the first hermit in late medieval England', in *Monks, Hermits and the Ascetic Tradition*, Studies in Church History, XXII (Oxford, 1985), pp. 203–14 (p. 206).

after God is created in righteousness and true holiness' (Ephesians 4:24).[10] For the author of the *Ancrene Wisse* clothing had another significance: plain clothing was the sign of a lack of vanity.[11] Above all, however, the change of clothing associated with entry into the religious life symbolised the rejection of family and society. Richard Rolle, the hermit of Hampole who wrote *Ego Dormio* for his 'dear sister in Christ', a woman who had just become or was considering becoming a nun at the Yorkshire convent of Yedingham, urged his reader that spiritual reward would follow 'if you abandon everything which you derive human pleasure from and cease to be preoccupied by your friends and relations'.[12] Human relationships were seen to distract from the religious vocation, and heavenly delights were to be preferred to earthly joys.

It is important not to exaggerate the divide between monastic and lay society or to underestimate the interaction between the two. Connections with family were often maintained, and monks and nuns might be given episcopal licence to visit their relatives. Monasteries and nunneries had a social function beyond the provision of intercession for humankind. They were places of hospitality; members of the gentry or mercantile classes purchased corrodies (the provision of lodging or food, often in their old age, in return for a lump sum); children were placed there to be educated; and the poor gathered to receive alms.

Hermits, too, could have a social function. Work was a part of their daily routine, and the rules surviving from late medieval England indicate that this might also bring them into contact with lay society. The repair of roads and bridges was one way in which the hermit could earn his keep. Even anchorites were not totally isolated. The *Ancrene Wisse*, for instance, assumes some contact, albeit regrettable, with the outside world:

They say about anchoresses that each has to have an old woman to feed her ears: a jabberer who jabbers to her all the stories of the area ... so that it is said in a proverb 'From mill and from market, from smithy and from anchor-hold people bring the news'. Christ knows, this is a sad saying, that the anchor-house, which should be the most solitary place of all, has to be linked with those three places in which there is most chatter.[13]

---

[10] *Ibid.*, p. 209.
[11] *Ancrene Wisse*, pp. 193–4.
[12] Quoted in F. Beer, *Women and Mystical Experience in the Middle Ages* (Woodbridge, 1992), p. 115.
[13] *Ancrene Wisse*, p. 46.

Moreover the legislation that restricted the size of the windows of anchorholds, forbade anchorites to hear confession or to use their cells to store valuables, suggests that, like hermits, those who had been immured and were 'dead to the world' still had a social function within it.

The exchange of spiritual and mystical literature reinforces this point. The *Book of Showings* of the Norwich recluse Julian was written for an outside audience, and Julian was visited by Margery Kempe. Richard Rolle wrote not only *Ego Dormio* for a would-be nun but also *The Commandment* for a nun of Hampole and *The Form of Living* for his disciple, the Richmondshire recluse Margaret Kirkby. It was mental and spiritual detachment rather than mere physical isolation that the late medieval recluse required. A striking illustration of such a search for solitude is found in the Carthusian order. Carthusian houses were group hermitages. The monastic complex – now best viewed at Mount Grace in Yorkshire – comprised a modest church for a limited number of communal services and, around a large cloister, individual cells where the monks lived, prayed, read, worked their garden and often wrote and copied mystical texts. The last employment constituted preaching and teaching, but without face-to-face contact. From their cells the monks were responsible for the transmission of major theological and devotional works. Although they had renounced the world, they still communicated with it. Paradoxically, the fourteenth-century burst of Carthusian foundations was encouraged by the patronage of men in the court circle of Richard II. Mount Grace, for instance, was founded by the king's nephew Thomas Holland, and Epworth by Thomas Mowbray, duke of Norfolk. Their support for the order arose from their admiration for the high standard of Carthusian observance and the order's great austerity. This not only guaranteed the efficacy of their prayers and intercessions but also in itself held a profound appeal for a materialistic society. The aristocratic patronage brought the Carthusians from their 'desert' to urban centres, and the London charterhouse was built adjacent to a burial ground of victims of the Black Death.

As part of the renunciation of self, the Rule of St Benedict demanded that a monk give up all personal goods. As an integrated member of a community, all his physical needs would be met by that community and there was no need for private possessions. The monastic ideal of communal living found one justification in the description in the earliest Christian community in Jerusalem, among whom all things were held in common (Acts 2:44–5). However, from the twelfth century, and increasingly in the thirteenth, the monastic orders faced challenges from less formal movements that interpreted the apostolic life not merely in terms of common ownership of property but as the observation of poverty and the act of preaching. The renewed emphasis on poverty was part of an antipathy towards an increasingly prosperous and economically complex society: St Francis, founder of the Franciscan friars, deliberately rejected his privileged upbringing. But the real novelty of the friars was that they rejected corporate as well as individual possessions. The *Regula Bullata*, the final version of Francis's rule, refers to the 'eminence of loftiest poverty', the virtue of serving God 'in poverty and humility', and a radical withdrawal from the world of buying and selling marked by a ban on handling money.[14] The aim of the friars was to be on terms of equality with the poorest of the poor. For Francis this poverty was absolute, extending to the denial of places to live and ownership of property. The Dominicans, who initially embraced poverty but accepted places to live, came to imitate the Franciscans in their interpretation of absolute poverty. The friars were wanderers, and they were to be sustained by begging. Labour was to be casual, rather than – as in the Rule of St Benedict – an essential component of the monastic life.

Such radical ideals were not easy to maintain, and in England as elsewhere a fierce debate emerged – almost from the death of Francis – on the nature of poverty and what it actually signified. The Franciscans saw poverty as an imitation of the poverty of Christ, as well as the renunciation of property in the search for evangelism. Just as Christ lived without a home and died without possessions, so too should the friars. However, differences soon emerged among the friars themselves about poverty and about the concepts of use and dominion, or ownership; and modifications were made to the rule. In 1230 the pope allowed the Franciscans to have 'spiritual friends' who could hold money on their behalf, and the further provision (in 1247) whereby the spiritual friend became a legal representative in all business matters undermined the very roots of the order.

Quite how things had changed in England over a generation can be seen in Thomas of Eccleston's account of the coming of the Franciscans to England, written in 1258–9. In many ways Thomas was looking back to a pioneering or golden age, and his remarks evoke an era when the friars embraced poverty absolutely. He held up as a shining example of the first Franciscan novices in England Brother Solomon, who

once visited his sister to beg alms. She brought him some bread, but turned away her face saying 'Cursed be the hour that I ever saw you'. But he joyfully accepted

---

[14] R. B. Brooke, *The Coming of the Friars* (1975), pp. 120–5.

the bread and went on his way. So strictly did he accept the rule of absolute poverty to which he was vowed that he would sometimes bring back in his cloak a little flour, salt, a few figs or an armful of wood for the benefit of some sick brother. But he was very careful never to accept or keep anything that was not an absolute necessity.[15]

Thomas also explained how the idea of 'spiritual friends' worked in England:

At Canterbury, Sir Alexander, warden of the priests' hospice, transferred to them a plot of ground and built them a chapel large enough for their present needs. And since the brethren refused to accept property as their own, it was held by the city council, and the brethren used it by the goodwill of the citizens.[16]

But a golden age it was, and in letting slip that 'in those days the friars were very strict about erecting buildings and possessing pictures', Thomas suggested that things were different in his own day.[17] His record makes clear the difficulties the friars had in reconciling success and their concept of poverty.

The debate about Franciscan poverty occupied a central place in medieval religious debate. The implications were far-reaching, for the Franciscan claim that Christ owned nothing set absolute poverty as the ultimate goal for all religious, both monastic and those in the hierarchy of the Church. This led to fierce controversy, in which English friars took a full part. In 1249–51 William of Nottingham, English prior provincial (that is, head of the Franciscans in England), took a stand against relaxations in the rule. Adam Marsh, a noted Franciscan and confessor of King Henry III, refused money, and in 1241 an English delegation petitioned the general, Haymo of Faversham, on behalf of the English province, to hold fast to the rule as composed by Francis. English friars, as Knowles wrote, 'united to preserve the first purity of the Rule'.[18] The culmination of the debate was the papal bull *Cum inter nonnullos* of 1323, which declared heretical the belief that Christ and his apostles owned nothing.

For all religious orders, however, the differentiation between personal and corporate poverty could be difficult to justify to the outside world. By the later middle ages the friars as well as the traditional monastic orders were facing criticism for their wealth. John Wyclif was of the opinion that

[15] Thomas of Eccleston, *The Coming of the Franciscans*, trans. L. Sherley-Price (1964), p. 8.
[16] *Ibid.*, p. 15.   [17] *Ibid.*, p. 33.
[18] D. Knowles, *The Religious Orders in England*, I: *1216–1340* (Cambridge, 1948), pp. 143–5.

'it would be to the advantage of the kingdom, were the expenses of which friars despoil kingdoms to be distributed to the poor for the building of humble houses'.[19]

Although it was not one of the formal vows taken by monks and nuns, chastity was a fundamental of the monastic life, as it was by this period for the secular clergy also. This meant renunciation of marriage and sexual relations. For some it meant lifelong virginity; for others the assumption of a life of self-denial after widowhood.[20] This is one area in which attitudes seem to have been gendered. Chastity and virginity might be invested with different meanings for men and women. There may have been men for whom denial of sex and sexuality was an important dynamic behind the decision to enter religion. Religious writing – and it is important to remember that this writing was for the most part by men – suggests that it was perceived, or represented, as even more important for women. Idung of Prufening, a twelfth-century Cluniac monk who converted to the Cistercians, drew attention to the difference between the sexes when he stated that a woman could lose her virginity by violence, 'a thing which in the masculine sex nature itself prevents'. A common way of describing female chastity was as a vessel that had to be guarded. For Idung a consecrated woman was 'a glass vessel' because of her fragility and a 'golden vessel' because of her virginity. The twelfth-century Cistercian abbot, Ailred of Rievaulx, whose letter to his sister influenced many writers on the religious life, spoke of 'an earthen vessel in which gold is stored for testing'. This imagery is carried into the *Ancrene Wisse*. When speaking of the need to 'flee the world', the author counsels thus:

the person who was carrying a costly liquid, a precious fluid, such as balsam is, in a fragile container, linctus in a brittle glass, would she not go out of the crowd, unless she were a fool? . . . This brittle container – that is, woman's flesh . . . is as brittle as any glass, for should it once be broken, it will never be mended, mended or whole as it was before, any more than glass.[21]

Solitude and strict enclosure were the means to preserve the fragile vessel.

For religious women – more than religious men – virginity was represented as the highest and most exalted aspect of the religious life. This was the message that the predominantly male-authored treatises on

[19] Quoted in M. Aston, *Faith and Fire: Popular and Unpopular Religion 1350–1600* (1993), p. 100.
[20] On these themes, see B. Newman, *From Virile Woman to Woman Christ: studies in medieval religion and literature* (Philadelphia, 1995), pp. 1–45.
[21] *Ancrene Wisse*, p. 80.

the religious life continued to promote to potential nuns. Not all insisted on spiritual motives, and the renunciation of sex and marriage could have practical advantages. The author of *Holy Virginity*, written around 1200, follows an established tradition in stressing the transitory joys of marriage and its many dangers and pains. A woman is urged to avoid marriage:

By God, woman, even if it were not at all for the love of God, or for the hope of heaven, or for the fear of hell, you should avoid this act [marriage] above all things, for the integrity of your flesh, for the sake of your body, and for your physical health.[22]

For a woman, the chaste life of the nun offered the opportunity to control her own body, an empowerment to escape the social control of marriage. In this instance renunciation was a positive, not a negative, choice.

Nunneries, however, were not just the refuge of the physical virgin. Women could enter religion as widows, and here we see a separate notion of virginity, spiritual virginity. The 'golden vessel' could not physically be restored, but a woman could be – as Margery Kempe, mother of fourteen put it – 'a virgin in her soul'. Virginity could now be possessed by wives and widows. It was not necessary even to enter the convent walls, and many widows in the later middle ages took a vow of chastity. The ceremony for profession of a vowess included the taking of a veil and receiving of a ring, but without retreat to a nunnery. The women known to have taken this route were generally wealthy enough to be self-supporting, such as Cecily, widow of Sir Thomas Gerard, who in 1491 took an oath of perpetual chastity and was invested with the veil, ring and mantle 'which customarily signify this state'.[23] Perhaps for such women part of the attraction of the move was that it ensured their future independence.

Renunciation of sex and marriage was therefore an important and enduring facet of the religious life. From the earliest days of Christianity a pervasive strand of thought had been that the woman who renounced marriage and child-bearing to serve Christ rose above her sex. She became a man, the virile woman.[24] However, in another important way religious women retained their sexuality as the brides of Christ. Again, this is quite gender-specific. *Holy Virginity* is one of many treatises to 'exploit the sexuality of the nuptial image. Christ is seen in graphically physical, male

---

[22] B. Millett and J. Wogan-Browne, eds., *Medieval English Prose for Women* (Oxford, 1990), p. 31.

[23] C. Harper-Bill, ed., *The Register of John Morton, Archbishop of Canterbury 1486–1500* (3 vols., Canterbury and York Soc., LXXV, LXXVIII, LXXXIX, 1987–2000), ii, p. 5.

[24] Newman, *Virile Woman*, pp. 1–45.

terms; he is ardent, generous, and far more attractive than any earthly counterpart could be'.[25] The nun remains chaste for her bridegroom. The *Life* of St Gilbert of Sempringham, written in and reflecting the attitudes of the early years of the thirteenth century, employs the same metaphors. The desire for sexual purity led to strict segregation. Those Gilbertine houses which accommodated both men and women were indeed 'double houses', with two cloisters, two sets of monastic buildings and a shared church divided down the centre by a high wall. The 'window house' in the passage which joined the male and female quarters was strictly guarded by a canon on one side and two nuns on the other. A small window allowed for necessary conversation (without eye contact) and a larger allowed for the food prepared on the women's side to be passed to the men.

This discussion has demonstrated different ways in which the concept of renunciation – of self-determination, of an individual place within society, of identity as a member of a family, of personal property, of materialism and of sex – set members of the religious orders apart from other members of society and was central to their existence. It was central, too, to lay perceptions of the role of the religious: those 'cowled champions' who prayed for them and commemorated them in institutions which would – it was thought – last for ever. Those who renounced the world enabled those who did not to live their lives in the hope of salvation. It is small wonder that in times of particular turbulence men and women turned to the monastic order for spiritual support. Walter Daniel described how Ailred as abbot of Revesby took advantage of the turbulence of King Stephen's reign to encourage knights to endow monasteries, since in so doing they would gain life rather than lose it.[26]

The numbers of men and women who in one way or another participated in the monastic life in medieval England is impossible to estimate. The numbers varied over the centuries; they were at their height in the twelfth and thirteenth centuries, and were badly hit by the crisis of the Black Death.[27] By 1530 there were in England and Wales at least 825 religious houses, comprising some 502 monasteries, 136 nunneries, and 187 friaries.[28] Together these housed in the region of 7,500 men and 1,800 women, which has been estimated as one in 375 of the population, and

---

[25] Beer, *Women and Mystical Experience*, p. 72. [26] Daniel, *Life of Ailred*, p. 28.
[27] See, for example, the suggested statistics in D. Knowles and R. N. Hadcock, *Medieval Religious Houses, England and Wales* (2nd edn, Cambridge, 1971), pp. 488–95.
[28] G. W. O. Woodward, *The Dissolution of the Monasteries* (1966), p. 2.

this figure does not include hermits and anchorites. Although the numbers were lower than they had been in the heyday of monasticism, renunciation was still a way of life for a significant proportion of the population and, as noted above, it was a way of life that commanded the respect of many who did not feel called to emulate it. As late as 1481–2 Edward IV founded a house for the Observant Franciscans at Greenwich.

By 1540, however, the monastic order had ceased to exist, and monasteries, nunneries and friaries were no longer a part of English society. Some historians have argued that the lack of opposition to the closure of the monasteries indicates that the very concept of renunciation was outmoded. When political strategy dictated the dissolution, there was little will to resist. To generalise about lay attitudes towards monasticism on the basis of the dissolution is difficult. By the later middle ages the monastic way of life had indeed come under criticism from a variety of sources for a variety of reasons. But the nature of that criticism suggests that renunciation was still important to people. What was being criticised was usually the *lack* of renunciation: the wealth of many houses and the alleged low level of observance within them. This was compatible with continuing lay support for local religious houses. Among early sixteenth-century testators in the York diocese, for instance, the favoured target for bequests was their parish church, but a quarter still left money to the friars for masses and prayers, and an eighth to monasteries; and the closure of the monasteries in the diocese met with opposition from within monastic and lay society.[29]

As this implies, it was not primarily awareness that men and women vowed to the religious life might fall short of their profession that hastened the end of the monastic order. Over the centuries monasteries had lost their monopoly on a number of functions: education, the production of manuscripts, pastoral responsibility and the commemoration of the dead. By the 1530s these could all be provided outside the walls of the monastery. But the problem can be seen as more fundamental. By the late middle ages ascetic renunciation of the world was no longer seen as the only, or indeed the best, way to salvation. It was not that the ideal of renunciation was rejected but that it began to take different forms. For the active Christian, life within society involved renunciation in different ways.

---

[29] C. Cross and N. Vickers, *Monks, Friars and Nuns in Sixteenth-Century Yorkshire* (Yorkshire Archaeological Society record series, CL, 1995), pp. 2–8.

CHAPTER 14

Ritual constructions of society

Charles Phythian-Adams

From 1429 at the latest, bystanders at the monastery town of Bury St Edmunds were accustomed to witness a curious annual sight on a feast day of its patronal saint. Led by monks and hung with garlands of flowers, a white bull (reared for the purpose on an adjacent manor of which the abbey was tenant-in-chief) would have been seen wending its way through the Southgate, via the edge of the Great Market, to the Great Gate of the abbey itself. The bull was accompanied each year by barren wives, who stroked its flanks as they processed, until they reached the abbey precinct. There they proceeded separately to offer at the shrine of St Edmund, 'glorious king, virgin and martyr', and to pray that after the performance of this ritual they might at last conceive.[1]

Such an observance may serve as a paradigm for the mechanisms of public ritual process to be discussed in what follows. As in this case, ritual contexts invariably reflect, first, both a specific time or occasion and a particularised spatial setting, each of these features thus helping to define the relevance of the occasion. Second, the participants too are deliberately distinguished through their positioning in the ritual, often by social status or age, though in this instance the contrasts are emphasised through gender and reproductive status. These focus on the married females who are nevertheless infertile. Then there are the unmarried adult males who are vowed abnormally to celibacy and chastity while dedicated to the service of a virgin male saint (who himself acts as intercessor with God the Father). Last is a male beast belonging to the saint, which is white and therefore appropriately 'pure', whilst paradoxically but unambiguously expressive of natural sexual potency. A third feature of contemporary ritual process is therefore the parade of potentially multiple meanings implicit, whether separately or together, in the nature of the contexts, the participants, the specific objects, costumes, actions, even decorations involved. Such

[1] W. C. Hazlitt, *Tenures of Land and Customs of Manors* (1874), p. 54.

meanings, fourth, frequently include direct or elliptical points of reference to, and interactions with, the perceived spheres of nature, magic or the supernatural. Finally, and above all, the same symbolic element may be differently deployed in other ritual contexts, whether public or private.

Belonging as ritual does to one extreme of a continuous spectrum of social behaviour, the isolation of it is to some extent an artificial exercise. What is clear, nevertheless, is that in a society so densely *ritualistic* in its social behaviour, ritual involves the varied mobilisation of a limited, but always developing, vocabulary of signs. The constant intermixing of different elements from the same vocabulary, but in contrasted circum-stances, ensures that in any one case there will be a degree of cross-referencing within this wider spectrum of meanings. The task of the historian of social ritual, therefore, is to seek as far as is practicable to understand such interlocking ritual patterns as underlying cultural con-structions of the society in question.

To expose something of the latent logic of such patterns, albeit in so short a compass here, it will be best to begin by briefly examining the fundamental vocabularies of the body, of gesturing and of physical positioning, before looking at ritual characterisations of social space and the interconnectedness of social time. In so doing, the discussion will move from a concentration on some basic elements of ritual to the consideration of whole rituals or groups of rituals.

The Bury observance was concerned overtly with the female body. Physical references designed to ensure the desired solution thus lay at the very core of the ritual performance. Having touched the live body of the bull, with the same hands the wives then offered to St Edmund and, we may confidently surmise, also touched the shrine containing his reputedly incorrupt cadaver. Before body language is discussed more generally, therefore, some stress should be placed on hands as the most conspicuous physical referents and, as a starting point, on the hand as supernatural conduit. Here, of course, the overarching symbol was 'the Hand of God', but it was the sacerdotal laying on of hands, and especially the anointing of bishops, priests and kings with different grades of oils, which empowered those so consecrated or ordained in the first case or those crowned in the second. Bishops and priests could themselves then anoint (to different degrees) and, since a priest was anointed specifically on his hands, he could now effect the mystery of the mass using those same hands in consecrating the elements. Kings might consequently heal scrofula through the royal touch, or other ailments with cramp rings worn by those afflicted. Originally forged from gold or silver coins offered manually by the sovereign for consecration on Good Friday and then redeemed for coins of lesser quality to the same value, these were later offered as already manufactured rings that were deliberately touched by him. At a more mundane level, according to a fifteenth-century custom of Romney, the withdrawal of the hand from the gospels by a suitor at law whilst swearing his oath could void the case. By so evading the divine contact necessary to ensure the truth, his testimony would be invalidated.

From a different supernatural angle, what was celestially imprinted upon everyone's inner hand might be divined through palmistry. More grisly was the magical power associated with 'the Hand of Glory', as it was later known: the severed hand and arm of a dead man (some potency clearly being thought to inhere in it) which needed to be buried for nine days and nights before use. Thereafter, it was claimed in 1439, with a burning candle placed in its clenched fingers by a night-time housebreaker, everyone in a dwelling, whether sleeping or waking, would be conveniently immobilised.[2]

If the hand could be employed as a direct link to the supernatural when certain rituals were observed, the perception of the whole body, together with its hierarchically understood members, as a model for society was central to medieval culture. It is hardly surprising therefore, that punitive ritual focused on the body of the individual deviant. When the stability of the body of Christian society itself was seen to have been threatened, indeed, the penalties could range from bodily mutilation – like branding, or nailing the ear of a thief to a post and letting him cut himself free – to the ritual destruction or total dismemberment of whole bodies in the most brutal ways. These extended from burning alive to pressing to death in the case of those who refused to plead; to hanging, disembowelment whilst still alive and then 'quartering' for the separate display of the parts.

The hand (and sometimes the glove as its surrogate) was the symbolic link between the whole society and its members and so between the highest and the lowest in it. It was no accident that some of the most basic social and legal terminology exploited the image of the hand as holding someone or something: maintenance, mainprise, mainour, mortmain or, in the case of marriage, hand-fasting. At the beginning of our period a serf knelt in public before his lord so that the latter could take the inferior's head between his hands, thereby taking the man symbolically into his physical possession. When he was released from the

---

[2] R. L. Storey, *The End of the House of Lancaster* (1966), p. 202.

hand of his lord, by contrast, the lord placed the weapon of a free man in the hands of the now 'manumitted' serf. For a vassal, the act of homage involved him kneeling before his seated lord and placing his hands, rather than his head, between those of his superior. For a lord the members of his own household, being fed effectively by him, were in his mainpast and, as his dependants, were to be produced in court by him if accused of felony. In the last resort a hand could be regarded as an offending member, and might be ceremonially amputated as the penalty for physical violence in the royal court or a court of justice.

More commonly, hands were the most expressive vehicles for gesturing and, in cases of physical proximity, therefore, were used to delimit body space in ways that helped to define relations of closeness or distance. It is by no means clear that the modern custom of handshaking as a greeting in Europe generally is any earlier than the seventeenth or eighteenth century. Before that in England, male handshaking, as elsewhere, may have been restricted to the sealing of bargains or conflict reconciliation. What forcibly struck late medieval foreign visitors was the English emphasis on greeting or departing with kisses, presumably on the cheek with hands on the upper arms. One Venetian observer in 1513, however, reported that when a woman met a friend (gender unspecified) in the street they shook hands (perhaps warmly grasped both each other's hands) and kissed on the mouth. Apart from the actions of gentlefolk when 'leading' ladies by the hand, kissing seems to have been the nearest that those who were broadly social equals could come on an agreed formal basis to invading someone else's body-space. In total contrast, the language of threat included seizing someone by the front of his garment and pulling him so close, in order to intimidate, that the two faces were almost touching.

In a society of distinct social gradations, body spacing was the means by which social relations of different sorts were instantly expressed in public. Apart from the obvious advantage of height given to a social superior on horseback, of whom a corresponding degree of 'port' or personal bearing was expected when unmounted, it is evident that ever more extreme degrees of relational positioning before a lord were necessary in order to ensure that inferiors signalled their acknowledgement of that reality. This might be through bowing: 'low obeisaunce' whilst looking him in the eye; making 'a running knee' – genuflecting on the move; or, whether male or female, kneeling before a lord or husband, perhaps for some time, in order to crave a favour. The most abject posture, that of total prostration face down on the floor with arms outstretched, could be adopted by priest, monarch or flagellant as a gesture of utter humility or contrition towards God. At close quarters, then, not only did inferiors thus seek, at least temporarily, to position themselves at a conspicuously lower physical level than a superior; they were otherwise also expected to keep a respectful distance. Even a town clerk of mid-fifteenth-century Exeter had to stand sufficiently far away so as not to overhear a crucial conversation concerning the city, and so had to accept that others would need to report on it 'for y was not all thyng so nye ham to hire and knowe alle thyng that was said and comyned, for my degree was not . . . '.[3] When the central space of a great hall was not cluttered by tables, and a lord wished to receive some private communication standing before the fire, his followers were clearly expected to stand well away around the walls.

Physical spaces generally were designed or exploited to reinforce customary social positioning. Close parallels between the arrangement of publicly shared interiors, whether secular or ecclesiastical, were very apparent. The royal court and lordly hall together with cathedral churches, for example, shared clearly defined upper ends marked by an elevated table or high altar (distinguished further by music), behind which in secular cases was traditionally located the seat or bench of the incumbent lord under a canopy. At the beginning of our period the removal of bishops' thrones from behind high altars to the south sides of choirs was a comparatively recent matter. In both these secular and ecclesiastical contexts the ritual focus was segregated: for the consumption of actual food or for the realisation of ritual food at the privileged ends of the buildings concerned, inferiors or laity were largely confined to the lower ends. Just as congregations had to stand aside to allow the passage of liturgical processions along the central space of a nave, so room had to be left in a hall for the ceremonial entry of the dishes for the lord's table from the screen end. As Mark Girouard has pointed out, moreover, in the case of a gentleman carver at a great man's banquet (whose ritualised dissection of *entire* cooked beasts or fowls comprised but a mannered extension of what had been ritually done in the field to prepare the carcass for the kitchen), even 'his towel, second napkin and girdle were worn in exactly the same way as a priest wears a stole, maniple and girdle for mass'.[4]

---

[3] S. A. Moore, ed., *Letters and Papers of John Shillingford, mayor of Exeter 1447–1459* (Camden Society, ns II, 1871), p. 37.
[4] M. Girouard, *Life in the English Country House* (1978), p. 47.

Usually adjacent to the dwelling of a lord was a ring-fenced area in which he and his favoured followers shared the 'quest' for game and incidentally provided some of the venison for his mainpast. Ordinary tenants being excluded, hunting grounds were the venues for socially restricted and highly specialised rituals which, in regularly pitting culture against nature in the pursuit of an exclusive meat (which it was customary to gift rather than sell), were more frequently practised by those of rank, including women, than the tournaments of which so much has been written. Each hunt followed a set sequence and climaxed with the ritual 'unmaking' of the dead beast – even by the lord personally – for subsequent cooking, the first external parts to be cut off a male carcass, and specially reserved on a forked stick, being the testicles, whether those of hart or buck (or even of boar or hare), all of which animals were reputed for their sexual potency. Significantly, these delicacies were regarded as 'the finest eating' for a hereditary ruling caste and were so reserved for 'the mouth of the lord'.[5]

Other social spaces, by contrast, more closely reflected the fraternal ideal of *communitas*, being occupied by whole bodies of people in self-identifying social groupings: parochial congregations; 'communities' of vill or town; urban councils; occupational fellowships and guilds, whether rural or urban. Church naves or yards, guildhalls, marketplaces or streets were variously used for oath-taking ceremonies as people joined or progressed in seniority through each particular group; for seasonal eating and drinking together, whether as adjuncts to meetings or to raise funds; and for processions. Processing two by two in ascending order of seniority, indeed, may normally have been a rather less solemn affair than might now be suspected, to judge from the need to issue injunctions entirely to set aside 'all idle chatter' on ad hoc propitiatory processions in the face of nothing less than the Black Death.[6]

The converse of such activities were the rituals involving social discipline in much the same public places. Most common were shaming rituals for moral offenders who might be ordered by the Church to do penance standing barefoot in the nave, churchyard or marketplace for set periods of time in their shirt or, in the case of women, in their shift with their hair let down, and sometimes to be whipped. Likewise the extreme humiliation of one throwing himself on the ground publicly to beg for mercy in the face of likely execution was further emphasised not only by

[5] J. Cummins, *The Hound and the Hawk: the art of medieval hunting* (1988), p. 47.
[6] R. Horrox, ed., *The Black Death* (Manchester, 1994), p. 117.

the similar stripping away of normal attire (the mark of an accepted member of society) but also by the addition of a yoke or halter to denote that the individual was no better than a beast. Even more pointed was a customary punishment of those, like cheating urban tradesmen, who had betrayed a public trust. The culprit was forced to ride through the streets to open derision, facing backwards on horseback, holding onto the tail, and hung front and back with symbols of the offence: two urine flasks in the case of one quack physician; rotten joints of meat for a butcher; or simply a placard where a London citizen had sought to sell a girl into prostitution.

If in all such cases normal external indicators of reputation in local society were displaced, in more extreme circumstances formal exclusion from it and its social space was possible. Leaving aside outlawry by the shire court and excommunication by the Church, dwindling numbers of lepers, for example, were still incarcerated in lazar houses after undergoing a form of ritual burial, during which they had to kneel under a black pall for mass to be recited over them, before having earth piled over their feet. The fugitive from justice who had taken unprivileged sanctuary for forty days would be ordered by a coroner to abjure the realm: to walk garbed as a penitent to an often distant port, to wade into the sea and to beg to be shipped to another country. So real and so symbolic a repudiation of a subject beyond the precise limits of the realm was echoed in customary modes of execution by towns along the coastline, whether the condemned were thrown into the sea with their hands tied over their shins, or buried alive on the foreshore, or simply lashed to a stake at low water so that the tides might flow and ebb over them twice.

More localised jurisdictional edges were delimited in different ways. On an expedition around Wales in 1188 to whip up recruitment for a crusade, the archbishop of Canterbury was courteously met at the limits of each native princely territory by its lord, entertained, and then escorted to the boundary of his next host. Probably from the fourteenth century, each new bishop of Durham was greeted on his first visit to the diocese midway across the Tees, the southern boundary of his palatinate, by his tenant, the lord of Sockburn, who there handed over the family falchion (a short curved sword) to be looked at by the bishop as a symbol of his new temporal authority before he handed it back again. The outer perimeter of the permanent sanctuary at Beverley was defined by sanctuary crosses, though the broad area concerned, like its equivalents at York or Ripon, was sub-divided into a series of precisely delimited concentric zones of increasing safety, narrowing in on the frithstool near the high altar where the seizure of a fugitive was regarded as an una-mendable crime.

In many cities as the middle ages progressed, moreover, there are signs that, perhaps beginning with London's Cheapside in the later thirteenth century, central spaces were developing as permanent arenas for proces-sions which publicly moved dignitaries or symbols through civic spaces for different purposes. Such occasions simultaneously flaunted the power of the current civic and guild officers whilst parading whole bodies of sworn, and therefore privileged, citizens in their formal groups before crowds of spectators. At Coventry, and close to the marketplace, the cathedral and two parish churches shared a single central graveyard which was surrounded by foci for different ritual occasions: a bishop's palace, halls for priests and the gaol, as well as the civic guildhall. The whole of this area was linked by 'procession ways'. In other towns like King's Lynn or Leicester, guildhall and civic church stood in deliberately close relationship to each other. Ritual was thus built into the medieval environment.

Contemporary perceptions of clearly defined spaces as variously pri-vileged bring us to a fundamental feature of ritual mechanisms which is best introduced through a particular example. From 1275 onwards, it would seem that annually on the feast of the Commemoration of St Paul (30 June) it was customary for Sir William le Baud or his heirs, the tenants of an Essex hunting chase held of the chapter of St Paul's Cathedral, to bring in the 'unmade' carcass of a fallow buck. This would be borne through the cathedral itself, in the wake of the liturgical pro-cession, even up to the steps of the high altar – as though to the saint's high table. There it was received by the canons, fully vested and with garlands of roses on their heads, who immediately dispatched the meat for cooking. As if to confirm that the offering was made to the patron saint of the cathedral through his mainpast, the canons, the head and antlers were then carried on a pole before the cross in the procession back to the west door of the cathedral. Here the lord's keeper blew 'the death of the Bucke' on his horn, to which similar horn calls replied from around the city.[7] In doing this, the participants simply replicated the practices of a customary home-coming by a hunt when the spoils were ceremonially accompanied to the castle gate or hall door. In other words, what was normally done in another, secular place was in this instance transposed to a new context where such activity was strictly abnormal.

---

[7] John Stow, *A Survey of London*, ed. C. L. Kingsford (2 vols., Oxford, 1971), i, p. 334.

For the duration of the ritual on St Paul's Day, therefore, what might otherwise have been regarded as a violation of sacred space was permitted.

This temporary ritual transgression into a zone of quite other normal usage is one of the hallmarks distinguishing the exceptional quality of ritual occasions. Indeed the same public space might be differently transformed according to separate moments in the local ritual cycle. The start of the route taken by the white bull into Bury, for example, was also that customarily used for royal entries when, doubtless, the house-fronts were hung with table-carpets or bed-coverings from the best rooms, as seems to have been the case for coronation processions in the capital. In probably all settlements, the seasonal decoration of house-fronts with masses of foliage brought in from the country at May Day helped temporarily to convert 'culture' into 'nature'. Most remarkable of all, from the fourteenth century to the Reformation, was the brief annual transformation of civic space into 'sacred' space at the feast of Corpus Christi. Parishioners, or guilds, or urban freemen in their fellowships, then solemnly escorted the host under a canopy of honour, in a tabernacle or crystal monstrance, from the church in which it had been consecrated out into the open air and then through the main thoroughfares of the built-up area.

If at York this *ommegang* or 'going about' with sacred *tableaux* (perhaps derived from the Low Countries) seems to have avoided the separate liberties that there fractured any sense of unified municipal space, at Coventry the procession and the pageants appear to have traversed the different jurisdictional elements that had until then been in conflict with one another, so underlining the 'one-body' symbolism of the event. Not that we should understand such occasions in isolation. At Durham there was a distinct pattern of interlinked processioning between the feast of St Mark (25 April) and Corpus Christi. Four processions in succession involved the prior and the monks going out from the cathedral to visit different parish churches in the city in turn. Three processions at Rogationtide then comprised virtual circuits of the priory precinct with portable shrines and relics including the banner of St Cuthbert. The climactic observance of Corpus Christi itself involved a reciprocal movement from the laity. In this case the host was brought by the bailiffs and occupations of the city with their craft banners and flaming torches from the civic church in the marketplace, up through the town to the north door of the cathedral. There it was greeted outside and reverenced by the prior and monks, probably kneeling so that their hands and heads might touch the ground, accompanied again by St Cuthbert's banner.

The body of Christ was then escorted inside by the augmented procession, and eventually to the shrine beyond the high altar, where lay the incorrupt body of St Cuthbert, and around the feretory, before the civic element moved out of doors again and so back to the other end of the town. Interconnections in social space, whether indoors or out of doors, between distinct gradations of sanctity and between sacred and secular, let alone between different all-male corporate groups, are here self-evident.

As Durham's ritual calendar indicates, the timings of ritual too need to be understood as parts of a whole: as linked punctuation marks within recognisable short-term cycles of social time – whether agrarian, customary or liturgical – or as points of annual emphasis that varied from community to community. It is impossible to do full justice to this complex and much misunderstood matter here. What must be stressed, however, is that, unlike historians of religion, students of the contrasted rituals of local societies and of localised social groupings – whether rural, urban or domestic – cannot focus only on the liturgical calendar. What is at issue are *communal* calendars which drew also on other sources of influence. Great households, for example, boasted their own individual calendars based on quarter days, the rhythms of the hunting seasons, adopted holy days and the timings of trips to distant parts of their lord's estates or the capital. For fixed urban and rural societies, by contrast, although the year was characterised by the blending of economic, administrative, popular *and* liturgical timings, which led to much variation from place to place, an underlying common pattern may nevertheless be discerned.

The three most popular seasonal celebrations – Christmas, May Day and midsummer – were, indeed, only partially assimilated into the liturgical calendar, the first and the last being residually linked to both the solstitial cycle and, it may be legitimately argued, even to shadowy remnants of the pre-Christian calendar. The absence of Carnival, so commonly celebrated on the continent as the prelude to the movable season of Lent, is one of the most marked features of the English scene. In Yorkshire, by contrast, it was the pagan midwinter season – in Bede, a double month ('before *Giuli*' and 'after *Giuli*')[8] – that seems to have been reflected in churches when, even in the seventeenth century, the parishioners danced and cried 'Yole' on Christmas Day; or when mistletoe, a plant held to be under the astrological governance of the sun, was placed on the high altar of York Minster. It was also when, as in the

---

[8] K. Harrison, *The Framework of Anglo-Saxon History to A.D. 900* (Cambridge, 1976), pp. 3–4.

early thirteenth century at the river port of Torksey (Lincs.), which had close trading links with York, a special amnesty for the suspension of disputes known as the 'Yule-gyrth' was declared.[9] At York by the end of the middle ages this was first proclaimed in the city centre on St Thomas's Day (21 December) but to the effect that 'all manner of whores and thieves, dice players, carders and other unthrifty folk be welcome ... att the reverence of the high feast of Youle, till the twelve days be passed', and then publicised with special horn fanfares at four entrances to the city.[10] This seems to have been succeeded by a carnivalesque 'riding' led by the sheriffs' serjeants, which featured a gluttonous 'Yule' facing backwards while carrying a shoulder of lamb with cakes hanging from his neck, and 'Yule's wife' bearing a distaff, denoting either women's employment – suspended for the season – or the mark of a scold. The casting about of 'draff' or processed brewers' grain (fit only to feed pigs), indeed, even suggests Tudor shaming rituals associated with husband-beaters, though to judge from local tradition both may have been guised as reputedly deceitful Jews. The presence of children 'crying after them' could indicate the promise of a new generation in the succeeding year. On Distaff Day, the day after Twelfth Night, the normal order was resumed.[11]

The inter-related fire ceremonies of the midsummer season, with their cognate residual references to the solstice, may also relate back ultimately to the other pagan double month which, despite a thin later Christian overlay of feast days, had formerly linked the latter part of what later became June with the early part of July. These interconnections are brought out by customs at Whitby, 'a havyn towne inhabyted with maryners' and at 'all other havyn townes, thereaboute'. Along this stretch of the Yorkshire coast, annually on the *eves* of the feasts of the Nativity of St John the Baptist (23 June), Sts Peter and Paul (28 June), and the Translation of St Thomas Becket (6 July) respectively

at the tyme of the bonefiers accustomed ... all maryners and masters of schippes, accompanyed with other yong peple, have used to have caried before them on a staf halfe a terbarell brennyng [tar-barrel burning], and the maryners

[9] R. E. G. Cole, 'The royal burgh of Torksey, its churches, monasteries and castle', *Associated Architectural Societies Reports and Papers*, 28 (1905–6), 478.

[10] J. Brand, *Observations on the Popular Antiquities of Great Britain*, ed. H. Ellis (3 vols., 1849), i, p. 477.

[11] A. F. Johnstone and M. Rogerson, eds., *York*, I: *Introduction: The Records*, Records of Early English Drama (Toronto, 1970), p. 174; M. Hufford, 'The sacred and profane: civic ceremonial at York, 1485–1585' (MA dissertation, University of Leicester, 1985), ch. 5.

to folowe too and too (having suche wepons in there handes as they please to bere . . .); and to syng throught the strettes, and to resort to every bonefier, and there to drynke and make mery with songes and honest pastymes.[12]

Elsewhere on such occasions we hear not only of neighbourhood bonfires, but also of burning wheels being launched down hills or of multitudes of torches being carried through city streets by armed watches marching under royal licence.

The period between the Christmas and midsummer seasons not only shared special days marked by the ubiquitous ritual importation into settlements of different classes of vegetation at different times: holly, ivy and mistletoe, Palm Sunday willow, May Day hawthorn, red roses at Corpus Christi, or midsummer birch. It also contained the major liturgical moments in the church calendar connected with Christ's life and resurrection and the impact of his ministry – most of them oscillating from year to year between 4 February and 24 June because of the movability of Easter. When Easter was at its latest the climax of the sequence, Corpus Christi, coincided with Midsummer Day. Echoing this bunching since before the Norman Conquest were the only extended annual holidays for ordinary people, at Christmas, Easter and Whitsuntide. Clearly as a result of these conjunctions, the same six-month block attracted to itself the greatest set-piece, communally *collective*, rituals of the year. In it also were compressed those rituals that were most expressive of the world turned temporarily upside down: boy bishops in great churches around Christmas; lords of misrule in great households, whether lordly or civic, during the twelve days; the customs associated with the young at Shrove Tuesday; the ritual assertion of wifely authority over husbands on Hock Tuesday; the May Day festival of youth; and the summertime lords of misrule with the attendant churchyard junketings of youth especially in market towns at, for example, Whitsuntide.

There was nothing to match this concentration of collective ritual occasions during the remaining half of the year. Certainly there were isolated days of liturgical significance, especially saints' days (notably those of the Virgin, who tended to be the object of individual veneration), as there were occasions for marking distinct stages in the agricultural, fair-time, municipal or exchequer years. It cannot be argued, however, that the character of the second half of the year replicated the

---

[12] W. Brown, ed., *Yorkshire Star Chamber Proceedings*, III (Yorkshire Archaeological Society record series, LI, 1914), p. 198.

extended holiday patterns, the ritual intensity, the regular communal involvement (as opposed to small-group participation) or the symbolic coherence of the first. For this reason it has been suggested that, despite local variations, communal customary calendars during the later middle ages generally shared this underlying temporal division into two halves which may be characterised respectively as predominantly 'ritualistic' and 'secular'. We need to appreciate that this contrast 'was more a matter of emphasis than of rigid demarcation'.[13]

Ritual did not simply entrench overall structures of medieval authority or the nationally derived hierarchies of superiority and inferiority so beloved of the textbook writers. It is also misleading to regard regular observances – often designed to raise money for local works – as indicating a 'Merry England' that never in fact existed. Rather, the study of ritual should refocus us on contemporary realities on the ground, many of them harsh in the extreme, by enabling us to follow the different ways in which ritual permeated all aspects of medieval life in a face-to-face society (private rituals and rituals of riot being but two of many issues that could not be covered here). Above all perhaps, medieval ritual involved techniques of sending, recognising and decoding a multiplicity of interpersonal visual signals from a limited vocabulary of meanings in a largely illiterate and predominantly outdoor world of small communities.

If there was effectively a common 'language' of ritual performance, its expression was infinitely varied geographically. Repetitive annual rituals involved everyone through a continuing process of public reiteration: the constant rearrangement, whether calendrically or through rites of passage, not only of signs but also of differently overlapping groups of people in particular places. Rituals regularly reminded the members of such groupings, even if they were in conflict with one another, that they interrelated nevertheless within locally specific customary structures, variously privileged social spaces and often within regionally identifiable cultural spheres (not least with regard to the cults of major saints like Edmund or Cuthbert). Even personal confrontation seems to have invoked a set sequence involving ritualised threat, symbolic signals of imminent violent action, and an expectation of customary intervention, as a built-in way of defusing conflict – though not necessarily always successfully. The serious breach of constantly reaffirmed customary norms, moreover, might invite implacable public reprisals and ultimately ritual expulsion or execution. Overall the structural interconnections peculiar to every community were

---

[13] C. V. Phythian-Adams, *Local History and Folklore* (1975), pp. 23–4.

ritualised annually through its own local calendar, which thus became the unique expression of its collective identity.

Customary ways, however, were never static. As time went on, from the fourteenth century in particular, not only were ritual details adjusted from place to place but society kept adding extra observances to existing repertoires. As communities shrank dramatically in size, especially in village and city England, it looks almost as though efforts were made to intensify the bonds of belonging amongst the survivors, and not least in the market towns that benefited most. It is a coincidence at least worth pondering that in English history ritual proliferation or re-emphasis by local societies (rather than by government choice) seem most often to be associated with periods of population contraction, whether nationally during the later middle ages or in post-Restoration England, or more specifically in the countryside of later Victorian Britain.

CHAPTER 15

Identities

Miri Rubin

Identity is as elusive as it is central to individual lives and collective experience.[1] People in the past, just as today, think about their identity even when they are least aware of it. When making a new acquaintance, when entering a settlement different from one's own, when seeking a marriage partner or taking leave of the dying: on all these occasions and more, a person is called to judge and reflect on choices and their consequences, on connections and affinities, all refracted through the sense of self. And the self is multi-layered, ever-changing, hardly ever totally knowable. We change, yet we change slowly and imperceptibly in most cases. We change through self-fashioning and through the expectations of others. In what follows identity will be discussed as an evolving entity; the self will be explored as both private and communal.

The insights of historians of gender can be extended to our understanding of identity: that it is relational, always measured and experienced through affinities to other men and women. These others may be private individuals – parents, siblings, neighbours – or they can represent public entities such as the Church or the state or a monastic order. Yet each offers a set of claims and expectations, enfolded in a narrative and a mode of being in the world, which forges the individual in the most personal ways. Think, for example, of the heads of a family: mother and father. To them were accorded powers, and of them were expected a whole range of actions, responses and responsibilities. Knowing what their roles entailed – from the example of others, from the teaching of priests, from popular tales – helped to create the sense of self as parents or family leaders. This does not mean that they had no other affinities and identities – occupational, social or religious – but for a while their role in the family may have been the defining one. As their children grew up,

[1] I am most grateful to the volume's editors for their searching suggestions, and to Liesbeth van Houts and Gareth Stedman Jones for reading and commenting on the chapter.

more of their leisure and resources could be devoted to other roles and a different set of identifications took precedence, so that not only is the sense of self – of duties and expectations – diverse and complex at any point in a life, but that very cluster of attributes is one that changes over time, a cocktail of a different blend and thus of a differing savour.

The perception that this sense of identity is the unique possession of an individual – even, in a very real sense, the creation of that individual – is one that has often been denied to medieval men and women. Historians have allowed themselves an alarming degree of condescension in accepting all too easily that people in the middle ages possessed no, or only a weak, sense of self. This has become in some debates the very definition of modernity, with the yardstick of a 'modern' society being the emergence of responsible and self-aware individuals. Following Lawrence Stone's assertion that families began to produce people with fully evolved emotional worlds only at the turn of the eighteenth century, even some medievalists, while arguing with the chronology, accepted the assumption that the 'self' was born at a specific date.[2] Sweeping narratives about the emergence of modernity habitually depend on the notion of a medieval time when the sense of selfhood was radically different. And even where the existence of 'self' is conceded to the middle ages, this is only with the qualification that such views of person and self, or of will and intention, 'are utterly different from what will be found by the time of the Renaissance'.[3]

This perception has two components. One is that the individual and his or her concerns were subsumed in and subordinated to the needs of the community. To be an individualist was thus frowned on. It was aberrant and, in a moral sense, lacking that concern for neighbourliness that was the essence of charity as understood by the medieval Church. The other is the belief that medieval society demanded conformity to stereotypes; that identity was a straitjacket, bringing with it immutable rules of behaviour and lifestyle. Up to a point, both these assumptions are true. The common weal (or public good) was a powerful element of late medieval political rhetoric, often with 'singular lucre' (private profit) as its counterpoint. There was also a sense, enshrined in the courtesy books discussed earlier in this volume, that people should conform to, and hence be identifiable in terms of, their social role.[4]

---

[2] L. Stone, *The Family, Sex and Marriage in England 1500–1800* (1977).
[3] T. J. Reiss, *The Discourse of Modernism* (Ithaca, NY, 1982), p. 72.
[4] See above, pp. 72, 115.

This is, however, an over-simplification. In practice the importance of community and the sense of what behaviour was appropriate to a particular role within that community co-existed with personal responsibility, entailing an awareness not only of self and identity but of purpose and aspiration. To take only a single example, the teaching and rituals of the medieval Church emphasised selfhood as the locus for moral choice and responsibility, the unit of salvation, even if they were based on the assumption that some men and women were more fully aware and some – like peasants, *rustici* – were less. Confession, enjoined on the laity by the fourth Lateran Council in 1215, required people to reflect on their individual actions and motivation.[5] Following ideas developed by St Augustine and re-elaborated by Peter Abelard (d.1142) *intention* was paramount. In Abelard's words, 'God considers only the mind in rewarding good or evil, not the results of deeds, and he thinks not what comes forth from fault or from our good will'.[6] Priests were trained and guided to use confession as an interrogatory occasion, at which a well-informed priest probed the subjectivity of an individual and produced better self-understanding. Robert of Flamborough composed one of the most influential penitential guidebooks of the middle ages, the *Liber poenitentialis* (*c.* 1208–13), which combined instruction and set questions for use at confession. This became the pervasive parochial practice, delivered to differing degrees of effectiveness. The arrival of the friars further boosted the importance of confession and its adjunct, penance. Above all, bishops composed and circulated a wide range of modest but useful penitential booklets, disseminated among the clergy at annual synods.

The acts of confession and penance – the first private, the second covering a range of possible acts of prayer, charity, chastisement and devotion (most, to some degree, 'public') – were followed by rituals of reconciliation, above all reception of the eucharist. The state of reincorporation into the community after confession and penance combined personal experience with public display, blending self-reflection and communal approval. It is interesting, in this context, to note the way in which contemporary writers, familiar with this ritual, used confession scenes in the construction of their vernacular narratives. In Chaucer's hands dramatic frames are made by the confessions of the Pardoner, the

---

[5] See above, pp. 301–2.
[6] Peter Abelard, *Ethics*, ed. and trans. D. E. Luscombe (Oxford, 1971), pp. 44–5.

Wife of Bath and the Canon's Yeoman – all of whom, in the modern sense of the word, are 'individuals'.

THE SOURCES FOR STUDYING IDENTITIES

The work of the historian in unearthing the ideas and practices that structured identities is not easy. Written sources that set out criteria for proper behaviour and the penalty for lapses, as well as many surviving visual and material traces, convey ideals of majesty, femininity, sanctity, virility, servility; in short, of all the roles and positions which may be inhabited. These convey the prevailing sense of the ideal types of personalities. And yet each individual is unique, and every blend of identities creates its own challenges and life dramas. How then may we penetrate beyond the, admittedly influential, structures of socialisation, education and influence, and reach experience as lived by some of the millions living in our period?

Historians have begun to identify 'ego-documents' beyond the easily recognised diary or letter, relatively few of which survive from the middle ages. Names are badges of identity; creative writing such as poetry or prayer, a will or an inscription on a tomb, even words spoken to a tribunal, are personal expressions within communal frames. Life dramas – the struggle of an individual with the consequences of identity – may sometimes be discerned from biography, and a common type is the sacred biography, that of the holy person, the saint to be. Although these stories are stereotypical in many ways, and follow a certain structure leading on to the unfolding of a saint's life, they nonetheless try to frame an essential dilemma within their narrative. The identity of daughter vies against that of religious, the identity of bishop with worldly responsibilities against a yearning towards sanctity. The role in family and in community clashes with aspirations for heightened religious commitment. The narrative of such a struggle is captured in the quasi-hagiographical *Book* of Margery Kempe, written down for her in about 1423. Here is a laywoman, mother of several children, struggling to put her life in the world aside and forge another life-identity for herself. At her disposal was the broad array of English pilgrimage sites and devotional traditions, and even these did not suffice. After finally imposing chastity in marriage-bed within her home, after exploring the variety of opportunities for self-expression within the churches of her home town of Bishop's Lynn (Norf.), she went on pilgrimage in the north of England, Prussia, Rome and Jerusalem. Her self-fashioning arises from the dramatic text, a heroine struggling against the conventions of marriage and religion. Beyond the bombast and self-congratulation there are dilemmas which the historian is privy to, rare glimpses into self-awareness and personal identity.

Margery, member of a mayoral family, ultimately rejected dynasty as a determinant of identity. But for many men and women dynasty offered a powerful mode of identification. From the very greatest nobles to the lesser gentry, coats of arms combined elements of heraldic grammar to convey the richness of family affinities to which they could lay claim. Edward III built the lilies of France into the royal arms of England when he laid claim to the French throne through his mother Queen Isabella. Lesser men recorded their participation on crusades or famous campaigns and their regional connections: for example, several Cheshire families adopted the wheatsheaf borne by the earls of Chester. The ability to 'read' such references was itself a mark of status. One fifteenth-century report says that Thomas Montagu, earl of Salisbury, chose three partridges as the arms given in reward to 'a certain gentleman' for service in battle; what the earl apparently did not tell the beneficiary was that he had chosen this emblem because of its medieval symbolism, which would imply that the holder was 'a great liar or a sodomite'.[7] In general, of course, heraldry was a representation of social success. If heraldry originated as a practical means of identification on battlefields, it developed into an intricate art of self-introduction and maintenance of identity.

Heraldry's importance in that respect can be seen in the vehemence of the quarrels which arose when two families found themselves bearing the same arms, as in the famous Scrope v. Grosvenor dispute resolved in 1389. It is also clearly displayed on tombstones and memorial brasses, which combine the assertion of the ideal with the individualisation of heraldry. Few English medieval funerary monuments, even the most naturalistic, are actual portraits. Instead they offer an image of the deceased as an exemplar of their proper estate: cleric, knight, merchant or judge; wife or widow. Other than heraldry, and the memorial inscription itself, glimpses of individuality on tombs are rare, although not non-existent. The brass of Hugh Hastings (d.1347) at Elsing (Norf.) incorporates representations of his companions at arms. More touchingly, the effigy of Dame Alice Cassy (*c.* 1400) in Deerhurst church (Glos.) rests her feet on her pet dog, whose collar identifies him as Terri. Sometimes style asserted individuality. Walter de Helyon, who had fought in France and was

---

[7] Quoted in M. Keen, *Chivalry* (1984), pp. 130–1.

buried at St Bartholomew's church, Much Marcle (Herefs.), around 1357 is commemorated by a simple wooden painted effigy of a knight with his belt and his sword and in a gesture of prayer.

Personal identity can also be discerned from wills, from the manner in which goods and revenues were allocated voluntarily by people for disposition after death. The disposal of most landed property was regulated by custom and law, but chattels were at the individual's disposal. Testators often followed convention, as in the standard bequests of a few pence to local religious houses, but they might also express desires, affinities and friendships. The will allowed them not only to summarise a life and its rich networks of associations, but also to make good lapses and fulfil wishes which had not been carried out in their lifetime, such as the pilgrimages to be performed by proxy discussed above.[8] Although the wording of the preliminaries, including the bequest of the testator's soul to God and the saints, was often formulaic, and is therefore problematic as evidence of personal belief, other elements more surely reflect the testator's own concerns. The choice of burial place might assert a regional or familial identity, as might endowments. The successful London merchant John Pyel (d.1382) remembered his natal Northamptonshire by founding and endowing a college of priests at Irthlingborough. Grants for commemoration expressed aspirations for a better self and a good afterlife. Gifts marked out circles of sociability. On the whole women tended to leave bequests to a larger and more diverse group of beneficiaries.[9] Wills clearly reveal the life-worlds of their makers and illustrate efforts to knit together, at the end of a life, a web of associations and memories.

It is not only in wills that we come close to subjectivity and its expression. Some of the groupings joined by individuals, such as religious fraternities, are expressive of a sense of self and place. Medieval English people knew how to associate; how to create occasions and frameworks, idioms and rituals which made a collection of individuals more than their sum.[10] Fraternities flourished in English towns and villages. It was within them that the intensive work of commemorating the dead was concentrated and organised but, like any social club, the fraternity served

---

[8] See above, p. 318.

[9] C. M. Barron, 'Introduction: the widow's world in later medieval London', in C. M. Barron and A. F. Sutton, eds., *Medieval London Widows, 1300–1500* (1994), pp. xiii–xxxiv, at p. xvi; P. H. Cullum, '"And hir name was charite": charity by and for women in late medieval Yorkshire', in P. J. P. Goldberg, ed., *Woman is a Worthy Wight: women in English society, c. 1200–c. 1500* (Stroud, 1992), pp. 182–211.

[10] D. Wallace, *Chaucerian Polity: absolutist lineages and associational forms in England and Italy* (Stanford, CA, 1997), pp. 65–82.

a variety of purposes. It expressed fashions in devotional life, the aspirations of a craft group or the wishes of an elite for an exclusive space. The London fraternity of the Holy Trinity and Sts Fabian and Sebastian in St Botolph's church, Aldgate, for instance, saw in 1408–9 an unusual entry of courtiers and distinguished prelates to their association. These were not – as one might expect – neighbours, but people who had perhaps come to know the fraternity while Henry IV spent time in the neighbourhood during the Smithfield jousts and tournaments of that year.[11] In contrast, some very modest folk of Norwich created their own fraternity, of St Augustine, which was prepared to admit members who could not enter more financially demanding and socially prestigious groups.[12] The choice of age-group as the focus for merriment and prayer, dance and celebration animated parish groupings of 'bachelors' and 'maidens', expressing aspects of identity at the formative and socially intensive stage of early adulthood and courtship.[13]

The intricate linguistic map of England forces a realisation of the vast variation in dialect and vocabulary which characterised English regions. England was criss-crossed by a network of small markets and towns, connected by road and river, rendering the English population, as Wendy Childs discusses above, highly mobile.[14] Yet it was also characterised by dialectal difference, which reflected layers of historical presence and assimilation of Celtic with Saxon and Saxon with Norman, together with a strong Danish contribution from Lincolnshire and the Midlands northwards. Following the Norman Conquest, settlers brought their own languages and dialects – Flemish, or Norman and Breton French – which blended locally into Anglo-Norman, the language of the landed and powerful. This temporarily eclipsed English as the literary language although, as Paul Strohm discusses below, English remained available to writers when they chose to use it.

Before the opening of our period language marked identity particularly strongly. In the generations following the Norman Conquest a process of settlement of members of continental Norman families created groups identified in a manner we may think of as ethnic – by language, habits, kin identification and, largely, by class. The 'Norman' group spoke

---

[11] P. Basing, ed., *Parish Fraternity Register: fraternity of the Holy Trinity and SS Fabian and Sebastian in the parish of St Botolph without Aldersgate* (London Record Society, 1982), pp. 15–16.

[12] H. F. Westlake, *The Parish Guilds of Mediaeval England* (1919), pp. 41, 202.

[13] K. L. French, *The People of the Parish: community life in a late medieval English parish* (Philadelphia, 2001), pp. 117–29.

[14] See above, pp. 260–75.

French and shared a ritual and social life; they worshipped particular saints and gave their sons names like Richard, Hugh and Nigel – in which, for reasons of prestige, they were soon followed by the English. Their marriage arrangements spanned the Channel, as did their inheritances. Although this multi-ethnic identity was weakening even before the loss of Normandy in 1214, a 'French' cultural identity continued to set apart the landed class from those who served them for at least another century after that. By the end of our period, however, this multi-ethnic identity had given way to a more pronounced English identity, inflected by regional tones and affiliations.

By the fourteenth century the emerging Middle English language and literature also carried regional character in the insular legacy of alliterative poetry. It was used by the poets who created *Sir Gawain and the Green Knight, Wynnere and Wastoure* and *Morte Arthure*: poems originating in the north-west but also known to have been widely disseminated. By the late fourteenth century alliterative poetry was used for the depiction of grotesque and satirical figures, having outgrown its original aim to praise and magnify. William Langland's great alliterative poem, *Piers Plowman*, describes *Covetise* (Avarice) as 'bitelbrowed and baberlipped' (beetle-browed and thick-lipped).[15] Alliteration also fed into Chaucer's poetry where it was blended into many other borrowings, and it enriched the parlance of courtiers, merchants, clerics and lawyers in London and the south-east.

So a variety of sources bearing traces of feelings and choices may provide the historian with an entry point into the sense of identity and self of people in the medieval past. They allow us to acquire a sense of the complex loyalties and dramatic dilemmas which people at all levels of society confronted. These sources are not evenly spread over our period. One might generalise by saying that between 1200 and 1500 the sources increasingly portray life further down the social scale, that the proportion of vernacular writing and art grows, and that urban material becomes more predominant, so that a diversity of voices can increasingly be heard.

At the same time, horizons were widening, which necessarily affected people's sense of belonging and identity. In the countryside manor-based living, in which customary tenancies grounded most people in a single settlement for life, came to co-exist with more diverse forms of work and production, entailing travel and encounters with a more varied array of folk and ways of life. Other examples discussed elsewhere in this book

---

[15] *Piers Plowman*, B-Text, Passus V, line 298.

include professional soldiering and long-distance trade, both of which created groups of people whose relationship with their own communities – their values and their identities – were tested and severed for long periods. And from the late fourteenth century another trend becomes evident among men and women: one of experimentation with alternative religious ideas, and a widespread and vernacular critique of the established ecclesiastical order. After 1380 religion became a hotly debated commitment, which was self-defining in new and sometimes dangerous ways.

THE CREATION OF IDENTITY

One might usefully think of identity as a set of overlapping circles. To each person there is a core of experiences – early, intimate and formative – to which are added possibilities and inclinations resulting from the gradual exercise of greater autonomy and the acquisition of skills. Identity was never a process of replacement, but of accumulation. Although education, for example, was designed to turn the child into an adult, sediments from earlier experience survived. Sediments such as these are crucial for the understanding of identity, and involve the laying down of strata of memories and attitudes. The young woman who became a nun did not forget her childlike play, her dalliances with boys, her delight in new clothes and good food, even if all these were to be given up after her consecration as a bride of Christ. A man who acquired scholarship and progressed through a rigorous learning of theology and law, could nonetheless practise the rhythms of popular belief, repeat the sayings of his locality, or venerate a saint who was little known outside his natal region.

By the beginning of our period baptism was an established ritual of entry into Christian life and was celebrated as soon as circumstances allowed. The importance attached to this sacrament is evident from the repeated complaints of parishioners about priests who are too frequently absent or otherwise negligent of their duty to baptise. In extreme circumstances midwives were allowed to pronounce the formula of baptism, but the normal celebration was more elaborate and momentous. It was at baptism that the infant became a child of God, cleansed of original sin. But it was also at baptism that the infant was received into human society. Three godparents were designated, whose relationship to the child was seen as analogous to that of the birth parents. The senior of them generally chose the child's name, although this might be over-ridden by tradition in aristocratic families. The Mortimers, for instance, maintained a commitment to the names of Roger and Edmund for their two eldest sons over several generations. As this implies, names made a statement about identity, even though names were relatively few. In *c.* 1280 28 per cent of the men of the village of Kibworth Harcourt (Leics.) were named Robert, and 16 per cent William. In fifteenth-century Warwickshire the political and social dominance of Richard Beauchamp, earl of Warwick, is reflected in a generation of local gentry who shared his first name. Occasionally names told other stories. The Beauchamps themselves adopted the name Guy in the late thirteenth century in a deliberate act of self-identification with the mythical hero Guy of Warwick. At a lower social level the descent of a Devonshire family from a Breton settler after the Conquest was remembered in the name Joel.[16] Surnames embodied identity too. Until the mid fourteenth century most were still fluid, conveying personal details. Some of the more entertaining ones are obvious to explain, others less so. It is easy to imagine why a Hull merchant at the end of the thirteenth century, John Herring, became universally known in the course of his career as John Rottenherring. But how did Adam Halfnaked, a man much involved in the custody of ecclesiastical estates in early fourteenth-century England, come about his odd surname? Of course, most surnames were altogether more prosaic: many derived from the family's place of origins or from an ancestor's occupation. And once surnames became fixed they asserted familial identity, with collateral heirs sometimes required to take the family name as a condition of their inheriting the land.[17]

From infancy, gender was a strong component of identity, as Jeremy Goldberg discusses below, and deviation from the expected norms was generally regarded as profoundly unnatural.[18] The inculcation of appropriate behaviour was thus a major concern of medieval educators. Instruction in the home, and the ethos inculcated within it, were crucial to the formation of any person. Women had a crucial role to play here, with preachers emphasising the centrality of women to the maintenance of family values. As the early thirteenth-century theologian Thomas of Chobham, quoted above, emphasised in his manual for confessors, this might be a matter of moulding the behaviour of husbands as well as children.[19] Although women were barred from preaching in public and

---

[16] D. A. Postles, 'The baptismal name in thirteenth-century England: processes and patterns', *Medieval Prosopography*, 13.2 (1992), 6, 12, 17, 19–20.

[17] For the case of Matthew Oxe, who changed his surname to deny his former identity as a serf, see above p. 68 n. 69.

[18] For some exceptions see below, pp. 401–2.

[19] See the discussion by Peter Coss, above, pp. 50, 58–9.

from holding any sacerdotal role in the Church, wives and mothers were accorded real importance as conduits for religious lore and as nurturers of religious sensibility. Christian identity was instilled in homes, and could include a very wide range of activities beyond the formal catechism. It introduced children to favoured local saints, to local places of worship and pilgrimage and to prayers for specific occasions. Girls learned to match food preparation not only to the seasons of the year, but to the religious calendar – fish on Fridays, no animal fat or meat during Lent – and all were warned about the ways in which feast days and Sundays intruded into the rhythms of work and leisure. A book of hours owned by Margaret Blackburn of York in the mid fifteenth century was probably used by a succession of mothers to teach their daughters to read. It is adorned by a whole-page image of St Sitha, the patron saint of servants, with her set of household keys, an apt reminder of female roles.[20] This is an intimate book, loved by families and used over generations in their daily lives, and in imparting gender, religious and family identity.

In rural Suffolk, women of middling social position but of some standing in their local communities, commissioned books for domestic worship and the instruction of their children, illustrated with images of innocence and purity, such as those associated with the alleged boy-martyr Robert of Bury.[21] Again, a local cult was being harnessed to family instruction. The household was also the repository of other forms of instruction. Anglo-Norman books of remedies and recipes circulated among the greatest families, but English versions of such materials were collected in the commonplace books of lesser folk, along with a variety of charms and means of prognostication.

Instruction was the central task of the Church. Eamon Duffy discusses above the new emphasis in this period on the Church's pastoral role and the ways in which priests were equipped to meet their obligation to instruct the laity in the essentials of their faith.[22] In many places it was also the parish clergy who were the providers of a further tier of education, this time directed only at boys: the ability to read and write in Latin which rendered them *literatus* and opened the door to further education and advancement. The involvement of individual clerics in this sort of

---

[20] P. Cullum and J. Goldberg, 'How Margaret Blackburn taught her daughters: reading devotional instruction in a book of hours', in J. Wogan-Browne et al., eds., *Medieval Women: texts and contexts in late medieval Britain. Essays for Felicity Riddy* (Turnhout, 2000), pp. 217–36, image at p. 226.

[21] M. Rubin, 'The body, whole and vulnerable, in fifteenth-century England', in B. A. Hanawalt and D. Wallace, eds., *Bodies and Disciplines. Intersections of literature and history in fifteenth-century England* (Minneapolis, 1996), pp. 19–28, at pp. 24–5.

[22] See above, pp. 301–5.

schooling is often unrecorded, but can be glimpsed, for example, in the campaign waged by the master of Beverley Minster school against local competitors at the beginning of the fourteenth century.[23] As his vigorous counter-measures suggest, there was money to be made in education, evidence of a demand for education which was to grow steadily throughout this period.

Some of the boys who availed themselves of this schooling might go on to university, usually when they were about fourteen. This was a break from the most familiar scenes of home and of locality, and also brought a distinct change of identity. Until the end of this period most scholars were in at least minor orders. The assumption of a clerical identity set a man apart from his lay peers – at least in theory. This was most marked in the case of priests, whose distinctiveness had been emphasised by the reformers of the late eleventh and early twelfth centuries and then intensified by the theological developments summed up in the decrees of the fourth Lateran Council. Priests could absolve from sin and thereby could determine an individual's salvation or damnation. They also, to use the contemporary phrase, 'made God' when, at the climax of the mass, the bread and wine consecrated by the priest became the body and blood of Christ. But they were at the same time an essential part of the local community, participating in most celebrations of family and lifecycle events, and cultivating their glebe much as their parishioners cultivated their holdings. The records of parochial visitations, where lay people's complaints against their clergy were voiced, reveal just how difficult the resulting balancing act could be. In 1519 the chaplain in charge at Surfleet (Lincs.), was accused of trading in hemp, grain and livestock, and pas-turing his sheep and horses in the churchyard.[24] The requirement of priestly celibacy could be particularly testing, although it is possible that parishioners found a discreet relationship with a 'housekeeper' an acceptable alternative to promiscuity.

A university education might also open other doors. At the BA level it taught a very specific set of skills: grammar (fluency in Latin), logic (the ability to develop an argument) and rhetoric (the skill to articulate that argument persuasively). This equipped the graduate for administrative tasks in Church and state through mastery of record-keeping, corre-spondence, debate and diplomacy. In turn these could lead to lucrative

[23] A. F. Leach, ed., *Memorials of Beverley Minster*, I (Surtees Society, XCVIII, 1897), pp. lx–lxi, 48, 114.
[24] A. Hamilton Thompson, ed., *Visitations in the Diocese of Lincoln 1517–1531*, I (Lincoln Record Society, XXXIII, 1940), p. 59. For further examples, see pp. xxxiv–xxxvi.

and prestigious jobs in the service of kings, magnates and cities. Within England this created a professional and highly mobile elite. University graduates became significantly more prominent both in the service of the state (especially in relation to international diplomacy) and in the high offices of the Church during the fourteenth and fifteenth centuries. The beneficiaries of patronage themselves, these men could in turn do favours for others and became powerful 'fixers' in an elaborate network of privileged preferment. The country was thus criss-crossed by associations which transcended locality but which might nonetheless co-exist with strong local and familial loyalties. Robert Stillington was only one of a number of late medieval bishops who founded schools in their home towns, in his case Acaster Selby (Yorks.), and he also helped his nephews in their studies abroad. Grammar-school training was still sufficient for most of the men recruited as clerks in royal and aristocratic service. But the lack of university training did not mean to say that these men did not have powerful networks of their own. For much of the fourteenth century the Westminster-based royal civil service included a very influential group of men from families based around the Humber in north Lincolnshire, north Nottinghamshire and parts of Yorkshire: as clerks, and therefore celibates, they nevertheless perpetuated these local links by regularly providing opportunities for cousins and nephews to join the staff of the royal Chancery and Exchequer.

For a small privileged group a clerical training opened up a Europe-wide vista of appointments and tasks. A man with good Latin and a powerful recommendation could reach as far as the papal curia and receive preferment there, as several Englishmen did. One, Nicholas Breakspear, had even become pope in 1154, and although this was not to be repeated, in other respects the period saw the growing integration of European elites of skill, which came to embrace not only the Latin-literate but also architects, artists and musicians. This pan-European artistic community transferred and transformed styles in literature, music and architecture to create gems of artistic assimilation.

THE POSSIBILITIES OF 'SELF-FASHIONING'

Inasmuch as all aspects of identity are cultural constructs of great complexity and potential richness, identity can be made particularly explicit and articulate through the provision of symbolic forms for its expression. Image and ritual practice were thus crucial to the formation of identity and the assumption of new aspects of identity. A concept which has been used for the understanding of such rituals is *rite de passage,* coined by the folklorist Arnold van Gennep in 1909. The rite of passage is a ceremony powerful in its symbolic impact and devised to mark a transition in lifecycle, which is always a change in identity: from maiden to wife, from layman to priest, from whole to leprous, from prince to king, from girl to nun. Anthropologists have traditionally studied rituals as age-old and static, as belonging to people 'without a history'. In the hands of historians the study of rites of passage has been transformed. They are invested with conflict and they are often devised within the political sphere with great deliberation – like the funeral for Edward II in 1327, at which no body was displayed, or the re-burial of the long-dead Richard II in 1413. Rituals could be designed with one end in mind and then transformed and re-made to another. While the Latin veiling ceremony for nuns was designed to hand them over to the authority of the abbess and the sacramental care of priests, vernacular manuals interpreted the occasion as an empowering choice for women to seize and enjoy.[25] Attention to ritual reveals the assumption as well as the ascription of identity. It can mark the terrain between expected behaviour, role and attitude, and that which participants choose for themselves or interpret within the recommended normative domain.

Self-fashioning is a term coined by Renaissance scholars to describe the many acts by which writers created an author's authority for themselves through the use of rhetorical devices, and the choice of genre. It has since been expanded to describe acts by which individuals choose to present themselves to the world – or even just to themselves – by nurturing a persona through literary and other representational devices: clothing, linguistic idiom, public gestures. Our consideration of men and women's progress through the lifecycle, formed by and around strict codes of behaviour related to age, status and gender, need not exclude processes of self-invention and attempts to make a specific place for oneself in the world. The opportunities were not unlimited, and offered a wider choice to men than to women, but they did exist in the later middle ages. Such making is also a process of self-discovery, since 'individuals take action in public to make a certain image of themselves recognisable to others, and in the process they come to recognise their own person in that image'.[26]

---

[25] N. Bradley Warren, *Spiritual Economies: female monasticism in later medieval England* (Philadelphia, 2001), pp. 33–44.
[26] R. C. Trexler, 'Introduction', in *Persons in Groups: social behaviour as identity formation in medieval and Renaissance Europe* (Binghamton, NY, 1985), p. 4.

Let us consider the rituals of civic life discussed in the previous chapter. In these townsmen forged performances which were meant to reflect and enhance their positions. The summer celebrations of the feast of Corpus Christi, which revolved around outdoor eucharistic processions, observed strict hierarchies which translated closeness to the eucharist carried by priests into the measure of status and wealth. In the larger cities, which boasted numerous craft and trade guilds, town officials determined an order that reflected wealth and influence among them. For this reason the issue of precedence was frequently tested and contested.[27] The procession also operated at another level of labelling: the participants were citizens, those with a recognised economic and political stake in the town. As interesting and significant were the identities of those who were not included: women, those workers whose craft was not sufficiently prestigious; foreigners (which in the middle ages meant any outsider, not only those from other countries); those too young or too old or too poor. Within the processions members of craft guilds marched in their livery and the town officials, at the heart of the procession and closest to its sacerdotal, sacramental heart, wore their robes of office. Related to the intense moment of public display were the celebrations which followed: religious services and feasting exclusive to the craftsmen and their families, further enhancing the identity related to work and worth.

People sported distinguishing marks either by choice or by ascription. The latter were designed to clarify identities that might not otherwise be obvious. Prostitutes were recognised in several cities by a striped hood, to avoid embarrassing confusion with 'respectable' women. Most male Jews of England in the thirteenth century were meant to wear a distinguishing badge, introduced in the aftermath of the fourth Lateran Council through the ecclesiastical legislation of local bishops. The badge, in the shape of the tablets of the law (*tabula*), was meant to mark out Jews, who might otherwise not be easily distinguishable from other groups such as the Lombards or Cahorsins who ran their businesses in London in very close proximity. This labelling was only poorly enforced, but probably most strikingly in dioceses with activist bishops, such as Lincoln and Norwich in the early thirteenth century.

Such imposed markers could shade into identification as a form of shaming: of distinguishing the aberrant. Branding was a punishment recognised in law in later medieval England, and literally marked the offender with a public sign of his offence. After 1361 fugitives outlawed

[27] M. Rubin, *Corpus Christi: the eucharist in late medieval culture* (Cambridge, 1991), esp. pp. 263–5.

under the labour legislation and who had been apprehended by sheriffs were liable to be branded on the forehead with the letter F, for falsity. A particular form of branding emerged in the late middle ages as anxieties emerged about the abuse of clerical privilege. An offender who could demonstrate that he was in orders – generally by reading a passage of the bible – would be handed over to the church courts for trial, where the penalties were far milder. It was recognised that this was being exploited by men who were not in fact priests, and in 1489 parliament tried to ensure that laymen could only enjoy benefit of clergy once by ordering the branding on the left thumb of any felon who could not produce supporting evidence of ordination.

Clergy were distinguished by a tonsure, which in some cases was minimal and discreet, so as to call little attention. Parish clergy were also expected to dress soberly and modestly when off duty. Members of religious orders were much more explicit in their self-presentation: the friars with their black or grey habits and their corded belts and sandalled feet; Augustinian canons in their white habits. Monastic habits were seen less in public since monks were meant to remain in their monasteries. But monks travelled for study and pilgrimage, to preach in parishes associated with their houses and on business, and contemporaries would have recognised their clothing. For all clergy, mass vestments marked out their sacred status and attacks on priests so vested were regarded as particularly heinous.

For lay people, weapons were a common status marker. Swords were worn by knights; indeed girding with a sword was part of the ritual of creating a knight. They were a potent image of authority, as can be seen in the various 'magic' swords like Excalibur in chivalric literature and in their role in royal coronations. Towards the end of our period a number of cities secured the right to have a sword borne before their mayor on public occasions. A broader social group carried daggers and knives: a symbol of freedom as well as an attribute of manliness. Arms were not worn by women or serfs, and were not meant to be worn by the clergy, who were not allowed to shed blood. In contemporary accounts of popular unrest the low social status and moral degeneracy of the insurgents is generally signalled by their use of household or agricultural implements as weapons.

The quality of clothing was also a strong marker of status and vocation. Fur and good cloth, embroidery and jewellery all bespoke status and wealth. At the other end of the scale, homespun was the cheapest and coarsest cloth. The russet cloth of Colchester was a dependable dull cloth chosen by working people and those who wished to appear humble such as friars and penitents. In *The Canterbury Tales*, his inimitable version of the age-long satire of social types – what is sometimes called estates satire – Geoffrey Chaucer was alert to the messages of appearance. Minute attention is paid to dress and accessories by a man who knew his merchandise well. Chaucer appreciated the registers in which clothing spoke and made them even more eloquent: dress could be a social mirror, reliably marking status or office, but also a badge of vanity, of aspiration. The Wife of Bath's clothing, which we encounter through two costumes – Sunday best and travel garments – was like a palimpsest of her life experiences and occupations: heavy long coverchiefs, red hose, new fine shoes, and for travel a brand new hat over a wimple. Her hard-won finery was her way of expressing her identity, the fruit of her toil and the legacy of her many marriages.

Clothing had always been about aspiration as well as actual status, but this became increasingly marked across this period. The deep economic and social changes brought about by the Black Death of 1348–9 meant that the disposable income of many in the lower tiers of society increased, allowing the purchase of a wider range of food and clothing and reducing the usefulness of clothing as a signifier of status. The first attempt to regulate clothing according to status was made in 1363, just fifteen years after the plague had first reached England.[28] A sub-text was the desire to limit the import of foreign goods, which is why, when the legislation (predictably) failed, subsequent reissues were strident about the damage done to the realm. But its avowed target was 'the outrageous and excessive apparel of many people, contrary to their estate and degree' and it spoke to the contemporary anxiety that the lower orders were getting above themselves. To rectify this situation a scale of entitlement was created by which, for example, craftsmen and yeomen could not wear cloth of above a certain price, or any sort of embroidered or decorated clothing. Now that labour was scarce and wages high, fussy and elaborate needlework bespoke cost just as eloquently as the nature of the fabric itself. The legislation continued to be revised and reissued into the fifteenth century, although by 1483 the framers of the legislation seem to have lost heart and mainly confined themselves to restricting the most sumptuous furs and fabrics to a tiny socio-political elite.

The sense that status had become more difficult to discern reverberates in the writings of moralists and the poetry of complaint in the decades

---

[28] *Statutes of the Realm*, I, pp. 380–2.

after the Black Death. Whereas twelfth-century chroniclers might bemoan the fact that the king preferred to employ men 'raised from dust', complaints about social malleability, dissimulation and transformation seem to intensify and become more varied in the later middle ages. In his *Piers Plowman*, WilliamLangland saw a society full of worldly advancement, but one in which simplicity and natural justice had been lost. An anonymous preacher gave an unsympathetic picture of the miseries of the ambitious, obsessed by status and its manifestations. Such a man knows no rest:

Indeed, how can he, when he does not know what new fashion to follow; when he worries about precedence, not knowing whether to ride before or behind or when he can carry a weapon; always terrified that someone will gain more admiration than he; and never having a moment's peace while he can see a neighbour who exceeds him in status or respect.[29]

It was not only moralists who felt uneasy. There could be more general hostility to people who seemed to have advanced beyond their proper status. Lawyers in particular seemed to trouble notions of order and justice. They possessed knowledge of the intricacies of government and the law that allowed them to make or break people greater than themselves, earning rich fees with which manors and the trappings of gentility could be purchased. And yet they were not much more than servants, and often of very modest birth without inherent lordship or inherited wealth. Other forms of professional advancement might also be problematic, particularly forms of service where the employee derived vicarious authority from the power of his master: bullying bailiffs or swaggering retainers.

For the beneficiaries of such advancement the relationship was worth marking. This was often done through the wearing of livery badges and clothes, which marked achievement and capacity, connection and privilege. They performed the dual work of affirming identity and signalling difference. They also asserted the power of the lord, since the possession of servants was an index of status. In late medieval England the proliferation of partisan badges and emblems raised a particular anxiety, reflected in the repeated attempts to regulate their use by statute. As the legislation reveals, the problem was not so much the acknowledged servant, since a lord would in that case be expected to take responsibility for his servant's behaviour, but the men over whom the lord's control was too

[29] R. Horrox, ed., *The Black Death* (Manchester, 1994), p. 339.

tenuous to act as a brake on bad behaviour. In representational terms this was the difference between the livery clothing of the household servant and the badges of base metal, or even fabric, distributed wholesale.

Royal service in the late middle ages was marked in similar ways, and could generate similar problems of representation and authority. Yeomen of the crown employed on the king's business wore a silver-gilt crown on one shoulder, signalling that they had royal authority behind them. There was an obvious temptation to wear the insignia when about their own concerns, allowing them an authority far greater than they could claim in their own right. Kings distributed livery badges too. When the post-coronation progress of Richard III took him to York in August 1483, the king ordered 13,000 fabric badges bearing his emblem of the white boar. The most famous royal badge is, however, the white hart of Richard II, the symbol displayed on so many artefacts and works of art of the Ricardian court, most beautifully in the Wilton Diptych where it is woven into the fabric of Richard's robe, worn as a jewel on the breasts of Richard and all the angels, and painted on the Diptych's outer panel.[30]

The exchange of such emblems, whether royal or aristocratic, was meant to signal the personal identification of recipient and donor. On one occasion Richard II wore his uncle John of Gaunt's collar as a sign of the 'good love heartfully felt between them'.[31] In the Wilton Diptych he is shown wearing the broom-cod collar of his father-in-law, the French king Charles VI. Nobles were proud to wear elaborate jewelled collars of the royal livery. The problems started when the personal dimension was stripped out and the symbol was used to claim a relationship that did not really exist – when the identification, and hence the claimed identity, was in effect fictitious. Then it became a sort of fraudulent self-fashioning, analogous to dressing or behaving above one's station and generating similar criticism.

Self-fashioning might also entail a deliberate subversion of identity. Medieval nobles and knights, themselves men of standing and influence, can be said to have adopted a submissive, 'feminine' role vis-à-vis their prince simply by subscribing to the hierarchical and cultural assumptions of his court. The religious devotion of powerful men might entail a similar transgression of sorts into the terrain of the feminine, by self-identification with the abject, the chaste, the circumscribed and the

[30] D. Gordon, L. Monnas and C. Elam, eds., *The Regal Image of Richard II and the Wilton Diptych* (1997), plates 1 and 9.

[31] A. Goodman, *John of Gaunt: the exercise of princely power in fourteenth-century Europe* (Harlow, 1992), p. 144.

enclosed. Henry of Grosmont, duke of Lancaster (d.1361) turned to the realm of Marian devotion and composed an imaginative devotional text, the *Livre des seintes medicines*, in which he humbled himself, wounded as he was by the sins that come so easily to a man of his stature. Duke Henry here appropriated a language of abjection through devotional appeal to Mary, seeking her nourishment and balm, her medicine. Richard Beauchamp, earl of Warwick, had an important association with Emma Rawghton, anchoress of the city of York. Emma consoled him at moments of political misfortune and reported to the earl significant messages received from the Virgin Mary.[32] A wide variety of styles of devotion – from the most austere to the most ostentatious, forms of self-help or experiences within groups – enabled men and women, above all those with means and leisure, to experiment in making and re-making themselves. In nunneries women were exploring the possibilities of self-governance, developing versions of official liturgies laid down for them by male clerics and experiencing some possibilities for self-fashioning which their equivalent location in landed society may not have offered so readily.[33]

IDENTITY AND COMMUNITY

The middle ages have frequently been used by theorists of modernity as a locus of cohesive community. Sociologists and anthropologists, historians and poets have found in medieval social relations – in the village, the guild, the monastery – units of intimate and bonded sociability of a particularly intensive kind. Max Weber identified in the dissolution of these ties the possibilities of individual self-assertion and the economic and political dynamism that followed from it. Early trade unionists sought in the collegiality of the guild a model for the modern organisation of labourers, and the socialist views of William Morris and his followers were deeply coloured by their view of the middle ages. 'Community' has featured in the titles of numerous studies of medieval social and political history, often aligned with another term, such as polity, locality or charity. It is, however, a notoriously slippery concept, as the debate about the legitimacy of the concept of the 'county community' has demonstrated, and in medieval usage was as much about exclusion as inclusion. The 'community of the realm' or the 'community of the shire' were the people who mattered. In a chapter on identity it is useful to

---

[32] Warren, *Spiritual Economies*, ch. 5.   [33] *Ibid.*, chs. 1 and 2.

reflect on the interlocking experiences of personal identity through participation in collective, communal endeavours, alongside a consideration of individual identity as an entity which places the person apart or at a distance from the aims and actions of groups.

Medieval people recognised shared aims and made alliances around specific aims and tasks: political, agrarian or devotional. At a grass-roots level, adult males who collected in tithings (groups of ten although the number varied in practice) were required to take responsibility for each other's actions and bring offenders within the group to justice. The growth of a central legal system, as discussed by Simon Walker above, in some respects eroded this self-determination, but its survival can be seen in the number of local men involved in the maintenance of law and order, whether by reporting offences or, as juries, giving their verdict on what had happened.[34] There also remained an abiding sense that communities, whether guilds, aristocratic retinues, households or universities, should discipline their own members. This went hand in hand with a dislike for external intervention. Guild regulations often stipulated that members should not go to law until the officers of the guild had attempted to arbitrate the dispute, and the University of Oxford (for a time) closed ranks in defence of John Wyclif.

For communities, self-regulation of this kind was a facet of their concern for their own interests. Traders and manufacturers came together in guilds in defence of their shared economic interests. Critics might claim that such guilds existed to create a monopoly and keep prices high. Their members insisted that their goal was the maintenance of high standards, by regulating apprenticeships or inspecting goods put on sale; that it was, in fact, for the public good rather than private interest. Religious fraternities were founded in honour of a particular saint, or to keep a light burning in the local church, but they also generally ensured that members received a good funeral and post-mortem prayers that they would probably not have been able to provide for themselves, as well as offering help to members fallen on hard times and providing occasions for sociability.

Such activities forged links and experiences which might be seen as 'social capital': a good which transcended men's capacity to act as individuals, and which might serve as model and inducement for future co-operation. Identity – both personal and collective – might be explored and expressed in response to external authority. Such acts – concerted efforts which elicited from an individual a choice and some risk – are

---

[34] See above, pp. 91–112.

evident in those areas of England which saw the strongest manorial lordship.[35] In those regions characterised by communities managing arable in a variety of joint ventures within a manorial system, the pooling of effort facilitated other forms of joint action. The period 1280–1310, which saw the greatest pressure on resources, brought a series of struggles between servile communities and their lords, most famously in the manor of Halesowen (Worcs.), where court rolls reveal deliberate and concerted peasant action in attempts to stabilise rents and protect access to communal resources.[36] Some 150 years later, in the midst of a deep economic crisis around 1450, the now much smaller community similarly came together in concerted action against landlords in south Worcestershire.[37]

Here is a level of action and mobilisation which is difficult to document except at times of crisis. If we gaze higher up the social scale at parish and county gentry – not the greatest men but those men who held manors and jurisdiction, whose duty it was to turn up to the county court and assist the sheriff in administration – we find that they too came together for political action over issues which affected their wellbeing. At the beginning of our period their complaints tended to address two issues: the remit of the sheriff's powers and forest law. In 1204 Devon men won from King John the curtailment of shrieval action, and the Forest Charter of 1217 coincided with the freeing of lands afforested under the previous two kings. Deliberation and organisation were local among the men who attended or were represented at the county court. Disafforestation of a local hundred brought together middling knights and the abbot of Peterborough in 1215.[38] When in the late thirteenth and fourteenth centuries judicial business passed increasingly into the hands of royal officials and judges, the county court still remained a central venue for the expression of political identity and action. It was large, it was expected to attract great men and small, and the growing importance of parliament created opportunities for it in selecting parliamentary representatives and in drafting petitions. Local political gatherings were sometimes large enough to be inclusive: in 1388 sixty-six townsmen and 330 'well-born

[35] Campbell, above pp. 209–13, discusses the various intensities of manorial lordship.

[36] Z. Razi, 'The struggle between the abbots of Halesowen and their tenants in the thirteenth and fourteenth centuries', in T. H. Aston, P. R. Coss, C. Dyer and J. Thirsk, eds., *Social Relations and Ideas: essays in honour of R. H. Hilton* (Cambridge, 1983), pp. 151–67.

[37] E. Fryde, 'Economic depression in England in the second and third quarters of the fifteenth century: effective resistance of tenants to landlords as one of its consequences', in R. W. Kaeuper, ed., *Violence in Medieval Society* (Woodbridge, 2000), pp. 215–26.

[38] J. R. Maddicott, 'Magna Carta and the local community 1215–1259', *P&P*, 102 (1984), 25–65, at 26–30, 37, 49.

men' met in Lincoln to proclaim their support for the Lords Appellants, a group of magnates who had opposed Richard II and his leading supporters. Local courts were the venue for royal proclamations, which grew in importance and frequency during the Hundred Years War.

Local experience of struggles and disputes became part of the memory and identity of local communities, at least for a while. The breaking up and distribution of millstones from the parlour of the abbot of Bury St Edmunds in 1381, discussed by Eamon Duffy, is a case in point.[39] Local memory and myth could retain its potency for a surprisingly long time. In later medieval Beverley the belief that King Athelstan in the early tenth century had granted freedom to the minster in the words 'As free make I thee, as heart can think or eye can see' was appropriated by the townsmen as an argument for their freedom from royal exactions. In Coventry, the story of Godiva's ride naked through the city to shame her husband Leofric into granting the city its freedom was appropriated in the 1490s by citizens protesting against a new toll on wool and cloth, who insisted 'This city should be free and now is bond / Dame good Eve made it free'. Such stories raised awareness of community, as did shared rituals, like the bawdy 'Yule Riding' at York or the Norwich pageant of St George. The people of Bury St Edmunds might remember the broken millstones; they also participated in the ritual described by Charles Phythian-Adams in the previous chapter, involving the leading of a white bull through the streets.[40]

Shared memory might also be written on the landscape. Ruins spoke of the passing of time. The shrunken towns of the fifteenth century, petitioning for relief from the crown, made much of the abandoned houses falling into ruin. Deserted settlements were now a feature of the countryside. Place names in both town and country preserved the memory of previous generations. Baynard's Castle, the great London mansion in Thames Street owned in the fifteenth century by the dukes of York, preserved the name of a private castle that had disappeared in the thirteenth century and was to carry the name forward into the early modern period. But even without such aides-memoire, local memory could stretch a long way back. When Edward I launched his great enquiry into land ownership in 1279, the findings of which were embodied in the Hundred Rolls, local juries apparently had no difficulty recounting property descent over four or five generations and the occasional error

---

[39] See above, pp. 334–5.
[40] D. Palliser, 'Urban society', in R. Horrox, ed., *Fifteenth-Century Attitudes: perceptions of society in late medieval England* (Cambridge, 1994), pp. 132–49, at 147–8; above, p. 369.

suggests that they were relying on memory rather than the written record. As this reveals, memories can falter and be lost. To be a member of a community is to share the sense of what is redundant as well as what is worthy of memory. The resulting sense of belonging creates a familiarity which can be both comforting and suffocating.

The accumulation of such memory, which is both local and broader, contributed over centuries to the making of an identity of the people of England. This was varied by region – through dialect, family structure, agricultural productivity, level of communication and ease of movement. It was also indelibly marked by relationships with people who would not have considered themselves English, even if they owed allegiance or paid taxes to the king of England. The generations following the Conquest saw the meaningful if varied attachment of a wide 'empire' to the English crown: through fealty (Brittany), through conquest (Ireland and later Wales), through marriage (Scotland), and through marriage and inheritance (Anjou and Poitou). In all these parts, even as in the regions of England, dialects and languages were meaningfully diverse, enough to set people apart and make interaction difficult. Between England and its neighbours borders were highly permeable, and so cultures of hybridity developed under military and tenurial regimes exploitative of local populations, characterised by attempts to define and separate by law the identities of English from other groups.

The anonymous *Libelle of Englysch Polycye*, written *c.*1436, demonstrates just how dependent the sense of Englishness was on a sense of otherness in neighbours as well as in more remote nations. It was written after the relief by Humphrey, duke of Gloucester of the siege of Calais by a Franco-Burgundian force, a feat followed by English raids into western Flanders. The well-informed Londoner who wrote the *Libelle* witnessed the impact of the events on London: riots that resulted in the burning of the houses of Flemish merchants. He proposes an alternative to England's embroilment in an economic and political situation which necessitated contact with Flemings, who were well known for treachery and deceit. An alternative might be Ireland and its natural, unexploited wealth:

> For of silver and gold there is the ore
> Among the wild Irish, though they be poor,
> For they are rude [primitive] and have therein no skill.[41]

---

[41] *The Libelle of Englyshe Polycye: a poem on the use of sea-power, 1436*, ed. G. Warner (Oxford, 1926), p. 35, lines 686–8. The section ends with an exhortation to maintain control of Wales, pp. 40–1.

Here something akin to a colonial enterprise is being put forth as a solution to English economic and moral decline. England had relied heavily on the export of wool to Flanders and the added value it could gain through monopolistic ventures of sale and distribution, which in turn had led to an experiment in overseas settlement in Calais. Now a new enterprise of conquest and exploitation was offered in the *Libelle*, one to engage the enterprise and energy of the English: the settlement of Ireland, the turn westwards. If the English were routed on the continent, they might triumph in their western hinterland. A national effort combining soldiers and merchants, churchmen and peasants, was put forward, as a project that would also reinvigorate the monarchy and provide a rallying call for crown and nobility.

The Irish, Scots or Welsh were not figures attached to a single place, along and beyond a border; rather these were identities which emerged out of the encounter, struggle and co-existence with neighbouring people, through the imagination as well as interaction.[42] The Jew was similarly imagined, as part of small communities which were first welcomed into England by William the Conqueror and finally expelled from it by Edward I in 1290. The beginning of our period saw a process of theological, legal and administrative discussion and codification, which defined Judaism increasingly as an antagonistic, threatening entity within a Christian world, and imputed to Jews varying degrees of ill-will and active hostility to Christians and their faith. In some communities in the thirteenth century English people enacted dramas by which Jews were accused of heinous crimes against children, through the ritual murder accusation that saw some of its earliest appearances in England. Jews were also accused of financial impropriety – coin-clipping, as well as more familiar complaints of usury[43] – and of the desecration of symbols of Christian worship and faith, such as the eucharist and images of the Virgin. The speed and agility with which these accusations unfolded in the thirteenth century, and the variety of genres within which they became enshrined, and continued to appear even after the expulsion of the Jews, testify to the centrality of this significant 'other' in the making of Christian identity, a central facet of the emergent sense of Englishness. In the wake of the Barons' War of 1264 the Jewish quarter of London was looted by the followers of Simon de Montfort and many Jews perished.

---

[42] These interactions are discussed further by Frame, below pp. 435–53.
[43] W. Johnson, 'Textual sources for the study of Jewish currency crimes in thirteenth-century England', *British Numismatic Journal*, 66 (1996), 21–31.

Similar acts were perpetrated in Worcester, Lincoln and elsewhere and fitted into the image of the barons' struggle as a triumph of Englishmen against foreigners. Recent scholarship underplays the idea that Edward I, in expelling the Jews in 1290, was merely interested in appropriating their wealth: a fervent and uncompromising religious zeal seems also to have been an important factor both for the king and for his advisors.

This trope of Englishness – triumphant Christian conformity – was also adopted by the kings of England in a variety of ways. Crusading was a theme which had animated the actions of kings and magnates from 1095, when Urban II had preached the first crusade at Clermont. Jerusalem, conquered on that crusade, was lost again in 1187 but remained a focus for the male imagination and kingly prestige. The third crusade, of which Richard I (d.1199) had been one of the leaders, came within sight of Jerusalem before turning back. Crusading themes inspired even those who remained at home. Henry III received the relic of the Holy Blood – brought from Jerusalem through Constantinople – as a gift from Louis IX of France, and housed it lavishly in Westminster Abbey. Henry never went on crusade, although he had vowed to do so, and the crusading mantle fell to his son Edward, who took the cross in 1268 and set out for the Holy Land in 1270. His crusade achieved little, although he retained crusading ambitions for the rest of his life and would presumably have valued one contemporary comment on his death: 'Jerusalem, you have lost the flower of all chivalry'.[44] In the second part of the fourteenth century English crusading ambitions focused rather on support for the reconquest of the Iberian peninsula and the struggle of the Teutonic Knights in the Baltic. But the Holy Land was never forgotten. Richard II's alliance with France was presented as the preliminary to a joint crusading effort and a number of Englishmen died on journeys to Palestine, among them John Lord Roos, Thomas Lord Clifford and Sir John Clanvowe. Thomas Mowbray, duke of Norfolk was on his way back from the Holy Land when he died at Venice in 1399. The crusading theme was to be re-shaped in the fifteenth century as Europe confronted the Turkish challenge, although it was somewhat dimmed during England's preoccupation with its civil wars.

By then, however, Christian conformity was also something that could be demonstrated nearer home, against the brand of religious enthusiasm that came to be known as Lollardy. This movement, associated with followers of the Oxford academic John Wyclif, also raised anxieties about

[44] M. Prestwich, *Edward I* (1988), p. 66.

dissimulation: the sort of fraudulent assumption of identity discussed in other contexts above. In the case of Lollardy the line between orthodoxy and heresy was often blurred. Among the landed classes, literate men with the confidence to pursue ideas and interests independently or through writers and priests in their households, exhibited an attraction to those aspects of self-scrutiny and pietism which reforming attitudes favoured. Some, like Sir John Clanvowe, wrote texts, others protected and supported notorious preachers, and all showed an interest in religious writings in the vernacular. None of this, however, necessarily amounted to heresy, although (as Margery Kempe was to find), in a society sensitised to the possibility of heterodoxy, extravagant piety or the possession of English texts was enough to arouse suspicion.

Wyclif's views had been condemned at the Blackfriars Council of 1382 but the Church moved slowly towards targeting his followers and the king, Richard II, although impeccably orthodox himself, showed no interest in doing otherwise. This was to change in the Lancastrian period, and here we encounter an interesting instance of political efforts to mould identity. For the Lancastrian kings sought to direct attention away from their own shaky disputed claim to the throne by constructing the sense of a loyal English subject. First Henry IV – crusader in his youth, then called to put down the Glyn Dŵr rebellion during a lull in the wars in France – then his son Henry V, each in his way contributed to the creation of an ideal English subject. This ideal was then disseminated through the operations of the system of ecclesiastical justice, and under the military leadership of a warrior king. State and Church combined here in novel ways to encourage people towards right belief and loyalty to the crown. This was achieved by collapsing the boundaries between religious probity and political allegiance. A person who held erroneous religious beliefs was presented as politically unsound, while those who rebelled against the king were often suspected of holding heterodox beliefs.[45] Views such as these were not only put forward in polemical works read by a small though influential elite, but were also spread through the public enactments of interrogations, accusation and sometimes (although rarely) executions.

The efforts to instil religious conformity involved community participation. Religious error among priests or neighbours was to be reported to Church officials by parishioners. The prominence given to the issue of

---

[45] P. Strohm, *England's Empty Throne: usurpation and the language of legitimation 1399–1422* (1998), esp. chs. 2 and 5.

religious conformity thereby gave occasion for the expression of disapproval against members of the community who lived 'unchristian', or
simply eccentric, lives. The denouncer of a 'Lollard' neighbour was also
proclaiming her or his own identity as a good Christian and a good
subject. Identifying such deviants, however, was not easy. A whole series
of questions – about the eucharist, images, clerical power – were, despite
their centrality, subjects of debate among people who were in no sense
heretics. The Church aimed to diminish occasion for error, or indeed
discussion of religious ideas, by increasingly limiting the subjects
appropriate for discussion, preaching and catechism. It also insisted that
the vernacular bible should not fall into the hands of lay people, although
rich patrons could commission any type of translation they wished with
impunity.

To say that the cluster of religion and loyalty to the crown became a
central preoccupation is not to say that all people internalised Christian
beliefs with the same degree of commitment and faith. It is rather to say
that communities and individuals spent a great deal of energy in debating
and reflecting on the boundaries of orthodoxy, on the manner in which
faith should be experienced and expressed, and on the relation between
public institutions and local styles of ritual, worship and celebration.
From all of these – from the struggle with doubt, the debate, the collective ritual, the display of zeal, and from the chastisement of others –
identities were made.

The more one tries to define and settle identity, the more complex are its
lineaments. A useful way of thinking about identity is through the image
of a cluster of co-existing attributes. Within that cluster, components can
gain or lose their relative importance over time. What is without doubt is
that a perceived threat to one of the components tends to raise awareness
of that component and to magnify its importance within the cluster.
A person might feel particularly aware of being a Christian when confronted by a Jew or a Muslim. National identity might be similarly
intensified. Welshness was acutely felt in Edwardian boroughs – like Flint
and Basingwerk in 1277 – planted in the north of Wales, which privileged
English burgesses after removing local Welsh farmers to a site ten miles
away in the valley of Rheidol.[46]

The role of the 'other' in defining identity should not blind one to the
existence of those who choose in effect to become 'the other'. The

---

[46] D. Walker, *Medieval Wales* (Cambridge, 1990), p. 57.

assumption of the role of an outsider was a device of writers from at least the twelfth century, allowing them a vantage point from which they could satirise or condemn their contemporaries. But this was not only a literary conceit. Individuals deliberately flouted convention or refused to conform. The heretic John Badby, the second man to be burned after the passing of the statute *De Heretico Comburendo* in 1401, was absolutely unyielding in upholding his own views. Indeed his answers at his trial in 1410 suggest the deliberate intention to outrage his eminent audience. He was, predictably in the circumstances, condemned to death. As the flames took hold Badby cried out, prompting the prince of Wales, the future Henry V, to halt the burning and offer a reprieve if Badby recanted. Badby refused and was put back into the flames.[47] Men and women might set themselves outside their community less dramatically by their behaviour. One fourteenth-century tenant of the bishop of Durham, William Standupryght, was reported to be so quarrelsome that he drove away all the other inhabitants of the village of Ricknall.[48] Others might feel themselves to be involuntary misfits, out of place in society, an experience poignantly described by the poet Hoccleve, who suffered some form of depressive illness *c.* 1414.

Such men were the exceptions, but in the search for identity it is often the nonconformists for whom historians are most willing to claim individuality. In part this is because the exceptional are visible in a way in which the typical are not. Will preambles offer an obvious example. Virtually all medieval testators bequeathed their souls to Almighty God, the Blessed Virgin and all the saints of heaven. Those who did *not* therefore immediately become the focus of attention, like the Daltons and their associates in Hull who adopted an unusual and elaborate version of the preamble at the end of our period. Their individuality is considered 'notable' while conformists are dismissed as 'mindless plagiarists'.[49]

The privileging of nonconformity in this way plays down the extent to which conformity can be chosen rather than being the default position for the unthinking. It thereby denies the commitment felt by many to the shared aspirations and assumptions of their society. The adoption of social conventions is not evidence of any lack of self-awareness. As this

---

[47] P. McNiven, *Heresy and Politics in the Reign of Henry IV. The burning of John Badby* (Woodbridge, 1987), ch. 11.

[48] R. H. Britnell, 'Feudal reaction after the Black Death in the palatinate of Durham', *P&P*, 128 (1990), 28–47, at p. 40.

[49] P. Heath, 'Urban piety in the later middle ages: the evidence of Hull wills', in R. B. Dobson, ed., *Church, Politics and Patronage in England and France in the Fifteenth Century* (Gloucester, 1984), pp. 209–34, at p. 215.

chapter has sought to emphasise, identity is the result of a complex interplay between personal and social forces, or between the individual and the community. It is about how people are seen, but also about how they see themselves, and the two are not the same thing. Hoccleve, who had particular cause to reflect on the nature of identity, was well aware of the disjunction but, unlike the historian, was looking at it from the inside rather than the outside. In his account of his illness he describes how he would sit in front of a mirror telling himself that he looked normal but would then remember that men cannot tell how they appear to others.[50]

[50] J. A. Burrow, ed., *Thomas Hoccleve's Complaint and Dialogue* (EETS, os CCCXIII, 1999), pp. 12–15.

CHAPTER 16

Life and death: the ages of man

P. J. P. Goldberg

It was a commonplace for educated people of the medieval era to think in terms of the ages of man, but the bewildering multiplicity of schemes for dividing the life-span into three, four, five, six, seven or some other number of divisions tells its own story. These are abstract conventions that cannot be read as simple mirrors of social practice. Thus, for example, within the tripartite scheme, the first stage may extend well into the third decade. The stages of childhood, adolescence, and early adulthood are here compressed into a single phase, but there is little reason to believe that people in the middle ages were unable to recognise these as distinctive and with their own needs. The terminology of the ages of man schema is likewise problematic. Latin terms such as *pueritia*, *adolescentia* and *iuventus* suggest obvious English equivalents, but these are in fact meaningless outside the philosophical framework to which they belong. It would be unwise, however, to dismiss these systems as of no practical relevance. They may not readily translate into evidence for social practice, but they may still have influenced the way people of the time thought about themselves and each other. The effect of the schemes tends to be that maturity was achieved only slowly, but that old age was reached at an earlier age than we would expect from the perspective of our own culture of longevity. The clue here is that the three score years and ten of the life course was regularly seen as characterised by a progression towards and then a falling away from a peak of physical and intellectual development achieved at the half-way stage. Indeed, this 'perfect age' corresponded with the thirty-three years that Christ achieved by the time of his crucifixion. It follows that people in the middle ages may not have thought themselves fully adult until well into their twenties, but may have considered themselves old at the point we in our own culture admit to middle age.

The 'ages of man' tends to be just that. It relates to the lives of men and hardly addresses the rather different circumstances of women. Phillips offers an alternative model for the 'ages of woman' that sees her perfect age as located not in the fourth, but in the second decade.[1] Here the model is not Christ, but Mary, who became a mother at fourteen, and the numerous virgin martyrs whose mortal lives ended in their mid to later teens. Again, it would be foolhardy to imagine that women were considered adult some years before men or old before their brothers had even entered the phase of 'youth'. What it does suggest, however, is that there was a particular cultural interest in the young unmarried woman in a way that was perhaps less true of men. Medieval societies socialised men and women differently. If we are to follow the life courses of men and women in medieval England, we must offer an account that is sensitive to gender difference. Though birth, reproduction and death are natural processes, the process of socialisation, the making of marriage, or provision for old age and death are culturally constructed and hence have their own histories. We need, therefore, also to be aware of change over time and differences in the experiences of different status groups.

This is a demanding agenda. Unfortunately the medievalist is not helped by the paucity of the evidence. This is an era before censuses and the collection of vital statistics; only in 1538 did Thomas Cromwell institute the recording of baptisms, marriages and burials, and most extant parish registers are from at least a generation later. The position regarding the more obvious personal sources – letters, diaries and autobiographical accounts – is not much more satisfactory. The last two hardly exist in our period, the first only for comparatively select groups and only really from the fifteenth century. The medievalist must look instead for otherwise less promising texts and adopt an essentially creative approach to sources that only indirectly relate to mapping the history of the human lifecycle. It follows also that more attention is given to some aspects of the lifecycle than others simply because some are better documented: much has been written on the making of marriage, but all too little on married life itself. Childhood, and particularly earlier childhood, is especially sparsely documented. The upper echelons of society, as always, are better recorded than those at the bottom of the social hierarchy.

The bringing of new life into the world was, and still is, an anxious time, but for people in the middle ages it had added cultural significance because the child represented a new and vulnerable soul. Depictions of childbirth invariably represent the mother assisted by numbers of other

---

[1] K. Phillips, 'Maidenhood as the perfect age of woman's life', in K. Lewis et al., eds., *Young Medieval Women* (Stroud, 2000), pp. 1–24.

women, and documentary evidence reinforces the view that what some scholars have dubbed the 'ceremony' of childbirth was exclusively women's territory. (Indeed it is tempting to conclude that the frequency of manuscript depictions of childbirth represents a form of voyeurism on the part of male artists and book owners.) The women helpers called to the mother in labour were probably largely friends, neighbours and kin rather than professionals, but equally it is likely that some of these women, through attending numbers of births, would have gained experience of the management of delivery. It follows that the woman who took the principal role in assisting the mother need not have been a professional midwife, in the way we might understand the term today, but rather an older and more experienced neighbour. Only larger towns could have generated enough births to support professional midwives – two midwives are, for example, listed in the poll tax returns for Reading in 1381 – though numbers of women may have acted on a semi-professional basis.[2]

Delivery, ideally, took place in a specially prepared room kept warm and dark. We know this best from post-medieval evidence, but it is also suggested from the chance description of births found in church court litigation. In one case from the later fourteenth century a gentlewoman, Ellen de Rouclif, gave birth in a basement room, which was implicitly not the family's regular bedchamber.[3] This attempt to mimic the womb may, however, have signified the social rank of the mother. Most mothers would have lived in houses comprising only one or two rooms and there would have been little scope to set space aside for the mother's confinement and delivery. Similarly we must be sceptical as to the degree to which mothers were formally segregated for the month after their delivery prior to their ritual reincorporation into the community by means of purification or 'churching', which involved the mother being sprinkled with holy water at the church door. That most mothers were churched, and so cleansed of the impurities of sexual intercourse and childbirth, is suggested by the large numbers of women recorded as paying fees for the ritual in surviving fifteenth-century parish accounts.[4] That we also have evidence that the day of the mother's churching might be accompanied

---

[2] C. C. Fenwick, ed., *The Poll Taxes of 1377, 1379 and 1381: Part 1*, Records of Social and Economic History, new series, XXVII (British Academy, 1998), p. 41.

[3] Borthwick Institute for Archives (hereafter BIA) (York), CP.E.89, deposition of Ellen Taliour, translated in P. J. P. Goldberg, ed., *Women in England c. 1275–1525* (Manchester, 1995), p. 78.

[4] P. Heath, *Medieval Clerical Accounts*, Borthwick Paper XXVI (1964); R. N. Swanson, ed., *Catholic England: faith, religion and observance before the Reformation* (Manchester, 1993), pp. 151–7; L. R. Poos, *A Rural Society after the Black Death: Essex 1350–1525* (Cambridge, 1991), pp. 121–7.

by family celebration, as was the case with Ellen de Rouclif, suggests, however, that the laity understood childbirth in more positive terms.

Much has been written of medieval scientific knowledge concerning obstetrics, but little is known of ordinary practice. The men who wrote the academic texts on the subject were not the women who delivered the children. Even those texts in the vernacular and supposedly addressed to women, such as *The Knowing of Womankind in Childing*, do not address the management of normal deliveries.[5] This strengthens our earlier suggestion that such knowledge was gained from experience, not from texts. Depictions of childbirth invariably show the mother lying in bed whilst other women wash the infant or fetch the mother nourishing food or 'caudle'. Sometimes a chair that looks remarkably like a delivery stool is placed next to the bed and it seems likely that such stools were indeed used for the actual delivery. The mother may have been aided in less tangible ways by the use of written prayers and charms or, not uncommonly, a girdle (fabric belt) borrowed from (and hence empowered by) an image of the Virgin in the parish church. The mother would also have invoked spiritual help during labour, notably from St Margaret, who, because she had escaped from the belly of a dragon, was regarded as the patroness of women in childbed.

Parents were anxious to see their newly born infants baptised quickly, often within forty-eight hours of delivery, lest the child, stained by original sin, be denied hope of salvation by dying unbaptised. In an emergency the baptism could be performed by the midwife and naming could follow subsequently. This shared concern with the sacrament of baptism suggests that parents were interested in and concerned for their children even as tiny babies, but that these sentiments co-existed with a pragmatic recognition of infants' vulnerability. Statistical evidence for perinatal and maternal mortality does not really exist, but the likelihood is that it was less acute than is popularly imagined. Archaeological evidence does provide harrowing examples of the skeletal remains of adult women with their babies still lodged at the pelvic opening. But because the bones of small infants do not generally survive, archaeology cannot give us an overall sense of infant mortality. Anecdotal evidence from the Rouclif case noted previously relates to the births of seventeen children. Of these, eight were still alive when aged about twelve years, four had died in the intervening years, one lived to at least eighteen months (and

[5] This text is discussed and short extracts published in A. Barrat, ed., *Women's Writing in Middle English* (1992), pp. 27–35.

may still have been alive at the time of the case), and of the remaining four nothing further is known. Of the four that had died, one is known to have lived a few months, another only a matter of days.

Early childhood may have been a hazardous time, but those scholars who have argued that parents chose not to invest emotionally in their offspring lest they die are hard pressed to find contemporary evidence to support this thesis. Babies were swaddled, normally nourished with their mothers' milk, sung lullabies, rocked in their cradles, and carried about where necessary. Primary childcare appears to have been very much within women's province. It may be that older female siblings and, in slightly better-off households, female servants assisted mothers to care for the very young, but wet nurses, who suckled the infant in place of the mother, seem not to have been employed below the ranks of the aristocracy (and perhaps more prosperous urban families). Maternal breastfeeding was probably extended well into the child's second year and so the infant was given some protection from various diseases through the mother. The practice of prolonged maternal breastfeeding would also have helped reduce the mother's fertility and so helped space births.

We have little evidence for infanticide or the abandonment of children. It may be unsurprising that an essentially secret crime should go undetected and unreported, but it is worth remarking that, unlike in the cities of northern Italy, there was no institutional provision for abandoned children, and the 1377 poll tax returns do not raise suspicions concerning the overall gender balance of the population. Had there been a marked cultural prejudice against girls and in favour of boys, we might expect to see the sort of skewed sex ratios found for early fifteenth-century Tuscan communities. The probability is that both infanticide and abandonment were comparatively rare occurrences, though a fourteenth-century pastoral manual, the *Memoriale presbiterorum*, advises confessors to ask of 'sexually experienced women' whether they have ever abandoned a child in a church or churchyard as a foundling.[6] One telling factor here is that there was perhaps not the same cultural stigma attached to mothers who gave birth outside wedlock as appears to have been true of southern Europe, where family honour demanded that daughters remained at home and guarded their virginity until they were married.

Hanawalt has made a pioneering attempt to throw light on early childhood using coroners' rolls: that is, evidence relating to homicides

---

[6] M. Haraven, 'Confession, social ethics and social discipline in the *Memoriale Presbiterorum*', in P. Biller and A. J. Minnis, eds., *Handling Sin: confession in the middle ages* (York, 1998), p. 161.

and accidental deaths.[7] This is clearly an oblique and problematic source. She has argued that these records show that male toddlers were much more likely to wander outside the house (and so fall into ditches and the like) than their sisters. This could reflect interesting gender differences whereby little girls were discouraged from leaving the house, but may only reflect the greater likelihood of the coroner being called to investigate the death of a male child than a female. Hanawalt has also argued that slightly older children were likely to imitate the tasks of their same-gender parent. Phillips has likewise noticed that mothers were more likely to find the bodies of daughters who had gone missing, whereas both parents were equally likely to find sons.[8] The implication is that parents were aware of, and children were taught, distinctive gender identities from quite an early age. These may also have been reflected in dress and in the games children played. We know that toys, such as spinning tops or lead-moulded knights, were made on a commercial basis, and hence that play was a recognised need of young children, but we know little of which children played with which toys.

Older children were probably allowed much freedom to play among themselves whether in the house, the fields or the street. Children may also have played near to where their parents were working. In the urban artisanal household the family and work groups were essentially the same, and fathers here may have played nearly as active a role in supervising children as mothers. Children probably assisted their parents initially as an extension of play. In the peasant economy, certain tasks were regularly assigned to children, notably tending livestock in the fields, scaring birds away from newly sown crops, gathering firewood, collecting nuts and berries. Mothers presumably taught their daughters to use the distaff from a young age; boys would have learnt how to use a bow and arrow.

The rudiments of the faith and the identity of some of the more important saints would have been taught to young children: mothers – as much as parochial clergy – probably played a key role here. In aristocratic, mercantile and substantial artisanal, and even some well-to-do peasant households mothers may also have instructed children in the basics of reading, though this was probably rare before the later fourteenth century. Older boys, particularly in an urban context, might go on to grammar school for instruction in Latin, and a small number of peasant

---

[7] B. A. Hanawalt, *The Ties that Bound: peasant families in medieval England* (New York, 1986), esp. pp. 156–87.

[8] K. M. Phillips, 'The Medieval Maiden: young womanhood in late medieval England', (D.Phil. thesis, University of York, 1997), p. 132.

boys would have been singled out to be trained as clergy. The most ubiquitous way in which youngsters learnt skills outside the home was, as we shall see, through the institution of 'lifecycle' service, whereby teenagers and young adults lived as part of the household and labour force of family acquaintances, distant kin and even strangers. Service and servants tended to be more a feature of urban than rural society and this is reflective of the generally more conservative nature of peasant society.

The peasant economy was characterised by a rather more marked gender division of labour than appears true of urban society. Though both sexes were involved of necessity in the grain and hay harvests, which even in the labour-abundant years of the earlier fourteenth century put real pressures on the rural labour force, some tasks were gender-specific. Ploughing and mowing, for example, were men's work, but weeding and dairying were women's work. Hanawalt has argued from her analysis of the spatial location of accidental deaths that men's work was outdoors, while women stayed within or close by the house. Our preceding observation shows that this interpretation does not hold water, but suggests another more subtle distinction. Weeding and dairying could be learnt from a comparatively early age since only some of the processes depended on the possession of a certain height and physical development. As such they could be learnt informally by girls tagging along beside their mothers. Ploughing and mowing using a scythe could only be attempted from a more advanced age since both were potentially dangerous and would require careful supervision. It follows that boys would have been taught these as teenagers and not as children and that the more conscious process of teaching would have imbued these activities with a certain kudos that we somewhat lazily label 'skill'. Girls, on the other hand, tended not to be initiated into new tasks on achieving their teens with the consequent result that women's work was seen to be inherently unskilled (or even 'natural' to women), and that women were seen always to occupy a category akin to children. The one qualification to this general pattern is that in pastoral areas some older girls would have learnt how to make butter and cheese or how to shear sheep. It is in this pastoral sector, also, that we find significant rural evidence for the employment of young women as live-in servants.[9]

---

[9] For example, using poll tax evidence, in pastoral Howdenshire (Yorks., E.R.) there were just under 100 male servants for every 100 female servants in 1379, but the equivalent proportion in arable Rutland (in 1377) was over 160 male servants to every 100 female.

The point at which children left home varied considerably, though it is unlikely that they normally left before they achieved their canonical majority (twelve for girls, fourteen for boys). Emmota Cokfeld's *famula*, noted in a matrimonial case of 1394 running an errand for her mistress, was twelve at the time.[10] Many children, however, particularly in the countryside, remained within the natal home into adulthood and may only have left, if at all, to marry. The principal factor pulling children away from the natal home prior to marriage was the demand for servants and this was always greater in towns, characterised by a multiplicity of crafts and services not found in peasant society, particularly in the century after the Black Death. The point remains, however, that from their early teens children were considered of sufficient age to leave home and to work for others. It follows that whether they remained with their natal families or otherwise, children of this age were considered old enough to be an integral part of the household labour force. Though not yet thought adult, they were no longer children.

Youngsters of both sexes can be found as servants and the later fourteenth-century poll taxes suggest that in towns the gender balance was fairly even. Many urban servants would be migrants from the surrounding countryside, but even rural servants, who tended to be predominantly males, moved about and did not necessarily work in their natal communities. Usually servants contracted for a year at a time, though half-year contracts are also found; parents probably contracted on behalf of younger servants, but older servants were free to negotiate terms for themselves. Certain days in the year were established as customary hiring dates, notably Martinmas (11 November) north of the Trent and Michaelmas (29 September) in the midlands and south, but other feast days, such as Pentecost (late spring or early summer) or the feast of St John the Baptist (29 August) are also commonly found. Alice Dalton, for example, remembered taking positions as a servant in York and neighbouring Poppleton variously at Martinmas and Pentecost when aged between fifteen and eighteen in the earlier years of the fifteenth century.[11] The exceptions to this pattern were apprentices who might contract at any time, but who normally served for a period of seven years. Most were male, but a few females were apprenticed to silkworkers, embroiderers and the like. Both servants and apprentices were primarily remunerated in terms of bed, board and clothing. Only some older servants are likely to have received anything approaching a wage paid at the

[10] BIA, CP.E.215. [11] BIA, CP.F.201.

conclusion of their term. At the end of the fourteenth century, for example, John, the servant of the Oxford brewer Thomas Chantour, was given a tunic with hood, a 'roket' [coat] and an apron, plus 10s, clearly an insufficient wage had he been expected to feed and house himself.[12]

Service provided an opportunity for youngsters to gain a variety of skills and be socialised in manners that could not readily be provided in the natal home or even in the natal community. The aristocracy seems commonly to have sent their children into service in households of the same or higher status as part of their upbringing. Anne, Elizabeth and Margery Paston, for example, members of a Norfolk gentry family, all spent time in the households of other aristocratic families. London mercantile families may have hoped to launch their children's careers in like fashion. Geoffrey Chaucer, for example, the son of a London vintner, began his career as a page in the household of the countess of Ulster.[13] Such service also provided a form of security for young people at around the age when they might lose one or both their parents, and there are examples of the children of deceased London citizens being placed as apprentices in order to provide them with quasi-parental nurture.

As youngsters gained skills, experience and strength, the temptation was to move on so as to learn more. Each time they did so they negotiated their terms of service afresh, always seeking some improvement in recognition of their growing experience. Moving on also meant servants were able to increase their contacts and, for older servants especially, the opportunities to enter into courtship and find a spouse. But although servants enjoyed a degree of independence and had a clear sense of the limits of their responsibilities to their employers and equally of their employers' obligations towards them, they remained dependants and as such quasi-adolescents.

Coming of age seems to have varied according to gender and to social rank. It should also be seen as a process, since children acquired different degrees of autonomy and different responsibilities at different ages. Children could be held criminally responsible once 'capable of trickery' – perhaps at about ten years – and in peasant society boys were entered into the tithing (a sort of self-policing organisation) at twelve. Young women, like weeds, were thought by nature to mature more quickly than their brothers. This is reflected in the earlier age of consent (canonical

[12] H. E. Salter, ed., *Medieval Archives of the University of Oxford*, Oxford Historical Society, LXXIII (1921), pp. 13–14.
[13] M. M. Crow and C. C. Olson, eds., *Chaucer Life Records* (Oxford, 1966), pp. 13–22.

majority) assigned to girls compared to boys, itself related to classical theories regarding sexual maturity. In fact girls probably achieved sexual maturity (menarche) at about fourteen or fifteen rather than at twelve years. Interestingly this coincides with feudal and customary under-standings of age of majority for women, since peasant girls and the daughters of the aristocracy alike were considered to come of age for purposes of inheritance at or about fifteen. Aristocratic men, in contrast, generally came of age at twenty-one, but for other levels of society custom was less clearly fixed. *Bracton*, written immediately prior to our period, relates legal majority to the capacity of young people to carry out the responsibilities appropriate to their level of society. Thus the son of a burgess achieves 'full age when he knows how properly to count money, measure cloths and perform other similar paternal business'. This is reflected in borough customs: at Shrewsbury a boy came of age at fifteen if he could measure cloth and tell a good penny from a bad. A woman of like status, according to *Bracton*, came of age when she knew how to order her house and do the things that belonged to its management. He adds that a girl will not have sufficient 'discretion and understanding' to manage these things before her fourteenth or fifteenth year.[14] In peasant society the position for males varied from manor to manor according to custom. On the manor of Halesowen (Worcs.), for example, it was twenty-one, but at Thornbury (Gloucs.) it was only fourteen. The urban male apprentice, on the other hand, would not normally complete his apprenticeship before twenty-one and there is plenty of evidence for young people of both sexes still in service, and hence in positions of dependency, well into their twenties. These observations have implica-tions for the ages at which young people married.

Marriage had different meanings for men and women. For males marriage represented social adulthood: in a culture in which couples set up a new home together, the man became a householder with authority over all others who came to reside within that household. For women marriage probably meant more in terms of reproduction and child-rearing. Margery Kempe's fourteen children, who are so conspicuously absent from her *Book*, were probably not atypical. Many mothers would have borne fewer, and of course the older children may have begun to leave home by the time the younger ones arrived. Nevertheless, most

---

[14] G. W. Woodbine, ed., *Bracton on the Laws and Customs of England* (4 vols., Cambridge, MA, 1968), ii, pp. 250–1. *Bracton* is here talking of girls holding property in socage, a form of free tenure found in both rural and urban contexts; M. Bateson, ed., *Borough Customs* (2 vols., Selden Society, XVIII and XXI, 1904–6), ii, pp. 158–9.

women would have passed much of their adulthood in repeated pregnancies and often with youngsters to nurse. Marriage also meant different
things at different levels of society. The majority of men probably looked
for a partner who could augment the labour needs of the household, just
as women may have looked for a man who promised a degree of economic stability. For the aristocracy, however, work was not an issue.
Rather the concern here was to make marriages that enhanced the
respective families' social position and which guaranteed the smooth
transmission of property from one generation to the next. It will
immediately be seen that here we pass from the concerns of the parties
marrying to those of their families, and this is reflected in what we know
about courtship and the making of marriage.

From the later twelfth century the Church taught that it was the
consent of the man and the woman alone that made a marriage: an
argument necessitated by the belief that the marriage of Joseph and the
Virgin was unconsummated. This was formally incorporated into the
provisions of the fourth Lateran Council of 1215, which also recognised
marriage as a sacrament of the Church. The primacy of consent appears
to have been respected without significant challenge, but in emphasising
consent the Church did not expect young people to make their own
decisions without due deference to their families. In fact autonomy was
one pole of a spectrum that at the other end encompassed a high degree
of parental persuasion. Most marriages fell somewhere within this spectrum. If parents or others exerted excessive pressure, the marriage could
be challenged because it violated the principles of consent, as happened in
1362 when Alice Belamy of Raskelf (Yorks., N.R.) claimed her great uncle
had threatened to pick her up by the ears and throw her down a well.[15]
Few young people, however, would have entered into matrimony in the
face of hostility from parents, family or their own peer group.

Other than for the aristocracy, our knowledge of the processes by
which marriages were made is largely limited to the evidence of litigation
within the church courts and hence to a tiny minority of disputed contracts. They can nevertheless provide us with clues to the nature of the
stages that went to make a marriage – for example, courtship, proposal,
publicity and solemnisation at the church door. Thus the relative frequency of cases alleging forced marriage emanating from the more
prosperous levels of peasant society and from the gentry may be indicative
of a higher degree of parental involvement and influence in the making of

---

[15] BIA, CP.E.85.

marriages (especially of daughters). Reading the evidence in this way, it would seem that parental influence in the making of marriages was strongest at all times among the more well-to-do peasantry and weakest among townsfolk in the century following the Black Death. Here the high demand for servants was sufficient to give young people an unusual degree of freedom to engage in courtship and ultimately select marriage partners without constant parental supervision. For example, when Richard Carter and Joan atte Enges, servants in neighbouring York households, exchanged vows in about 1370, their employers, but not members of their families, were present. This was much less likely to have been the case before the plague and again by the second half of the fifteenth century. Thus when in 1470 Elizabeth Isaak of London agreed to marry John Bolde, she did so on condition that her brother consent, her father being dead; and Bolde on another occasion asked her mother for her good will.[16]

The likelihood is that well-to-do peasants shared the concerns of their social superiors and looked to make marriages for their children that enhanced the family's standing and contacts within the community. They may also have adopted a conservative attitude towards their daughters' 'honour', regularly understood in sexual terms, and so been more chary of allowing their daughters to engage in courtship. The proliferation of maidens' guilds, and even young men's guilds, during the later fifteenth century in rural parishes may represent one attempt to socialise the children of the more well-to-do in this conservative morality. We may also illustrate these values tangentially by reference to cases where a young woman's brothers forced a wavering male suitor to contract marriage, and also by the case of Isabella Alan living in the Yorkshire Wolds in the mid fifteenth century who was allegedly paid 20 marks compensation by the man who had seduced her.[17] This concern with honour accords with a number of other observations, notably the relative paucity of females found in service in the countryside (but the high proportion of adolescent and young adult women living at home) even at the time of the poll taxes. The daughters of the well-to-do are likewise much less likely to be presented within the manor court for fornication (and hence liable for the leyrwite fine) than their poorer sisters. Peasant women also probably married at an earlier age than their urban counterparts. Razi suggests that

---

[16] BIA, CP.E.155, translated in Goldberg, *Women in England*, p. 137; S. McSheffrey, *Love and Marriage in late Medieval London* (Kalamazoo, MI, 1995), pp. 53–4.

[17] BIA, CP.F.189.

on the large West Midlands manor of Halesowen in the century or more from the 1270s, villein women who paid the marriage fine (merchet) appear to have done so when aged about eighteen.[18] Razi's evidence relates primarily to more well-to-do families, but that is our interest here. Women who live at home, who are protected from associating freely with the opposite sex and who marry when they are still in their teens (albeit late teens) are not going to be making their own marriage decisions. For these women, consent meant going along with their parents' plans.

This pattern of parental initiative was at least as true of the aristocracy. At this level of society it was customary for the bride's father to pay a dowry to the groom – at other levels of society some kind of matching of gifts on the part of both families to help set up the young couple in their new home appears more normal. Fathers consequently had an immediate financial stake in their daughters' marriages. Aristocratic society likewise laid considerable weight on the 'honour' of their womenfolk and, although they might go into service in other aristocratic households, daughters were socialised from an early age to shun all intimate contact with the opposite sex and guard their virginity from the continuous snares and allurements of the male. This is the world of *The Book of the Knight of the Tower*, a later fourteenth-century French conduct book addressed to aristocratic girls which is known to have been popular in England and was printed by Caxton. Conversely, aristocratic males, especially younger sons, were allowed some freedom to seek out prospective marriage partners, though no marriage was possible without the good will of the woman's family. There is much evidence from the various fifteenth-century gentry and mercantile letter collections of brothers exchanging information on possible spouses. Thus Richard Cely wrote in 1481 to the younger George Cely of John Dalton's sister that 'she is as goodly a young woman, as fair, as well-bodied and as serious as any I have seen these seven years, and a good height'.[19] Oldest sons, to whom the family title and property would descend, probably enjoyed much less autonomy.

The balance between the influence of parents and kin and the autonomy allowed to young people themselves in the making of marriages is reflected in the ages at which couples married. Unfortunately clear statistical evidence for age at marriage is either lacking or problematic. It is easy to produce anecdotal examples of aristocratic child marriages – the need to spell out provision for brides marrying as children

---

[18] Z. Razi, *Life, Marriage and Death in a Medieval Parish* (Cambridge, 1980), pp. 60–4.
[19] A. Hanham, ed., *The Cely Letters 1472–1488* (EETS, os CCLXXIII, 1975), p. 106.

in marriage contracts accentuates this picture – but the likelihood is that such marriages were the exception in our period. Hollingsworth's evidence for the marriage of the daughters of dukes in the period 1330–1479 suggests that though some third had already married by their sixteenth birthday, another third only married at some point in their early twenties (and even then not all had married). Sons of dukes married at varying ages from about fifteen, although only half had married by twenty-five years. Fleming found that a sample of males who subsequently served as members of parliament married at a mean age of just under twenty-two years.[20] Here it is tempting to suggest some correlation between legal majority, the inheritance of property and matrimony.

Outside the ranks of the aristocracy, child marriage was rarer still, though we do find the odd case from the church courts relating to the upper ranks of peasant society. In a marriage case from the first decades of the fourteenth century, Alice Crane of Cropwell Butler (Notts.) was only fourteen when she contracted William Crane, but he was himself allegedly even younger.[21] Razi's analysis of the Halesowen court rolls suggests peasant men normally married at about twenty to brides of a similar or slightly younger age, but his data are probably only reliable for better-off peasant families and, in relation to the marriage of males, the heir. Younger peasant sons may have married a little later. The same may be generally true of poorer peasant families. Poos's analysis of the Essex poll tax returns for 1381 would support this: he found that a significantly higher proportion of husbandmen (the more substantial peasants) were married than was true of labourers (poor peasants).[22] This is also apparent from the rather better 1379 Howdenshire (Yorks., E.R.) returns. This would translate into later marriage for the families of labourers and even a significant proportion of labourers opting out of marriage, having neither the means to support children nor the land that would benefit from the labour of those children. It should be noted that in Howdenshire these single labourers were as likely to be women as men.

For urban society we effectively have no evidence before the later fourteenth century, but an analysis of age and marital status from the deposition evidence cited earlier would suggest males marrying at some point in their mid twenties women only a couple of years younger, a

[20] T. H. Hollingsworth, 'A demographic study of the British ducal families', *Population Studies*, 11 (1957), 13–14; P. Fleming, *Family and Household in Medieval England* (Basingstoke, 2001), p. 22.

[21] BIA, CP.E.23; R. H. Helmholz, *Marriage Litigation in Medieval England* (Cambridge, 1974), pp. 201–4.

[22] Razi, *Life, Marriage and Death*, pp. 63, 136; Poos, *A Rural Society*, pp. 155–7.

pattern that falls clearly within what demographic historians call a north-west European pattern, but which differs somewhat from the earlier pattern of marriage associated with (at least better-off) peasants. The Essex and Howdenshire poll tax evidence again reinforces this view. Age at marriage, particularly for women, may have fallen slightly, though still within the parameters of a north-western model, by the later fifteenth century since we have more evidence of familial involvement in marriages by this date. The implication is that a north-west European marriage regime emerged during the course of the English later middle ages and that it may have developed most precociously in towns and cities. Interestingly we begin to find some London authors at the end of the fourteenth and beginning of the fifteenth century actively advocating love as a motivation for marriage. Thus Hoccleve wrote of his wife in an autobiographical passage in his *Regiment of Princes* that 'I chose her as my mate for love alone'. He goes on to suggest – a comment on the frequency of separation – that those who marry for love stick together.[23] This same precocious development may also be true of the developing economy of East Anglia. Smith has, for example, hypothesised that the Spalding serf lists (genealogical listings of the priory's servile tenants) are compatible with such a marriage regime as early as the 1260s.[24]

Whereas the making of marriages is comparatively well documented, the nature of married life is much less so. Again we have more evidence for mercantile and gentry families from the fifteenth-century letter collections. Marriage meant the beginning of a sexual, and hence reproductive, relationship, though couples may often have begun this relationship prior to any actual solemnisation. Only at the end of our period does it appear that the upper echelons of peasant and urban society started to disapprove of sex before solemnisation and this itself may indicate that, for this level of society at least, the ceremony at the church door had come to be identified as symbolic of marriage rather than merely the final, and to some extent optional, stage in a longer process. Medieval men and women had some knowledge of contraceptive techniques. Biller, for example, has argued for the possibility of a widespread awareness of coitus interruptus (withdrawal), and the author of the *Memoriale presbiterorum* writes of the use of potions and herbs to impede

---

[23] F. J. Furnivall, ed., *Hoccleve's Works*, III: *The Regement of Princes* (EETS, es LXXII, 1897), pp. 57 (l. 1561), 59 (ll. 1625–8).

[24] R. M. Smith, 'Hypothèses sur la nuptialité en Angleterre aux XIIIe et XIVe siècles', *Annales: ESC*, 38 (1983), 120–4.

conception or induce abortion.[25] Nevertheless, it is likely that age at marriage and the practice of extended maternal breastfeeding were the most significant influences on how many children couples had. The clergy had much to say on the inappropriateness of sex at certain times – such as on Sundays, feast days or during Lent – in any position other than the missionary, and on the sinfulness of contraceptive practices. Some of this teaching may have been disseminated through preaching and the hearing of confession, but we cannot know how far the laity responded. What is apparent is that certain groups in lay society by the end of our period were beginning to articulate an increasingly conservative sexual morality and to demand the same of the clergy. This is reflected in accusations levelled by churchwardens at parochial visitations against neighbours who failed to keep their marriage vows and priests who were incontinent. Not all couples were faithful, and some married men used the services of prostitutes or fathered illegitimate children. The York merchant, John Goddysbruk, for example, asked in his will of 1407 that 20s be given 'to Emmot with whom I had a daughter ... and that it be sent to her secretly'.[26] A minority of couples – perhaps one in ten – would, however, have been unable to conceive and so remained childless. Since, culturally and theologically, becoming a mother and rearing children was so important to a woman's identity, such childlessness must often have been a cause of distress, hinted at in the sad case of the couple who were reported at the parish visitation for idolatry because they slept with an empty cradle by their bed 'as if there were an infant in it'.[27] Pregnancy and repeated childbirth would, nevertheless, have been the lot of most wives and the support of numbers of children the responsibility of most couples.

Clerical commentators and sermonisers regularly reiterated the authority of husbands over wives and the need for wives to be dutiful. The biblical understanding of husband and wife as one body, but with the husband at the head, is mirrored in legal notions. A husband was normally responsible for his wife's debts, and a wife was exempt from responsibility for criminal actions if acting on her husband's commandment. Conversely, the murder of a husband by his wife was considered 'petty treason'. Husbands were expected to exercise authority over their wives as over their children and servants and could lawfully chastise a disobedient wife. In a

---

[25] P. P. A. Biller, 'Birth-control in the West in the thirteenth and early fourteenth centuries', *P&P*, 94 (1982), 16–23; Haraven, 'Confession, social ethics and social discipline', p. 161.
[26] Goldberg, *Women in England*, p. 144.   [27] *Ibid.*, p. 135.

society that freely used violence as a means of resolving disputes, a certain level of 'domestic' violence should be no surprise, but neighbours expected certain limits and would not necessarily tolerate abusive husbands. Limited redress for abused wives was also provided by the church courts, which in extreme cases might sanction the separation of the couple subject to the payment of maintenance on the part of the husband. The normal experience, however, rarely impinges on the record. Most wives probably deferred to their husbands in public, but may have been less submissive privately. We have, moreover, plenty of evidence, from urban society especially, of women acting independently of their husbands, particularly in respect of economic activity.

The partnership between husband and wife was central to the household as an economic unit. In peasant society work activities, as we have already observed, tended to be more gender-specific, but husbands and wives would work together as a team cutting and binding during harvest. At other times husbands would plough, sow, ditch and hedge, whilst wives minded poultry, prepared flax, brewed ale or took goods to market. Poorer peasant couples were probably dependent on both parties selling their labour, though women may also have brought in additional income through spinning, keeping poultry or petty retailing. In urban society, wives were an integral part of the artisanal workshop. When in 1390–1, for example, the York founders' guild moved to limit masters to a single apprentice at a time, special exemption was allowed to Giles de Benoyne 'because he has no wife'.[28] But in addition to assisting in the workshop and to serving customers from behind the counter, wives also contributed through a variety of other activities such as spinning, brewing, making candles (as in the case of butchers' wives) or even on occasion running their own business (as must have been true of the London silkwomen, who were often married). Again, we know less about labouring couples, whose lives probably mirrored those of their rural counterparts.

The mutual dependence of most husbands and wives, the shared burden of responsibility for young children, the fact that husbandmen (peasants with sufficient land to support themselves) and artisans would have spent much of their days in their wives' company, must have required couples to get on. Aristocratic and labouring couples may have spent less time together, but gentry correspondence suggests at least a high degree of mutual respect between husbands and wives, occasionally hints of real affection. The problem is that few conventional sources allow

[28] *Ibid.*, p. 203.

much scope for the expression of feeling. We need to be careful not to see these silences as evidence of a lack of affective bond between spouses; nor should our own rather different cultural prejudices lead us to conclude that later medieval marriages were essentially loveless because the majority were not initiated solely by the young people making them.

Medieval marriages could not be terminated by divorce, a concept not recognised within canon law. Marriages could be annulled – declared never to have been valid – because bigamous, made without consent or between persons too closely related to one another; but this was rare. It does not follow, however, that couples always co-habited and remained faithful to one another. There are various scattered hints that couples sometimes separated by mutual consent – by the end of our period such couples were sometimes reported by the churchwardens at parish visitations – and it is apparent from disputed marriage cases that couples might even enter new relationships though strictly already married. The author of the *Memoriale presbiterorum* comments admonishingly that 'many women despise their husbands and withdraw from them, dwelling apart'.[29] How often such arrangements occurred is not known, but it was probably more common at the lower echelons of society than elsewhere.

Most marriages, however, were terminated not by human agency but by the death of a spouse. Remarriage seems to have been acceptable for both men and women, and a few prosperous individuals married more than twice. An analysis of York wills over the later fourteenth and fifteenth centuries suggests that widowers were much more likely to remarry than widows: between one in three and one in two widowers remarried as against only one in six or seven widows. How representative these trends are is hard to tell, though widow remarriage was probably more common before the plague. In the land-hungry years of the later thirteenth and early fourteenth centuries, peasant widows holding land were especially sought after in marriage. In some instances lords obliged widows to remarry in order to secure the considerable merchet (marriage) fine that landless males were prepared to offer. At other times, widows may have preferred not to remarry unless they had young children to support. A few wealthier widows, notably from the ranks of the gentry, took vows of chastity. In some instances, Cullum has argued, this was to protect them against familial pressures to remarry.[30]

---

[29] Haraven, 'Confession, social ethics and social discipline', pp. 157, 159.
[30] P. H. Cullum, 'Vowesses and female lay piety in the province of York, 1300–1530', *Northern History*, 32 (1996), 35–6.

Too often scholars have explored widow remarriage from a male perspective: widows will remarry if still young and attractive or have property to their name. In fact we need also to consider the woman's perspective. Whereas men would regularly seek to find a new partner to care for them in their declining years, women were more capable of looking after themselves and many were in an economic position to do so. In urban society, at least before the late fifteenth century, widows of artisans seem regularly to have taken over workshops and to have continued to trade with the assistance of apprentices or other servants. Thus in 1458 Emmot Pannal, a York saddler's widow, left all the tools of her workshop to her servant Richard Thorpp.[31] In rural (and aristocratic) society jointure, whereby title to a holding was in the name of husband and wife, increasingly displaced customary arrangements for dower. The consequence was that widows enjoyed control over the entire holding, where previously they had merely a life interest in a third or half the holding.

Peasant couples and widows alike were able to use their possession of land as a means of purchasing security in old age. In the decades before the Black Death manor court rolls often record maintenance agreements whereby older peasants effectively passed their holdings to a younger generation in return for accommodation and regular provision of food. Such arrangements were made both with kin and non-kin, even at the cost of disinheriting the tenant's own children. The more well-to-do might purchase corrodies, a sort of annuity or retirement plan, from a religious house. For a lump payment in advance of need, support in old age was purchased at levels that varied from simple provision of food to sheltered accommodation. From the later fourteenth century we also see a proliferation, especially, but not exclusively, in towns, of small hospitals or almshouses (sometimes also known as *maisonsdieu* or God's houses). Their particular concern was with the 'respectable' poor: those too old, feeble or handicapped to support themselves.

For the poor in general, funerary and anniversary doles, casual almsgiving and the outdoor relief provided by some hospitals, religious houses and guilds provided a safety net. In rural society peasant holdings were sometimes given to support the poor and needy and so supplement (perhaps significantly) the alms supposed to be provided out of the parochial living. The lack of this provision could become a particular bone of contention where churches had been appropriated and the parish revenue thus diverted to a religious house. At all times, however, both in

---

[31] Goldberg, *Women in England*, p. 197.

town and country, the lot of the very poor was probably very hard, in spite of the tendency in the post-plague world for moralists to equate begging with wilful idleness.

Before the registration of baptisms and burials it is often hard to gauge average expectation of life. We have comparatively good evidence for the greater aristocracy and for numbers of monks, evidence that is thus skewed towards the better off, adults and males. The same is true of Razi's data in respect of manorial tenants. Some attempts have been made to use cemetery evidence but these are often hampered by the problem of linking skeletal remains (aged not in years, but relative maturity) from a cemetery used over several centuries to a specific period. Lastly there is the evidence of the ages of witnesses or deponents attesting to proofs of age (where witnesses testified that a feudal heir was of age to inherit) or giving testimony within the church courts. Here we can find numerous old men (even the odd alleged centenarian), but no clear sense of how representative this evidence is of the general population structure.

For the manor of Halesowen between 1270 and 1400, Razi found that male tenants who survived to adulthood might on average live to fifty or thereabouts. This compares quite favourably with Russell's evidence for tenants-in-chief, an exclusively aristocratic population, though here the mean life expectation dips to nearer forty for the cohorts born either side of the Black Death, whereas Razi's sample actually shows a slight improvement in the half-century following the plague. It also compares with evidence for the monks, themselves often of peasant stock, of Christchurch (Canterbury) and Westminster around the middle of the fifteenth century.[32] The monks' expectation of life declined, however, later in the century (and at Westminster continued to decline until the end of the century). The congruence of these different pieces of evidence is encouraging, but only the monastic evidence is good enough to show up clearly real shifts over time.

What the monastic evidence also shows is that by the fifteenth century tuberculosis had become a major killer alongside the plague introduced by the first pandemic of 1348–9 and thereafter endemic. Conventionally this last disease has been understood by historians to be bubonic plague, although this view is periodically challenged.[33] The evidence we have for

---

[32] Razi, *Life, Marriage and Death*, p. 130; J. C. Russell, *British Medieval Population* (Albuquerque, 1948), table 8.1, p. 176; J. Hatcher, 'Mortality in the fifteenth century: some new evidence', *EcHR*, 2nd ser., 39 (1986), 19–38; B. F. Harvey, *Living and Dying in England, 1100–1540: the monastic experience* (Oxford, 1993), pp. 127–9.

[33] Most recently by S. K. Cohn, *The Black Death Transformed* (2002).

disease before the advent of plague is even sketchier. Skeletal evidence tells of the prevalence of such chronic conditions as arthritis or deformities caused by failure properly to set fractures, but rarely of life-threatening diseases. Leprosy, which can show up, was endemic at the beginning of the period, as witnessed by the ubiquity of leper hospitals founded during the central middle ages, but seems to have been in decline before the plague. The hungry years of the late thirteenth century and more particularly the first two decades of the fourteenth century probably saw a high incidence of malnutrition-related disease, including typhus, which no doubt translated into diminished life expectancy for poorer members of society. Child mortality was probably particularly high in those periods and again in the post-plague era. The major respiratory diseases, including pneumonia, were probably significant killers at all times, especially for the elderly. The absence of evidence relating to the morbidity of women is frustrating. There is slight evidence, however, that they were less vulnerable to plague, and that the hazards of childbearing, though real, have probably been overstated.

People in the middle ages were encouraged to think of death as an ever-present possibility. The clergy repeatedly reminded their flocks of the transitory nature of earthly existence. By the end of the middle ages some were even learning how to conduct themselves in their final hour through books on the 'art of dying' (*ars moriendi*). Images of the three living and the three dead warned of the vanity of worldly wealth and the inevitability of death. The late medieval fashion among the wealthy devout for tombs with representations of the decaying cadaver, like that commissioned by John Baret in St Mary's church, Bury St Edmunds, pushed home the same message. They also solicited the help of the living. The doctrine of purgatory, the belief (discussed by Eamon Duffy above) that souls stained by sin could still ultimately be saved once purged of that sin, created a new need for people to be remembered – and be prayed for – long after their deaths. Those with sufficient wealth could purchase the remembrance of strangers by their elaborate sepulchral monuments or the endowment of perpetual chantries. Alternative forms of commemoration included the gifting of vestments or furnishings within the parish church marked with the donor's arms or labelled with texts asking for the prayers of the living. The less prosperous could hope to be remembered by their parish guild, a form of collectivity that became especially popular after the plague. The very poor, however, were reliant on the memory of family and friends.

Such a brief analysis of so broad a theme can do scant justice to the diversity of experience over a comparatively long and highly eventful period. Whereas medieval theories of the ages of man obscure gender differences, modern scholars have tended to emphasise gender and marital status at the expense of thinking about social status, age or dynamic change. Thus some writers talk of the ways in which wives and daughters were subordinated within a patriarchal society, but widows, freed from the bonds of matrimony, were 'liberated'. We should be sensitive to the hierarchical nature of medieval society, of which gender hierarchy was but one dimension. Children and adolescents were supposed to be respectful to their elders, obedient to their parents or employers, and firmly (but not harshly) disciplined if they were not. During their teens, however, young people of both sexes took on more obligations and responsibilities as part of their socialisation into what was necessary to run a household. This process culminated in matrimony, associated in English culture with setting up a new household. Legally wives remained quasi-dependants, but in fact a more egalitarian relationship may have been common, especially in urban society; peasant society seems to have been much more conservative in respect of gender ideology. Another striking feature of English culture, at least below the level of the aristocracy, is provided by the comparatively weak ties between parents and children beyond the period of socialisation. Indeed, children were socialised to be able to support themselves and make their own way in the world. Children do not seem to have felt a strong obligation to provide for their parents in old age. Rather their parents made, so far as they were able, their own arrangements, even to the extent, on occasion, of disinheriting their children.

CHAPTER 17

The wider world

Robin Frame

The answer to the question of where the 'wider world' begins is always subjective. People inhabit a variety of overlapping worlds, contoured by status and role as much as by geography. The horizons of a well-travelled English aristocrat, conscious of belonging to an international chivalric culture, of an educated cleric whose physical and mental habitat was western Christendom, or of a London merchant with contacts from Genoa to Reykjavik, were very different from those of lesser people. Yet it would be misleading to imagine that the awareness of any inhabitant of England stopped at the county or parish boundary. As the tens of thousands of mariners and military recruits show, wealth was not a necessary precondition of wider experience, and even the untravelled could absorb perceptions and prejudices. It was within this context that a sense of 'Englishness' was formulated.

England was, it is true, an agglomeration of overlapping 'countries': counties and broader regions. Contemporary comments convey images of particular areas and their inhabitants. A thirteenth-century satire, 'A Description of the Norfolk people', mocked the supposed naivety and crudity of its subjects, provoking a Norfolk man, John of St Omer, to respond with 'A Refutation of the Description of Norfolk'.[1] In the mid-fourteenth century, John de Grandisson, the bishop of Exeter, reaching for a handy cliché, portrayed Cornwall and Devon as at 'the end of the world'.[2] Writers frequently commented on the supposed barren wildness of the north. Geoffrey of Monmouth, whose fantastical *History of the Kings of Britain* was composed in the 1130s, set the tone by describing Britain north of the Humber as 'a land frightful to live in, more or less

---

[1] T. Turville-Petre, *England the Nation: language, literature and national identity, 1290–1340* (Oxford, 1996), pp. 142–3.
[2] F. C. Hingeston-Randolph, ed., *Register of John de Grandisson, Bishop of Exeter (A.D. 1327–1369),* (3 vols., 1894–99), i, pp. 97–8. I owe this reference to Professor R. A. Griffiths.

uninhabited'.[3] Nor were such views confined to inveterate southerners. They were shared by Ranulf Higden (d.1363), a Benedictine of Chester who compiled a widely read *Universal Chronicle*. Higden's comments are a warning that perceptions were as complicated at this period as at any other.

Any attempt to pinpoint the division between 'north' and 'south' soon exposes complex regional interlockings, and also the slipperiness of terminology. The crown used the Trent, the boundary between the ecclesiastical provinces of Canterbury and York, as a convenient line of administrative division. But, while rivers might mark organisational boundaries, they were centres of social and economic regions. The Tees, far from marking the southern limits of a distinctive 'north-east', was at the heart of a single world, embracing south Durham and north Yorkshire. Students at Oxford were divided into 'northerners' and 'southerners', but the 'northerners' included Scots, Welsh and Irish. The prominence of northern barons and knights in the opposition to King John led chroniclers to apply the label 'northerners' to the opposition movement as a whole. At the other end of the period, Richard III's affinity could be characterised as 'the northern men' by hostile southerners. But there was no impermeable north–south political division. The Percys, as well as lording it at Alnwick and in Yorkshire, held estates in Sussex. It was the same in the west, where the greater Welsh marcher lordships had always been held by English aristocrats.

The close integration of the outer parts of the kingdom confirms that England, while containing *pays* and regions, cannot be represented as divided into them. As Simon Walker discusses above, royal government penetrated the entire land. A common law of England was applied throughout the country, and law was perhaps the most significant marker of identity in the medieval world.[4] Taxation and military service drew men together, in complaint and comradeship. The 'countries' of particular lords formed zones of influence, but they were constantly reshaped by accidents of inheritance and politics, and were firmly caught within the patronage field of the crown. The boundaries of the kingdom were also fairly clear. The sea answered most questions. Before the outbreak of the Anglo-Scottish wars in 1296, the border with Scotland was certainly porous, with aristocrats holding lands in both kingdoms, and market

---

[3] Geoffrey of Monmouth, *History of the Kings of Britain*, trans. L. Thorpe (Harmondsworth, 1966), p. 189.
[4] See pp. 92–5.

towns such as Selkirk or Morpeth, as well as the regional centres of Newcastle upon Tyne, Carlisle and Berwick-upon-Tweed (the richest borough of the Scottish crown), attracting people from both kingdoms. But the political frontier, agreed in 1237, was well understood. There remained a small 'debateable land' in the Eden Valley to the north of Carlisle, just as there were local disputes over where the competence of the sheriffs of Shropshire or Herefordshire ended and those of neighbouring marcher lords began. But such uncertainties are notable mainly for their triviality. There was, however, a significant complication, to which we shall return at the end of the chapter: not all those who regarded themselves as English lived within the kingdom itself.

An image of England in relation to its neighbours and in the world at large, which was familiar not just to the highly educated, is presented in *mappae mundi* (world maps).[5] These were based on outlines which went back to classical times. Many were produced in England. Henry III had world maps painted on the walls of his palaces at Westminster and Winchester, and the St Albans chronicler Matthew Paris (d. *c.* 1259), himself a cartographer, was aware of another at Waltham Abbey. The most famous survivor is the elaborate map dating from the reign of Edward I, now in the cathedral library at Hereford. The Hereford *Mappa Mundi* has the characteristic features of such maps. The world is shown as a disc. East is placed at the top, where Christ presides in majesty over creation; here too is paradise, shown as an island. Jerusalem lies at the centre of the earth, as befits the focal point of the Christian faith. The three known continents are shown. Asia occupies the upper half of the map; the Mediterranean divides the lower half into two quarters, with Europe on the left and Africa on the right. Around the perimeter lie the islands, with those of the Atlantic, including Britain and Ireland, at the bottom left, opposite Sri Lanka, which was well known by 1300 as a source of spices. In the remoter parts of Asia and Africa appear a selection of the strange beings that were believed, on the evidence of classical and early medieval writers, to inhabit the margins of the known world.

The same cosmographical scheme permeates the *Travels of Sir John Mandeville*. It was once believed that Mandeville was, as the preface claims, an English knight, and that his book was stimulated by journeys he made in the second quarter of the fourteenth century. However, the

---

[5] The maps referred to in the succeeding paragraphs are conveniently reproduced in P. D. A. Harvey, *Mappa Mundi. The Hereford World Map* (1996).

author's name, like the content of the book, is almost certainly fictional. *Mandeville* is based on familiar classical and medieval texts, among them the vast *Speculum Mundi* of Vincent of Beauvais (d.1264), though it does show some awareness of recent writings by western visitors to India and China. *Mandeville* may have been written in northern France or the Netherlands, but it was widely circulated in England. The first part deals with the Near East and the Holy Land, whose topography was familiar from classical works, the bible and pilgrim literature. The second part takes the reader to India and China ('Cathay'), Ethiopia and Turkey. The author then proceeds further into the world of the imagination, with Gog and Magog and the ten Jewish tribes believed to have been penned up by Alexander the Great beyond the Carpathian Mountains, the idealised kingdom of Prester John, and the 'Valley Perilous'. Here the normal rules of nature ceased to apply. The traveller encounters giants, troglodytes, cyclopses, headless races with eyes beneath their shoulders, and *sciapods* – 'whose foot is so large that it shadeth all the body against the sun when they wish to lie and rest themselves'.[6] Mandeville, nevertheless, made it clear to his readers that the earth was spherical and circumnavigable, a view propounded by Bede (d.735) and more recently by the English polymath, Roger Bacon (d.1266): 'the land and sea are of a round shape and form, for the part of the heavens that is visible in one country is not visible in another country . . . and if a man took passages by ships that would go to explore the world, men could go by ship all about the earth, both above and beneath'.[7]

The primary purpose of the world maps was spiritual and didactic; they delineated the divinely ordered cosmos. Nevertheless, however crudely, they provided an image of England's relationship to her immediate neighbours. The Hereford map has an elongated outline of England (labelled 'Britannia') and Wales, the latter almost separated from the former by rivers. Scotland is broader than England, and is shown as a separate island. Ireland lies to the west, parallel to England and Wales; it is even more elongated, extending south beyond Cornwall. Despite the errors and the lack of proportion and perspective, the map shows some awareness of contemporary realities. It shows Edward I's recently built Welsh castle-boroughs of Conway and Carnarvon, together with his city of Dublin. The Isle of Wight is shown midway between the English south coast and Aquitaine, which lie closer to each other than England does to

---

[6] P. Hamelius, ed., *Mandeville's Travels, from MS Cotton Titus C. XVI in the British Museum* (2 vols., EETS, os CLIII–IV, 1919–23), i, p. 104.
[7] *Ibid.*, pp. 119–20.

Ireland: but this may reflect contemporary perceptions of the relationship between the English crown and its duchy in south-west France.

In the minds of its inhabitants England was clearly positioned historically as well as geographically. The antiquity and coherence of the kingdom made the English identity less problematical than that of many other peoples. At times of political turbulence, and in border regions in times of war, Englishmen could face awkward choices. But they were spared the continuing dilemmas over loyalty and identity that afflicted people in Aquitaine, or those who had to combine the roles of 'bons Bretons' and 'bons Francoys'.[8] Even so, the English identity was not without its historical ambiguities, paradoxes and tensions. Contemporaries knew that the inhabitants of England were of varied origin. A shared past had to be manufactured – consciously or not – out of awkward materials.

Already by 1200 the descendants of the Norman settlers had accommodated themselves within the history of England, a process eased by the eagerness of the Norman kings to present themselves as the legitimate inheritors of an ancient kingly tradition. Chroniclers such as William of Malmesbury and Henry of Huntingdon, writing in the time of Henry I, seamlessly continued the story of English kings and people under God first set forth by Bede. Differences of opinion exist about the speed and thoroughness of this Norman appropriation of the English past. But it was well advanced by the time of the conquests and settlements in Ireland, which began in 1169–70. Those who participated in these ventures were normally described as 'English', both by themselves and by the Irish. Their Englishness was formed within the context of twelfth-century European cultural developments: one mark of a cultivated Englishman was knowledge of French, which was already by 1200 becoming a 'learned language' in England. The point is neatly made by a verse-chronicle celebrating the achievements of the conquerors in Ireland. The work is in French; its heroes are throughout described as *li engleis*.[9]

A second piece of inventiveness rebranded Arthur, and the 'British' history he symbolised, as 'English'. It is impossible to over-estimate the influence and popularity of Geoffrey of Monmouth's *History*. Geoffrey had told the story of the struggle of the Britons against the Anglo-Saxon invaders. The obvious resonances of his work for the Welsh, who looked

[8] M. Jones, '"Bons Bretons et Bons Francoys": the language and meaning of treason in later medieval France', *TRHS* 5th ser., 32 (1982), 91–112.
[9] G. H. Orpen, ed., *Song of Dermot and the Earl* (Oxford, 1892). The range of languages available to the English is discussed by Strohm, below, chapter 18.

forward to an apocalyptic revenge on the English, did not stop its appropriation in England itself, where the distinction between Britons and English was brazenly elided. Edward I and Edward III were Arthurian enthusiasts, for whom 'The Matter of Britain' provided a counterpoise to the Charlemagne legend which was used as an endorsement by the French monarchy. Arthur was adaptable to most situations. As well as ruling all Britain, according to Geoffrey his authority had extended over Ireland and into France as well. The power of these ideas is visible in the chronicle of Peter Langtoft, canon of Bridlington. Writing in French, at a time when Edward I appeared to have subdued the Scots as well as the Welsh, Langtoft portrayed him as out-doing Arthur:

> Now are the islanders all brought together
> and Albania is rejoined to its regalities
> of which King Edward is proclaimed lord.
> Cornwall and Wales are in his power
> and Ireland the great is at his will.
> There is no longer any king of all the countries
> except King Edward who has united them.
> Arthur had never so fully the allegiances.[10]

Like Edward's, Langtoft's horizons were not bounded by the British Isles. He presents the revived Arthurian overlordship of the islands as a preliminary to a reconquest of the Plantagenet lands in France, after which Edward would take the cross to the Holy Land.

The twin themes – of a Christian English people with a continuous history, who were the true inheritors of the Arthurian tradition into the bargain – were widely diffused in the later middle ages. Some scholars had reservations about Geoffrey's wilder imaginative flights; but the mutually contradictory nature of the narratives does not appear to have been a problem. They lay behind the two most influential historical works of the fourteenth century: Higden's *Polychronicon*, translated from Latin into English by John Trevisa around 1387, and the Brut chronicles, which exist in French and English versions. Some fifty manuscripts of the French Brut survive, and double that number of the English Brut. Both works were printed by Caxton in the 1480s. These narratives seeped into the national consciousness; they were familiar far beyond the circles where books were handled and read.

---

[10] P. Coss, ed., *Thomas Wright's Political Songs of England, from the Reign of John to that of Edward II* (Cambridge, 1996), p. 308.

English history was not, however, a smooth, consensual construct. There was also a history of friction: the story of the English at odds with their rulers, who might still be presented as foreign. This interpretation is present in two of the earliest histories composed in English, the verse chronicle of Robert of Gloucester, written in the West Country in the time of Edward I, and the chronicle attributed to Robert Mannyng of Bourne in Lincolnshire, who completed a translation and continuation of Langtoft around 1338. Both fail to fold the Normans comfortably into the national story. Instead, picking up a line of interpretation pursued by the Anglo-Saxon chronicle until it petered out around 1150, they present them as interlopers, ancestors of an oppressive government and aristocracy, which burdens 'the Englyssh' with taxes and feudal dues.[11] These ideas, which find echoes in fourteenth-century poems protesting against royal exactions and abuses, were not peculiar to those who wrote in English. Langtoft himself was disillusioned by Edward I's later years. Higden deplores the adulteration of the English language by Norman-French influences. And the notion that the national stock was weakened through the foreign blood of the aristocracy was a commonplace found in the Brut and elsewhere. Such paradoxes cannot be resolved by imagining that the two interpretations played to different audiences. The same gentry, clergy and freemen who warmed to stories of national solidarity and a heroic past under heroic leaders were receptive to denunciations of a distant and exploitative political class. The political elites, depending on circumstances and context, could be viewed either as patriotic English leaders of an English people, or as outsiders, against whom 'the English' sharpened an identity of a more resentful sort.

The 'alien' motif appeared early in the domestic political context. Matthew Paris condemned Henry III for the favour shown to foreigners at the expense of native-born barons. He targeted the Savoyard relatives of Queen Eleanor of Provence who came to England after Henry's marriage in 1236, and the Poitevins, led by Henry's half-brothers, who made careers in England from the following decade. The political analysis is simplistic. In 1258 the Savoyards were mostly aligned with the English barons in opposition to the Poitevin group; and, of course, Simon de Montfort, the champion of the cause of the 'native-born', was himself a Frenchman. But these illogicalities do not detract from the underlying assumption that the kingdom belonged rightfully to those who were born

---

[11] Turville-Petre, *England the Nation*, pp. 91–103. For further discussion of Robert of Gloucester and Robert Mannyng see pp. 457–9 below.

within it. This view even led Matthew to praise the hated Welsh when it suited his rhetorical purpose: he presents them as leaguing together to defend 'the liberty of their country and the laws of their ancestors', in stark contrast to the craven English, who bent their necks to a foreign yoke.[12] Similar views are expressed in the *Song of Lewes*, a poem written by a supporter of the baronial opposition, which condemns those who 'had studied to erase the name of the English', praises the de Montforts for 'condoling the lamentable lot of the English', and urges the king to favour the native-born and cease promoting greedy outsiders: 'let strangers arrive only to depart swiftly, like men of a moment, not permanent fixtures'.[13] The *Song* was, admittedly, written for an elite audience. But there is no doubt that the sentiments it expressed were widely shared.

Anti-alien sentiment recurred throughout the period, in various guises. The hatred of outsiders in authority encompassed the papacy and its representatives. Controversial issues included ecclesiastical taxation, the proceeds of which pope and king shared, and papal provision of clergy – especially foreign (usually Italian) clergy – to English benefices, which limited the opportunities of native clergy and cut across aristocratic rights of church patronage. The gradual deterioration of the English position in France from the 1430s intensified the general hostility towards aliens resident in England. In 1440 a tax of 16d was imposed on all alien households and 6d on individual foreigners. There was also recurrent animus against foreign merchants and financiers, who were thought to be damaging the interests of their English counterparts, and draining the country of bullion. The Italians were a well-established target, and the collapse of the Anglo-Burgundian alliance in 1435 intensified suspicions of the Flemings.

Comments on England's enemies are characteristically crude. Chief Justice Fortescue, writing in praise of the English system of government in the 1470s, was at the more sophisticated end of the spectrum of abuse when he wrote that 'it is not poverty which keeps Frenchmen from rising, but it is cowardice and lack of hearts and courage, which no Frenchman has like an Englishman'.[14] Hostility to the French and delight at English successes were fanned by royal propaganda, which found its way to the public by numerous routes. Edward I and Edward III informed their

---

[12] Matthew Paris, *Chronica Majora*, ed. H. R. Luard (7 vols., RS, 1872–83), v, pp. 596–8, cf. pp. 616, 639–40.

[13] C. L. Kingsford, ed., *The Song of Lewes* (Oxford, 1890), lines 68–9, 281–2, 315–17.

[14] John Fortescue, *On the Laws and Governance of England*, ed. S. Lockwood (Cambridge, 1997), p. 111.

subjects that the French king had plans to conquer England and extirpate the English tongue. The chronicler Henry Knighton elaborated Edward III's claim in 1346 that an invasion plan had been discovered, saying that the French king's son would have given 'the lands which he won in England to the nobles who went with him, to each according to his degree, and in that way the lands of England would be permanently secured for France'.[15] There were stage-managed celebrations, notably in London upon Henry V's return from Agincourt, when the king was welcomed as 'another David coming from the slaying of Goliath (who might appropriately be represented by the arrogant French)'.[16]

From the point of view of its neighbours, later medieval England appeared a bellicose state – conquering the Welsh, attempting to subjugate the Scots and the Irish, and maintaining armies in France in pursuit of preposterous claims. It is easy to underestimate the extent to which the English felt threatened and surrounded. In 1216–17, during the civil war that marked the end of John's reign, the future Louis VIII brought an army to England in support of John's opponents, Alexander II occupied Carlisle and Llywelyn the Great, who had been in negotiations with France in 1212, took many castles in south Wales. During the Hundred Years War the fear of invasion and encirclement was well founded. The French attacked Southampton and the Isle of Wight in 1339. Scottish invasions of the north, as in 1346 and 1357, were timed to coincide with English campaigns on the continent. The coastal counties, like those of the north, were often in a state of military preparedness, which placed obligations on the population at large. Particularly in the late fourteenth and early fifteenth centuries, the seas were infested by pirates associated with hostile powers. This gave the maintenance of an English presence on the other side of the Channel a defensive rationale with wide appeal. Mercantile interests in London, Southampton or Bristol, for whom the North Sea and Biscay routes were vital, could identify themselves readily, not just with the need to hold Calais, Brest or Bordeaux, but with the recovery of the duchy of Normandy by Henry V, and even with the possession by Henry VI of the crown of France itself.

Anti-French sentiment co-existed with a continuing sense of cultural unity between the elites of the two countries. To some extent the same could be said of Scotland. Jean Froissart (*c.* 1337–*c.* 1410), the Flemish chronicler who spent time at the French and English courts, recorded the

---

[15] G. H. Martin, ed., *Knighton's Chronicle, 1337–1396* (Oxford, 1995), p. 59.
[16] F. Taylor and J. S. Roskell, eds., *Gesta Henrici Quinti* (Oxford, 1975), pp. 108–11.

chivalric deeds of knights of all three kingdoms. David II (1329–71) and James I (1406–37) spent comfortable periods of captivity in England. The latter, author of *The Kingis Quair*, advanced the literary use of English in Scotland. The lack of a linguistic barrier at the border facilitated the sense of membership of a common cultural world, though the growing link between language and nationality could lead to questioning of Scotland's right to be a separate kingdom. In the fourteenth and fifteenth centuries substantial numbers of Scots lived, as traders and migrant labourers, not just in northern England, but down the entire east coast as far as London. They attracted hostility during times of military crisis, but often attempts to expose and indict them seem to have sprung from the resentment of their neighbours at the very ease with which 'enemies' could live and profit among them. False accusations that people were Scots (which would be considered libellous in York) confirm that there was little observable difference between the English and the sort of Scotsmen who settled across the border.

Matters were not, however, so straightforward as this suggests. Even in the twelfth century, English writers had contrasted the kings of Scots and their Anglo-French entourage with the savage troops from the outer provinces who committed atrocities during Scottish invasions of northern England. In the later fourteenth century Scottish writers themselves, notably the chronicler John Fordun, began to portray Scotland as culturally polarised between the Gaelic-speaking highlands, inhabited by 'wild Scots', and the more civilised, anglophone lowlands. This distinction was also made by men from south of the border. Froissart referred to 'a city called Aberdeen, on the borders of wildest Scotland'.[17] These finer distinctions may have been lost on less expert observers, who could imagine that the Scottish leaders all spoke Gaelic. In 1464 William Gregory, a London merchant, was content to remark of the Scots in general 'it is hard to put trust in them, for they are ever found full of guile and deceit'.[18]

If the subjects of the kings of Scots were believed to include barbarians, the Welsh and Irish were unambiguously stigmatised as such. By far the most influential writer on this subject was Gerald of Wales (*c.* 1146–*c.* 1223), whose works became the standard handbooks on these peoples. Gerald's outlook was not straightforward. He was one-quarter Welsh by blood, and

[17] J. Froissart, *Chronicles*, trans. G. Brereton (Harmondsworth, 1968), p. 335.
[18] J. Gairdner, ed., *The Historical Collections of a Citizen of London in the Fifteenth Century* (Camden Soc., 2nd ser. XVII, 1876), p. 224.

not slow to play up his connections with Welsh royalty. But essentially he wrote as an outsider, portraying exotic and barbarous peoples for a metropolitan audience:

> while man usually progresses from the woods to the fields, and from the fields to settlements and communities of citizens, this people [the Irish] despises work on the land, has little use for the money-making of towns, contemns the rights and privileges of citizenship, and desires neither to abandon, nor lose respect for, the life which it has been accustomed to lead in the woods and countryside.[19]

The Welsh and Irish lacked stable central authorities, were given to internecine wars and inheritance disputes, were brave but lacked staying power in battle, were unreliable in their dealings and ignorant of chivalric conventions. While they were hospitable, 'their external characteristics of beard and dress, and internal cultivation of the mind, are so barbarous that they cannot be said to have any culture'.[20] These traits were seen as character flaws: their economic arrangements amounted to 'idleness', their unstable politics to 'oath-breaking', 'treachery' and 'fickleness' (*levitas*). Above all, as a Paris-educated religious reformer, Gerald disapproved of married clergy, hereditary benefices and the lax marriage arrangements of the population, which failed to draw the proper line between legitimate children and bastards. They were, in short, 'a filthy people, wallowing in vice'.[21] Ireland's position on the edges of the known world also predisposed Gerald to locate strange beings there – including some who were half-man, half-ox, as a result of the habit of sexual congress with cows.

The influence of Gerald's works on later commentators was pervasive. Higden's characterisation of Ireland and its human and animal inhabitants was lifted almost entirely from Gerald, whose views thereby attained wider currency than they might otherwise have done. During the thirteenth century these assumptions of Welsh and Irish barbarity, unreliability and lack of morality had passed from academic to political discourse. The codification of English law enshrined a set of norms to which the Celtic peoples failed to conform. In 1277 Edward I, having received petitions from some Irish bishops seeking the extension of English law to the Irish, condemned Irish laws as 'detestable to God, and

---

[19] Gerald of Wales, *The History and Topography of Ireland*, trans. J. J. O'Meara (Harmondsworth, 1982), pp. 100–1.
[20] *Ibid.*, p. 101. [21] *Ibid.*, p. 106.

so contrary to all law that they ought not to be deemed laws'.[22] By 1284, in the wake of the conquest of north Wales, the king and his advisers were busy extirpating the unacceptable features of Welsh law and replacing them with enlightened English practices, such as the law of felony and associated capital punishment. Similar opinions and stereotypes constantly recur. As R. R. Davies said, 'the image of the Welsh had taken a firm shape, so that when the master-builders of Beaumaris castle remarked in a letter in 1296 to Edward I that "as you will know, Welshmen are Welshmen", there was no need to elaborate the point. The image did the rest'.[23] In 1351 the king's council in Ireland considered that settlers who lived in frontier areas were beset by the 'fickleness [*levitas*] of an unconquered people'.[24] In 1419 the Yorkshire Franciscan Nicholas Warter, who had been provided to the Ulster bishopric of Dromore by Pope Martin V, immediately petitioned successfully to be excused residence because of the insuperable difficulties of ministering 'among the native Irish [*meros Ybernicos*]'.[25]

Thus presented, it might seem that the outlook of the English was formed by a mixture of bad history, xenophobic propaganda, resentment and crude ethnic prejudice. When attention shifts from what some men wrote to what many people did, a more complex picture emerges. In 1270 the future Edward I and his brother Edmund of Lancaster set out on a crusade which was to keep Edward abroad, in France, Italy, Cyprus and the Holy Land itself, until 1274. Accompanying the expedition were some 300 members of the English elite, about half of them knights, whose landed interests stretched into every county of the kingdom. These men did not travel alone; the numbers on the move were much increased by the presence of their households and servants. Occasionally the results could be startling. Hamo Lestrange, from a Shropshire baronial family, married the heiress of the lordship of Beirut, though he survived only until 1273 to pursue his Levantine ambitions. Another figure who set out with Edward better exemplifies the range of experiences that could be acquired by a well-born Englishman. Thomas de Clare (d.1287) was a younger brother of the earl of Gloucester. After some education at Oxford, he did well out of the spoils of the Barons' War of 1263–5. He was with Edward at Paris in 1269, during the preparations for the

[22] H. S. Sweetman, ed., *Calendar of Documents relating to Ireland* (5 vols., 1875–86), ii, no. 1408.
[23] R. R. Davies, 'Buchedd a Moes y Cymry', *Welsh History Review*, 12 (1984), 179.
[24] R. Frame, 'Thomas Rokeby, Sheriff of Yorkshire, Justiciar of Ireland', *Peritia*, 10 (1996), 284.
[25] M. Robson, 'Nicholas Warter, Franciscan bishop of Dromore, c.1372–1448', *Collectanea Hibernica*, 42 (2000), 24.

expedition. After he returned in 1272, he was used as a diplomat in Gascony and in dealings with the French court. The last phase of his life was focused on Ireland, where the earls of Gloucester were lords of Kilkenny. He received a speculative grant of lands and rights beyond the Shannon, in Thomond. His last years were spent fighting, castle-building and honing his diplomatic skills among the O'Briens and others whom he sought to make tributary.

Like so many rulers of the period, Edward I had a genuine enthusiasm for the crusade, but European politics had a habit of getting in the way. Even so, his reign was punctuated by communications with distant places. While in Palestine in 1271, he had sent envoys to the Mongol khan in the hope of forging an alliance against Islam. After his return to the west, spasmodic contacts were maintained, partly through the English Dominican David of Ashby, author of *The Deeds of the Tartars* (as westerners called the Mongols), who had spent time at the Mongol court. Some fifteen embassies from the east made contact with the English court during Edward's reign, six from the Mongol rulers themselves. In 1291, just before news arrived of the fall of Acre, which was to end the possibility of crusading in the Holy Land itself, Geoffrey of Langley, a knight who had been on the 1270 crusade, went on a crusading journey which took him to Trebizond. During it he sent messengers to the khan at Tabriz.

Despite the collapse of the crusader states, the area that was to be the subject of the first part of Mandeville's *Travels* remained open. There were new possibilities too for those who sought adventure and spiritual merit. Edward I's great-nephew, Henry of Grosmont, duke of Lancaster (d.1361), participated in campaigns in southern Spain; he was present at the siege of Algeçiras and on a naval expedition against the Moorish town of Ceuta in North Africa. In 1351–2 he followed fashion by organising an expedition in support of the Teutonic Order against the pagans on the frontiers of northern Germany, visiting Stettin and possibly reaching Estonia and Lithuania. After this he seems to have visited Cyprus and Rhodes. His grandson, the future Henry IV, followed in his footsteps. In 1390 Henry sailed from Boston in Lincolnshire to eastern Germany, landing near Danzig, from where he rode through Brandenburg to Vilna on the River Neva. A second expedition in 1392 was followed by an excursion through Prague, Vienna and Venice to Rhodes and Jerusalem; his return journey took him to Cyprus, Milan and Paris.

English people also travelled abroad as pilgrims. In the early fifteenth century the *Life* of Margery Kempe, the Norfolk mystic, shows her covering startling amounts of ground on journeys driven by religious fervour. The places she visited included Danzig, Aachen, Santiago de Compostela, Constance, Venice, Assisi, Rome, Jerusalem, Jericho and Bethlehem. Few others were so extensively travelled, but pilgrim routes were well worn. Froissart tells of two English knights who underwent the rigours of the journey to St Patrick's Purgatory, a cavern at Lough Derg in Fermanagh.[26] More familiar to English men and women was the taxing journey across southern France and northern Spain to the shrine of St James at Compostela. Many also visited Rome, whether on pilgrimage or on business at the papal curia. Throughout the period, but particularly from the 1290s to the 1450s, hundreds of thousands of Englishmen soldiered on the continent; at least as many more were engaged in transporting them and in attending in non-combatant roles. The largest expedition was probably that for the Crécy–Calais campaign of 1346–7, when close on 30,000 troops were involved. In between the major campaigns there were dozens of smaller expeditions. Nor were military enterprises confined to the nearer continent. The Black Prince's 1355–6 expedition to Gascony saw English and Gascon forces penetrate deep into Languedoc, bypassing Toulouse, sacking Carcassonne and occupying the *bourg* of Nîmes. During the following decades, the prince and his brother John of Gaunt campaigned extensively in Spain. Success could lead to troops assuming a garrison role which kept them in France for long periods. Some were given land there. Henry V's conquest of Normandy turned Caen in particular into a veritable English town.

The relationship between the English and the outside world was complicated by the fact that not all English people lived within England itself. The settlement in Normandy, where grants were made on condition that they could be sold on only to other Englishmen, was merely the last and most temporary creation of an English community rooted elsewhere. English settlers had encroached on the borders of Wales since the Anglo-Saxon period. The conquests of marcher lords after 1066 had scattered English-speaking garrisons, burgesses, peasants and churchmen from Flint and Montgomery to Glamorgan, Gower and Pembrokeshire. A further wave of settlement followed Edward I's conquest of north Wales, symbolised by plantation boroughs such as Denbigh, Ruthin and Carnarvon. Self-interest, displayed in defence of their legal privileges, together with periodic Welsh uprisings, preserved the sense of ethnic difference, despite some intermarriage and considerable cultural exchange.

---

[26] Froissart, *Chronicles*, pp. 405–6.

The connection of Welsh outposts of Englishness with the metropolis remained close and relatively unproblematical. Where the English were not the direct subjects of the prince of Wales (or, in the absence of a prince, of the king), they were subjects of marcher lords, themselves English nobles. From Bristol and Hereford well-ridden roads led to centres of colonial administration such as Brecon, Monmouth, Cardiff and Carmarthen. English magnates came frequently to their Welsh lordships on hunting expeditions, or to receive fealties and gifts, as Roger Mortimer, fourth earl of March did upon coming of age in 1393. Cattle were driven to the households of marcher lords in midland and eastern England; salmon caught in the River Usk were served at the table of Elizabeth de Clare in Suffolk. Except in the period of Owain Glyn Dŵr's rising, Wales functioned as a familiar satellite to the English world. Its management at local level depended heavily on Welshmen who ran their own communities; but they did so under the supervision of English officials, and the network of colonial centres in the lowlands formed a bridge to the metropolis.

The relationship with Ireland was more difficult. The south and east of the country was part of the English world, and anything but cut off. The eastern ports from Dundalk and Drogheda to Dublin and beyond were in constant communication with Chester. Wexford, Waterford, Cork and other south-coast towns were linked to Bristol, Bridgwater and Southampton. All were ruled by English-speaking elites, with a sense of distinctness from the Irish, which showed itself in Waterford by-laws forbidding the use of the Gaelic language. The coastal lowlands and river valleys of the same regions contained small towns and manorial villages dominated by elites whose origins lay outside Ireland. Stretching across and beyond these zones of heavy settlement was a society of settler lords and gentry, holding their lands by English law (a privilege that was denied to their Irish neighbours), conscious of their English descent, and describing themselves as English.

People came and went between the two islands. Into Ireland sailed governors and other officials from England with substantial retinues, agents of English aristocrats and religious houses that held Irish lands, clergy taking up Irish benefices, together, of course, with merchants and mariners from English ports. Although the deterioration of security in Ireland, together with adverse economic conditions, led some English landowners to sell up in the later fourteenth century, not all did so. Bath Abbey was still managing property in Waterford in the late fifteenth century. Some important interests remained alive and even expanded, notably those of the Mortimer and Talbot families. It remained possible for English newcomers to establish themselves. In the fourteenth century the Prestons, a merchant dynasty from Lancashire, grew rich on the commissariat trade promoted by the Scottish wars. Members of the family entered the Irish judiciary and made advantageous marriages; the creation of the viscountcy of Gormanston for Sir Robert Preston in 1478 completed their success. For Michael Tregory, archbishop of Dublin from 1449, who had been rector of the university founded in Caen under Henry VI, English Ireland proved an alternative to the collapsing English Normandy.

From the later fourteenth century there was movement in the opposite direction as traders, professional men, artisans and rural labourers migrated from the beleaguered colony to England. Measures to force the Irish-born to return to Ireland at the time of Richard II's 1394 Irish expedition produced more than 500 recorded exemptions, and these do not reveal migrants at the bottom of the socio-economic scale. As with the Scots, there is little to suggest that there were cultural barriers to assimilation. Men born in Ireland could rise high. John Toky or Bannebury, originally from Limerick, was sheriff and mayor of Bristol during the 1390s; in the 1420s William Overy from Ireland was mayor and MP for Southampton.

Despite these exchanges of people, there were tensions and uncertainties in both countries over the status and national identity of the settlers. In what sense were they English? They were undoubtedly subjects of the king, and English in their own estimation. In the fourteenth century clashes between the existing establishment in Dublin and the circles of governors newly arrived from England were debated in terms of identity and allegiance. In 1341 the nobles and higher clergy, with representatives of the Irish shires and royal boroughs, angered by what they saw as maltreatment by officials from England, drew Edward III's attention to the loyalty of his 'English liege people of Ireland'.[27] Later, such jealousies led to ordinances prohibiting quarrels between 'the English born in Ireland' and 'the English born in England', and insisting on what might today be described as parity of esteem.[28] The anxieties of a colonial population, whose privileges depended on differentiation from the native population and identification with the metropolis, are also visible in the 1366 Statutes of Kilkenny, which sought to

---

[27] H. F. Berry, ed., *Statutes of Ireland, John–Henry V* (Dublin, 1907), pp. 342–3.
[28] *Ibid.*, pp. 417 (1357), 436–7 (1366).

prevent intermarriage and cultural exchange with the Irish. Officials from England and the inhabitants of the core settled areas were agreed that such interactions undermined the English identity and the loyalty of those who lived on the frontiers of the colony.

That Ireland stretched the boundaries of Englishness wider than some found comfortable is also apparent from reactions in England to residents from Ireland. Orders concerning the Irish in England often made no explicit distinction between the 'two nations' in Ireland, a distinction that was fundamental to life within the colony itself. From the 1420s the Irish-born – in this case almost by definition men of English descent and status, since only they were entitled to use English law – suffered a period of exclusion from the Inns of Court. In 1440 they were briefly swept up in the anti-alien feelings that led to the imposition of taxation on foreigners. This may have been an administrative error made in a period of financial difficulty rather than the product of considered hostility. But it is significant that the mistake could be made, and that it prompted the earl of Ormond, the settler lord with the best connections in England, to petition in favour of 'the English lieges'. The loss of most of the French lands by 1453, together with the shrinkage of the colony in Ireland, may have contributed to the ending of some of these ambiguities. By the 1480s the (loyal) inhabitants of all the diminished territories outside England were explicitly defined as 'denizens' for English purposes.

Thus the line between English and non-English was not absolutely clear-cut. Even so, there is something to be said for the view that the critical divide lay not so much between England and its insular neighbours as between the extended English world and the uncivilised zones that lay beyond: the Scottish highlands and islands, native Wales and Gaelic Ireland. As we have seen, outsiders were aware of a difference between 'wild Scots' and lowlanders. The chronicler Adam of Usk, a Welshman variously in the service of the Mortimers, the crown and the papacy, drew a sharp distinction between his own anglicised region of south-east Wales and the north. In 1403 he describes how Owain Glyn Dŵr 'emerged with his manikins from the caves and the woods ... [and] taking enormous quantities of booty with him, he returned to the safety of Snowdonia in the north of Wales, the source of all the evils in Wales, while the people silently cursed his flagrant barbarities'.[29] Despite the looseness of labelling in England, descriptions of the 'barbarity' of the Irish took for granted the (less interesting) fact that there were English zones in the island. Thomas

[29] C. Given-Wilson, ed., *The Chronicle of Adam of Usk* (Oxford, 1997), p. 173.

Walsingham, the St Albans chronicler, reporting the repatriation measure of 1394, stated that 'such a multitude had come to England in the hope of gain, that [Ireland] was almost emptied of cultivators and defenders, through which the native Irish, enemies of the English, had almost destroyed the part of the island which obeyed the king of England, and had subjected it to their abominable rule'.[30]

Yet just as some 'English' were more unambiguously English than others, the supposedly barbarous outbacks were far from impenetrable to Englishmen, and perhaps not so exotic as journalistic observers suggested. Owain Glyn Dŵr himself had served on Richard II's 1385 campaign against the Scots, joined the household of the earl of Arundel, and possibly even served a period of legal apprenticeship in the courts at Westminster. He followed in an honourable tradition. In Edward II's time Sir Gruffudd Llwyd and Sir Rhys ap Gruffudd, leaders of the Welsh of north Wales, had been closely attached to the royal court. John Rous (d.1491), the Warwickshire antiquary, saw nothing odd about travelling to Anglesey in order to consult chronicles.

Ireland too constantly belies the image of separate worlds. John Colton, the Norfolk-born archbishop of Armagh (1383–1404), who reached the archbishopric after periods spent as head of Gonville Hall in Cambridge and in high posts in the Dublin administration, ruled a diocese and province that lay mostly 'among the Irish'. Like his predecessors and successors, he normally resided in the English enclaves in counties Louth and Meath. Armagh itself was dominated by the Gaelic Irish dean and chapter, and provincial councils were normally held, not there, but at the church of St Peter at Drogheda. Yet this is not the whole story. Colton visited Armagh, and clergy from the Irish districts attended councils at Drogheda. He had close dealings with the Gaelic lords of Ulster, counselling them on their submissions to Richard II in 1395. In 1397 he journeyed north to exercise his jurisdiction during a vacancy in the bishopric of Derry. We glimpse him, amid a clerical and lay entourage of mixed origin, receiving the renders and hospitality of the erenaghs, heads of the hereditary ecclesiastical families, deep in the Gaelic interior. At sites near Derry, such as 'the vill of Dermot O'Cahan', he heard marital cases involving native dynasties whose power lay on this remote Atlantic coast.[31]

---

[30] H. T. Riley, ed., *Chronica Monasterii S. Albani Johannis de Trokelowe et Henrici de Blaneforde* (RS, XXVIII, 1866), p. 171.
[31] W. Reeves, ed., *Acts of Archbishop Colton in his Metropolitan Visitation of the Diocese of Derry, 1397* (Dublin, 1850), pp. 35–8.

This vignette may serve as a final illustration of the gulf that lies between the images presented in descriptive sources and practical relationships, between words and deeds. The English had a clear view of their place in space and time, and of their identity as a people. They equipped their neighbours, whom they often resented or feared, with fixed characteristics, verging upon caricature. At the same time, some English lived permanently intermingled with outsiders, and many spent time, successfully enough, in distant places. The wider scenes on which they commented, and which many experienced in person, were for the most part set within a common west European home.

CHAPTER 18

Writing and reading

Paul Strohm

Various narratives of 'emergence' and 'growth' have both advanced and hindered knowledge about writing and reading in the medieval period. Such narratives – all of which possess some truth but also require some modification – include the movement from a multi-lingual culture to the primacy of English as a spoken and written language; a broad increase in literacy, and especially vernacular literacy; the continued encroachment of writing upon the domain of orality; and the emergence of printing and the appearance of the printed book.

No-one looking at the beginning of our period and then at its end could fail to notice enormous changes in all these areas. Between 1200 and 1500, English had routed Latin and French in the rolls of parliament and at least in the oral side of legal pleading; had long since prevailed in the literary arena; and (despite determined resistance) had already sporadically been and was about to become the premier language even of religious controversy. Especially when one considers the full range of literacies – including the more pragmatic forms of literacy specific to commerce and trade – the number of literate citizens had vastly multiplied. An optimistic judgement from Sir Thomas More (though negatively expressed) was that in 1533, just after the end of our period, 'far more than four parts of all the whole divided into ten could never read English yet' – that is, that practically 60 per cent of the people could read English at some level.[1] Despite the persistence of drama and other kinds of oral presentation and performance, the practice of private and silent reading was now predominant. Printed books were available in numbers, and the largely dispersed and 'bespoke' business of professional scribal production was giving way to the more intensive,

---

[1] Quoted in J. W. Adamson, 'The extent of literacy in England in the fifteenth and sixteenth centuries', *The Library*, 4th ser. 10 (1929–30), 162–93; quotation at p. 171. More's judgement has recently been sustained by J. B. Trapp, 'Literacy, books and readers', in L. Hellinga and J. B. Trapp, eds., *The Cambridge History of the Book in Britain*, III: *1400–1557* (Cambridge, 1999), pp. 31–43, at pp. 39–40.

speculative and assiduously promoted activities of the bookseller. Writing, no longer simply a device of administrative and cultural domination wielded by a narrow institutional elite, was now the common possession of all those urban and commercial groups included in what we might call the 'middle strata' of the realm, with important penetrations into the countryside and varied rural vocational groupings as well.

Such developmental narratives notwithstanding, the most fruitful scholarship of recent decades has devoted itself to modifying or overthrowing them. Among their demonstrated inadequacies has been their inability to address redundancies and persistences of older practices, to accommodate mixed situations and modes, or to recognise variation according to vocational or social level or geographical difference. An essential corrective step requires us to acknowledge the co-existence of different literate practices previously supposed to succeed one another in time. This acknowledgement undoubtedly complicates the saga of emerging literacy, and threatens some previously favoured ideas. Yet the introduction of such complications is also productive, in its revelation and appreciation of the creativity with which people and cultures respond to new communicative technologies.

Replacement of Latin and French by English was obviously occurring apace, but we must recall the continuing ecclesiastical and literary prestige of Latin, and the predominance of French in legal recordkeeping, throughout the period. The celebrated fifteenth-century document announcing the intention of the London brewers' company to keep their records in English is written in Latin, even as their record-book itself begins in French.[2] Arguments for a sudden late medieval expansion of participation in literate culture have now been modified by an understanding that even technically non-literate persons of the thirteenth and fourteenth centuries always possessed an active understanding of writing and its power.[3] Assumptions about the replacement of oral and collective forms of literary composition by private, silent reading of written texts have been amended to allow for a range of intermediate practices, such as the reading out of written texts to groups of hearers in a situation of aural–oral enjoyment.[4] Accounts of late fifteenth-century

---

[2] R. W. Chambers and M. Daunt, eds., *A Book of London English, 1384–1425* (Oxford, 1931), p. 16.

[3] As fruitfully explored by Susan Crane, 'The writing lesson of 1381', in B. Hanawalt, ed., *Chaucer's England: literature in historical context* (Minneapolis, 1992), pp. 201–19, and S. Justice, *Writing and Rebellion: England in 1381* (Berkeley, 1994).

[4] For references on this subject see the Further Reading. I am indebted to Vincent Gillespie for conversation and advice on these matters.

transition from a manuscript to a print culture are now altered by an understanding that scribal organisation in the fourteenth and fifteenth centuries allowed for collaborative scribal endeavours, anthologisations, circulating libraries, private ownership and other partial anticipations of the commercialised printshop. Conversely, late fifteenth-century printers imitated the appearance and physical arrangement of manuscripts, relied upon existing patronage practices and upon occasion bound printed booklets and manuscript pages into the same volume. Scriveners did not simply go out of business with the invention of the printing press, but continued to find employment as copyists well into the seventeenth century. In each of these cases, a situation of stimulating co-existence is to be presumed. Radically differing literacies and competencies flourished side by side. Public performance and private reading exerted competing claims. Manuscripts and printed books co-existed on a single owner's shelves.

Each depiction – of radical transformation and of persistently mixed practice – possesses its own kind of truth, depending on whether our approach is longitudinal or diachronic on the one hand, or latitudinal or synchronic on the other. Even as the longitudinal analyst observes and describes a broad pattern of change over time, so the latitudinal analyst notes local peculiarities, redundancies and overlaps. The design of this chapter attempts a compromise between these two modes of analysis. It will select for particular attention five transitional moments in the history of medieval English writing and reading when a larger developmental pattern emerges obstinately or even inescapably into view. Yet its consideration of these moments will also attend to what might be considered their 'non-progressive' aspects – the senses in which past practice or local variation somehow paved the way for, co-existed with, or even found shelter within, the most prepossessing aspects of the new.

At the beginning of our period, in the thirteenth and earlier fourteenth centuries, Latin was still the principal language of disputation and record-keeping, as well as of serious historical and literary effort. With respect to written language, Anglo-Norman French was clearly the second resort, and even took primacy in some areas. It not only enjoyed pre-eminence in legal and judicial record-keeping but also in literary and narrative expression (including chronicle-writing, hagiography and romance-writing, where it displayed vastly greater innovative energies than did English throughout the twelfth and thirteenth centuries). A handful of sophisticated texts in Middle English does survive from the late twelfth or beginning of the thirteenth century, including Layaman's

Brut, a verse chronicle drawing extensively on Wace's French original; the saints' lives of the 'Katherine Group', steeped in Latin hagiographical tradition; and the debonair debate-poem *The Owl and the Nightingale*, rich in Latin and French antecedents. All these works suggest that talented, multi-lingual writers had the ability to produce texts in English *when they chose* – when, that is, the invention of tradition (Layamon), or motives of spiritual education and direction (the Katherine Group) or the amusement of sheer virtuosity (*The Owl and the Nightingale*) happened to offer a suitable incentive. Yet, in the thirteenth century, circumstances propitious for English rarely prevailed, and, even when English was chosen, its use often seemed to require some special circumstance or explanation. Each of the three texts mentioned, for example, seems fully aware of its special circumstances: Layamon of his act of *translation* from French and Latin historiographical traditions into an indigenous (alliterative) English form; the Katherine Group of its responsibilities to an audience of cloistered women; the author of *The Owl and the Nightingale* of its literary appropriation of French and Latin debate poems into a work which takes 'the literary' as a subject of self-conscious discussion.

Since chronicles were normally written in Latin or French, the first of the authors known collectively as 'Robert of Gloucester' was taking a leap when he set out in the later thirteenth century to write a metrical chronicle in English, and his own comments reflect an awareness of the singularity of his enterprise. Writing on the Norman arrival, 'Robert' takes the occasion to insert some tart remarks on the provinces of French and English. Explaining that the Normans showed up speaking French, and that they continued teaching it to their children, he proposes an explanation for England's dual-language situation:

> Vor bote a man conne frenss . me[n] telth of him lute.
> Ac lowe men holdeth to engliss . & to hor owe speche yute.
> Ich wene ther ne beth in al the world . contreyes none.
> That ne holdeth to hor owe speche . bote engelond one.[5]

(For unless a man knows French, men esteem him little, but the lower classes still cling to English and to their own speech. I suppose there are no countries in all the world that do not uphold their own language, except only England.)

Robert's model is at once historical (in its links with the Conquest) and sociological (in his 'class'-based explanation for linguistic difference),

---

[5] W. A. Wright, ed., *The Metrical Chronicle of Robert of Gloucester* (2 vols., RS, 1886–7), ii, pp. 543–4. For 'Robert', see A. Gransden, *Historical Writing in England c. 550–c. 1307* (Ithaca, 1974), pp. 432–8.

though its equation of English-speaking with low social status must obviously be regarded as something of a stylisation. Robert himself is an erudite man, possibly monastic or at least with the learned resources of a good monastic library, and hardly as deeply peasant-identified as his lines might imply. Furthermore, despite his indictment of England for deserting its speech, he shifts to a rather bland endorsement of diglossia as a prudent linguistic approach:

> Ac wel me wot uor to conne . bothe wel it is .
> Vor the more that a mon can . the more wurthe he is.

(And it seems to me a good thing to learn both languages, since the more that a man learns the more worthy he is.)

Having opted for a 'conflict' model of the linguistic situation, Robert thus rather quickly declares a truce; indeed, his use of Latin learning and his emulation of French rhymed verse are already implicitly conciliatory. His choice of English itself may actually be less conflictual and more opportune than it seems. As we know from the sporadic survival of earlier works like *The Owl and the Nightingale*, a large and still partly concealed secular audience of English speakers – some, like Robert himself, quite well educated – was waiting in the wings, and Robert appears to have made an early but pragmatic decision to address them. This decision is implicit, not only in his choice of English, but also in the affiliations of his chronicle with romance (as distinct from monastic) chronicle traditions, and also the fact that none of the known manuscripts of his work is of monastic provenance.

Although Robert's implied audience seems rather well educated, he adopts the stance that English is the language of 'lewd' or unlearned persons, and the declared intention of reaching such persons was one of the early rationales for the choice of English. Thus, in the first half of the fourteenth century, Robert Mannyng justified his choice of English for his *Historia* by associating it with the concerns or interests of one segment of the populace – the 'lewed' or unlearned:

> All the story of Inglande
> As Robert Mannyng wryten it fand,
> And on Inglysch has it schewed
> Not for the lerid bot for the lewed.[6]

---

[6] H. Phillips, ed., extract from Robert Mannyng, *Chronicle*: prologue in J. Wogan-Browne et al., eds., *The Idea of the Vernacular: an anthology of Middle English literary theory, 1280–1520* (Pennsylvania, 1999), pp. 20–4.

(All the story of England, as Robert Mannyng found it written, and has revealed it in English, not for the learned but for the unlearned.)

Even the most vigorous later fourteenth-century argument for the use of English – John Trevisa's 'Dialogue between the Lord and the Clerk on Translation' (prefacing his translation of a chronicle by Ranulf Higden) – partially accepts this rather apologetic definition of the possible audience for English. Trevisa argues that his choice of English will benefit some who may not learn Latin:

for somme may nought for other maner bisynes, somme for elde, somme for defaute of witte, somme for defaaute of catel other of frendes to fynde hem to scole, and somme for other diverse defautes and lettes.[7]

(for some may not because they are too busy, some because of old age, some for lack of intelligence, some because they lack the means or else friends to provide them with education, and some because of other failures and hindrances.)

But, as early as the mid-century, a less concessive argument was also being made. The author of a work of religious instruction entitled *Speculum vitae* argues simply that English is the best choice on all accounts in which to address a diverse audience, learned as well as unlearned:

Bot lered and lewed, alde and yonnge
All understandes Inglysche tonng.[8]

(But learned and unlearned, old and young, all understand the English tongue.)

Once English was established as a viable possibility, an author's linguistic choice might be based upon a variety of considerations, including the linguistic associations of a particular genre of writing, or the contours of the particular audience to be reached. Obviously, for example, works of popular religious instruction were more likely to be written in English than were works of abstruse theological speculation. Michael Clanchy's observation about twelfth- and thirteenth-century England was equally true of the century that followed: 'English, French and Latin performed distinct social and intellectual functions'.[9] Thus in the second half of the

---

[7] S. Shepherd, ed., extract from John Trevisa, *Dialogue* in Wogan-Browne et al., *The Idea of the Vernacular*, p. 132.

[8] Quoted in Wogan-Browne et al., *The Idea of the Vernacular*, p. 337.

[9] M. T. Clanchy, *From Memory to Written Record: England 1066–1307* (2nd edn, Oxford, 1993), p. 200.

fourteenth century, when John Gower chose to write long works in French, then Latin and then English, his choices were based less on the 'triumph' of English, than the nature of those works: first *Mirour de l'omme*, a work of religious instruction; then *Vox clamantis*, written within traditions of Latin satire; then *Confessio amantis*, a work of varied English narrative, written in a deliberate middle style, for a general audience similar to that of Chaucer's *Canterbury Tales*. (The proof that Gower's choices were based more on considerations of genre and tradition than on the triumph of English is that he returned to Latin for his final work, a historical and polemical endorsement of the Lancastrian succession, entitled *Cronica tripertita*.)

Writers choosing to write in English after the mid-century were less likely to offer special justification. At times, though, a special case might still be made. Writing *c.*1385 (and thus contemporaneously with Chaucer and Gower and Langland), Thomas Usk still felt moved to comment upon his choice of English for his *Testament of Love*. Observing that some of his contemporaries who attempt poetry or 'poysye-mater' in French conduct themselves no better than do Frenchmen in English, he proposes that Latin continue to enjoy its clerical sphere, and that Frenchmen and Englishmen stick to their proper spheres:

Let than clerkes endyten in Latyn, for they have the propertie of science and the knowynge in that facultie; and lette Frenchmen in their Frenche also endyten their queynt termes, for it is kyndely to their mouthes; and let us shewe our fantasyes in suche wordes as we lerneden of our dames tonge.[10]

(Then let clerks compose in Latin, for they have the attribute of learning and knowledge of that skill; and let Frenchmen also compose their ingenious phrases in their French, for it comes naturally to their lips; and let us set down our creations in such words as we learned from our mothers' tongues.)

Yet Usk's endeavour seems less that of claiming space for himself, than of consolidating an accomplished situation. English, he observes in his rather self-conscious art-prose, *is* our natural tongue – for literary expression as well as for more mundane areas of life – and let us simply acknowledge the fact.

Chaucer's decision to write in English helped to confirm its status, but even he, who seems to spring into English in the least premeditated of ways, had deliberate choices to make. His first poems were written in emulation of French models, and his early, and now lost, ballads and lays

---

[10] Thomas Usk, *The Testament of Love*, ed. R. A. Shoaf (Kalamazoo, MI, 1998), p. 49.

may have been written in that language.[11] Further, when turning to his essay in science-writing, *A Treatise on the Astrolabe*, Chaucer shows definite trepidation about employing his 'light English' in place of the more conventional Latin, even declaring the king the 'lord of this language' and disclaiming any personal attempt to 'usurp' an inappropriate role.

These are, however, special cases and conditions. By the end of the fourteenth century, a general presumption had shifted; English was no longer just employed for discrete sallies into areas traditionally reserved for Latin or French, but (excepting a very few enclaves in scholarly and historical writing, learned disputation and record-keeping) had become the language of first resort for the widest variety of writing occasions.

Shadowing Robert of Gloucester's references to our 'own' speech, and the various discussions of the prerogatives of the 'lewd', is a sense of English as a wedge opening up other sorts of social struggle. However natural the 'triumph of English' might retrospectively seem, the fact remains that its early history is indeed intermingled with occasions of political and religious turmoil – not just Robert's crude shorthand of Normans versus the rest of 'us', but other kinds of local and very urgent struggles among and between segments of the fourteenth- and fifteenth-century populace. When a politically or doctrinally based party mounts an urgent appeal to win hearts and minds, then practical considerations of audience-building come to the fore. A decorum-breaking turn to English was always likely when loyalties were at stake – including the manoeuvres of urban factions, competition between different religious tendencies, and the politics of kingship itself.

Later medieval London was, for example, awash with written materials of all kinds – banns, broadsides, bulls, schedules, accusations, postings, lists of traitors and felons, promulgations of surprising doctrines, proclamations of all sorts – and the external and internal walls of St Paul's, the doors of Westminster Hall and the gates of Westminster Abbey would have been festooned with them, as were the gates and church doors of other cities and towns. Most were, given their communicative purpose, written in English. Thus, when a particular contention came into high focus, it was likely to be aired in the form of a street-level, English, script. One such crucial juncture in later fourteenth-century London life was the series of contentions around the mayoralty, involving John Northampton (mayor 1381–3) and his arch-rival Nicholas Brembre (mayor 1383–6).

---

[11] R. H. Robbins, 'Geoffroi Chaucier, poète français', *Chaucer Review*, 13 (1978), 93–115.

Shortly after gaining office in a highly disputatious election battle with his rival, Brembre and pro-Brembre aldermen issued a proclamation, preserved as the first English document in the city's Letter-Books:

> that no man make none congregaciouns, conuenticules, ne assembles of poeple in priue nen apert, ne no more craftes than other men, with-oute leue of the mair; ne ouermore in none manere ne make alliances, confederacies, conspiracies, ne obligaciouns for to bynde men to-gidre, for to susteyne eny quereles in lyuyngge and deyengge to-gidre, vpon peyne of enpresonement.[12]
>
> (that no one make congregations, unlawful gatherings, or private or open assemblies of people, or craft guilds either, without the mayor's permission. Nor additionally in any manner make alliances, confederations, conspiracies, or sworn oaths to bind men together, to further any quarrels in living and dying together, upon pain of imprisonment.)

Oaths about 'living and dying' together draw upon conventional language and might not be quite as melodramatic as they sound; but the proclamation was issued at a time when John Northampton, under arrest for treason, seemed likely to forfeit his life. Northampton's appeal to his followers 'to stand by him in right and wrong' seemed calculated to provoke considerable turmoil, and a sympathy strike did occur, resulting in the arrest and condemnation of Northampton's supporter John Constantine.[13] This, then, propelled the city council into the direct avenue of an English proclamation, to be followed in close succession by Thomas Usk's English 'Appeal' against John Northampton, by other proclamations against rumour and night-walking, by a 1388 guild petition to parliament, and in 1389 by royally mandated guild returns in which guilds and fraternities furnished their records (in some cases already kept in English) in order to exonerate themselves from political suspicion.

A few other proclamations and petitions in English precede this London flurry,[14] but this is the largest-scale and most sustained fourteenth-century entry of English into civil documents. As Caroline Barron has observed, civic English – far more common than contemporary survivals would suggest – may be said to have originated less in civic-minded plans for the 'common profit' of all, and more in the urgencies of political faction.[15]

Equally conflict-oriented was the bold entry into English precipitated by the Lollards – reform-minded followers of John Wyclif in the 1380s

---

[12] Chambers and Daunt, *Book of London English*, p. 31.   [13] *Ibid.*, p. 30.   [14] *Ibid.*, pp. 271–2.
[15] Unpublished talks, New Chaucer Society, Seattle, 1988; London History Seminar, Senate House, June 2000.

and 1390s – who enacted their convictions by preparing and circulating biblical translations, written sermons and argumentative treatises. Decrying Wyclif's sponsorship of biblical translations, the chronicler Henry Knighton conveys some of the oppositional flavour of the early Lollard movement:

Master John Wyclif translated [the gospel] from Latin into the language not of angels but of Englishmen [*in Anglicam linguam non angelicam*], so that he made that common and open to the laity, and to women who were able to read, which used to be for literate and perceptive clerks [*admodum literatis et bene intelligentibus*], and spread the Evangelists' pearls to be trampled by swine.[16]

Knighton powerfully conveys the shocked sense of transgression when previously reserved materials, in a language with limited access, are suddenly made more broadly available.

'Broadly available' seems almost an understatement. Lollard sermons in English – copied in formats suitable for public delivery, and not just private reading – exist in profusion. The standard English collection contains 294 sermons, and exists in thirty-one surviving manuscripts.[17] Different versions of the Wycliffite bible are to be found in some 250 existing manuscripts, giving a bare hint of the breadth of fifteenth-century circulation. The tumultuous confusion of the situation is indicated by the ironical fact that English gospels were read by Lollards and non-Lollards alike, many of the latter presumably unaware of the provenance of their reading materials. Additionally, many tracts and treatises were placed in circulation, including the Wycliffite *Lanterne of Light*, which consists of English arguments supported by quotations from the Vulgate then rendered into English.[18]

This 'unfitting' outpouring, supported by travelling preachers and Lollard conventicles or schools, had a potential for the encouragement and multiplication of heretical views which the clerical establishment could hardly ignore. Major condemnation and proscription of Wyclif's views commenced in 1382. Efforts at suppression culminated in Archbishop Arundel's *Constitutions* of 1407–9, aimed specifically at Lollards, but catching a good many more fish in their net. Nicholas Watson has observed of this legislation that it 'constitutes one of the most draconian

---

[16] G. H. Martin, ed., *Knighton's Chronicle, 1337–1396* (Oxford, 1995), pp. 242–5.
[17] A. Hudson, *The Premature Reformation. Wycliffite texts and Lollard history* (Oxford, 1988), p. 197.
[18] Ed. L. M. Swinburn (EETS, os CLI, 1917). Only a handful of copies now survive from what was probably a wide distribution.

pieces of censorship in English history, going far beyond its ostensible aim of destroying the Lollard heresy and effectively attempting to curtail all sorts of theological thinking and writing in the vernacular'.[19] With regard to biblical translation it forbids the Englishing of the bible and ownership of any translation made without episcopal approval: 'No one henceforth shall translate any text of Holy Scripture into the English language on his own authority, by way of book, booklet or tract . . . under pain of the greater excommunication, until it shall have been approved by the diocesan of the place, or, if the occasion demands it, by the provincial council'.[20]

Supplementing the negativism of the *Constitutions* was a propaganda offensive of substantial proportions, designed to counter the Lollards' own promulgation of a body of approved texts. At the forefront of sponsored orthodox production was *Mirrour of the Blessed Lyf of Jesu Christ* by the Carthusian Nicholas Love, a free rendering of the pseudo-Bonaventuran *Meditationes Vitae Christi*, including several tart rejoinders to Lollard anti-sacramentalism. Seeking to direct its readers back from the thickets of inappropriate theological speculation, this treatise proposes meditation on the scenes of Christ's life as the proper form of Christian devotion. It was probably the most popular book of the fifteenth century, and it is still extant in forty-seven complete copies.[21] Of most interest in the present context is the fact that Love submitted the translation to Archbishop Arundel himself, 'Who after examining it for several days, returning it to the above mentioned author, commended and approved it personally, and further decreed . . . that it rather be published universally for the edification of the faithful and the confutation of heretics or lollards'.[22]

As Anne Hudson has argued, Lollardy not only made opportunistic use of literacy but was in fact a 'literate' heresy, founded on the seemingly paradoxical emergence of a new religious subject, the *laicus litteratus* or literate layman.[23] Measures such as Arundel's represented responses in kind – attempts to deprive Lollards and other potential heretics of access

---

[19] N. Watson, 'Censorship and cultural change in late-medieval England: vernacular theology, the Oxford translation debate, and Arundel's Constitutions of 1409', *Speculum*, 70 (1995), 822–64, quotation from 826. For a different emphasis see p. 330 above.

[20] A. R. Myers, ed., *English Historical Documents*, IV: *1337–1485* (1969), p. 856.

[21] M. Deanesley, *The Lollard Bible* (Cambridge, 1920), p. 353; B. Nolan, 'Nicholas Love', in A. S. G. Edwards, ed., *Middle English Prose* (New Brunswick, NJ, 1984), p. 86.

[22] Cited in Nicholas Love, *Mirror of the Blessed Life of Jesus Christ*, ed. Michael G. Sargent (New York, 1992), p. xlv.

[23] A. Hudson, '*Laicus litteratus*: the paradox of Lollardy', in P. Biller and A. Hudson, eds., *Heresy and Literacy, 1000–1530* (Cambridge, 1994), pp. 222–36.

to the written word. And the argument may be taken a step further, to the observation that literacy and manuscript circulation not only provided a new and advanced means of contention but also opened a new arena of contention. Writing provided a place where different currents of orthodoxy and heterodoxy, previously implicit or commingled, sprang vividly into view, in forms that demanded immediate action.

John Claydon and his book may stand as an example.[24] Charged in 1415 as a lapsed heretic, Claydon, a skinner of London, admitted to owning books written in English, including one covered in red leather, well bound and written in a good English hand on calfskin. This was the recently written (1409–15) Lollard tract *Lanterne of Light*, which turned out to be the principal basis of the charges against him. Having seized the books, the mayor of London declared them the worst and most perverse that he had ever read or seen ('pessimi et perversissimi libri quos unquam legit vel vidit'). Claydon confessed that he had caused the book to be written for him by scribe John Grime, and later testimony established that Grime had brought the volume to his home in four quires, and that Claydon's literate servant John Fuller had worked with Grime and Claydon to correct the volume prior to binding it. Fuller frequently read aloud to Claydon in his home. Also aware of these readings were former servant David Berde (who seems to have been present at some of them) and servants Sander Philip and Balthazar Mero (whose memories are less vivid, but who represent themselves as well aware of the book and its importance in the household). Additionally, such prominent Lollards as Richard Baker (alias Richard Gurmyn) – himself burnt for heresy – and one 'Montfort' also participated in such occasions, hearing this book read and discussing and frequently disputing its contents and other articles of faith.

Excepting Grime, who wrote out the manuscript, and Fuller, who read it aloud to different parties, Claydon and the other members of his household were illiterate. Claydon explained in his own testimony that he was unable to read, and relied upon Fuller ('nescivit legere, set audivit fere quartam partem illius libri legi per quendam qui vocabatur Johannes Fuller'), and Berde, Philip and Mero are flatly designated *illiteratus*. Nevertheless, a considerable amount of 'borderline' or 'transitional' literacy is exhibited in these testimonies. Claydon was able to participate actively, not only in the procurement of this volume, but in correcting its

---

[24] For what follows see E. F. Jacob, ed., *The Register of Henry Chichele* (4 vols., Oxford, 1943–7), iv, pp. 132–8.

proofs and in discussing its contents. He had formed his own opinion of the volume, diametrically opposed to the mayor's, declaring many things he had heard in it to be useful and good and healthful to his soul ('saluti anime sue valde utilia et bona') and describing himself as sufficiently satisfied with the book that he would have been happy to have paid three times the price. His ability to assess the parts read aloud to him was based in part upon the book's relation to his own previous (and aural) experiences. One of his reasons for esteeming it was that it contained a sermon he already knew, having previously heard it preached aloud. His illiterate servant Berde was also able to demonstrate familiarity with the contents of the book, testifying (correctly) that it contained an exposition of the ten commandments in English, along with other materials which he could not recall.

Here we have a splendid example of what Brian Stock has called a 'textual community'. The elements of such a community, according to Stock, are a text (which need not be literally present, but which, present or absent, serves as a point of reference), an 'interpreter' who employs it as a basis for reforming a group's thoughts, and additional modifications of behaviour or action, leading inevitably to a situation of conflict with other religious groups or with the society at large. One of Stock's most striking points – well borne out here – is that inability to read need not prevent participation in a literate system, since such systems invariably allow orality to retain its functions alongside graphic representation.[25] In Claydon's case a set of interlocking circumstances – including his respect for the written word, the co-operation of literate persons, and situations of oral performance – allow an illiterate man to participate in bookish experiences.

The status and importance of the book in late medieval England is, incidentally, confirmed by the fact that the *Lanterne of Light* was no less on trial than Claydon himself. Examined by a panel of doctors, the *Lanterne* was found heretical on fifteen counts, and, together with Claydon's other books, found guilty and condemned to be burned by fire. So, too, was Claydon to die soon after. A letter survives from mayor Fauconer to the king, Henry V, unctuously praising his conquests and offering to burn Claydon as 'arch-parent of this heretical depravity'.[26] King Henry obviously concurred, and several chronicles record Claydon's death by burning in London that year.

---

[25] B. Stock, *The Implications of Literacy* (Princeton, NJ, 1983), esp. pp. 42–59, 90–92.
[26] H. T. Riley, ed., *Memorials of London Life* (1868), pp. 617–18.

Literacy also emerges as a multi-faceted presence in the fifteenth-century letters of those materially and culturally aspirational Norfolk gentry, the Pastons. We know of the Pastons mainly through their written and dictated correspondence, and the rich archive of their letters allows us to share in their efforts to consolidate and hold their properties, make marriages and sustain themselves during periods of separation. The letters also reveal a reliance upon more cultivated forms of literacy – mainly in English but also in Latin and French – reflected in book ownership and in an imaginative centrality of books and bookishness within their forms of daily life. In 1434 Agnes Paston had custody of a copy of the *Stimulus Conscientiae* – probably the Middle English *Prick of Conscience*.[27] We encounter Margaret Paston writing in 1449 to her husband John, requesting that he arrange for his brother William (then at Cambridge) to receive a nominale (or service-book) and a book of sophistry (probably by Aristotle) at Cambridge (I:234);[28] a book of French was taken from the Pastons' manor house in 1465 by the duke of Suffolk's men (I:326); a courtier friend of John II promises in 1467 to return his borrowed copy of Ovid's *De Arte Amandi*, but jests that the womanising John might do better to read Ovid's Remedy of Love (*De Remedio*), unless he proposes to fall into the lap ('white as whale's bone') of Lady Anne P. (II:379); in 1472 John II sought the return from John III of 'my Temple of Glass', by John Lydgate (I:447); John III wrote to John II in 1472 seeking (from yet another borrower, the earl of Arran) his sister Anne's copy of Lydgate's *Siege of Thebes* (I:575); John III wrote to John II in the same year, seeking to trace the whereabouts of 'the book of seven sages', evidently in possession of their brother Walter (I:576); John III sought from John II in 1474 'my book of the meeting of the duke and of the emperor' (I:592); in 1510 Agnes, wife of John III, bequeathed 'my great book of prayers' (II:616).

Such passages suggest the presence of a culture in which books figured prominently, and this impression is more than sustained by the existence of an inventory (1475–9) of John II's books (I:516–18). It consists of some seventeen items, mostly compilations, mainly in English but also in Latin. Secular poems are well represented, but there is a strong admixture of heraldic writings, and some statutes and philosophical and religious texts. Included among them are romances of Arthur, Guy of Warwick and

---

[27] H. S. Bennett, *The Pastons and their England* (Cambridge, 1922), pp. 110–11.
[28] This and subsequent references to the letters are to Norman Davis, ed., *Paston Letters and Papers of the Fifteenth Century* (2 vols., Oxford, 1971–6), and are to volume and page number.

Richard Coeur de Lyon, a chronicle, Chaucer's *Troilus, Legend of Good Women* and *Parliament of Fowls*, Lydgate's *Temple of Glass*, an English translation of Christine de Pizan's *Othea*, and more.

Also noted as a memorandum attached to the inventory is a compilation volume, 'my book of knighthood', in which John II was much involved, as is attested by surviving progress reports and bills from scribe William Ebesham (for which see II:386–7, 391–2). According to John's inventory, and to Ebesham's fuller accounting, this volume contained such works as a coronation treatise, materials on jousting, statutes of war, and a copy of a book of advice to princes, *De Regimine Principum*.

If John II's book holdings, and the volumes which most claimed his attention, show a certain disposition toward courtly fictions, they indicate an even more specific interest in what commentator G. A. Lester calls *noriture* or nurture: the passport afforded by literature to the courtly life to which John II seems increasingly to have aspired.[29] Beginning, in the opinion of his uncle, as an unadept courtier in youth (I:199–200), John seems increasingly to have fallen under the spell of courtly life. Several comments in his letters suggest that the imaginative support for these strides was literary as well as pragmatic. So, too, was even his more practical younger brother John III dazzled by a glimpse of the court life which his older brother afforded him – in this case, the pageantry of the Burgundian court, which seemed to unite activities and precepts previously encountered only in books of romance:

And they that haue jostyd ... in-to thys day haue ben as rychely beseyn ... as clothe of gold and sylk and syluyr and goldsmythys werk myght mak hem ... And asfor the Dwkys coort, as of lordys, ladys, and gentylwomen, knytys, sqwyirs, and gentyllmen, I herd neuer of non lyek to it saue Kyng Artourys cort (I:539).

(And they that have jousted until this day have appeared as richly provided as cloth of gold and silk and silver and goldsmiths' work might make them. And as for the lords, ladies, gentlewomen, knights, esquires and gentlemen of the duke's court, I never heard of anything to compare with it except the court of King Arthur.)

The array of literate skills and proclivities demonstrated by the Paston family and so many of their contemporaries argues for a significant growth in educational opportunities in the course of the fifteenth century. Later medieval education occurred in a variety of formats and venues,

[29] G. A. Lester, *Sir John Paston's 'Grete Boke'* (Cambridge, 1984), p. 8.

including households, noble courts, apprenticeships, grammar and other schools, religious foundations, heretical or unauthorised 'conventicles', and, of course, the burgeoning universities at Oxford and Cambridge. Formal literate education still normally meant education in Latin, but home schooling, apprenticeships and conventicles could and did instil a foundation of vernacular literacy.

William Paston, sergeant-at-law and founder of the family's fortunes, was evidently educated in a local school and then at the Inns of Court; as described by an unfriendly mid-century 'Remembraunce':

Clement had a sone William qwych ... he sett to schole, and oftyn he borowyd mony to fynd hym to scole; and aftr that he yede to Courte wyth the helpe of ... hese uncle and lerned the lawe (I.xlii).

(Clement had a son William whom he put to school, and often he borrowed money to keep him there, and then he went to court with the help of his uncle, and studied the law.)

William's son, John I, also progressed to the Inns of Court, in his case after Cambridge, and John's two brothers studied at least briefly at Cambridge as well. John I's sons, John II and John III, seem to have depended upon home schooling, presumably, as H. S. Bennett suggests, supplied by the family's chaplain,[30] before John II was placed in the royal household, and John III in the household of the duke of Norfolk. Their brothers Walter and William studied at Oxford and Eton respectively. As for their wives and sisters, some functional English literacy may, at least, be presumed, as well as an interest in the books in their possession. But their writing and reading appear to have been limited in scope. The women of the family appear to have employed scribes for their correspondence, and their books may have been read to them. In any case, they must have been reliant upon home schooling. Thus, at various levels – uneven by circumstance and even more radically so by gender – education progressed.

Among the books of John Paston II was one not mentioned above: 'a boke jn preente off the Pleye of the ...'. This now-incomplete entry evidently refers to *The Game of Chess*, the second of the books to come from Caxton's press. The date of this book's publication, 1474, is the earliest possible date for Paston's list; the latest is 1479, the year of his death. That a book so recently printed found its way into Paston's library might be read either as a sign of printing's easy accommodation with existing manuscript culture, or as a sign of printing's transformative

---

[30] Bennett, *Pastons and their England*, p. 103.

infiltration of that same culture. Each observation is, of course, equally true.

The argument for continuity is well served by the presence of Paston's 'book in print' among his manuscript books and quires; so too in libraries and elsewhere did written manuscripts and printed books sit side by side, innocent of the distinctions observed in libraries and archives today. The very idea of 'the book' as an object of veneration long pre-dated the arrival of the printed book, and many aspects of the book as artefact were established in the manuscript era – including such matters as its division into folio and quarto and hand-sized formats, as well as a sense of the different genres (such as books of hours, lives of saints and romance narratives) appropriate to bookishness itself and to the different formats of the book. Silent reading had already established itself as a possible practice in the manuscript era, creating a new and highly personal form of relation to the book. Prior to the introduction of the typeset book, printed images had already attained general circulation in the form of block books, a form of proto-print. Persons involved in manuscript circulation, such as John Shirley, had already experimented with the audience-building and promotional activities often attributed to early printers, and distribution networks were already in place. The rise of standardised dialects (and, in particular, the linkage of the dialect of London with a more extensive central midlands standard dialect around 1400) was another important precondition of broadened circulation. Inexpensive paper was already used in manuscript culture (although it would not be produced in England until the end of the fifteenth century). In all these ways the manuscript culture of the earlier fifteenth century prepared the way for the untroubled reception of the printed book in the last quarter of the century.

Once printing was launched, it did not cease to rely upon the suppositions and practices of the manuscript culture. William Caxton was, for example, much involved with manuscripts, not only using them as copy-texts for his printed books, but probably offering them for sale as well. Whether or not he employed in-house scribes, Caxton certainly had sections of manuscripts copied for presentation, as in the case of the so-called Caxton Ovid. Far from deserting their trade upon the introduction of the printing press, scribes continued to perform complementary and supplementary tasks throughout the period and beyond. Handwriting hardly died out, nor has it; and other practices associated with the pre-print era continued to flourish in the printshop culture. Caxton continued to rely upon established forms of aristocratic patronage. Early printed books also relied on presentational conventions established in manuscript culture: choices of typeface, reliance upon quires marked with signature letters instead of foliation, and other indebtednesses ensured a form of protective mimicry of the old by the new. Such mimicry was enhanced by practices of illumination. Although sparingly used by Caxton, early printers on the continent freely indulged in the hand-illumination of capitals, borders, rubrications and sometimes even illustrations, giving their printed books the look and style of manuscript productions.

Thus by 1500 printing had effected only minor perturbation of existing practice. The situation might be likened to Michael Clanchy's brilliant observation about the earlier encroachment of literacy upon the domain of orality – a transition which instituted itself 'by ensuring that it changed the old ways . . . as little as possible'.[31] On however modest a scale it was first introduced, the potential of printing to effect enormous changes was there from the beginning. Most consequential, perhaps, is the subtle but all-important shift between a diffuse scribal enterprise, which relied on home workshops and independent artisans who awaited 'bespoke' or special orders, and a shop-based printing trade which sought to create its own demand by cultivating an external market. Even if the number of copies in question is small – one informal estimate treats 250 as a substantial run for an early Caxton volume – a market remained to be sought in a new way.[32]

The new literary market of the later middle ages may be usefully defined in relation to Malcolm Parkes' distinction between the 'professional reader' (who possesses the specialised literacy of the scholar or theologian), the 'cultivated reader' (who reads recreationally), and the 'pragmatic reader' (who reads or writes in the course of business transactions).[33] By this standard, Caxton's principal overtures were to the cultivated reader. In this regard, he was a man of his century. As we have already seen in the case of the Pastons, motives of nurture and self-enhancement were predominant in the choices of those members of the aristocracy and gentry and the mercantile classes who formed the bulk of the elective fifteenth-century readership. Ford comments that people tended to own books they 'needed', but 'need' in this case must be culturally rather than pragmatically understood: the concept of 'cultural capital' or symbolic self-aggrandisement is actively relevant here, reflected

---

[31] Clanchy, *Memory to Written Record*, p. 293.
[32] N. F. Blake, *Caxton: England's first publisher* (New York, 1975), p. 29.
[33] M. B. Parkes, 'The literacy of the laity', in D. Daiches and A. Thorlby, eds., *The Mediaeval World* (1973), pp. 555–78.

both in a pride in book ownership for its own sake and an active interest in the contribution of books to personal refinement.[34]

Caxton's interest in English works promising edification and refinement inclined him to works of literature (such as poems by Chaucer and Lydgate), courtesy (such as *The Book of the Knight of the Tower*), popular history (*Chronicles of England, Polychronicon, History of Troy*), morality (*Game of Chess*, Aesop), chivalry (*Feats of Arms, Order of Chivalry*), and general religious instruction (*Golden Legend*, John Mirk's *Festial, Speculum Vitae Christi*). These works may have attracted somewhat different audiences. Blake points out that the *Speculum Vitae Christi* was found particularly within monastic and aristocratic houses, whereas the *Festial* (a book of sermons) was more popular with parish priests.[35] Nevertheless, an attempt at the definition of a general, secular and genteel audience is evident in these contours. Missing from the list, for example, are works like *Piers Plowman* (whose alliterative style was perhaps now thought 'rude'), religious controversy (including the writing of Pecock and other works tainted by heresy) or intense mystical devotion (such as Julian of Norwich, or even the softer-core *Scale of Perfection*, later printed by Wynkyn de Worde).

Caxton's appeal to readers on the basis of self-betterment is clear in the prose of his prefaces. Naturally enough, his *Book of Good Manners* presents itself in such terms, translated 'so that it might be had and used among the people to amend their manners and increase virtuous living'. A similar appeal accompanies his *Order of Chivalry*, proposing that those of noble blood 'thereafter keep the lore and commandments contained therein'.[36] Similar claims for improvement are, however, made for other genres as well. Malory's *King Arthur*, for example, teaches us 'to exercise and follow virtue, by which we may come to and attain good fame and renown in this life' and Higden's history describes things which 'by experience are greatly conducive to a righteous life'.[37]

The conflictual dimension of printing was therefore effectively masked in its earliest days, when printing was more often employed for purposes of social consolidation than change. Early in the next century, printing would cede its role as a servant of genial consensus. The new technology, and the proselytising possibilities it helped to create, were to be increasingly enlisted in the religious and state controversies of the Reformation era.

---

[34] M. L. Ford, 'Private ownership of printed books', in *The Cambridge History of the Book in Britain*, iii, pp. 205–28.
[35] Blake, *Caxton*, p. 183. [36] N. F. Blake, ed., *Caxton's Own Prose* (1973), pp. 60, 127.
[37] *Ibid.*, pp. 109, 131.

CHAPTER 19

Conclusion

Rosemary Horrox

All historical boundaries are problematic. The dates chosen as the limits for this volume, 1200–1500, are arbitrary – as the choice of round numbers was designed to signal and as was stressed in the Preface. None of the contributors would claim that these three centuries represent a self-contained period. The exploration of their themes has meant looking back to earlier developments that were still working themselves out when this period opens, but also glancing forward to suggest how changes continued to unfold in the next century. No-one is in the business of trying to identify some medieval/modern divide, and although, through convention and convenience, most of us continue to use the term 'the late middle ages' it is with no intention of implying that the period should be characterised as liminal, let alone autumnal.

One consequence of this perspective is that the Black Death, as in other recent work, is denied its traditional status as the earthquake that reduced medieval certainties to rubble and allowed the building of the modern world. This model was firmly established by Cardinal Gasquet in the first major English study of the plague, published in 1893. Gasquet was particularly interested in the possibility that the plague might explain the Protestant Reformation, but he was also convinced that it brought about a complete social revolution as well. Other historians have linked it more specifically with the rise of capitalism, individualism, the middle classes and the modern state. These ideas fell out of favour in the course of the twentieth century, partly because many of the arguments amounted to little more than *post hoc, propter hoc*, but also because it became fashionable in the mid twentieth century to insist that medieval chroniclers had exaggerated the scale of the mortality and that the death rate was far less than the one in two claimed by Gasquet. Since then estimates of plague mortality have been creeping back towards (and in some cases beyond) the one in two mark and some historians are evidently beginning to feel that it is unreasonable to claim that such massive mortality had *no*

473

long-term consequences beyond the quantifiably economic (upon which most writers are now agreed). What is clear, at least, is that the unfolding of those consequences was far more complex than the old model would allow and that their fruitful exploration demands acknowledgement of the striking continuities rather than merely a determination to hunt out 'change'.

The readiness to see the plague as the agent of modernity was driven by two largely unstated assumptions: that the middle ages were profoundly different from 'modern' society and that medieval ways of doing things were so entrenched that it would take a major catastrophe to bring about significant change. Attention focused, therefore, on trying to identify that upheaval. In the political sphere the same approach generated the belief, now also generally abandoned, that it was the bloodbath of the Wars of the Roses that destroyed the 'feudal' nobility and ushered in the new monarchy as well as an upwardly mobile middle class. The rejection of that approach thus has as a corollary not only the assertion of continuities, but also an acceptance of incremental, ongoing change: what the current jargon would define as endogenous rather than exogenous change. Many examples could be offered: among them, the shift from memory to written record, the growth of the common law and the new pastoral imperatives that grew out of contritionist theology. There is also now much greater recognition that such developments were not simply imposed on medieval society from above but were at least in part a response to demand from below.

The earlier tacit denial that change could be self-generated in the middle ages was founded in a sense that the past was primitive and progress is an attribute of modernity. But it also drew encouragement from the ways in which medieval writers sought to present their own world. The most admired attribute in the middle ages was order: the quality which brought fallen humanity closest to the perfection envisaged by its creator. *Dis*order, although the inevitable consequence of mankind's fall from grace, was aberrant and to be corrected. Both qualities were seen in the widest terms. Order entailed a sense of what was right and fitting: the natural law of which all human laws were imperfect reflections but also the 'reason' to which contemporaries endlessly appealed in justification or explanation. Malory's King Arthur, for instance, celebrating his marriage to Guinevere, promised to grant any man's wish 'except it were unreasonable'.[1] No more definition was

---

[1] Thomas Malory, *Works*, ed. E. Vinaver (2nd edn, Oxford, 1969), p. 61.

necessary, although Arthur subsequently offered one: he would grant any wish that did not impair his realm or his estate. The maintenance of order, in all its senses, was the prerequisite of harmony: the state of man living in peace with man, but also of man living in peace with God. Disorder was disharmony, and writers and preachers reached instinctively for images of the out-of-tune instrument centuries before Shakespeare's Ulysses asserted, 'Take but degree away, untune that string, and hark what discord follows'.[2]

Ulysses' target, with which his predecessors would have sympathised, was those who showed a lack of deference towards their betters, and it is easy to see how the commitment to order could be deployed as an argument against change in general and social change in particular. There were plenty of medieval writers who were prepared to argue that order required acceptance of the status quo. As the first prayer book of Edward VI (1549) phrased it, as part of the response to the question 'What is my duty towards my neighbours?': 'To submit myself to all my governors, teachers, spiritual pastors and masters. To order myself lowly and reverently to all my betters'. This assumed that one could identify one's betters, and the medieval emphasis on hierarchy seems to play into the same set of values. The formulation and articulation of hierarchies was just one example of the love of patterning in which the intellectual commitment to order could manifest itself. The courtesy books cited by several of the contributors to this volume recognised the problems inherent in establishing precedence, but took it as axiomatic that the exercise should be undertaken.

This equation of order with stasis is, however, misleading. As several contributors to this volume have pointed out, individuals could change their social standing or their role. They could also be markedly undeferential, as indeed the contemporary emphasis on the importance of deference itself betrays. A more fruitful way into the question is the equation of order with a sense of what was appropriate. Men and women were indeed expected to behave in conformity with their status, recognising where they were placed in the scheme of things. The tag *nosce teipsum* (know thyself), rendered by Chaucer with rather more cynicism as 'Full wise is he that can know himself', was an injunction to look outwards as well as inwards.[3] Improving one's placing was not, except by some moralists, frowned on. The growing demand for education across

---

[2] William Shakespeare, *Troilus and Cressida*, i.3.
[3] The Riverside edition of *The Canterbury Tales*, The Monk's Tale, line 2139.

this period demonstrates as much. Although medieval education was generally directed at fitting its recipients for the niche they were expected to fill, there was always an underlying sense that it was a route to betterment. Even the sons and daughters of the gentry, sent to other households to learn the behaviour and skills requisite for their social position, would be sent where possible to the households of their parents' social superiors, rather than their equals. The fact that this is relatively rarely articulated is evidence of the extent to which it was taken for granted rather than of its novelty. Thus a contemporary account of the rise of the Pastons could comment baldly that Clement Paston, characterised as a good husbandman who followed the plough and whose wife was unfree, sent his son William to school 'and often he borrowed money to find him to school'.[4] William ended up as a royal justice and although, as Philippa Maddern reminds us above, the speed and permanence of his elevation is atypical, the hope of similar advancement fuelled the demand for schooling. When in 1439 William Bingham petitioned for licence to found God's House in Cambridge to address 'the great scarcity of masters of grammar' this was less an expression of the parlous state of education than a reflection of consumer demand.[5]

Viewed in this context, the late medieval sumptuary laws were not evidence of hostility to social mobility per se, but of discomfort when people could not be 'placed' securely. By attempting to regulate appearance they reveal a world in which social standing was in practice what one could support, not just financially but behaviourally. It is significant that William of Wykeham, the founder of Winchester and New College, Oxford took as his motto the proverb 'Manners maketh man', with the clear implication that not only can behaviour be learned but that this is a desirable state of affairs. Writers hostile to the whole notion of social mobility predictably took issue with this view, insisting that behaviour was, on the contrary, innate, but their vehemence suggests that they were fighting a losing battle. There was indeed in medieval England a continuing sense that status derived from birth was the best sort of status – it could hardly be otherwise when the defining attributes of the elite, land and title, were largely hereditary. But widespread acceptance of the doctrine of primogeniture, leaving younger sons with 'that which the cat left on the malt heap' demanded a pragmatic recognition of the

---

[4] N. Davis, ed., *Paston Letters and Papers of the Fifteenth Century* (2 vols., Oxford, 1971–6), ii, pp. xli–xlii.
[5] R. Willis and J. W. Clark, *The Architectural History of the University of Cambridge* (3 vols., Cambridge, 1988), i, p. lvi.

very different lifestyle and social standing that might be experienced by siblings.[6]

Another respect in which the middle ages created its own reputation for stasis was the insistence that what was done in the present was legitimated by what had been done in the past; indeed that what had been done in the past *should* be what was done in the present. Generations of later authors have mocked medieval scholars for their reliance on 'authorities', especially when, as in the medieval Bestiary, received wisdom seemed to fly in the face of common observation. That misses the point of the Bestiaries, which were allegories rather than scientific treatises: the medieval equivalent, one could say, of the C. S. Lewis *Narnia* stories rather than of David Attenborough's *Life on Earth*. More generally, the criticism overlooks the fact that the deployment of authorities entailed authorial choice. Similarly, custom and precedent were immensely powerful forces but they were inevitably selective, constituting (although not generally admitting) a choice about what aspects of the past should be upheld. Such choices were fluid, although the increasing reliance on written records did something to limit that fluidity. Even so, self-conscious change remained possible, albeit often signalled by the very urgency with which its proponents insisted that it represented a return to the good old days. The radicalism of the mendicant orders, or of the most vociferous sixteenth-century critics of the Church, was presented as a stripping away of new and unjustified accretions to the body instituted by Christ and his apostles. If all else failed, change could be justified, especially in the political arena, by presenting it as the fulfilment of prophecy.

'Novelty' or 'new fangledness' retained negative connotations, and the latter in particular did so well beyond the middle ages. But advance did not always have to be camouflaged as return and some writers were prepared to use 'novelty' in a positive sense. The medieval cliché that men were 'dwarves on the shoulders of giants' is also testimony to acceptance of progress. Writers of plague treatises insisted that they were better able than their authorities to discuss the terrifying new disease because they were experienced in it and their predecessors were not. Among the various innovations mentioned in earlier chapters and recognised at the time as improvements were developments in agricultural technology,

---

[6] The quotation is from Thomas Wilson, describing the state of England in 1600, cited by D. A. L. Morgan, 'The individual style of the English gentleman', in M. Jones, ed., *Gentry and Lesser Nobility in Medieval Europe* (Gloucester, 1986), p. 21.

ship-building and mapping. One could probably add improvements in building – fewer high-status buildings seem to have fallen down in the late middle ages, although builders were prepared to cut corners in their cheaper developments. And the public response to 'novelty' was not always negative. The commercialisation of the medieval economy brought more choice for those consumers who could afford it. The disapprobation of moralists makes it clear that there was a sense of what was fashionable and that this was spreading beyond the elite. For its critics 'fashionable' seems often to have been identified with 'foreign': another reason for damning it in their eyes, but offering more evidence of the openness of medieval men and women to the possibility of new ways of doing things.

Of course change could be a source of conflict. The notorious breakdown of lord/peasant relations in Halesowen (Worcs.) had its roots in a new lord's attempt to subvert custom. The post-plague world saw wider conflict as lords and employers struggled to block the economic changes consequent upon demographic collapse: reduced competition for land and higher wages. Some writers inveighed against a 'world turned upside down' in which, in John Gower's Orwellian image of the 1381 rising, farm animals became ravening beasts. The rising was undoubtedly profoundly shocking – the chronicler Thomas Walsingham evoked apocalyptic imagery to convey his outrage – and, could we see the views of the rebels rather than their critics, we might see a burning optimism on their side that the world could be renewed. But in the event that did not happen. The social order was reasserted and tensions seem gradually to have subsided. In the course of the fifteenth century the rhetoric of common petitions in parliament moved away from blaming the idle and feckless English workman for the economic malaise and towards accusations that foreign competition was taking work away from honest English tradesmen. By the mid century the royal government was even emboldened to resume experiments in widening the tax base although there was no move to reinstitute the poll tax, the immediate trigger of the 1381 rising.

Change might be uncomfortable at times, it might even generate overt hostility in some quarters, but it was incremental and could generally be absorbed. It is striking in this context that the most recent work on the Reformation of the sixteenth century – another traditional 'turning point' – is inclined to emphasise that this too was a gradual process: gradual, that is, in the sense that it was a long way down the line before contemporaries fully realised how far they had come, but also in the sense that underlying assumptions changed more slowly than public observance. Although reliance on public pronouncements can obscure the fact, change is never definitive; it always has to be negotiated (in both senses) by individuals and communities. How medieval men and women negotiated the world in which they lived has been the theme of this book.

Further reading

The place of publication is London unless otherwise stated.

CHAPTER 1 INTRODUCTION

Astill, G. and Langdon, J., eds., *Medieval Farming and Technology: the impact of agricultural change in northwest Europe* (Leiden, 1997).

Aston, T. H. and Philpin, C. H. E., eds., *The Brenner Debate: agrarian class structure and economic development in pre-industrial Europe* (Cambridge, 1985).

Bailey, M., *A Marginal Economy? East Anglian Breckland in the later middle ages* (Cambridge, 1989).

'Demographic decline in late medieval England: some thoughts on recent research', *EcHR*, 2nd series, 49 (1996), 1–19.

'The commercialisation of the English economy, 1086–1500', *JMH*, 24 (1998), 297–311.

'Peasant welfare in England, 1290–1348', *EcHR*, 2nd series, 51 (1998), 223–51.

Barron, C. M., 'The "golden age" of women in medieval London', *Reading Medieval Studies*, 15 (1989), 35–58.

Bennett, J. M., *Women in the Medieval English Countryside: gender and household in Brigstock before the plague* (Oxford, 1987).

'Medieval women, modern women: across the great divide', in D. Aers, ed., *Culture and History, 1350–1600: essays on English communities, identities and writing* (New York, 1992), pp. 147–75.

Bolton, J. L., *The Medieval English Economy, 1150–1500* (1980).

'"The world upside down": plague as an agent of social and economic change', in W. M. Ormrod and P. G. Lindley, eds., *The Black Death in England* (Stamford, 1996), pp. 17–78.

Brenner, R., 'Agrarian class structure and economic development in pre-industrial Europe', *P&P*, 70 (1976), 30–75.

'The agrarian roots of European capitalism', *P&P*, 97 (1982), 16–113.

'The rises and declines of serfdom in medieval and early modern Europe', in M. L. Bush, ed., *Serfdom and Slavery: studies in legal bondage* (Harlow, 1996), pp. 247–76.

'Property relations and the growth of agricultural productivity in late medieval and early modern Europe', in A. Bhaduri and R. Skarstein, eds., *Economic Development and Agricultural Productivity* (Cheltenham, 1997), pp. 9–41.

Britnell, R. H., 'Commerce and capitalism in late medieval England: problems of description and theory', *Journal of Historical Sociology*, 6 (1993), 359–76.

The Commercialisation of English Society, 1000–1500 (2nd edn, Manchester, 1996).

Britnell, R. H. and Campbell, B. M. S., eds., *A Commercialising Economy: England 1086 to c. 1300* (Manchester, 1995).

Britnell, R. H. and Hatcher, J., eds., *Progress and Problems in Medieval England: essays in honour of Edward Miller* (Cambridge, 1996).

Britton, E., *The Community of the Vill: a study in the history of the family and village life in fourteenth-century England* (Toronto, 1977).

Campbell, B. M. S., 'Agricultural progress in medieval England: some evidence from eastern Norfolk', *EcHR*, 2nd series, 36 (1983), 26–46.

English Seigniorial Agriculture, 1250–1450 (Cambridge, 2000).

Campbell, B. M. S., Galloway, J. A., Keene, D. and Murphy, M., *A Medieval Capital and its Grain Supply: agrarian production and distribution in the London region c. 1300* (Institute of British Geographers, Historical Geography Research Series, XXX, 1993).

Campbell, B. M. S. and Overton, M., eds., *Land, Labour and Livestock: historical studies in European agricultural productivity* (Manchester, 1991).

Chambers, J. D., *Population, Economy and Society in Pre-Industrial England* (Oxford, 1972).

Crone, P., *Pre-Industrial Societies* (Oxford, 1989).

Day, J., *The Medieval Market Economy* (Oxford, 1987).

DeWindt, A. R., 'Peasant power structures in fourteenth-century King's Ripton', *Mediaeval Studies*, 38 (1976), 236–67.

'Redefining the peasant community in medieval England: the regional perspective', *Journal of British Studies*, 26 (1987), 163–207.

DeWindt, E. B., *Land and People in Holywell-cum-Needingworth: structures of tenure and patterns of social organisation in an East Midlands village, 1252–1457* (Toronto, 1972).

Doyle, W., 'Myths of order and ordering myths', in M. L. Bush, ed., *Social Orders and Social Classes in Europe since 1500: studies in social stratification* (1992), pp. 218–29.

Du Boulay, F. R. H., *An Age of Ambition: English society in the late middle ages* (1970).

Duby, G., *The Three Orders: feudal society imagined*, trans. A. Goldhammer (Chicago, 1980).

Dyer, A., *Decline and Growth in English Towns 1400–1640* (Basingstoke, 1991).

Dyer, C., 'A redistribution of incomes in fifteenth century England?', in R. H. Hilton, ed., *Peasants, Knights and Heretics* (Cambridge, 1981), pp. 192–215.

Standards of Living in the later Middle Ages: social change in England, c. 1200–1520 (Cambridge, 1989).

'How urbanized was medieval England?', in J. M. Duvosquel and E. Thoen, eds., *Peasants and Townsmen in Medieval Europe: studia in honorem Adriaan Verhulst* (Gent, 1995), pp. 169–83.

Making a Living in the Middle Ages: the people of Britain, 850–1520 (New Haven, CT, 2002).

Eiden, H., 'Joint action against "bad lordship" in the Peasants' Revolt in Essex and Norfolk', *History*, 83 (1998), 5–30.

Epstein, S. R., *Freedom and Growth: the rise of states and markets in Europe, 1300–1750* (2000).

Fourquin, G., *The Anatomy of Popular Rebellion in the Middle Ages*, trans. A. Chesters (Amsterdam, 1978).

Galloway, J. A., 'Town and country in England, 1300–1750', in S. R. Epstein, ed., *Town and Country in Europe, 1300–1800* (Cambridge, 2001), pp. 106–31.

Glasscock, R. E., 'England *circa* 1334', in H. C. Darby, ed., *A New Historical Geography of England before 1600* (Cambridge, 1976), pp. 136–85.

Goldberg, P. J. P., 'Female labour, service and marriage in the late medieval urban north', *Northern History*, 22 (1986), 18–38.

'Mortality and economic change in the diocese of York, 1390–1514', *Northern History*, 24 (1988), 38–55.

'Women in fifteenth-century town life', in J. A. F. Thomson, ed., *Towns and Townspeople in the Fifteenth Century* (Gloucester, 1988), pp. 107–28.

Women, Work and Life Cycle in a Medieval Economy: women in York and Yorkshire, c. 1300–1520 (Oxford, 1992).

Hajnal, J., 'European marriage patterns in perspective', in D. V. Glass and D. E. C. Eversley, eds., *Population in History: essays in historical demography* (1965), pp. 101–43.

Hallam, H. E., *Rural England, 1066–1348* (1981).

Hanawalt, B. A., ed., *Chaucer's England: literature in historical context* (Minneapolis, MN, 1992).

Harvey, B. F., 'The population trend in England between 1300 and 1348', *TRHS*, 5th series, 16 (1966), 23–42.

Hatcher, J., *Plague, Population and the English Economy, 1348–1530* (1977).

'English serfdom and villeinage: towards a reassessment', *P&P*, 90 (1981), 3–39.

Hatcher, J. and Bailey, M., *Modelling the Middle Ages: the history and theory of England's economic development* (Oxford, 2001).

Hilton, R. H., *The English Peasantry in the later Middle Ages* (Oxford, 1975).

Bond Men Made Free: medieval peasant movements and the English Rising of 1381 (1977).

Class Conflict and the Crisis of Feudalism: essays in medieval social history (1985).

English and French Towns in Feudal Society: a comparative study (Cambridge, 1992).

Hilton, R. H. and Aston, T. H., eds., *The English Rising of 1381* (Cambridge, 1984).

Holton, R. J., *The Transition from Feudalism to Capitalism* (Basingstoke, 1985).

Horrox, R., ed., *Fifteenth-Century Attitudes: perceptions of society in late medieval England* (Cambridge, 1994).

Jones, E. D., 'The exploitation of its serfs by Spalding priory before the Black Death', *Nottingham Mediaeval Studies*, 43 (1999), 126–51.

Keen, M., *English Society in the later Middle Ages 1348–1500* (Harmondsworth, 1990).

Kermode, J., *Medieval Merchants: York, Beverley and Hull in the later middle ages* (Cambridge, 1998).

Kitsikopoulos, H., 'Standards of living and capital formation in pre-plague England: a peasant budget model', *EcHR*, 2nd series, 53 (2000), 237–61.

Langdon, J., *Horses, Oxen and Technological Innovation: the use of draught animals in English farming from 1066 to 1500* (Cambridge, 1986).

Maddicott, J. R., 'The English peasantry and the demands of the Crown 1294–1341', *P&P* supplement 1 (1975).

Masschaele, J., *Peasants, Merchants and Markets: inland trade in medieval England, 1150–1350* (Basingstoke, 1997).

Mate, M. E., *Daughters, Wives and Widows after the Black Death: women in Sussex, 1350–1535* (Woodbridge, 1998).

Mayhew, N. J., 'Numismatic evidence and falling prices in the fourteenth century', *EcHR*, 2nd series, 27 (1974), 1–15.

Miller, E. and Hatcher, J., *Medieval England: rural society and economic change, 1086–1348* (1978).

Medieval England: towns, commerce and crafts, 1086–1348 (1995).

Moore, J. S., '"Quot homines?": the population of Domesday England', *Anglo-Norman Studies* 19 (1997), 307–34.

Mousnier, R., *Social Hierarchies: 1450 to the present*, trans. P. Evans (1973).

Mundill, R. R., *England's Jewish Solution: experiment and expulsion, 1262–1290* (Cambridge, 1998).

Nightingale, P., 'England and the European depression of the mid-fifteenth century', *Journal of European Economic History*, 26 (1997), 631–56.

Ossowski, S., *Class Structure in the Social Consciousness*, trans. S. Patterson (1963).

Persson, K. G., *Pre-Industrial Economic Growth: social organization and technological progress in Europe* (Oxford, 1988).

Phythian-Adams, C. V., 'Rituals of personal confrontation in late medieval England', *Bulletin of the John Rylands University Library of Manchester*, 73 (1991), 65–90.

Pirenne, H., *Economic and Social History of Medieval Europe* (1933).

Medieval Cities: their origins and the revival of trade, trans. F. D. Halsey (Princeton, NJ, 1974; first edn, 1925).

Platt, C., *King Death: the Black Death and its aftermath in late-medieval England* (1996).

Poos, L. R., *A Rural Society after the Black Death: Essex 1350–1525* (Cambridge, 1991).

Postan, M. M., 'Medieval agrarian society in its prime: England', in M. M. Postan, ed., *The Cambridge Economic History of Europe*, I, *The Agrarian Life of the Middle Ages* (Cambridge, 1966), pp. 549–632.

The Medieval Economy and Society: an economic history of Britain in the middle ages (1972).

Essays on Medieval Agriculture and General Problems of the Medieval Economy (Cambridge, 1973).

Raftis, J. A., *Peasant Economic Development within the English Manorial System* (Montreal, 1996).

Razi, Z., 'The Toronto School's reconstitution of medieval peasant society: a critical view', *P&P*, 85 (1979), 141–58.

Life, Marriage and Death in a Medieval Parish: economy, society and demography in Halesowen 1270–1400 (Cambridge, 1980).

'The struggles between the abbots of Halesowen and their tenants in the thirteenth and fourteenth centuries', in T. H. Aston, P. R. Coss, C. Dyer, and J. Thirsk, eds., *Social Relations and Ideas: essays in honour of R. H. Hilton* (Cambridge, 1983), pp. 151–67.

Razi, Z. and Smith, R. M., eds., *Medieval Society and the Manor Court* (Oxford, 1996).

Reynolds, S., *An Introduction to the History of English Medieval Towns* (Oxford, 1977).

'Medieval urban history and the history of political thought', *Urban History Yearbook* (1982), 14–23.

Rigby, S. H., *English Society in the later Middle Ages: class, status and gender* (Basingstoke, 1995).

Chaucer in Context: society, allegory and gender (Manchester, 1996).

Marxism and History: a critical introduction (2nd edn, Manchester, 1998).

'Approaches to pre-industrial social structure', in J. Denton, ed., *Orders and Hierarchies in late Medieval and Renaissance Europe* (Basingstoke, 1999), pp. 6–25.

'Gendering the Black Death: women in later medieval England', in P. Stafford and A. B. Mulder-Bakker, eds., *Gendering the Middle Ages* (Oxford, 2001), pp. 745–54.

ed., *A Companion to Britain in the later Middle Ages* (Oxford, 2003).

'Historical materialism: social structure and social change in the middle ages', *Journal of Medieval and Early Modern Studies*, 34 (2004), 473–522.

Rigby, S. H. and Ewan, E., 'Government, power and authority, 1300–1540', in D. Palliser, ed., *The Cambridge Urban History of Britain*, I: *600–1540* (Cambridge, 2000), pp. 291–312.

Runciman, W. G., 'Towards a theory of social stratification', in F. Parkin, ed., *The Social Analysis of Class Structure* (1974), pp. 55–101.

Smith, R. M., 'Hypothèses sur la nuptialité en Angleterre aux XIIIe–XIVe siècles', *Annales*, 38 (1983), 107–36.

Spufford, P., *Money and its use in Medieval Europe* (Cambridge, 1988).

Stone, D., 'The productivity of hired and customary labour: evidence from Wisbech Barton in the fourteenth century', *EcHR*, 2nd series, 50 (1997), 640–56.

Thrupp, S. L., *The Merchant Class of Medieval London* (Chicago, 1948).

Titow, J. Z., *English Rural Society 1200–1350* (1969).

Waugh, S. L., *England in the Reign of Edward III* (Cambridge, 1991).

Wrigley, E. A., *Population and History* (1969).

CHAPTER 2 AN AGE OF DEFERENCE

Alcock, N. W. and Woodfield, C. T. P., 'Social pretensions in architecture and ancestry: Hall House, Sawbridge, Warwickshire and the Andrewe family', *The Antiquaries Journal*, 76 (1996), 51–72.

Archer, R. E., '"How ladies . . . who live on their manors ought to manage their households and estates": women as landholders and administrators in the later middle ages', in P. J. P. Goldberg, ed., *Woman is a Worthy Wight: women in English society, c. 1200–1500* (Stroud, 1992), pp. 149–81.

Bellamy, J. G., *The Law of Treason in England in the later Middle Ages* (Cambridge, 1970).

Brand, P., *The Origins of the English Legal Profession* (Oxford, 1992).

'The age of Bracton', in J. Hudson, ed., *The History of English Law: centenary essays on 'Pollock and Maitland'* (British Academy, 1996), pp. 65–89.

Britnell, R. H., *The Commercialisation of English Society, 1000–1500* (2nd edn, Manchester, 1996).

Carpenter, C., 'The Beauchamp affinity: a study of bastard feudalism at work', *EHR*, 95 (1980), 514–33.

Lordship and Polity: a study of Warwickshire landed society, 1401–1499 (Cambridge, 1992).

Carpenter, D. A., Coss, P. R. and Crouch, D. D., 'Debate: bastard feudalism revised', *P&P*, 131 (1991), 165–203.

Cherry, M., 'The Courtenay earls of Devon: the formation and disintegration of a late medieval aristocratic affinity', *Southern History*, 1 (1979), 71–97.

Coss, P. R., 'Literature and social terminology: the vavasour in England', in T. H. Aston et al., eds., *Social Relations and Ideas: essays in honour of R. H. Hilton* (Cambridge, 1983), pp. 109–50.

'Bastard feudalism revised', *P&P*, 125 (1989), 27–64.

Lordship, Knighthood and Locality: a study in English society c. 1180–c. 1280 (Cambridge, 1991).

The Knight in Medieval England, 1000–1400 (Stroud, 1993).

The Lady in Medieval England, 1000–1500 (Stroud, 1998).

The Origins of the English Gentry (Cambridge, 2003).

Coss, P. R. and Keen, M., eds., *Heraldry, Pageantry and Social Display in Medieval England* (Woodbridge, 2002).

Crouch, D., *The Image of Aristocracy in Britain 1000–1300* (1992).

Cullum, P. and Goldberg, P. J. P., 'How Margaret Blackburn taught her daughters: reading devotional instruction in a book of hours', in J. Wogan-Browne et al., eds., *Medieval Women: texts and contexts in medieval Britain: essays for Felicity Riddy* (Turnhout, 2000), pp. 217–36.

Dyer, C., 'Were there any capitalists in fifteenth-century England?', in J. Kermode, ed., *Enterprise and Individuals in Fifteenth-Century England* (Stroud, 1991), pp. 1–24.

'How urbanized was medieval England?', in J.-M. Duvosquel and E. Thoen, eds., *Peasants and Townsmen in Medieval Europe: studia in honorem Adriaan Verhulst* (Ghent, 1995), pp. 169–83.

Emmerson, R. K. and Goldberg, P. J. P., 'The Lord Geoffrey had me made: lordship and labour in the Luttrell Psalter', in J. Bothwell, P. J. P. Goldberg and W. M. Ormrod, eds., *The Problem of Labour in Fourteenth-Century England* (York, 2000), pp. 43–63.

Farmer, S., 'Persuasive voices: clerical images of medieval wives', *Speculum*, 61 (1986), 517–43.

Faulkner, K., 'The transformation of knighthood in early thirteenth-century England', *EHR*, III (1996), 1–23.

Given-Wilson, C., *The English Nobility in the late Middle Ages* (1987).

Hanawalt, B. A., ed., *Chaucer's England: literature in historical context* (Minneapolis, MN, 1992).

Hicks, M., *Bastard Feudalism* (1995).

The English Peasantry in the later Middle Ages (Oxford, 1975).

Hilton, R. H., 'Freedom and villeinage in England', in R. H. Hilton, ed., *Peasants, Knights and Heretics* (Cambridge, 1976), pp. 174–91.

Bond Men Made Free: medieval peasant movements and the English Rising of 1381 (1977).

The Decline of Serfdom in Medieval England (2nd edn, 1983).

Class Conflict and the Crisis of Feudalism: essays in medieval social history (1985).

Hilton, R. H. and Aston, T. H., eds., *The English Rising of 1381* (Cambridge, 1984).

Horrox, R., 'The urban gentry in the fifteenth century', in J. A. F. Thomson, ed., *Towns and Townspeople in the Fifteenth Century* (Gloucester, 1988), pp. 22–44.

ed., *Fifteenth-Century Attitudes: perceptions of society in late medieval England* (Cambridge, 1994).

Keen, M., *Chivalry* (New Haven, CT, 1984).

Mann, J., *Chaucer and Medieval Estates Satire: the literature of social classes and the General Prologue to the Canterbury Tales* (Cambridge, 1973).

Mertes, K., *The English Noble Household 1250–1600: good governance and politic rule* (Oxford, 1988).

Miller, E., 'Rulers of thirteenth-century towns: the cases of York and Newcastle-upon-Tyne', in P. R. Coss and S. D. Lloyd, eds., *Thirteenth Century England*, I (Woodbridge, 1986), pp. 128–41.

Richmond, C., *John Hopton: a fifteenth century Suffolk gentleman* (Cambridge, 1981).

The Paston Family in the Fifteenth Century: the first phase (Cambridge, 1990).

Saul, N., 'The social status of Chaucer's Franklin: a reconsideration', *Medium Aevum*, 52 (1983), 10–26.

Strohm, P., *Hochon's Arrow: the social imagination of fourteenth-century texts* (Princeton, 1992).

Storey, R. L., 'Gentlemen-bureaucrats', in C. H. Clough, ed., *Profession, Vocation and Culture in later Medieval England* (Liverpool, 1982), pp. 90–129.

Walker, S., *The Lancastrian Affinity 1361–1399* (Oxford, 1990).

Waugh, S. L., 'Tenure to contract: lordship and clientage in thirteenth-century England', *EHR*, 101 (1986), 813–39.

'The third century of English feudalism', in M. Prestwich, R. Britnell and R. Frame, eds., *Thirteenth Century England* VII (Woodbridge, 1999), pp. 47–59.

Woolgar, C. M., *The Great Household in late Medieval England* (New Haven, CT, 1999).

CHAPTER 3 THE ENTERPRISE OF WAR

Ayton, A., *Knights and Warhorses: military service and the English aristocracy under Edward III* (Woodbridge, 1994).

Barber, R. *The Knight and Chivalry* (Woodbridge, 1974).

Barker, J. R. V., *The Tournament in England 1100–1400* (Woodbridge, 1986).

Bradbury, J., *The Medieval Archer* (Woodbridge, 1985).

Coss, P. R., *The Knight in Medieval England, 1000–1400* (Stroud, 1993).

Curry, A. and Hughes, M., eds., *Arms, Armies and Fortifications in the Hundred Years War* (Woodbridge, 1994).

Hewitt, H. J., *The Organisation of War under Edward III, 1338–62* (Manchester, 1966).

Keen, M. H., *The Laws of War in the Late Middle Ages* (1965).

Chivalry (New Haven, CT, 1984).

Powicke, M., *Military Obligation in Medieval England: a study in liberty and duty* (Oxford, 1962).

Prestwich, M., *Armies and Warfare in the Middle Ages: the English experience* (New Haven, CT, 1996).

Strickland, M., *War and Chivalry: the conduct and perception of war in England and Normandy, 1066–1217* (Cambridge, 1996).

ed., *Armies, Chivalry and Warfare in Medieval Britain and France: proceedings of the 1995 Harlaxton Symposium* (Stamford, 1998).

Vale, M. G. A., *War and Chivalry: warfare and aristocratic culture in England, France and Burgundy at the end of the Middle Ages* (1981).

CHAPTER 4 ORDER AND LAW

Baker, J. H., *An Introduction to English Legal History* (3rd edn, 1990).

Beckerman, J. S., 'Procedural innovation and institutional change in medieval English manorial courts', *Law and History Review*, 10 (1992), 197–252.

Bellamy, J. G., *The Criminal Trial in later Medieval England: felony before the courts from Edward I to the sixteenth century* (Stroud, 1998).

Brand, P., *The Origins of the English Legal Profession* (Oxford, 1992).

Kings, Barons and Justices: the making and enforcement of legislation in thirteenth-century England (Cambridge, 2003).

Brooks, C. W., 'Litigation and society in England, 1200–1996', in C. W. Brooks, ed., *Lawyers, Litigation and English Society since 1450* (1998), pp. 63–128.

Fryde, N., 'A medieval robber baron: Sir John Molyns of Stoke Poges, Buckinghamshire', in R. F. Hunnisett and J. B. Post, eds., *Medieval Legal Records Edited in Memory of C. A. F. Meekings* (1978), pp. 198–207.

Green, R. F., *A Crisis of Truth: literature and law in Ricardian England* (Philadelphia, 1999).

Guth, D. J., 'Enforcing late medieval law: patterns in litigation during Henry VII's reign', in J. H. Baker, ed., *Legal Records and the Historian* (1978), pp. 80–96.

Hanawalt, B. A., *'Of Good and Ill Repute': gender and social control in medieval England* (Oxford, 1998).

Hastings, M., *The Court of Common Pleas in Fifteenth-Century England: a study of legal administration and procedure* (Ithaca, NY, 1947).

Helmholz, R. H., *Marriage Litigation in Medieval England* (Cambridge, 1974).

Holt, J. C., *Robin Hood* (1982).

Ives, E. W., *The Common Lawyers of Pre-Reformation England* (Cambridge, 1983).

Kaeuper, R. W., *War, Justice and Public Order: England and France in the later middle ages* (Oxford, 1988).

Maddern, P. C., *Violence and Social Order: East Anglia 1422–1442* (Oxford, 1992).

Maddicott, J. R., *Law and Lordship: royal justices as retainers in thirteenth- and fourteenth-century England*, *P&P* supplement 4 (1978).

McIntosh, M. K., *Controlling Misbehavior in England, 1370–1600* (Cambridge, 1998).

Milsom, S. F. C., *Historical Foundations of the Common Law* (2nd edn, 1981).

Moreton, C. E., *The Townshends and their World: gentry, law, and land in Norfolk c. 1450–1551* (Oxford, 1992).

Musson, A., *Medieval Law in Context: the growth of legal consciousness from Magna Carta to the Peasants' Revolt* (Manchester, 2001).

Musson, A. and Ormrod, W. M., *The Evolution of English Justice: law, politics and society in the fourteenth century* (Basingstoke, 1999).

Palmer, R. C., *The Whilton Dispute, 1264–1380: a socio-legal study of dispute settlement in medieval England* (Princeton, NJ, 1984).

Powell, E., 'Arbitration and the law in England in the later middle ages, *TRHS*, 5th series, 13 (1983), 49–67.

Kingship, Law and Society: criminal justice in the reign of Henry V (Oxford, 1989).

Pronay, N., 'The chancellor, the chancery, and the council at the end of the fifteenth century', in H. Hearder and H. R. Loyn, eds., *British Government and Administration: studies presented to S. B. Chrimes* (Cardiff, 1974), pp. 87–103.

Putnam, B. H., *The Place in Legal History of Sir William Shareshull, Chief Justice of the King's Bench 1350–1361: a study of judicial and administrative methods in the reign of Edward III* (Cambridge, 1950).

Razi, Z. and Smith, R. M., eds., *Medieval Society and the Manor Court* (Oxford, 1996).

Summerson, H., 'The enforcement of the statute of Winchester, 1285–1327', *Journal of Legal History*, 13 (1992), 232–50.

Walker, S., 'Yorkshire justices of the peace, 1389–1413', *EHR*, 108 (1993), 281–313.

CHAPTER 5 SOCIAL MOBILITY

Barron, C. M. and Sutton, A. F., eds., *Medieval London Widows, 1300–1500* (1994).

Bennett, J. M., *Ale, Beer and Brewsters in England: women's work in a changing world, 1300–1600* (Oxford, 1996).

A Medieval Life: Cecilia Penifader of Brigstock, c. 1295–1344 (Boston, MA, 1999).

Bennett, M. J., *Community, Class and Careerism: Cheshire and Lancashire society in the age of Sir Gawain and the Green Knight* (Cambridge, 1983).

Carpenter, C., *Lordship and Polity: a study of Warwickshire landed society, 1401–1499* (Cambridge, 1992).

Carpenter, D. A., 'Was there a crisis of the knightly class in the thirteenth century? The Oxfordshire evidence', *EHR*, 95 (1980), 721–52.

Crook, D., 'A dying queen and a declining knight: Sir Richard de Weston of Weston, Nottinghamshire (d.1301), and his family', in C. Richmond and I. Harvey, eds., *Recognitions: essays presented to Edmund Fryde* (Aberystwyth, 1996), pp. 89–124.

Coss, P. R., *Lordship, Knighthood and Locality: a study in English society c. 1180–c. 1280* (Cambridge, 1991).

Curry, A. and Matthew, E., eds., *Concepts and Patterns of Service in the later Middle Ages* (Woodbridge, 2000).

Dyer, C., *Standards of Living in the later Middle Ages: social change in England, c. 1200–c. 1520* (Cambridge, 1989).

Fryde, E. B., *William de la Pole: merchant and king's banker (†1366)* (1988).

Peasants and Landlords in later Medieval England (Stroud, 1996).

Haines, R. M., *The Church and Politics in Fourteenth-Century England: the career of Adam Orleton, c. 1275–c. 1345* (Cambridge, 1978).

Hammer, C. I., 'Anatomy of an oligarchy: the Oxford town council in the fifteenth and sixteenth centuries', *Journal of British Studies*, 18 (1978), 1–27.

Hanawalt, B. A., 'Remarriage as an option for urban and rural widows in late medieval England', in S. S. Walker, ed., *Wife and Widow in Medieval England* (Ann Arbor, MI, 1993), pp. 141–64.

Holt, J. C., *Robin Hood* (1982).

Horrox, R. E., 'The urban gentry in the fifteenth century', in J. A. F. Thomson, ed., *Towns and Townspeople in the Fifteenth Century* (Gloucester, 1988), pp. 22–44.

Kermode, J., *Medieval Merchants: York, Beverley and Hull in the later middle ages* (Cambridge, 1998).

Kowaleski, M., 'The commercial dominance of a medieval provincial oligarchy: Exeter in the late fourteenth century', *Mediaeval Studies*, 46 (1984), 355–84.

McHardy, A., 'Careers and disappointment in the late medieval Church: some English evidence', in W. J. Sheils and D. Wood, eds., *The Ministry: clerical and lay* (Oxford, 1989), pp. 111–30.

Morgan, D. A. L., 'The individual style of the English gentleman', in M. Jones, ed., *Gentry and Lesser Nobility in late Medieval Europe* (Gloucester, 1986), pp. 15–35.

Moreton, C. E., *The Townshends and their World: gentry, law, and land in Norfolk c. 1450–1551* (Oxford, 1992).

Oliva, M., *The Convent and the Community in late Medieval England: female monasteries in the diocese of Norwich, 1350–1540* (Woodbridge, 1998).

Palmer, R. C., *English Law in the Age of the Black Death 1348–81: a transformation of governance and law* (Chapel Hill, NC, 1993).

Richmond, C., *John Hopton: a fifteenth century Suffolk gentleman* (Cambridge, 1981).

Rigby, S. H. and Ewan, E., 'Government, power and authority, 1300–1540', in D. Palliser, ed., *The Cambridge Urban History of Britain*, 1: 600–1540 (Cambridge, 2000), pp. 291–312.

Saul, N., *Knights and Esquires: the Gloucestershire gentry in the fourteenth century* (Oxford, 1981).

Smith, R. M., ed., *Land, Kinship and Life-Cycles* (Cambridge, 1984).

Storey, R. L., 'Gentlemen-bureaucrats', in C. H. Clough, ed., *Profession, Vocation and Culture in later Medieval England* (Liverpool, 1982), pp. 90–129.

CHAPTER 6 TOWN LIFE

Bartlett, J. N., 'The expansion and decline of York in the later middle ages', *EcHR*, 2nd series, 12 (1959–60), 17–33.

Bennett, J. M., *Ale, Beer and Brewsters in England: women's work in a changing world, 1300–1600* (Oxford, 1996).

Beresford, M., *New Towns of the Middle Ages: town plantation in England, Wales and Gascony* (1967).

Britnell, R. H., *Growth and Decline in Colchester, 1300–1525* (Cambridge, 1986).

ed., *Daily Life in the late Middle Ages* (Stroud, 1998).

Carlin, M., *Medieval Southwark* (1996).

Dyer, A., *Decline and Growth in English Towns 1400–1640* (Basingstoke, 1991).

Dyer, C., 'The consumer and the market in the later middle ages', *EcHR*, 2nd series, 42 (1989), 305–27.

'How urbanized was medieval England?', in J.-M. Duvosquel and E. Thoen, eds., *Peasants and Townsmen in Medieval Europe: studia in honorem Adriaan Verhulst* (Ghent, 1995), pp. 169–83.

Goldberg, P. J. P., *Women, Work and Life Cycle in a Medieval Economy: women in York and Yorkshire, c. 1300–1520* (Oxford, 1992).

Hammer, C. I., 'Anatomy of an oligarchy: the Oxford town council in the fifteenth and sixteenth centuries', *Journal of British Studies*, 18 (1978), 1–27.

Hilton, R. H., 'Small town society in England before the Black Death', *P&P*, 105 (1984), 53–78.

Holt, R. and Rosser, G., eds., *The Medieval Town: a reader in English urban history, 1200–1540* (1990).

Keene, D., *Survey of Medieval Winchester* (2 vols., Oxford, 1985).

Kermode, J., *Medieval Merchants: York, Beverley and Hull in the later middle ages* (Cambridge, 1998).

Kowaleski, M., *Local Markets and Regional Trade in Medieval Exeter* (Cambridge, 1995).

Masschaele, J., *Peasants, Merchants and Markets: inland trade in medieval England, 1150–1350* (Basingstoke, 1997).

McRee, B. R., 'Peacemaking and its limits in late medieval Norwich', *EHR*, 109 (1994), 831–66.

Miller, E. and Hatcher, J., *Medieval England: towns, commerce and crafts, 1086–1348* (1995).

Nightingale, P., *A Medieval Mercantile Community: the grocers' company and the politics and trade of London, 1000–1485* (New Haven, CT, 1995).

Palliser, D., ed., *The Cambridge Urban History of Britain, I: 600–1540* (Cambridge, 2000).

Phythian-Adams, C., *Desolation of a City: Coventry and the urban crisis of the late middle ages* (Cambridge, 1979).

Platt, C., *Medieval Southampton: the port and trading community, A.D. 1000–1600* (1973).

Reynolds, S., *An Introduction to the History of English Medieval Towns* (Oxford, 1977).

'Medieval urban history and the history of political thought', *Urban History Yearbook*, 1982, 14–23.

Rigby, S. H., *Medieval Grimsby, Growth and Decline* (Hull, 1993).

Rosser, G., *Medieval Westminster, 1200–1540* (Oxford, 1989).

'Myth, image and social process in the English medieval town', *Urban History*, 23 (1996), 5–25.

Shaw, D. G., *The Creation of a Community: the city of Wells in the middle ages* (Oxford, 1993).

Slater, T. R., ed., *Towns in Decline AD 100–1600* (Aldershot, 2000).

Swanson, H., *Medieval Artisans: an urban class in late medieval England* (Oxford, 1989).

Medieval British Towns (Basingstoke, 1999).

Thomson, J. A. F., ed., *Towns and Townspeople in the Fifteenth Century* (Gloucester, 1988).

Thrupp, S. L., *The Merchant Class of Medieval London* (Chicago, 1948).

CHAPTER 7 THE LAND

Astill, G. and Grant, A., eds., *The Countryside of Medieval England* (Oxford, 1988).

Astill, G. and Langdon, J., eds., *Medieval Farming and Technology: the impact of agricultural change in northwest Europe* (Leiden, 1997).

Aston, T. H. and Philpin, C. H. E., eds., *The Brenner Debate: agrarian class structure and economic development in pre-industrial Europe* (Cambridge, 1985).

Bailey, M., *A Marginal Economy? East Anglian Breckland in the later middle ages* (Cambridge, 1989).

Bartley, K. C. and Campbell, B. M. S., *Lay Lordship, Land and Wealth: a socio-economic atlas of England, 1300–49* (Manchester, 2004).

Beresford, M. W. and Hurst, J. G., *Deserted Medieval Villages: studies* (1971).

Brenner, R., 'Agrarian class structure and economic development in pre-industrial Europe', *P&P*, 70 (1976), 30–75.

'The agrarian roots of European capitalism', *P&P*, 97 (1982), 16–113.

'The rises and declines of serfdom in medieval and early modern Europe', in M. L. Bush, ed., *Serfdom and Slavery: studies in legal bondage* (Harlow, 1996), pp. 247–76.

'Property relations and the growth of agricultural productivity in late medieval and early modern Europe', in A. Bhaduri and R. Skarstein, eds., *Economic Development and Agricultural Productivity* (Cheltenham, 1997), pp. 9–41.

Campbell, B. M. S., *English Seigniorial Agriculture, 1250–1450* (Cambridge, 2000).

Campbell, B. M. S., Galloway, J. A., Keene, D. and Murphy, M., *A Medieval Capital and its Grain Supply: agrarian production and distribution in the London region c. 1300* (Institute of British Geographers, Historical Geography Research Series, XXX, 1993).

Campbell, B. M. S. and Overton, M., eds., *Land, Labour and Livestock: historical studies in European agricultural productivity* (Manchester, 1991).

Darby, H. C., Glasscock, R. E., Sheail, J. and Versey, G. R., 'The changing geographical distribution of wealth in England 1086–1334–1525', *Journal of Historical Geography*, 5 (1979), 247–62.

DeWindt, A. R., 'Peasant power structures in fourteenth-century King's Ripton', *Mediaeval Studies*, 38 (1976), 236–67.

'A peasant land market and its participants: King's Ripton, 1280–1400', *Midland History*, 4 (1978), 142–59.

Dyer, C., *Lords and Peasants in a Changing Society: the estates of the bishopric of Worcester, 680–1540* (Cambridge, 1980).

Everyday Life in Medieval England (1994).

Hallam, H. E., ed., *The Agrarian History of England and Wales,* II: *1042–1350* (Cambridge, 1988).

Harvey, B. F., *Westminster Abbey and its Estates in the Middle Ages* (Oxford, 1977).

Hatcher, J., 'English serfdom and villeinage: towards a reassessment', *P&P*, 90 (1981), 3–39.

Hilton, R. H., *The Decline of Serfdom in Medieval England* (2nd edn, 1983).

Howell, C., *Land, Family and Inheritance in Transition: Kibworth Harcourt 1280–1700* (Cambridge, 1983).

Kershaw, I., 'The great famine and agrarian crisis in England 1315–22', *P&P*, 59 (1973), 3–50.

Kosminsky, E. A., *Studies in the Agrarian History of England in the Thirteenth Century,* ed. R. H. Hilton, trans. R. Kisch (Oxford, 1956).

Maddicott, J. R., 'The English peasantry and the demands of the Crown 1294–1341', *P&P* supplement 1 (1975).

McIntosh, M. K., *Autonomy and Community: the royal manor of Havering, 1200–1500* (Cambridge, 1986).

Miller, E., *The Agrarian History of England and Wales,* III: *1348–1500* (Cambridge, 1991).

Miller, E. and Hatcher, J., *Medieval England: rural society and economic change, 1086–1348* (1978).

Postan, M. M., 'Medieval agrarian society in its prime: England', in M. M. Postan, ed., *The Cambridge Economic History of Europe,* I: *The Agrarian Life of the Middle Ages* (Cambridge, 1966), pp. 549–632.

Raftis, J. A., *Peasant Economic Development within the English Manorial System* (Montreal, 1996).

Razi, Z., *Life, Marriage and Death in a Medieval Parish: economy, society and demography in Halesowen 1270–1400* (Cambridge, 1980).

Razi, Z. and Smith, R. M., eds., *Medieval Society and the Manor Court* (Oxford, 1996).

Rigby, S. H., ed., *A Companion to Britain in the later Middle Ages* (Oxford, 2003).

Stone, D., 'The productivity of hired and customary labour: evidence from Wisbech Barton in the fourteenth century', *EcHR*, 2nd series, 50 (1997), 640–56.

Smith, R. M., ed., *Land, Kinship and Life-cycles* (Cambridge, 1984).

Sweeney, D., ed., *Agriculture in the Middle Ages: technology, practice and representation* (Philadelphia, 1995).

Titow, J. Z., *English Rural Society 1200–1350* (1969).

Whittle, J., *The Development of Agrarian Capitalism: land and labour in Norfolk, 1440–1580* (Oxford, 2000).

CHAPTER 8 A CONSUMER ECONOMY

Astill, G. and Grant, A., eds., *The Countryside of Medieval England* (Oxford, 1988).

Baldwin, F. E., *Sumptuary Legislation and Personal Regulation in England* (Baltimore, MD, 1926).

Biddle, M., ed., *Object and Economy in Medieval Winchester. Artefacts from medieval Winchester,* II (Oxford, 1990).

Blair, J. and Ramsey, N., eds., *English Medieval Industries: craftsmen, techniques, products* (1991).

Britnell, R. H., *The Commercialisation of English Society, 1000–1500* (2nd edn, Manchester, 1996).

ed., *Daily Life in the late Middle Ages* (Stroud, 1998).

Dyer, C., *Standards of Living in the later Middle Ages: social change in England, c. 1200–1520* (Cambridge, 1989).

Everyday Life in Medieval England (1994).

Egan, G., *The Medieval Household: daily living c. 1150–c. 1450,* Medieval Finds from Excavations in London, VI (HMSO, 1998).

Gaimster, D. and Stamper, P., eds., *The Age of Transition: the archaeology of English culture 1400–1600,* Society for Medieval Archaeology monograph XV (Oxford, 1997).

Grenville, J., *Medieval Housing* (1997).

Harvey, B., *Living and Dying in England 1100–1540: the monastic experience* (Oxford, 1993).

Hellinga, L. and Trapp, J. B., eds., *The Cambridge History of the Book in Britain,* III: *1400–1557* (Cambridge, 1999).

Hicks, M. A., ed., *Revolution and Consumption in late Medieval England* (Woodbridge, 2001).

Hunt, A., *Governance of the Consuming Passions: a history of sumptuary law* (Basingstoke, 1996).

Johnson, M., *An Archaeology of Capitalism* (Oxford, 1996).

Kowaleski, M., *Local Markets and Regional Trade in Medieval Exeter* (Cambridge, 1995).

Newton, S. M., *Fashion in the Age of the Black Prince: a study of the years 1340–1365* (Woodbridge, 1980).

Piponnier, F. and Mane, P., *Dress in the Middle Ages,* trans. C. Beamish (New Haven, CT, 1997).

Schofield, J., *Medieval London Houses* (New Haven, CT, 1994).

Woolgar, C. M., *The Great Household in late Medieval England* (New Haven, CT, 1999).

CHAPTER 9 MOVING AROUND

Britnell, R. H., *The Commercialisation of English Society, 1000–1500* (2nd edn, Manchester, 1996).

Childs, W. R., 'The perils, or otherwise, of maritime pilgrimage to Santiago de Compostela in the fifteenth century', in J. Stopford, ed., *Pilgrimage Explored* (Woodbridge, 1999), pp. 123–43.

Clark, J., ed., *The Medieval Horse and its Equipment c. 1150–c. 1450*, Medieval Finds from Excavations in London, V (HMSO, 1995).

Friel, I., *The Good Ship: ships, shipbuilding and technology in England, 1200–1520* (1995).

Hindle, B. P., 'The road network of medieval England and Wales', *Journal of Historical Geography*, 2 (1976), 207–21.

Hutchinson, G., *Medieval Ships and Shipping* (Leicester, 1994).

Jusserand, J. J., *English Wayfaring Life in the Middle Ages* (4th edn, 1950).

Kowaleski, M., *Local Markets and Regional Trade in Medieval Exeter* (Cambridge, 1995).

Langdon, J., *Horses, Oxen and Technological Innovation: the use of draught animals in English farming from 1066 to 1500* (Cambridge, 1986).

Lopez, R. S., 'The evolution of land transport in the middle ages', *P&P*, 9 (1956), 17–29.

Masschaele, J., *Peasants, Merchants and Markets: inland trade in medieval England, 1150–1350* (Basingstoke, 1997).

Miller, E. and Hatcher, J., *Medieval England: towns, commerce and crafts, 1086–1348* (1995).

Moore, E. W., *The Fairs of Medieval England: an introductory study* (Toronto, 1985).

Ohler, N., *The Medieval Traveller*, trans. C. Hiller (Woodbridge, 1989).

Phillips, J.R.S., *The Medieval Expansion of Europe* (Oxford, 1988).

Salzman, L. F., *English Trade in the Middle Ages* (Oxford, 1931).

Stenton, F. M., 'The road system of medieval England', *EcHR*, 7 (1936), 1–21.

Taylor, C., *Roads and Tracks of Britain* (1979).

Willan, T. S., *The Inland Trade: studies in English internal trade in the sixteenth and seventeeth centuries* (Manchester, 1976).

Willard, J. F., 'Inland transportation in England during the fourteenth century', *Speculum*, 1 (1926), 361–74.

Woolgar, C. M., *The Great Household in late Medieval England* (New Haven, CT, 1999).

CHAPTER 10 WORK AND LEISURE

Bardsley, S., 'Women's work reconsidered: gender and wage differentiation in late medieval England', *P&P*, 165 (1999), 3–29.

Beier, A. L., *Masterless Men: the vagrancy problem in England 1560–1640* (1985).

Burke, P., 'The invention of leisure in early modern Europe', *P&P*, 146 (1995), 136–50.

Carter, J. M., *Medieval Games: sports and recreations in feudal society* (Westport, CT, 1982).

Dyer, C., 'Leisure among the peasantry in the later middle ages,' in *Il tempo libero: economia e società secc xiii–xvii*, Istituto Internazionale di Storia Economica, F. Datini (Prato, 1995), pp. 291–306.

'Work ethics in the fourteenth century' in J. Bothwell et al., eds., *The Problem of Labour in Fourteenth-century England* (Woodbridge, 2000), pp. 21–41.

Dymond, D., 'A lost social institution: the camping close', *Rural History*, 1 (1990), 165–92.

Given-Wilson, C., 'Service, serfdom and English labour legislation, 1350–1500', in A. Curry and E. Matthew, eds., *Concepts and Patterns of Service in the later Middle Ages* (Woodbridge, 2000), pp. 21–37.

Hajnal, J., 'European marriage patterns in perspective', in D. V. Glass and D. E. C. Eversley, eds., *Population in History: essays in historical demography* (1965), pp. 101–43.

Harvey, B., 'Work and *festa ferianda* in medieval England', *JEH*, 23 (1972), 289–308.

Hatcher, J., 'Labour, leisure and economic thought before the nineteenth century', *P&P*, 160 (1998), 64–115.

Hoffman, R. C., 'Fishing for sport in medieval Europe: new evidence', *Speculum*, 60 (1985), 877–902.

Kowaleski, M. and Bennett, J., 'Crafts, gilds and women in the middle ages: fifty years after Marian K. Dale', in J. M. Bennett et al., eds., *Sisters and Workers in the Middle Ages* (Chicago, 1989), pp. 11–25.

McIntosh, M. K., *Controlling Misbehavior in England, 1370–1600* (Cambridge, 1998).

Ovitt, G., Jr., 'The cultural context of western technology: early Christian attitudes toward manual labour', in A. J. Frantzen and D. Moffat, eds., *The Work of Work: servitude, slavery and labor in medieval England* (Glasgow, 1994), pp. 71–94.

Penn, S. A. C. and Dyer, C. C., 'Wages and earnings in late medieval England: evidence from the enforcement of the labour laws', *EcHR*, 2nd series, 43 (1990), 356–76.

Reeves, A. C., *Pleasures and Pastimes in Medieval England* (Stroud, 1995).

Stone, D., 'The productivity of hired and customary labour: evidence from Wisbech Barton in the fourteenth century', *EcHR*, 2nd series, 50 (1997), 640–56.

Swanson, H., *Medieval Artisans: an urban class in late medieval England* (Oxford, 1989).

Woodward, D., *Men at Work: labourers and building craftsmen in the towns of northern England, 1450–1750* (Cambridge, 1995).

CHAPTER 11 RELIGIOUS BELIEF

Alexander, J. and Binski, P., eds., *The Age of Chivalry: art in Plantagenet England 1200–1400* (1987).

Aston, M., *Lollards and Reformers: images and literacy in late medieval religion* (1984).

Atkinson, C., *Mystic and Pilgrim: the book and the world of Margery Kempe* (Ithaca, NY, 1983).

Bossy, J., *Christianity in the West, 1400–1700* (Oxford, 1985).

Brown, A. D., *Popular Piety in late Medieval England: the diocese of Salisbury 1250–1550* (Oxford, 1995).

Duffy, E., *The Stripping of the Altars: traditional religion in England 1400–1580* (New Haven, CT, 1992).

Gibson, G. McM., *The Theater of Devotion: East Anglian drama and society in the late middle ages* (Chicago, 1989).

Goodman, A., *Margery Kempe and her World* (Harlow, 2002).

Hudson, A., *The Premature Reformation: Wycliffite texts and Lollard history* (Oxford, 1988).

Hughes, J., *Pastors and Visionaries: religion and secular life in late medieval Yorkshire* (Woodbridge, 1988).

Knowles, D., *The Religious Orders in England* (3 vols., Cambridge, 1948–59).

McFarlane, K. B., *John Wycliffe and the Beginnings of English Nonconformity* (1952).

Marks, R., *Image and Devotion in late Medieval England* (Stroud, 2004).

Marks, R. and Williamson, P., eds., *Gothic: art for England 1400–1547* (2003).

Pantin, W. A., *The English Church in the Fourteenth Century* (Cambridge, 1955).

Rex, R., *The Lollards* (Basingstoke, 2002).

Shinners, J. and Dohar, W. J., eds., *Pastors and the Care of Souls in Medieval England* (Notre Dame, IN, 1998).

Simpson, J., *Reform and Cultural Revolution, 1350–1547* (Oxford, 2002).

Swanson, R. N., *Church and Society in late Medieval England* (Oxford, 1989).

  ed., *Catholic England: faith, religion and observance before the Reformation* (Manchester, 1993).

Wallace, D., ed., *The Cambridge History of Medieval English Literature* (Cambridge, 1999).

Wogan-Browne, J. et al., eds., *The Idea of the Vernacular, an anthology of Middle English literary theory, 1280–1520* (Exeter, 1999).

CHAPTER 12 A MAGIC UNIVERSE

Bailey, M. D., 'From sorcery to witchcraft: clerical conceptions of magic in the later middle ages', *Speculum*, 76 (2001), 960–90.

Braekman, W. L., *Studies on Alchemy, Diet, Medicine and Prognostication in Middle English* (Brussels, 1986).

Burnett, C., ed., *Adelard of Bath: an English scientist and arabist of the early twelfth century* (1987).

  Magic and Divination in the Middle Ages: texts and techniques in the Islamic and Christian worlds (Aldershot, 1996).

Carey, H. M., *Courting Disaster: astrology at the English court and university in the later middle ages* (Basingstoke, 1992).

Eamon, W., *Science and the Secrets of Nature: books of secrets in medieval and early modern culture* (Princeton, NJ, 1994).

Fanger, C., ed., *Conjuring Spirits: texts and traditions of late medieval ritual magic* (Stroud, 1999).

Ferreiro, A., ed., *The Devil, Heresy and Witchcraft in the Middle Ages: essays in honor of Jeffrey B. Russell* (Leiden, 1998).

Flint, V. I. J., *The Rise of Magic in Early Medieval Europe* (Oxford, 1991).

Grant, E., 'Medieval and Renaissance scholastic conceptions of the influence of the celestial region on the terrestrial', *Journal of Medieval and Renaissance Studies*, 17 (1987), 1–23.

Kieckhefer, R., *Magic in the Middle Ages* (Cambridge, 1989).

'The specific rationality of medieval magic', *AmHR*, 99 (1994), 813–36.

Forbidden Rites: a necromancer's manual of the fifteenth century (Stroud, 1997).

Linden, S. J., *Darke Hierogliphicks: alchemy in English literature from Chaucer to the Restoration* (Lexington, KY, 1996).

Martels, Z. R. W. M. von, *Alchemy Revisited* (Leiden, 1990).

North, J. D., *Chaucer's Universe* (Oxford, 1988).

Owst, G. R., 'Sortilegium in English homiletic literature of the fourteenth century', in J. Conway Davies, ed., *Studies Presented to Sir Hilary Jenkinson* (1957), pp. 272–303.

Rawcliffe, C., *Medicine and Society in later Medieval England* (Stroud, 1995).

Thorndike, L., *A History of Magic and Experimental Science* (8 vols., New York, 1923–58).

CHAPTER 13 RENUNCIATION

Burton, J., *Monastic and Religious Orders in Britain, 1000–1300* (Cambridge, 1994).

Coppack, G., *The White Monks: the Cistercians in Britain 1128–1540* (Stroud, 1998).

Golding, B., *Gilbert of Sempringham and the Gilbertine Order c. 1130–c. 1300* (Oxford, 1995).

Greene, J. P., *Medieval Monasteries* (Leicester, 1992).

Harvey, B., *Living and Dying in England 1100–1540: the monastic experience* (Oxford, 1993).

Knowles, D., *The Religious Orders in England* (3 vols., Cambridge, 1948–59).

The Monastic Order in England: a history of its development from the times of St Dunstan to the fourth Lateran council, 940–1216 (2nd edn, Cambridge, 1963).

Lambert, M. D., *Franciscan Poverty: the doctrine of the absolute poverty of Christ and the apostles in the Franciscan order, 1210–1323* (1961).

Lawrence, C. H., *Medieval Monasticism: forms of religious life in Western Europe in the Middle Ages* (3rd edn, 2001).

The Friars: the impact of the early mendicant movement on Western society (1994).

Newman, B., *From Virile Woman to Woman Christ: studies in medieval religion and literature* (Philadelphia, 1995).

Norton, C. and Park, D., eds., *Cistercian Art and Architecture in the British Isles* (1986).

Oliva, M., *The Convent and the Community in late Medieval England: female monasteries in the diocese of Norwich 1350–1540* (Woodbridge, 1998).

Warren, A. K., *Anchorites and their Patrons in Medieval England* (Berkeley, 1986).

Woodward, G. W. O., *The Dissolution of the Monasteries* (1966).

CHAPTER 14 RITUAL CONSTRUCTIONS OF SOCIETY

Benson, R. G., *Medieval Body Language: a study of the use of gesture in Chaucer's poetry*, Anglistica xxi (Copenhagen, 1980).

Bloch, M., *The Royal Touch: sacred monarchy and scrofula in England and France*, trans. J. E. Anderson (1973).

Bremmer, J. and Roodenburg, H., eds., *A Cultural History of Gesture: from antiquity to the present day* (Cambridge, 1991).

Duffy, E., *The Stripping of the Altars: traditional religion in England 1400–1580* (New Haven, CT, 1992).

Gibson, G. McM., *The Theater of Devotion: East Anglian drama and society in the late middle ages* (Chicago, 1989).

Harvey, B., 'Work and *festa ferianda* in medieval England', *JEH*, 23 (1972), 289–308.

Homans, G. C., 'The husbandsman's year', in *English Villagers of the Thirteenth Century* (Cambridge, MA., 1942), chapter 23.

Humphrey, C., *The Politics of Carnival: festive misrule in medieval England* (Manchester, 2001).

Hutton, R., *The Rise and Fall of Merry England: the ritual year 1400–1700* (Oxford, 1994).

Ingram, M., 'Juridical folklore in England illustrated by rough music', in C. Brooks and B. Lobban, eds., *Communities and Courts in Britain, 1150–1900* (1997), pp. 61–81.

James, M., 'Ritual, drama and social body in the late medieval English town', in M. James, *Society, Politics and Culture: studies in early modern England* (Cambridge, 1986), pp. 16–47.

Mellinkoff, R., 'Riding backwards: theme of humiliation and symbol of evil', *Viator*, 4 (1973), 153–76.

Phythian-Adams, C. V., 'Ceremony and the citizen: the communal year at Coventry 1450–1550', in P. Clark and P. Slack, eds., *Crisis and Order in English Towns, 1500–1700* (1972), pp. 57–85.

'Milk and soot: the changing vocabulary of a popular ritual in Stuart and Hanoverian London', in D. Fraser and A. Sutcliffe, eds., *The Pursuit of Urban History* (1983), pp. 84–104.

'Rituals of personal confrontation in late medieval England', *Bulletin of the John Rylands University Library of Manchester*, 73 (1991), 65–90.

Rubin, M., *Corpus Christi: the eucharist in late medieval culture* (Cambridge, 1991).

Sacks, H. S., 'The demise of the martyrs: the feasts of St Clement and St Katherine in Bristol, 1400–1600', *Social History*, 11 (1986), 141–69.

Twycross, M., 'Some approaches to dramatic festivity, especially processions', in M.Twycross, ed., *Festive Drama* (Cambridge, MA, 1996), pp. 1–33.

CHAPTER 15 IDENTITIES

Aers, D., ed., *Culture and History 1350–1600: essays on English communities, identities and writing* (Hemel Hempstead, 1992).

Anderson, B. R. O'G., *Imagined Communities: reflections on the origin and spread of nationalism* (revised edn, 1991).

Baldwin, F. E. *Sumptuary Legislation and Personal Regulation in England* (Baltimore, MD, 1926).

Barrell, A. D. M. and Brown, M. H., 'A settler community in post-conquest rural Wales: the English of Dyffryn Clwyd, 1294–1399', *Welsh History Review*, 17 (1995), 332–55.

Davies, R. R., 'The peoples of Britain and Ireland: I. Identities'; 'II. Names, boundaries and regional solidarities'; 'III. Laws and customs'; 'IV. Language and historical mythology', *TRHS*, 6th series, 4 (1994), 1–20; 5 (1995), 1–20; 6 (1996), 1–23; 7 (1997), 1–24.

The First English Empire: power and identities in the British Isles 1093–1343 (Oxford, 2000).

'Kinsmen, neighbours and communities in Wales and the western British Isles, *c.*1100–*c.*1400', in P. Stafford, J. L. Nelson and J. Martindale, eds., *Law, Laity and Solidarities: essays in honour of Susan Reynolds* (Manchester, 2001) pp. 172–87.

'The identity of "Wales" in the thirteenth century', in R. R. Davies and G. H. Jenkins, eds., *From Medieval to Modern Wales: historical essays in honour of Kenneth O. Morgan and Ralph A. Griffiths* (Cardiff, 2004), pp. 45–63.

Forde, S., Johnson, L. and Murray, A. V., eds., *Concepts of National Identity in the Middle Ages* (Leeds, 1995).

Gillingham, J., *The English in the Twelfth Century: imperialism, national identity and political values* (Woodbridge, 2000).

Greenblatt, S., *Renaissance Self-Fashioning: from More to Shakespeare* (Chicago, 1980).

Hastings, A., *The Construction of Nationhood: ethnicity, religion and nationalism* (Cambridge, 1997).

McDonald, N. F. and Ormrod, W. M., eds., *Rites of Passage: cultures of transition in the fourteenth century* (Woodbridge, 2004).

Macfarlane, A., *The Origins of English Individualism* (1978).

McRee, B. R., 'Religious gilds and regulation of behavior in late medieval towns', in J. Rosenthal and C. Richmond, eds., *People, Politics and Community in the later Middle Ages* (Gloucester, 1987), pp. 108–22.

Maddicott, J. R., 'The county community and the making of public opinion in fourteenth-century England', *TRHS*, 5th series, 27 (1977), 27–43.

Mann, J., *Chaucer and Medieval Estates Satire: the literature of social classes and the General Prologue to the Canterbury Tales* (Cambridge, 1973).

Morris, C., *The Discovery of the Individual, 1050–1200* (1972).

Richmond, C., 'Englishness and medieval Anglo-Jewry', in S. Delany, ed., *Chaucer and the Jews: sources, contexts, meanings* (2002), pp. 213–28.

Rubin, M., 'Small groups: identity and solidarity in the late middle ages', in J. Kermode, ed., *Enterprise and Individuals in Fifteenth-Century England* (Stroud, 1991), pp. 132–50.

Short, I., ' "*Tam Angli tam Franci*": self-definition in Anglo Norman England', *Anglo Norman Studies*, 18 (1992), 153–75.

Strohm, P., *Social Chaucer* (Cambridge, MA, 1989).

Thomas, H. M., *The English and the Normans: ethnic hostility, assimilation and identity 1066–c. 1220* (Oxford, 2003).

Turville-Petre, T., *England the Nation: language, literature and national identity 1290–1340* (Oxford, 1996).

CHAPTER 16 LIFE AND DEATH: THE AGES OF MAN

Barratt, A., ed., *Women's Writing in Middle English* (1992).

Bennett, J. M., *Women in the Medieval English Countryside: gender and household in Brigstock before the plague* (Oxford, 1987).

Biller, P. P. A., 'Birth-control in the west in the thirteenth and early fourteenth centuries', *P&P*, 94 (1982), 3–26.

Binski, P., *Medieval Death: ritual and representation* (1996).

Brooke, C., *The Medieval Idea of Marriage* (Oxford, 1989).

Burrow, J. A., *The Ages of Man: a study in medieval writing and thought* (Oxford, 1988).

Fleming, P., *Family and Household in Medieval England* (Basingstoke, 2001).

Goldberg, P. J. P., *Women, Work and Life Cycle in a Medieval Economy: women in York and Yorkshire, c. 1300–1520* (Oxford, 1992).

    ed., *Women in England c. 1275–1525* (Manchester, 1995).

Hanawalt, B. A., *The Ties that Bound: peasant families in medieval England* (New York, 1986).

    Growing up in Medieval London: the experience of childhood in history (Oxford, 1993).

Harvey, B., *Living and Dying in England 1100–1540: the monastic experience* (Oxford, 1993).

Hatcher, J., *Plague, Population and the English Economy, 1348–1530* (1977).

Helmholz, R. H., *Marriage Litigation in Medieval England* (Cambridge, 1974).

Horrox, R., ed., *The Black Death* (Manchester, 1994).

Lewis, K., Menuge, N. J. and Phillips, K. M., eds., *Young Medieval Women* (Stroud, 1999).

Mate, M. E., *Daughters, Wives and Widows after the Black Death: women in Sussex, 1350–1535* (Woodbridge, 1998).

McSheffrey, S., *Love and Marriage in late Medieval London* (Kalamazoo, MI, 1995).

Orme, N., *Medieval Children* (New Haven, CT, 2001).

Penn, S. A. C., 'Female wage-earners in late fourteenth-century England', *Ag. Hist. Rev.*, 35 (1987), 1–14.

Poos, L. R., *A Rural Society after the Black Death: Essex 1350–1525* (Cambridge, 1991).

Razi, Z., *Life, Marriage and Death in a Medieval Parish: economy, society and demography in Halesowen 1270–1400* (Cambridge, 1980).

CHAPTER 17 THE WIDER WORLD

Allmand, C. T., *Lancastrian Normandy 1415–1450: the history of a mediaeval occupation* (Oxford, 1983).

Barnie, J., *War in Medieval Society: social values and the Hundred Years War 1337–99* (1974).

Bartlett, R., *Gerald of Wales 1146–1223* (Oxford, 1982).

Childs, W. R., 'Irish merchants and seamen in late medieval England', *Irish Historical Studies*, 32 (2000), 22–43.

Cosgrove, A., ed., *A New History of Ireland, II: Medieval Ireland 1169–1534* (Oxford, 1987).

Davies, R. R., *Conquest, Coexistence and Change: Wales, 1063–1415* (Oxford, 1987).

'The peoples of Britain and Ireland: I. Identities'; 'II. Names, boundaries and regional solidarities'; 'III. Laws and customs'; 'IV. Language and historical mythology', *TRHS*, 6th series, 4 (1994), 1–20; 5 (1995), 1–20; 6 (1996), 1–23; 7 (1997), 1–24.

The First English Empire: power and identities in the British Isles 1093–1343 (Oxford, 2000).

Du Boulay, F. R. H., 'Henry of Derby's expeditions to Prussia 1390–1 and 1392', in F. R. H. Du Boulay and C. M. Barron, eds., *The Reign of Richard II: essays in honour of May McKisack* (1971), pp. 153–72.

Frame, R., *Ireland and Britain, 1170–1450* (1998).

Gillingham, J., *The English in the Twelfth Century: imperialism, national identity and political values* (Woodbridge, 2000).

Gransden, A., *Historical Writing in England c. 550–c. 1307* (1974).

Historical Writing in England, II: c. 1307 to the early sixteenth century (1982).

Grant, A., *Independence and Nationhood: Scotland 1306–1469* (1984; reprinted Edinburgh, 1991).

Griffiths, R. A., *King and Country: England and Wales in the fifteenth century* (1991).

Harvey, M., *The English in Rome 1362–1420: portrait of an expatriate community* (Cambridge, 1999).

Harvey, P. D. A., *Mappa Mundi: the Hereford world map* (1996).

Jones, M. and Vale, M., eds., *England and her Neighbours 1066–1453: essays in honour of Pierre Chaplais* (1989).

Lloyd, S., *English Society and the Crusade 1216–1307* (Oxford, 1988).

Neville, C. J., 'Local sentiment and the "national" enemy in northern England in the later middle ages', *Journal of British Studies*, 35 (1996), 419–37.

Phillips, J. R. S., *The Medieval Expansion of Europe* (Oxford, 1988).

Pollard, A. J., *North-Eastern England during the Wars of the Roses: lay society, war, and politics 1450–1500* (Oxford, 1990).

Taylor, J., *The Universal Chronicle of Ranulf Higden* (Oxford, 1966).

Turville-Petre, T., *England the Nation: language, literature and national identity 1290–1340* (Oxford, 1996).

Vale, M. G. A., *English Gascony 1399–1453: a study of war, government and politics during the later stages of the Hundred Years' War* (Oxford, 1970).

Vaughan, R., *Matthew Paris* (Cambridge, 1958).

Webb, D., *Pilgrimage in Medieval England* (2000).

CHAPTER 18 WRITING AND READING

Blake, N. F., *Caxton: England's first publisher* (1976).

Briggs, C. F., 'Literacy, reading and writing in the medieval west', *JMH*, 26 (2000), 397–420.

Clanchy, M. T., *From Memory to Written Record: England, 1066–1307* (2nd edn, Oxford, 1993).

Coleman, J., *English Literature in History, 1350–1400: medieval readers and writers* (1981).

   Public Reading and the Reading Public in late medieval England and France (Cambridge, 1996).

Griffiths, J. and Pearsall, D., eds., *Book Production and Publishing in Britain, 1373–1475* (Cambridge, 1989).

Hellinga, L. and Trapp, J. B., eds., *The Cambridge History of the Book in Britain, III: 1400–1557* (Cambridge, 1999).

Hudson, A., *Lollards and their Books* (1985).

   The Premature Reformation: Wycliffite texts and Lollard history (Oxford, 1988).

Olson, L. and Kerby-Fulton, K., eds., *Voices in Dialogue: reading women in the middle ages* (Chicago, 2005).

Ormrod, W. M., 'The use of English: language, law and political culture in fourteenth-century England', *Speculum*, 78 (2003), 750–87.

Parkes, M. B., 'The literacy of the laity', in D. Daiches and A. Thorlby, eds., *Literature and Western Civilisation*, II: *The Mediaeval World* (1973), pp. 555–77.

Saenger, P., *The Space between Words: the origins of silent reading* (Stanford, 1997).

Simpson, J., *Reform and Cultural Revolution, 1350–1547* (Oxford, 2002).

Stock, B., *The Implications of Literacy: written language and models of interpretation in the eleventh and twelfth centuries* (Princeton, NJ, 1983).

Turville-Petre, T, *England the Nation: language, literature and national identity 1290–1340* (Oxford, 1996).

Wallace, D., ed., *The Cambridge History of Medieval English Literature* (Cambridge, 1999).

Watson, N., 'Censorship and cultural change in late-medieval England: vernacular theology, the Oxford translation debate and Arundel's constitutions of 1409', *Speculum*, 70 (1995), 822–64.

Wogan-Browne, J. et al., eds., *The Idea of the Vernacular, an anthology of Middle English literary theory, 1280–1520* (Exeter, 1999).

Index